**W9-BIK-925**

# VOLVO
## COUPES/SEDANS/WAGONS
## 1990-98 REPAIR MANUAL

**Covers all U.S. and Canadian models of Volvo Coupe, 240 series, 740/760/780 series, 850 series, 940/960 series, C70, S70/S90 series and V70/V90 series, including Cross Country**

**by Eric Michael Mihalyi,** A.S.E., S.T.S., S.A.E.

**CHILTON** *Automotive Books*

PUBLISHED BY **HAYNES NORTH AMERICA.** Inc.

Manufactured in USA
© 1999 Haynes North America, Inc.
ISBN 0-8019-9095-5
Library of Congress Catalog Card No. 99-072522
3456789012  9876543210

**Haynes Publishing Group**
Sparkford Nr Yeovil
Somerset BA22 7JJ England

**Haynes North America, Inc**
861 Lawrence Drive
Newbury Park
California 91320 USA

ABCDE
FGHIJ
KLMNO
P

# Contents

# Contents

## DRIVE TRAIN 7

## SUSPENSION AND STEERING 8

## BRAKES 9

## BODY AND TRIM 10

## GLOSSARY

## MASTER INDEX

## SAFETY NOTICE

Proper service and repair procedures are vital to the safe, reliable operation of all motor vehicles, as well as the personal safety of those performing repairs. This manual outlines procedures for servicing and repairing vehicles using safe, effective methods. The procedures contain many NOTES, CAUTIONS and WARNINGS which should be followed, along with standard procedures to eliminate the possibility of personal injury or improper service which could damage the vehicle or compromise its safety.

It is important to note that repair procedures and techniques, tools and parts for servicing motor vehicles, as well as the skill and experience of the individual performing the work vary widely. It is not possible to anticipate all of the conceivable ways or conditions under which vehicles may be serviced, or to provide cautions as to all possible hazards that may result. Standard and accepted safety precautions and equipment should be used when handling toxic or flammable fluids, and safety goggles or other protection should be used during cutting, grinding, chiseling, prying, or any other process that can cause material removal or projectiles.

Some procedures require the use of tools specially designed for a specific purpose. Before substituting another tool or procedure, you must be completely satisfied that neither your personal safety, nor the performance of the vehicle will be endangered.

Although information in this manual is based on industry sources and is complete as possible at the time of publication, the possibility exists that some car manufacturers made later changes which could not be included here. While striving for total accuracy, the authors or publishers cannot assume responsibility for any errors, changes or omissions that may occur in the compilation of this data.

## PART NUMBERS

Part numbers listed in this reference are not recommendations by Haynes North America, Inc. for any product brand name. They are references that can be used with interchange manuals and aftermarket supplier catalogs to locate each brand supplier's discrete part number.

## SPECIAL TOOLS

Special tools are recommended by the vehicle manufacturer to perform their specific job. Use has been kept to a minimum, but where absolutely necessary, they are referred to in the text by the part number of the tool manufacturer. These tools can be purchased, under the appropriate part number, from your local dealer or regional distributor, or an equivalent tool can be purchased locally from a tool supplier or parts outlet. Before substituting any tool for the one recommended, read the SAFETY NOTICE at the top of this page.

## ACKNOWLEDGMENTS

The publisher expresses appreciation to Volvo North America for their generous assistance, and to Gordon Louiscious Tobias, S.A.E. for his technical consultation.

# 1

## GENERAL INFORMATION AND MAINTENANCE

## HOW TO USE THIS BOOK

Chilton's Total Car Care manual for 1990–98 Volvo cars is intended to help you learn more about the inner workings of your vehicle while saving you money on its upkeep and operation.

The beginning of the book will likely be referred to the most, since that is where you will find information for maintenance and tune-up. The other sections deal with the more complex systems of your vehicle. Operating systems from engine through brakes are covered to the extent that the average do-it-yourselfer becomes mechanically involved. This book will not explain such things as rebuilding a differential for the simple reason that the expertise required and the investment in special tools make this task uneconomical. It will, however, give you detailed instructions to help you change your own brake pads and shoes, replace spark plugs, and perform many more jobs that can save you money, give you personal satisfaction and help you avoid expensive problems.

A secondary purpose of this book is a reference for owners who want to understand their vehicle and/or their mechanics better. In this case, no tools at all are required.

### Where to Begin

Before removing any bolts, read through the entire procedure. This will give you the overall view of what tools and supplies will be required. There is nothing more frustrating than having to walk to the bus stop on Monday morning because you were short one bolt on Sunday afternoon. So read ahead and plan ahead. Each operation should be approached logically and all procedures thoroughly understood before attempting any work.

All sections contain adjustments, maintenance, removal and installation procedures, and in some cases, repair or overhaul procedures. When repair is not considered practical, we tell you how to remove the part and then how to install the new or rebuilt replacement. In this way, you at least save labor costs. "Backyard" repair of some components is just not practical.

### Avoiding Trouble

Many procedures in this book require you to "label and disconnect . . . " a group of lines, hoses or wires. Don't be lulled into thinking you can remember where everything goes—you won't. If you hook up vacuum or fuel lines incorrectly, the vehicle may run poorly, if at all. If you hook up electrical wiring incorrectly, you may instantly learn a very expensive lesson.

You don't need to know the official or engineering name for each hose or line. A piece of masking tape on the hose and a piece on its fitting will allow you to assign your own label such as the letter A or a short name. As long as you remember your own code, the lines can be reconnected by matching similar letters or names. Do remember that tape will dissolve in gasoline or other fluids; if a component is to be washed or cleaned, use another method of identification. A permanent felt-tipped marker or a metal scribe can be very handy for marking metal parts. Remove any tape or paper labels after assembly.

### Maintenance or Repair?

It's necessary to mention the difference between maintenance and repair. Maintenance includes routine inspections, adjustments, and replacement of parts which show signs of normal wear. Maintenance compensates for wear or deterioration. Repair implies that something has broken or is not working. A need for repair is often caused by lack of maintenance. Example: draining and refilling the automatic transmission fluid is maintenance recommended by the manufacturer at specific mileage intervals. Failure to do this can shorten the life of the transmission/transaxle, requiring very expensive repairs. While no maintenance program can prevent items from breaking or wearing out, a general rule can be stated: MAINTENANCE IS CHEAPER THAN REPAIR.

Two basic mechanic's rules should be mentioned here. First, whenever the left side of the vehicle or engine is referred to, it is meant to specify the driver's side. Conversely, the right side of the vehicle means the passenger's side. Second, screws and bolts are removed by turning counterclockwise, and tightened by turning clockwise unless specifically noted.

Safety is always the most important rule. Constantly be aware of the dangers involved in working on an automobile and take the proper precautions. See the information in this section regarding SERVICING YOUR VEHICLE SAFELY and the SAFETY NOTICE on the acknowledgment page.

### Avoiding the Most Common Mistakes

Pay attention to the instructions provided. There are 3 common mistakes in mechanical work:

1. Incorrect order of assembly, disassembly or adjustment. When taking something apart or putting it together, performing steps in the wrong order usually just costs you extra time; however, it CAN break something. Read the entire procedure before beginning disassembly. Perform everything in the order in which the instructions say you should, even if you can't immediately see a reason for it. When you're taking apart something that is very intricate, you might want to draw a picture of how it looks when assembled at one point in order to make sure you get everything back in its proper position. We will supply exploded views whenever possible. When making adjustments, perform them in the proper order. One adjustment possibly will affect another.

2. Overtorquing (or undertorquing). While it is more common for overtorquing to cause damage, undertorquing may allow a fastener to vibrate loose causing serious damage. Especially when dealing with aluminum parts, pay attention to torque specifications and utilize a torque wrench in assembly. If a torque figure is not available, remember that if you are using the right tool to perform the job, you will probably not have to strain yourself to get a fastener tight enough. The pitch of most threads is so slight that the tension you put on the wrench will be multiplied many times in actual force on what you are tightening. A good example of how critical torque is can be seen in the case of spark plug installation, especially where you are putting the plug into an aluminum cylinder head. Too little torque can fail to crush the gasket, causing leakage of combustion gases and consequent overheating of the plug and engine parts. Too much torque can damage the threads or distort the plug, changing the spark gap.

There are many commercial products available for ensuring that fasteners won't come loose, even if they are not torqued just right (a very common brand is Loctite®). If you're worried about getting something together tight enough to hold, but loose enough to avoid mechanical damage during assembly, one of these products might offer substantial insurance. Before choosing a threadlocking compound, read the label on the package and make sure the product is compatible with the materials, fluids, etc. involved.

3. Crossthreading. This occurs when a part such as a bolt is screwed into a nut or casting at the wrong angle and forced. Crossthreading is more likely to occur if access is difficult. It helps to clean and lubricate fasteners, then to start threading the bolt, spark plug, etc. with your fingers. If you encounter resistance, unscrew the part and start over again at a different angle until it can be inserted and turned several times without much effort. Keep in mind that many parts, especially spark plugs, have tapered threads, so that gentle turning will automatically bring the part you're threading to the proper angle. Don't put a wrench on the part until it's been tightened a couple of turns by hand. If you suddenly encounter resistance, and the part has not seated fully, don't force it. Pull it back out to make sure it's clean and threading properly.

Be sure to take your time and be patient, and always plan ahead. Allow yourself ample time to perform repairs and maintenance. You may find maintaining your car a satisfying and enjoyable experience.

## TOOLS AND EQUIPMENT

▶ **See Figures 1 thru 15**

Naturally, without the proper tools and equipment it is impossible to properly service your vehicle. It would also be virtually impossible to catalog every tool that you would need to perform all of the operations in this book. Of course, It

would be unwise for the amateur to rush out and buy an expensive set of tools on the theory that he/she may need one or more of them at some time.

The best approach is to proceed slowly, gathering a good quality set of those tools that are used most frequently. Don't be misled by the low cost of bargain

TCCS1200

Fig. 1 All but the most basic procedures will require an assortment of ratchets and sockets

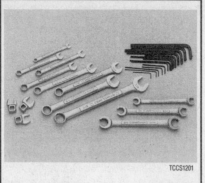

TCCS1201

Fig. 2 In addition to ratchets, a good set of wrenches and hex keys will be necessary

TCCS1202

Fig. 3 A hydraulic floor jack and a set of jackstands are essential for lifting and supporting the vehicle

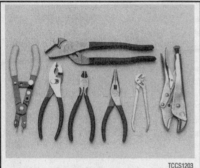

TCCS1203

Fig. 4 An assortment of pliers, grippers and cutters will be handy for old rusted parts and stripped bolt heads

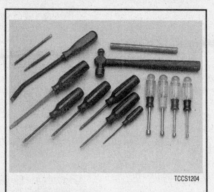

TCCS1204

Fig. 5 Various drivers, chisels and prybars are great tools to have in your toolbox

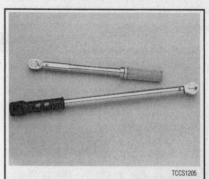

TCCS1205

Fig. 6 Many repairs will require the use of a torque wrench to assure the components are properly fastened

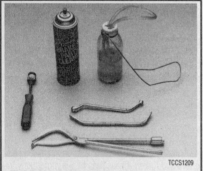

TCCS1209

Fig. 7 Although not always necessary, using specialized brake tools will save time

TCCS1210

Fig. 8 A few inexpensive lubrication tools will make maintenance easier

TCCS1211

Fig. 9 Various pullers, clamps and separator tools are needed for many larger, more complicated repairs

TCCS1212

Fig. 10 A variety of tools and gauges should be used for spark plug gapping and installation

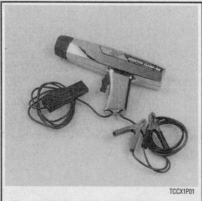

TCCX1P01

Fig. 11 Inductive type timing light

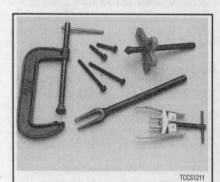

TCCX1P02

Fig. 12 A screw-in type compression gauge is recommended for compression testing

**Fig. 13 A vacuum/pressure tester is necessary for many testing procedures**

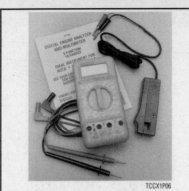

**Fig. 14 Most modern automotive multimeters incorporate many helpful features**

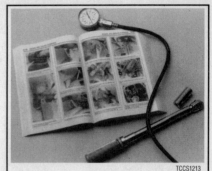

**Fig. 15 Proper information is vital, so always have a Chilton Total Car Care manual handy**

tools. It is far better to spend a little more for better quality. Forged wrenches, 6 or 12-point sockets and fine tooth ratchets are by far preferable to their less expensive counterparts. As any good mechanic can tell you, there are few worse experiences than trying to work on a vehicle with bad tools. Your monetary savings will be far outweighed by frustration and mangled knuckles.

Begin accumulating those tools that are used most frequently: those associated with routine maintenance and tune-up. In addition to the normal assortment of screwdrivers and pliers, you should have the following tools:
- Wrenches/sockets and combination open end/box end wrenches in sizes 3mm–19mm $^{13}\!/_{16}$ in. or $^5\!/_8$ in. spark plug socket (depending on plug type).

➡**If possible, buy various length socket drive extensions. Universal-joint and wobble extensions can be extremely useful, but be careful when using them, as they can change the amount of torque applied to the socket.**

- Jackstands for support.
- Oil filter wrench.
- Spout or funnel for pouring fluids.
- Grease gun for chassis lubrication (unless your vehicle is not equipped with any grease fittings—for details, please refer to information on Fluids and Lubricants, later in this section).
- Hydrometer for checking the battery (unless equipped with a sealed, maintenance-free battery).
- A container for draining oil and other fluids.
- Rags for wiping up the inevitable mess.

In addition to the above items there are several others that are not absolutely necessary, but handy to have around. These include Oil Dry( (or an equivalent oil absorbent gravel—such as cat litter) and the usual supply of lubricants, antifreeze and fluids, although these can be purchased as needed. This is a basic list for routine maintenance, but only your personal needs and desire can accurately determine your list of tools.

After performing a few projects on the vehicle, you'll be amazed at the other tools and non-tools on your workbench. Some useful household items are: a large turkey baster or siphon, empty coffee cans and ice trays (to store parts), ball of twine, electrical tape for wiring, small rolls of colored tape for tagging lines or hoses, markers and pens, a note pad, golf tees (for plugging vacuum lines), metal coat hangers or a roll of mechanic's wire (to hold things out of the way), dental pick or similar long, pointed probe, a strong magnet, and a small mirror (to see into recesses and under manifolds).

A more advanced set of tools, suitable for tune-up work, can be drawn up easily. While the tools are slightly more sophisticated, they need not be outrageously expensive. There are several inexpensive tach/dwell meters on the market that are every bit as good for the average mechanic as a professional model.

Just be sure that it goes to a least 1200–1500 rpm on the tach scale and that it works on 4, 6 and 8-cylinder engines. The key to these purchases is to make them with an eye towards adaptability and wide range. A basic list of tune-up tools could include:
- Tach/dwell meter
- Spark plug wrench and gapping tool
- Feeler gauges for valve adjustment
- Timing light

The choice of a timing light should be made carefully. A light which works on the DC current supplied by the vehicle's battery is the best choice; it should have a xenon tube for brightness. On any vehicle with an electronic ignition system, a timing light with an inductive pickup that clamps around the No. 1 spark plug cable is preferred.

In addition to these basic tools, there are several other tools and gauges you may find useful. These include:
- Compression gauge. The screw-in type is slower to use, but eliminates the possibility of a faulty reading due to escaping pressure.
- Manifold vacuum gauge
- 12V test light
- Combination volt/ohmmeter
- Induction Ammeter. This is used for determining whether or not there is current in a wire. These are handy for use if a wire is broken somewhere in a wiring harness.

As a final note, you will probably find a torque wrench necessary for all but the most basic work. The beam type models are perfectly adequate, although the newer click types (breakaway) are easier to use. The click type torque wrenches tend to be more expensive. Also keep in mind that all types of torque wrenches should be periodically checked and/or recalibrated. You will have to decide for yourself which better fits your pocketbook, and purpose.

## Special Tools

Normally, the use of special factory tools is avoided for repair procedures, since these are not readily available for the do-it-yourself mechanic. When it is possible to perform the job with more commonly available tools, it will be pointed out, but occasionally, a special tool was designed to perform a specific function and should be used. Before substituting another tool, you should be convinced that neither your safety nor the performance of the vehicle will be compromised.

Special tools can usually be purchased from an automotive parts store or from your dealer. In some cases special tools may be available directly from the tool manufacturer.

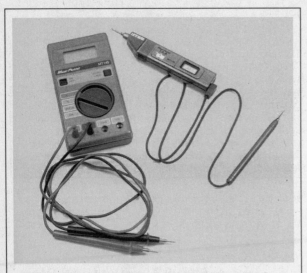

**Digital multimeters** come in a variety of styles and are a "must-have" for any serious home mechanic. Digital multimeters measure voltage (volts), resistance (ohms) and sometimes current (amperes). These versatile tools are used for checking all types of electrical or electronic components

Modern vehicles equipped with computer-controlled fuel, emission and ignition systems require modern electronic tools to diagnose problems. Many of these tools are designed solely for the professional mechanic and are too costly and difficult to use for the average do-it-yourselfer. However, various automotive aftermarket companies have introduced products that address the needs of the average home mechanic, providing sophisticated information at affordable cost. Consult your local auto parts store to determine what is available for your vehicle.

**Trouble code tools** allow the home mechanic to extract the "fault code" number from an on-board computer that has sensed a problem (usually indicated by a Check Engine light). Armed with this code, the home mechanic can focus attention on a suspect system or component

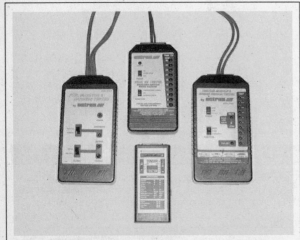

**Sensor testers** perform specific checks on many of the sensors and actuators used on today's computer-controlled vehicles. These testers can check sensors both on or off the vehicle, as well as test the accompanying electrical circuits

**Hand-held scanners** represent the most sophisticated of all do-it-yourself diagnostic tools. These tools do more than just access computer codes like the code readers above; they provide the user with an actual interface into the vehicle's computer. Comprehensive data on specific makes and models will come with the tool, either built-in or as a separate cartridge

## SERVICING YOUR VEHICLE SAFELY

▶ **See Figures 16, 17, 18 and 19**

It is virtually impossible to anticipate all of the hazards involved with automotive maintenance and service, but care and common sense will prevent most accidents.

The rules of safety for mechanics range from "don't smoke around gasoline," to "use the proper tool(s) for the job." The trick to avoiding injuries is to develop safe work habits and to take every possible precaution.

### Do's

- Do keep a fire extinguisher and first aid kit handy.
- Do wear safety glasses or goggles when cutting, drilling, grinding or prying, even if you have 20–20 vision. If you wear glasses for the sake of vision, wear safety goggles over your regular glasses.
- Do shield your eyes whenever you work around the battery. Batteries contain sulfuric acid. In case of contact with the eyes or skin, flush the area with water or a mixture of water and baking soda, then seek immediate medical attention.
- Do use safety stands (jackstands) for any undervehicle service. Jacks are for raising vehicles; jackstands are for making sure the vehicle stays raised until

you want it to come down. Whenever the vehicle is raised, block the wheels remaining on the ground and set the parking brake.
- Do use adequate ventilation when working with any chemicals or hazardous materials. Like carbon monoxide, the asbestos dust resulting from some brake lining wear can be hazardous in sufficient quantities.
- Do disconnect the negative battery cable when working on the electrical system. The secondary ignition system contains EXTREMELY HIGH VOLTAGE. In some cases it can even exceed 50,000 volts.
- Do follow manufacturer's directions whenever working with potentially hazardous materials. Most chemicals and fluids are poisonous if taken internally.
- Do properly maintain your tools. Loose hammerheads, mushroomed punches and chisels, frayed or poorly grounded electrical cords, excessively worn screwdrivers, spread wrenches (open end), cracked sockets, slipping ratchets, or faulty droplight sockets can cause accidents.
- Likewise, keep your tools clean; a greasy wrench can slip off a bolt head, ruining the bolt and often harming your knuckles in the process.
- Do use the proper size and type of tool for the job at hand. Do select a wrench or socket that fits the nut or bolt. The wrench or socket should sit straight, not cocked.
- Do, when possible, pull on a wrench handle rather than push on it, and adjust your stance to prevent a fall.
- Do be sure that adjustable wrenches are tightly closed on the nut or bolt and pulled so that the force is on the side of the fixed jaw.
- Do strike squarely with a hammer; avoid glancing blows.
- Do set the parking brake and block the drive wheels if the work requires a running engine.

### Don'ts

- Don't run the engine in a garage or anywhere else without proper ventilation—EVER! Carbon monoxide is poisonous; it takes a long time to leave the human body and you can build up a deadly supply of it in your system by simply breathing in a little every day. You may not realize you are slowly poisoning yourself. Always use power vents, windows, fans and/or open the garage door.
- Don't work around moving parts while wearing loose clothing. Short sleeves are much safer than long, loose sleeves. Hard-toed shoes with neoprene soles protect your toes and give a better grip on slippery surfaces. Jewelry such as watches, fancy belt buckles, beads or body adornment of any kind is not safe working around a vehicle. Long hair should be tied back under a hat or cap.
- Don't use pockets for toolboxes. A fall or bump can drive a screwdriver deep into your body. Even a rag hanging from your back pocket can wrap around a spinning shaft or fan.
- Don't smoke when working around gasoline, cleaning solvent or other flammable material.
- Don't smoke when working around the battery. When the battery is being charged, it gives off explosive hydrogen gas.
- Don't use gasoline to wash your hands; there are excellent soaps available. Gasoline contains dangerous additives which can enter the body through a cut or through your pores. Gasoline also removes all the natural oils from the skin so that bone dry hands will suck up oil and grease.

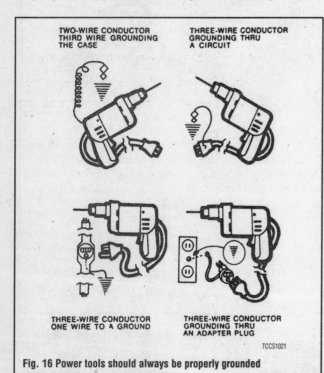

**TWO-WIRE CONDUCTOR THIRD WIRE GROUNDING THE CASE**

**THREE-WIRE CONDUCTOR GROUNDING THRU A CIRCUIT**

**THREE-WIRE CONDUCTOR ONE WIRE TO A GROUND**

**THREE-WIRE CONDUCTOR GROUNDING THRU AN ADAPTER PLUG**

TCCS1021

**Fig. 16 Power tools should always be properly grounded**

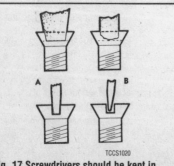

TCCS1020

**Fig. 17 Screwdrivers should be kept in good condition to prevent injury or damage which could result if the blade slips from the screw**

TCCS1022

**Fig. 18 Using the correct size wrench will help prevent the possibility of rounding off a nut**

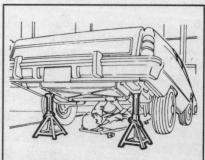

TCCS1023

**Fig. 19 NEVER work under a vehicle unless it is supported using safety stands (jackstands)**

• Don't service the air conditioning system unless you are equipped with the necessary tools and training. When liquid or compressed gas refrigerant is released to atmospheric pressure it will absorb heat from whatever it contacts. This will chill or freeze anything it touches.

• Don't use screwdrivers for anything other than driving screws! A screwdriver used as an prying tool can snap when you least expect it, causing injuries. At the very least, you'll ruin a good screwdriver.

• Don't use an emergency jack (that little ratchet, scissors, or pantograph jack supplied with the vehicle) for anything other than changing a flat! These jacks are only intended for emergency use out on the road; they are NOT designed as a maintenance tool. If you are serious about maintaining your vehicle yourself, invest in a hydraulic floor jack of at least a 1½ ton capacity, and at least two sturdy jackstands.

## FASTENERS, MEASUREMENTS AND CONVERSIONS

### Bolts, Nuts and Other Threaded Retainers

▶ See Figures 20, 21, 22 and 23

Although there are a great variety of fasteners found in the modern car or truck, the most commonly used retainer is the threaded fastener (nuts, bolts, screws, studs, etc.). Most threaded retainers may be reused, provided that they are not damaged in use or during the repair. Some retainers (such as stretch bolts or torque prevailing nuts) are designed to deform when tightened or in use and should not be reinstalled.

Whenever possible, we will note any special retainers which should be replaced during a procedure. But you should always inspect the condition of a retainer when it is removed and replace any that show signs of damage. Check all threads for rust or corrosion which can increase the torque necessary to achieve the desired clamp load for which that fastener was originally selected. Additionally, be sure that the driver surface of the fastener has not been compromised by rounding or other damage. In some cases a driver surface may become only partially rounded, allowing the driver to catch in only one direction. In many of these occurrences, a fastener may be installed and tightened, but the driver would not be able to grip and loosen the fastener again. (This

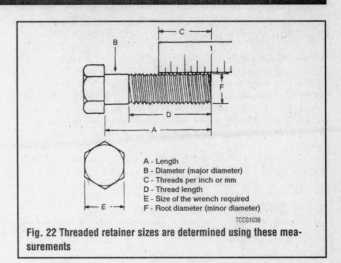

A - Length
B - Diameter (major diameter)
C - Threads per inch or mm
D - Thread length
E - Size of the wrench required
F - Root diameter (minor diameter)

TCCS1038

**Fig. 22 Threaded retainer sizes are determined using these measurements**

T - INTERNAL DRIVE
E - EXTERNAL

TCCS1016

**Fig. 23 Special fasteners such as these Torx® head bolts are used by manufacturers to discourage people from working on vehicles without the proper tools**

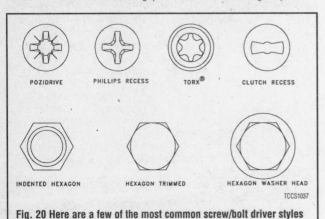

POZIDRIVE   PHILLIPS RECESS   TORX®   CLUTCH RECESS

INDENTED HEXAGON   HEXAGON TRIMMED   HEXAGON WASHER HEAD

TCCS1037

**Fig. 20 Here are a few of the most common screw/bolt driver styles**

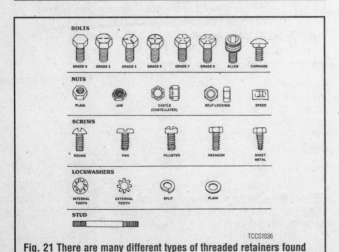

BOLTS
GRADE 0   GRADE 2   GRADE 5   GRADE 6   GRADE 7   GRADE 8   ALLEN   CARRIAGE

NUTS
PLAIN   JAM   CASTLE (CASTELLATED)   SELF-LOCKING   SPEED

SCREWS
ROUND   PAN   FILLISTER   HEXAGON   SHEET METAL

LOCKWASHERS
INTERNAL TOOTH   EXTERNAL TOOTH   SPLIT   PLAIN

STUD

TCCS1036

**Fig. 21 There are many different types of threaded retainers found on vehicles**

could lead to frustration down the line should that component ever need to be disassembled again).

If you must replace a fastener, whether due to design or damage, you must ALWAYS be sure to use the proper replacement. In all cases, a retainer of the same design, material and strength should be used. Markings on the heads of most bolts will help determine the proper strength of the fastener. The same material, thread and pitch must be selected to assure proper installation and safe operation of the vehicle afterwards.

Thread gauges are available to help measure a bolt or stud's thread. Most automotive and hardware stores keep gauges available to help you select the proper size. In a pinch, you can use another nut or bolt for a thread gauge. If the bolt you are replacing is not too badly damaged, you can select a match by finding another bolt which will thread in its place. If you find a nut which threads properly onto the damaged bolt, then use that nut to help select the replacement bolt. If however, the bolt you are replacing is so badly damaged (broken or drilled out) that its threads cannot be used as a gauge, you might start by looking for another bolt (from the same assembly or a similar location on your vehicle) which will thread into the damaged bolt's mounting. If so, the other bolt can be used to select a nut; the nut can then be used to select the replacement bolt.

In all cases, be absolutely sure you have selected the proper replacement. Don't be shy, you can always ask the store clerk for help.

## ✼✼ WARNING

Be aware that when you find a bolt with damaged threads, you may also find the nut or drilled hole it was threaded into has also been damaged. If this is the case, you may have to drill and tap the hole, replace the nut or otherwise repair the threads. NEVER try to force a replacement bolt to fit into the damaged threads.

## Torque

Torque is defined as the measurement of resistance to turning or rotating. It tends to twist a body about an axis of rotation. A common example of this would be tightening a threaded retainer such as a nut, bolt or screw. Measuring torque is one of the most common ways to help assure that a threaded retainer has been properly fastened.

When tightening a threaded fastener, torque is applied in three distinct areas, the head, the bearing surface and the clamp load. About 50 percent of the measured torque is used in overcoming bearing friction. This is the friction between the bearing surface of the bolt head, screw head or nut face and the base material or washer (the surface on which the fastener is rotating). Approximately 40 percent of the applied torque is used in overcoming thread friction. This leaves only about 10 percent of the applied torque to develop a useful clamp load (the force which holds a joint together). This means that friction can account for as much as 90 percent of the applied torque on a fastener.

### TORQUE WRENCHES

▶ See Figures 24, 25 and 26

In most applications, a torque wrench can be used to assure proper installation of a fastener. Torque wrenches come in various designs and most automotive supply stores will carry a variety to suit your needs. A torque wrench should be used any time we supply a specific torque value for a fastener. A torque wrench can also be used if you are following the general guidelines in the accompanying charts. Keep in mind that because there is

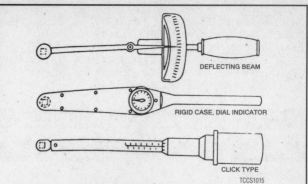

Fig. 25 Various styles of torque wrenches are usually available at your local automotive supply store

| Class | Diameter mm | Pitch mm | Specified torque | | | | | |
|---|---|---|---|---|---|---|---|---|
| | | | Hexagon head bolt | | | Hexagon flange bolt | | |
| | | | N·m | kgf·cm | ft·lbf | N·m | kgf·cm | ft·lbf |
| 4T | 6 | 1 | 5 | 55 | 48 in.·lbf | 6 | 60 | 52 in.·lbf |
| | 8 | 1.25 | 12.5 | 130 | 9 | 14 | 145 | 10 |
| | 10 | 1.25 | 26 | 260 | 19 | 29 | 290 | 21 |
| | 12 | 1.25 | 47 | 480 | 35 | 53 | 540 | 39 |
| | 14 | 1.5 | 74 | 760 | 55 | 84 | 850 | 61 |
| | 16 | 1.5 | 115 | 1,150 | 83 | — | — | — |
| 5T | 6 | 1 | 6.5 | 65 | 56 in.·lbf | 7.5 | 75 | 65 in.·lbf |
| | 8 | 1.25 | 15.5 | 160 | 12 | 17.5 | 175 | 13 |
| | 10 | 1.25 | 32 | 330 | 24 | 36 | 360 | 26 |
| | 12 | 1.25 | 59 | 600 | 43 | 65 | 670 | 48 |
| | 14 | 1.5 | 91 | 930 | 67 | 100 | 1,050 | 76 |
| | 16 | 1.5 | 140 | 1,400 | 101 | — | — | — |
| 6T | 6 | 1 | 8 | 80 | 69 in.·lbf | 9 | 90 | 78 in.·lbf |
| | 8 | 1.25 | 19 | 195 | 14 | 21 | 210 | 15 |
| | 10 | 1.25 | 39 | 400 | 29 | 44 | 440 | 32 |
| | 12 | 1.25 | 71 | 730 | 53 | 80 | 810 | 59 |
| | 14 | 1.5 | 110 | 1,100 | 80 | 125 | 1,250 | 90 |
| | 16 | 1.5 | 170 | 1,750 | 127 | — | — | — |
| 7T | 6 | 1 | 10.5 | 110 | 8 | 12 | 120 | 9 |
| | 8 | 1.25 | 25 | 260 | 19 | 28 | 290 | 21 |
| | 10 | 1.25 | 52 | 530 | 38 | 58 | 590 | 43 |
| | 12 | 1.25 | 95 | 970 | 70 | 105 | 1,050 | 76 |
| | 14 | 1.5 | 145 | 1,500 | 108 | 165 | 1,700 | 123 |
| | 16 | 1.5 | 230 | 2,300 | 166 | — | — | — |
| 8T | 8 | 1.25 | 29 | 300 | 22 | 33 | 330 | 24 |
| | 10 | 1.25 | 61 | 620 | 45 | 68 | 690 | 50 |
| | 12 | 1.25 | 110 | 1,100 | 80 | 120 | 1,250 | 90 |
| 9T | 8 | 1.25 | 34 | 340 | 25 | 37 | 380 | 27 |
| | 10 | 1.25 | 70 | 710 | 51 | 78 | 790 | 57 |
| | 12 | 1.25 | 125 | 1,300 | 94 | 140 | 1,450 | 105 |
| 10T | 8 | 1.25 | 38 | 390 | 28 | 42 | 430 | 31 |
| | 10 | 1.25 | 78 | 800 | 58 | 88 | 890 | 64 |
| | 12 | 1.25 | 140 | 1,450 | 105 | 155 | 1,600 | 116 |
| 11T | 8 | 1.25 | 42 | 430 | 31 | 47 | 480 | 35 |
| | 10 | 1.25 | 87 | 890 | 64 | 97 | 990 | 72 |
| | 12 | 1.25 | 155 | 1,600 | 116 | 175 | 1,800 | 130 |

TCCS1241

Fig. 26 Typical bolt torque for metric fasteners—WARNING: use only as a guide

no worldwide standardization of fasteners, the charts are a general guideline and should be used with caution. Again, the general rule of "if you are using the right tool for the job, you should not have to strain to tighten a fastener" applies here.

### Beam Type

▶ See Figure 27

The beam type torque wrench is one of the most popular types. It consists of a pointer attached to the head that runs the length of the flexible beam (shaft) to a scale located near the handle. As the wrench is pulled, the beam bends and the pointer indicates the torque using the scale.

| | Mark | Class | | Mark | Class |
|---|---|---|---|---|---|
| Hexagon head bolt | Bolt head No. 4—, 5—, 6—, 7—, 8—, 9—, 10—, 11— | 4T, 5T, 6T, 7T, 8T, 9T, 10T, 11T | Stud bolt | No mark | 4T |
| | No mark | 4T | | Grooved | 6T |
| Hexagon flange bolt w/ washer hexagon bolt | No mark | 4T | | | |
| Hexagon head bolt | Two protruding lines | 5T | | | |
| Hexagon flange bolt w/ washer hexagon bolt | Two protruding lines | 6T | Welded bolt | | 4T |
| Hexagon head bolt | Three protruding lines | 7T | | | |
| Hexagon head bolt | Four protruding lines | 8T | | | |

TCCS1240

Fig. 24 Determining bolt strength of metric fasteners—NOTE: this is a typical bolt marking system, but there is not a worldwide standard

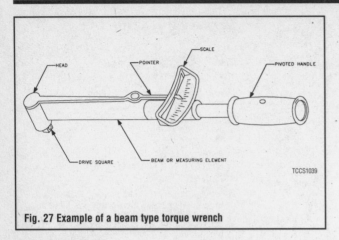

**Fig. 27 Example of a beam type torque wrench**

## Click (Breakaway) Type

▶ See Figure 28

Another popular design of torque wrench is the click type. To use the click type wrench you pre-adjust it to a torque setting. Once the torque is reached, the wrench has a reflex signaling feature that causes a momentary breakaway of the torque wrench body, sending an impulse to the operator's hand.

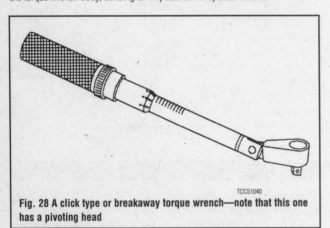

**Fig. 28 A click type or breakaway torque wrench—note that this one has a pivoting head**

## Pivot Head Type

▶ See Figures 28 and 29

Some torque wrenches (usually of the click type) may be equipped with a pivot head which can allow it to be used in areas of limited access. BUT, it must be used properly. To hold a pivot head wrench, grasp the handle lightly, and as

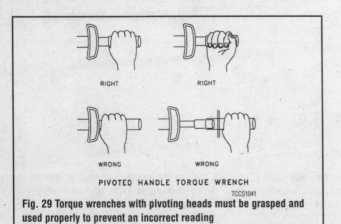

**Fig. 29 Torque wrenches with pivoting heads must be grasped and used properly to prevent an incorrect reading**

you pull on the handle, it should be floated on the pivot point. If the handle comes in contact with the yoke extension during the process of pulling, there is a very good chance the torque readings will be inaccurate because this could alter the wrench loading point. The design of the handle is usually such as to make it inconvenient to deliberately misuse the wrench.

➡**It should be mentioned that the use of any U-joint, wobble or extension will have an effect on the torque readings, no matter what type of wrench you are using. For the most accurate readings, install the socket directly on the wrench driver. If necessary, straight extensions (which hold a socket directly under the wrench driver) will have the least effect on the torque reading. Avoid any extension that alters the length of the wrench from the handle to the head/driving point (such as a crow's foot). U-joint or wobble extensions can greatly affect the readings; avoid their use at all times.**

### Rigid Case (Direct Reading)

▶ See Figure 30

A rigid case or direct reading torque wrench is equipped with a dial indicator to show torque values. One advantage of these wrenches is that they can be held at any position on the wrench without affecting accuracy. These wrenches are often preferred because they tend to be compact, easy to read and have a great degree of accuracy.

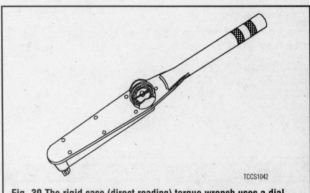

**Fig. 30 The rigid case (direct reading) torque wrench uses a dial indicator to show torque**

## TORQUE ANGLE METERS

▶ See Figure 31

Because the frictional characteristics of each fastener or threaded hole will vary, clamp loads which are based strictly on torque will vary as well. In most

**Fig. 31 Some specifications require the use of a torque angle meter (mechanical protractor)**

applications, this variance is not significant enough to cause worry. But, in certain applications, a manufacturer's engineers may determine that more precise clamp loads are necessary (such is the case with many aluminum cylinder heads). In these cases, a torque angle method of installation would be specified. When installing fasteners which are torque angle tightened, a predetermined seating torque and standard torque wrench are usually used first to remove any compliance from the joint. The fastener is then tightened the specified additional portion of a turn measured in degrees. A torque angle gauge (mechanical protractor) is used for these applications.

## Standard and Metric Measurements

▶ See Figure 32

Throughout this manual, specifications are given to help you determine the condition of various components on your vehicle, or to assist you in their installation. Some of the most common measurements include length (in. or cm/mm), torque (ft. lbs., inch lbs. or Nm) and pressure (psi, in. Hg, kPa or mm Hg). In most cases, we strive to provide the proper measurement as determined by the manufacturer's engineers.

Though, in some cases, that value may not be conveniently measured with what is available in your toolbox. Luckily, many of the measuring devices which are available today will have two scales so the Standard or Metric measurements may easily be taken. If any of the various measuring tools which are available to you do not contain the same scale as listed in the specifications, use the accompanying conversion factors to determine the proper value.

The conversion factor chart is used by taking the given specification and multiplying it by the necessary conversion factor. For instance, looking at the first line, if you have a measurement in inches such as "free-play should be 2 in." but your ruler reads only in millimeters, multiply 2 in. by the conversion factor of 25.4 to get the metric equivalent of 50.8mm. Likewise, if the specification was given only in a Metric measurement, for example in Newton Meters (Nm), then look at the center column first. If the measurement is 100 Nm, multiply it by the conversion factor of 0.738 to get 73.8 ft. lbs.

### CONVERSION FACTORS

**LENGTH–DISTANCE**

| | | | | |
|---|---|---|---|---|
| Inches (in.) | x 25.4 | = Millimeters (mm) | x .0394 | = Inches |
| Feet (ft.) | x .305 | = Meters (m) | x 3.281 | = Feet |
| Miles | x 1.609 | = Kilometers (km) | x .0621 | = Miles |

**VOLUME**

| | | | | |
|---|---|---|---|---|
| Cubic Inches (in3) | x 16.387 | = Cubic Centimeters | x .061 | = in3 |
| IMP Pints (IMP pt.) | x .568 | = Liters (L) | x 1.76 | = IMP pt. |
| IMP Quarts (IMP qt.) | x 1.137 | = Liters (L) | x .88 | = IMP qt. |
| IMP Gallons (IMP gal.) | x 4.546 | = Liters (L) | x .22 | = IMP gal. |
| IMP Quarts (IMP qt.) | x 1.201 | = US Quarts (US qt.) | x .833 | = IMP qt. |
| IMP Gallons (IMP gal.) | x 1.201 | = US Gallons (US gal.) | x .833 | = IMP gal. |
| Fl. Ounces | x 29.573 | = Milliliters | x .034 | = Ounces |
| US Pints (US pt.) | x .473 | = Liters (L) | x 2.113 | = Pints |
| US Quarts (US qt.) | x .946 | = Liters (L) | x 1.057 | = Quarts |
| US Gallons (US gal.) | x 3.785 | = Liters (L) | x .264 | = Gallons |

**MASS–WEIGHT**

| | | | | |
|---|---|---|---|---|
| Ounces (oz.) | x 28.35 | = Grams (g) | x .035 | = Ounces |
| Pounds (lb.) | x .454 | = Kilograms (kg) | x 2.205 | = Pounds |

**PRESSURE**

| | | | | |
|---|---|---|---|---|
| Pounds Per Sq. In. (psi) | x 6.895 | = Kilopascals (kPa) | x .145 | = psi |
| Inches of Mercury (Hg) | x .4912 | = psi | x 2.036 | = Hg |
| Inches of Mercury (Hg) | x 3.377 | = Kilopascals (kPa) | x .2961 | = Hg |
| Inches of Water ($H_2O$) | x .07355 | = Inches of Mercury | x 13.783 | = $H_2O$ |
| Inches of Water ($H_2O$) | x .03613 | = psi | x 27.684 | = $H_2O$ |
| Inches of Water ($H_2O$) | x .248 | = Kilopascals (kPa) | x 4.026 | = $H_2O$ |

**TORQUE**

| | | | | |
|---|---|---|---|---|
| Pounds–Force Inches (in–lb) | x .113 | = Newton Meters (N·m) | x 8.85 | = in–lb |
| Pounds–Force Feet (ft–lb) | x 1.356 | = Newton Meters (N·m) | x .738 | = ft–lb |

**VELOCITY**

| | | | | |
|---|---|---|---|---|
| Miles Per Hour (MPH) | x 1.609 | = Kilometers Per Hour (KPH) | x .621 | = MPH |

**POWER**

| | | | | |
|---|---|---|---|---|
| Horsepower (Hp) | x .745 | = Kilowatts | x 1.34 | = Horsepower |

**FUEL CONSUMPTION***

| | | | |
|---|---|---|---|
| Miles Per Gallon IMP (MPG) | x .354 | = Kilometers Per Liter (Km/L) | |
| Kilometers Per Liter (Km/L) | x 2.352 | = IMP MPG | |
| Miles Per Gallon US (MPG) | x .425 | = Kilometers Per Liter (Km/L) | |
| Kilometers Per Liter (Km/L) | x 2.352 | = US MPG | |

*It is common to covert from miles per gallon (mpg) to liters/100 kilometers (1/100 km), where mpg (IMP) x 1/100 km = 282 and mpg (US) x 1/100 km = 235.

**TEMPERATURE**

Degree Fahrenheit (°F) = (°C x 1.8) + 32
Degree Celsius (°C) = (°F − 32) x .56

TCCS1044

**Fig. 32 Standard and metric conversion factors chart**

## SERIAL NUMBER IDENTIFICATION

### Vehicle

▶ See Figures 33, 34 and 35

The Vehicle Identification Number (VIN) is an identification code comprised of a seventeen-digit combination of numbers and letters. Each letter, number or combination represents different items, such as manufacturer, type of restraint system, line, series and body type, engine, model year and consecutive unit number.

The VIN plate is located at the top left corner of the dashboard, just under the bottom of the windshield. The VIN number is also stamped on the right door pillar, on the certification label located on the driver's door, and on the emission control label located on the underside of the hood. On some models, there is a vehicle plate on the passenger side shock tower or the driver's side fender in the engine compartment that includes the VIN number, engine type, emission equipment, vehicle weights, and color codes.

**Fig. 33 The VIN plate as located on the dash panel**

90951P06

90951P37

**Fig. 34 This plate, located on the driver's side fender in the engine compartment, also contains the VIN number**

90951P05

**Fig. 35 The certification label located on the driver's door also contains the VIN number**

## VEHICLE IDENTIFICATION CHART

| Engine Code | | | | | | Model Year | |
|---|---|---|---|---|---|---|---|
| Engine Series (ID/VIN) | Engine Displacement Liters (cc) | Cubic Inches | No. of Cylinders | Fuel System | Eng. Mfg. | Code | Year |
| B5234T3/53 | 2.3 (2319) | 144 | 5 | EFI | VOLVO | L | 1990 |
| B5254S/55 | 2.4 (2435) | 151 | 5 | EFI | VOLVO | M | 1991 |
| B5254T/56 | 2.4 (2435) | 151 | 5 | EFI | VOLVO | N | 1992 |
| B5234T/57 | 2.3 (2319) | 144 | 5 | EFI | VOLVO | P | 1993 |
| B5254FT/58 | 2.3 (2319) | 144 | 5 | EFI | VOLVO | R | 1994 |
| B280F/69 | 2.8 (2849) | 175 | 6 | EFI | VOLVO | S | 1995 |
| B230FT/87 | 2.3 (2316) | 144 | 4 | EFI | VOLVO | T | 1996 |
| B234F/89 | 2.3 (2316) | 144 | 4 | EFI | VOLVO | U | 1997 |
| B230F/88 | 2.3 (2316) | 144 | 4 | EFI | VOLVO | V | 1998 |
| B6304F/95 | 2.9 (2922) | 181 | 6 | EFI | VOLVO | | |
| B6304S/96 | 2.9 (2922) | 181 | 6 | EFI | VOLVO | | |

EFI = Electronic Fuel Injection

90951C01

## Engine

♦ **See Figures 36, 37 and 38**

The engine serial number is stamped onto the engine block on the driver's side, just below the cylinder head. An identification tag or plate is also affixed to the timing cover. The engine size can also be identified by reading the sixth and seventh digits of the VIN and using charts in this manual or other similar information to decode the VIN.

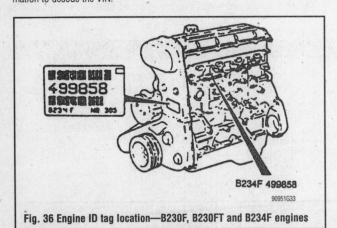

Fig. 36 Engine ID tag location—B230F, B230FT and B234F engines

90951G33

## Transmission/Transaxle

The transmission type designation, serial number and part number appear on a metal plate affix to the left-hand side of the transmission, just above the transmission pan on automatic transmissions/transaxles.

The manual transmission can be identified by referring to the Service Designation Number plate, found on the upper right side radiator support. A 10-digit Vehicle Identification Code (VIC), located in the upper right-hand corner of the Service Designation Number plate, contains information on the type of transmission used. The 9th digit of the VIC designates the transmission type.

## Drive Axle

♦ **See Figure 39**

The rear axle ratio and identification number (part number) are found on a label, located on the left-hand side of the axle housing.

## Transfer Case

The transfer case or bevel gear as Volvo refers to it, has a stamped steel tag attached on the side.

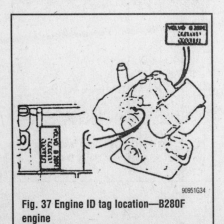

Fig. 37 Engine ID tag location—B280F engine

90951G34

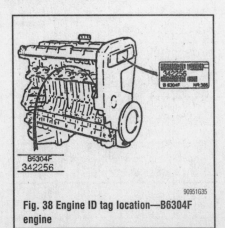

Fig. 38 Engine ID tag location—B6304F engine

90951G35

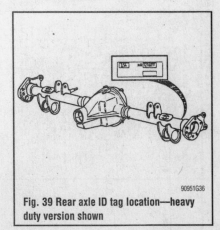

Fig. 39 Rear axle ID tag location—heavy duty version shown

90951G36

## ENGINE IDENTIFICATION AND SPECIFICATIONS

| Year | Model | Engine ID/VIN | Engine Displacement Liters (cc) | No. of Cyl. | Engine Type | Fuel System Type | Net Horsepower @ rpm | Net Torque @ rpm (ft. lbs.) | Bore x Stroke (in.) | Compression Ratio | Oil Pressure @ rpm |
|---|---|---|---|---|---|---|---|---|---|---|---|
| 1997 | 850 | B5254S/55 | 2.4(2435) | 5 | DOHC | EFI | 168@6100 | 162@4700 | 3.27 x 3.54 | 10.5:1 | 49.8@4000 |
| | 850GLT | B5254T/56 | 2.4(2435) | 5 | DOHC | EFI | 190@5200 | 191@1800 | 3.27 x 3.54 | 10.5:1 | 49.8@4000 |
| | 850T-5 | B5234T/57 | 2.3(2319) | 5 | DOHC | EFI | 222@5200 | 221@2100 | 3.19 x 3.54 | 8.5:1 | 49.8@4000 |
| | 850R | B5254FT/58 | 2.3(2319) | 5 | DOHC | EFI | 240@5600 | 221@2100 | 3.19 x 3.54 | 8.5:1 | 49.8@4000 |
| | 960 | B6304S/96 | 2.9(2922) | 6 | DOHC | EFI | 181@5200 | 199@4100 | 3.27 x 3.54 | 10.7:1 | 36@2000 |
| 1998 | S70 | B5254S/55 | 2.4(2435) | 5 | DOHC | EFI | 168@6100 | 162@4700 | 3.27 x 3.54 | 10.5:1 | 49.8@4000 |
| | S70GLT | B5254T/56 | 2.4(2435) | 5 | DOHC | EFI | 190@5200 | 199@1800 | 3.27 x 3.54 | 10.5:1 | 49.8@4000 |
| | S70T-5 | B5234T/57 | 2.3(2319) | 5 | DOHC | EFI | 236@5100 | 243@2100 | 3.19 x 3.54 | 8.5:1 | 49.8@4000 |
| | S90 | B6304T3/53 | 2.9(2922) | 6 | DOHC | EFI | 181@5200 | 199@4100 | 3.27 x 3.54 | 10.7:1 | 36@2000 |
| | C70 | B5254S/55 | 2.4(2435) | 5 | DOHC | EFI | 168@6100 | 162@4700 | 3.27 x 3.54 | 10.5:1 | 49.8@4000 |
| | V70 | B5254S/55 | 2.4(2435) | 5 | DOHC | EFI | 168@6100 | 162@4700 | 3.27 x 3.54 | 10.5:1 | 49.8@4000 |
| | V70GLT | B5254T/56 | 2.4(2435) | 5 | DOHC | EFI | 190@5200 | 199@1800 | 3.27 x 3.54 | 10.5:1 | 49.8@4000 |
| | V70T-5 | B5234T/57 | 2.3(2319) | 5 | DOHC | EFI | 236@5100 | 243@2100 | 3.19 x 3.54 | 8.5:1 | 49.8@4000 |
| | V70R AWD | B5254T/56 | 2.4(2435) | 5 | DOHC | EFI | 236@5100 | 243@2100 | 3.27 x 3.54 | 10.5:1 | 49.8@4000 |
| | V70XC AWD | B5234T/57 | 2.3(2319) | 5 | DOHC | EFI | 236@5200 | 243@2700 | 3.19 x 3.54 | 8.5:1 | 49.8@4000 |
| | V90 | B6304S/96 | 2.9(2922) | 6 | DOHC | EFI | 181@5200 | 199@4100 | 3.27 x 3.54 | 10.7:1 | 36@2000 |

SOHC = Single Overhead Camshaft
DOHC = Double Overhead Camshaft
EFI = Electronic Fuel Injection

90951C03

## ENGINE IDENTIFICATION AND SPECIFICATIONS

| Year | Model | Engine ID/VIN | Engine Displacement Liters (cc) | No. of Cyl. | Engine Type | Fuel System Type | Net Horsepower @ rpm | Net Torque @ rpm (ft. lbs.) | Bore x Stroke (in.) | Compression Ratio | Oil Pressure @ rpm |
|---|---|---|---|---|---|---|---|---|---|---|---|
| 1990 | 240 | B230F/88 | 2.3(2316) | 4 | SOHC | EFI | 114@5400 | 136@2750 | 3.78 x 3.15 | 9.8:1 | 35-85 @ 2000 |
| | 240DL | B230F/88 | 2.3(2316) | 4 | SOHC | EFI | 114@5400 | 136@2750 | 3.78 x 3.15 | 9.8:1 | 35-85 @ 2000 |
| | 740 | B230F/88 | 2.3(2316) | 4 | SOHC | EFI | 114@5400 | 136@2750 | 3.78 x 3.15 | 9.8:1 | 35-85@2000 |
| | 740GL | B230F/88 | 2.3(2316) | 4 | SOHC | EFI | 114@5400 | 136@2750 | 3.78 x 3.15 | 9.8:1 | 35-85@2000 |
| | 740GLE | B234F/89 | 2.3(2316) | 4 | DOHC | EFI | 150@5700 | 150@4450 | 3.78 x 3.15 | 10.0:1 | 73@3000 |
| | 740Turbo | B230FT/87 | 2.3(2316) | 4 | SOHC | EFI | 160@5300 | 187@2900 | 3.78 x 3.15 | 9.8:1 | 35-85@2000 |
| | 760GLE | B280F/69 | 2.8(2849) | 6 | SOHC | EFI | 146@5100 | 173@3750 | 3.58 x 2.86 | 9.5:1 | 57@3000 |
| | 760Turbo | B230FT/87 | 2.3(2316) | 4 | SOHC | EFI | 160@5300 | 187@2900 | 3.78 x 3.15 | 8.7:1 | 35-85@2000 |
| | 780 | B280F/69 | 2.8(2849) | 6 | SOHC | EFI | 146@5100 | 173@3750 | 3.58 x 2.86 | 9.5:1 | 57@3000 |
| | 780Turbo | B230FT/87 | 2.3(2316) | 4 | SOHC | EFI | 175@5300 | 187@2900 | 3.78 x 3.15 | 8.7:1 | 35-85@2000 |
| 1991 | 240GL | B230F/88 | 2.3(2316) | 4 | SOHC | EFI | 114@5400 | 136@2750 | 3.78 x 3.15 | 9.8:1 | 35-85@2000 |
| | 240DL | B230F/88 | 2.3(2316) | 4 | SOHC | EFI | 114@5400 | 136@2750 | 3.78 x 3.15 | 9.8:1 | 35-85@2000 |
| | 740GL | B230F/88 | 2.3(2316) | 4 | SOHC | EFI | 114@5400 | 136@2750 | 3.78 x 3.15 | 9.8:1 | 35-85@2000 |
| | 740Turbo | B230FT/87 | 2.3(2316) | 4 | SOHC | EFI | 162@5300 | 195@2900 | 3.78 x 3.15 | 8.7:1 | 35-85@2000 |
| | 940SE | B230FT/87 | 2.3(2316) | 4 | SOHC | EFI | 162@4800 | 195@3450 | 3.78 x 3.15 | 8.7:1 | 35-85@2000 |
| | 940Turbo | B230FT/87 | 2.3(2316) | 4 | SOHC | EFI | 162@4800 | 195@3450 | 3.78 x 3.15 | 8.7:1 | 35-85@2000 |
| | 940GLE | B234F/89 | 2.3(2316) | 4 | DOHC | EFI | 153@5700 | 150@4450 | 3.78 x 3.15 | 10.0:1 | 73@3000 |
| | 960 | B6304F/95 | 2.9(2922) | 6 | DOHC | EFI | 201@6000 | 197@4300 | 3.27 x 3.54 | 10.7:1 | 36@2000 |
| | Coupe | B230FT/87 | 2.3(2316) | 4 | SOHC | EFI | 175@5300 | 187@2900 | 3.78 x 3.15 | 8.7:1 | 35-85@2000 |
| 1992 | 240 | B230F/88 | 2.3(2316) | 4 | SOHC | EFI | 114@5400 | 136@2750 | 3.78 x 3.15 | 9.8:1 | 35-85@2000 |
| | 850 | B5254S/55 | 2.4(2435) | 5 | DOHC | EFI | 168@6200 | 162@3300 | 3.27 x 3.54 | 10.5:1 | 49.8@4000 |
| | 940 | B230F/88 | 2.3(2316) | 4 | SOHC | EFI | 114@5400 | 136@2750 | 3.78 x 3.15 | 9.8:1 | 35-85@2000 |
| | 940 Turbo | B230FT/87 | 2.3(2316) | 4 | SOHC | EFI | 162@4800 | 195@3450 | 3.78 x 3.15 | 8.7:1 | 35-85@2000 |
| | 960 | B6304F/95 | 2.9(2922) | 6 | DOHC | EFI | 201@6000 | 197@4300 | 3.27 x 3.54 | 10.7:1 | 36@2000 |
| 1993 | 240 | B230F/88 | 2.3(2316) | 4 | SOHC | EFI | 114@5400 | 136@2750 | 3.78 x 3.15 | 9.8:1 | 35-85@2000 |
| | 850 | B5254S/55 | 2.4(2435) | 5 | DOHC | EFI | 168@6200 | 162@3300 | 3.27 x 3.54 | 10.5:1 | 49.8@4000 |
| | 940 | B230F/88 | 2.3(2316) | 4 | SOHC | EFI | 114@5400 | 136@2750 | 3.78 x 3.15 | 9.8:1 | 35-85@2000 |
| | 850Turbo | B5234T/57 | 2.3(2319) | 5 | DOHC | EFI | 222@5200 | 221@2100 | 3.19 x 3.54 | 8.5:1 | 49.8@4000 |
| | 960 | B6304F/95 | 2.9(2922) | 6 | DOHC | EFI | 201@6000 | 197@4300 | 3.27 x 3.54 | 10.7:1 | 36@2000 |
| 1994 | 940 | B230F/88 | 2.3(2316) | 4 | SOHC | EFI | 114@5400 | 136@2750 | 3.78 x 3.15 | 9.8:1 | 35-85@2000 |
| | 940Turbo | B230FT/87 | 2.3(2316) | 4 | SOHC | EFI | 162@4800 | 195@3450 | 3.78 x 3.15 | 8.7:1 | 35-85@2000 |
| | 850 | B5254S/55 | 2.4(2435) | 5 | DOHC | EFI | 168@6200 | 162@3300 | 3.27 x 3.54 | 10.5:1 | 49.8@4000 |
| | 850Turbo | B5234T/57 | 2.3(2319) | 5 | DOHC | EFI | 222@5200 | 221@2100 | 3.19 x 3.54 | 8.5:1 | 49.8@4000 |
| | 960 | B6304F/95 | 2.9(2922) | 6 | DOHC | EFI | 201@6000 | 197@4300 | 3.27 x 3.54 | 10.7:1 | 36@2000 |
| 1995 | 940 | B230F/88 | 2.3(2316) | 4 | SOHC | EFI | 114@5400 | 136@2750 | 3.78 x 3.15 | 9.8:1 | 35-85@2000 |
| | 940Turbo | B230FT/87 | 2.3(2316) | 4 | SOHC | EFI | 162@4800 | 195@3450 | 3.78 x 3.15 | 8.7:1 | 35-85@2000 |
| | 850 | B5254S/55 | 2.4(2435) | 5 | DOHC | EFI | 168@6200 | 162@3300 | 3.27 x 3.54 | 10.5:1 | 49.8@4000 |
| | 850GLT | B5234T/57 | 2.3(2319) | 5 | DOHC | EFI | 222@5200 | 221@2100 | 3.19 x 3.54 | 8.5:1 | 49.8@4000 |
| | 960 | B6304S/95 | 2.9(2922) | 6 | DOHC | EFI | 201@6000 | 197@4300 | 3.27 x 3.54 | 10.7:1 | 36@2000 |
| 1996 | 850 | B5254S/55 | 2.4(2435) | 5 | DOHC | EFI | 168@6100 | 162@4700 | 3.27 x 3.54 | 10.5:1 | 49.8@4000 |
| | 850GLT | B5254T/56 | 2.4(2435) | 5 | DOHC | EFI | 190@5200 | 191@1800 | 3.27 x 3.54 | 10.5:1 | 49.8@4000 |
| | 850T-5 | B5234T/57 | 2.3(2319) | 5 | DOHC | EFI | 222@5200 | 221@2100 | 3.19 x 3.54 | 8.5:1 | 49.8@4000 |
| | 850R | B5254FT/58 | 2.3(2319) | 5 | DOHC | EFI | 240@5600 | 221@2100 | 3.19 x 3.54 | 8.5:1 | 49.8@4000 |
| | 960 | B6304S/96 | 2.9(2922) | 6 | DOHC | EFI | 181@5200 | 199@4100 | 3.27 x 3.54 | 10.7:1 | 36@2000 |

EFI = Electronic Fuel Injection

90951C02

**ROUTINE MAINTENANCE AND TUNE-UP**

### UNDERHOOD MAINTENANCE COMPONENT LOCATIONS—2.3L 5-CYLINDER TURBOCHARGED ENGINE

1. Oil fill cap
2. Brake master cylinder reservoir
3. Power steering pump reservoir
4. Coolant expansion tank
5. Washer fluid bottle
6. Fuse box
7. Transaxle dipstick (under hose)
8. Engine oil dipstick
9. Battery
10. Air cleaner housing
11. PCV valve (throttle pulley cover must be removed)

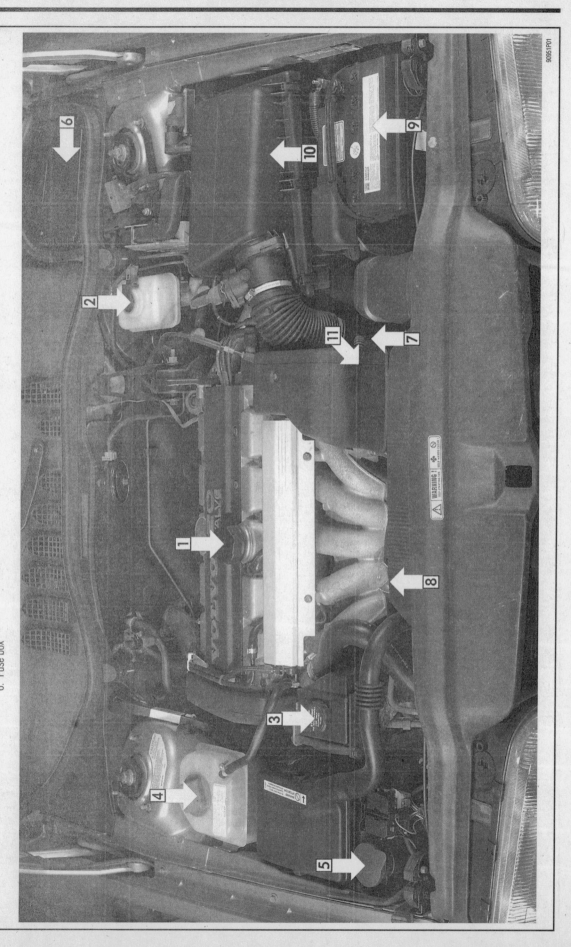

**UNDERHOOD MAINTENANCE COMPONENT LOCATIONS—2.4L 5-CYLINDER ENGINE**

1. Oil fill cap
2. Brake master cylinder reservoir
3. Power steering pump reservoir
4. Coolant expansion tank
5. Washer fluid bottle
6. Fuse box
7. Transaxle dipstick
8. Engine oil dipstick
9. Battery
10. Air cleaner housing
11. PCV valve (throttle pulley cover must be removed)

Proper maintenance and tune-up are the key to long and trouble-free vehicle life, and the work can yield its own rewards. Studies have shown that a properly tuned and maintained vehicle can achieve better gas mileage than an out-of-tune vehicle. As a conscientious owner and driver, set aside a Saturday morning, say once a month, to check or replace items that could cause major problems later. Keep your own personal log to jot down which services you performed, how much the parts cost you, the date, and the exact odometer reading at the time. Keep all receipts for such items as engine oil and filters, so that they may be referred to in case of related problems or to determine operating expenses. As a do-it-yourselfer, these receipts are the only proof you have that the required maintenance was performed. In the event of a warranty problem, these receipts will be invaluable.

The literature provided with your vehicle when it was originally delivered includes the factory recommended maintenance schedule. If you no longer have this literature, replacement copies are usually available from the dealer. A maintenance schedule is provided later in this section, in case you do not have the factory literature.

## Air Cleaner (Element)

### REMOVAL & INSTALLATION

#### ▶ See Figures 40, 41 and 42

The air cleaner assembly, on non-turbocharged engines, is located on the driver's side of the vehicle, near the radiator. On turbocharged engine, the air cleaner assembly is located on the passenger side of the vehicle, near the radiator.

1. Disconnect the negative battery cable.
2. Unsnap the clips retaining the air cleaner housing halves.
3. Separate the air cleaner housing halves.
4. Remove the air cleaner cartridge.

**To install:**

5. Install the air cleaner cartridge in the lower housing.
6. Place housing halves together and snap retaining clips into place.
7. Connect the negative battery cable.

## Fuel Filter

### REMOVAL & INSTALLATION

#### ▶ See Figures 43 thru 48

The fuel filter is located underneath the vehicle near the fuel tank, or on the driver's side of the firewall. It is recommended that the fuel filter be replaced every 60,000 miles (96,000 km). The fuel filter should be replaced, immediately, upon evidence of dirt in the fuel system.

1. Properly relieve the fuel system pressure, as outlined in Section 5.
2. Disconnect the negative battery cable.
3. Raise and safely support the vehicle.
4. Remove the fuel filter cover (if equipped).

➡**Have a container ready when loosening the fuel lines. Residual fuel in the lines will come out.**

5. Place a suitable container in position.
6. Loosen the fuel filter connections. If your vehicle has threaded type fittings:
    a. Remove the lines from the filter using the proper size wrenches.

### ✳✳ WARNING

**Always use flared wrenches (special hex wrench) to grip fuel lines or filter connections, when loosening.**

7. If your vehicle is equipped with quick-connect fittings:
    a. Using a 17mm wrench, depress the retaining tab on the fitting, and remove the line. Repeat for the filter's other line.
8. Remove the clamp retaining the fuel filter to the bracket.

**To install:**

9. Transfer the bracket to the new filter.
10. Note the direction on the fuel filter and install the filter to the bracket.

Fig. 40 Unsnap the retaining clips . . .
90951P16

Fig. 41 . . . and lift up the air cleaner lid . . .
90951P17

Fig. 42 . . . then remove the filter from the housing
90951P18

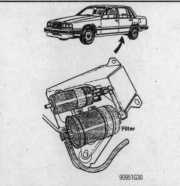
Fig. 43 Typical fuel filter location near the fuel tank
90951G30

Fig. 44 A Schrader valve is installed in the fuel feed line to relieve fuel pressure before changing the filter
90951P83

Fig. 45 Use a 17mm wrench to depress the tabs on the quick-connect fittings
90951P84

Fig. 46 Plugging the line and filter will result in less fuel being spilled, as well as prevent dirt from entering

Fig. 47 Unfasten the clamp holding the filter . . .

Fig. 48 . . . and remove the filter

11. Connect the fuel lines to the fuel filter. If your vehicle has threaded type fittings:

    a. Install the lines on the filter.
    b. Check to ensure that the copper seals are correctly installed.
    c. Tighten the lines to the proper torque.

12. If your vehicle has quick-connect fittings:

    a. Push the fittings onto the ends of the filter.
    b. There should be an audible click when the fittings are engaged.

13. Install the fuel filter cover (if equipped).
14. Lower the vehicle.
15. Reconnect the negative battery cable.

## PCV Valve

Volvo refers to the filter element in the Crankcase Ventilation system as the flame guard.

### REMOVAL & INSTALLATION

#### B230F, B230FT and B280F Engines

▶ See Figure 49

➡ Replace the flame guard at stated intervals.

1. Disconnect the negative battery cable.
2. Remove the hose from the nipple on the intake manifold.
3. Check the hoses and nipples for condition and clogging. Failure to do so can result in loss of oil.
4. Remove the flame guard.

**To install:**

5. Clean out the nipple in the intake manifold.
6. Install the flame guard in the nipple.
7. Install the hose on the nipple.
8. Connect the negative battery cable.

#### B5254S, B5234T, B5254T, B5254FT and B5234T3 Engines

▶ See Figures 50, 51, 52 and 53

1. Disconnect the negative battery cable.
2. Remove the throttle pulley cover.
3. Undo the hose clamp and remove the inlet hose to air cleaner housing.
4. Remove the flame trap from the hose by rotating it 0.59 inches (15mm) to the left.
5. Remove the flame trap from the inlet hose using a small screwdriver or pick.

**To install:**

6. Inspect the hoses for clogs, and clean out if necessary.
7. Insert a new flame trap into the inlet hose and rotate it back to the original position.
8. Install the inlet hose onto the air cleaner housing and install the hose clamp.

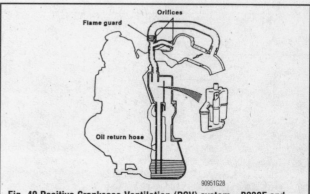

Fig. 49 Positive Crankcase Ventilation (PCV) system—B230F and B230FT engines

Fig. 50 Unfasten the retaining bolt from the throttle pulley cover and remove the cover

Fig. 51 Rotate the flame trap housing to remove it from the intake hose

Fig. 52 Remove the flame trap from its housing

Fig. 53 Inspect the O-ring in the intake hose before installing the flame trap

9. Install the throttle pulley cover.
10. Connect the negative battery cable.

### B6304F and B234F Engines

♦ See Figure 54

1. Disconnect the negative battery cable.
2. Rotate the flame trap outer casing 0.59 inches (15mm) to the left and remove the inlet hose.
3. Remove the flame trap from the inlet hose.

**To install:**
4. Inspect the hoses for clogs, and clean out if necessary.
5. Insert a new flame trap into the inlet hose.
6. Install the inlet hose onto the manifold and rotate the outer casing back to its original position.
7. Connect the negative battery cable.

## Evaporative Canister

### SERVICING

♦ See Figure 55

➡ For more information on the Evaporative Emissions system, please refer to Section 4 of this manual.

The fuel evaporative emission control system stores gasoline vapors which rise from the sealed fuel tank. The system prevents these unburned hydrocarbons from polluting the atmosphere. It consists of a charcoal vapor storage canister, check or purge valves and the interconnecting vapor lines.

The canister is located in the engine compartment, or under the wheelwell trim. The canister and vapor lines should be inspected for damage or leaks at least every 24,000 miles (38,600 km). Repair or replace any old or cracked hoses. Replace the canister if it is cracked or damaged in any way. Other than inspecting the lines and the canister for damage, there is no periodic maintenance for this item.

## Battery

### PRECAUTIONS

Always use caution when working on or near the battery. Never allow a tool to bridge the gap between the negative and positive battery terminals. Also, be careful not to allow a tool to provide a ground between the positive cable/terminal and any metal component on the vehicle. Either of these conditions will cause a short circuit, leading to sparks and possible personal injury.

Do not smoke, have an open flame or create sparks near a battery; the gases contained in the battery are very explosive and, if ignited, could cause severe injury or death.

All batteries, regardless of type, should be carefully secured by a battery hold-down device. If this is not done, the battery terminals or casing may crack from stress applied to the battery during vehicle operation. A battery which is not secured may allow acid to leak out, making it discharge faster; such leaking corrosive acid can also eat away at components under the hood.

Always visually inspect the battery case for cracks, leakage and corrosion. A white corrosive substance on the battery case or on nearby components would indicate a leaking or cracked battery. If the battery is cracked, it should be replaced immediately.

### GENERAL MAINTENANCE

♦ See Figure 56

A battery that is not sealed must be checked periodically for electrolyte level. You cannot add water to a sealed maintenance-free battery (though not all maintenance-free batteries are sealed); however, a sealed battery must also be checked for proper electrolyte level, as indicated by the color of the built-in hydrometer "eye."

Always keep the battery cables and terminals free of corrosion. Check these components about once a year. Refer to the removal, installation and cleaning procedures outlined in this section.

Keep the top of the battery clean, as a film of dirt can help completely discharge a battery that is not used for long periods. A solution of baking soda and water may be used for cleaning, but be careful to flush this off with clear water. DO NOT let any of the solution into the filler holes. Baking soda neutralizes battery acid and will de-activate a battery cell.

Batteries in vehicles which are not operated on a regular basis can fall victim to parasitic loads (small current drains which are constantly drawing current from the battery). Normal parasitic loads may drain a battery on a vehicle that is in storage and not used for 6–8 weeks. Vehicles that have additional accessories such as a cellular phone, an alarm system or other devices that increase parasitic load may discharge a battery sooner. If the vehicle is to be stored for 6–8 weeks in a secure area and the alarm system, if present, is not necessary, the negative battery cable should be disconnected at the onset of storage to protect the battery charge.

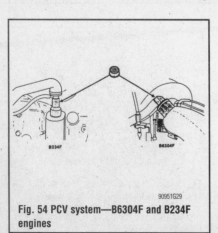

Fig. 54 PCV system—B6304F and B234F engines

Fig. 55 The evaporative canister is accessed from underneath the vehicle— 850 series

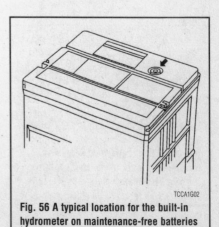

Fig. 56 A typical location for the built-in hydrometer on maintenance-free batteries

Remember that constantly discharging and recharging will shorten battery life. Take care not to allow a battery to be needlessly discharged.

## BATTERY FLUID

Check the battery electrolyte level at least once a month, or more often in hot weather or during periods of extended vehicle operation. On non-sealed batteries, the level can be checked either through the case on translucent batteries or by removing the cell caps on opaque-cased types. The electrolyte level in each cell should be kept filled to the split ring inside each cell, or the line marked on the outside of the case.

If the level is low, add only distilled water through the opening until the level is correct. Each cell is separate from the others, so each must be checked and filled individually. Distilled water should be used, because the chemicals and minerals found in most drinking water are harmful to the battery and could significantly shorten its life.

If water is added in freezing weather, the vehicle should be driven several miles to allow the water to mix with the electrolyte. Otherwise, the battery could freeze.

Although some maintenance-free batteries have removable cell caps for access to the electrolyte, the electrolyte condition and level on all sealed maintenance-free batteries must be checked using the built-in hydrometer "eye." The exact type of eye varies between battery manufacturers, but most apply a sticker to the battery itself explaining the possible readings. When in doubt, refer to the battery manufacturer's instructions to interpret battery condition using the built-in hydrometer.

➥**Although the readings from built-in hydrometers found in sealed batteries may vary, a green eye usually indicates a properly charged battery with sufficient fluid level. A dark eye is normally an indicator of a battery with sufficient fluid, but one which may be low in charge. And a light or yellow eye is usually an indication that electrolyte supply has dropped below the necessary level for battery (and hydrometer) operation. In this last case, sealed batteries with an insufficient electrolyte level must usually be discarded.**

### Checking the Specific Gravity

▶ **See Figures 57, 58 and 59**

A hydrometer is required to check the specific gravity on all batteries that are not maintenance-free. On batteries that are maintenance-free, the specific gravity is checked by observing the built-in hydrometer "eye" on the top of the battery case. Check with your battery's manufacturer for proper interpretation of its built-in hydrometer readings.

### ❊❊❊ CAUTION

**Battery electrolyte contains sulfuric acid. If you should splash any on your skin or in your eyes, flush the affected area with plenty of clear water. If it lands in your eyes, get medical help immediately.**

The fluid (sulfuric acid solution) contained in the battery cells will tell you many things about the condition of the battery. Because the cell plates must be kept submerged below the fluid level in order to operate, maintaining the fluid level is extremely important. And, because the specific gravity of the acid is an indication of electrical charge, testing the fluid can be an aid in determining if the battery must be replaced. A battery in a vehicle with a properly operating charging system should require little maintenance, but careful, periodic inspection should reveal problems before they leave you stranded.

As stated earlier, the specific gravity of a battery's electrolyte level can be used as an indication of battery charge. At least once a year, check the specific gravity of the battery. It should be between 1.20 and 1.26 on the gravity scale. Most auto supply stores carry a variety of inexpensive battery testing hydrometers. These can be used on any non-sealed battery to test the specific gravity in each cell.

The battery testing hydrometer has a squeeze bulb at one end and a nozzle at the other. Battery electrolyte is sucked into the hydrometer until the float is lifted from its seat. The specific gravity is then read by noting the position of the float. If gravity is low in one or more cells, the battery should be slowly charged and checked again to see if the gravity has come up. Generally, if after charging, the specific gravity between any two cells varies more than 50 points (0.50), the battery should be replaced, as it can no longer produce sufficient voltage to guarantee proper operation.

## CABLES

▶ **See Figures 60, 61, 62, 63 and 64**

Once a year (or as necessary), the battery terminals and the cable clamps should be cleaned. Loosen the clamps and remove the cables, negative cable first. On batteries with posts on top, the use of a puller specially made for this purpose is recommended. These are inexpensive and available in most auto parts stores. Side terminal battery cables are secured with a small bolt.

Clean the cable clamps and the battery terminal with a wire brush, until all corrosion, grease, etc., is removed and the metal is shiny. It is especially important to clean the inside of the clamp thoroughly (an old knife is useful here), since a small deposit of foreign material or oxidation there will prevent a sound electrical connection and inhibit either starting or charging. Special tools are available for cleaning these parts, one type for conventional top post batteries and another type for side terminal batteries. It is also a good idea to apply some dielectric grease to the terminal, as this will aid in the prevention of corrosion.

After the clamps and terminals are clean, reinstall the cables, negative cable last; DO NOT hammer the clamps onto battery posts. Tighten the clamps securely, but do not distort them. Give the clamps and terminals a thin external coating of grease after installation, to retard corrosion.

Check the cables at the same time that the terminals are cleaned. If the cable insulation is cracked or broken, or if the ends are frayed, the cable should be replaced with a new cable of the same length and gauge.

TCCA1P07

**Fig. 57 On non-maintenance-free batteries, the fluid level can be checked through the case on translucent models; the cell caps must be removed on other models**

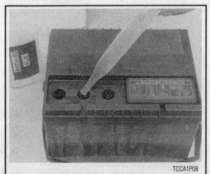

TCCA1P08

**Fig. 58 If the fluid level is low, add only distilled water through the opening until the level is correct**

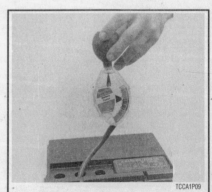

TCCA1P09

**Fig. 59 Check the specific gravity of the battery's electrolyte with a hydrometer**

Fig. 60 Maintenance is performed with household items and with special tools like this post cleaner

Fig. 61 The underside of this special battery tool has a wire brush to clean post terminals

Fig. 62 Place the tool over the battery posts and twist to clean until the metal is shiny

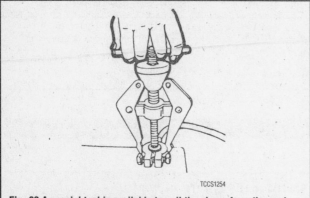

Fig. 63 A special tool is available to pull the clamp from the post

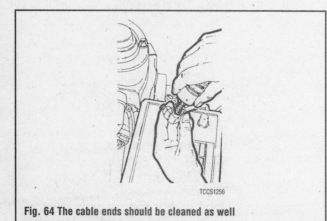

Fig. 64 The cable ends should be cleaned as well

## CHARGING

> ※※ CAUTION
>
> **The chemical reaction which takes place in all batteries generates explosive hydrogen gas. A spark can cause the battery to explode and splash acid. To avoid serious personal injury, be sure there is proper ventilation and take appropriate fire safety precautions when connecting, disconnecting, or charging a battery and when using jumper cables.**

A battery should be charged at a slow rate to keep the plates inside from getting too hot. However, if some maintenance-free batteries are allowed to discharge until they are almost "dead," they may have to be charged at a high rate to bring them back to "life." Always follow the charger manufacturer's instructions on charging the battery.

## REMOVAL & INSTALLATION

♦ **See Figures 65 thru 70**

1. Disconnect the negative and then the positive battery cables.
2. Loosen the hold-down clamp or strap retainers.
3. Remove the battery hold-down device.
4. Remove the battery from the vehicle.

While the battery is removed, it is a good idea and opportunity to check the condition of the battery tray. Clear it of any debris, and check it for soundness (the battery tray can be cleaned with a baking soda and water solution). Rust should be wire brushed away, and the metal given a couple coats of anti-rust paint.

**To install:**

5. Install the battery and tighten the hold-down clamp or strap securely. Do not overtighten, as this can crack the battery case.
6. Connect the positive and then the negative battery cables.

Fig. 65 Loosen the battery hold-down device retainer . . .

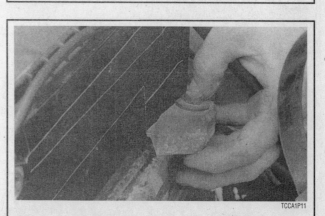

Fig. 66 . . . then remove the battery hold-down device

Fig. 67 Remove the battery from the vehicle

Fig. 68 Use a wire brush to clean any rust from the battery tray

Fig. 69 Brush on a solution of baking soda and water to clean the tray

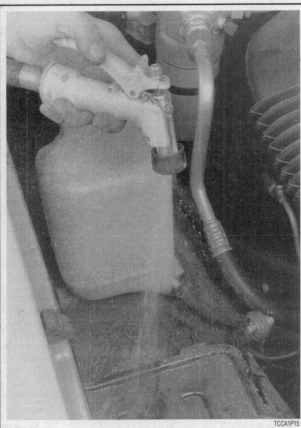

Fig. 70 After cleaning the tray thoroughly, wash it off with some water

## REPLACEMENT

When it becomes necessary to replace the battery, select one with an amperage rating equal to or greater than the battery originally installed. Deterioration and just plain aging of the battery cables, starter motor, and associated wires makes the battery's job harder in successive years. The slow increase in electrical resistance over time makes it prudent to install a new battery with a greater capacity than the old.

## Belts

### INSPECTION

▶ **See Figures 71, 72, 73, 74 and 75**

Inspect the belts for signs of glazing or cracking. A glazed belt will be perfectly smooth from slippage, while a good belt will have a slight texture of fabric

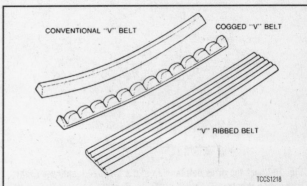

Fig. 71 There are typically 3 types of accessory drive belts found on vehicles today

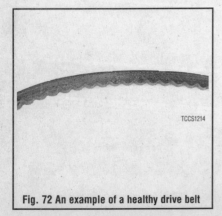

Fig. 72 An example of a healthy drive belt

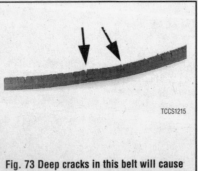

Fig. 73 Deep cracks in this belt will cause flex, building up heat that will eventually lead to belt failure

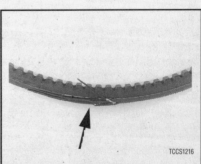

Fig. 74 The cover of this belt is worn, exposing the critical reinforcing cords to excessive wear

TCCS1217

**Fig. 75 Installing too wide a belt can result in serious belt wear and/or breakage**

visible. Cracks will usually start at the inner edge of the belt and run outward. All worn or damaged drive belts should be replaced immediately. It is best to replace all drive belts at one time, as a preventive maintenance measure, during this service operation.

Tension of the drive belts is done by depressing a flat part of the belt, midway between two components. If the belt moves $1/4$—$3/8$ of an inch, it has proper tension, if not, proceed to adjustment or replacement if the belt is old and stretched.

## ADJUSTMENT

### V-Belts

▶ **See Figure 76**

1. Perform the inspection before adjusting the drive belts.
2. Loosen the adjusting bolt(s) and using a suitable tool, rotate the accessory in the proper direction to increase belt tension.

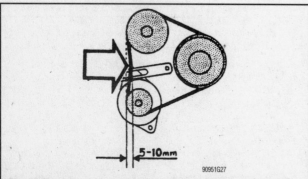

5-10mm

90951G27

**Fig. 76 Check the drive belt tension at the arrowed location on vehicles with a V-belt**

3. Check the tension while still supporting the accessory; if the tension is okay, tighten the adjusting bolts, then recheck the tension.

### Serpentine Belt

All engines with a serpentine belt use an automatic drive belt tensioner. No adjustment is necessary.

## REMOVAL & INSTALLATION

### V-Belts

1. Disconnect the negative battery cable.
2. Loosen the mounting and adjusting bolts on the accessory and move it to its extreme loosest position, generally by moving it toward the center of the motor.
3. Remove the old belt. Some belts run around a third or idler pulley, which acts as an additional pivot in the belt's path. It may be possible to loosen the idler pulley as well as the main component, making your job much easier. Depending on which belt(s) you are changing, it may be necessary to loosen or remove other interfering belts to get at the one(s) you want.
4. Check the pulleys for dirt or built-up material which could affect belt contact.
5. Carefully install the new belt. Gentle pressure in the direction of rotation is helpful.
6. Adjust the belt tension.
7. Retighten the mounting bolts and recheck the tension.
8. Connect the negative battery cable.

### Serpentine Belt

▶ **See Figures 77, 78 and 79**

1. Disconnect the negative battery cable.
2. Using a suitable tool attached to the drive belt tensioner pulley, rotate the tensioner to release the tension.
3. Remove the drive belt from the pulley, and remove the drive belt from the accessory and crank pulleys, noting its proper routing.
   **To install:**
4. Install the new belt (if being replaced) around the accessories and the crankshaft.
5. Rotate the automatic tensioner to release the tension and slip the belt under the tensioner pulley.
6. Check the belt for proper routing and tension.
7. Connect the negative battery cable.

## Timing Belts

### SERVICING

Most Volvo engines utilize a timing belt to drive the camshaft from the crankshaft's turning motion and to maintain proper valve timing. Some manufacturers schedule periodic timing belt replacement to assure optimum engine perfor-

90951P36

**Fig. 77 The automatic belt tensioner is tough to access; a special serpentine belt tool may be helpful**

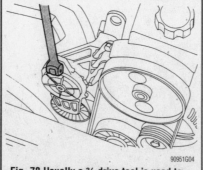

90951G04

**Fig. 78 Usually a $3/8$ drive tool is used to relieve the belt tensioner on the 2.9L 6-cylinder engine**

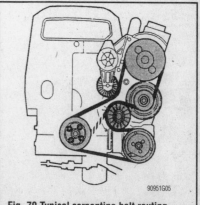

90951G05

**Fig. 79 Typical serpentine belt routing**

mance, to make sure the motorist is never stranded should the belt break (as the engine will stop instantly) and, for some (manufacturers with interference motors), to prevent the possibility of severe internal engine damage should the belt break.

Volvo recommends replacing the belt at different times on different models; refer to the maintenance charts to cross reference the vehicle you own or are working on.

Whether or not you decide to replace it, you would be wise to check it periodically to make sure it has not become damaged or worn. Generally speaking, a severely worn belt may cause engine performance to drop dramatically, but a damaged belt (which could give out suddenly) may not give as much warning. In general, anytime the engine timing cover(s) is (are) removed, you should inspect the belt for premature parting, severe cracks or missing teeth.

## Hoses

### REMOVAL & INSTALLATION

▶ **See Figures 80, 81, 82 and 83**

Upper and lower radiator hoses, along with the heater hoses, should be checked for deterioration, leaks and loose hose clamps at least every 15,000 miles (24,000 km). It is also wise to check the hoses periodically in early spring and at the beginning of the fall or winter when you are performing other maintenance. A quick visual inspection could discover a weakened hose which might have left you stranded if it had remained unrepaired.

Whenever you are checking the hoses, make sure the engine and cooling system are cold. Visually inspect for cracking, rotting or collapsed hoses, and replace as necessary. Run your hand along the length of the hose. If a weak or swollen spot is noted when squeezing the hose wall, the hose should be replaced.

1. Disconnect the negative battery cable.
2. Remove the radiator pressure cap.

Fig. 80 The cracks developing along this hose are a result of age-related hardening

TCCS1219

**✳✳ CAUTION**

**Never remove the pressure cap while the engine is running, or personal injury from scalding hot coolant or steam may result. If possible, wait until the engine has cooled to remove the pressure cap. If this is not possible, wrap a thick cloth around the pressure cap and turn it slowly to the stop. Step back while the pressure is released from the cooling system. When you are sure all the pressure has been released, use the cloth to turn and remove the cap.**

3. Position a clean container under the radiator and/or engine draincock or plug, then open the drain and allow the cooling system to drain to an appropriate level. For some upper hoses, only a little coolant must be drained. To remove hoses positioned lower on the engine, such as a lower radiator hose, the entire cooling system must be emptied.

**✳✳ CAUTION**

**When draining coolant, keep in mind that cats and dogs are attracted by ethylene glycol antifreeze, and are quite likely to drink any that is left in an uncovered container or in puddles on the ground. This will prove fatal in sufficient quantity. Always drain coolant into a sealable container. Coolant may be reused unless it is contaminated or several years old.**

4. Loosen the hose clamps at each end of the hose requiring replacement. Clamps are usually either of the spring tension type (which require pliers to squeeze the tabs and loosen) or of the screw tension type (which require screw or hex drivers to loosen). Pull the clamps back on the hose away from the connection.
5. Twist, pull and slide the hose off the fitting, taking care not to damage the neck of the component from which the hose is being removed.

➡If the hose is stuck at the connection, do not try to insert a screwdriver or other sharp tool under the hose end in an effort to free it, as the connection and/or hose may become damaged. Heater connections especially may be easily damaged by such a procedure. If the hose is to be replaced, use a single-edged razor blade to make a slice along the portion of the hose which is stuck on the connection, perpendicular to the end of the hose. Do not cut deep so as to prevent damaging the connection. The hose can then be peeled from the connection and discarded.

6. Clean both hose mounting connections. Inspect the condition of the hose clamps and replace them, if necessary.
   **To install:**
7. Dip the ends of the new hose into clean engine coolant to ease installation.
8. Slide the clamps over the replacement hose, then slide the hose ends over the connections into position.
9. Position and secure the clamps at least ¼ in. (6.35mm) from the ends of the hose. Make sure they are located beyond the raised bead of the connector.
10. Close the radiator or engine drains and properly refill the cooling system with the clean drained engine coolant or a suitable mixture of ethylene glycol coolant and water.

Fig. 81 A hose clamp that is too tight can cause older hoses to separate and tear on either side of the clamp

TCCS1220

Fig. 82 A soft spongy hose (identifiable by the swollen section) will eventually burst and should be replaced

TCCS1221

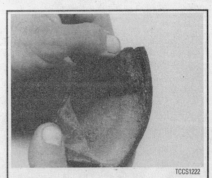

Fig. 83 Hoses are likely to deteriorate from the inside if the cooling system is not periodically flushed

TCCS1222

11. If available, install a pressure tester and check for leaks. If a pressure tester is not available, run the engine until normal operating temperature is reached (allowing the system to naturally pressurize), then check for leaks.

### ☀ CAUTION

**If you are checking for leaks with the system at normal operating temperature, BE EXTREMELY CAREFUL not to touch any moving or hot engine parts. Once temperature has been reached, shut the engine OFF, and check for leaks around the hose fittings and connections which were removed earlier.**

12. Connect the negative battery cable.

### CV-Boots

#### INSPECTION

#### ▶ See Figures 84, 85 and 86

The CV (Constant Velocity) boots should be checked for damage each time the oil is changed and any other time the vehicle is raised for service. These boots keep water, grime, dirt and other damaging-matter from entering the CV-joints. Any of these could cause early CV-joint failure which can be expensive to repair. Heavy grease thrown around the inside of the front wheel(s) and on the brake caliper/drum can be an indication of a torn boot. Thoroughly check the boots for missing clamps and tears. If the boot is damaged, it should be replaced immediately. Please refer to Section 7 for procedures.

### Spark Plugs

#### ▶ See Figure 87

A typical spark plug consists of a metal shell surrounding a ceramic insulator. A metal electrode extends downward through the center of the insulator

and protrudes a small distance. Located at the end of the plug and attached to the side of the outer metal shell is the side electrode. The side electrode bends in at a 90° angle so that its tip is just past and parallel to the tip of the center electrode. The distance between these two electrodes (measured in thousandths of an inch or hundredths of a millimeter) is called the spark plug gap.

The spark plug does not produce a spark, but instead provides a gap across which the current can arc. The coil produces anywhere from 20,000 to 50,000 volts (depending on the type and application) which travels through the wires to the spark plugs. The current passes along the center electrode and jumps the gap to the side electrode, and in doing so, ignites the air/fuel mixture in the combustion chamber.

### SPARK PLUG HEAT RANGE

#### ▶ See Figure 88

Spark plug heat range is the ability of the plug to dissipate heat. The longer the insulator (or the farther it extends into the engine), the hotter the plug will operate; the shorter the insulator (the closer the electrode is to the block's cooling passages) the cooler it will operate. A plug that absorbs little heat and remains too cool will quickly accumulate deposits of oil and carbon since it is not hot enough to burn them off. This leads to plug fouling and consequently to misfiring. A plug that absorbs too much heat will have no deposits but, due to the excessive heat, the electrodes will burn away quickly and might possibly lead to preignition or other ignition problems. Preignition takes place when plug tips get so hot that they glow sufficiently to ignite the air/fuel mixture before the actual spark occurs. This early ignition will usually cause a pinging during low speeds and heavy loads.

The general rule of thumb for choosing the correct heat range when picking a spark plug is: if most of your driving is long distance, high speed travel, use a colder plug; if most of your driving is stop and go, use a hotter plug. Original equipment plugs are generally a good compromise between the 2 styles and most people never have the need to change their plugs from the factory-recommended heat range.

Fig. 84 CV-boots must be inspected periodically for damage

Fig. 85 A torn boot should be replaced immediately

Fig. 86 This CV-boot is leaking; notice the wet residue on the inside part of the boot

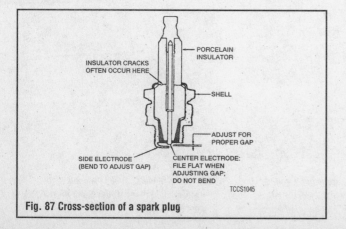

Fig. 87 Cross-section of a spark plug

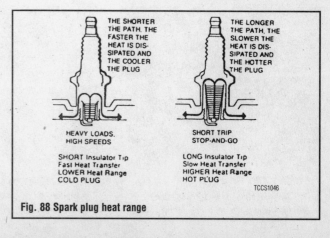

Fig. 88 Spark plug heat range

## REMOVAL & INSTALLATION

▶ **See Figures 89 thru 97**

A set of spark plugs usually requires replacement after about 20,000–30,000 miles (32,000–48,000 km), depending on your style of driving. In normal operation plug gap increases about 0.001 in. (0.025mm) for every 2500 miles (4000 km). As the gap increases, the plug's voltage requirement also increases. It requires a greater voltage to jump the wider gap and about two to three times as much voltage to fire the plug at high speeds than at idle. The improved air/fuel ratio control of modern fuel injection combined with the higher voltage output of modern ignition systems will often allow an engine to run significantly longer on a set of standard spark plugs, but keep in mind that efficiency will drop as the gap widens (along with fuel economy and power).

When you're removing spark plugs, work on one at a time. Don't start by removing the plug wires all at once, because, unless you number them, they may become mixed up. Take a minute before you begin and number the wires with tape.

1. Disconnect the negative battery cable, and if the vehicle has been run recently, allow the engine to thoroughly cool.
2. If equipped, remove the spark plug cover.
3. Carefully twist the spark plug wire boot to loosen it, then pull upward and remove the boot from the plug. Be sure to pull on the boot and not on the wire, otherwise the connector located inside the boot may become separated.
4. Using compressed air, blow any water or debris from the spark plug well to assure that no harmful contaminants are allowed to enter the combustion chamber when the spark plug is removed. If compressed air is not available, use a rag or a brush to clean the area.

➡ **Remove the spark plugs when the engine is cold, if possible, to prevent damage to the threads. If removal of the plugs is difficult, apply a few drops of penetrating oil or silicone spray to the area around the base of the plug, and allow it a few minutes to work.**

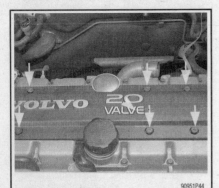
Fig. 89 The spark plug cover is usually retained by six bolts . . .

Fig. 90 . . . which normally are removed with a T25 Torx® head bit

Fig. 91 After the bolts are removed, lift the cover off and carefully set it aside

Fig. 92 Remove the spark plug wire by first gently twisting the boot loose

Fig. 93 After the plug wire is loosened, carefully lift it out of the cylinder head

Fig. 94 The spark plug as mounted in the cylinder head—B5254S engine

Fig. 95 Typically, the spark plugs are removed using a ⅝ inch spark plug socket

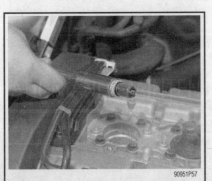
Fig. 96 Inspect the plugs, even if you are replacing them, as they will reveal information about the condition of your engine

Fig. 97 A piece of hose is a good tool for starting the threads of the spark plugs upon installation

5. Using a spark plug socket that is equipped with a rubber insert to properly hold the plug, turn the spark plug counterclockwise to loosen and remove the spark plug from the bore.

## ✳✳ WARNING

**Be sure not to use a flexible extension on the socket. Use of a flexible extension may allow a shear force to be applied to the plug. A shear force could break the plug off in the cylinder head, leading to costly and frustrating repairs.**

**To install:**

6. Inspect the spark plug boot for tears or damage. If a damaged boot is found, the spark plug wire must be replaced.

7. Using a wire feeler gauge, check and adjust the spark plug gap. When using a gauge, the proper size should pass between the electrodes with a slight drag. The next larger size should not be able to pass while the next smaller size should pass freely.

8. Carefully thread the plug into the bore by hand. If resistance is felt before the plug is almost completely threaded, back the plug out and begin threading again. In small, hard to reach areas, an old spark plug wire and boot could be used as a threading tool. The boot will hold the plug while you twist the end of the wire and the wire is supple enough to twist before it would allow the plug to crossthread.

## ✳✳ WARNING

**Do not use the spark plug socket to thread the plugs. Always carefully thread the plug by hand or using an old plug wire to prevent the possibility of crossthreading and damaging the cylinder head bore.**

9. Carefully tighten the spark plug. If the plug you are installing is equipped with a crush washer, seat the plug, then tighten about ¼ turn to crush the washer. If you are installing a tapered seat plug, tighten the plug to specifications provided by the vehicle or plug manufacturer.

10. Apply a small amount of silicone dielectric compound to the end of the spark plug lead or inside the spark plug boot to prevent sticking, then install the boot to the spark plug and push until it clicks into place. The click may be felt or heard, then gently pull back on the boot to assure proper contact.

11. Install the spark plug cover (if equipped).

12. Connect the negative battery cable.

### INSPECTION & GAPPING

▶ **See Figures 98, 99, 100, 101 and 102**

Check the plugs for deposits and wear. If they are not going to be replaced, clean the plugs thoroughly. Remember that any kind of deposit will decrease the efficiency of the plug. Plugs can be cleaned on a spark plug cleaning machine, which can sometimes be found in service stations, or you can do an acceptable job of cleaning with a stiff brush. If the plugs are cleaned, the electrodes must be filed flat. Use an ignition points file, not an emery board or the like, which will leave deposits. The electrodes must be filed perfectly flat with sharp edges; rounded edges reduce the spark plug voltage by as much as 50%.

Check spark plug gap before installation. The ground electrode (the L-shaped one connected to the body of the plug) must be parallel to the center electrode and the specified size wire gauge (please refer to the Tune-Up Specifications chart for details) must pass between the electrodes with a slight drag.

## ✳✳ CAUTION

**NEVER adjust the gap on a used platinum type spark plug.**

Always check the gap on new plugs as they are not always set correctly at the factory. Do not use a flat feeler gauge when measuring the gap on a used plug, because the reading may be inaccurate. A round-wire type gapping tool is the best way to check the gap. The correct gauge should pass through the electrode gap with a slight drag. If you're in doubt, try one size smaller and one larger. The smaller gauge should go through easily, while the larger one shouldn't go through at all. Wire gapping tools usually have a bending tool attached. Use that to adjust the side electrode until the proper distance is obtained. Absolutely never attempt to bend the center electrode. Also, be careful not to bend the side electrode too far or too often as it may weaken and break off within the engine, requiring removal of the cylinder head to retrieve it.

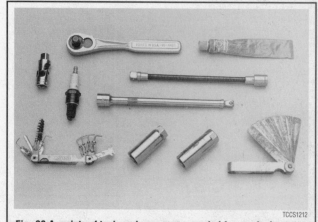

TCCS1212

**Fig. 98 A variety of tools and gauges are needed for spark plug service**

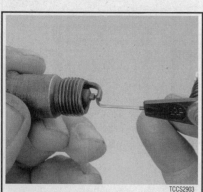

TCCS2903

**Fig. 99 Checking the spark plug gap with a feeler gauge**

TCCS2904

**Fig. 100 Adjusting the spark plug gap**

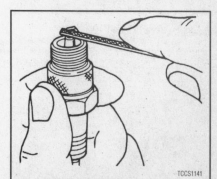

TCCS1141

**Fig. 101 If the standard plug is in good condition, the electrode may be filed flat—WARNING: do not file platinum plugs**

A **normally worn** spark plug should have light tan or gray deposits on the firing tip.

A **carbon fouled** plug, identified by soft, sooty, black deposits, may indicate an improperly tuned vehicle. Check the air cleaner, ignition components and engine control system.

This spark plug has been **left in the engine too long**, as evidenced by the extreme gap. Plugs with such an extreme gap can cause misfiring and stumbling accompanied by a noticeable lack of power.

An **oil fouled** spark plug indicates an engine with worn poston rings and/or bad valve seals allowing excessive oil to enter the chamber.

A **physically damaged** spark plug may be evidence of severe detonation in that cylinder. Watch that cylinder carefully between services, as a continued detonation will not only damage the plug, but could also damage the engine.

A **bridged or almost bridged** spark plug, identified by a build-up between the electrodes caused by excessive carbon or oil build-up on the plug.

TCCA1P40

**Fig. 102 Used spark plugs which show damage may indicate engine problems**

## Spark Plug Wires

### TESTING

▶ **See Figures 103 and 104**

Visually inspect the spark plug cables for burns, cuts, or breaks in the insulation. Check the spark plug boots and the nipples on the distributor cap and coil. Replace any damaged wiring. If no physical damage is obvious, the wires can be checked with an ohmmeter for excessive resistance.

Every 50,000 miles (80,000 km) or 60 months, the resistance of the wires should be checked with an ohmmeter. Wires with excessive resistance will cause misfiring, and may make the engine difficult to start in damp weather.

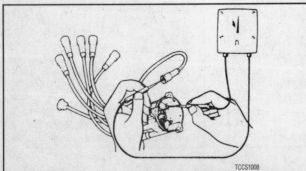

TCCS1008

**Fig. 103 Checking plug wire resistance through the distributor cap with an ohmmeter**

90951P61

**Fig. 104 Checking individual plug wire resistance with a digital ohmmeter**

1. Remove the spark plug wires one at a time.
2. Measure the length of the spark plug wire with a suitable tool. Write down the length.
3. Connect one lead of an ohmmeter to one end of the spark plug wire on the metal conductor, and the other lead to the other end.
4. Replace any wire which shows over 5,000–7,000 ohms per foot.

## REMOVAL & INSTALLATION

The best possible method for installing a new set of wires is to replace ONE AT A TIME, so there can be no mix-up. On distributor equipped engines, don't rely on wiring diagrams or sketches, since the position of the distributor can be changed (unless the distributor is keyed for installation in only one position). Start by replacing the longest wire first. Install the boot firmly over the spark plug. Route the wire in exactly the same path as the original and connect it to the distributor or coil pack (as applicable). Repeat the process for each successively shorter wire.

## Distributor Cap and Rotor

### REMOVAL & INSTALLATION

▶ See Figures 105 thru 115

➡Depending on the reason you have for removing the distributor cap, it may (in some cases) make more sense to leave the spark plug wires attached. This is the case, for example, if you are testing spark plug wires, or if removal is necessary to access other components (and wire play allows you to reposition the cap out of the way).

1. Disconnect the negative battery cable.
2. On some models, it is necessary to remove the air cleaner housing and attaching hoses.
3. Remove the retaining screws for the distributor cap.

Fig. 105 To remove the air cleaner housing, remove the heated air intake tube from the exhaust manifold . . .

Fig. 106 . . . and the air intake pickup tube from the front of the vehicle, next to the radiator . . .

Fig. 107 . . . along with the air cleaner retaining bolt, then lift the housing out of the engine compartment

Fig. 108 A flat bladed screwdriver usually works best to remove the distributor cap retaining screws

Fig. 109 Gently pull the cap outward to remove it from the distributor

Fig. 110 Matchmark the plug wires to avoid confusion during installation

Fig. 111 Rotate the wires to loosen them, then separate them from the cap

Fig. 112 Remove the rotor cover before unfastening the bolts

Fig. 113 The rotor is attached to the shaft by three bolts

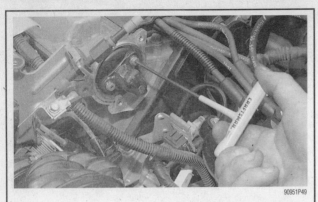
Fig. 114 Typically, a 3mm Allen wrench is used to remove the bolts

Fig. 116 Inspect the distributor cap for cracks, burns, wear and damage

Fig. 115 After the bolts are removed, separate the rotor from the distributor

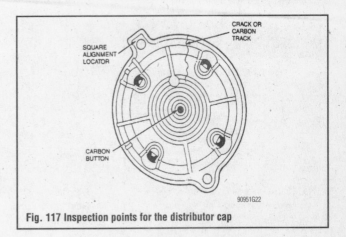
Fig. 117 Inspection points for the distributor cap

4. Carefully lift the distributor cap STRAIGHT up and off the distributor, in order to prevent damage to the rotor blade.

5. Remove and label the spark plug wires from the distributor cap.

6. If equipped, remove the screws retaining the rotor to the distributor shaft.

7. Remove the rotor from the distributor shaft, noting its position for reinstallation.

8. Inspect both the distributor cap and rotor for damage; replace as necessary.

**To install:**

9. Install the rotor on the distributor shaft, in the correct position.

10. Install and tighten the retaining bolt on the rotor (if equipped).

11. Install the distributor cap on the distributor.

12. Install and tighten the distributor cap retaining screws.

13. Install the spark plug wires in the correct locations on the distributor cap.

14. Install the air cleaner housing and hoses if removed.

15. Start the vehicle and ensure that it starts and runs normally.

16. Connect the negative battery cable.

### INSPECTION

▶ **See Figures 116, 117 and 118**

After removing the distributor cap and rotor, clean the components (both inside and outside of the cap) using soap and water. If compressed air is available, carefully dry the components (wearing safety goggles) or allow the parts to air dry. You can dry them with a clean, soft cloth, but don't leave any lint or moisture behind.

Once the cap and rotor have been thoroughly cleaned, check for cracks, carbon tracks, burns or other physical damage. Make sure the distributor cap's carbon button is free of damage. Check the cap terminals for dirt or corrosion. Always check the rotor blade and spring closely for damage. Replace any components where damage is found.

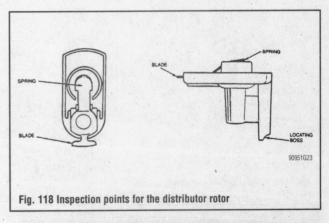
Fig. 118 Inspection points for the distributor rotor

## Ignition Timing

### GENERAL INFORMATION

Ignition timing is the measurement, in degrees of crankshaft rotation, of the point at which the spark plugs fire in each of the cylinders. It is measured in degrees before or after Top Dead Center (TDC) of the compression stroke.

Ideally, the air/fuel mixture in the cylinder will be ignited by the spark plug just as the piston passes TDC of the compression stroke. If this happens, the piston will be at the beginning of the power stroke just as the compressed and ignited air/fuel mixture forces the piston down and turns the crankshaft. Because it takes a fraction of a second for the spark plug to ignite the mixture in the cylinder, the spark plug must fire a little before the piston reaches TDC. Otherwise, the mixture will not be completely ignited as the piston passes TDC and the full power of the explosion will not be used by the engine.

The timing measurement is given in degrees of crankshaft rotation before the piston reaches TDC (BTDC). If the setting for the ignition timing is 10 BTDC, each spark plug must fire 10 degrees before each piston reaches TDC. This only holds true, however, when the engine is at idle speed. As the engine speed increases, the pistons go faster. The spark plugs have to ignite the fuel even sooner if it is to be completely ignited when the piston reaches TDC.

If the ignition is set too far advanced (BTDC), the ignition and expansion of the fuel in the cylinder will occur too soon and tend to force the piston down while it is still traveling up. This causes engine ping. If the ignition spark is set too far retarded, or after TDC (ATDC), the piston will have already started on its way down when the fuel is ignited. The piston will be forced down for only a portion of its travel, resulting in poor engine performance and lack of power.

Timing marks or scales can be found on the rim of the crankshaft pulley and the timing cover. The marks on the pulley correspond to the position of the piston in the No. 1 cylinder. A stroboscopic (dynamic) timing light is hooked onto the No. 1 cylinder spark plug wire. Every time the spark plug fires, the timing light flashes. By aiming the light at the timing marks while the engine is running, the exact position of the piston within the cylinder can be easily read (the flash of light makes the mark on the pulley appear to be standing still). Proper timing is indicated when the mark and scale are in specified alignment.

## ✳✳ WARNING

**When checking timing with the engine running, take care not to get the timing light wires tangled in the fan blades and/or drive belts.**

## INSPECTION & ADJUSTMENT

Although the timing may be checked on the Bosch Motronic system, it is not adjustable. All timing functions are carried out by the ECU. The ignition timing may be checked with a conventional inductive timing light.

Ignition timing on vehicles equipped with the EZ115K, EZ116K, or REX-1 ignition system may be checked with a conventional timing light. The timing, however, cannot be adjusted. If the ignition setting is wrong, use the following procedure:

1. Check the throttle switch.
2. Check that the wiring to the crank sensor is correctly connected at the connector in the firewall.
3. Open the cover of the test connector and connect the cable to terminal 6.
4. Turn the ignition **ON**. Select Test Function 1 by pushing button once for more than 1 second and count the number of blinks. Note the number and press again in case there are more fault codes (up to 3). Note the fault codes to begin troubleshooting.
   - **Code 1–1–1**—No fault codes in memory.
   - **Code 1–4–2**—Fault in control unit. Engine runs with safety-retarded ignition timing (approximately 10 degrees).
   - **Code 1–4–3**—Knock sensor faulty. Engine runs with safety-retarded ignition timing (approximately 10 degrees).
   - **Code 1–4–4**—Load signal missing (from fuel system control unit). Control unit selects full-load ignition.
   - **Code 2–1–4**—Engine speed sensor faulty.
   - **Code 2–2–4**—Coolant temperature sensor inoperative.
   - **Code 2–3–4**—Throttle switch for idling faulty. Engine runs with safety-retarded ignition timing (does not apply to REX 1 ignition system).
   - **Code 3–3–4**—Throttle switch in idle position—okay (REX 1 ignition only).
5. If fault Code 1–1–1 (no fault in memory) appears, check the fuel system.
6. If the LED does not light when the button is pressed, or no code is blinked out, check the connection at the ECU.

## Valve Lash

The recommended maintenance interval for valve clearance adjustment is 30,000 miles (48,000 km). The clearance may be checked with the engine hot or cold.

### ADJUSTMENT

➥**Not all Volvo engines have adjustable valves. The following engines have adjustable valves, all others use hydraulic tappets and are non-adjustable.**

#### B230F and B230FT Engines

◆ **See Figures 119 thru 125**

Valve clearance adjustment requires the following special tools:
- Valve tappet depressor tool (Volvo tool 5022 or equivalent) to push down the tappet sufficiently to remove the adjusting disc.
- A special designed pair of pliers (Volvo tool 5026 or equivalent) to actually remove and install the valve adjusting disc.
- A set of varying-thickness valve adjusting discs (sometimes called shims) to make the necessary corrections.
- Feeler gauge to check valve clearance.

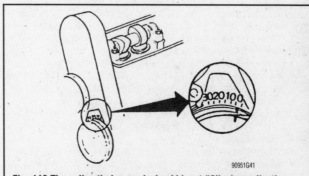

Fig. 119 The pulley timing mark should be at "0" when adjusting the valves—B230F and B230FT engines

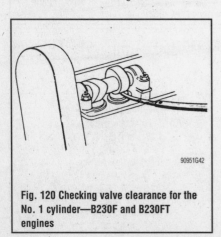

Fig. 120 Checking valve clearance for the No. 1 cylinder—B230F and B230FT engines

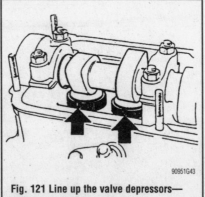

Fig. 121 Line up the valve depressors—B230F and B230FT engines

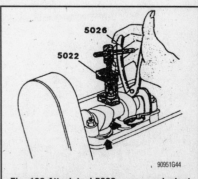

Fig. 122 Attach tool 5022, or an equivalent valve depressor, and remove the disc—B230F and B230FT engines

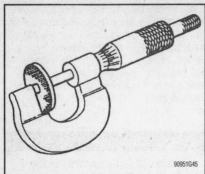

**Fig. 123 Measure the disc thickness using a micrometer—B230F and B230FT engines**

**Fig. 124 View of a typical disc—B230F and B230FT engines**

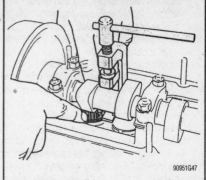

**Fig. 125 Positioning a new disc—B230F and B230FT engines**

### ✳✳ WARNING

**The use of the correct special tools or their equivalent is required for this procedure.**

1. Disconnect the negative battery cable.
2. Remove the valve cover.
3. Rotate the engine, using the crankshaft center bolt, until the No. 1 cylinder is at Top Dead Center (TDC). Both cam lobes for the No. 1 cylinder should point up at equally large angles, and the pulley timing mark should be at 0 degrees.
4. Insert the correct size feeler gauge, as indicated, and check the No. 1 cylinder valve clearance.

➡**Always check valve clearance with cylinder at TDC. Always turn ¼ turn after TDC to set.**

5. If the clearance is incorrect, line up valve depressors. Turn the valve depressors so that the notches are at right angle to the engine center line.
6. Attach valve depressor tool 5022 or equivalent and depress the valve. Screw down the tool spindle until the depressor groove is just above the edge and accessible with the pliers. Use tool 5026 or equivalent to remove the disc.
7. Using a micrometer, measure the disc thickness. Calculate the thickness of disc to be used. Discs are available from 0.130–0.180 inch (3.30–4.50mm), in increments of 0.001 inch (0.05mm). Use the following example:

    a. The measured clearance is 0.02 in. (0.50mm), and the correct clearance is 0.016 inch (0.40mm); therefore, the difference is 0.004 inch (0.10mm).

    b. The measured thickness of the existing disc is 0.150 inch (3.80mm). Therefore, the correct thickness of the new disc will be 0.150 + 0.004 inch = 0.154 inch (3.80 + 0.10mm = 3.90mm).

➡**It is advisable to use metric measurements to simplify calculations.**

8. Lubricate the new disc with clean engine oil and place into position.
9. Remove valve depressor tool 5022 or equivalent.

➡**Install the discs with their marks facing DOWN.**

10. Rotate the engine crankshaft until the No. 3 cylinder is at the correct position. Both cam lobes for the No. 3 cylinder should point up at equally large angles. Check and adjust the clearance as described previously.
11. Repeat Step 7 for cylinder No. 4 and then for cylinder No. 2.
12. Rotate the engine a few turns, then recheck all cylinders.
13. Install the valve cover, using a new valve cover gasket.
14. Connect the negative battery cable.
15. Check engine operation.

**B280F Engine**

▶ **See Figures 126, 127, 128 and 129**

1. Disconnect the negative battery cable.
2. On right side of engine:

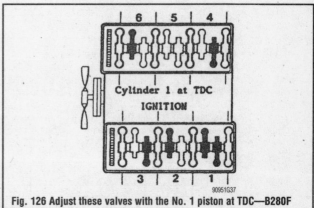

**Fig. 126 Adjust these valves with the No. 1 piston at TDC—B280F engine**

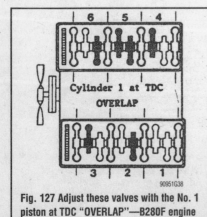

**Fig. 127 Adjust these valves with the No. 1 piston at TDC "OVERLAP"—B280F engine**

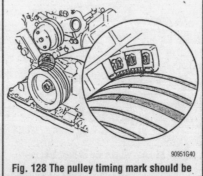

**Fig. 128 The pulley timing mark should be at the "0" mark on the engine shoulder when adjusting the valves—B280F engine**

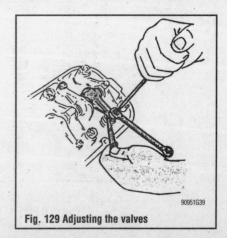

**Fig. 129 Adjusting the valves**

a. Remove the oil filler cap with hoses.
b. Remove the air conditioning compressor with bracket, and position aside.
c. Remove the oil dipstick.
d. Disconnect the wire bundle from the clamps on the valve cover.
3. On left side of engine:
a. Disconnect the air inlet hose.
b. Disconnect the main wiring harness clamp from the valve cover.
c. Remove the spark plug wires and fuel lines from the valve cover.
4. Remove the valve covers.
5. Using a 36mm hex socket on the crankshaft pulley bolt, rotate the crankshaft until the mark on the pulley is opposite the **0** mark on the engine shoulder. Both rocker arms for No. 1 cylinder should have clearance.
6. Insert the proper size feeler gauge between the valve and adjusting screw. Check and, if necessary, adjust the following valves: Intake 1, 2 and 4 and Exhaust 1, 3 and 6.

7. Rotate the crankshaft one complete turn (valve overlapping No. 1 cylinder), so that the mark on the pulley is again opposite **0** mark on the engine shoulder.
8. Check and if necessary, adjust the following valves: Intake 3, 5 and 6 and Exhaust 2, 4 and 5.
9. Install the valve covers, using a new valve cover gaskets.
10. Reinstall all removed components.
11. Connect the negative battery cable.
12. Check engine operation.

## Idle Speed and Mixture Adjustments

Although the idle speed may be checked, it is not adjustable. All idle speed functions are carried out by the ECU.

### GASOLINE ENGINE TUNE-UP SPECIFICATIONS

| | Engine ID/VIN | Engine Displacement Liters (cc) | Spark Plugs Gap (in.) | Ignition Timing (deg.) MT | AT | Fuel Pump (psi) | Idle Speed (rpm) MT | AT | Valve Clearance In. | Ex. |
|---|---|---|---|---|---|---|---|---|---|---|
| 1990 | B-230F/88 | 2.3 (2316) | 0.028 | 12B | 12B | 43 | 775 | 775 | 0.016 | 0.016 |
| | B-230FT/87 | 2.3 (2316) | 0.028-0.032 | 12B | 12B | 43 | 750 | 750 | 0.014-0.018 | 0.014-0.018 |
| | B-234F/89 | 2.3 (2316) | 0.028 | 15B | 15B | 42 | 850 | 850 | HYD | HYD |
| | B-280F/69 | 2.8 (2849) | 0.024-0.028 | — | 16B | 36 | — | 750 | 0.006-0.008 | 0.012-0.014 |
| 1991 | B-230F/88 | 2.3 (2316) | 0.028 | 12B | 12B | 43 | 775 | 775 | 0.016 | 0.016 |
| | B-230FT/87 | 2.3 (2316) | 0.028-0.032 | 12B | 12B | 43 | 750 | 750 | 0.014-0.018 | 0.014-0.018 |
| | B-234F/89 | 2.3 (2316) | 0.028 | 15B | 15B | 42 | 850 | 850 | HYD | HYD |
| 1992 | B-230F/88 | 2.3 (2316) | 0.028 | 12B | 12B | 43 | 775 | 775 | 0.014-0.018 | 0.014-0.018 |
| | B-230FT/87 | 2.3 (2316) | 0.028-0.032 | — | 12B | 43 | — | 750 | 0.014-0.018 | 0.014-0.018 |
| | B-234F/89 | 2.3 (2316) | 0.028 | — | 15B | 42 | — | 850 | HYD | HYD |
| | B-6304F/95 | 2.9 (2922) | 0.024-0.028 | — | 16B | 43 | — | 700-800 | HYD | HYD |
| 1993 | B-230F/88 | 2.3 (2316) | 0.028 | 12B | 12B | 43 | 775 | 775 | 0.014-0.018 | 0.014-0.018 |
| | B-230FT/87 | 2.3 (2316) | 0.028-0.032 | — | 12B | 43 | — | 750 | 0.014-0.018 | 0.014-0.018 |
| | B-6304F/95 | 2.9 (2922) | 0.024-0.028 | — | 16B | 43 | — | 700-800 | HYD | HYD |
| | B-5254S/55 | 2.4 (2435) | 0.028 | — | 10B | 43 | — | 750-850 | HYD | HYD |
| 1994 | B-230F/88 | 2.3 (2316) | 0.028 | — | 12B | 43 | 775 | 775 | 0.014-0.018 | 0.014-0.018 |
| | B-230FT/87 | 2.3 (2316) | 0.028-0.032 | — | 12B | 43 | — | 750 | 0.014-0.018 | 0.014-0.018 |
| | B-6304F/95 | 2.9 (2922) | 0.024-0.028 | — | 16B | 43 | — | 700-800 | HYD | HYD |
| | B-5254S/55 | 2.4 (2435) | 0.028 | — | 10B | 43 | — | 750-850 | HYD | HYD |
| | B-5234T/57 | 2.3 (2319) | 0.028 | — | 6B | 58 | — | 800-900 | HYD | HYD |
| 1995 | B-230F/88 | 2.3 (2316) | 0.028 | — | 12B | 43 | 775 | 775 | 0.014-0.018 | 0.014-0.018 |
| | B-230FT/87 | 2.3 (2316) | 0.028-0.032 | — | 12B | 43 | — | 750 | 0.014-0.018 | 0.014-0.018 |
| | B-6304F/95 | 2.9 (2922) | 0.024-0.028 | — | 16B | 43 | — | 700-800 | HYD | HYD |
| | B-5254S/55 | 2.4 (2435) | 0.028 | — | 10B | 43 | — | 750-850 | HYD | HYD |
| | B-5234T/57 | 2.3 (2319) | 0.028 | — | 6B | 58 | — | 800-900 | HYD | HYD |
| 1996 | B-5254S/55 | 2.4 (2435) | 0.028 | 3-7B | 10B | 43 | 750-850 | 750-850 | HYD | HYD |
| | B-5254T/56 | 2.4 (2435) | 0.028 | 3-7B | 6B | 58 | 800-900 | 800-900 | HYD | HYD |
| | B-5234T/57 | 2.3 (2319) | 0.028 | 3-7B | 6B | 58 | 800-900 | 800-900 | HYD | HYD |
| | B-5254FT/58 | 2.3 (2319) | 0.028 | 3-7B | 6B | 58 | 800-900 | 800-900 | HYD | HYD |
| | B-6304F/96 | 2.9 (2922) | 0.024-0.028 | — | 16B | 43 | — | 700-800 | HYD | HYD |
| 1997 | B-5254S/55 | 2.4 (2435) | 0.028 | 3-7B | 10B | 43 | 750-850 | 750-850 | HYD | HYD |
| | B-5254T/56 | 2.4 (2435) | 0.028 | 3-7B | 6B | 58 | 800-900 | 800-900 | HYD | HYD |
| | B-5234T/57 | 2.3 (2319) | 0.028 | 3-7B | 6B | 58 | 800-900 | 800-900 | HYD | HYD |
| | B-5254FT/58 | 2.3 (2319) | 0.028 | 3-7B | 6B | 58 | 800-900 | 800-900 | HYD | HYD |
| | B-6304F/96 | 2.9 (2922) | 0.024-0.028 | — | 16B | 43 | — | 700-800 | HYD | HYD |
| 1998 | B-5234T3/53 | 2.3 (2319) | 0.028 | 3-7B | 6B | 58 | 800-900 | 800-900 | HYD | HYD |
| | B-5254S/55 | 2.4 (2435) | 0.028 | 3-7B | 10B | 43 | 750-850 | 750-850 | HYD | HYD |
| | B-5254T/56 | 2.4 (2435) | 0.028 | 3-7B | 6B | 58 | 800-900 | 800-900 | HYD | HYD |
| | B-5234T/57 | 2.3 (2319) | 0.028 | 3-7B | 6B | 58 | 800-900 | 800-900 | HYD | HYD |
| | B-6304F/96 | 2.9 (2922) | 0.024-0.028 | — | 16B | 43 | — | 700-800 | HYD | HYD |

B = Before Top Dead Center (TDC)
HYD = Hydraulic valve tappets

90951CA6

## Air Conditioning System

### SYSTEM SERVICE & REPAIR

▶ See Figure 130

➡It is recommended that the A/C system be serviced by an EPA Section 609 certified automotive technician utilizing a refrigerant recovery/recycling machine.

The do-it-yourselfer should not service his/her own vehicle's A/C system for many reasons, including legal concerns, personal injury, environmental damage and cost. The following are some of the reasons why you may decide not to service your own vehicle's A/C system.

According to the U.S. Clean Air Act, it is a federal crime to service or repair (involving the refrigerant) a Motor Vehicle Air Conditioning (MVAC) system for money without being EPA certified. It is also illegal to vent R-12 and R-134a refrigerants into the atmosphere. Selling or distributing A/C system refrigerant (in a container which contains less than 20 pounds of refrigerant) to any person who is not EPA 609 certified is also not allowed by law.

State and/or local laws may be more strict than the federal regulations, so be sure to check with your state and/or local authorities for further information. For further federal information on the legality of servicing your A/C system, call the EPA Stratospheric Ozone Hotline.

➡Federal law dictates that a fine of up to $25,000 may be levied on people convicted of venting refrigerant into the atmosphere. Additionally, the EPA may pay up to $10,000 for information or services leading to a criminal conviction of the violation of these laws.

When servicing an A/C system you run the risk of handling or coming in contact with refrigerant, which may result in skin or eye irritation or frostbite. Although low in toxicity (due to chemical stability), inhalation of concentrated refrigerant fumes is dangerous and can result in death; cases of fatal cardiac arrhythmia have been reported in people accidentally subjected to high levels of refrigerant. Some early symptoms include loss of concentration and drowsiness.

➡Generally, the limit for exposure is lower for R-134a than it is for R-12. Exceptional care must be practiced when handling R-134a.

Also, refrigerants can decompose at high temperatures (near gas heaters or open flame), which may result in hydrofluoric acid, hydrochloric acid and phosgene (a fatal nerve gas).

R-12 refrigerant can damage the environment because it is a Chlorofluorocarbon (CFC), which has been proven to add to ozone layer depletion, leading to increasing levels of UV radiation. UV radiation has been linked with an increase in skin cancer, suppression of the human immune system, an increase in cataracts, damage to crops, damage to aquatic organisms, an increase in ground-level ozone, and increased global warming.

R-134a refrigerant is a greenhouse gas which, if allowed to vent into the atmosphere, will contribute to global warming (the Greenhouse Effect).

It is usually more economically feasible to have a certified MVAC automotive technician perform A/C system service on your vehicle. Some possible reasons for this are as follows:

- While it is illegal to service an A/C system without the proper equipment,

the home mechanic would have to purchase an expensive refrigerant recovery/recycling machine to service his/her own vehicle.
- Since only a certified person may purchase refrigerant—according to the Clean Air Act, there are specific restrictions on selling or distributing A/C system refrigerant—it is legally impossible (unless certified) for the home mechanic to service his/her own vehicle. Procuring refrigerant in an illegal fashion exposes one to the risk of paying a $25,000 fine to the EPA.

#### R-12 Refrigerant Conversion

If your vehicle still uses R-12 refrigerant, one way to save A/C system costs down the road is to investigate the possibility of having your system converted to R-134a. The older R-12 systems can be easily converted to R-134a refrigerant by a certified automotive technician by installing a few new components and changing the system oil.

The cost of R-12 is steadily rising and will continue to increase, because it is no longer imported or manufactured in the United States. Therefore, it is often possible to have an R-12 system converted to R-134a and recharged for less than it would cost to just charge the system with R-12.

If you are interested in having your system converted, contact local automotive service stations for more details and information.

### PREVENTIVE MAINTENANCE

▶ See Figures 131 and 132

Although the A/C system should not be serviced by the do-it-yourselfer, preventive maintenance can be practiced and A/C system inspections can be performed to help maintain the efficiency of the vehicle's A/C system. For preventive maintenance, perform the following:

- The easiest and most important preventive maintenance for your A/C system is to be sure that it is used on a regular basis. Running the system for five minutes each month (no matter what the season) will help ensure that the seals and all internal components remain lubricated.

➡Some newer vehicles automatically operate the A/C system compressor whenever the windshield defroster is activated. When running, the compressor lubricates the A/C system components; therefore, the A/C system would not need to be operated each month.

- In order to prevent heater core freeze-up during A/C operation, it is necessary to maintain proper antifreeze protection. Use a hand-held coolant tester (hydrometer) to periodically check the condition of the antifreeze in your engine's cooling system.

➡Antifreeze should not be used longer than the manufacturer specifies.

- For efficient operation of an air conditioned vehicle's cooling system, the radiator cap should have a holding pressure which meets manufacturer's specifications. A cap which fails to hold these pressures should be replaced.
- Any obstruction of or damage to the condenser configuration will restrict air flow which is essential to its efficient operation. It is, therefore, a good rule to keep this unit clean and in proper physical shape.

➡Bug screens which are mounted in front of the condenser (unless they are original equipment) are regarded as obstructions.

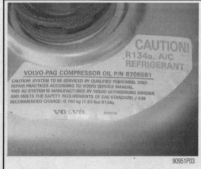

Fig. 130 The A/C identification label should be checked before any repairs are made

Fig. 131 A coolant tester can be used to determine the freezing and boiling levels of the coolant in your vehicle

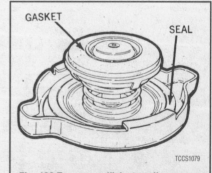

Fig. 132 To ensure efficient cooling system operation, inspect the radiator cap gasket and seal

• The condensation drain tube expels any water which accumulates on the bottom of the evaporator housing into the engine compartment. If this tube is obstructed, the air conditioning performance can be restricted and condensation buildup can spill over onto the vehicle's floor.

## SYSTEM INSPECTION

▶ **See Figure 133**

The easiest and often most important check for the air conditioning system consists of a visual inspection of the system components. Visually inspect the air conditioning system for refrigerant leaks, damaged compressor clutch, abnormal compressor drive belt tension and/or condition, plugged evaporator drain tube, blocked condenser fins, disconnected or broken wires, blown fuses, corroded connections and poor insulation.

A refrigerant leak will usually appear as an oily residue at the leakage point in the system. The oily residue soon picks up dust or dirt particles from the surrounding air and appears greasy. Through time, this will build up and appear to be a heavy dirt impregnated grease.

For a thorough visual and operational inspection, check the following:
• Check the surface of the radiator and condenser for dirt, leaves or other material which might block air flow.
• Check for kinks in hoses and lines.
• Check the system for leaks.
• Make sure the drive belt is properly tensioned. When the air conditioning is operating, make sure the drive belt is free of noise or slippage.
• Make sure the blower motor operates at all appropriate positions, then check for distribution of the air from all outlets with the blower on **HIGH** or **MAX**.

➡**Keep in mind that under conditions of high humidity, air discharged from the A/C vents may not feel as cold as expected, even if the system is working properly. This is because vaporized moisture in humid air retains heat more effectively than dry air, thereby making humid air more difficult to cool.**

• Make sure the air passage selection lever is operating correctly. Start the engine and warm it to normal operating temperature, then make sure the temperature selection lever is operating correctly.

## Windshield Wiper (Elements)

### ELEMENT (REFILL) CARE & REPLACEMENT

▶ **See Figures 134 thru 143**

For maximum effectiveness and longest element life, the windshield and wiper blades should be kept clean. Dirt, tree sap, road tar and so on will cause streaking, smearing and blade deterioration if left on the glass. It is advisable to wash the windshield carefully with a commercial glass cleaner at least once a month. Wipe off the rubber blades with the wet rag afterwards. Do not attempt to move wipers across the windshield by hand; damage to the motor and drive mechanism will result.

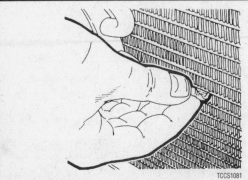

**Fig. 133 Periodically remove any debris from the condenser and radiator fins**

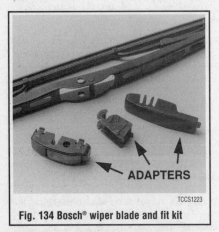

TCCS1223

**Fig. 134 Bosch® wiper blade and fit kit**

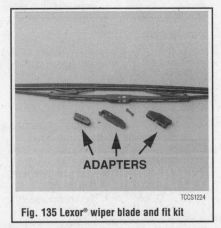

TCCS1224

**Fig. 135 Lexor® wiper blade and fit kit**

TCCS1225

**Fig. 136 Pylon® wiper blade and adapter**

TCCS1226

**Fig. 137 Trico® wiper blade and fit kit**

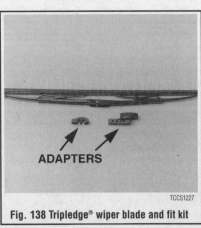

TCCS1227

**Fig. 138 Tripledge® wiper blade and fit kit**

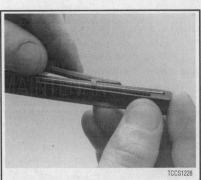

TCCS1228

**Fig. 139 To remove and install a Lexor® wiper blade refill, slip out the old insert and slide in a new one**

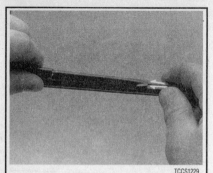

Fig. 140 On Pylon® inserts, the clip at the end has to be removed prior to sliding the insert off

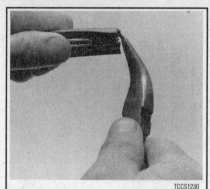

Fig. 141 On Trico® wiper blades, the tab at the end of the blade must be turned up . . .

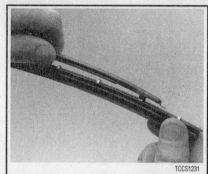

Fig. 142 . . . then the insert can be removed. After installing the replacement insert, bend the tab back

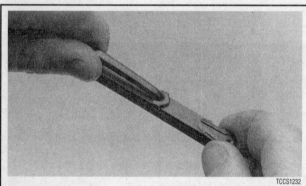

Fig. 143 The Tripledge® wiper blade insert is removed and installed using a securing clip

To inspect and/or replace the wiper blade elements, place the wiper switch in the **LOW** speed position and the ignition switch in the **ACC** position. When the wiper blades are approximately vertical on the windshield, turn the ignition switch to **OFF**.

Examine the wiper blade elements. If they are found to be cracked, broken or torn, they should be replaced immediately. Replacement intervals will vary with usage, although ozone deterioration usually limits element life to about one year. If the wiper pattern is smeared or streaked, or if the blade chatters across the glass, the elements should be replaced. It is easiest and most sensible to replace the elements in pairs.

If your vehicle is equipped with aftermarket blades, there are several different types of refills and your vehicle might have any kind. Aftermarket blades and arms rarely use the exact same type blade or refill as the original equipment. Here are some typical aftermarket blades; not all may be available for your vehicle:

The Anco® type uses a release button that is pushed down to allow the refill to slide out of the yoke jaws. The new refill slides back into the frame and locks in place.

Some Trico® refills are removed by locating where the metal backing strip or the refill is wider. Insert a small screwdriver blade between the frame and metal backing strip. Press down to release the refill from the retaining tab.

Other types of Trico® refills have two metal tabs which are unlocked by squeezing them together. The rubber filler can then be withdrawn from the frame jaws. A new refill is installed by inserting the refill into the front frame jaws and sliding it rearward to engage the remaining frame jaws. There are usually four jaws; be certain when installing that the refill is engaged in all of them. At the end of its travel, the tabs will lock into place on the front jaws of the wiper blade frame.

Another type of refill is made from polycarbonate. The refill has a simple locking device at one end which flexes downward out of the groove into which the jaws of the holder fit, allowing easy release. By sliding the new refill through all the jaws and pushing through the slight resistance when it reaches the end of its travel, the refill will lock into position.

To replace the Tridon® refill, it is necessary to remove the wiper blade. This refill has a plastic backing strip with a notch about 1 in. (25mm) from the end. Hold the blade (frame) on a hard surface so that the frame is tightly bowed. Grip the tip of the backing strip and pull up while twisting counterclockwise. The backing strip will snap out of the retaining tab. Do this for the remaining tabs until the refill is free of the blade. The length of these refills is molded into the end and they should be replaced with identical types.

Regardless of the type of refill used, be sure to follow the part manufacturer's instructions closely. Make sure that all of the frame jaws are engaged as the refill is pushed into place and locked. If the metal blade holder and frame are allowed to touch the glass during wiper operation, the glass will be scratched.

## Tires and Wheels

Common sense and good driving habits will afford maximum tire life. Fast starts, sudden stops and hard cornering are hard on tires and will shorten their useful life span. Make sure that you don't overload the vehicle or run with incorrect pressure in the tires. Both of these practices will increase tread wear.

➡**For optimum tire life, keep the tires properly inflated, rotate them often and have the wheel alignment checked periodically.**

Inspect your tires frequently. Be especially careful to watch for bubbles in the tread or sidewall, deep cuts or underinflation. Replace any tires with bubbles in the sidewall. If cuts are so deep that they penetrate to the cords, discard the tire. Any cut in the sidewall of a radial tire renders it unsafe. Also look for uneven tread wear patterns that may indicate the front end is out of alignment or that the tires are out of balance.

### TIRE ROTATION

▶ **See Figures 144, 145 and 146**

Tires must be rotated periodically to equalize wear patterns that vary with a tire's position on the vehicle. Tires will also wear in an uneven way as the front steering/suspension system wears to the point where the alignment should be reset.

Rotating the tires will ensure maximum life for the tires as a set, so you will not have to discard a tire early due to wear on only part of the tread. Regular rotation is required to equalize wear.

When rotating "unidirectional tires," make sure that they always roll in the same direction. This means that a tire used on the left side of the vehicle must not be switched to the right side and vice-versa. Such tires should only be rotated front-to-rear or rear-to-front, while always remaining on the same side of the vehicle. These tires are marked on the sidewall as to the direction of rotation; observe the marks when reinstalling the tire(s).

Some styled or "mag" wheels may have different offsets front to rear. In these cases, the rear wheels must not be used up front and vice-versa. Furthermore, if these wheels are equipped with unidirectional tires, they cannot be rotated unless the tire is remounted for the proper direction of rotation.

➡**The compact or space-saver spare is strictly for emergency use. It must never be included in the tire rotation or placed on the vehicle for everyday use.**

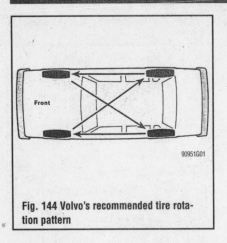

**Fig. 144 Volvo's recommended tire rotation pattern**

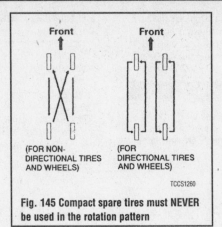

**Fig. 145 Compact spare tires must NEVER be used in the rotation pattern**

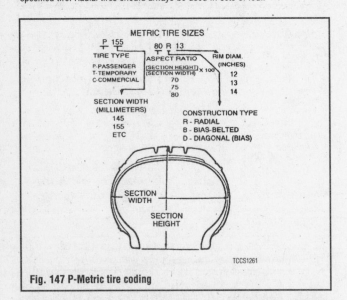

**Fig. 146 Unidirectional tires are identifiable by sidewall arrows and/or the word "rotation"**

## TIRE DESIGN

**♦ See Figure 147**

For maximum satisfaction, tires should be used in sets of four. Mixing of different types (radial, bias-belted, fiberglass belted) must be avoided. In most cases, the vehicle manufacturer has designated a type of tire on which the vehicle will perform best. Your first choice when replacing tires should be to use the same type of tire that the manufacturer recommends.

When radial tires are used, tire sizes and wheel diameters should be selected to maintain ground clearance and tire load capacity equivalent to the original specified tire. Radial tires should always be used in sets of four.

**Fig. 147 P-Metric tire coding**

> ❋ CAUTION

**Radial tires should never be used on only the front axle.**

When selecting tires, pay attention to the original size as marked on the tire. Most tires are described using an industry size code sometimes referred to as P-Metric. This allows the exact identification of the tire specifications, regardless of the manufacturer. If selecting a different tire size or brand, remember to check the installed tire for any sign of interference with the body or suspension while the vehicle is stopping, turning sharply or heavily loaded.

### Snow Tires

Good radial tires can produce a big advantage in slippery weather, but in snow, a street radial tire does not have sufficient tread to provide traction and control. The small grooves of a street tire quickly pack with snow and the tire behaves like a billiard ball on a marble floor. The more open, chunky tread of a snow tire will self-clean as the tire turns, providing much better grip on snowy surfaces.

To satisfy municipalities requiring snow tires during weather emergencies, most snow tires carry either an M + S designation after the tire size stamped on the sidewall, or the designation "all-season." In general, no change in tire size is necessary when buying snow tires.

Most manufacturers strongly recommend the use of 4 snow tires on their vehicles for reasons of stability. If snow tires are fitted only to the drive wheels, the opposite end of the vehicle may become very unstable when braking or turning on slippery surfaces. This instability can lead to unpleasant endings if the driver can't counteract the slide in time.

Note that snow tires, whether 2 or 4, will affect vehicle handling in all non-snow situations. The stiffer, heavier snow tires will noticeably change the turning and braking characteristics of the vehicle. Once the snow tires are installed, you must re-learn the behavior of the vehicle and drive accordingly.

➡ **Consider buying extra wheels on which to mount the snow tires. Once done, the "snow wheels" can be installed and removed as needed. This eliminates the potential damage to tires or wheels from seasonal removal and installation. Even if your vehicle has styled wheels, see if inexpensive steel wheels are available. Although the look of the vehicle will change, the expensive wheels will be protected from salt, curb hits and pothole damage.**

## TIRE STORAGE

If they are mounted on wheels, store the tires at proper inflation pressure. All tires should be kept in a cool, dry place. If they are stored in the garage or basement, do not let them stand on a concrete floor; set them on strips of wood, a mat or a large stack of newspaper. Keeping them away from direct moisture is of paramount importance. Tires should not be stored upright, but in a flat position.

## INFLATION & INSPECTION

**♦ See Figures 148 thru 157**

The importance of proper tire inflation cannot be overemphasized. A tire employs air as part of its structure. It is designed around the supporting strength of the air at a specified pressure. For this reason, improper inflation drastically reduces the tire's ability to perform as intended. A tire will lose some air in day-to-day use; having to add a few pounds of air periodically is not necessarily a sign of a leaking tire.

Two items should be a permanent fixture in every glove compartment: an accurate tire pressure gauge and a tread depth gauge. Check the tire pressure (including the spare) regularly with a pocket type gauge. Too often, the gauge on the end of the air hose at your corner garage is not accurate because it suffers too much abuse. Always check tire pressure when the tires are cold, as pressure increases with temperature. If you must move the vehicle to check the tire inflation, do not drive more than a mile before checking. A cold tire is generally one that has not been driven for more than three hours.

A plate or sticker is normally provided somewhere in the vehicle (door post, hood, tailgate or trunk lid) which shows the proper pressure for the tires. Never counteract excessive pressure build-up by bleeding off air pressure (letting some air out). This will cause the tire to run hotter and wear quicker.

### ✲✲ CAUTION

**Never exceed the maximum tire pressure embossed on the tire! This is the pressure to be used when the tire is at maximum loading, but it is rarely the correct pressure for everyday driving. Consult the owner's manual or the tire pressure sticker for the correct tire pressure.**

Once you've maintained the correct tire pressures for several weeks, you'll be familiar with the vehicle's braking and handling personality. Slight adjustments in tire pressures can fine-tune these characteristics, but never change the cold pressure specification by more than 2 psi. A slightly softer tire pressure will give a softer ride but also yield lower fuel mileage. A slightly harder tire will give crisper dry road handling but can cause skidding on wet surfaces. Unless you're fully attuned to the vehicle, stick to the recommended inflation pressures.

Fig. 148 The tire label on the fuel filler door should be consulted for various tire information

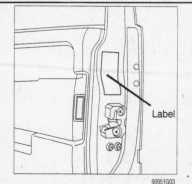

Fig. 149 Some Volvos have a tire label on the passenger side front door

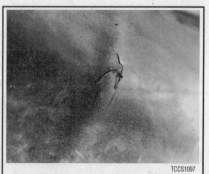

Fig. 150 Tires should be checked frequently for any sign of puncture or damage

Fig. 151 Tires with deep cuts, or cuts which bulge, should be replaced immediately

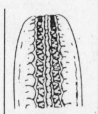

- DRIVE WHEEL HEAVY ACCELERATION
- OVERINFLATION

- HARD CORNERING
- UNDERINFLATION
- LACK OF ROTATION

Fig. 152 Examples of inflation-related tire wear patterns

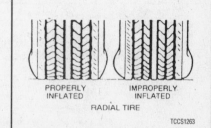

PROPERLY INFLATED    IMPROPERLY INFLATED
RADIAL TIRE

Fig. 153 Radial tires have a characteristic sidewall bulge; don't try to measure pressure by looking at the tire. Use a quality air pressure gauge

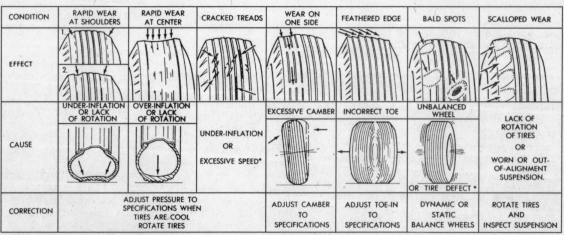

| CONDITION | RAPID WEAR AT SHOULDERS | RAPID WEAR AT CENTER | CRACKED TREADS | WEAR ON ONE SIDE | FEATHERED EDGE | BALD SPOTS | SCALLOPED WEAR |
|---|---|---|---|---|---|---|---|
| EFFECT | | | | | | | |
| CAUSE | UNDER-INFLATION OR LACK OF ROTATION | OVER-INFLATION OR LACK OF ROTATION | UNDER-INFLATION OR EXCESSIVE SPEED* | EXCESSIVE CAMBER | INCORRECT TOE | UNBALANCED WHEEL OR TIRE DEFECT * | LACK OF ROTATION OF TIRES OR WORN OR OUT-OF-ALIGNMENT SUSPENSION. |
| CORRECTION | ADJUST PRESSURE TO SPECIFICATIONS WHEN TIRES ARE COOL ROTATE TIRES | | | ADJUST CAMBER TO SPECIFICATIONS | ADJUST TOE-IN TO SPECIFICATIONS | DYNAMIC OR STATIC BALANCE WHEELS | ROTATE TIRES AND INSPECT SUSPENSION |

*HAVE TIRE INSPECTED FOR FURTHER USE.

Fig. 154 Common tire wear patterns and causes

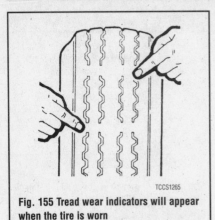

Fig. 155 Tread wear indicators will appear when the tire is worn

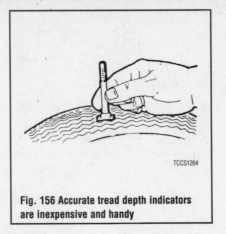

Fig. 156 Accurate tread depth indicators are inexpensive and handy

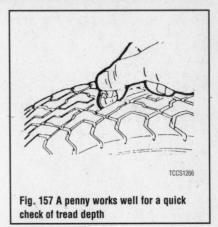

Fig. 157 A penny works well for a quick check of tread depth

All tires made since 1968 have built-in tread wear indicator bars that show up as ½ in. (13mm) wide smooth bands across the tire when 1/16 in. (1.5mm) of tread remains. The appearance of tread wear indicators means that the tires should be replaced. In fact, many states have laws prohibiting the use of tires with less than this amount of tread.

You can check your own tread depth with an inexpensive gauge or by using a Lincoln head penny. Slip the Lincoln penny (with Lincoln's head upside-down) into several tread grooves. If you can see the top of Lincoln's head in 2 adjacent grooves, the tire has less than 1/16 in. (1.5mm) tread left and should be replaced. You can measure snow tires in the same manner by using the "tails" side of the Lincoln penny. If you can see the top of the Lincoln memorial, it's time to replace the snow tire(s).

## CARE OF SPECIAL WHEELS

If you have invested money in magnesium, aluminum alloy or sport wheels, special precautions should be taken to make sure your investment is not wasted and that your special wheels look good for the life of the vehicle.

Special wheels are easily damaged and/or scratched. Occasionally check the rims for cracking, impact damage or air leaks. If any of these are found, replace the wheel. But in order to prevent this type of damage and the costly replacement of a special wheel, observe the following precautions:

- Use extra care not to damage the wheels during removal, installation, balancing, etc. After removal of the wheels from the vehicle, place them on a mat or other protective surface. If they are to be stored for any length of time, support them on strips of wood. Never store tires and wheels upright; the tread may develop flat spots.
- When driving, watch for hazards; it doesn't take much to crack a wheel.
- When washing, use a mild soap or non-abrasive dish detergent (keeping in mind that detergent tends to remove wax). Avoid cleansers with abrasives or the use of hard brushes. There are many cleaners and polishes for special wheels.
- If possible, remove the wheels during the winter. Salt and sand used for snow removal can severely damage the finish of a wheel.

- Make certain the recommended lug nut torque is never exceeded or the wheel may crack. Never use snow chains on special wheels; severe scratching will occur.

## Maintenance Lights

### RESETTING

#### 1990 740 and 780; 1990–92 240

♦ See Figure 158

The Service Reminder Indicator (SRI) zeroing knob is located at the rear of the instrument panel. The indicator light illuminates after approximately 5,000 miles (8,000 km). It goes on for 2 minutes each time the engine is started until the oil and filter have been changed and the counter reset.

Reach up behind the dashboard and push the knob to reset the reminder light.

#### 760 and All 1991–95 Models Except 850 and 1991–92 240

♦ See Figure 159

The SRI zeroing knob is located on the front of the instrument cluster, underneath a rubber grommet. Remove the rubber grommet; then using a small screwdriver, depress the knob to reset.

#### 1993–95 850

♦ See Figures 160, 161, 162 and 163

The SRI is reset using the Data Link Connector (DLC). The procedure is as follows:
1. Turn the ignition switch to the **ON** position.
2. At the DLC, select position 7 and place the diagnostic connector in the socket.
3. Depress the button on the DLC four times.

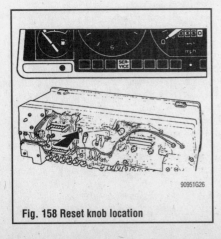

Fig. 158 Reset knob location

Fig. 159 Service reminder light reset button location on the front of the instrument cluster

Fig. 160 The Data Link Connector (DLC) is located in the passenger side front of the engine compartment

Fig. 161 Remove the cover to reveal the socket and button on the DLC

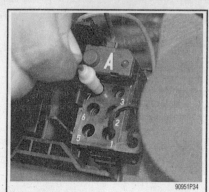

Fig. 162 Install the diagnostic connector in socket 7 . . .

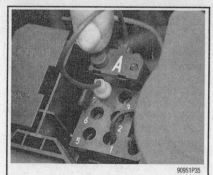

Fig. 163 . . . and press the button in the sequence listed in the procedure to reset the light

4. When the Light Emitting Diode (LED) glows steadily, the system is ready to be reset.
5. Depress the button once, and wait for the LED to light again.
6. Depress the button five times, and wait for the LED to light again.
7. Depress the button once again, and wait for the LED to light again.
8. Turn the ignition **OFF**.
9. Start the engine and verify the maintenance light goes out.

### 1996–98 Vehicles (OBD-II)

1996–98 models incorporate the OBD-II diagnostic system. The SRI is reset using the Volvo Scan tool or equivalent. Follow the scan tool manufacturer's instructions to reset the SRI.

## FLUIDS AND LUBRICANTS

### Fluid Disposal

Used fluids such as engine oil, transmission fluid, antifreeze and brake fluid are hazardous wastes and must be disposed of properly. Before draining any fluids, consult with your local authorities; in many areas, waste oil, antifreeze, etc. is being accepted as a part of recycling programs. A number of service stations and auto parts stores are also accepting waste fluids for recycling.

Be sure of the recycling center's policies before draining any fluids, as many will not accept different fluids that have been mixed together.

### Fuel and Engine Oil Recommendations

FUEL

➡**Some fuel additives contain chemicals that can damage the catalytic converter and/or oxygen sensor. Read all of the labels carefully before using any additive in the engine or fuel system.**

All vehicles covered by this manual are designed to run on unleaded fuel. The use of a leaded fuel in a vehicle requiring unleaded fuel will plug the catalytic converter and render it inoperative. It will also increase exhaust backpressure to the point where engine output will be severely reduced. Obviously, use of leaded fuel should not be a problem, since most companies have stopped selling it for quite some time.

The minimum octane rating of the unleaded fuel being used must be at least 87 (as listed on the pumps), which usually means regular unleaded. Some areas may have even lower octane available, which would make 87 a midgrade fuel. In these cases a minimum fuel octane of 87 should STILL be used.

Fuel should be selected for the brand and octane which performs best with your engine. Judge a gasoline by its ability to prevent pinging, its engine starting capabilities (cold and hot) and general all weather performance. The use of a fuel too low in octane (a measurement of anti-knock quality) will result in spark knock. Since many factors such as altitude, terrain, air temperature and humidity affect operating efficiency, knocking may result even though the recommended fuel is being used. If persistent knocking occurs, it may be necessary to switch to a different brand or grade of fuel. Continuous or heavy knocking may result in engine damage.

➡**Your engine's fuel requirement can change with time, mainly due to carbon buildup, which will in turn change the compression ratio. If your engine pings or knocks switch to a higher grade of fuel. Sometimes just changing brands will cure the problem.**

The other most important quality you should look for in a fuel is that it contains detergents designed to keep fuel injection systems clean. Many of the major fuel companies will display information right at the pumps telling you that their fuels contain these detergents. The use of a high-quality fuel which contains detergents will help assure trouble-free operation of your vehicle's fuel system.

OIL

#### ▶ See Figure 164

The recommended oil viscosity for sustained temperatures ranging from below -20°F (-30°C) to above 100°F (40°C) are listed in the section. The only oil type shown is multi-viscosity. Multi-viscosity oils are recommended because of their wider range of acceptable temperatures and driving conditions.

When adding oil to the crankcase or changing the oil and filter, it is important that oil of an equal quality to original equipment be used in your vehicle. The use of inferior oils may void the warranty, damage your engine, or both.

The Society of Automotive Engineers (SAE) grade number of the oil indicates the viscosity of the oil—its ability to lubricate at a given temperature. The lower the SAE number, the lighter the oil; the lower the viscosity, the easier it is to crank the engine in cold weather, but the less the oil will lubricate and protect the engine at high temperatures. This number is marked on every oil container.

When using engine oil, there are two types of ratings with which you should be familiar: viscosity and service (quality). There are several service ratings, resulting from tests established by the American Petroleum Institute. The most current rating, SJ, is recommended for use in all engines. The SJ rating supersedes all other ratings.

Oil viscosity should be chosen from those oils recommended for the lowest anticipated temperatures during the oil change interval. Due to the need for an oil that embodies both good lubrication at high temperature and easy cranking in cold weather, multi-grade oils have been developed. Basically, a multi-grade oil is thinner at low temperatures and thicker at high temperatures. For example, a 10W-40 oil (the W stands for winter) exhibits the characteristics of a 10-weight (SAE 10) oil when the vehicle is first started and the oil is cold. Its lighter weight allows it to travel to the lubricating surfaces quicker and offer less resistance to starter motor cranking than a heavier oil. But after the engine reaches operating temperature, the 10W-40 oil begins acting like straight 40-weight (SAE 40) oil. It behaves as a heavier oil, providing greater lubrication and protection against foaming than lighter oils.

The American Petroleum Institute (API) designations, also found on oil containers, indicates the classification of engine oil used for given operating con-

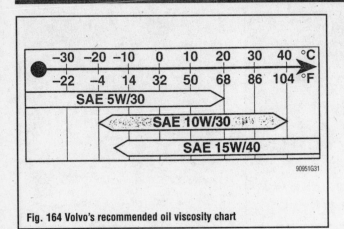

**Fig. 164 Volvo's recommended oil viscosity chart**

ditions. Only oils designated Service SJ (or the latest superseding designation) heavy-duty detergent should be used in your vehicle. Oils of the SJ-type perform many functions inside the engine besides their basic lubrication. Through a balanced system of metallic detergents and polymeric dispersants, the oil prevents high and low temperature deposits and also keeps sludge and dirt particles in suspension. Acids, particularly sulfuric, as well as other by-products of engine combustion are neutralized by the oil. If these acids are allowed to concentrate, they can cause corrosion and rapid wear of the internal engine parts.

## Engine

### OIL LEVEL CHECK

♦ See Figures 165, 166 and 167

### ✳✳ CAUTION

**The EPA warns that prolonged contact with used engine oil may cause a number of skin disorders, including cancer! You should make every effort to minimize your exposure to used engine oil. Protective gloves should be worn when changing the oil. Wash your hands and any other exposed skin areas as soon as possible after exposure to used engine oil. Soap and water, or waterless hand cleaner should be used.**

It is a good idea to check the engine oil each time or at least every other time you fill your fuel tank. Check the engine oil level with the vehicle on level ground and the transmission in **PARK**. When checking fluid level, use a clean rag that will not leave lint.

1. Be sure the vehicle is on level surface.
2. Shut **OFF** the engine and wait a few minutes to allow the oil to drain back into the oil pan.
3. Remove the engine oil dipstick and wipe clean with a lint-free rag.
4. Reinstall the dipstick and push it down until it is fully seated in the tube.
5. Once again, remove the dipstick and note the level on the indicator. If necessary, fill to the normal level.

### OIL & FILTER CHANGE

♦ See Figures 168 thru 177

The engine oil and filter should be replaced according to your driving habits. Consult the maintenance intervals chart later in this section.

1. Operate the engine for a few minutes. This increases the engine oil temperature and allows the oil to flow more rapidly.

### ✳✳ CAUTION

**The EPA warns that prolonged contact with used engine oil may cause a number of skin disorders, including cancer! You should make every effort to minimize your exposure to used engine oil. Protective gloves should be worn when changing the oil. Wash your hands and any other exposed skin areas as soon as possible after exposure to used engine oil. Soap and water, or waterless hand cleaner should be used.**

2. Raise and support the vehicle safely.
3. Position a suitable drain pan under the engine oil pan drain plug.
4. On most Volvos, use a 17mm wrench to remove the oil pan drain plug.
5. Allow the oil to drain completely.
6. Reinstall and tighten the drain plug. DO NOT OVERTIGHTEN. Make sure you install the drain plug gasket before tighten the drain plug.
7. Position the drain pan under the engine oil filter.
8. Clean around the oil filter mounting surface with a shop rag.
9. Using the an oil filter wrench, remove the oil filter.
10. Lubricate the rubber oil seal of the new filter. Screw the filter on by hand; retighten with a wrench only if necessary.
11. Lower the vehicle.
12. Refill the crankcase to the normal oil level.
13. Replace the filler cap.
14. Start the engine and check for leaks.
15. Shut **OFF** the engine. Wait a few minutes and check the oil level. Add oil if necessary.
16. Reset the service indicator, as described earlier in this section.

### ✳✳ WARNING

**Operating the engine without the proper amount and type of engine oil will result in severe engine damage.**

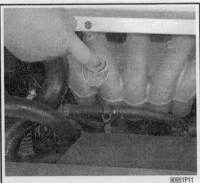

**Fig. 165 Remove the dipstick from the engine**

**Fig. 166 The tag on the dipstick indicates that the oil level should be between the . . .**

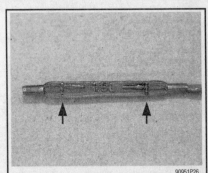

**Fig. 167 . . . MIN and MAX markings on the dipstick, as shown by the arrowed range**

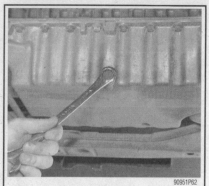

Fig. 168 Use a 17mm wrench to loosen the drain plug

Fig. 169 Unscrew the drain plug by hand, while keeping inward pressure on it to prevent leakage

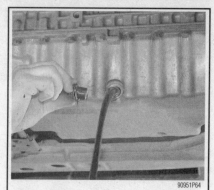

Fig. 170 Make sure the drain pan is positioned before you remove the drain plug

Fig. 171 Inspect the drain plug gasket for cracks; it should be replaced if necessary, or an oil leak will occur

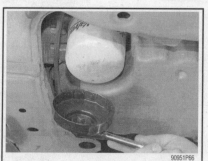

Fig. 172 Use an appropriate size oil filter wrench to remove the filter. (A cap type wrench is shown, but a strap type is also okay)

Fig. 173 Loosen the filter slowly until . . .

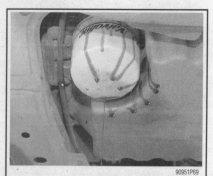

Fig. 174 . . . oil starts to drain out; remove the wrench and let the filter drain, then unscrew the filter by hand

Fig. 175 After the filter is removed, inspect the threads on the filter mounting boss (1) and clean the gasket surface (2)

Fig. 176 Remove the oil filler cap . . .

Fig. 177 . . . and place a funnel in the opening to fill the crankcase with oil

## Manual Transmission/Transaxle

### FLUID RECOMMENDATIONS

Automatic Transmission Fluid (ATF) type F is recommended for manual transmissions. On the M46, engine oil SAE 10W-40 is recommended for use in areas where temperature seldom drops below 14°F (10°C).

### LEVEL CHECK

◆ **See Figures 178 and 179**

The fluid level should be checked at 10,000 mile (16,000 km) intervals.
1. Raise and support the vehicle safely.
2. Remove the transmission level plug.

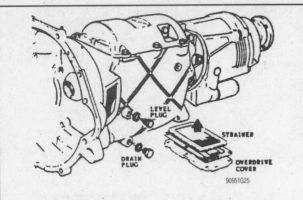

Fig. 178 Level (fill) and drain plug locations—M46 transmission

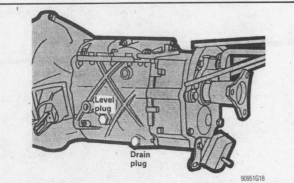

Fig. 179 Level (fill) and drain plug locations—M47 and M90 transmissions

3. Check that the oil level is up to the filler hole. Top up, if necessary.
4. Install the transmission level plug and lower the vehicle.

## DRAIN & REFILL

**M46 Transmission**

1. Raise and support the vehicle safely.
2. Place a suitable container into position.
3. Drain the oil by removing the transmission drain plug and overdrive cover.
4. After the oil is completely drained, reinstall the drain plug.
5. Clean the strainer before reinstalling the overdrive cover.
6. Remove the level plug, then fill the transmission with the recommended lubricant through the filler hole. The oil level should be up to the filler hole.
7. Install the level plug.
8. Lower the vehicle.

**M47 and M90 Transmissions**

1. Raise and support the vehicle safely.
2. Place a suitable container into position.
3. Drain the oil by removing the transmission drain plug.
4. After the oil is completely drained, reinstall the drain plug.
5. Remove the level plug, then fill the transmission with the recommended lubricant through the filler hole. The oil level should be up to the filler hole.
6. Install the level plug.
7. Lower the vehicle.
8. Road test the vehicle and check for leaks.

## Automatic Transmission/Transaxle

### FLUID RECOMMENDATIONS

Dexron III® type Automatic Transmission Fluid (ATF) is recommended for all automatic transmissions/transaxles.

### LEVEL CHECK

▶ **See Figures 180 and 181**

The fluid level should be checked at 10,000 mile (16,000 km) intervals.
1. Check the transmission fluid level with the vehicle on level ground, with the transmission/transaxle in the **Park** position, with the engine idling.
2. Remove the dipstick and wipe it clean, using a lint-free rag.

➡ **The dipstick has graduations for hot and cold transmission/transaxle fluid levels.**

3. Reinstall the dipstick. Remove it and check the dipstick markings.
    a. Cold fluid: At fluid temperatures below 105°F (40°C), the level may be below the **MIN** mark.
    b. Operating temperature: At fluid temperatures above 195°F (90°C), the level may be above the **MAX** mark.
4. Check the condition of the ATF. Discoloration and smell can be caused by heavy engine loads, such as towing. In this case, remove and clean oil pan, oil strainer and magnet. Refer to the Pan & Filter Service procedure later in this section.
5. If topping up is necessary, fill through the dipstick tube.

### DRAIN & REFILL

▶ **See Figures 182 thru 188**

### ✳ CAUTION

**Do not immediately drain the transmission fluid, if the vehicle was recently driven. Oil can be scalding hot.**

1. Disconnect the negative battery cable.
2. Raise and support the vehicle safely.

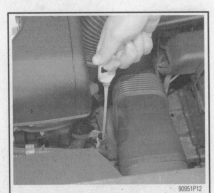

Fig. 180 Remove the dipstick from the tube and check the fluid level

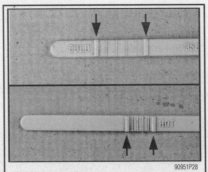

Fig. 181 The dipstick is marked on both sides; one side is for checking while cold, the other side while hot

Fig. 182 The drain plug on most Volvo transaxles is loosened with a 22mm wrench

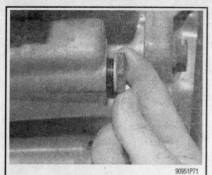

Fig. 183 After the drain plug is loose, unscrew it by hand while keeping inward pressure against the plug

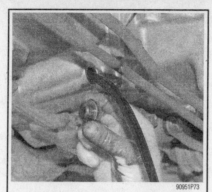

Fig. 184 Remove the drain plug and let the fluid drain into a suitable container

Fig. 185 Inspect the drain plug gasket for cracks; replace if necessary, or a leak could occur

Fig. 186 Some drain plugs are magnetic and will attract metallic particles. If the magnet is full, serious problems are likely

Fig. 187 With the dipstick removed, install a funnel into the dipstick tube to refill the transmission/transaxle

Fig. 188 Pour the proper ATF into the funnel and fill the transmission/transaxle

3. Place a suitable drain pan beneath the transmission/transaxle.
4. Remove the drain plug and drain the fluid.
5. Reinstall the drain plug.
6. Lower the vehicle.
7. Fill the transmission with the proper fluid.
8. Connect the negative battery cable.
9. Firmly apply the parking brake and block the drive wheel. Start the engine and allow it to reach operating temperature. Check for leaks.
10. Move the gear selector lever through all ranges.
11. Wait approximately 2 minutes and check the fluid level with the engine running and the gear selector in the **Park** position. Adjust the fluid level as required.

### PAN & FILTER SERVICE

▶ **See Figures 189, 190 and 191**

➡ Automatic transmissions contain a strainer (filter), but automatic transaxles do not. Removal of the pan is only required for repair. Refer to the preceding drain and refill procedure.

#### ❊ CAUTION

Do not immediately drain the transmission fluid, if the vehicle was recently driven. Oil can be scalding hot.

1. Disconnect the negative battery cable.
2. Raise and support the vehicle safely.
3. Place a suitable drain pan beneath the transmission.
4. Remove the drain plug and drain the fluid.
5. Install the drain plug.

➡ On some models, it may be necessary to remove the dipstick tube from the pan for access.

6. Unfasten the oil pan retaining bolts and remove the pan.
7. Unfasten the strainer retaining bolts.
8. Remove the strainer from the valve body.

**To install:**

9. Clean the oil pan and particle magnet(s).

➡ **According to the manufacturer, the strainer can be cleaned, but we at Chilton recommend replacement with a new one.**

10. Install the replacement strainer onto the valve body and tighten the bolts.
11. Install the particle magnet(s) into the pan.
12. Place a new gasket onto the transmission pan.
13. Place the pan into position on the transmission, and tighten the bolts.
14. If removed, install the dipstick tube.
15. Lower the vehicle.

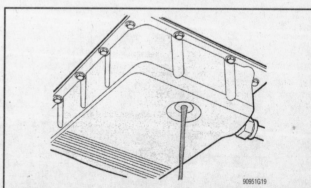

Fig. 189 Remove the drain plug and allow the transmission fluid to drain

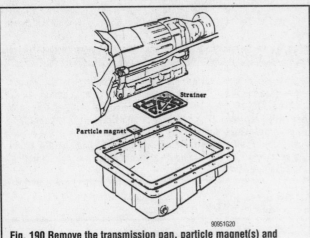

**Fig. 190 Remove the transmission pan, particle magnet(s) and strainer**

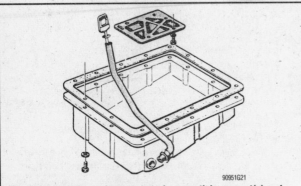

**Fig. 191 Install the replacement strainer, particle magnet(s) and pan, along with the dipstick tube, if removed**

16. Fill the transmission with the proper fluid.
17. Connect the negative battery cable.
18. Firmly apply the parking brake and block the drive wheel. Start the engine and allow it to reach operating temperature. Check for leaks.
19. Move the gear selector lever through all ranges.
20. Wait approximately 2 minutes and check the fluid level in **Park** position. Adjust as required.

## Transfer Case

### FLUID RECOMMENDATIONS

The recommended oil for the transfer case is API-GL-5/SAE 80W, or equivalent.

### LEVEL CHECK

There is a plug to the left side of the flange for the rear wheel driveshaft. The level is checked by removing this plug and checking the fluid level. The fluid should be no more than ½ inch (13mm) below this plug. If your finger is unable to fit in this opening, a small screwdriver works.

### DRAIN & REFILL

The transfer case cannot be drained while still attached to the transmission. However, an alternative method is to use a hand-held vacuum pump with a piece of hose and suck out the fluid. Refill with the appropriate grade of oil.

## Drive Axle

### FLUID RECOMMENDATIONS

#### ♦ See Figure 192

The rear axle should be serviced with API GL-5, MIL-L-2105 B or C or equivalent, with a viscosity rating of SAE 90. When temperatures are below 15°F (-10°C), use SAE 80.

Use oils with the proper additives for vehicles equipped with a limited slip differential.

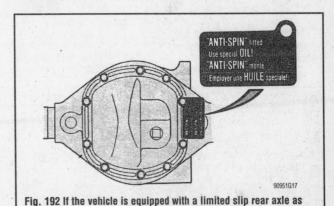

**Fig. 192 If the vehicle is equipped with a limited slip rear axle as noted by this tag, the proper oil or additive must be used**

### LEVEL CHECK

#### ♦ See Figure 193

The fluid level should be checked at 10,000 mile (16,000 km) intervals.
1. Raise and support the vehicle safely.
2. Remove the rear axle level plug.
3. Check that the oil level is up to the level plug hole. Top up, if necessary.
4. Reinstall the rear axle level plug.
5. Lower the vehicle.

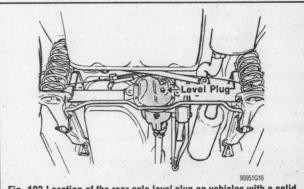

**Fig. 193 Location of the rear axle level plug on vehicles with a solid rear axle**

### DRAIN & REFILL

Drain and refill the rear axle housing every 100,000 miles (161,000 km) or any time the vehicle is driven in high water (up to the axle). Although some fluid can be removed using a suction gun, the best method is to remove the rear cover to ensure that all of any present contaminants are removed. As with any fluid change, the oil should be at normal operating temperature to ensure the best flow/removal of fluid and contaminants.

1. Drive the vehicle until the lubricant reaches normal operating temperature.

2. If necessary for access, raise and support the vehicle safely using jackstands, but be sure that the vehicle is level so you can properly refill the axle when you are finished.

3. Use a wire brush to clean the area around the differential. This will help prevent dirt from contaminating the differential housing while the cover is removed.

4. Position a drain pan under the rear axle.

5. Loosen and remove all but one or two of the rear cover upper or side retaining bolts. The remaining bolt(s) should then be loosened to within a few turns of complete removal. Use a small prytool to carefully break the gasket seal at the base of the cover and allow the lubricant to drain. Be VERY careful not to force or damage the cover and gasket mating surface.

6. Once most of the fluid has drained, remove the final retaining bolt(s) and separate the cover from the housing.

**To fill the differential:**

7. Carefully clean the gasket mating surfaces of the cover and axle housing of any remaining gasket or sealer. A putty knife is a good tool to use for this. You may want to cover the differential gears using a rag or piece of plastic to prevent contaminating them with dirt or pieces of the old gasket.

8. Install the rear cover using a new gasket and sealant. Tighten the retaining bolts using a crisscross pattern.

➡**Make sure the vehicle is level before attempting to add fluid to the rear axle, otherwise an incorrect fluid level will result.**

9. Refill the rear axle housing using the proper grade and quantity of lubricant, then install the filler plug.

10. Lower the vehicle, if applicable, then operate the vehicle and check for any leaks.

## Cooling System

### FLUID RECOMMENDATIONS

▶ **See Figures 194 and 195**

Volvo's all-weather antifreeze Type C (blue-green color) or equivalent should be used on a year round basis. The cooling system should always contain 50% antifreeze solution and 50% water. Studies have shown that extremely weak antifreeze solutions (10–20%) provide poor rust protection, while antifreeze solutions in excess of 70% provide less effective boil over protection.

### LEVEL CHECK

▶ **See Figure 196**

The coolant level should be checked at every 5,000 mile (8,000 km) intervals. The level should appear between the maximum and minimum marks of the translucent expansion tank. Do not remove the expansion tank filler cap except to top up the system, as air might become trapped in the system and reduce cooling efficiency. Top up the system with a mixture of 50% anti-freeze and 50% water; use this mixture all year round. If the engine is warm when you top up the cooling system, remove the filler cap slowly in order to allow any excess pressure to escape.

### ✳✳ CAUTION

**Never open, service or drain the radiator or cooling system when hot; serious burns can occur from the steam and hot coolant. Also, when draining engine coolant, keep in mind that cats and dogs are attracted to ethylene glycol antifreeze and could drink any that is left in an uncovered container or in puddles on the ground. This will prove fatal in sufficient quantities. Always drain coolant into a sealable container. Coolant should be reused unless it is contaminated or is several years old.**

### DRAIN & REFILL

▶ **See Figures 197, 198, 199, 200 and 201**

It is recommended that the coolant be replaced at 30,000 mile (48,000 km) intervals. Perform this operation with the engine cold.

1. Remove the expansion tank cap and set the heater controls to **HOT**.

2. Raise the vehicle and support it safely.

3. Open the petcock on the bottom of the radiator. If the coolant is to be reused, collect it in a clean container.

4. Completely drain the radiator of all the coolant.

5. Close the petcock and lower the vehicle.

6. On models with an expansion tank, either use a siphon or unfasten the tank and hold it up so that all of the coolant in it flows into the radiator.

7. Add coolant to the expansion tank until coolant is level with the **MAX** mark on the tank.

8. Start the engine and let it idle until normal operating temperature is reached and check for leaks.

9. Bleed the cooling system by leaving the cap off the expansion tank and the vehicle reaches normal operating temperature. The atmospheric pressure will aid in the removal of air pockets from the system.

10. Check the coolant level and refill if necessary.

11. Install the expansion tank cap.

### FLUSHING & CLEANING THE SYSTEM

1. Proceed with draining the system as previously outlined.

2. When the system has drained, reconnect the hoses and secure as necessary.

3. Move the temperature control for the heater to its hottest position; this allows the heater core to be flushed as well.

4. Using a garden hose, fill the radiator and allow the water to run out the engine draincocks. Continue until the water runs clear.

5. Be sure to clean the expansion tank as well.

➡**If the system is badly contaminated with rust or scale, you can use a commercial flushing solution to clean it out. Follow the manufacturer's instructions. Some causes of rust are air in the system, failure to**

Fig. 194 A tag is usually placed on the expansion tank or the strut tower indicating the type of coolant to be used

Fig. 195 Volvo recommends mixing 50% coolant and 50% water to fill the cooling system

Fig. 196 The expansion tank is marked with MIN/MAX levels; the fluid should be between them

Fig. 197 The radiator petcock is accessible through an opening in the gravel shield

Fig. 198 Loosen the petcock using the proper size tool; most vehicles require a 6mm Allen head wrench

Fig. 199 After the petcock is loose, coolant will start to drain out

Fig. 200 When the coolant is drained, remove the petcock, then clean and inspect it before installation

Fig. 201 Pour the proper 50/50 coolant mixture into the expansion tank to refill the system

change the coolant regularly, use of excessively hard or soft water, and/or failure to use the correct mix of antifreeze and water.

6. After the system has been flushed, continue with the refill procedures outlined above.

7. Check the condition of the radiator cap and its gasket, replacing the cap if anything looks improper.

## Brake Master Cylinder

### FLUID RECOMMENDATIONS

It is recommended that only brake fluid meeting the specification DOT 4+ (DOT 4) be used in the brake system. AVOID mixing different types of brake fluid.

### LEVEL CHECK

▶ See Figures 202, 203 and 204

The fluid level should be checked at every 5,000 mile (8,000 km) intervals. It is recommended that the fluid be replaced at 30,000 mile (48,000 km) intervals. If the vehicle is subjected to particularly hard wear, such as driving in mountainous regions, it should be changed at least once a year or every 15,000 miles (24,000 km).

### ❊❊ CAUTION

**Brake fluid contains polyglycol ethers and polyglycols. Avoid contact with the eyes and wash your hands thoroughly after handling brake fluid. If you do get brake fluid in your eyes, flush your eyes with clean, running water for 15 minutes. If eye irritation persists, or if you have taken brake fluid internally, IMMEDIATELY seek medical assistance.**

Fig. 202 The master cylinder reservoir is marked with MIN and MAX levels

Fig. 203 Wipe the top of the master cylinder reservoir clean before opening the cap to prevent contamination

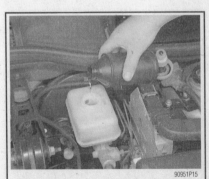

Fig. 204 Pour the proper brake fluid directly into the reservoir; if you use a funnel, be sure not to mix fluids

1. Position the vehicle on a level surface.
2. Locate the brake fluid reservoir in the engine compartment. Check the fluid reservoir and brake lines for leaks.
3. Check the brake fluid without removing the cap. Adjust the level if necessary, using the recommended fluid. When filling the master cylinder, extreme cleanliness should be observed to prevent dirt entering the system.

➡**Low fluid level may indicate worn brakes.**

## Clutch Master Cylinder

### FLUID RECOMMENDATIONS

The clutch master cylinder is located on the firewall, below the brake master cylinder, and adjacent to the power brake booster.

On some models, the clutch and brake fluid share the same reservoir and, therefore, the same fluid requirements. The clutch fluid level is checked when the brake fluid level is checked. The fluid level in the reservoir has **MIN** and **MAX** markings, and the fluid level is OK if it is between these two lines.

➡**Low fluid level may indicate worn brakes.**

### ✷✷ CAUTION

**Brake fluid contains polyglycol ethers and polyglycols. Avoid contact with the eyes and wash your hands thoroughly after handling brake fluid. If you do get brake fluid in your eyes, flush your eyes with clean, running water for 15 minutes. If eye irritation persists, or if you have taken brake fluid internally, IMMEDIATELY seek medical assistance.**

On models with a separate clutch master cylinder, the fluid should be in between the **MIN** and **MAX** levels.

## Power Steering Pump

### FLUID RECOMMENDATIONS

Automatic Transmission Fluid (ATF) type F is recommended for the power steering system.

### LEVEL CHECK

◆ **See Figures 205, 206 and 207**

The fluid level should be checked at every 5,000 mile (8,000 km) intervals.
1. Operate the vehicle until normal operating temperature is reached.
2. Check the fluid level, with the engine idling, while fluid is still hot.
3. Wipe the reservoir housing clean.
4. Check that the fluid level is within the markings (MIN/MAX) on the dipstick which is attached to the cover.
5. Adjust if necessary.

## Chassis Greasing

◆ **See Figure 208**

Check the suspension and driveline every 10,000 miles (16,000 km) intervals. Use regular chassis lube on applicable joints if binding is noticed.

Ball joints, suspension bushings and driveline joints are permanently lubricated at the factory and require no periodic lubrication. However, check the rubber seals of these parts for cracking or damage. Replace any damaged seal with a new one, making sure to pack the new seal with multipurpose chassis grease. Many aftermarket parts used to replace these components will contain a provision for lubrication. The easiest way to determine if a component can be lubricated is to look for a grease (Zerk®) fitting.

On most models the steering stops require lubricating or a noise will be heard when the vehicle is turned all the way in either direction. To grease the stops, simply spread some a multi-purpose grease, usually bearing grease over the surface.

### PROCEDURE

1. Raise and support the vehicle safely.
2. Locate all grease fittings on the vehicle. They are usually located on the at ball joints, suspension bushings and universal joints.

➡**Some grease fittings may be obscured by road dirt or grease from an over zealous chassis lubrication.**

3. Inspect the boot or seal for damage and replace as necessary. It is useless to attempt filling a damaged boot with grease as it will probably leak out.
4. Remove the grease fitting cap.
5. Clean the area around the grease fitting with a rag.
6. Connect a grease gun to the fitting and pump grease into the joint until the boot or seal swells slightly. On a well maintained vehicle, this should be no more than 3–4 pumps.

➡**Do not overfill the component with grease. If grease exits the boot or seal, it is overfill.**

Fig. 205 The dipstick is built into the filler cap, located on top of the reservoir

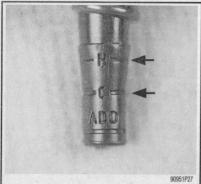

Fig. 206 The dipstick is marked with H (for Hot), C (for Cold) and an ADD range

Fig. 207 Pour the fluid directly into the reservoir, using a funnel if necessary

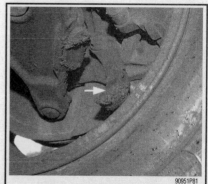

Fig. 208 Lubricate the steering stops at every oil change interval

7. Remove the grease gun and install the grease fitting cap.

8. Lower the vehicle.

## Body Lubrication and Maintenance

### LUBRICATION

▶ See Figures 209, 210, 211, 212 and 213

The body has several points that require periodic lubrication to maintain their quality operation. These points include the following:

• Hood hinges: lubricate every 10,000 miles (16,000 km), use heavy oil.

• Hood latch mechanism: lubricate every 10,000 miles (16,000 km), use general purpose grease.

• Door hinges, stop and striker plates: lubricate every 10,000 miles (16,000 km). Lubricate the door hinges with heavy oil. Use door wax to lubricate the striker plates. Check that the latches lock in both outer and inner positions.

• Check that the door stops are in working order and provide positive locking in intermediate and outer positions.

• Power Antenna: service the power antenna every 5,000 miles (8,000 km). Clean the antenna rod with ATF or other suitable lubricating oil. Wipe the rod clean and apply more oil on the antenna; then run the antenna up/down a few times. Repeat as necessary, until the antenna is clean and functions properly.

### CAR WASHING

The car should be washed at regular intervals to remove dirt, dust, insects, and tar and other possibly damaging stains that can adhere to the paint and may cause damage. Proper exterior maintenance also helps in the resale value of the vehicle by maintaining its like-new appearance.

➡ It is particularly important to frequently wash the car in the wintertime to prevent corrosion, when salt has been used on the roads.

There are many precautions and tips on washing, including the following:

• When washing the car, do not expose it do direct sunlight.

• Use lukewarm water to soften the dirt before you wash with a sponge, and plenty of water, to avoid scratching.

• A detergent can be used to facilitate the softening of dirt and oil.

• A water-soluble grease solvent may be used in cases of sticky dirt. However, use a washplace with a drainage separator.

• Dry the car with a clean chamois and remember to clean the drain holes in the doors and rocker panels.

• If equipped with a power radio antenna, it must be dried after washing.

### ✳✳ CAUTION

**Never clean the bumpers with gasoline or paint thinner, always use the same agent as used on the painted surfaces of the vehicle.**

• Tar spots can be removed with tar remover or kerosene after the car has been washed.

• A stiff-bristle brush and lukewarm soapy water can be used to clean the wiper blades. Frequent cleaning improves visibility when using the wipers considerably.

• Wash off the dirt from the underside (wheel housings, fenders, etc.).

• In areas of high industrial fallout, more frequent washing is recommended.

### ✳✳ CAUTION

**During high pressure washing the spray nozzle must never be closer to the vehicle than 13 inches (30 cm). Do not spray into the locks.**

• When washing or steam cleaning the engine, avoid spraying water or steam directly on the electrical components or near the distributor or ignition components. After cleaning the engine, the spark plug wells should be inspected for water and blown dry if necessary.

• Special car washing detergent is the best to use. Liquid dishwashing

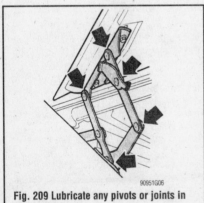

Fig. 209 Lubricate any pivots or joints in the hood hinges

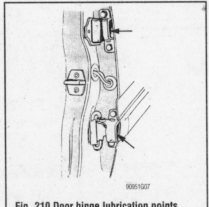

Fig. 210 Door hinge lubrication points

Fig. 211 Use a heavy oil to lubricate the door hinges

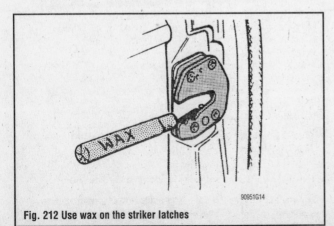

Fig. 212 Use wax on the striker latches

Fig. 213 Wipe the antenna clean and lightly lubricate with a mild lubricant such as ATF to increase antenna motor life

detergent can remove wax and leave the car's paint unprotected and in addition some liquid detergents contains abrasives which can scratch the paint.

• Bird droppings should be removed from the paintwork as soon as possible, otherwise the finish may be permanently stained.

**※※ WARNING**

**When the car is driven immediately after being washed, apply the brakes several times in order to remove any moisture from the braking surfaces.**

**※※ WARNING**

**Engine cleaning agents should not be used when the engine is warm, a fire risk is present as most engine cleaning agents are highly flammable.**

Automatic car washing is a simple and quick way to clean your car, but it is worth remembering that it is not as thorough as when you yourself clean the car. Keeping the underbody clean is vitally important, and some automatic washers do not contain equipment for washing the underside of the car.

When driving into an automatic was, make sure the following precautions have been taken:

• Make sure all windows are up, and no objects that you do not want to get wet are exposed.

• In some cases, rotating the side view mirrors in can help to avoid possible damage.

• If your car is equipped with a power antenna, lower it. If your vehicle has a solid mounted, non-power antenna, it is best to remove it, but this is not always practical. Inspect the surroundings to reduce the risk of possible damage, and check to see if the antenna can be manually lowered.

**※※ WARNING**

**Most manufacturers do not recommend automatic car washing in the first six months due to the possibility of insufficient paint curing; a safe bet is to wait until after six months of ownership (when purchased new) to use an automatic car wash.**

## WAXING

➡**Before applying wax, the vehicle must be washed and thoroughly dried.**

Waxing a vehicle can help to preserve the appearance of your vehicle. A wide range of polymer-based car waxes are available today. These waxes are easy to use and produce a long-lasting, high gloss finish that protects the body and paint against oxidation, road dirt, and fading.

Sometimes, waxing a neglected vehicle, or one that has sustained chemical or natural element damage (such as acid rain) require more than waxing, and a light-duty compound can be applied. For severely damaged surfaces, it is best to consult a professional to see what would be required to repair the damage.

Waxing procedures differ according to manufacturer, type, and ingredients, so it is best to consult the directions on the wax and/or polish purchased.

## INTERIOR CLEANING

### Upholstery

Fabric can usually be cleaned with soapy water or a proper detergent. For more difficult spots caused by oil, ice cream, soda, etc., use a fabric cleaner available at most parts stores. Be sure when purchasing the cleaner to read the label to ensure it is safe to use on your type of fabric. A safe method of testing the cleaner is to apply a small amount to an area usually unseen, such as under a seat, or other areas. Wait a while, perhaps even a day to check the spot for fading, discoloring, etc., as some cleaners will only cause these problems after they have dried.

Leather upholstery requires special care, it can be cleaned with a mild soap and a soft cloth. It is recommended that a special leather cleaner be used to clean but also treat the leather surfaces in your vehicle. Leather surfaces can age quickly and can crack if not properly taken care of, so it is vital that the leather surfaces be maintained.

### Floor Mats and Carpet

The floor mats and carpet should be vacuumed or brushed regularly. They can be cleaned with a mild soap and water. Special cleaners are available to clean the carpeted surfaces of your vehicle, but take care in choosing them, and again it is best to test them in a usually unseen spot.

### Dashboard, Console, Door Panels, Etc.

The dashboard, console, door panels, and other plastic, vinyl, or wood surfaces can be cleaned using a mild soap and water. Caution must be taken to keep water out of electronic accessories and controls to avoid shorts or ruining the components. Again special cleaners are available to clean these surfaces, as with other cleaners care must taken in purchasing and using such cleaners.

There are protectants available which can treat the various surfaces in your car giving them a "shiny new look", however some of these protectants can cause more harm than good in the long run. The shine that is placed on your dashboard attracts sunlight accelerating the aging, fading and possibly even cracking the surfaces. These protectants also attract more dust to stick to the surfaces they treat, increasing the cleaning you must do to maintain the appearance of your vehicle. Personal discretion is advised here.

## Wheel Bearings

### REPACKING

➡**Sodium based grease is not compatible with lithium based grease. Read the package labels and be careful not to mix the two types. If there is any doubt as to the type of grease used, completely clean the old grease from the bearing and hub before replacing.**

Before handling the bearings, there are a few things that you should remember to do and not to do.

**DO the following:**

• Remove all outside dirt from the housing before exposing the bearing.
• Treat a used bearing as gently as you would a new one.
• Work with clean tools in clean surroundings.
• Use clean, dry gloves, or at least clean, dry hands.
• Clean solvents and flushing fluids are a must.
• Use clean paper when laying out the bearings to dry.
• Protect disassembled bearings from rust and dirt. Cover them up.
• Use clean, lint-free rags to wipe the bearings.
• Keep the bearings in oil-proof paper when they are to be stored or are not in use.
• Clean the inside of the housing before replacing the bearing.

**Do NOT do the following:**

• Do not work in dirty surroundings.
• Do not use dirty, chipped or damaged tools.
• Do not work on wooden work benches or use wooden mallets.
• Do not handle bearings with dirty or moist hands.
• Do not use gasoline for cleaning. Use a safe solvent.
• Do not spin dry bearings with compressed air. They will be damaged.
• Do not use cotton waste or dirty cloths to wipe bearings.
• Do not scratch or nick bearing surfaces.
• Do not allow the bearing to come in contact with dirt or rust at any time.

The front wheel bearings only on rear drive Volvo models require periodic maintenance. A premium high melting point grease or equivalent must be used. Long fiber type greases must not be used. This service is recommended every 30,000 miles (48,000 km).

➡**For information on Wheel Bearing removal and installation, refer to Section 8 of this manual.**

1. Remove the wheel bearing.
2. Clean all parts in a non-flammable solvent and let them air dry.

➡**Only use lint-free rags to dry the bearings. Never spin-dry a bearing with compressed air, as this will damage the rollers.**

3. Check for excessive wear and damage. Replace the bearing as necessary.

➡**Packing wheel bearings with grease is best accomplished by using a wheel bearing packer (available at most automotive parts stores).**

4. If a wheel bearing packer is not available, the bearings may be packed by hand.

 a. Place a "healthy" glob of grease in the palm of one hand.

 b. Force the edge of the bearing into the grease so that the grease fills the space between the rollers and the bearing cage.

 c. Keep rotating the bearing while continuing to push the grease through.

 d. Continue until the grease is forced out the other side of the bearing.

5. Place the packed bearing on a clean surface and cover it until it is time for installation.

6. Install the wheel bearing.

## TRAILER TOWING

### General Recommendations

Your vehicle was primarily designed to carry passengers and cargo. It is important to remember that towing a trailer will place additional loads on your vehicle's engine, drive train, steering, braking and other systems. However, if you decide to tow a trailer, using the prior equipment is a must.

Local laws may require specific equipment such as trailer brakes or fender mounted mirrors. Check your local laws.

### Trailer Weight

The weight of the trailer is the most important factor. A good weight-to-horsepower ratio is about 35:1, 35 lbs. of Gross Combined Weight (GCW) for every horsepower your engine develops. Multiply the engine's rated horsepower by 35 and subtract the weight of the vehicle passengers and luggage. The number remaining is the approximate ideal maximum weight you should tow, although a numerically higher axle ratio can help compensate for heavier weight.

### Hitch (Tongue) Weight

▶ **See Figure 214**

Calculate the hitch weight in order to select a proper hitch. The weight of the hitch is usually 9–11% of the trailer gross weight and should be measured with the trailer loaded. Hitches fall into various categories: those that mount on the frame and rear bumper, the bolt-on type, or the weld-on distribution type used for larger trailers. Axle mounted or clamp-on bumper hitches should never be used.

Check the gross weight rating of your trailer. Tongue weight is usually figured as 10% of gross trailer weight. Therefore, a trailer with a maximum gross weight of 2000 lbs. will have a maximum tongue weight of 200 lbs. Class I trailers fall into this category. Class II trailers are those with a gross weight rating of 2000–3000 lbs., while Class III trailers fall into the 3500–6000 lbs. category. Class IV trailers are those over 6000 lbs. and are for use with fifth wheel trucks, only.

When you've determined the hitch that you'll need, follow the manufacturer's installation instructions, exactly, especially when it comes to fastener torque. The hitch will subjected to a lot of stress and good hitches come with hardened bolts. Never substitute an inferior bolt for a hardened bolt.

### Engine

One of the most common, if not THE most common, problems associated with trailer towing is engine overheating. If you have a cooling system without an expansion tank, you'll definitely need to get an aftermarket expansion tank kit, preferably one with at least a 2 quart capacity. These kits are easily installed on the radiator's overflow hose, and come with a pressure cap designed for expansion tanks.

Aftermarket engine oil coolers are helpful for prolonging engine oil life and reducing overall engine temperatures. Both of these factors increase engine life. While not absolutely necessary in towing Class I and some Class II trailers, they are recommended for heavier Class II and all Class III towing. Engine oil cooler systems usually consist of an adapter, screwed on in place of the oil filter, a remote filter mounting and a multi-tube, finned heat exchanger, which is mounted in front of the radiator or air conditioning condenser.

### Transmission/Transaxle

An automatic transmission/transaxle is usually recommended for trailer towing. Modern automatics have proven reliable and, of course, easy to operate, in trailer towing. The increased load of a trailer, however, causes an increase in the temperature of the automatic transmission fluid. Heat is the worst enemy of an automatic transmission. As the temperature of the fluid increases, the life of the fluid decreases.

It is essential, therefore, that you install an automatic transmission cooler. The cooler, which consists of a multi-tube, finned heat exchanger, is usually installed in front of the radiator or air conditioning compressor, and hooked in-line with the transmission cooler tank inlet line. Follow the cooler manufacturer's installation instructions.

Select a cooler of at least adequate capacity, based upon the combined gross weights of the vehicle and trailer.

Cooler manufacturers recommend that you use an aftermarket cooler in addition to, and not instead of, the present cooling tank in your radiator. If you do want to use it in place of the radiator cooling tank, get a cooler at least two sizes larger than normally necessary.

➡**A transmission cooler can, sometimes, cause slow or harsh shifting in the transmission during cold weather, until the fluid has a chance to come up to normal operating temperature. Some coolers can be purchased with or retrofitted with a temperature bypass valve which will allow fluid flow through the cooler only when the fluid has reached above a certain operating temperature.**

### Handling a Trailer

Towing a trailer with ease and safety requires a certain amount of experience. It's a good idea to learn the feel of a trailer by practicing turning, stopping and backing in an open area such as an empty parking lot.

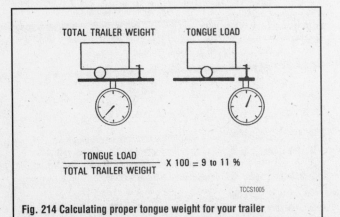

$$\frac{\text{TONGUE LOAD}}{\text{TOTAL TRAILER WEIGHT}} \times 100 = 9 \text{ to } 11 \%$$

TCCS1005

**Fig. 214 Calculating proper tongue weight for your trailer**

## TOWING THE VEHICLE

### Preferred Towing Method—Flatbed

♦ **See Figure 215**

For maximum safety to the components of your drive train and chassis, it is most desirable to have your vehicle towed on a flatbed or whole vehicle trailer. The only way to properly place the vehicle on a flatbed is to have it pulled on from the front.

**Fig. 215 Towing hooks are provided; they are exposed when the trim cover is removed**

## JUMP STARTING A DEAD BATTERY

♦ **See Figure 216**

Whenever a vehicle is jump started, precautions must be followed in order to prevent the possibility of personal injury. Remember that batteries contain a small amount of explosive hydrogen gas which is a by-product of battery charging. Sparks should always be avoided when working around batteries, especially when attaching jumper cables. To minimize the possibility of accidental sparks, follow the procedure carefully.

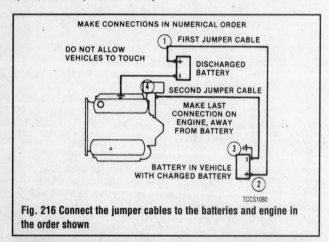

**Fig. 216 Connect the jumper cables to the batteries and engine in the order shown**

### ❉❉ CAUTION

**NEVER hook the batteries up in a series circuit or the entire electrical system will go up in smoke, including the starter!**

Vehicles equipped with a diesel engine may utilize two 12 volt batteries. If so, the batteries are connected in a parallel circuit (positive terminal to positive terminal, negative terminal to negative terminal). Hooking the batteries up in parallel circuit increases battery cranking power without increasing total battery voltage output. Output remains at 12 volts. On the other hand, hooking two 12 volt batteries up in a series circuit (positive terminal to negative terminal, posi-

### Alternate Towing Method—T-Hook

If a flatbed is unavailable, your vehicle can be towed using a T-hook wrecker. In this case, it is best to tow with the drive axle off the ground, as this will prevent wear and tear on the drive train. Tow vehicle speed should not exceed 35 mph (56 km/h) when using this method.

### ❉❉ WARNING

**This method CANNOT be used on an AWD vehicle.**

### Last Chance Towing Method—Dolly

If absolutely necessary, you can tow your vehicle with either the front or rear wheels on a dolly. Again, the preferred method would be to have the drive axle on the dolly, so the drive train is not turning. All conditions which apply to the T-hook method also apply for the dolly method.

### ❉❉ WARNING

**This method CANNOT be used on an AWD vehicle.**

tive terminal to negative terminal) increases total battery output to 24 volts (12 volts plus 12 volts).

### Jump Starting Precautions

• Be sure that both batteries are of the same voltage. Vehicles covered by this manual and most vehicles on the road today utilize a 12 volt charging system.

• Be sure that both batteries are of the same polarity (have the same terminal, in most cases NEGATIVE grounded).

• Be sure that the vehicles are not touching or a short could occur.

• On serviceable batteries, be sure the vent cap holes are not obstructed.

• Do not smoke or allow sparks anywhere near the batteries.

• In cold weather, make sure the battery electrolyte is not frozen. This can occur more readily in a battery that has been in a state of discharge.

• Do not allow electrolyte to contact your skin or clothing.

### Jump Starting Procedure

1. Make sure that the voltages of the 2 batteries are the same. Most batteries and charging systems are of the 12 volt variety.

2. Pull the jumping vehicle (with the good battery) into a position so the jumper cables can reach the dead battery and that vehicle's engine. Make sure that the vehicles do NOT touch.

3. Place the transmissions of both vehicles in **Neutral** (MT) or **P** (AT), as applicable, then firmly set their parking brakes.

➡**If necessary for safety reasons, the hazard lights on both vehicles may be operated throughout the entire procedure without significantly increasing the difficulty of jumping the dead battery.**

4. Turn all lights and accessories OFF on both vehicles. Make sure the ignition switches on both vehicles are turned to the **OFF** position.

5. Cover the battery cell caps with a rag, but do not cover the terminals.

6. Make sure the terminals on both batteries are clean and free of corrosion or proper electrical connection will be impeded. If necessary, clean the battery terminals before proceeding.

7. Identify the positive (+) and negative (-) terminals on both batteries.

8. Connect the first jumper cable to the positive (+) terminal of the dead

battery, then connect the other end of that cable to the positive (+) terminal of the booster (good) battery.

9. Connect one end of the other jumper cable to the negative (-) terminal on the booster battery and the final cable clamp to an engine bolt head, alternator bracket or other solid, metallic point on the engine with the dead battery. Try to pick a ground on the engine that is positioned away from the battery in order to minimize the possibility of the 2 clamps touching should one loosen during the procedure. DO NOT connect this clamp to the negative (-) terminal of the bad battery.

### ✳✳ CAUTION

**Be very careful to keep the jumper cables away from moving parts (cooling fan, belts, etc.) on both engines.**

10. Check to make sure that the cables are routed away from any moving parts, then start the donor vehicle's engine. Run the engine at moderate speed for several minutes to allow the dead battery a chance to receive some initial charge.

11. With the donor vehicle's engine still running slightly above idle, try to start the vehicle with the dead battery. Crank the engine for no more than 10 seconds at a time and let the starter cool for at least 20 seconds between tries. If the vehicle does not start in 3 tries, it is likely that something else is also wrong or that the battery needs additional time to charge.

12. Once the vehicle is started, allow it to run at idle for a few seconds to make sure that it is operating properly.

13. Turn ON the headlights, heater blower and, if equipped, the rear defroster of both vehicles in order to reduce the severity of voltage spikes and subsequent risk of damage to the vehicles' electrical systems when the cables are disconnected. This step is especially important to any vehicle equipped with computer control modules.

14. Carefully disconnect the cables in the reverse order of connection. Start with the negative cable that is attached to the engine ground, then the negative cable on the donor battery. Disconnect the positive cable from the donor battery and finally, disconnect the positive cable from the formerly dead battery. Be careful when disconnecting the cables from the positive terminals not to allow the alligator clips to touch any metal on either vehicle or a short and sparks will occur.

## JACKING

Your vehicle was supplied with a jack for emergency road repairs. This jack is fine for changing a flat tire or other short term procedures not requiring you to go beneath the vehicle. If it is used in an emergency situation, carefully follow the instructions provided either with the jack or in your owner's manual. Do not attempt to use the jack on any portions of the vehicle other than specified by the vehicle manufacturer. Always block the diagonally opposite wheel when using a jack.

A more convenient way of jacking is the use of a garage or floor jack. You may use the floor jack at the illustrated jacking locations.

Never place the jack under the radiator, engine or transmission components. Severe and expensive damage will result when the jack is raised. Additionally, never jack under the floorpan or bodywork; the metal will deform.

When raising the vehicle with a floor jack, position the jack under the crossmember at the front of the vehicle or under the differential case (if equipped) of the rear axle at the rear. When jacking at the front of the vehicle, do not position the jack under the gravel shield or the engine oil pan or you will damage these components.

Do not position the support stands under lower control arms or other slanted surfaces as they might slip and allow the vehicle to fall. The support stands can be placed beneath the rear axle tubes at the rear of the vehicle and beneath the reinforced areas of the rocker panels or front frame members. The vehicle's weight should push vertically (downward) on the stands; the stands should be on a level and solid base.

Whenever you plan to work under the vehicle, you must support it on jackstands or ramps. Never use cinder blocks or stacks of wood to support the vehicle, even if you're only going to be under it for a few minutes. Never crawl under the vehicle when it is supported only by the tire-changing jack or other floor jack.

➡**Always position a block of wood or small rubber pad on top of the jack or jackstand to protect the lifting point's finish when lifting or supporting the vehicle.**

Small hydraulic, screw, or scissors jacks are satisfactory for raising the vehicle. Drive-on trestles or ramps are also a handy and safe way to both raise and support the vehicle. Be careful though, some ramps may be too steep to drive your vehicle onto without scraping the front bottom panels. Never support the vehicle on any suspension member (unless specifically instructed to do so by a repair manual) or by an underbody panel.

### Jacking Precautions

▶ **See Figures 217, 218 and 219**

The following safety points cannot be overemphasized:
• Always block the opposite wheel or wheels to keep the vehicle from rolling off the jack.
• When raising the front of the vehicle, firmly apply the parking brake.
• When the drive wheels are to remain on the ground, leave the vehicle in gear to help prevent it from rolling.
• Always use jackstands to support the vehicle when you are working underneath. Place the stands beneath the vehicle's jacking brackets. Before climbing underneath, rock the vehicle a bit to make sure it is firmly supported.

Fig. 217 Position the jack in the middle to raise both wheels, and jack up the front of the vehicle by its subframe

Fig. 218 Place the jackstands beneath the rear end of the subframe to support the front of the vehicle

Fig. 219 Raise the rear by jacking at the rear spring perch, then place the jackstand under the frame rail; raise only one side at a time

## SCHEDULED MAINTENANCE INTERVALS

| TO BE SERVICED | TYPE OF SERVICE | 5 | 10 | 20 | 30 | 40 | 50 | 60 | 70 | 80 | 90 | 100 | 110 | 120 |
|---|---|---|---|---|---|---|---|---|---|---|---|---|---|---|
| Engine oil & filter① | R | ✓ | ✓ | ✓ | ✓ | ✓ | ✓ | ✓ | ✓ | ✓ | ✓ | ✓ | ✓ | ✓ |
| Automatic transmission fluid⑥ | S/I | | ✓ | ✓ | ✓ | ✓ | ✓ | ✓ | ✓ | ✓ | ✓ | ✓ | ✓ | ✓ |
| Fluid levels (all) | S/I | ✓ | ✓ | ✓ | ✓ | ✓ | ✓ | ✓ | ✓ | ✓ | ✓ | ✓ | ✓ | ✓ |
| Rotate tires | S/I | | ✓ | ✓ | ✓ | ✓ | ✓ | ✓ | ✓ | ✓ | ✓ | ✓ | ✓ | ✓ |
| Automatic transmission shift control | S/I | | ✓ | ✓ | ✓ | ✓ | ✓ | ✓ | ✓ | ✓ | ✓ | ✓ | ✓ | ✓ |
| Brake pads & parking brake | S/I | | ✓ | ✓ | ✓ | ✓ | ✓ | ✓ | ✓ | ✓ | ✓ | ✓ | ✓ | ✓ |
| Driveshaft boots (850) | S/I | | ✓ | ✓ | ✓ | ✓ | ✓ | ✓ | ✓ | ✓ | ✓ | ✓ | ✓ | ✓ |
| Engine & transmission (check for leaks) | S/I | | ✓ | ✓ | ✓ | ✓ | ✓ | ✓ | ✓ | ✓ | ✓ | ✓ | ✓ | ✓ |
| Exhaust system | S/I | | | ✓ | ✓ | ✓ | ✓ | ✓ | ✓ | ✓ | ✓ | ✓ | ✓ | ✓ |
| Grease link arm stops (1994-97 850) | S/I | | | ✓ | ✓ | ✓ | ✓ | ✓ | ✓ | ✓ | ✓ | ✓ | ✓ | ✓ |
| Reset service reminder① | S/I | | | ✓ | ✓ | ✓ | ✓ | ✓ | ✓ | ✓ | ✓ | ✓ | ✓ | ✓ |
| Driveshaft, U-joints | S/I | | | | ✓ | ✓ | ✓ | ✓ | ✓ | ✓ | ✓ | ✓ | ✓ | ✓ |
| Driveshaft joints (850) | S/I | | | | ✓ | | | ✓ | | | ✓ | | | ✓ |
| Clutch | S/I | | | ✓ | | ✓ | | ✓ | | ✓ | | ✓ | | ✓ |
| Kickdown cable (240/940) | S/I | | | | ✓ | | | ✓ | | | ✓ | | | ✓ |
| Brake & fuel lines & hoses | S/I | | | | ✓ | | | ✓ | | | ✓ | | | ✓ |
| Steering & suspension | S/I | | | | ✓ | | | ✓ | | | ✓ | | | ✓ |
| Air cleaner filter | R | | | | ✓ | | | ✓ | | | ✓ | | | ✓ |
| Spark plugs | R | | | | ✓ | | | ✓ | | | ✓ | | | ✓ |
| Timing belt (1993 960) | R | | | | ✓ | | | ✓ | | | ✓ | | | ✓ |
| Timing belt (1994-95 960) | R | | | | | | ✓ | | | | | ✓ | | |
| Timing belt (850 & 1996-97 960) | R | | | | | | | | ✓ | | | | | |

90951C08

## SCHEDULED MAINTENANCE INTERVALS

| TO BE SERVICED | TYPE OF SERVICE | 5 | 10 | 20 | 30 | 40 | 50 | 60 | 70 | 80 | 90 | 100 | 110 | 120 |
|---|---|---|---|---|---|---|---|---|---|---|---|---|---|---|
| Timing belt (B230F, FT)③ | R | | | | | | ✓ | | | | | ✓ | | |
| Timing belt (B230F, FT)③ | S/I | | | | | | | ✓ | | | | | ✓ | |
| Timing belt (B230F, FT) | S/I | | ✓ | | | | | | | | | | | |
| Timing belt (B230FD) | S/I | | | | | | | | | | | | ✓ | |
| Timing belt (B230FD)④ | R | | | | | | | | | | | ✓ | | |
| Timing gear belt tensioner pivot bearing (1993 960) | S/I | | | | ✓ | | | ✓ | | | | | | ✓ |
| Timing gear belt tensioner pivot bearing (1993 850) | R | | | | | | ✓ | | | | | | | |
| Valve clearance (240/740) | S/I | | | | ✓ | | | ✓ | | | ✓ | | | ✓ |
| Drive belt tensioner (850) | S/I | | | | ✓ | | | ✓ | | | ✓ | | | ✓ |
| Drive belts⑧ | S/I | | | | ✓ | | | ✓ | | | ✓ | | | ✓ |
| Fuel line filter⑨ | R | | | | | | | ✓ | | | | | | |
| EGR system | S/I | | | | | | | ✓ | | | | ✓ | | |
| PCV nipple (orifice)/hoses | S/I | | | | | | | ✓ | | | | ✓ | | |
| Check suspension torques⑦ | S/I | ✓ | | | | | | | | | | | | |
| Brake fluid② | R | | | | | | | | | | | | | |

90951C09

① Perform operation every 5000 miles on turbocharged models.
② Replace every 2 years or 30,000 miles, whichever comes first under normal conditions, more frequently in mountainous areas or moist climates.
③ Except 850 shown. 850 (1993) - perform at 1500 miles.
④ 1993-95 shown; replace every 100,000 miles (1996-97)
⑤ 850, 960: replace at 60,000 miles.
⑥ Replace as follows: 1993 240/940 - every 20,000 miles; 1994 940 - every 40,000 miles.
R – Replace    S/I – Service or Inspect

### FREQUENT OPERATION MAINTENANCE (SEVERE SERVICE)

If a vehicle is operated under any of the following conditions it is considered severe service:
- Extremely dusty areas.
- 50% or more of the vehicle operation is in 32°C (90°F) or higher temperatures, or constant operation in temperatures below 0°C (32°F).
- Prolonged idling (vehicle operation in stop and go traffic).
- Frequent short running periods (engine does not warm to normal operating temperatures).
- Police, taxi, delivery usage or trailer towing usage.
Oil & oil filter change – (all models) change every 5000 miles.
Air filter element – service or inspect every 15,000 miles.

## CAPACITIES

| Year | Model | Engine ID/VIN | Engine Displacement Liters (cc) | Engine Oil with Filter (qts.)②③ | Transmission (pts.) 4-Spd | Transmission (pts.) 5-Spd | Transmission (pts.) Auto. | Transfer Case (pts.) | Drive Axle Front (pts.) | Drive Axle Rear (pts.) | Fuel Tank (gal.) | Cooling System (qts.) |
|---|---|---|---|---|---|---|---|---|---|---|---|---|
| 1990 | 240 | B-230F/88 | 2.3 (2316) | 4.0 | — | 3.2 | 15.6② | — | ① | — | 15.8 | 10.0 |
| | 240DL | B-230F/88 | 2.3 (2316) | 4.0 | — | 3.2 | 15.6② | — | ① | — | 15.8 | 10.0 |
| | 740 | B-230F/88 | 2.3 (2316) | 4.0 | — | 3.2 | 15.6② | — | ① | — | 15.8 | 10.0 |
| | 740GL | B-230F/88 | 2.3 (2316) | 4.0 | — | 3.2 | 15.6② | — | ① | — | 15.8 | 10.0 |
| | 740GLE | B-234F/89 | 2.3 (2316) | 4.0 | 4.8 | — | 15.6② | — | ① | — | 15.8 | 10.0 |
| | 740Turbo | B-230FT/87 | 2.3 (2316) | 4.0 | 4.8 | — | 15.6② | — | ① | — | 15.8 | 10.0 |
| | 760GLE | B-280F/69 | 2.8 (2849) | 6.0 | — | — | 15.6② | — | ① | — | 21.0 | 10.0 |
| | 760Turbo | B-230FT/87 | 2.3 (2316) | 4.0 | — | — | 15.6② | — | ① | — | 21.0 | 10.0 |
| | 780 | B-280F/69 | 2.8 (2849) | 6.0 | — | — | 15.6② | — | ① | — | 21.0 | 10.5 |
| | 780Turbo | B-230FT/87 | 2.3 (2316) | 4.0 | — | — | 15.6② | — | ① | — | 21.0 | 10.5 |
| 1991 | 240DL | B-230F/88 | 2.3 (2316) | 4.0 | — | 3.2 | 15.6② | — | ① | — | 15.8 | 10.0 |
| | 240GL | B-230F/88 | 2.3 (2316) | 4.0 | — | 3.2 | 15.6② | — | ① | — | 15.8 | 10.0 |
| | 740GL | B-230F/88 | 2.3 (2316) | 4.0 | — | 3.2 | 15.6② | — | ① | — | 15.8 | 10.0 |
| | 740Turbo | B-230FT/87 | 2.3 (2316) | 4.0 | — | — | 15.6② | — | ① | — | 15.8 | 10.0 |
| | 940GL | B-230FT/87 | 2.3 (2316) | 4.0 | — | — | 15.6② | — | ① | — | 15.8 | 10.0 |
| | 940GLE | B-234F/89 | 2.3 (2316) | 4.0 | — | — | 15.6② | — | ① | — | 15.8 | 10.5 |
| | Coupe | B-230FT/87 | 2.3 (2316) | 4.0 | — | — | 15.6② | — | ① | — | 21.0 | 10.5 |
| 1992 | 240DL | B-230F/88 | 2.3 (2316) | 4.0 | — | 3.2 | 15.6② | — | ① | — | 15.8 | 10.0 |
| | 240GL | B-230F/88 | 2.3 (2316) | 4.0 | — | 3.2 | 15.6② | — | ① | — | 15.8 | 10.0 |
| | 740GL | B-230F/88 | 2.3 (2316) | 4.0 | — | 3.2 | 15.6② | — | ① | — | 15.8 | 10.0 |
| | 940SE | B-230FT/87 | 2.3 (2316) | 4.0 | — | — | 15.6② | — | ① | — | 15.8 | 10.0 |
| | 940Turbo | B-234F/89 | 2.3 (2316) | 4.0 | — | — | 15.6② | — | ① | — | 15.8 | 10.0 |
| | 940GLE | B-6304F/95 | 2.9 (2922) | 6.0 | — | — | 15.6② | — | ① | — | 19.8 | 11.3 |
| 1993 | 240 | B-230F/88 | 2.3 (2316) | 4.0 | — | 3.2 | 15.6② | — | ① | — | 15.8 | 10.0 |
| | 940 | B-230FT/87 | 2.3 (2316) | 4.0 | — | — | 15.6② | — | ① | — | 19.8 | 10.0 |
| | 940Turbo | B-6304F/95 | 2.9 (2922) | 6.0 | — | — | 15.6② | — | ① | — | 19.8 | 11.3 |
| | 960 | B-5254S/55 | 2.4 (2435) | 5.6 | — | 4.4 | 8.4 | — | ① | — | 19.3 | 7.6 |
| 1994 | 940 | B-230F/88 | 2.3 (2316) | 4.0 | — | — | 15.6② | — | ① | — | 19.8 | 10.0 |
| | 940Turbo | B-230FT/87 | 2.3 (2316) | 4.0 | — | — | 15.6② | — | ① | — | 19.8 | 10.0 |
| | 850 | B-5254S/55 | 2.4 (2435) | 5.6 | — | 4.4 | 8.4 | — | ① | — | 19.3 | 7.6 |
| | 850Turbo | B-5234T/57 | 2.3 (2319) | 5.6 | — | 4.4 | 8.4 | — | ① | — | 19.3 | 7.6 |
| | 960 | B6304F/95 | 2.9 (2922) | 6.0 | — | — | 16.4 | — | ① | — | 21.8 | 10.0 |
| 1995 | 940 | B-230F/88 | 2.3 (2316) | 4.0 | — | — | 15.6② | — | ① | — | 19.8 | 10.0 |
| | 940Turbo | B-230FT/87 | 2.3 (2316) | 4.0 | — | — | 15.6② | — | ① | — | 19.8 | 10.0 |
| | 850 | B-5254S/55 | 2.4 (2435) | 5.6 | — | 4.4 | 8.4 | — | ① | — | 19.3 | 7.6 |
| | 850Turbo | B-5234T/57 | 2.3 (2319) | 5.6 | — | 4.4 | 8.4 | — | ① | — | 19.3 | 7.6 |
| | 960 | B6304F/95 | 2.9 (2922) | 6.0 | — | — | 16.4 | — | ① | — | 21.8 | 10.0 |

90951C04

## CAPACITIES

| Year | Model | Engine ID/VIN | Engine Displacement Liters (cc) | Engine Oil with Filter (qts.)② | Transmission (pts.) 4-Spd | Transmission (pts.) 5-Spd | Transmission (pts.) Auto. | Transfer Case (pts.) | Drive Axle Front (pts.) | Drive Axle Rear (pts.) | Fuel Tank (gal.) | Cooling System (qts.) |
|---|---|---|---|---|---|---|---|---|---|---|---|---|
| 1996 | 850 | B-5254S/55 | 2.4 (2435) | 5.6 | — | 4.4 | 8.4 | — | — | — | 19.3 | 7.6 |
| | 850GLT | B-5254T/56 | 2.4 (2435) | 5.6 | — | 4.4 | 8.4 | — | — | — | 19.3 | 7.6 |
| | 850T-5 | B-5234T/57 | 2.3 (2319) | 5.6 | — | 4.4 | 8.4 | — | — | — | 19.3 | 7.6 |
| | 850R | B-5254FT/58 | 2.3 (2319) | 5.6 | — | — | 8.4 | — | — | — | 19.3 | 7.6 |
| | 960 | B-6304S/96 | 2.9 (2922) | 6.0 | — | — | 16.4 | — | — | ① | 21.8 | 10.0 |
| 1997 | 850 | B-5254S/55 | 2.4 (2435) | 5.6 | — | 4.4 | 8.4 | — | — | — | 19.3 | 7.6 |
| | 850GLT | B-5254T/56 | 2.4 (2435) | 5.6 | — | 4.4 | 8.4 | — | — | — | 19.3 | 7.6 |
| | 850T-5 | B-5234T/57 | 2.3 (2319) | 5.6 | — | 4.4 | 8.4 | — | — | — | 19.3 | 7.6 |
| | 850R | B-5254FT/58 | 2.3 (2319) | 5.6 | — | 4.4 | 8.4 | — | — | — | 19.3 | 7.6 |
| | 960 | B-630AS/96 | 2.9 (2922) | 6.0 | — | — | 16.4 | — | — | ① | 21.8 | 10.0 |
| 1998 | S70 | B5254S/55 | 2.4 (2435) | 6.1 | — | 4.4 | 8.4 | — | — | — | 18.5 | 7.6 |
| | S70GLT | B-5254T/56 | 2.4 (2435) | 6.1 | — | 4.4 | 8.4 | — | — | — | 18.5 | 7.6 |
| | S70T-5 | B-5234T/57 | 2.3 (2319) | 6.1 | — | 4.4 | 8.4 | — | — | — | 18.5 | 7.6 |
| | S90 | B-630AS/95 | 2.9 (2922) | 6.0 | — | — | 16.4 | — | — | ① | 21.8 | 10.0 |
| | C70 | B-5234T3/53 | 2.3 (2319) | 6.1 | — | 4.4 | 8.4 | — | — | — | 18.5 | 7.6 |
| | V70 | B-5254S/55 | 2.4 (2435) | 6.1 | — | 4.4 | 8.4 | — | — | — | 18.5 | 7.6 |
| | V70GLT | B-5254T/56 | 2.4 (2435) | 6.1 | — | 4.4 | 8.4 | — | — | — | 18.5 | 7.6 |
| | V70T-5 | B-5234T/57 | 2.3 (2319) | 6.1 | — | 4.4 | 8.4 | — | — | — | 18.5 | 7.6 |
| | V70 AWD | B-5254T/56 | 2.4 (2435) | 6.1 | — | 4.4 | 8.4 | 1.7 | — | 2.9 | 18.5 | 7.6 |
| | V70R AWD | B-5234T/57 | 2.3 (2319) | 6.1 | — | — | 8.4 | 1.7 | — | 2.9 | 18.5 | 7.6 |
| | V70XC AWD | B-5254T/56 | 2.4 (2435) | 6.1 | — | — | 8.4 | 1.7 | — | 2.9 | 18.5 | 7.6 |
| | V90 | B-630AS/96 | 2.9 (2922) | 6.1 | — | — | 16.4 | — | — | ① | 21.8 | 10.0 |

90951C05

① 1030 axle-2.8
1031 axle-3.4
1035 axle-2.9
1041 axle-3.1
1045 axle-2.8
1055 axle-3.2
1065 axle-2.9

② On turbocharged engines, add 0.7 US qts. if the cooler is drained

③ Total fluid capacity cannot be drained. 3.6 qts (3.4 liters) can be drained, the rest remains in the torque converter and control systems

④ 4 door - 21.0
5 door - 15.8

## ENGLISH TO METRIC CONVERSION: LENGTH

To convert inches (ins.) to millimeters (mm): multiply number of inches by 25.4
To convert millimeters (mm) to inches (ins.): multiply number of millimeters by .04

| Inches | Decimals | Millimeters | Inches to millimeters (inches) | mm | Inches | Decimals | Millimeters | Inches to millimeters (inches) | millimeters mm |
|---|---|---|---|---|---|---|---|---|---|
| 1/64 | 0.015625 | 0.3969 | 0.0001 | 0.00254 | 33/64 | 0.515625 | 13.0969 | 0.6 | 15.24 |
| 1/32 | 0.03125 | 0.7937 | 0.0002 | 0.00508 | 17/32 | 0.53125 | 13.4937 | 0.7 | 17.78 |
| 3/64 | 0.046875 | 1.1906 | 0.0003 | 0.00762 | 35/64 | 0.546875 | 13.8906 | 0.8 | 20.32 |
| 1/16 | 0.0625 | 1.5875 | 0.0004 | 0.01016 | 9/16 | 0.5625 | 14.2875 | 0.9 | 22.86 |
| 5/64 | 0.078125 | 1.9844 | 0.0005 | 0.01270 | 37/64 | 0.578125 | 14.6844 | 1 | 25.4 |
| 3/32 | 0.09375 | 2.3812 | 0.0006 | 0.01524 | 19/32 | 0.59375 | 15.0812 | 2 | 50.8 |
| 7/64 | 0.109375 | 2.7781 | 0.0007 | 0.01778 | 39/64 | 0.609375 | 15.4781 | 3 | 76.2 |
| 1/8 | 0.125 | 3.1750 | 0.0008 | 0.02032 | 5/8 | 0.625 | 15.8750 | 4 | 101.6 |
| 9/64 | 0.140625 | 3.5719 | 0.0009 | 0.02286 | 41/64 | 0.640625 | 16.2719 | 5 | 127.0 |
| 5/32 | 0.15625 | 3.9687 | 0.001 | 0.0254 | 21/32 | 0.65625 | 16.6687 | 6 | 152.4 |
| 11/64 | 0.171875 | 4.3656 | 0.002 | 0.0508 | 43/64 | 0.671875 | 17.0656 | 7 | 177.8 |
| 3/16 | 0.1875 | 4.7625 | 0.003 | 0.0762 | 11/16 | 0.6875 | 17.4625 | 8 | 203.2 |
| 13/64 | 0.203125 | 5.1594 | 0.004 | 0.1016 | 45/64 | 0.703125 | 17.8594 | 9 | 228.6 |
| 7/32 | 0.21875 | 5.5562 | 0.005 | 0.1270 | 23/32 | 0.71875 | 18.2562 | 10 | 254.0 |
| 15/64 | 0.234375 | 5.9531 | 0.006 | 0.1524 | 47/64 | 0.734375 | 18.6531 | 11 | 279.4 |
| 1/4 | 0.25 | 6.3500 | 0.007 | 0.1778 | 3/4 | 0.75 | 19.0500 | 12 | 304.8 |
| 17/64 | 0.265625 | 6.7469 | 0.008 | 0.2032 | 49/64 | 0.765625 | 19.4469 | 13 | 330.2 |
| 9/32 | 0.28125 | 7.1437 | 0.009 | 0.2286 | 25/32 | 0.78125 | 19.8437 | 14 | 355.6 |
| 19/64 | 0.296875 | 7.5406 | 0.01 | 0.254 | 51/64 | 0.796875 | 20.2406 | 15 | 381.0 |
| 5/16 | 0.3125 | 7.9375 | 0.02 | 0.508 | 13/16 | 0.8125 | 20.6375 | 16 | 406.4 |
| 21/64 | 0.328125 | 8.3344 | 0.03 | 0.762 | 53/64 | 0.828125 | 21.0344 | 17 | 431.8 |
| 11/32 | 0.34375 | 8.7312 | 0.04 | 1.016 | 27/32 | 0.84375 | 21.4312 | 18 | 457.2 |
| 23/64 | 0.359375 | 9.1281 | 0.05 | 1.270 | 55/64 | 0.859375 | 21.8281 | 19 | 482.6 |
| 3/8 | 0.375 | 9.5250 | 0.06 | 1.524 | 7/8 | 0.875 | 22.2250 | 20 | 508.0 |
| 25/64 | 0.390625 | 9.9219 | 0.07 | 1.778 | 57/64 | 0.890625 | 22.6219 | 21 | 533.4 |
| 13/32 | 0.40625 | 10.3187 | 0.08 | 2.032 | 29/32 | 0.90625 | 23.0187 | 22 | 558.8 |
| 27/64 | 0.421875 | 10.7156 | 0.09 | 2.286 | 59/64 | 0.921875 | 23.4156 | 23 | 584.2 |
| 7/16 | 0.4375 | 11.1125 | 0.1 | 2.54 | 15/16 | 0.9375 | 23.8125 | 24 | 609.6 |
| 29/64 | 0.453125 | 11.5094 | 0.2 | 5.08 | 61/64 | 0.953125 | 24.2094 | 25 | 635.0 |
| 15/32 | 0.46875 | 11.9062 | 0.3 | 7.62 | 31/32 | 0.96875 | 24.6062 | 26 | 660.4 |
| 31/64 | 0.484375 | 12.3031 | 0.4 | 10.16 | 63/64 | 0.984375 | 25.0031 | 27 | 690.6 |
| 1/2 | 0.5 | 12.7000 | 0.5 | 12.70 | | | | | |

TCCS1C02

## ENGLISH TO METRIC CONVERSION: TORQUE

To convert foot-pounds (ft. lbs.) to Newton-meters: multiply the number of ft. lbs. by 1.3
To convert inch-pounds (in. lbs.) to Newton-meters: multiply the number of in. lbs. by .11

| in lbs | N-m | in lbs | N-m | in lbs | N-m | in lbs | N-m | in lbs | N-m |
|---|---|---|---|---|---|---|---|---|---|
| 0.1 | 0.01 | 1 | 0.11 | 10 | 1.13 | 19 | 2.15 | 28 | 3.16 |
| 0.2 | 0.02 | 2 | 0.23 | 11 | 1.24 | 20 | 2.26 | 29 | 3.28 |
| 0.3 | 0.03 | 3 | 0.34 | 12 | 1.36 | 21 | 2.37 | 30 | 3.39 |
| 0.4 | 0.04 | 4 | 0.45 | 13 | 1.47 | 22 | 2.49 | 31 | 3.50 |
| 0.5 | 0.06 | 5 | 0.56 | 14 | 1.58 | 23 | 2.60 | 32 | 3.62 |
| 0.6 | 0.07 | 6 | 0.68 | 15 | 1.70 | 24 | 2.71 | 33 | 3.73 |
| 0.7 | 0.08 | 7 | 0.78 | 16 | 1.81 | 25 | 2.82 | 34 | 3.84 |
| 0.8 | 0.09 | 8 | 0.90 | 17 | 1.92 | 26 | 2.94 | 35 | 3.95 |
| 0.9 | 0.10 | 9 | 1.02 | 18 | 2.03 | 27 | 3.05 | 36 | 4.0 |

## ENGLISH TO METRIC CONVERSION: MASS (WEIGHT)

Current mass measurement is expressed in pounds and ounces (lbs. & ozs.). The metric unit of mass (or weight) is the kilogram (kg). Even although this table does not show conversion of masses (weights) larger than 15 lbs, it is easy to calculate larger units by following the data immediately below.

To convert ounces (oz.) to grams (g): multiply th number of ozs. by 28
To convert grams (g) to ounces (oz.): multiply the number of grams by .035
To convert pounds (lbs.) to kilograms (kg): multiply the number of lbs. by .45
To convert kilograms (kg) to pounds (lbs.): multiply the number of kilograms by 2.2

| lbs | kg | lbs | kg | oz | kg | oz | kg |
|---|---|---|---|---|---|---|---|
| 0.1 | 0.04 | 0.9 | 0.41 | 0.1 | 0.003 | 0.9 | 0.024 |
| 0.2 | 0.09 | 1 | 0.4 | 0.2 | 0.005 | 1 | 0.03 |
| 0.3 | 0.14 | 2 | 0.9 | 0.3 | 0.008 | 2 | 0.06 |
| 0.4 | 0.18 | 3 | 1.4 | 0.4 | 0.011 | 3 | 0.08 |
| 0.5 | 0.23 | 4 | 1.8 | 0.5 | 0.014 | 4 | 0.11 |
| 0.6 | 0.27 | 5 | 2.3 | 0.6 | 0.017 | 5 | 0.14 |
| 0.7 | 0.32 | 10 | 4.5 | 0.7 | 0.020 | 10 | 0.28 |
| 0.8 | 0.36 | 15 | 6.8 | 0.8 | 0.023 | 15 | 0.42 |

## ENGLISH TO METRIC CONVERSION: TEMPERATURE

To convert Fahrenheit (°F) to Celsius (°C): take number of °F and subtract 32; multiply result by 5; divide result by 9
To convert Celsius (°C) to Fahrenheit (°F): take number of °C and multiply by 9; divide result by 5; add 32 to total

| Fahrenheit (°F) | Celsius (°C) | Celsius (°C) | Fahrenheit (°F) |
|---|---|---|---|
| -40 | -40 | -38 | -36.4 |
| -35 | -37.2 | -36 | -32.8 |
| -30 | -34.4 | -34 | -29.2 |
| -25 | -31.7 | -32 | -25.6 |
| -20 | -28.9 | -30 | -22 |
| -15 | -26.1 | -28 | -18.4 |
| -10 | -23.3 | -26 | -14.8 |
| -5 | -20.6 | -24 | -11.2 |
| 0 | -17.8 | -22 | -7.6 |
| 1 | -17.2 | -20 | -4 |
| 2 | -16.7 | -18 | -0.4 |
| 3 | -16.1 | -16 | 3.2 |
| 4 | -15.6 | -14 | 6.8 |
| 5 | -15.0 | -12 | 10.4 |
| 10 | -12.2 | -10 | 14 |
| 15 | -9.4 | -8 | 17.6 |
| 20 | -6.7 | -6 | 21.2 |
| 25 | -3.9 | -4 | 24.8 |
| 30 | -1.1 | -2 | 28.4 |
| 35 | 1.7 | 0 | 32 |
| 40 | 4.4 | 2 | 35.6 |
| 45 | 7.2 | 4 | 39.2 |
| 50 | 10.0 | 6 | 42.8 |
| 55 | 12.8 | 8 | 46.4 |
| 60 | 15.6 | 10 | 50 |
| 65 | 18.3 | 12 | 53.6 |
| 70 | 21.1 | 14 | 57.2 |
| 75 | 23.9 | 16 | 60.8 |
| 80 | 26.7 | 18 | 64.4 |
| 85 | 29.4 | 20 | 68 |
| 90 | 32.2 | 22 | 71.6 |
| 95 | 35.0 | 24 | 75.2 |
| 100 | 37.8 | 26 | 78.8 |
| 105 | 40.6 | 28 | 82.4 |
| 110 | 43.3 | 30 | 86 |
| 115 | 46.1 | 32 | 89.6 |
| 120 | 48.9 | 34 | 93.2 |
| 125 | 51.7 | 36 | 96.8 |
| 130 | 54.4 | 38 | 100.4 |
| 135 | 57.2 | 40 | 104 |
| 140 | 60.0 | 42 | 107.6 |
| 145 | 62.8 | 44 | 111.2 |
| 150 | 65.6 | 46 | 114.8 |
| 155 | 68.3 | 48 | 118.4 |
| 160 | 71.1 | 50 | 122 |
| 165 | 73.9 | 52 | 125.6 |
| 170 | 76.7 | 54 | 129.2 |
| 175 | 79.4 | 56 | 132.8 |
| 180 | 82.2 | 58 | 136.4 |
| 185 | 85.0 | 60 | 140 |
| 190 | 87.8 | 62 | 143.6 |
| 195 | 90.6 | 64 | 147.2 |
| 200 | 93.3 | 66 | 150.8 |
| 205 | 96.1 | 68 | 154.4 |
| 210 | 98.9 | 70 | 158 |
| 212 | 100.0 | 75 | 167 |
| 215 | 101.7 | 80 | 176 |
| 220 | 104.4 | 85 | 185 |
| 225 | 107.2 | 90 | 194 |
| 230 | 110.0 | 95 | 202 |
| 235 | 112.8 | 100 | 212 |
| 240 | 115.6 | 105 | 221 |
| 245 | 118.3 | 110 | 230 |
| 250 | 121.1 | 115 | 239 |
| 255 | 123.9 | 120 | 248 |
| 260 | 126.6 | 125 | 257 |
| 265 | 129.4 | 130 | 266 |
| 270 | 132.2 | 135 | 275 |
| 275 | 135.0 | 140 | 284 |
| 280 | 137.8 | 145 | 293 |
| 285 | 140.6 | 150 | 302 |
| 290 | 143.3 | 155 | 311 |
| 295 | 146.1 | 160 | 320 |
| 300 | 148.9 | 165 | 329 |
| 305 | 151.7 | 170 | 338 |
| 310 | 154.4 | 175 | 347 |
| 315 | 157.2 | 180 | 356 |
| 320 | 160.0 | 185 | 365 |
| 325 | 162.8 | 190 | 374 |
| 330 | 165.6 | 195 | 383 |
| 335 | 168.3 | 200 | 392 |
| 340 | 171.1 | 205 | 401 |
| 345 | 173.9 | 210 | 410 |
| 350 | 176.7 | 215 | 414 |

TCCS1C01

## ENGLISH TO METRIC CONVERSION: TORQUE

Torque is now expressed as either foot-pounds (ft./lbs.) or inch-pounds (in./lbs.). The metric measurement unit for torque is the Newton-meter (Nm). This unit—the Nm—will be used for all SI metric torque references, both the present ft./lbs. and in./lbs.

| ft lbs | N-m | ft lbs | N-m | ft lbs | N-m | ft lbs | N-m |
|---|---|---|---|---|---|---|---|
| 0.1 | 0.1 | 33 | 44.7 | 74 | 100.3 | 115 | 155.9 |
| 0.2 | 0.3 | 34 | 46.1 | 75 | 101.7 | 116 | 157.3 |
| 0.3 | 0.4 | 35 | 47.4 | 76 | 103.0 | 117 | 158.6 |
| 0.4 | 0.5 | 36 | 48.8 | 77 | 104.4 | 118 | 160.0 |
| 0.5 | 0.7 | 37 | 50.7 | 78 | 105.8 | 119 | 161.3 |
| 0.6 | 0.8 | 38 | 51.5 | 79 | 107.1 | 120 | 162.7 |
| 0.7 | 1.0 | 39 | 52.9 | 80 | 108.5 | 121 | 164.0 |
| 0.8 | 1.1 | 40 | 54.2 | 81 | 109.8 | 122 | 165.4 |
| 0.9 | 1.2 | 41 | 55.6 | 82 | 111.2 | 123 | 166.8 |
| 1 | 1.3 | 42 | 56.9 | 83 | 112.5 | 124 | 168.1 |
| 2 | 2.7 | 43 | 58.3 | 84 | 113.9 | 125 | 169.5 |
| 3 | 4.1 | 44 | 59.7 | 85 | 115.2 | 126 | 170.8 |
| 4 | 5.4 | 45 | 61.0 | 86 | 116.6 | 127 | 172.2 |
| 5 | 6.8 | 46 | 62.4 | 87 | 118.0 | 128 | 173.5 |
| 6 | 8.1 | 47 | 63.7 | 88 | 119.3 | 129 | 174.9 |
| 7 | 9.5 | 48 | 65.1 | 89 | 120.7 | 130 | 176.2 |
| 8 | 10.8 | 49 | 66.4 | 90 | 122.0 | 131 | 177.6 |
| 9 | 12.2 | 50 | 67.8 | 91 | 123.4 | 132 | 179.0 |
| 10 | 13.6 | 51 | 69.2 | 92 | 124.7 | 133 | 180.3 |
| 11 | 14.9 | 52 | 70.5 | 93 | 126.1 | 134 | 181.7 |
| 12 | 16.3 | 53 | 71.9 | 94 | 127.4 | 135 | 183.0 |
| 13 | 17.6 | 54 | 73.2 | 95 | 128.8 | 136 | 184.4 |
| 14 | 18.9 | 55 | 74.6 | 96 | 130.2 | 137 | 185.7 |
| 15 | 20.3 | 56 | 75.9 | 97 | 131.5 | 138 | 187.1 |
| 16 | 21.7 | 57 | 77.3 | 98 | 132.9 | 139 | 188.5 |
| 17 | 23.0 | 58 | 78.6 | 99 | 134.2 | 140 | 189.8 |
| 18 | 24.4 | 59 | 80.0 | 100 | 135.6 | 141 | 191.2 |
| 19 | 25.8 | 60 | 81.4 | 101 | 136.9 | 142 | 192.5 |
| 20 | 27.1 | 61 | 82.7 | 102 | 138.3 | 143 | 193.9 |
| 21 | 28.5 | 62 | 84.1 | 103 | 139.6 | 144 | 195.2 |
| 22 | 29.8 | 63 | 85.4 | 104 | 141.0 | 145 | 196.6 |
| 23 | 31.2 | 64 | 86.8 | 105 | 142.4 | 146 | 198.0 |
| 24 | 32.5 | 65 | 88.1 | 106 | 143.7 | 147 | 199.3 |
| 25 | 33.9 | 66 | 89.5 | 107 | 145.1 | 148 | 200.7 |
| 26 | 35.2 | 67 | 90.8 | 108 | 146.4 | 149 | 202.0 |
| 27 | 36.6 | 68 | 92.2 | 109 | 147.8 | 150 | 203.4 |
| 28 | 38.0 | 69 | 93.6 | 110 | 149.1 | 151 | 204.7 |
| 29 | 39.3 | 70 | 94.9 | 111 | 150.5 | 152 | 206.1 |
| 30 | 40.7 | 71 | 96.3 | 112 | 151.8 | 153 | 207.4 |
| 31 | 42.0 | 72 | 97.6 | 113 | 153.2 | 154 | 208.8 |
| 32 | 43.4 | 73 | 99.0 | 114 | 154.6 | 155 | 210.2 |

TCCS1C03

## ENGLISH TO METRIC CONVERSION: FORCE

Force is presently measured in pounds (lbs.). This type of measurement is used to measure spring pressure, specifically how many pounds it takes to compress a spring. Our present force unit (the pound) will be replaced in SI metric measurements by the Newton (N). This term will eventually see use in specifications for electric motor brush spring pressures, valve spring pressures, etc.

To convert pounds (lbs.) to Newton (N): multiply the number of lbs. by 4.45

| lbs | N | lbs | N | lbs | N | oz | N |
|---|---|---|---|---|---|---|---|
| 0.01 | 0.04 | 21 | 93.4 | 59 | 262.4 | 1 | 0.3 |
| 0.02 | 0.09 | 22 | 97.9 | 60 | 266.9 | 2 | 0.6 |
| 0.03 | 0.13 | 23 | 102.3 | 61 | 271.3 | 3 | 0.8 |
| 0.04 | 0.18 | 24 | 106.8 | 62 | 275.8 | 4 | 1.1 |
| 0.05 | 0.22 | 25 | 111.2 | 63 | 280.2 | 5 | 1.4 |
| 0.06 | 0.27 | 26 | 115.6 | 64 | 284.6 | 6 | 1.7 |
| 0.07 | 0.31 | 27 | 120.1 | 65 | 289.1 | 7 | 2.0 |
| 0.08 | 0.36 | 28 | 124.6 | 66 | 293.6 | 8 | 2.2 |
| 0.09 | 0.40 | 29 | 129.0 | 67 | 298.0 | 9 | 2.5 |
| 0.1 | 0.4 | 30 | 133.4 | 68 | 302.5 | 10 | 2.8 |
| 0.2 | 0.9 | 31 | 137.9 | 69 | 306.9 | 11 | 3.1 |
| 0.3 | 1.3 | 32 | 142.3 | 70 | 311.4 | 12 | 3.3 |
| 0.4 | 1.8 | 33 | 146.8 | 71 | 315.8 | 13 | 3.6 |
| 0.5 | 2.2 | 34 | 151.2 | 72 | 320.3 | 14 | 3.9 |
| 0.6 | 2.7 | 35 | 155.7 | 73 | 324.7 | 15 | 4.2 |
| 0.7 | 3.1 | 36 | 160.1 | 74 | 329.2 | 16 | 4.4 |
| 0.8 | 3.6 | 37 | 164.6 | 75 | 333.6 | 17 | 4.7 |
| 0.9 | 4.0 | 38 | 169.0 | 76 | 338.1 | 18 | 5.0 |
| 1 | 4.4 | 39 | 173.5 | 77 | 342.5 | 19 | 5.3 |
| 2 | 8.9 | 40 | 177.9 | 78 | 347.0 | 20 | 5.6 |
| 3 | 13.4 | 41 | 182.4 | 79 | 351.4 | 21 | 5.8 |
| 4 | 17.8 | 42 | 186.8 | 80 | 355.9 | 22 | 6.1 |
| 5 | 22.2 | 43 | 191.3 | 81 | 360.3 | 23 | 6.4 |
| 6 | 26.7 | 44 | 195.7 | 82 | 364.8 | 24 | 6.7 |
| 7 | 31.1 | 45 | 200.2 | 83 | 369.2 | 25 | 7.0 |
| 8 | 35.6 | 46 | 204.6 | 84 | 373.6 | 26 | 7.2 |
| 9 | 40.0 | 47 | 209.1 | 85 | 378.1 | 27 | 7.5 |
| 10 | 44.5 | 48 | 213.5 | 86 | 382.6 | 28 | 7.8 |
| 11 | 48.9 | 49 | 218.0 | 87 | 387.0 | 29 | 8.1 |
| 12 | 53.4 | 50 | 222.4 | 88 | 391.4 | 30 | 8.3 |
| 13 | 57.8 | 51 | 226.9 | 89 | 395.9 | 31 | 8.6 |
| 14 | 62.3 | 52 | 231.3 | 90 | 400.3 | 32 | 8.9 |
| 15 | 66.7 | 53 | 235.8 | 91 | 404.8 | 33 | 9.2 |
| 16 | 71.2 | 54 | 240.2 | 92 | 409.2 | 34 | 9.4 |
| 17 | 75.6 | 55 | 244.6 | 93 | 413.7 | 35 | 9.7 |
| 18 | 80.1 | 56 | 249.1 | 94 | 418.1 | 36 | 10.0 |
| 19 | 84.5 | 57 | 253.6 | 95 | 422.6 | 37 | 10.3 |
| 20 | 89.0 | 58 | 258.0 | 96 | 427.0 | 38 | 10.6 |

TCCS1C04

## ENGLISH TO METRIC CONVERSION: LIQUID CAPACITY

Liquid or fluid capacity is presently expressed as pints, quarts or gallons, or a combination of all of these. In the metric system the liter (l) will become the basic unit. Fractions of a liter would be expressed as deciliters, centiliters, or most frequently (and commonly) as milliliters.

To convert pints (pts.) to liters (l): multiply the number of pints by .47
To convert liters (l) to pints (pts.): multiply the number of liters by 2.1
To convert quarts (qts.) to liters (l): multiply the number of quarts by .95

To convert liters (l) to quarts (qts.): multiply the number of liters by 1.06
To convert gallons (gals.) to liters (l): multiply the number of gallons by 3.8
To convert liters (l) to gallons (gals.): multiply the number of liters by .26

| gals | liters | qts | liters | pts | liters |
|---|---|---|---|---|---|
| 0.1 | 0.38 | 0.1 | 0.10 | 0.1 | 0.05 |
| 0.2 | 0.76 | 0.2 | 0.19 | 0.2 | 0.10 |
| 0.3 | 1.1 | 0.3 | 0.28 | 0.3 | 0.14 |
| 0.4 | 1.5 | 0.4 | 0.38 | 0.4 | 0.19 |
| 0.5 | 1.9 | 0.5 | 0.47 | 0.5 | 0.24 |
| 0.6 | 2.3 | 0.6 | 0.57 | 0.6 | 0.28 |
| 0.7 | 2.6 | 0.7 | 0.66 | 0.7 | 0.33 |
| 0.8 | 3.0 | 0.8 | 0.76 | 0.8 | 0.38 |
| 0.9 | 3.4 | 0.9 | 0.85 | 0.9 | 0.43 |
| 1 | 3.8 | 1 | 1.0 | 1 | 0.5 |
| 2 | 7.6 | 2 | 1.9 | 2 | 1.0 |
| 3 | 11.4 | 3 | 2.8 | 3 | 1.4 |
| 4 | 15.1 | 4 | 3.8 | 4 | 1.9 |
| 5 | 18.9 | 5 | 4.7 | 5 | 2.4 |
| 6 | 22.7 | 6 | 5.7 | 6 | 2.8 |
| 7 | 26.5 | 7 | 6.6 | 7 | 3.3 |
| 8 | 30.3 | 8 | 7.6 | 8 | 3.8 |
| 9 | 34.1 | 9 | 8.5 | 9 | 4.3 |
| 10 | 37.8 | 10 | 9.5 | 10 | 4.7 |
| 11 | 41.6 | 11 | 10.4 | 11 | 5.2 |
| 12 | 45.4 | 12 | 11.4 | 12 | 5.7 |
| 13 | 49.2 | 13 | 12.3 | 13 | 6.2 |
| 14 | 53.0 | 14 | 13.2 | 14 | 6.6 |
| 15 | 56.8 | 15 | 14.2 | 15 | 7.1 |
| 16 | 60.6 | 16 | 15.1 | 16 | 7.6 |
| 17 | 64.3 | 17 | 16.1 | 17 | 8.0 |
| 18 | 68.1 | 18 | 17.0 | 18 | 8.5 |
| 19 | 71.9 | 19 | 18.0 | 19 | 9.0 |
| 20 | 75.7 | 20 | 18.9 | 20 | 9.5 |
| 21 | 79.5 | 21 | 19.9 | 21 | 9.9 |
| 22 | 83.2 | 22 | 20.8 | 22 | 10.4 |
| 23 | 87.0 | 23 | 21.8 | 23 | 10.9 |
| 24 | 90.8 | 24 | 22.7 | 24 | 11.4 |
| 25 | 94.6 | 25 | 23.6 | 25 | 11.8 |
| 26 | 98.4 | 26 | 24.6 | 26 | 12.3 |
| 27 | 102.2 | 27 | 25.5 | 27 | 12.8 |
| 28 | 106.0 | 28 | 26.5 | 28 | 13.2 |
| 29 | 110.0 | 29 | 27.4 | 29 | 13.7 |
| 30 | 113.5 | 30 | 28.4 | 30 | 14.2 |

TCCS1C05

## ENGLISH TO METRIC CONVERSION: PRESSURE

The basic unit of pressure measurement used today is expressed as pounds per square inch (psi). The metric unit for psi will be the kilopascal (kPa). This will apply to either fluid pressure or air pressure, and will be frequently seen in tire pressure readings, oil pressure specifications, fuel pump pressure, etc.

To convert pounds per square inch (psi) to kilopascals (kPa): multiply the number of psi by 6.89

| Psi | kPa | Psi | kPa | Psi | kPa | Psi | kPa |
|-----|-----|-----|-----|-----|-----|-----|-----|
| 0.1 | 0.7 | 37 | 255.1 | 82 | 565.4 | 127 | 875.6 |
| 0.2 | 1.4 | 38 | 262.0 | 83 | 572.3 | 128 | 882.5 |
| 0.3 | 2.1 | 39 | 268.9 | 84 | 579.2 | 129 | 889.4 |
| 0.4 | 2.8 | 40 | 275.8 | 85 | 586.0 | 130 | 896.3 |
| 0.5 | 3.4 | 41 | 282.7 | 86 | 592.9 | 131 | 903.2 |
| 0.6 | 4.1 | 42 | 289.6 | 87 | 599.8 | 132 | 910.1 |
| 0.7 | 4.8 | 43 | 296.5 | 88 | 606.7 | 133 | 917.0 |
| 0.8 | 5.5 | 44 | 303.4 | 89 | 613.6 | 134 | 923.9 |
| 0.9 | 6.2 | 45 | 310.3 | 90 | 620.5 | 135 | 930.8 |
| 1 | 6.9 | 46 | 317.2 | 91 | 627.4 | 136 | 937.7 |
| 2 | 13.8 | 47 | 324.0 | 92 | 634.3 | 137 | 944.6 |
| 3 | 20.7 | 48 | 331.0 | 93 | 641.2 | 138 | 951.5 |
| 4 | 27.6 | 49 | 337.8 | 94 | 648.1 | 139 | 958.4 |
| 5 | 34.5 | 50 | 344.7 | 95 | 655.0 | 140 | 965.2 |
| 6 | 41.4 | 51 | 351.6 | 96 | 661.9 | 141 | 972.2 |
| 7 | 48.3 | 52 | 358.5 | 97 | 668.8 | 142 | 979.0 |
| 8 | 55.2 | 53 | 365.4 | 98 | 675.7 | 143 | 985.9 |
| 9 | 62.1 | 54 | 372.3 | 99 | 682.6 | 144 | 992.8 |
| 10 | 69.0 | 55 | 379.2 | 100 | 689.5 | 145 | 999.7 |
| 11 | 75.8 | 56 | 386.1 | 101 | 696.4 | 146 | 1006.6 |
| 12 | 82.7 | 57 | 393.0 | 102 | 703.3 | 147 | 1013.5 |
| 13 | 89.6 | 58 | 399.9 | 103 | 710.2 | 148 | 1020.4 |
| 14 | 96.5 | 59 | 406.8 | 104 | 717.0 | 149 | 1027.3 |
| 15 | 103.4 | 60 | 413.7 | 105 | 723.9 | 150 | 1034.2 |
| 16 | 110.3 | 61 | 420.6 | 106 | 730.8 | 151 | 1041.1 |
| 17 | 117.2 | 62 | 427.5 | 107 | 737.7 | 152 | 1048.0 |
| 18 | 124.1 | 63 | 434.4 | 108 | 744.6 | 153 | 1054.9 |
| 19 | 131.0 | 64 | 441.3 | 109 | 751.5 | 154 | 1061.8 |
| 20 | 137.9 | 65 | 448.2 | 110 | 758.4 | 155 | 1068.7 |
| 21 | 144.8 | 66 | 455.0 | 111 | 765.3 | 156 | 1075.6 |
| 22 | 151.7 | 67 | 461.9 | 112 | 772.2 | 157 | 1082.5 |
| 23 | 158.6 | 68 | 468.8 | 113 | 779.1 | 158 | 1089.4 |
| 24 | 165.5 | 69 | 475.7 | 114 | 786.0 | 159 | 1096.3 |
| 25 | 172.4 | 70 | 482.6 | 115 | 792.9 | 160 | 1103.2 |
| 26 | 179.3 | 71 | 489.5 | 116 | 799.8 | 161 | 1110.0 |
| 27 | 186.2 | 72 | 496.4 | 117 | 806.7 | 162 | 1116.9 |
| 28 | 193.0 | 73 | 503.3 | 118 | 813.6 | 163 | 1123.8 |
| 29 | 200.0 | 74 | 510.2 | 119 | 820.5 | 164 | 1130.7 |
| 30 | 206.8 | 75 | 517.1 | 120 | 827.4 | 165 | 1137.6 |
| 31 | 213.7 | 76 | 524.0 | 121 | 834.3 | 166 | 1144.5 |
| 32 | 220.6 | 77 | 530.9 | 122 | 841.2 | 167 | 1151.4 |
| 33 | 227.5 | 78 | 537.8 | 123 | 848.0 | 168 | 1158.3 |
| 34 | 234.4 | 79 | 544.7 | 124 | 854.9 | 169 | 1165.2 |
| 35 | 241.3 | 80 | 551.6 | 125 | 861.8 | 170 | 1172.1 |
| 36 | 248.2 | 81 | 558.5 | 126 | 868.7 | 171 | 1179.0 |

TCCS1C06

## ENGLISH TO METRIC CONVERSION: PRESSURE

The basic unit of pressure measurement used today is expressed as pounds per square inch (psi). The metric unit for psi will be the kilopascal (kPa). This will apply to either fluid pressure or air pressure, and will be frequently seen in tire pressure readings, oil pressure specifications, fuel pump pressure, etc.

To convert pounds per square inch (psi) to kilopascals (kPa): multiply the number of psi by 6.89

| Psi | kPa | Psi | kPa | Psi | kPa | Psi | kPa |
|-----|-----|-----|-----|-----|-----|-----|-----|
| 172 | 1185.9 | 216 | 1489.3 | 260 | 1792.6 | 304 | 2096.0 |
| 173 | 1192.8 | 217 | 1496.2 | 261 | 1799.5 | 305 | 2102.9 |
| 174 | 1199.7 | 218 | 1503.1 | 262 | 1806.4 | 306 | 2109.8 |
| 175 | 1206.6 | 219 | 1510.0 | 263 | 1813.3 | 307 | 2116.7 |
| 176 | 1213.5 | 220 | 1516.8 | 264 | 1820.2 | 308 | 2123.6 |
| 177 | 1220.4 | 221 | 1523.7 | 265 | 1827.1 | 309 | 2130.5 |
| 178 | 1227.3 | 222 | 1530.6 | 266 | 1834.0 | 310 | 2137.4 |
| 179 | 1234.2 | 223 | 1537.5 | 267 | 1840.9 | 311 | 2144.3 |
| 180 | 1241.0 | 224 | 1544.4 | 268 | 1847.8 | 312 | 2151.2 |
| 181 | 1247.9 | 225 | 1551.3 | 269 | 1854.7 | 313 | 2158.1 |
| 182 | 1254.8 | 226 | 1558.2 | 270 | 1861.6 | 314 | 2164.9 |
| 183 | 1261.7 | 227 | 1565.1 | 271 | 1868.5 | 315 | 2171.8 |
| 184 | 1268.6 | 228 | 1572.0 | 272 | 1875.4 | 316 | 2178.7 |
| 185 | 1275.5 | 229 | 1578.9 | 273 | 1882.3 | 317 | 2185.6 |
| 186 | 1282.4 | 230 | 1585.8 | 274 | 1889.2 | 318 | 2192.5 |
| 187 | 1289.3 | 231 | 1592.7 | 275 | 1896.1 | 319 | 2199.4 |
| 188 | 1296.2 | 232 | 1599.6 | 276 | 1903.0 | 320 | 2206.3 |
| 189 | 1303.1 | 233 | 1606.5 | 277 | 1909.8 | 321 | 2213.2 |
| 190 | 1310.0 | 234 | 1613.4 | 278 | 1916.7 | 322 | 2220.1 |
| 191 | 1316.9 | 235 | 1620.3 | 279 | 1923.6 | 323 | 2227.0 |
| 192 | 1323.8 | 236 | 1627.2 | 280 | 1930.5 | 324 | 2233.9 |
| 193 | 1330.7 | 237 | 1634.1 | 281 | 1937.4 | 325 | 2240.8 |
| 194 | 1337.6 | 238 | 1641.0 | 282 | 1944.3 | 326 | 2247.7 |
| 195 | 1344.5 | 239 | 1647.8 | 283 | 1951.2 | 327 | 2254.6 |
| 196 | 1351.4 | 240 | 1654.7 | 284 | 1958.1 | 328 | 2261.5 |
| 197 | 1358.3 | 241 | 1661.6 | 285 | 1965.0 | 329 | 2268.4 |
| 198 | 1365.2 | 242 | 1668.5 | 286 | 1971.9 | 330 | 2275.3 |
| 199 | 1372.0 | 243 | 1675.4 | 287 | 1978.8 | 331 | 2282.2 |
| 200 | 1378.9 | 244 | 1682.3 | 288 | 1985.7 | 332 | 2289.1 |
| 201 | 1385.8 | 245 | 1689.2 | 289 | 1992.6 | 333 | 2295.9 |
| 202 | 1392.7 | 246 | 1696.1 | 290 | 1999.5 | 334 | 2302.8 |
| 203 | 1399.6 | 247 | 1703.0 | 291 | 2006.4 | 335 | 2309.7 |
| 204 | 1406.5 | 248 | 1709.9 | 292 | 2013.3 | 336 | 2316.6 |
| 205 | 1413.4 | 249 | 1716.8 | 293 | 2020.2 | 337 | 2323.5 |
| 206 | 1420.3 | 250 | 1723.7 | 294 | 2027.1 | 338 | 2330.4 |
| 207 | 1427.2 | 251 | 1730.6 | 295 | 2034.0 | 339 | 2337.3 |
| 208 | 1434.1 | 252 | 1737.5 | 296 | 2040.8 | 240 | 2344.2 |
| 209 | 1441.0 | 253 | 1744.4 | 297 | 2047.7 | 341 | 2351.1 |
| 210 | 1447.9 | 254 | 1751.3 | 298 | 2054.6 | 342 | 2358.0 |
| 211 | 1454.8 | 255 | 1758.2 | 299 | 2061.5 | 343 | 2364.9 |
| 212 | 1461.7 | 256 | 1765.1 | 300 | 2068.4 | 344 | 2371.8 |
| 213 | 1468.7 | 257 | 1772.0 | 301 | 2075.3 | 345 | 2378.7 |
| 214 | 1475.5 | 258 | 1778.8 | 302 | 2082.2 | 346 | 2385.6 |
| 215 | 1482.4 | 259 | 1785.7 | 303 | 2089.1 | 347 | 2392.5 |

TCCS1C07

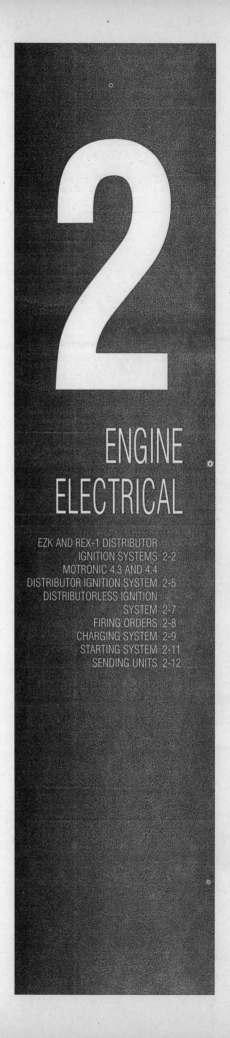

# 2

# ENGINE
# ELECTRICAL

## EZK AND REX-1 DISTRIBUTOR IGNITION SYSTEMS

### General Information

▶ **See Figures 1 and 2**

➡**For information on understanding electricity and troubleshooting electrical circuits, please refer to Section 6 of this manual.**

The EZ115K, EZ116K, EZ129K, and REX-1 ignition systems, used on Coupe, 240, 700 series, 1993–94 850, and 940 models are like most engine management systems currently in use, in that ignition functions are closely integrated with the fuel system. Various sensors feed information to an on-board computer which makes necessary adjustments.

The EZK ignition systems are used on vehicles utilizing Bosch LH-Jetronic electronic engine controls. The REX-1 system is used on vehicles with the Bendix Regina electronic engine control system. Both systems have separate control modules for the ignition and engine controls. The inputs are similar on both; knock sensor, crankshaft position sensor, engine coolant temperature sensor, throttle position sensor or switch, and inputs from the electronic engine control module.

### Diagnosis and Testing

#### SERVICE PRECAUTIONS

▶ **See Figure 3**

• The ignition system operates with a very high output and there are hazardous voltages in the low and high voltage circuits.
• Always turn the ignition **OFF**, before separating connectors.
• Before detaching the control unit connector, remove fuse 1 (740/940 models) or fuse 31 (760 models) to deactivate the ignition system.
• Never disconnect the battery while the engine is running.
• Always disconnect the battery when quick charging the battery.
• Never use a boost charger or voltage higher than 16 volts to start the engine.
• Always remove the control unit if the vehicle is to be stove or if welding is to be carried out. The control unit must not be exposed to temperatures above 176°F (80°C).
• Do not replace a control unit without first correcting the original fault, or the same fault may damage the new control unit.

• Do not be hasty in condemning the ECM. This system uses voltages and resistances that are very small. Examine the sensors, wiring and connectors carefully. The sensors operate in more harsh conditions than the ECM which is generally in a more protected location.
• Check all ground connections before condemning the ECM.
• Use care when working around vehicles equipped with Supplementary Restraint System (SRS), often known as "air bags." Vehicles equipped with SRS are generally recognized by the letters **SRS** molded into the steering wheel cover. Follow all precautions to avoid personal injury.
• A spare location in the fuse panel is used as a test terminal for SRS diagnostics. Never install a fuse in this position or connect accessories to this terminal.

Before performing any component testing, check for and, if necessary, repair the following:

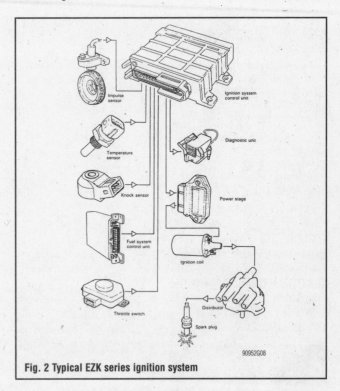

**Fig. 2 Typical EZK series ignition system**

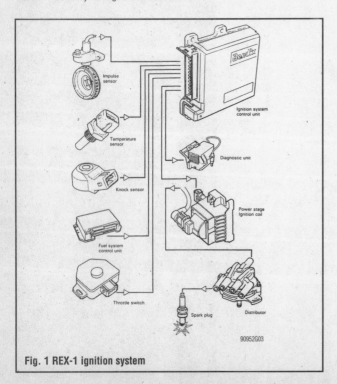

**Fig. 1 REX-1 ignition system**

**Fig. 3 Take care in working around the ignition system; high voltage is present and electrical shock can occur**

- Damaged, corroded, contaminated, carbon tracked or worn distributor cap and rotor
- Damaged, fouled, improperly seated or gapped spark plug(s)
- Damaged or improperly engaged electrical connections, spark plug wires, etc.
- Discharged battery
- Blown fuses

## SECONDARY SPARK TEST

The best way to perform this procedure is to use a spark tester (available at most automotive parts stores). Two types of spark testers are commonly available. The Neon Bulb type is connected to the spark plug wire and flashes with each ignition pulse. The Air Gap type must be adjusted to the individual spark plug gap specified for the engine. This type of tester allows the user to not only detect the presence of spark, but also the intensity (orange/yellow is weak, blue is strong).

1. Disconnect a spark plug wire at the spark plug end.
2. Connect the plug wire to the spark tester and ground the tester to an appropriate location on the engine.
3. Crank the engine and check for spark at the tester.
4. If spark exists at the tester, the ignition system is functioning properly.
5. If spark does not exist at the spark plug wire, remove the distributor cap and ensure that the rotor is turning when the engine is cranked.
6. If the rotor is turning, perform the spark test again using the ignition coil wire.
7. If spark does not exist at the ignition coil wire, test the ignition coil, and other distributor related components or wiring. Repair or replace components as necessary.

## Adjustments

Ignition system functions are controlled by the control module, so no adjustment is necessary.

To check or adjust the ignition timing, refer to Section 1 of this manual.

## Ignition Coil

### TESTING

#### EZ115K and EZ116K Systems

*PRIMARY WINDING TEST*

1. Disconnect the negative battery cable.
2. Remove fuse No. 1 (740 and 940 models) or fuse No. 31 (model 760) from the fuse box. Note that these fuses must be removed whenever any connector to or from the ECU is removed or installed.
3. Remove the air cleaner assembly.
4. Remove the connector from the power stage.
5. Remove the rubber cover from the connector to expose the terminals. Never test the terminals from the front. This could result in damage to the terminals and make any faults worse.
6. Connect an ohmmeter between the power stage amplifier connector terminal 1 and terminal 15 of the ignition coil. Resistance should be 0.6–1.0 ohms.
7. If resistance is low, replace the ignition coil.
8. If resistance is too high, connect an ohmmeter directly to terminals 1 and 15 of the ignition coil. If resistance is still too high, replace the ignition coil.
9. If resistance is correct (0.6–1.0 ohm), check the wire between the ignition coil and power stage amplifier connector terminal 1. Replace/repair the wire as needed.
10. Install the air cleaner assembly.
11. Connect the negative battery cable.

*SECONDARY WINDING TEST*

▶ See Figure 4

1. Disconnect the negative battery cable.
2. Remove the air cleaner assembly.
3. Remove the connector from the power stage.
4. Remove the rubber cover from the connector to expose the terminals. Never test the terminals from the front. This could result in damage to the terminals and make any faults worse.
5. Connect an ohmmeter between the power stage amplifier connector terminal 1 and the ignition coil high tension terminal (coil tower). Resistance should be 6.5–9.0 kilohms.
6. If resistance is higher or lower, replace the ignition coil.
7. Install the air cleaner assembly.
8. Connect the negative battery cable.

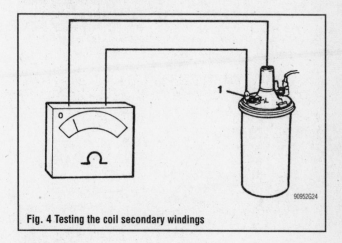

**Fig. 4 Testing the coil secondary windings**

#### EZ129K System

*PRIMARY WINDING TEST*

1. Disconnect the negative battery cable.
2. Remove the air cleaner assembly.
3. Connect an ohmmeter between the primary windings connectors on the outside of the coil.
4. Resistance should be 0.5–1.5 ohms.
5. Install the air cleaner assembly.
6. Connect the negative battery cable.

*SECONDARY WINDING TEST*

1. Disconnect the negative battery cable.
2. Remove the air cleaner assembly.
3. Remove the coil wire from the coil.
4. Connect an ohmmeter between one of the primary windings connectors on the outside of the coil and the coil wire tower on the coil.
5. Resistance should be 8–9 kilohms.
6. Install the air cleaner assembly.
7. Connect the negative battery cable.

#### REX-1 System

➡To check the ignition coil/power stage unit on REX-1 systems, make sure the ignition switch is OFF.

1. Remove the air cleaner assembly.
2. Unplug the connectors from the coil/power stage unit.
3. Remove the ignition coil from the power stage by removing the 2 Torx® head screws and lifting off the ignition coil.
4. Measure the resistance between the terminals of the ignition coil by

connecting an ohmmeter between the low voltage terminals (+) and (-). Resistance should be 0.5 ohms.

5. Connect an ohmmeter between the high tension terminal and a low voltage terminal. Resistance should be approximately 5000 ohms.

6. Check that voltage is present at the ignition coil/power stage unit by first turning the ignition **ON**. Connect a voltmeter between ground and terminal A in the 3-way connector. There should be 12 volts. If the voltage is low, or none at all, check the point where the feed wire branches to the ECU and ignition coil/power stage unit.

7. Check that the voltage does not fall below 10.5 volts when the starter motor is operated.

8. Turn the ignition key **OFF**.

9. Check the ground connections of the ignition coil/power stage unit by connecting an ohmmeter between ground and terminal B of the 3-way connector. The resistance should not exceed 0.1 ohm. If the resistance is too high, check for bad ground connection.

10. Connect an ohmmeter between ground and terminal A of the 2-way connector. If resistance is more than 0.1 ohm, check for a bad ground connection.

11. Check the signal line between the ignition coil/power stage unit and ECU. Check for power on this circuit. Connecting a shop-made buzzer between terminal B of the 2-way connector and terminal 16 of the ECU may be helpful. If the line is problem-free, the buzzer should sound.

12. Install the air cleaner assembly.

### REMOVAL & INSTALLATION

#### EZ115K and EZ116K Systems

▶ **See Figure 5**

1. Disconnect the negative battery cable.
2. Remove the air cleaner assembly.
3. Disconnect and tag the coil primary leads.
4. Carefully remove the coil wire from the coil tower.
5. Remove the mounting bolt(s) from the retaining bracket and remove the ignition coil.

**To install:**

6. Install the coil and tighten the bracket retaining bolts.
7. Install the coil wire on the coil tower.
8. Connect the coil primary leads.
9. Install the air cleaner assembly.
10. Connect the negative battery cable.

#### EZ129K System

1. Disconnect the negative battery cable.
2. Remove the air cleaner assembly.
3. Disconnect and tag the coil primary leads.
4. Carefully remove the coil wire from the coil tower.
5. Unplug the power stage connector.
6. Remove the mounting bolt(s) from the retaining bracket and remove the ignition coil and power stage.

**To install:**

7. Install the coil and power stage and tighten the retaining bolts.
8. Plug the power stage connector in.
9. Install the coil wire on the coil tower.

10. Connect the coil primary leads.
11. Install the air cleaner assembly.
12. Connect the negative battery cable.

#### REX-1 System

▶ **See Figure 6**

1. Disconnect the negative battery cable.
2. Remove the air cleaner assembly.
3. Carefully remove the coil wire from the coil tower.
4. Unplug the connectors.
5. Remove the mounting bolt(s) from the retaining bracket and remove the ignition coil and power stage.

**To install:**

6. Install the coil and power stage and tighten the retaining bolts.
7. Plug the connectors in.
8. Install the coil wire on the coil tower.
9. Install the air cleaner assembly.
10. Connect the negative battery cable.

### Power Stage (Ignition Module)

The power stage on the REX-1 and EZ129K systems is combined with the ignition coil into a single unit (Power Stage/Ignition Coil). Refer to the ignition coil removal and installation procedure earlier in this section.

### REMOVAL & INSTALLATION

#### EZ115K and EZ116K Systems

▶ **See Figure 7**

1. Disconnect the negative battery cable.
2. Unplug the power stage connector.
3. Unfasten the mounting bolt(s) from the retaining bracket, then remove the ignition coil and power stage.

**To install:**

4. Install the coil and power stage and tighten the retaining bolts.
5. Plug in the power stage connector.
6. Connect the negative battery cable.

### Distributor

The only function of the distributor is to distribute voltage to the spark plugs. There are no advance functions built into the distributor. It is no longer possible to adjust ignition timing through the distributor.

### REMOVAL & INSTALLATION

#### EZ115K, EZ116K and REX-1 Systems

▶ **See Figure 8**

1. Disconnect the negative battery cable.
2. Label and remove the spark plug wires.

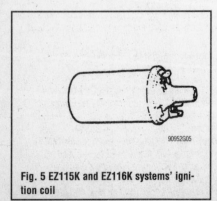

**Fig. 5 EZ115K and EZ116K systems' ignition coil**

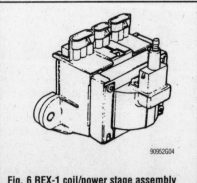
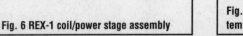

**Fig. 6 REX-1 coil/power stage assembly**

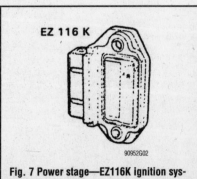

**Fig. 7 Power stage—EZ116K ignition system**

3. Label and remove the distributor cap.
4. Remove the rotor, dust cover and O-ring.
5. Remove the camshaft center bolt and rotor holder. Pull the distributor housing forward until its base rests against the rotor holder. Tap the distributor housing lightly, with a hammer, to release the rotor holder from the shaft.

**To install:**
6. Install the distributor.
7. Tighten the rotor holder to 52–66 ft. lbs. (70–90 Nm).
8. Install the rotor, dust cover, and O-ring.
9. Install the distributor cap.
10. Install the spark plug wires.
11. Connect the negative battery cable.
12. If possible, check the ignition timing.

### EZ129K System

On this system, the distributor is essentially a rotor bolted onto the end of the intake camshaft. There is no distributor housing to remove. Once the distributor cap is removed, the rotor can be removed from the camshaft. Refer to Section 1 for Distributor Cap and Rotor removal and installation.

### Crankshaft Position Sensor

The Crankshaft position sensor is covered in Section 4, under Electronic Engine Controls.

### Camshaft Position Sensor

The Camshaft position sensor is covered in Section 4, under Electronic Engine Controls.

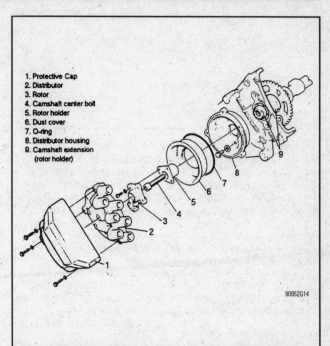

1. Protective Cap
2. Distributor
3. Rotor
4. Camshaft center bolt
5. Rotor holder
6. Dust cover
7. O-ring
8. Distributor housing
9. Camshaft extension (rotor holder)

**Fig. 8 Exploded view of the distributor assembly—EZ115K, EZ116K and REX-1 ignition systems**

## MOTRONIC 4.3 AND 4.4 DISTRIBUTOR IGNITION SYSTEM

### General Information

▸ See Figure 9

The Motronic 4.3 and 4.4 system on 850/C70/S70/V70 models is a total control system. Both engine and ignition controls are incorporated into one system with one control module. The control module receives the inputs from various sensors and controls all the outputs together.

The inputs that directly affect ignition include the RPM sensor (crankshaft position sensor), Camshaft Position (CMP) sensor, knock sensors, Engine Coolant Temperature (ECT) sensor, Mass Air Flow (MAF) sensor, acceleration sensor, Throttle Position (TP) sensor and, on vehicles equipped with an automatic transaxle, a Transmission Control Module (TCM). The RPM and CMP sensors determine engine speed and directly affect ignition timing control. The

TP and MAF sensors, as well as the TCM, determine engine load. The knock sensor determines if the ignition timing is correct by detecting engine knocks or "pre-ignition," and the acceleration sensor determines if the vehicle is being driven on a bumpy or uneven surface, possibly causing faulty knock sensor readings.

The system has a fail safe or "limp home mode" where it defaults to a predetermined timing and voltage level if an input device fails. The Malfunction Indicator Lamp (MIL) will illuminate and the vehicle may exhibit more driveability problems; it should be diagnosed as soon as possible.

### Diagnosis and Testing

#### SERVICE PRECAUTIONS

- The ignition system operates with a very high output and there are hazardous voltages in the low and high voltage circuits.
- Always turn the ignition **OFF**, before separating connectors.
- Never disconnect the battery while the engine is running.
- Always disconnect the battery when quick charging the battery.
- Never use a boost charger or voltage higher than 16 volts to start the engine.
- Always remove the control unit if the vehicle is to be stove or if welding is to be carried out. The control unit must not be exposed to temperatures above 176°F (80°C).
- Do not replace a control unit without first correcting the original fault, or the same fault may damage the new control unit.
- Do not be hasty in condemning the ECM. This system uses voltages and resistances that are very small. Examine the sensors, wiring and connectors carefully. The sensors operate in more harsh conditions than the ECM which is generally in a more protected location.
- Check all ground connections before condemning the ECM.
- Use care when working around vehicles equipped with Supplementary Restraint System (SRS), often known as "air bags." Vehicles equipped with SRS are generally recognized by the letters **SRS** molded into the steering wheel cover. Follow all precautions to avoid personal injury.

Before performing any component testing, check for and, if necessary, repair the following:

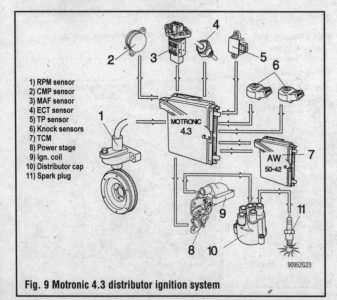

1) RPM sensor
2) CMP sensor
3) MAF sensor
4) ECT sensor
5) TP sensor
6) Knock sensors
7) TCM
8) Power stage
9) Ign. coil
10) Distributor cap
11) Spark plug

**Fig. 9 Motronic 4.3 distributor ignition system**

- Damaged, corroded, contaminated, carbon tracked or worn distributor cap and rotor
- Damaged, fouled, improperly seated or gapped spark plug(s)
- Damaged or improperly engaged electrical connections, spark plug wires, etc.
- Discharged battery
- Blown fuses

## SECONDARY SPARK TEST

The best way to perform this procedure is to use a spark tester (available at most automotive parts stores). Two types of spark testers are commonly available. The Neon Bulb type is connected to the spark plug wire and flashes with each ignition pulse. The Air Gap type must be adjusted to the individual spark plug gap specified for the engine. This type of tester allows the user to not only detect the presence of spark, but also the intensity (orange/yellow is weak, blue is strong).

1. Disconnect a spark plug wire at the spark plug end.
2. Connect the plug wire to the spark tester and ground the tester to an appropriate location on the engine.
3. Crank the engine and check for spark at the tester.
4. If spark exists at the tester, the ignition system is functioning properly.
5. If spark does not exist at the spark plug wire, remove the distributor cap and ensure that the rotor is turning when the engine is cranked.
6. If the rotor is turning, perform the spark test again using the ignition coil wire.
7. If spark does not exist at the ignition coil wire, test the ignition coil, and other distributor related components or wiring. Repair or replace components as necessary.

## Adjustments

Ignition system functions are controlled by the ECM, so no adjustment is necessary. To check or adjust the ignition timing, refer to Section 1 of this manual.

## Ignition Coil

### TESTING

#### Primary Winding Test

▶ See Figures 10, 11 and 12

1. Disconnect the negative battery cable.
2. Remove the air cleaner assembly.
3. Remove the coil primary leads.
4. Connect an ohmmeter between the primary windings connectors on the outside of the coil.
5. Resistance should be 0.5–1.5 ohms.

#### Secondary Winding Test

▶ See Figure 13

1. Disconnect the negative battery cable.
2. Remove the air cleaner assembly.
3. Remove the coil wire from the coil.
4. Connect an ohmmeter between one of the primary winding connectors on the outside of the coil and the coil wire tower on the coil.
5. Resistance should be 8–9 kilohms.

### REMOVAL & INSTALLATION

▶ See Figures 14, 15, 16 and 17

The ignition coil and power stage are an assembly.
1. Disconnect the negative battery cable.
2. Remove the air cleaner assembly.
3. Carefully remove the coil wire from the coil tower.

Fig. 10 Remove the coil primary leads

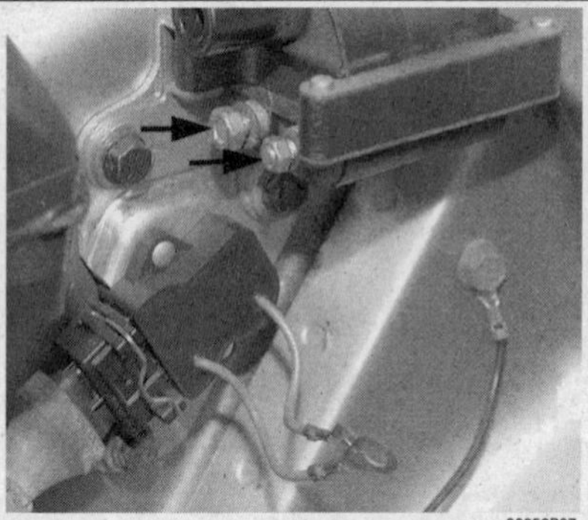

Fig. 11 Attach the ohmmeter probes to the studs after removing the primary leads

Fig. 12 Testing the primary windings of the ignition coil

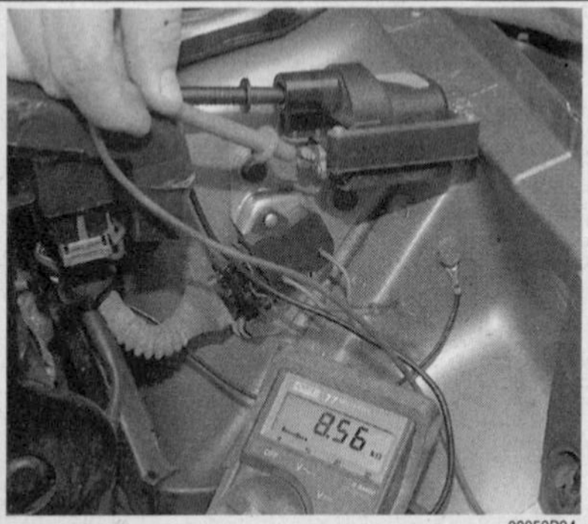

Fig. 13 Testing the secondary windings of the ignition coil

Fig. 14 Remove the coil wire from the coil

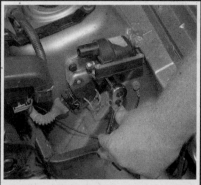

Fig. 15 Unfasten the mounting bolts . . .

Fig. 16 . . . then remove the assembly from the strut tower

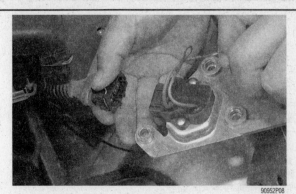

Fig. 17 Unplug the power stage connector and remove the assembly from the vehicle

4. Remove the mounting bolt(s) from the retaining bracket and remove the ignition coil and power stage.
5. Unplug the power stage connector.

**To install:**

6. Install the coil and power stage and tighten the retaining bolts.
7. Plug the power stage connector in.
8. Install the coil wire on the coil tower.
9. Install the air cleaner assembly.
10. Connect the negative battery cable.

## Power Stage (Ignition Module)

### REMOVAL & INSTALLATION

The ignition coil and power stage are an assembly. Refer to the Ignition Coil removal and installation procedure in this section.

# DISTRIBUTORLESS IGNITION SYSTEM

## General Information

▶ See Figure 18

The B6304 engine is the only engine equipped with a distributorless ignition system. Each cylinder is equipped with an individual ignition coil. The coil is located over the spark plug, just like a spark plug boot; this style is referred to as "coil over plug". Using separate coils for each plug guarantees a very high voltage (approximately 49 kV) and rapid power build-up. This results in effective initiation of the combustion process and improves cold start performance.

The ignition coils are controlled by two power stages (ignition modules). One module is connected to cylinders 1, 3, and 5 and the other to 2, 4, and 6. The power stages each incorporate three separate drivers, one for each ignition coil. The power stages are controlled by the ECM, which receives inputs from various sensors and other components.

The ECM computes ignition timing and activates the power stage controlling current to the ignition coils. During start-up, the ECM ensures a fixed timing and ignition voltage, but, after start-up, the ECM continually computes optimum ignition requirements based on engine speed, engine load, engine temperature, and combustion timing.

The engine speed is monitored by the crankshaft position (RPM) sensor and the Camshaft Position (CMP) sensor. The engine load is monitored by the Mass Air Flow (MAF) sensor, Throttle Position (TP) sensor, and by inputs from the Transmission Control Module (TCM), which sends a torque reduction signal to the ECM when a gear change is imminent. The engine temperature is determined by the Engine Coolant Temperature (ECT) sensor. The knock sensor determines if the ignition timing is correct by detecting engine knocks or "pre-ignition."

The system has a fail safe or "limp home mode" where it defaults to a predetermined timing and voltage level if an input device fails. The Malfunction Indicator Lamp (MIL) will illuminate and the vehicle may exhibit more driveability problems; it should be diagnosed as soon as possible.

## Distributor

On these Motronic systems, the distributor is essentially a rotor bolted onto the end of the intake camshaft. There is no distributor housing to remove. Once the distributor cap is removed, the rotor can be removed from the camshaft. See Section 1 for Distributor Cap and Rotor removal and installation.

## Crankshaft Position Sensor

The Crankshaft position sensor is covered in Section 4, under Electronic Engine Controls.

## Camshaft Position Sensor

The Camshaft position sensor is covered in Section 4, under Electronic Engine Controls.

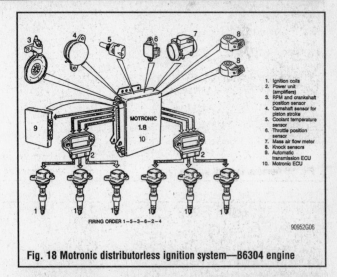

1. Ignition coils
2. Power unit (amplifiers)
3. RPM and crankshaft position sensor
4. Camshaft sensor for piston stroke
5. Coolant temperature sensor
6. Throttle position sensor
7. Mass air flow meter
8. Knock sensors
9. Automatic transmission ECU
10. Motronic ECU

FIRING ORDER 1–5–3–6–2–4

Fig. 18 Motronic distributorless ignition system—B6304 engine

## Diagnosis and Testing

The best way to perform this procedure is to use a spark tester (available at most automotive parts stores). The Air Gap type must be adjusted to the individual spark plug gap specified for the engine. This type of tester allows the user to not only detect the presence of spark, but also the intensity (orange/yellow is weak, blue is strong).

1. Remove a coil from a cylinder.
2. Connect the coil to the spark tester and ground the tester to an appropriate location on the engine.

➡ **The coil must be connected to the harness during this test.**

3. Crank the engine and check for spark at the tester.
4. If spark exists at the tester, the ignition system is functioning properly.
5. If spark does not exist at the spark tester, there is a fault in the ignition system. Further testing of the ignition system is needed. refer to component testing procedures.

## Adjustments

All adjustments in the ignition system are controlled by the Engine Control Module (ECM) for optimum performance. No adjustments are possible.

## Ignition Coil

### TESTING

▸ **See Figure 19**

With the ignition **OFF**, disconnect the harness from the ignition coil, then place the leads of an ohmmeter across terminals 1 and 2 of the ignition coil. Resistance should be approximately 1 ohm; if out of range, replace the ignition coil.

**Fig. 19 Connect an ohmmeter across the two terminals of the ignition coil to test the coil**

### REMOVAL & INSTALLATION

▸ **See Figure 20**

1. Disconnect the negative battery cable.
2. Disconnect the harness from the ignition coil.
3. Remove the retaining bolt from the ignition coil-to-upper cylinder head.
4. Lift the coil off of the spark plug and from the cylinder.
**To install:**
5. Place the ignition coil into the correct cylinder and onto the spark plug. Push gently downward until a click is either felt or heard; the coil is now attached to the spark plug.
6. Install and tighten the retaining bolt on the ignition coil-to-upper cylinder head.

## FIRING ORDERS

▸ **See Figures 21, 22, 23 and 24**

➡ **To avoid confusion, remove and tag the spark plug wires one at a time, for replacement.**

If a distributor is not keyed for installation with only one orientation, it could have been removed previously and rewired. The resultant wiring would

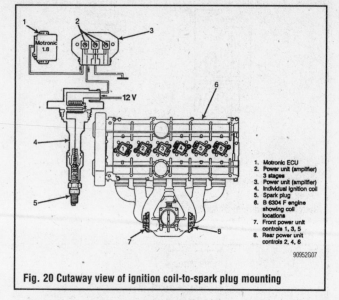

**Fig. 20 Cutaway view of ignition coil-to-spark plug mounting**

1. Motronic ECU
2. Power unit (amplifier) 3 stages
3. Power unit (amplifier)
4. Individual ignition coil
5. Spark plug
6. B 6304 F engine showing coil locations
7. Front power unit controls 1, 3, 5
8. Rear power unit controls 2, 4, 6

7. Connect the harness to the ignition coil.
8. Connect the negative battery cable.

## Power Stage (Ignition Module)

### REMOVAL & INSTALLATION

The power stages are located on the intake manifold for increased cooling.
1. Disconnect the negative battery cable.
2. Disconnect the harness from the power stage(s).
3. For each power stage to be removed, unfasten the two bolts retaining the power stage to the intake manifold.
4. Remove the power stage(s).
**To install:**
5. Install the power stage(s) and tighten the retaining bolts.
6. Connect the harness to the power stage(s).
7. Connect the negative battery cable.

## Crankshaft Position Sensor

The Crankshaft position sensor is covered in Section 4, under Electronic Engine Controls.

## Camshaft Position Sensor

The Camshaft position sensor is covered in Section 4, under Electronic Engine Controls.

hold the correct firing order, but could change the relative placement of the plug towers in relation to the engine. For this reason, it is imperative that you label all wires before disconnecting any of them. Also, before removal, compare the current wiring with the accompanying illustrations. If the current wiring does not match, make notes in your book to reflect how your engine is wired.

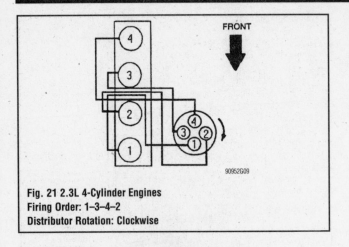

Fig. 21 2.3L 4-Cylinder Engines
Firing Order: 1–3–4–2
Distributor Rotation: Clockwise

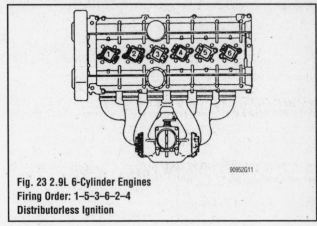

Fig. 23 2.9L 6-Cylinder Engines
Firing Order: 1–5–3–6–2–4
Distributorless Ignition

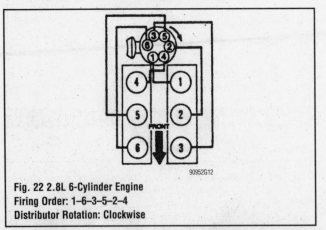

Fig. 22 2.8L 6-Cylinder Engine
Firing Order: 1–6–3–5–2–4
Distributor Rotation: Clockwise

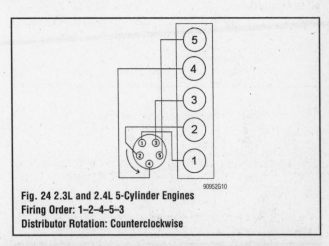

Fig. 24 2.3L and 2.4L 5-Cylinder Engines
Firing Order: 1–2–4–5–3
Distributor Rotation: Counterclockwise

## CHARGING SYSTEM

### General Information

The automobile charging system provides electrical power for operation of the vehicle's ignition and starting systems and all the electrical accessories. The battery services as an electrical surge or storage tank, storing (in chemical form) the energy originally produced by the engine driven generator. The system also provides a means of regulating generator output to protect the battery from being overcharged and to avoid excessive voltage to the accessories.

The storage battery is a chemical device incorporating parallel lead plates in a tank containing a sulfuric acid/water solution. Adjacent plates are slightly dissimilar, and the chemical reaction of the 2 dissimilar plates produces electrical energy when the battery is connected to a load such as the starter motor. The chemical reaction is reversible, so that when the generator is producing a voltage (electrical pressure) greater than that produced by the battery, electricity is forced into the battery, and the battery is returned to its fully charged state.

The vehicle's alternator is driven mechanically, by a belt(s) that is driven by the engine crankshaft. In an alternator, the field rotates while all the current produced passes only through the stator winding. The brushes bear against continuous slip rings rather than a commutator. This causes the current produced to periodically reverse the direction of its flow. Diodes (electrical one-way switches) block the flow of current from traveling in the wrong direction. A series of diodes is wired together to permit the alternating flow of the stator to be converted to a pulsating, but unidirectional flow at the alternator output. The alternator's field is wired in series with the voltage regulator.

The regulator consists of several circuits. Each circuit has a core, or magnetic coil of wire, which operates a switch. Each switch is connected to ground through one or more resistors. The coil of wire responds directly to system voltage. When the voltage reaches the required level, the magnetic field created by the winding of wire closes the switch and inserts a resistance into the generator field circuit, thus reducing the output. The contacts of the switch cycle open and close many times each second to precisely control voltage.

### Alternator Precautions

Several precautions must be observed when performing work on alternator equipment.

• If the battery is removed for any reason, make sure that it is reconnected with the correct polarity. Reversing the battery connections may result in damage to the one-way rectifiers.

• Never operate the alternator with the main circuit broken. Make sure that the battery, alternator, and regulator leads are not disconnected while the engine is running.

• Never attempt to polarize an alternator.

• When charging a battery that is installed in the vehicle, disconnect the negative battery cable.

• When utilizing a booster battery as a starting aid, always connect it in parallel; negative to negative, and positive to positive.

• When arc (electric) welding is to be performed on any part of the vehicle, disconnect the negative battery cable and alternator leads.

• Never unplug the ECM while the engine is running or with the ignition in the **ON** position. Severe and expensive damage may result within the solid state equipment.

### Alternator

TESTING

**Voltage Test**

1. Make sure the engine is **OFF**, and turn the headlights on for 15–20 seconds to remove any surface charge from the battery.
2. Using a DVOM set to volts DC, probe across the battery terminals.
3. Measure the battery voltage.
4. Write down the voltage reading and proceed to the next test.

### No-Load Test

1. Connect a tachometer to the engine.

> ✳✳ **CAUTION**

**Ensure that the transmission is in PARK and the emergency brake is set. Blocking a wheel is optional and an added safety measure.**

2. Turn off all electrical loads (radio, blower motor, wipers, etc.)
3. Start the engine and increase engine speed to approximately 1500 rpm.
4. Measure the voltage reading at the battery with the engine holding a steady 1500 rpm. Voltage should have raised at least 0.5 volts, but no more than 2.5 volts.
5. If the voltage does not go up more than 0.5 volts, the alternator is not charging. If the voltage goes up more than 2.5 volts, the alternator is overcharging.

➡Usually under and overcharging is caused by a defective alternator, or its related parts (regulator), and replacement will fix the problem; however, faulty wiring and other problems can cause the charging system to malfunction. Further testing, which is not covered by this book, will reveal the exact component failure. Many automotive parts stores have alternator bench testers available for use by customers. An alternator bench test is the most definitive way to determine the condition of your alternator.

6. If the voltage is within specifications, proceed to the next test.

### Load Test

1. With the engine running, turn on the blower motor and the high beams (or other electrical accessories to place a load on the charging system).
2. Increase and hold engine speed to 2000 rpm.
3. Measure the voltage reading at the battery.
4. The voltage should increase at least 0.5 volts from the voltage test. If the voltage does not meet specifications, the charging system is malfunctioning.

➡Usually under and overcharging is caused by a defective alternator, or its related parts (regulator), and replacement will fix the problem; however, faulty wiring and other problems can cause the charging system to malfunction. Further testing, which is not covered by this book, will reveal the exact component failure. Many automotive parts stores have alternator bench testers available for use by customers. An alternator bench test is the most definitive way to determine the condition of your alternator.

### REMOVAL & INSTALLATION

➡On some models, it will be necessary to remove the air pump and position it to one side to gain access to the alternator.

### Except 850/C70/S70/V70

1. Disconnect the negative battery cable.
2. Loosen the alternator adjusting bolts (if equipped).
3. Remove the drive belt from the alternator pulley.
4. Disconnect the electrical leads to the alternator.
5. Remove the alternator adjusting bolts (if equipped) and mounting bolts.
6. Remove the alternator from the vehicle.

**To install:**

7. Install the alternator into the bracket.
8. Install the mounting bolts and the adjusting bolts (if equipped).
9. Tighten the mounting bolts only and, if equipped, leave the adjusting bolts loose.
10. Connect the electrical leads to the alternator.
11. Install the drive belt around the alternator pulley.
12. Adjust the tension on the belt (non-serpentine) as outlined in Section 1 and tighten the adjusting bolts (if equipped).
13. Connect the negative battery cable.
14. Verify the operation of the alternator.

### 850/C70/S70/V70

▶ See Figures 25 thru 34

1. Disconnect the negative battery cable.
2. Remove the drive belt from the engine.
3. Remove the power steering pump and tensioner bracket mounting bolts, then lift the assembly up and rest it on top of the engine.
4. Disconnect the electrical leads to the alternator.
5. Remove the alternator mounting bolts.
6. Remove the alternator from the vehicle.

**To install:**

7. Install the alternator onto the engine and tighten the mounting bolts:
8. Connect the electrical leads to the alternator.
9. Install the power steering pump and tensioner bracket and tighten the mounting bolts.
10. Install the drive belt.
11. Connect the negative battery cable.
12. Verify the operation of the alternator.

## Regulator

### REMOVAL & INSTALLATION

➡The following procedure applies only to externally mounted regulators; on vehicles whose alternators have integral regulators, the alternator must be removed for service or replacement.

1. Disconnect the negative battery cable.
2. Disconnect the harness from the regulator.

Fig. 25 Release the tensioner . . .

Fig. 26 . . . and remove the drive belt

Fig. 27 Remove the mounting bolts from the bracket . . .

Fig. 28 . . . and note their location for installation (they are different lengths)

Fig. 29 After the bolts are removed, lift the bracket and place the alternator on top of the engine

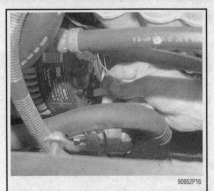

Fig. 30 Detach the electrical connectors from the back of the alternator

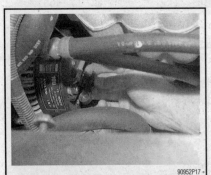

Fig. 31 Remove the cover from the battery cable connection on the rear of the alternator . . .

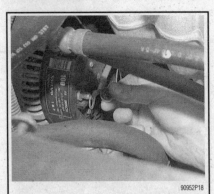

Fig. 32 . . . then unfasten and remove the cable from the alternator

Fig. 33 Unfasten the alternator mounting bolts . . .

Fig. 34 . . . and remove the alternator

3. Remove the regulator retaining screws.
4. Remove the regulator from the vehicle.

**To install:**

5. Install the regulator into place and tighten the retaining screws.
6. Connect the harness to the regulator.
7. Connect the negative battery cable.

## STARTING SYSTEM

### General Information

The starting system includes the battery, starter motor, solenoid, ignition switch, circuit protection and wiring connecting the components. An inhibitor switch is included in the starting system to prevent the vehicle from being started with the vehicle in gear.

When the ignition key is turned to the **START** position, current flows and energizes the starter's solenoid coil. The solenoid plunger and clutch shift lever are activated and the clutch pinion engages the ring gear on the flywheel. The switch contacts close and the starter cranks the engine until it starts.

To prevent damage caused by excessive starter armature rotation when the engine starts, the starter incorporates an over-running clutch in the pinion gear.

### Starter

TESTING

The easiest way to test the performance of the starter is to perform a voltage drop test.

➡**The battery must be in good condition and fully charged prior to performing this test.**

1. Connect a voltmeter between the positive and negative terminals of the battery.

2. Turn the ignition key to the **START** position and note the voltage drop on the meter.

3. If voltage drops below 11.5 volts, there is high resistance in the starting system.

4. Check for proper connections at the battery and starter.

5. Check the resistance of the battery cables and replace as necessary.

6. If all other components in the system are functional, the starter may be faulty.

→**Many automotive parts stores have starter bench testers available for use by customers. A starter bench test is the most definitive way to determine the condition of your starter.**

### REMOVAL & INSTALLATION

▶ See Figures 35, 36, 37 and 38

1. Disconnect the negative battery cable at the battery.
2. Disconnect the leads from the starter motor.
3. Remove the starter motor retaining bolts.
4. Remove the starter motor from the vehicle.

**To install:**

5. Position the starter motor to the flywheel housing.

6. Apply locking compound to the bolt threads and install the retaining bolts finger-tight.

7. Tighten the bolts to approximately 25 ft. lbs. (34 Nm).

8. Connect the starter motor leads and the negative battery cable.

Fig. 35 Unfasten the nut retaining the starter cables . . .

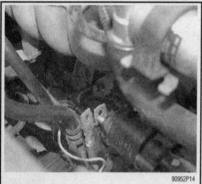

Fig. 36 . . . and remove the starter cables

Fig. 37 Unfasten the starter retaining bolts . . .

Fig. 38 . . . and remove the starter from the engine

## SENDING UNITS

→**This section describes the operating principles of sending units, warning lights and gauges. Sensors which provide information to the Electronic Control Module (ECM) are covered in Section 4 of this manual.**

Instrument panels contain a number of indicating devices (gauges and warning lights). These devices are composed of two separate components. One is the sending unit, mounted on the engine or other remote part of the vehicle, and the other is the actual gauge or light in the instrument panel.

Several types of sending units exist, however most can be characterized as being either a pressure type or a resistance type. Pressure type sending units convert liquid pressure into an electrical signal which is sent to the gauge. Resistance type sending units are most often used to measure temperature and use variable resistance to control the current flow back to the indicating device. Both types of sending units are connected in series by a wire to the battery (through the ignition switch). When the ignition is turned **ON**, current flows from the battery through the indicating device and on to the sending unit.

### Coolant Temperature Sender

▶ See Figure 39

The Engine Coolant Temperature (ECT) sensor is used as the sending unit on Volvos. Please refer to Section 4 of this manual for information.

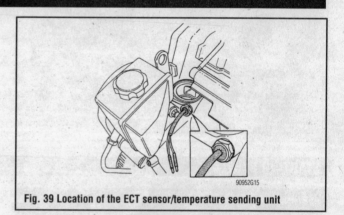

Fig. 39 Location of the ECT sensor/temperature sending unit

## Oil Pressure Sender

### TESTING

▶ See Figure 40

1. Unplug sensor connector and insert a jumper wire between terminals 1 and 2.

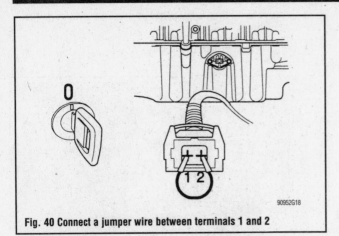

**Fig. 40 Connect a jumper wire between terminals 1 and 2**

2. Start the vehicle.
3. If the light is on, check the harness and dashboard light.
4. If the light is off, replace the sensor and recheck the light operation.

## REMOVAL & INSTALLATION

▶ **See Figures 41, 42 and 43**

1. Raise and safely support the vehicle.
2. Unplug the connector from the sensor.
3. Unfasten the sensor mounting bolts and remove the sensor from the oil pan.

**To install:**
4. Install the sensor into the oil pan.
5. Tighten the sensor mounting bolts.
6. Plug in the sensor connector.
7. Lower the vehicle.

## Fuel Level Sender

### TESTING

The easiest way to test the fuel level sender is to use an assistant and remove the sending unit from the fuel tank. Turn the ignition **ON**, but leave the engine **OFF**. While your assistant watches the fuel gauge, slowly move the sending unit arm upward and have your assistant check if the fuel gauge responds accordingly. If the gauge does not move, check the circuit to the gauge, and check the gauge; if both are OK, replace the sending unit.

### REMOVAL & INSTALLATION

▶ **See Figures 44, 45, 46 and 47**

On the Coupe, 240, 700 Series, and 940 models, the sending unit is attached to the fuel pump. See Section 5 for service information.

On the 850/C70/S70/V70 and 960/S90/V90 models, the sending unit has an access panel located in the trunk/hatch area. The procedure is as follows:
1. Relieve the fuel system pressure.
2. Disconnect the negative battery cable.
3. Tilt the rear seat forward and remove or fold back the trunk compartment carpet over the right-hand wheelwell panel. Remove any access panels or covers as necessary.
4. Disconnect the sending unit electrical wiring.
5. Remove the sending unit's plastic retaining nut using a socket wrench and tool 999-5486 or equivalent.
6. Lift the sending unit out carefully and remove the rubber seal.

### ✳✳ WARNING

**Install the retaining nut while the sending unit is removed, otherwise the tank connection may swell and the nut will be difficult to install.**

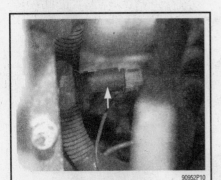

**Fig. 41 The oil pressure sensor is mounted to the side of the oil pan—850 model shown**

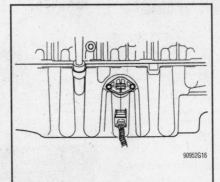

**Fig. 42 Unplug the connector from the oil pressure sensor**

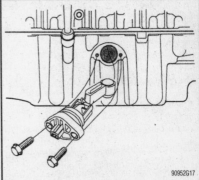

**Fig. 43 Unfasten the retaining bolts and remove the sensor**

**Fig. 44 Remove the trunk/hatch trim**

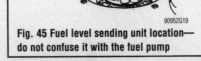

**Fig. 45 Fuel level sending unit location— do not confuse it with the fuel pump**

**Fig. 46 Unfasten the fuel level sending unit's connector**

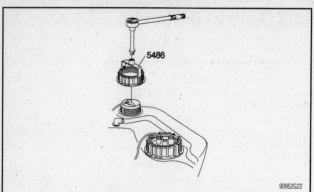

**Fig. 47 Using a socket wrench and tool 999-5486 or equivalent, remove the retaining ring and lift the sending unit out of the tank**

**To install:**

7. Install a new dry seal, making sure that it is seated properly. Lubricate the top and outer side of the seal with petroleum jelly.

8. Install the sending unit with the wiring harness facing towards the passenger side of the vehicle.

9. Remove the retaining nut from the tank and install the retaining nut on the sending unit. Tighten it to 30 ft. lbs. (40 Nm) using tool 999-5486 or equivalent.

10. Connect the wiring, then install the panels, covers and carpet.
11. Connect the negative battery cable.
12. Run the engine and check for leaks.

## Electric Fan Switch

### TESTING

The electric fan switch, or thermal switch, can be checked by placing the element in a bucket of water using an ohmmeter. Heat the water to approximately 207°–216°F (97°–102°C) and connect the switch leads to an ohmmeter. The switch should have no continuity until the temperature reaches this level. Let the water cool off below 207°F (97°C) and the switch should lose continuity. If the switch has no continuity at any temperature, replace it.

### REMOVAL & INSTALLATION

▶ **See Figure 48**

The thermal switch is located on the top of the radiator, usually on the passenger side.

1. Disconnect the negative battery cable.
2. Drain and recycle the engine coolant.

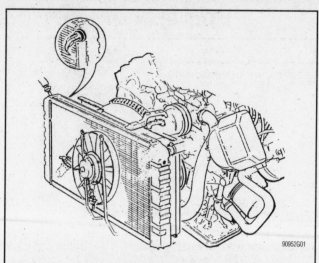

**Fig. 48 The cooling fan switch is located at the upper corner of the radiator**

### ❋❋ CAUTION

**Never open, service or drain the radiator or cooling system when hot; serious burns can occur from the steam and hot coolant. Also, when draining engine coolant, keep in mind that cats and dogs are attracted to ethylene glycol antifreeze and could drink any that is left in an uncovered container or in puddles on the ground. This will prove fatal in sufficient quantities. Always drain coolant into a sealable container. Coolant should be reused unless it is contaminated or is several years old.**

3. Unplug the electrical connector from the switch.
4. Using a suitable size socket or wrench, loosen the switch.
5. Remove the switch by hand.

**To install:**

6. Install the switch into the radiator, and start the threads by hand.
7. Tighten the switch into the radiator, but take care not to overtighten or you will break the switch or radiator.
8. Plug the electrical connector in.
9. Connect the negative battery cable.
10. Refill the coolant and start the engine.
11. Let the vehicle warm up and check the operation of the fan switch.
12. Check the level of the coolant.

### ❋❋ CAUTION

**Never open, service or drain the radiator or cooling system when hot; serious burns can occur from the steam and hot coolant.**

## Troubleshooting Basic Starting System Problems

| Problem | Cause | Solution |
|---|---|---|
| Starter motor rotates engine slowly | • Battery charge low or battery defective | • Charge or replace battery |
| | • Defective circuit between battery and starter motor | • Clean and tighten, or replace cables |
| | • Low load current | • Bench-test starter motor. Inspect for worn brushes and weak brush springs. |
| | • High load current | • Bench-test starter motor. Check engine for friction, drag or coolant in cylinders. Check ring gear-to-pinion gear clearance. |
| Starter motor will not rotate engine | • Battery charge low or battery defective | • Charge or replace battery |
| | • Faulty solenoid | • Check solenoid ground. Repair or replace as necessary. |
| | • Damaged drive pinion gear or ring gear | • Replace damaged gear(s) |
| | • Starter motor engagement weak | • Bench-test starter motor |
| | • Starter motor rotates slowly with high load current | • Inspect drive yoke pull-down and point gap, check for worn end bushings, check ring gear clearance |
| | • Engine seized | • Repair engine |
| Starter motor drive will not engage (solenoid known to be good) | • Defective contact point assembly | • Repair or replace contact point assembly |
| | • Inadequate contact point assembly ground | • Repair connection at ground screw |
| | • Defective hold-in coil | • Replace field winding assembly |
| Starter motor drive will not disengage | • Starter motor loose on flywheel housing | • Tighten mounting bolts |
| | • Worn drive end busing | • Replace bushing |
| | • Damaged ring gear teeth | • Replace ring gear or driveplate |
| | • Drive yoke return spring broken or missing | • Replace spring |
| Starter motor drive disengages prematurely | • Weak drive assembly thrust spring | • Replace drive mechanism |
| | • Hold-in coil defective | • Replace field winding assembly |
| Low load current | • Worn brushes | • Replace brushes |
| | • Weak brush springs | • Replace springs |

TCCS2C01

## Troubleshooting Basic Charging System Problems

| Problem | Cause | Solution |
| --- | --- | --- |
| Noisy alternator | • Loose mountings<br>• Loose drive pulley<br>• Worn bearings<br>• Brush noise<br>• Internal circuits shorted (High pitched whine) | • Tighten mounting bolts<br>• Tighten pulley<br>• Replace alternator<br>• Replace alternator<br>• Replace alternator |
| Squeal when starting engine or accelerating | • Glazed or loose belt | • Replace or adjust belt |
| Indicator light remains on or ammeter indicates discharge (engine running) | • Broken belt<br>• Broken or disconnected wires<br>• Internal alternator problems<br>• Defective voltage regulator | • Install belt<br>• Repair or connect wiring<br>• Replace alternator<br>• Replace voltage regulator/alternator |
| Car light bulbs continually burn out— battery needs water continually | • Alternator/regulator overcharging | • Replace voltage regulator/alternator |
| Car lights flare on acceleration | • Battery low<br>• Internal alternator/regulator problems | • Charge or replace battery<br>• Replace alternator/regulator |
| Low voltage output (alternator light flickers continually or ammeter needle wanders) | • Loose or worn belt<br>• Dirty or corroded connections<br>• Internal alternator/regulator problems | • Replace or adjust belt<br>• Clean or replace connections<br>• Replace alternator/regulator |

TCCS2C02

# 3

# ENGINE AND ENGINE OVERHAUL

## ENGINE MECHANICAL

### ENGINE MECHANICAL SPECIFICATIONS

| Description | English Specifications | Metric Specifications |
|---|---|---|
| **General Information** | | |
| Engine Type | | |
| B230F and FT | OHC In-line 4-cylinder | |
| B234F | OHC In-line 4-cylinder | |
| B280F | OHC 90 degree V-6 | |
| B254S, T, and FT | OHC In-line 5-cylinder | |
| B234T and T3 | OHC In-line 5-cylinder | |
| B6304 | OHC In-line 6-cylinder | |
| Bore & Stroke | | |
| B230F and FT | 3.78 x 3.15 in. | 96.0 x 80.0 mm |
| B234F | 3.78 x 3.15 in | 96.0 x 80.0 mm |
| B280F | 3.58 x 2.87 in. | 90.9 x 72.9 mm |
| B254S, T, and FT | 3.27 x 3.54 in. | 83.0 x 89.9 mm |
| B234T and T3 | 3.19 x 3.54 in. | 81.0 x 89.9 mm |
| B6304 | 3.27 x 3.54 in. | 83.0 x 89.9 mm |
| Displacement | | |
| B230F and FT | 144 c.i. | 2.3L |
| B234F | 144 c.i. | 2.3L |
| B280F | 175 c.i. | 2.8L |
| B254S, T, and FT | 151 c.i. | 2.4L |
| B234T and T3 | 144 c.i. | 2.3L |
| B6304 | 181 c.i. | 2.9L |
| Compression Ratio | | |
| B230F | 9.8:1 | |
| B230FT | 8.7:1 | |
| B234F | 10.0:1 | |
| B280F | 9.5:1 | |
| B254S, T, and FT | 10.5:1 | |
| B234T and T3 | 8.5:1 | |
| B6304 | 10.7:1 | |
| Firing Order | | |
| B230F and FT | 1-3-4-2 | |
| B234F | 1-3-4-2 | |
| B280F | 1-6-3-5-2-4 | |
| B254S, T, and FT | 1-2-4-5-3 | |
| B234T and T3 | 1-2-4-5-3 | |
| B6304 | 1-5-3-6-2-4 | |
| Lubrication | Pressure Feed - Full Flow Filtration | |
| Cooling System | Liquid Cooled - Forced Circulation | |
| **Crankshaft** | | |
| End-Play | | |
| B230F and FT | 0.004 - 0.016 in. | 0.102 - 0.406 mm |
| B234F | 0.004 - 0.016 in. | 0.102 - 0.406 mm |
| B280F | 0.0028 - 0.0106 in. | 0.0711 - 0.2692 mm |
| B254S, T, and FT | 0.003-0.007 in. | 0.08 - 0.19 mm |
| B234T and T3 | 0.003-0.007 in. | 0.08 - 0.19 mm |
| B6304 | 0.003-0.007 in. | 0.08 - 0.19 mm |
| Run-out | | |
| B230F and FT | 0.013 in. | 0.032 mm |
| B234F | 0.013 in. | 0.032 mm |
| B280F | 0.013 in. | 0.032 mm |
| B254S, T, and FT | 0.013 in. | 0.032 mm |
| B234T and T3 | 0.013 in. | 0.032 mm |
| B6304 | 0.013 in. | 0.032 mm |

90953C03

### ENGINE MECHANICAL SPECIFICATIONS

| Description | English Specifications | Metric Specifications |
|---|---|---|
| **Rod Journal** | | |
| Diameter | | |
| B230F and FT | 2.1255 - 2.1260 in. | 53.9877 - 54.0004 mm |
| B234F | 2.0472 - 2.0476 in. | 51.9989 - 52.0090 mm |
| B280F | 2.3611 - 2.3618 in. | 59.9719 - 59.9897 mm |
| B254S, T, and FT | 1.96 in. | 50.0 mm |
| B234T and T3 | 1.96 in. | 50.0 mm |
| B6304 | 1.96 in. | 50.0 mm |
| Out-of-Round | | |
| B230F and FT | 0.00016 in. | 0.004 mm |
| B234F | 0.00016 in. | 0.004 mm |
| B280F | 0.0002 in. | 0.004 mm |
| B254S, T, and FT | 0.0002 in. | 0.004 mm |
| B234T and T3 | 0.0002 in. | 0.004 mm |
| B6304 | 0.0002 in. | 0.004 mm |
| Taper | | |
| B230F and FT | 0.00016 in. | 0.004 mm |
| B234F | 0.00016 in. | 0.004 mm |
| B280F | 0.0002 in. | 0.004 mm |
| B254S, T, and FT | 0.0002 in. | 0.004 mm |
| B234T and T3 | 0.0002 in. | 0.004 mm |
| B6304 | 0.0002 in. | 0.004 mm |
| **Main Bearing Journal** | | |
| Diameter | | |
| B230F and FT | 2.4981 - 2.4986 in. | 63.4517 - 63.4644 mm |
| B234F | 2.4803 in. | 63.0 mm |
| B280F | 2.7576 - 2.7583 in. | 70.0434 - 70.0608 mm |
| B254S, T, and FT | 2.5 in. | 65.0 mm |
| B234T and T3 | 2.5 in. | 65.0 mm |
| B6304 | 2.5 in. | 65.0 mm |
| Out-of-Round | | |
| B230F and FT | 0.00016 in. | 0.004 mm |
| B234F | 0.00016 in. | 0.004 mm |
| B280F | 0.0002 in. | 0.004 mm |
| B254S, T, and FT | 0.0002 in. | 0.004 mm |
| B234T and T3 | 0.0002 in. | 0.004 mm |
| B6304 | 0.0002 in. | 0.004 mm |
| Taper | | |
| B230F and FT | 0.00016 in. | 0.004 mm |
| B234F | 0.00016 in. | 0.004 mm |
| B280F | 0.0002 in. | 0.004 mm |
| B254S, T, and FT | 0.0002 in. | 0.004 mm |
| B234T and T3 | 0.0002 in. | 0.004 mm |
| B6304 | 0.0002 in. | 0.004 mm |
| Bearing Clearance | | |
| B230F and FT | 0.0011 - 0.0033 in. | 0.0279 - 0.0838 mm |
| B234F | 0.0011 - 0.0033 in. | 0.0279 - 0.0838 mm |
| B280F | 0.0035 in. | 0.0889 mm |
| B254S, T, and FT | .001 - .002 in. | .02 - .04 mm |
| B234T and T3 | .001 - .002 in. | .02 - .04 mm |
| B6304 | .001 - .002 in. | .02 - .04 mm |
| **Connecting Rod** | | |
| Bearing Clearance | | |
| B230F and FT | 0.0009 - 0.0026 in. | 0.23 - 0.26 mm |
| B234F | 0.0009 - 0.0026 in. | 0.23 - 0.26 mm |
| B280F | 0.0079 - 0.0150 in. | 0.2007 - 0.3810 mm |
| B254S, T, and FT | N/A | N/A |
| B234T and T3 | N/A | N/A |
| B6304 | N/A | N/A |

90953C04

## ENGINE MECHANICAL SPECIFICATIONS

| Description | English Specifications | Metric Specifications |
|---|---|---|
| **Side Clearance** | | |
| B230F and FT | 0.006 - 0.0014 in. | 0.1524 - 0.3556 mm |
| B234F | 0.006 - 0.0018 in. | 0.1524 - 0.4572 mm |
| B280F | 0.0079 - 0.0150 in. | 0.2007 - 0.3810 mm |
| B6254S, T, and FT | 0.006 - 0.0018 in. | 0.1524 - 0.4572 mm |
| B6234T and T3 | 0.006 - 0.0018 in. | 0.1524 - 0.4572 mm |
| B6304 | 0.006 - 0.0018 in. | 0.1524 - 0.4572 mm |
| **Cylinder Block** | | |
| **Cylinder Bore Diameter** | | |
| B230F and FT and B234F | | |
| Standard "C" | 3.7795 - 3.7799 in. | 96.00 - 96.01 mm |
| Standard "D" | 3.7799 - 3.7803 in. | 96.01 - 96.02 mm |
| Standard "E" | 3.7803 - 3.7807 in. | 96.02 - 96.03 mm |
| Standard "G" | 3.7811 - 3.7815 in. | 96.04 - 96.05 mm |
| Oversize 1 | 3.7913 in. | 96.3 mm |
| Oversize 2 | 3.8031 in. | 96.6 mm |
| B280F | 3.5827 - 3.5639 in. | 91.13 - 91.16 mm |
| B6254S, T, and FT | | |
| Standard "C" | 3.2677 - 3.2681 in. | 83.00 - 83.01 mm |
| Standard "D" | 3.2681 - 3.2685 in. | 83.01 - 83.02 mm |
| Standard "E" | 3.2685 - 3.2689 in. | 83.02 - 83.03 mm |
| Standard "G" | 3.2692 - 3.2696 in. | 83.04 - 83.05 mm |
| Oversize 1 | 3.2755 - 3.2759 in. | 83.20 - 83.21 mm |
| Oversize 2 | 3.2834 - 3.2838 in. | 83.40 - 83.41 mm |
| B6234T and T3 | | |
| Standard "C" | 3.1889 - 3.1893 in. | 81.00 - 81.01 mm |
| Standard "D" | 3.1893 - 3.1897 in. | 81.01 - 81.02 mm |
| Standard "E" | 3.1897 - 3.1901 in. | 81.02 - 81.03 mm |
| Standard "G" | 3.1905 - 3.1909 in. | 81.04 - 81.05 mm |
| Oversize 1 | 3.1968 - 3.1972 in. | 81.20 - 81.21 mm |
| Oversize 2 | 3.2047 - 3.2051 in. | 81.40 - 81.41 mm |
| B6304 | | |
| Standard "C" | 3.2677 - 3.2681 in. | 83.00 - 83.01 mm |
| Standard "D" | 3.2681 - 3.2685 in. | 83.01 - 83.02 mm |
| Standard "E" | 3.2685 - 3.2689 in. | 83.02 - 83.03 mm |
| Standard "G" | 3.2692 - 3.2696 in. | 83.04 - 83.05 mm |
| Oversize 1 | 3.2755 - 3.2759 in. | 83.20 - 83.21 mm |
| Oversize 2 | 3.2834 - 3.2838 in. | 83.40 - 83.41 mm |
| **Maximum Taper** | | |
| All engines | 0.004 in. | 0.10 mm |
| **Maximum Out-of Round** | | |
| All engines | 0.004 in. | 0.10 mm |
| **Deck Height** | | |
| B230F and FT | 5.73 in. | 145.6 mm |
| B234F | 5.73 in. | 145.6 mm |
| B280F | N/A | N/A |
| B6254S, T, and FT | 5.20 in. | 132.1 mm |
| B6304 | 5.20 in. | 132.1 mm |
| **Maximum Deck Warpage** | | |
| **Length** | | |
| All engines | .020 in | .50 mm |
| **Width** | | |
| All engines | .008 in. | .20 mm |

90953C05

## ENGINE MECHANICAL SPECIFICATIONS

| Description | English Specifications | Metric Specifications |
|---|---|---|
| **Pistons, Pins, and Rings** | | |
| **Piston-to-Cylinder Clearance** | | |
| B230F and FT | 0.0004 - 0.0012 in. | 0.0101 - 0.0305 mm |
| B234F | 0.0004 - 0.0012 in. | 0.0101 - 0.0305 mm |
| B280F | 0.0007 - 0.0015 in. | 0.0177 - 0.0381 mm |
| B6254S, T, and FT | 0.0003 - 0.0011 in. | 0.010 - 0.030 mm |
| B6234T and T3 | 0.0003 - 0.0011 in. | 0.010 - 0.030 mm |
| B6304 | 0.0003 - 0.0011 in. | 0.010 - 0.030 mm |
| **Piston Diameter** | | |
| B230F and FT and B234F | | |
| Standard "C" | 3.7787 - 3.7791 in. | 95.978 - 95.989 mm |
| Standard "D" | 3.7791 - 3.7795 in. | 95.989 - 95.999 mm |
| Standard "E" | 3.7795 - 3.7799 in. | 95.999 - 96.009 mm |
| Standard "G" | 3.7811 - 3.7815 in. | 96.039 - 96.050 mm |
| Oversize 1 | 3.7905 - 3.7909 in. | 96.278 - 96.288 mm |
| Oversize 2 | 3.8024 - 3.8028 in. | 96.581 - 96.591 mm |
| B280F | 3.5796 - 3.5807 in. | 91.051 - 91.083 mm |
| B6254S, T, and FT | | |
| Standard "C" | 3.2669 - 3.2673 in. | 82.980 - 82.990 mm |
| Standard "D" | 3.2673 - 3.2677 in. | 82.990 - 83.000 mm |
| Standard "E" | 3.2677 - 3.2681 in. | 83.000 - 83.010 mm |
| Standard "G" | 3.2683 - 3.2689 in. | 83.017 - 83.032 mm |
| Oversize 1 | 3.2746 - 3.2752 in. | 83.177 - 83.192 mm |
| Oversize 2 | 3.2825 - 3.2831 in. | 83.377 - 83.392 mm |
| B6234T and T3 | | |
| Standard "C" | 3.1881 - 3.1885 in. | 80.980 - 80.990 mm |
| Standard "D" | 3.1885 - 3.1889 in. | 80.990 - 81.000 mm |
| Standard "E" | 3.1889 - 3.1893 in. | 81.000 - 81.010 mm |
| Standard "G" | 3.1896 - 3.1902 in. | 81.017 - 81.032 mm |
| Oversize 1 | 3.1959 - 3.1965 in. | 81.177 - 81.192 mm |
| Oversize 2 | 3.2038 - 3.2044 in. | 81.377 - 81.392 mm |
| B6304 | | |
| Standard "C" | 3.2669 - 3.2673 in. | 82.980 - 82.990 mm |
| Standard "D" | 3.2673 - 3.2677 in. | 82.990 - 83.000 mm |
| Standard "E" | 3.2677 - 3.2681 in. | 83.000 - 83.010 mm |
| Standard "G" | 3.2683 - 3.2689 in. | 83.017 - 83.032 mm |
| Oversize 1 | 3.2746 - 3.2752 in. | 83.177 - 83.192 mm |
| Oversize 2 | 3.2825 - 3.2831 in. | 83.377 - 83.392 mm |
| **Piston Pin Diameter** | | |
| B230F and FT | .9055 in. | 23.0 mm |
| B234F | .9055 in. | 23.0 mm |
| B280F | .9055 in. | 23.0 mm |
| B6254S, T, and T3 | 0.9 in. | 23.0 mm |
| B6304 | 0.9 in. | 23.0 mm |
| **Piston Ring End Gap** | | |
| B230F and FT | | |
| No. 1 Compression | 0.0118 - 0.0217 in. | 0.2997 - 0.5512 mm |
| No. 2 Compression | 0.0118 - 0.0217 in. | 0.2997 - 0.5512 mm |
| Oil Control | 0.0118 - 0.0256 in. | 0.2997 - 0.5512 mm |
| B234F | | |
| No. 1 Compression | 0.0118 - 0.0217 in. | 0.2997 - 0.5512 mm |
| No. 2 Compression | 0.0118 - 0.0217 in. | 0.2997 - 0.5512 mm |
| Oil Control | 0.0118 - 0.0256 in. | 0.2997 - 0.5512 mm |
| B280F | | |
| No. 1 Compression | 0.0158 - 0.0236 in. | 0.4013 - 0.5994 mm |
| No. 2 Compression | 0.0158 - 0.0236 in. | 0.4013 - 0.5994 mm |
| Oil Control | 0.0158 - 0.0571 in. | 0.4013 - 1.4503 mm |

90953C06

## ENGINE MECHANICAL SPECIFICATIONS

| Description | English Specifications | Metric Specifications |
|---|---|---|
| **B6254S, T, and FT** | | |
| No. 1 Compression | 0.012 - 0.022 in. | 0.30 - 0.55 mm |
| No. 2 Compression | 0.012 - 0.022 in. | 0.30 - 0.55 mm |
| Oil Control | 0.012 - 0.024 in. | 0.30 - 0.60 mm |
| **B234T and T3** | | |
| No. 1 Compression | 0.012 - 0.022 in. | 0.30 - 0.55 mm |
| No. 2 Compression | 0.012 - 0.022 in. | 0.30 - 0.55 mm |
| Oil Control | 0.012 - 0.024 in. | 0.30 - 0.60 mm |
| **B6304** | | |
| No. 1 Compression | 0.012 - 0.022 in. | 0.30 - 0.55 mm |
| No. 2 Compression | 0.012 - 0.022 in. | 0.30 - 0.55 mm |
| Oil Control | 0.012 - 0.024 in. | 0.30 - 0.60 mm |
| **Piston Ring Side Clearance** | | |
| **B230F and FT** | | |
| No. 1 Compression | 0.0024 - 0.0036 in. | 0.060 - 0.092 mm |
| No. 2 Compression | 0.0016 - 0.0028 in. | 0.040 - 0.072 mm |
| Oil Control | 0.0012 - 0.0025 in. | 0.030 - 0.063 mm |
| **B234F** | | |
| No. 1 Compression | 0.0024 - 0.0036 in. | 0.060 - 0.092 mm |
| No. 2 Compression | 0.0016 - 0.0028 in. | 0.040 - 0.072 mm |
| Oil Control | 0.0012 - 0.0025 in. | 0.030 - 0.063 mm |
| **B280F** | | |
| No. 1 Compression | 0.0021 - 0.0029 in. | 0.053 - 0.074 mm |
| No. 2 Compression | 0.0010 - 0.0021 in. | 0.025 - 0.053 mm |
| Oil Control | 0.0004 - 0.0009 in. | 0.010 - 0.023 mm |
| **B6254S, T, and FT** | | |
| No. 1 Compression | 0.0024 - 0.0036 in. | 0.060 - 0.092 mm |
| No. 2 Compression | 0.0016 - 0.0028 in. | 0.040 - 0.072 mm |
| Oil Control | 0.0012 - 0.0025 in. | 0.030 - 0.063 mm |
| **B234T and T3** | | |
| No. 1 Compression | 0.0024 - 0.0036 in. | 0.060 - 0.092 mm |
| No. 2 Compression | 0.0016 - 0.0028 in. | 0.040 - 0.072 mm |
| Oil Control | 0.0012 - 0.0025 in. | 0.030 - 0.063 mm |
| **B6304** | | |
| No. 1 Compression | 0.0024 - 0.0036 in. | 0.060 - 0.092 mm |
| No. 2 Compression | 0.0016 - 0.0028 in. | 0.040 - 0.072 mm |
| Oil Control | 0.0012 - 0.0025 in. | 0.030 - 0.063 mm |
| **Balance Shaft (B234F only)** | | |
| Front Bearing Inside Diameter | 1.8512 - 1.8523 in. | 47.020 - 47.060 mm |
| Front Journal Outside Diameter | 1.8494 - 1.8504 in. | 46.975 - 47.000 mm |
| Center Bearing Inside Diameter | 1.6957 - 1.6969 in. | 43.070 - 43.100 mm |
| Center Journal Outside Diameter | 1.6939 - 1.6949 in. | 43.025 - 43.050 mm |
| Rear Bearing Inside Diameter | 1.6917 - 1.6929 in. | 43.970 - 43.000 mm |
| Rear Journal Outside Diameter | 1.6900 - 1.6909 in. | 42.925 - 42.950 mm |
| Bearings Oil Clearance | 0.0008 - 0.0030 in. | .020 - 0.075 mm |
| **Camshaft and Lifters** | | |
| **Journal Diameter** | | |
| B230F and FT | 1.179 - 1.180 in. | 29.950 - 29.972 mm |
| B280F | 1.179 - 1.180 in. | 29.950 - 29.972 mm |
| No. 1 | 1.592 - 1.593 in. | 40.436 - 40.462 mm |
| No. 2 | 1.616 - 1.617 in. | 41.046 - 41.071 mm |
| No. 3 | 1.639 - 1.640 in. | 41.630 - 41.656 mm |
| No. 4 | 1.663 - 1.664 in. | 42.240 - 42.265 mm |
| B6254S, T, and FT | N/A | N/A |
| B234T and T3 | N/A | N/A |
| B6304 | N/A | N/A |

90953C07

## ENGINE MECHANICAL SPECIFICATIONS

| Description | English Specifications | Metric Specifications |
|---|---|---|
| **Lobe Lift** | | |
| **B230F and FT** | | |
| Intake | 0.374 in. | 9.499 mm |
| Exhaust | 0.414 in. | 10.515 mm |
| **B234F** | | |
| Intake | 0.370 in. | 9.398 mm |
| Exhaust | 0.370 in. | 9.398 mm |
| **B280F** | | |
| Intake | 0.235 in. | 5.969 mm |
| Exhaust | 0.214 in. | 5.436 mm |
| **B6254S, T, and FT** | | |
| Intake | 0.333 in. | 8.470 mm |
| Exhaust | 0.333 in. | 8.470 mm |
| **B234T and T3** | | |
| Intake | 0.313 in. | 7.961 mm |
| Exhaust | 0.313 in. | 7.961 mm |
| **B6304** | | |
| Intake | 0.354 in. | 9.004 mm |
| Exhaust | 0.354 in. | 9.004 mm |
| **Bearing Clearance** | | |
| B230F and FT | 0.0012 - 0.0028 in. | 0.0304 - 0.0711 mm |
| B234F | 0.0014 - 0.0034 in. | 0.0356 - 0.0864 mm |
| B280F | 0.0012 - 0.0028 in. | 0.0304 - 0.0711 mm |
| B6254S, T, and FT | 0.0012 - 0.0028 in. | 0.0304 - 0.0711 mm |
| B234T and T3 | 0.0012 - 0.0028 in. | 0.0304 - 0.0711 mm |
| B6304 | 0.0012 - 0.0028 in. | 0.0304 - 0.0711 mm |
| **End-play** | | |
| B230F and FT | 0.004 - 0.0016 in. | 0.102 - 0.406 mm |
| B234F | 0.004 - 0.0016 in. | 0.102 - 0.406 mm |
| B280F | N/A | N/A |
| B6254S, T, and FT | 0.002 - 0.008 in. | 0.05 - 0.20 mm |
| B234T and T3 | 0.002 - 0.008 in. | 0.05 - 0.20 mm |
| B6304 | 0.002 - 0.008 in. | 0.05 - 0.20 mm |
| **Lifter Diameter** | | |
| B230F and FT | 1.4567 - 1.4565 in. | 36.975 - 36.995 mm |
| B234F | 1.4567 - 1.4565 in. | 36.975 - 36.995 mm |
| B280F | 1.4567 - 1.4565 in. | 36.975 - 36.995 mm |
| B6254S, T, and FT | 1.3750 - 1.3780 in. | 34.950 - 35.020 mm |
| B234T and T3 | 1.3750 - 1.3780 in. | 34.950 - 35.020 mm |
| B6304 | 1.3750 - 1.3780 in. | 34.950 - 35.020 mm |
| **Lifter Height** | | |
| B230F and FT | 1.180 - 1.220 in. | 29.97 - 30.99 mm |
| B234F | 1.180 - 1.220 in. | 29.97 - 30.99 mm |
| B280F | N/A | N/A |
| B6254S, T, and FT | N/A | N/A |
| B234T and T3 | N/A | N/A |
| B6304 | N/A | N/A |
| **Oil Clearance** | | |
| B230F and FT | 0.0012 - 0.0030 in. | 0.030 - 0.076 mm |
| B234F | 0.0012 - 0.0030 in. | 0.030 - 0.076 mm |
| B280F | 0.0012 - 0.0030 in. | 0.030 - 0.076 mm |
| B6254S, T, and FT | N/A | N/A |
| B234T and T3 | N/A | N/A |
| B6304 | N/A | N/A |
| **Cylinder Head** | | |
| **Cylinder Head Height** | | |
| B230F and FT | 5.752 in. | 146.1 mm |
| B234F | 5.752 in. | 146.1 mm |
| B280F | N/A | N/A |
| B6254S, T, and FT | 5.076 - 5.080 in. | 128.95 - 129.05 mm |

90953C08

## ENGINE MECHANICAL SPECIFICATIONS

| Description | English Specifications | Metric Specifications |
|---|---|---|
| B5234T and T3 | 5.076 - 5.080 in. | 128.95 - 129.05 mm |
| B6304 | 5.076 - 5.080 in. | 128.95 - 129.05 mm |
| Maximum Warpage | | |
| Width | | |
| All Engines | 0.020 in. | 0.50 mm |
| Length | | |
| All Engines | 0.008 in. | 0.20 mm |
| Valve Seat Width | | |
| B230F and FT | | |
| Intake | 0.049 - 0.075 in. | 1.27 - 1.91 mm |
| Exhaust | 0.066 - 0.066 in. | 1.68 - 2.31 mm |
| B234F | | |
| Intake | 0.049 - 0.075 in. | 1.27 - 1.91 mm |
| Exhaust | 0.066 - 0.066 in. | 1.68 - 2.31 mm |
| B260F | | |
| Intake | 0.049 - 0.075 in. | 1.27 - 1.91 mm |
| Exhaust | 0.066 - 0.066 in. | 1.68 - 2.31 mm |
| B5254S, T, and FT | | |
| Intake | 0.055 - 0.070 in. | 1.40 - 1.80 mm |
| Exhaust | 0.070 - 0.086 in. | 1.80 - 2.20 mm |
| B5234T and T3 | | |
| Intake | 0.055 - 0.070 in. | 1.40 - 1.80 mm |
| Exhaust | 0.070 - 0.086 in. | 1.80 - 2.20 mm |
| B6304 | | |
| Intake | 0.055 - 0.070 in. | 1.40 - 1.80 mm |
| Exhaust | 0.070 - 0.086 in. | 1.80 - 2.20 mm |
| Valve Seat Angle | | |
| All Engines | | |
| Intake | 45 degrees | |
| Exhaust | 45 degrees | |
| Valve Guide Diameter | | |
| B230F and FT | | |
| Intake | 0.3150 - 0.3158 in. | 8.00 - 8.02 mm |
| Exhaust | 0.3150 - 0.3158 in. | 8.00 - 8.02 mm |
| B234F | | |
| Intake | 0.3150 - 0.3158 in. | 8.00 - 8.02 mm |
| Exhaust | 0.3150 - 0.3158 in. | 8.00 - 8.02 mm |
| B260F | | |
| Intake | 0.3150 - 0.3158 in. | 8.00 - 8.02 mm |
| Exhaust | 0.3150 - 0.3158 in. | 8.00 - 8.02 mm |
| B5254S, T, and FT | | |
| Standard | 0.472 in. | 12.0 mm |
| Oversize 1 | 0.476 in. | 12.1 mm |
| Oversize 2 | 0.480 in. | 12.2 mm |
| B5234T and T3 | | |
| Standard | 0.472 in. | 12.0 mm |
| Oversize 1 | 0.476 in. | 12.1 mm |
| Oversize 2 | 0.480 in. | 12.2 mm |
| B6304 | | |
| Standard | 0.472 in. | 12.0 mm |
| Oversize 1 | 0.476 in. | 12.1 mm |
| Oversize 2 | 0.480 in. | 12.2 mm |
| Valve Stem-to-guide Clearance | | |
| All Engines | 0.0012 - 0.0024 in. | 0.030 - 0.060 mm |
| **Valves and Springs** | | |
| Valve Face Angle | | |
| All Engines | 44.5 degrees | |

90953C09

## ENGINE MECHANICAL SPECIFICATIONS

| Description | English Specifications | Metric Specifications |
|---|---|---|
| Valve Head Diameter | | |
| B230F and FT | | |
| Intake | 1.73 in. | 44 mm |
| Exhaust | 1.38 in. | 35 mm |
| B234F | | |
| Intake | 1.73 in. | 44 mm |
| Exhaust | 1.38 in. | 35 mm |
| B260F | | |
| Intake | 1.81 - 1.85 in. | 46.04 - 47.05 mm |
| Exhaust | 1.45 - 1.49 in. | 36.88 - 37.90 mm |
| B5254S, T, and FT | | |
| Intake | 1.568 - 1.580 in. | 39.85 - 40.15 mm |
| Exhaust | 1.568 - 1.580 in. | 39.85 - 40.15 mm |
| B5234T and T3 | | |
| Intake | 1.568 - 1.580 in. | 39.85 - 40.15 mm |
| Exhaust | 1.568 - 1.580 in. | 39.85 - 40.15 mm |
| B6304 | | |
| Intake | 1.568 - 1.580 in. | 39.85 - 40.15 mm |
| Exhaust | 1.568 - 1.580 in. | 39.85 - 40.15 mm |
| Valve Stem Diameter | | |
| B230F and FT | | |
| Intake | 0.3132 - 0.3138 in. | 7.955 - 7.970 mm |
| Exhaust | 0.3128 - 0.3134 in. | 7.945 - 7.960 mm |
| B234F | | |
| Intake | 0.3132 - 0.3138 in. | 7.955 - 7.970 mm |
| Exhaust | 0.3128 - 0.3134 in. | 7.945 - 7.960 mm |
| B260F | | |
| Intake | Tapered | Tapered |
| Exhaust | Tapered | Tapered |
| B5254S, T, and FT | | |
| Intake | 0.273 - 0.274 in. | 6.95 - 6.97 mm |
| Exhaust | 0.274 - 0.275 in. | 6.97 - 6.99 mm |
| B5234T and T3 | | |
| Intake | 0.273 - 0.274 in. | 6.95 - 6.97 mm |
| Exhaust | 0.274 - 0.275 in. | 6.97 - 6.99 mm |
| B6304 | | |
| Intake | 0.273 - 0.274 in. | 6.95 - 6.97 mm |
| Exhaust | 0.274 - 0.275 in. | 6.97 - 6.99 mm |
| Valve Spring Height | | |
| B230F and FT | 1.79 in. | 45.5 mm |
| B234F | 1.79 in. | 45.5 mm |
| B260F | 1.85 in. | 47.1 mm |
| B5254S, T, and FT | 1.70 in. | 43.2 mm |
| B5234T and T3 | 1.70 in. | 43.2 mm |
| B6304 | 1.70 in. | 43.2 mm |
| Valve Spring Test Pressure | | |
| B230F and FT | 158 lbs. @ 1.08 in. | 703 N @ 27.5 mm |
| B234F | 158 lbs. @ 1.08 in. | 703 N @ 27.5 mm |
| B260F | 165 lbs. @ 1.08 in. | 734 N @ 27.5 mm |
| B5254S, T, and FT | | |
| Intake | 150 lbs. @ 1.00 in. | 667 N @ 25.4 mm |
| Exhaust | 61 lbs. @ 1.34 in. | 271 N @ 34.1 mm |
| B5234T and T3 | | |
| Intake | 150 @ 1.00 in. | 667 N @ 25.4 mm |
| Exhaust | 61 lbs. @ 1.34 in. | 271 N @ 34.1 mm |
| B6304 | | |
| Intake | 150 @ 1.00 in. | 667 N @ 25.4 mm |
| Exhaust | 61 lbs. @ 1.34 in. | 271 N @ 34.1 mm |

90953C10

## Engine

### REMOVAL & INSTALLATION

In the process of removing the engine, you will come across a number of steps which call for the removal of a separate component or system, such as "disconnect the exhaust system" or "remove the radiator." In most instances, a detailed removal procedure can be found elsewhere in this manual.

It is virtually impossible to list each individual wire and hose which must be disconnected, simply because so many different model and engine combinations have been manufactured. Careful observation and common sense are the best possible approaches to any repair procedure.

Removal and installation of the engine can be made easier if you follow these basic points:

- If you have to drain any of the fluids, use a suitable container.
- Always tag any wires or hoses and, if possible, the components they came from before disconnecting them.
- Because there are so many bolts and fasteners involved, store and label the retainers from components separately in muffin pans, jars or coffee cans. This will prevent confusion during installation.
- After unbolting the transmission or transaxle, always make sure it is properly supported.
- If it is necessary to disconnect the air conditioning system, have this service performed by a qualified technician using a recovery/recycling station. If the system does not have to be disconnected, unbolt the compressor and set it aside.
- When unbolting the engine mounts, always make sure the engine is properly supported. When removing the engine, make sure that any lifting devices are properly attached to the engine. It is recommended that if your engine is supplied with lifting hooks, your lifting apparatus be attached to them.
- Lift the engine from its compartment slowly, checking that no hoses, wires or other components are still connected.
- After the engine is clear of the compartment, place it on an engine stand or workbench.
- After the engine has been removed, you can perform a partial or full teardown of the engine using the procedures outlined in this manual.

➡**Although Volvo recommends removing the engine and transmission as an assembly, we at Chilton have found the transmission can be left in the vehicle if desired. If choosing to remove the engine only and leave the transmission in the vehicle, disregard the transmission, shifter, cables, driveshaft, and mount removal procedures. In place of these procedures, the bell housing bolts must be removed, as well as the torque converter bolts, if equipped with an automatic transmission. Also, a floorjack or other suitable support must be placed under the transmission.**

#### 2.3L 4-Cylinder Engine

1. Properly relieve the fuel system pressure.
2. Disconnect the battery cables, negative lead first.
3. Remove the battery.
4. If equipped with a manual transmission, remove the shifter.
5. Disconnect the windshield washer hose and engine compartment light wire.
6. Scribe marks around the hood mount brackets on the underside of the hood for later alignment.
7. Remove the hood.
8. Remove the overflow tank cap.
9. Remove the gravel shield from the underside of the radiator.
10. Drain the cooling system.
11. Remove the upper and lower radiator hoses.
12. Disconnect the overflow hoses at the radiator.
13. Disconnect the PCV hose at the cylinder head.
14. If equipped with an automatic transmission, disconnect the oil cooler lines at the radiator.
15. Remove the fan assembly.
16. Remove the radiator and fan shroud.
17. Remove the air cleaner.
18. If equipped, disconnect the hoses at the air pump.

19. Remove the air pump and drive belt.
20. Remove the vacuum pump and hoses.
21. Disconnect the power brake booster vacuum hose.
22. Remove the power steering pump, drive belt and bracket. Position aside without disconnecting the hydraulic lines.
23. If equipped with A/C, remove the crankshaft pulley and compressor drive belt. Then install the pulley again for reference.
24. Disconnect the air conditioning wiring and remove the compressor from the bracket. Position the compressor aside without disconnecting the hoses.
25. Remove the bracket.
26. Disconnect the vacuum hoses from the engine.
27. Disconnect the carbon canister hoses.
28. Remove the distributor wire connector, high tension lead, starter cables and the clutch cable clamp.
29. Disconnect the wiring harness at the voltage regulator.
30. Disconnect the throttle cable at the pulley and the wire for the A/C at the manifold solenoid.
31. Remove the gas cap.
32. Disconnect the fuel lines at the filter and return pipe.
33. At the firewall, remove the electrical connectors for the ballast resistor and relays.
34. Disconnect the heater hoses.
35. Unplug the micro-switch connectors at the intake manifold and all remaining harness connectors to the engine.
36. If equipped, disconnect the cruise control cables and hoses.
37. Drain the engine oil.
38. Remove the exhaust manifold flange retaining nuts. Loosen the exhaust pipe clamp bolts and remove the bracket for the front exhaust pipe mount.
39. Remove the exhaust manifolds from the cylinder head.
40. Raise and safely support the vehicle.
41. From underneath, remove the front motor mount bolts.
42. If equipped with an automatic transmission, place the gear selector lever in **PARK** and disconnect the gear shift control rod from the transmission.
43. On manual transmission vehicles, disconnect the clutch controls.
44. Disconnect the speedometer cable and mark and remove the driveshaft from the transmission.
45. On overdrive equipped vehicles, disconnect the control wire from the shifter.
46. Use a floor jack and a wooden block and support the weight of the engine beneath the transmission.
47. Remove the bolts for the rear transmission mount.
48. Remove the transmission support crossmember.
49. Lift out the engine using the proper lifting equipment.

➡**When removing the engine and transmission as an assembly, they must be removed at slightly an angle to clear the engine compartment.**

50. Separate the engine from the transmission.
**To install:**
51. If the engine was rebuilt, install any components removed such as engine mounts, lifting eyelets, etc.
52. Install the engine to the transmission.
53. Attach the engine and transmission to the hoist, and carefully raise the engine.
54. Place the engine into the engine compartment carefully, and guide into the mounting position.
55. Install and tighten the engine mounts to 37 ft. lbs. (50 Nm).
56. Install the transmission crossmember.
57. Install the rear transmission mount.
58. Remove the hoist.
59. Installation of the remaining components is the reverse of removal.

#### 2.8L 6-Cylinder Engine

1. Properly relieve the fuel system pressure.
2. Disconnect the negative battery cable.
3. If equipped with manual transmission, remove the shifter assembly.
4. Remove the battery.
5. Disconnect the windshield washer hose and engine compartment light wire.
6. Scribe marks around the hood mount brackets on the underside of the hood for later hood alignment.

7. Remove the hood.
8. Remove the air cleaner assembly.
9. Remove the splash guard under the engine.
10. Remove the overflow tank cap.
11. Drain the cooling system.
12. Remove the upper and lower radiator hoses and disconnect the overflow hoses at the radiator.
13. If equipped with automatic transmission, disconnect the transmission cooler lines at the radiator.
14. Remove the fan assembly.
15. Remove the radiator and fan shroud.
16. Disconnect the heater hoses, power brake hose at the intake manifold and the vacuum pump hose at the pump.
17. Remove the vacuum pump and O-ring in the valve cover.
18. Remove the gas cap.
19. Properly relieve the fuel system pressure.
20. At the firewall remove the fuel lines at the filter and return pipe, remove the relay connectors and all other wire connectors.
21. Disconnect the distributor wires.
22. Disconnect the evaporative control carbon canister hoses and the vacuum hose at the EGR valve.
23. Remove the voltage regulator wire connector.
24. Disconnect the throttle cable and kickdown cable, on automatic transmission vehicles, the vacuum amplifier hose at the T-pipe and the hoses at the thermostat.
25. If equipped, disconnect the cruise control cables and hoses.
26. Disconnect the air pump hose at the backfire valve, the solenoid valve wire and the micro-switch wire.
27. Remove the exhaust manifold flange retaining nuts (both sides).
28. If equipped with air conditioning, remove the compressor and drive belt and place it aside. Do not disconnect the refrigerant hoses.
29. Drain the crankcase.
30. Remove the power steering pump, drive belt and bracket. Position aside.
31. From underneath, remove the retaining nuts for the front motor mounts.
32. Remove, as required, the front exhaust pipe.
33. On 49 states vehicles, remove the front exhaust pipe hangers and clamps and allow the system to hang.
34. If equipped with automatic transmission, place the shift lever in **P**.
35. Disconnect the shift control lever at the transmission.
36. On manual transmission vehicles, disconnect the clutch cylinder from the bell housing. Leave the cylinder connected; secure it to the vehicle.
37. Disconnect the shifter linkage.
38. Disconnect the speedometer cable and mark and remove the driveshaft.
39. Raise and safely support the vehicle. Place jackstands under the reinforced box member area to the rear of each front jacking attachment. Then, using a floor jack and a thick, wide wooden block, support the weight of the engine under the oil pan.
40. Remove the bolts for the rear transmission mount.
41. Remove the transmission support crossmember.
42. Lift out the engine and transmission as a unit.

➡**When removing the engine and transmission as an assembly, they must be removed at slightly an angle to clear the engine compartment.**

43. Separate the engine from the transmission.
**To install:**
44. If the engine was rebuilt, install any components removed such as engine mounts, lifting eyelets, etc.
45. Install the engine to the transmission.
46. Attach the engine and transmission to the hoist; and carefully raise the engine.
47. Place the engine into the engine compartment carefully, and guide into the mounting position.
48. Install and tighten the engine mounts to 37 ft. lbs. (50 Nm).
49. Install the transmission crossmember.
50. Install the rear transmission mount.
51. Remove the hoist.
52. Installation of the remaining components is the reverse of removal.

## 2.9L 6-Cylinder Engine

1. Properly relieve the fuel system pressure.
2. Disconnect the negative battery cable.
3. Remove the battery.
4. Remove the ground lead connection to the body at the top of side member.
5. Remove the drive belt.
6. Remove the cooling fan.
7. Release the upper bolts and unfasten the connector at the relay in front of the battery.
8. Disconnect the ground lead at the right-hand ground terminal.
9. Remove the splash shield from the underside of the radiator.
10. Drain the cooling system.
11. Remove the upper and lower radiator hoses from the engine.
12. Remove the radiator overflow hose.
13. Remove the transmission cooler lines from the radiator.
14. Remove the top nut on both left and right side engine mounts.
15. Remove and remove the large and small crankcase ventilation hoses and the idle air hose.
16. Disconnect the idle air valve wiring.
17. Disconnect and remove the two EVAP valve hoses at the intake manifold.
18. Unplug the air mass meter connector, air preheater hose and throttle pulley cover.
19. Remove the air intake hose from the throttle body.
20. Remove the servo pump mounting bolts.
21. Disconnect and remove the fuel return line at the regulator and fuel line at the firewall.
22. Remove the throttle cable, cruise control vacuum hose and fuel line snap catches.
23. Remove the engine wiring harness cover and disconnect the harness. Remove the relay connector. Remove the harness duct retaining nuts.
24. Disconnect the heater hoses at the firewall, ECC hoses at the intake manifold and brake servo vacuum hose.
25. Remove the timing pick up and camshaft sensor connectors.
26. Support the engine at the rear using engine removal tool assembly 5033, 5006, 5115, 5428 and 5429, or equivalent that will support the engine from above.
27. Remove the radiator.
28. Drain the engine oil.
29. Disconnect the hose at the oil thermostat in the cylinder block.
30. Disconnect the A/C compressor wiring. Remove the compressor from the mount and set it aside without disconnecting the hoses.
31. Remove the exhaust pipe flanges at the manifold. Remove the lower section of the air preheater pipe and remove the exhaust pipe shield.
32. Remove the oil pipe connections at the gearbox. Plug the openings.
33. Remove the clips between the gear selector lever and control rod/reaction arm. Withdraw the rods from their mounting.

➡**Before separating the driveshaft, mark the coupling halves for reassembly.**

34. Disconnect the driveshaft and transmission support member.
35. Install engine lifting tool (2810 or equivalent) and adjust the lifting yoke to ensure the engine is balanced. Position the wiring harnesses so as to avoid damage when lifting.
36. Remove the engine and transmission assembly from the vehicle.
37. Separate the engine from the transmission.
**To install:**
38. If the engine was rebuilt, install any components removed such as engine mounts, lifting eyelets, etc.
39. Install the engine to the transmission.
40. Attach the engine and transmission to the hoist, and carefully raise the engine.
41. Place the engine into the engine compartment carefully, and guide into the mounting position.
42. Install and tighten the engine mounts to 37 ft. lbs. (50 Nm).
43. Install the transmission crossmember.
44. Install the rear transmission mount.
45. Remove the hoist.
46. Installation of the remaining components is the reverse of removal.

**2.3L and 2.4L 5-Cylinder Engines**

▶ See Figure 1

> ❋❋ WARNING

**After the engine is removed, do not move the vehicle or the wheel bearings will be damaged.**

1. Properly relieve the fuel system pressure.
2. Disconnect the negative battery cable.
3. Remove the battery and tray.
4. Raise and safely support vehicle.
5. On vehicles with automatic transaxles, remove the air baffle from below the engine.
6. Remove the radiator expansion cap.
7. Drain the coolant into a suitable container.
8. Remove the front wheels and disconnect both track rods from the axle.
9. Remove both ball joints from the control arm.
10. Remove the ABS/brake hose bracket bolt.
11. Remove both halfshafts.
12. Remove the right side engine mount retainer bolts.
13. Remove the torque rod bolt in the gearbox.

➡**Install plugs in the axle shaft holes to prevent fluid leakage.**

14. Remove the front exhaust pipe lower nut and bolt from the bracket.
15. Remove the two carriage bolts and skid plate.
16. Remove the speedometer connection and remove the front and rear lower engine mount bolts.
17. Lower the vehicle.
18. Remove the fresh air intake to the air cleaner, coil wires, throttle pulley cover and throttle cable from the pulley.
19. Tag and remove the throttle body inlet hose, idle air control valve, crankcase ventilation, preheat hoses and mass air flow sensor connector.
20. Disconnect the torque rod from the bracket and firewall.
21. Disconnect the ground strap from the firewall.
22. Unfasten the heated oxygen sensors and clips.
23. Remove the brake booster hose from the engine.
24. Remove the upper air charge pipe and fresh air intake from the radiator then disconnect the vacuum hoses to the turbocharger and EGR regulator.
25. Remove the radiator and coolant hoses
26. Remove the clutch slave cylinder retaining ring, if equipped. Make sure that the piston does not slip out.
27. Remove the gear cable selector, after marking the position.
28. On automatic transaxle, mark the position and then remove the gear selector cable.
29. Remove the accessory drive belt
30. Remove the A/C compressor without disconnecting the lines and set it aside
31. Properly relieve the fuel system pressure.
32. Remove the fuel distribution manifold cover, injector covers, upper and lower fuel line clips and engine ground strap.
33. Install holders 999-5533 or equivalent on the injectors.
34. Disconnect the fuel pressure regulator vacuum hose. Lift the fuel distribution manifold off and lay it aside.

➡**Make sure that the injectors and needles are not damaged.**

35. Disconnect and remove the wiring harness from the engine.
36. Lift up the air pump and lay it to one side.
37. Install engine lifting yoke 999-2810 and arm 999-5428, or equivalents, and connect to hoist.
38. Remove the front engine mount when the engine/transaxle is secured.
39. Lift the engine out of the vehicle.
40. On vehicles with automatic transaxles remove the turbo oil cooler lines and valve (if equipped) from the right side of the oil sump.
41. Separate the engine from the transaxle.
**To install:**
42. If the engine was rebuilt, install any components removed such as engine mounts, lifting eyelets, etc.

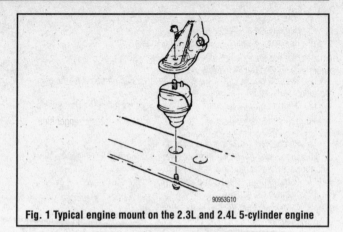

**Fig. 1 Typical engine mount on the 2.3L and 2.4L 5-cylinder engine**

43. Install the engine to the transaxle.
44. Install the valve and turbo oil cooler lines to the oil sump.
45. Attach the engine and transaxle to the hoist, and carefully raise the engine.
46. Place the engine into the engine compartment carefully, and guide into the mounting position.
47. Install and tighten the engine mounts to 37 ft. lbs. (50 Nm).
48. Installation of the remaining components is the reverse of removal.

## Rocker Arm (Valve) Cover

REMOVAL & INSTALLATION

**2.3L 4-Cylinder Engines**

▶ See Figure 2

1. Disconnect the negative battery cable.
2. Label and remove the spark plug wires.
3. Remove the attaching bolts for the valve cover.
4. Remove the valve cover from the cylinder head. If necessary, lightly tap the valve cover with a soft hammer to aid in removal.
**To install:**
5. Thoroughly clean the valve cover and cylinder head gasket mating surfaces.
6. Install the valve cover on the cylinder head using a new gasket.
7. Tighten the valve cover bolts to 14 ft. lbs. (20 Nm) in a crisscross pattern.
8. Install the spark plug wires.
9. Connect the negative battery cable.
10. Start the engine and check for leaks.

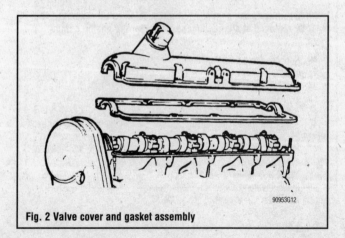

**Fig. 2 Valve cover and gasket assembly**

## 2.8L 6-Cylinder Engine

1. Disconnect the negative battery cable.
2. The following steps are necessary if your car has A/C and if you are removing the passenger side valve cover, if you do not need to remove the passenger side valve cover, skip them.

   a. Remove the A/C compressor belt and the compressor from the mounting bracket located on the passenger side of the engine. Do not remove the lines from the compressor.

   b. Place the compressor with the lines attached on the passenger side front shock tower and secure.

   c. Remove the compressor bracket.

3. Remove the air cleaner-to-throttle body hose.
4. Label and remove all necessary electrical and vacuum connections.
5. Remove the attaching bolts for the valve cover(s).
6. Remove the valve cover(s) from the cylinder head(s). If necessary, lightly tap the valve cover with a soft hammer to aid in removal.

### To install:

7. Thoroughly clean the valve cover(s) and cylinder head gasket mating surfaces.
8. Install the valve cover(s) on the cylinder head(s) using new gaskets.
9. Tighten the valve cover bolts to 11 ft. lbs. (15 Nm) in a crisscross pattern.
10. Install all necessary electrical and vacuum connections.
11. Install the air cleaner assembly.
12. Install the A/C bracket (if removed).
13. Install the A/C compressor and belt (if removed).
14. Connect the negative battery cable.
15. Start the engine and check for leaks.

## 2.3L and 2.4L 5-Cylinder, and 2.9L 6-Cylinder Engines

▶ See Figures 3, 4, 5, 6 and 7

The 2.3L and 2.4L 5-cylinder, and 2.9L 6-cylinder engines have a two-piece cylinder head, the upper half and the lower half. The upper half is basically the same as a valve cover, except that it incorporates the bearing caps for the camshafts into the underside.

1. Disconnect the negative battery cable.
2. Remove the spark plug access cover.
3. Label and remove the ignition coils and vent hoses or the distributor cap and wires if equipped.
4. Check the cam alignment before removing the cylinder head.
5. Remove the bolts attaching the upper cylinder head.
6. Remove the upper cylinder head, lightly tap with a soft hammer if necessary.

### To install:

7. Thoroughly clean the upper and lower cylinder head gasket mating surfaces.
8. Apply liquid sealing compound to the upper cylinder head mating surface.

### ✳✳ WARNING

**Use a roller or your finger to spread sealant, do not use an excessive amount of sealant, or the oil passages could become clogged.**

9. Place the upper cylinder head onto the lower cylinder head.
10. Check the cam alignment before tightening the cylinder head.
11. Install Volvo tool number 5454 or equivalent to the upper cylinder head.

**Fig. 3 Remove the clamp and detach the vent hose**

**Fig. 4 Remove the spark plug cover and the plug wires or ignition coils to access the retaining bolts**

**Fig. 5 Remove the retaining bolts**

**Fig. 6 A light tap with a soft-faced hammer is usually required to loosen the valve cover**

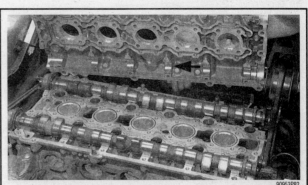

**Fig. 7 Carefully lift the upper cylinder head up and off the lower section. Note the integral camshaft bearing caps in the casting**

12. Tighten the nut on the tools to seat the upper cylinder head.

13. Tighten the upper cylinder head bolts, beginning from the center out to 13 ft. lbs. (17 Nm).

14. Install the ignition coils and hoses or the distributor cap and wires.

15. Install the spark plug access cover.

16. Connect the negative battery cable.

17. Start the vehicle and check for leaks.

## Rocker Arm/Shafts

### REMOVAL & INSTALLATION

The 2.8L V6 engine (B280F) is the only engine that contains rocker arms and/or shafts.

#### 2.8L 6-Cylinder Engine

▶ See Figure 8

1. Properly relieve the fuel system pressure.
2. Disconnect the negative battery cable.
3. Remove the air cleaner-to-throttle body hose.
4. Disconnect the air pump bracket
5. Remove the driver's side valve cover (if removing the driver's side rocker shaft assembly).
6. Tie the upper radiator hose aside and remove the oil filler cap and carbon canister hose.
7. The following steps are necessary if your car has A/C and if you are removing the passenger side valve cover. If you do not need to remove the passenger side valve cover, skip them.

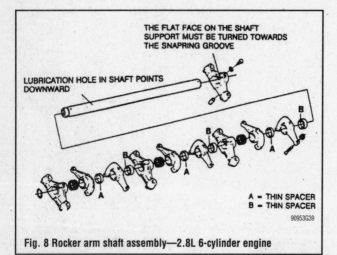

Fig. 8 Rocker arm shaft assembly—2.8L 6-cylinder engine

a. Remove the A/C compressor belt and the compressor from the mounting bracket located on the passenger side of the engine. Do not remove the lines from the compressor.

b. Place the compressor with the lines attached on the passenger side front shock tower and secure.

c. Remove the compressor bracket.

8. Remove the EGR valve.
9. Remove the control pressure regulator.
10. Disconnect any hoses or wires in the way. Remove the right valve cover, if necessary.

➡**Do not jar the head while the rocker and bolts are loose, as the cylinder liner O-ring seals may break, requiring engine disassemble.**

11. The rocker arm bolts double as cylinder head bolts. Loosen the head bolts by reversing the torque sequence. If removing both rocker shafts, mark them left and right.

**To install:**

12. Install the rocker shafts. Follow cylinder head installation procedure for proper torque specification and sequence.
13. Adjust the valve lash.
14. Install the valve covers, EGR valve, control pressure regulator, air conditioning compressor and bracket and air pump.
15. Attach all fuel, coolant and vacuum lines previously disconnected.
16. Attach all electrical connections previously removed.
17. Connect the negative battery cable.
18. Start the engine and allow it to reach operating temperature.
19. Adjust the timing and check for leaks.

## Thermostat

### REMOVAL & INSTALLATION

▶ See Figures 9, 10 and 11

1. Disconnect the negative battery cable.
2. Drain the cooling system into a suitable container.
3. Disconnect the coolant hose attached to the thermostat housing.
4. Remove the thermostat housing retaining bolts.
5. Remove the thermostat housing, thermostat and gasket. Some thermostats require alignment with certain marks or are "clocked" (only fit in the housing a certain way), so be sure to pay close attention while removing.

**To install:**

6. Before installing the thermostat, thoroughly clean the mating surfaces.
7. Fit a new gasket and place the thermostat into position.
8. Install the thermostat housing and tighten bolts to proper torque (refer to torque specifications in the back of this section).
9. Fill the cooling system through the expansion tank.
10. Connect the negative battery cable.
11. Start the engine and allow to reach normal operating temperature.
12. Bleed the cooling system.
13. Top up with coolant and check for leaks.

Fig. 9 Remove the radiator hose

Fig. 10 Unfasten the retaining bolts and remove the thermostat housing

Fig. 11 Remove the thermostat from the engine

## Intake Manifold

### REMOVAL & INSTALLATION

#### 2.3L 4-Cylinder Engine

1. Properly relieve the fuel system pressure.
2. Disconnect the negative battery cable.
3. Remove the air cleaner-to-throttle body hose.
4. If equipped, disconnect the cruise control cables and hoses.
5. Remove the PCV valve.
6. Disconnect the wiring and the fuel hose from the cold start injector. If necessary, remove the cold start injector.
7. Disconnect the wiring and the hoses at the auxiliary valve. If necessary, remove the auxiliary valve.
8. Remove the intake manifold brace.
9. Label and disconnect the vacuum hoses at the intake manifold.
10. Loosen the clamp for the rubber connecting pipe on the air-fuel control unit and remove the boot from the manifold.
11. Remove the manifold bolts and manifold.

**To install:**

12. Clean the gasket mating surfaces thoroughly.
13. Install the intake manifold, using new gaskets, and tighten the bolts to 15 ft. lbs. (20 Nm).
14. Install the intake manifold brace and the air-fuel control unit connecting pipe.
15. Install and connect the auxiliary valve, cold start injector using a new gasket, and the PCV valve.
16. Connect all vacuum hoses and electrical connectors.
17. Connect the negative battery cable.
18. Start the engine and bring it to normal operating temperature.

#### 2.8L 6-Cylinder Engine

▶ **See Figure 12**

1. Properly relieve the fuel system pressure.
2. Disconnect the negative battery cable.
3. Remove the air cleaner-to-throttle body hose.
4. Drain the radiator coolant.
5. Remove the throttle cable from the pulley and bracket.
6. If equipped, disconnect the cruise control cables and hoses.
7. On automatic transmission vehicles, remove the throttle cable that is connected to the transmission.
8. Remove the EGR pipe from the EGR valve to the manifold.
9. Disconnect the EGR vacuum line.
10. Remove the PCV valve.

➡ **Cover the oil cap opening with a rag to keep dirt out.**

11. Remove the front manifold bolts and remove the front section of the manifold.
12. Unplug the cold start connector, fuel line and injector.
13. Remove the pressure control regulator vacuum lines, fuel lines and the connector.
14. Remove the auxiliary valve and its necessary piping.
15. Unplug the electrical connections at the air fuel control unit.
16. Remove all 6 spark plug wires.
17. Remove all 6 injectors.
18. Move the wiring harness to the outside of the manifold.
19. Disconnect the vacuum hose at the distributor and the intake manifold.
20. Disconnect the heater hose at the intake manifold.
21. Disconnect the hose to the diverter valve.
22. Disconnect the vacuum hose to the power brake booster.
23. Disconnect the throttle cable link.
24. Disconnect the wires to the micro-switch.
25. Pull the wires away from the intake manifold.
26. Remove the fuel filter line and the return line.
27. Remove the air control unit.
28. Disconnect the vacuum hose from the throttle valve housing.
29. Remove the pipe and cold start injector assembly.
30. Remove the intake manifold from the vehicle.

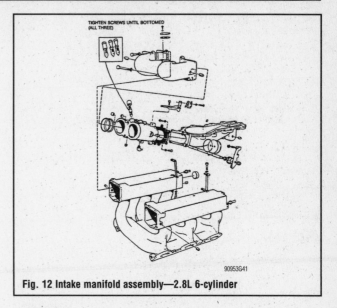

**Fig. 12 Intake manifold assembly—2.8L 6-cylinder**

**To install:**

31. Clean all gasket mating surfaces thoroughly.
32. Install the intake manifold using new gaskets and tighten the bolts to 7–11 ft. lbs. (10–15 Nm).
33. Install the cold start injector assembly using a new gasket, air control unit, fuel filter and return line, throttle cable, EGR valve, diverter valve, heater hose, injectors and spark plug wires.
34. Install all vacuum, fuel and coolant hoses previously removed.
35. Attach all electrical connections previously removed.
36. Fill the radiator with coolant and check the engine and transmission oil.
37. Connect the negative battery cable.
38. Start the engine and bring to operating temperature.
39. Bleed the cooling system.
40. Check for leaks.

#### 2.9L 6-Cylinder Engine

1. Properly relieve the fuel system pressure.
2. Disconnect the negative battery lead.
3. Remove the air cleaner-to-throttle body hose.
4. Remove the throttle pulley cover.
5. Disconnect and remove the throttle switch wiring, throttle cable and bracket, cruise control vacuum servo and vacuum hoses at throttle the housing.
6. Remove the injector cover plate and distribution manifold retaining bolts (3).
7. Disconnect the pressure regulator vacuum hose and fuel line bracket.
8. Carefully lift out the injector and distribution manifold assembly.
9. Remove the air preheater hose.
10. Remove the left and right side power stage connectors on the bottom of the manifold.
11. Remove the manifold bottom mounting.
12. Disconnect the brake servo hose and vacuum hoses under the manifold.
13. Cut away the clamps securing the rubber sleeves between the manifold sections, and lift out the outer manifold section.
14. Remove the upper bolts and loosen the lower bolts.
15. Remove the inner section of the manifold.

**To install:**

16. Install the inner section of the manifold, using a new gasket.
17. Install the rubber sleeves on the inner section and lubricate the free ends with petroleum jelly.
18. Install the mounting bolts and torque to 15 ft. lbs. (20 Nm).
19. Route the wiring between the second and third branches of the outer manifold section.
20. Place the manifold against the lower section and connect the crankcase ventilation hoses.
21. Insert the manifold branches in the rubber sleeves. Secure with new Oetiker clamps.
22. Tighten the manifold lower mounting.

23. Reconnect the vacuum hoses, brake servo hose, power stage connectors and air preheater hose.
24. Inspect the injector O-rings. Lubricate with petroleum jelly.
25. Reconnect the fuel pressure regulator vacuum hose.
26. Press the fuel distribution manifold into position.
27. Tighten the manifold retaining bolts to 15 ft. lbs. (20 Nm).
28. Reconnect the injector harnesses and EGR vacuum hoses.
29. Install the injector cover.
30. Install the throttle cable, throttle pulley cover and vacuum hoses (cruise control and throttle housing).
31. Install the cable bracket at the throttle pulley.
32. Reconnect the PCV, idling valve wiring, air hose, air mass meter and throttle housing connector.
33. Connect the negative battery lead.
34. Start the engine and check operation.

### 2.3L and 2.4L 5-Cylinder Engines

▶ **See Figures 13 thru 18**

1. Properly relieve the fuel system pressure.
2. Disconnect the negative battery cable.
3. Remove the injector cover.
4. Unfasten the connectors and clips from the injectors.
5. Remove the two clips holding the fuel line.
6. Remove the distribution manifold mounting bolts.
7. Carefully remove the fuel rail with the fuel injectors by pulling upward evenly over the entire rail assembly to unseat the injector O-rings.
8. Disconnect the hose to the purge valve.
9. Carefully lay the distribution manifold and injectors on the engine.

### ✳✳ WARNING

**Make sure that the injectors and needles are not damaged.**

10. Remove the throttle pulley cover.
11. Disconnect the throttle linkage from the pulley.
12. Disconnect the intake air hose to the throttle body.
13. Remove the multi-nipple.
14. Remove the EGR hose clamp on turbo models.
15. Remove the pressure line to turbo instrumentation/EGR valve control.
16. Disconnect the vacuum hose.
17. Disconnect the brake booster hose.
18. Loosen the dipstick bracket and intake manifold lower bracket bolt.

➡**If additional room is necessary, you may remove the electric cooling fan.**

19. Loosen the lower intake manifold bolts several turns.

➡**The lower intake manifold bolts are not through-bolts.**

20. Remove the upper intake manifold bolts.
21. Remove the intake manifold.
22. Make sure the mating surfaces of the cylinder head and intake manifold is clean.

**To install:**
23. If removed, install the throttle body with a new gasket.
24. Install a new intake gasket.
25. Install the intake manifold and upper bolts. Tighten all bolts from inside to outside to 15 ft. lbs. (20 Nm).
26. Install the EGR valve (if equipped) with a new gasket.
27. Install the throttle body with a new gasket.
28. Install the multi-nipple and connect the hoses.
29. Install the fuel distribution manifold.
30. Install the wiring and injector cover.
31. Install the remaining components.
32. Connect the negative battery cable.
33. Test run engine and check for leaks.

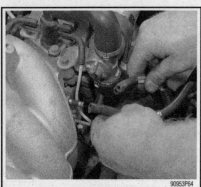

**Fig. 13 Label and remove the various vacuum lines from the intake manifold**

**Fig. 14 Some hoses are more easily removed from their sources than at the intake manifold**

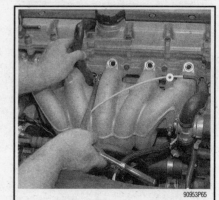

**Fig. 15 Remove the retaining bolts . . .**

**Fig. 16 . . . and carefully lift the intake manifold from the cylinder head**

**Fig. 17 Remove the old intake gasket from the cylinder head and thoroughly clean the mating surfaces**

**Fig. 18 You can see the valves through the intake ports. Inspect the valves for carbon build-up while the intake manifold is off**

## Exhaust Manifold

### REMOVAL & INSTALLATION

➡️Before working on the exhaust system, it is a good idea to soak the retaining hardware with a quality rust penetrant prior to attempting to remove them. After the penetrant is applied, wait at least 10–15 minutes to let the penetrant begin to work.

#### 2.3L 4-Cylinder Engine

1. Disconnect the negative battery cable.
2. Remove the air cleaner and all necessary hoses.
3. Remove the EGR valve pipe from the manifold.
4. Remove the exhaust pipe from the exhaust manifold.
5. Remove the turbo, turbo pipes, and attaching hardware.
6. Remove the manifold nuts and manifold.

**To install:**

7. Position and install the manifold using a new gasket.
8. Tighten the manifold bolts to 10–20 ft. lbs. (14–27 Nm).
9. Install the turbo, turbo pipes, and attaching hardware.
10. Install the EGR valve pipe.
11. Install the air cleaner and any necessary hoses.
12. Connect the negative battery cable.
13. Start the vehicle and check for leaks.

#### 2.8L 6-Cylinder Engine

♦ **See Figure 19**

1. Disconnect the negative battery cable.
2. Raise and support the vehicle safely.
3. Unbolt the crossover pipe from the left and right side of the exhaust manifolds, if equipped.

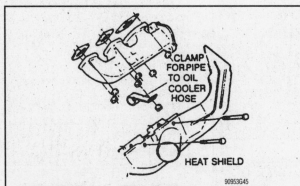

**Fig. 19 Exploded view of the exhaust manifold assembly—2.8L 6-cylinder engine**

➡️If the vehicle has the Y-type exhaust pipe disconnect this pipe at the left and right manifolds.

4. Remove any other necessary hardware.
5. Remove the manifold nuts.
6. Remove the manifold(s) from the cylinder head(s).

**To install:**

7. Install the manifold(s) on the cylinder head(s).

➡️Always use new gaskets when reinstalling the manifolds.

8. Tighten the manifold bolts to 7–11 ft. lbs. (10–15 Nm).
9. Connect the Y or crossover pipe.
10. Install any removed hardware.
11. Lower the vehicle.
12. Connect the negative battery cable.
13. Start the vehicle and check for leaks.

#### 2.9L 6-Cylinder Engine

1. Disconnect the negative battery lead.
2. Remove the exhaust pipe mounting nuts at the manifold joints.
3. Remove the heat shield retaining bolts and heat shield.
4. Remove the exhaust manifold mounting nuts.
5. Remove the exhaust manifold and gasket.

**To install:**

6. Before installation, clean the manifold and cylinder head mating surfaces.
7. Fit a new gasket and place the exhaust manifold into position.
8. Install the mount lifting lug on the studs between the 3rd and 4th exhaust branches.
9. Tighten the mounting nuts to 18 ft. lbs. (25 Nm).
10. Install the heat shield to the rear manifold. Tighten to 11 ft. lbs. (15 Nm).
11. Install the front exhaust pipe to manifold. Using threadlocking compound, tighten to 44 ft. lbs. (60 Nm).

➡️Loosen the joint at the catalytic converter and re-tighten to 18 ft. lbs. (25 Nm). This is necessary to prevent stress on the system.

12. Connect the negative battery lead.
13. Start the engine and check for leaks.

#### 2.3L and 2.4L 5-Cylinder Engines

♦ **See Figures 20 thru 28**

1. Disconnect the negative battery cable.
2. Raise and safely support the vehicle.
3. Disconnect the exhaust pipe from the manifold by removing the nuts on the flanged joint.
4. If equipped, remove the turbo, turbo pipes, and attaching components.
5. Remove the carriage bolts from the manifold.
6. Remove the two heat shields from the exhaust manifold.
7. Remove the exhaust manifold bolts.
8. Push the manifold toward the firewall and lift it out from the top.

**Fig. 20 Remove the exhaust pipe-to-manifold flange retaining hardware . . .**

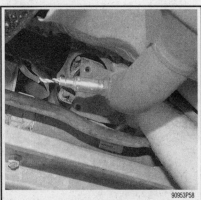

**Fig. 21 . . . and disconnect the flange**

**Fig. 22 Remove the manifold heat shield**

Fig. 23 The EGR tube is connected on the driver's side of the manifold

Fig. 24 Use two wrenches to remove the EGR tube fitting

Fig. 25 The EGR valve and tube are located beneath the throttle body

Fig. 26 Unfasten the fitting on the EGR valve and remove the tube from the vehicle

Fig. 27 Unfasten the retaining bolts and remove the manifold from the engine

Fig. 28 The exhaust manifold uses individual gaskets around each port in the head; replace them before manifold installation

### ✱✱ WARNING

When removing or installing the exhaust manifold, be careful not to damage the air conditioning pressure switch, if so equipped.

**To install:**

9. Check the gasket surface of the cylinder head, clean if necessary.
10. Install the exhaust manifold using new gaskets.
11. Line up the exhaust manifold with the pipe using the carriage bolts.
12. Install the exhaust manifold bolts using a locking compound on the threads.
13. Tighten the bolts to 18 ft. lbs. (25 Nm).
14. Install the turbo, turbo pipes, and attaching components.
15. Install the heat shields.
16. Tighten the carriage bolts using thread sealing compound.
17. Tighten the nuts to no more than 86 inch lbs. (10 Nm). Remember to install the springs and washers with the nuts.
18. Connect the negative battery cable.
19. Run the engine and check for leaks.

## Turbocharger

### REMOVAL & INSTALLATION

➡ Before working on the exhaust system, it is a good idea to soak the retaining hardware with a quality rust penetrant prior to attempting to remove them. After the penetrant is applied, wait at least 10–15 minutes to let the penetrant begin to work.

### 2.3L 4-Cylinder Engine

▸ See Figures 29, 30 and 31

1. Disconnect the negative battery cable.
2. Remove preheater hose to the air cleaner.
3. Remove the pipe and rubber bellows between the air/fuel control unit and the turbocharger unit.
4. Pull out the crankcase ventilation hose from the pipe.

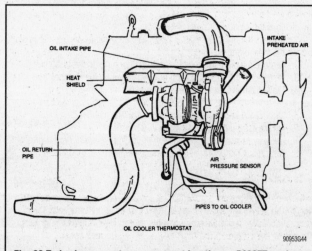

Fig. 29 Turbocharger system component locations—B230FT engine

**Fig. 30 Disconnect the turbo unit from the exhaust manifold**

**Fig. 31 Lubricating the exhaust manifold bolts with a proper rust penetrant or lubricant aids their installation into the cylinder head. Note the manifold bolt locations**

5. Remove the pipe and pipe connector between the turbocharger unit and the intake manifold.

➡**Cover the turbocharger intake and outlet ports to keep dirt out of the system.**

6. Disconnect the exhaust pipe and place aside.
7. Remove the upper heat shield.
8. Remove the brace between the turbocharger unit and the manifold.
9. Remove the lower heat shield by removing the retaining screw under the manifold.
10. Remove the oil pipe clamp, retaining screws on the turbo unit and the pipe connection screw in the cylinder block under the manifold. Do not allow any dirt to enter the oil passages.
11. Remove the manifold retaining nuts and washers. Leave one nut in place to keep the manifold in position.
12. Remove the oil delivery pipe. Cover the opening on the turbo unit.
13. Disconnect the air/fuel control unit by loosening the clamps.
14. Move the unit with the lower section of the air cleaner up to the right side wheel housing. Place a cover over the wheel housing as protection.
15. Remove the remaining nut and washer on the manifold.
16. Lift the assembly forward and up.
17. Remove the manifold gaskets.
18. Disconnect the return oil pipe O-ring from the cylinder block.
19. Disconnect the turbocharger unit from the manifold.

**To install:**

➡**Be sure to use a new gasket for the exhaust manifold and a new O-ring to the return oil pipe. Coat the O-ring with oil prior to installing. Keep everything clean during assembly and use extreme care to keep dirt out of the various turbo inlet and outlet pipes and hoses.**

20. Install the turbocharger on the exhaust manifold and tighten the bolts as follows:
    a. Step 1—7 ft. lbs. (10 Nm)
    b. Step 2—30 ft. lbs. (40 Nm)
    c. Step 3—Tighten all bolts an additional 120 degrees (⅓ turn).

21. Install the exhaust manifold and turbocharger assembly on the engine.
22. Connect all oil pipes from and to the turbocharger using new O-rings.
23. Install the air/fuel control unit and air cleaner.
24. Install the heat shields, spark plug wires, exhaust pipes, preheater assembly and expansion tank.
25. Connect the negative battery cable.
26. Disconnect the wire at terminal 15 (brown) of the ignition coil. Use the ignition key to crank the engine for about 30 seconds. This circulates oil to the turbocharger, providing proper start-up lubrication.
27. Turn the ignition **OFF**, reconnect the coil wire, start the engine and allow it to idle for a few minutes prior to test driving.

### 2.3L and 2.4L 5-Cylinder Engines

▶ **See Figure 32**

1. Disconnect the negative battery cable.
2. Drain and recycle the engine coolant.
3. Drain the engine oil.
4. Remove the heat shield from over the exhaust manifold.
5. Remove the upper air charge pipe and rubber hose from the turbo and move it to one side.
6. Remove the fresh air intake hose and inner heat shield.
7. Disconnect the upper turbo coolant return pipe and clamp off the hose, move it to the side.
8. Disconnect the oil inlet pipe nipple.
9. Raise and safely support the vehicle.
10. Remove or disconnect the following from under side:
- clamp between the pipes
- oil return pipe
- exhaust pipe bracket and bolt
- exhaust pipe to turbo nut
- exhaust manifold to turbo nuts
11. From the top side remove the exhaust pipe to turbo nuts.
12. Disconnect the coolant inlet pipe to the turbo.
13. Remove the turbo/exhaust manifold nuts.
14. Disconnect the following hoses from the turbo:
- red boost pressure
- white bypass valve
- yellow pressure regulator
15. Remove the turbo and the old pin bolts from the exhaust manifold.
16. Coat new O-rings with oil, and install them in the pipes.

**To install:**

17. Remove the old O-rings from the pipes.
18. Install new pin bolts with threadlocking compound and tighten to 15 ft. lbs. (20 Nm).
19. Install the turbo and connect the red, white, and yellow hoses to it.
20. Install the upper exhaust manifold nuts and tighten them lightly.

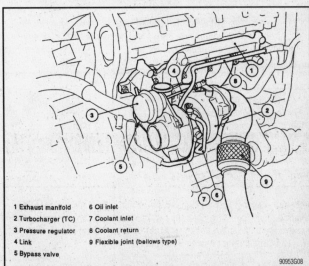

| 1 Exhaust manifold | 6 Oil inlet |
| 2 Turbocharger (TC) | 7 Coolant inlet |
| 3 Pressure regulator | 8 Coolant return |
| 4 Link | 9 Flexible joint (bellows type) |
| 5 Bypass valve | |

**Fig. 32 Turbocharger assembly and related components—2.3L and 2.4L 5-cylinder engines**

21. Working from under the vehicle, install the lower exhaust manifold nuts and tighten them to 18 ft. lbs. (25 Nm).

22. On the top side, tighten the upper exhaust manifold nuts to 18 ft. lbs. (25 Nm).

23. Tighten the exhaust manifold/turbo nuts to 22 ft. lbs. (30 Nm) and check that they are mated properly.

24. Under the vehicle install the oil pipe, grease the O-ring.

25. Install the exhaust pipe bracket bolt.

26. Lower the vehicle and install or connect the following:

- oil inlet pipe
- inlet and outlet coolant pipes (make sure the clamps are removed)
- fresh air intake hose
- inner heat shield
- upper air charge pipe
- outer heat shield

➡**Replace the copper coolant pipe and upper oil pipe washers.**

27. Raise the vehicle and remove the clamp from coolant return hose.

28. Connect the negative battery cable.

29. Run the engine to check the boost pressure.

30. Check oil and coolant levels.

➡**It may be necessary to reset a fault code after replacing the turbocharger.**

## Radiator

### REMOVAL & INSTALLATION

◆ **See Figures 33 thru 43**

➡**Perform this work only on a cold engine.**

1. Disconnect the negative battery cable.
2. Set the heater control to MAX heat.

3. Remove the expansion tank cap.

4. Place a suitable drain pan into position. Open the cock on the right-hand side of the engine block. Fit a hose to the cock to collect the coolant. Open the radiator draincock.

5. Close the drain cocks when the coolant is completely drained.

6. Remove the cooling fan.

7. Remove the cooling fan shroud.

8. Disconnect the upper and lower radiator hoses

9. On vehicles equipped with automatic transmissions, disconnect the transmission oil cooler lines at the radiator. Plug the lines immediately. Catch the spillage from the radiator in a separate pan.

10. Some vehicles are equipped with a temp sensor on the driver's side top of the radiator, if equipped remove the connector.

11. Remove the radiator retaining bolts and brackets.

12. Remove the radiator assembly from the vehicle.

➡**On 850/C70/S70/V70 models, the radiator comes out the bottom of the vehicle.**

**To install:**

13. Place the radiator into position and install the retaining bolts.

14. On automatic transmission vehicles, connect the oil cooler lines.

15. Install the fan and shroud.

16. Install the lower and upper radiator hoses.

17. Connect the expansion tank hose. Make sure that the overflow hose is clear of the fan and is free of any sharp bends.

18. Fill the cooling system through the expansion tank, with a 50 percent antifreeze, 50 percent water solution.

19. Connect the negative battery cable.

20. Run the engine until normal operating temperature is reached.

21. Bleed the cooling system.

22. Check for leaks.

23. Top up the cooling system, as required.

24. Replace the cap.

25. Check and top up the automatic transmission fluid level.

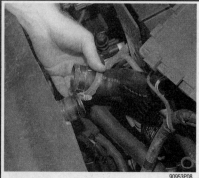

Fig. 33 Undo the clamps and remove the radiator hoses

Fig. 34 A pair of retaining ring pliers can be used to release the quick-connect fittings on the transmission cooler lines

Fig. 35 Remove the line from the radiator; fluid will most likely spill, so placing a pan underneath is advised

Fig. 36 Plug the cooler line . . .

Fig. 37 . . . and the cooler fitting on the radiator to prevent contamination

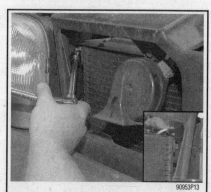

Fig. 38 Remove the condenser and radiator upper mounting bolts

Fig. 39 The condenser must be supported after the upper mounting bolts are removed (two pieces of rope or tiestraps are helpful)

Fig. 40 Remove the lower mounting bolt on the passenger side . . .

Fig. 41 . . . as well as that on the driver's side of the radiator

Fig. 42 After the radiator support brackets are removed . . .

Fig. 43 . . . the radiator can be removed. (On some models such as this 850, you remove it from below)

## Engine Fan

### REMOVAL & INSTALLATION

#### Belt Driven Type

1. Disconnect the negative battery cable.
2. If equipped with a two-piece shroud, remove the top section of the fan shroud.
3. Loosen the adjusting bolts and slacken the drive belts.
4. Remove the fan mounting bolts.
5. Remove the fan assembly.
**To install:**
6. Install the engine fan.
7. Tighten the fan mounting bolts.

8. Adjust the drive belt(s) to the specified tension.
9. If removed, install the top half of the fan shroud.
10. Connect the negative battery cable.

#### Electric Cooling Fan

Some models are equipped with electric cooling fans. The fan function is controlled by a thermocontact placed in the upper right corner of the radiator. Some vehicles may be equipped with a thermal switch in the radiator end tank or lower radiator hose. The fan, on most models, will generally switch ON when coolant temperatures are 190–212°F (88–100°C).

B6304F engines are fitted with a fully electric radiator fan. The 2-speed fan is mounted behind the radiator. The fan is controlled by a relay, in response to either temperature signal sent to the Motronic control unit or directly by the pressure switches mounted in the A/C high-pressure circuit. The relay is mounted on a bracket in front of the battery.

#### Except 850/C70/S70/V70

1. Disconnect the negative and positive battery cables.
2. Remove the battery holder, as required.
3. Remove the harness connector on the crossmember.
4. Undo the relay and remove the ground lead from the terminal on the right-hand wheel housing in the engine compartment.
5. Remove the fan shroud, if required.
6. Remove the cooling fan mounting bolts.
7. Remove the fan assembly from the vehicle.
**To install:**
8. Install the fan assembly in the vehicle.
9. Tighten the mounting bolts.
10. Install the fan shroud and tighten the bolts.
11. Connect the ground lead, and attach the relay connector.
12. Attach the connector on the crossmember.
13. Install the battery holder as required.
14. Connect the battery cables.
15. Start the engine and check cooling fan operation.

#### 850/C70/S70/V70

▶ See Figures 44 thru 50

1. Disconnect the negative battery cable.
2. Remove the two retaining bolts on relay holder from the top of the radiator.
3. Remove the control module and air intake hoses.
4. Remove the four fan mounting bolts.
5. Pull the fan up and unplug the relay and fan connectors.
6. Remove the fan from the vehicle.
**To install:**
7. Place the fan into the engine compartment and attach the relay and connectors.
8. Tighten the four fan retaining bolts.
9. Install the air hoses.
10. Tighten the relay holder retaining bolts.
11. Connect the negative battery cable.

Fig. 44 Remove the retaining bolts on the driver's side . . .

Fig. 45 . . . and passenger side of the radiator

Fig. 46 Slide the relay holder toward the engine

Fig. 47 Remove the air hoses from the control module box and the air cleaner

Fig. 48 Remove the connectors from the fan assembly

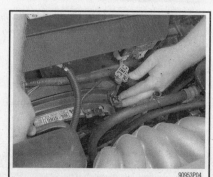

Fig. 49 After the retaining bolts are removed, carefully maneuver the fan up . . .

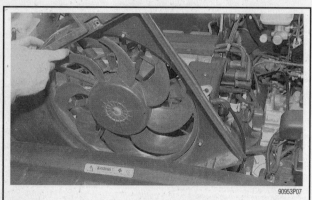

Fig. 50 . . . and out of the engine compartment

## Water Pump

### REMOVAL & INSTALLATION

#### 2.3L 4-Cylinder Engine

▶ See Figure 51

1. Disconnect the negative battery cable.
2. Set the heater control to MAX heat.
3. Remove the expansion tank cap.
4. Open the draincocks on the right-hand side of the engine block and on the radiator, and drain the coolant into a suitable container.
5. Close the draincocks when the coolant is completely drained.
6. Remove the radiator shroud and fan.

7. Remove the lower radiator hose at the water pump.
8. If required, remove the retaining bolt for the coolant pipe beneath the exhaust manifold and pull the pipe rearward.
9. Remove the drive belts and water pump pulleys.
10. Remove the water pump bolts, washers and nuts.
11. Remove the water pump assembly.

**To install:**

12. Clean the gasket contact surfaces thoroughly and use a new gasket and O-rings. Coat the O-rings with coolant prior to installing them. Install a thin layer of gasket sealer on the water pump to help the gasket stay in place during installation.

### ✳✳ CAUTION

**Make sure that the water pump is aligned before tightening the retaining bolts, it is extremely easy to misalign the pump and break it.**

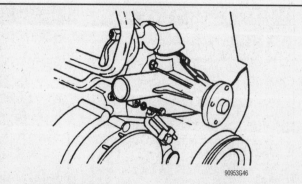

Fig. 51 Water pump installation on the 2.3L 4-cylinder

13. Install the water pump and tighten the bolts to 11–15 ft. lbs. (15–20 Nm) in a crisscross pattern.

14. Install the coolant pipe and lower radiator hose.

15. Install the accessory drive belts and water pump pulley.

16. Install the fan and shroud.

17. Connect the negative battery cable.

18. Fill the cooling system with coolant.

19. Start the engine and allow it to reach normal operating temperature.

20. Check for leaks.

21. Add coolant as necessary.

## 2.8L 6-Cylinder Engine

▶ See Figure 52

1. Disconnect the negative battery cable.

➡On some variants of this engine, it may be necessary to remove the front and main sections of the intake manifold.

2. Remove the overflow tank cap and drain the cooling system.

3. Disconnect both radiator hoses.

4. On automatic transmission vehicles, disconnect the transmission cooler lines at the radiator.

5. Disconnect the fan shroud.

6. Remove the radiator and fan shroud.

7. Remove the fan.

8. Remove the hoses from the water pump to each cylinder head.

9. Remove the fan belts.

10. Remove the water pump pulley.

11. Loosen the hose clamps at the rear of the water pump.

12. Remove the water pump from the block (3 bolts).

**To install:**

13. Transfer the thermal sender and temperature sensor to the new water pump.

14. Transfer the thermostat cover, thermostat and rear pump cover to the new pump.

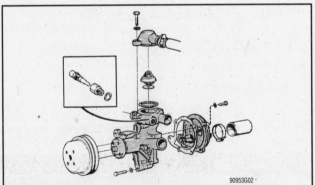

Fig. 52 Exploded view of the water pump assembly on the 2.8L 6-cylinder engine

15. Install the new pump and tighten the bolts to 11–15 ft. lbs. (15–20 Nm).

16. Install the clamps, water pump pulley and fan belts.

17. Install the hoses that reach to each cylinder head.

18. Install the fan, shroud and radiator.

19. If equipped with an automatic transmission, connect the transmission cooler lines.

20. Install the intake manifold, as necessary.

21. Connect the negative battery cable.

22. Fill the radiator with coolant if necessary.

23. Start the engine and allow it to reach operating temperature.

24. Check for leaks.

## 2.9L 6-Cylinder Engine

1. Disconnect the negative battery cable.

2. Drain the cooling system by opening the draincock on the right side of the cylinder block.

3. Remove the timing belt.

4. Remove the water pump retaining bolts (7) and remove the water pump.

**To install:**

5. Before installing the water pump, clean the mating surfaces.

6. Install the water pump, using a new gasket.

7. Tighten the mounting bolts to 15 ft. lbs. (20 Nm).

8. Install the timing belt.

9. Fill the cooling system.

10. Connect the negative battery cable.

11. Start the engine and check for leaks.

## 2.3L and 2.4L 5-Cylinder Engines

▶ See Figures 53, 54 and 55

1. Properly relieve the fuel system pressure.

2. Disconnect the negative battery cable.

3. Raise and safely support vehicle.

4. Remove the splashguard from below the engine.

5. Drain the cooling system.

6. Remove the following:
- Fuel line clips
- Expansion tank
- Front timing cover
- Accessory belts

7. Remove the timing belt.

8. Remove the water pump retaining bolts and remove the water pump from the block.

9. Clean the cylinder block where the two mate.

**To install:**

➡The replacement pump may look different than your original, this is normal as Volvo redesigned the pump on later models and the replacement pump is the new design.

10. Install the new water pump and gasket, and tighten the bolts to 15 ft. lbs. (20 Nm).

11. Install the timing belt.

Fig. 53 The water pump is retained by eight bolts (some are hidden in photo)

Fig. 54 Unfasten the retaining bolts and carefully remove the water pump from the engine

Fig. 55 Position a new gasket on the pump before installing it

12. Install the following:
- The two fuel line clips
- Front timing cover
- Accessory belts
- Spark plug cover
- Vibration damper guard
- Wheel well panel
- Wheel
13. Connect the negative battery cable.
14. Fill the cooling system.
15. Run the engine to normal operating temperature.
16. Top off as necessary and check for leaks.

## Cylinder Head

### REMOVAL & INSTALLATION

#### 2.3L 4-Cylinder Engine

▶ **See Figures 56 and 57**

1. Disconnect the negative battery cable.
2. Drain the engine oil.
3. Remove the overflow tank cap and drain the coolant.
4. Disconnect the upper radiator hose.
5. Remove the distributor cap and wires.
6. Remove the PCV hoses.
7. Remove the EGR valve and vacuum pump.
8. Remove the air pump, if equipped, and air injection manifold.
9. Disconnect and remove all hoses to the turbocharger, if equipped. Plug all open hoses and holes immediately.
10. Remove the exhaust manifold and header pipe bracket.
11. Remove the intake manifold.
12. Remove the fuel injectors.

Fig. 56 Positioning the cylinder head and gasket on the engine block. Check that the water pump O-ring sits correctly in the groove

13. Remove the valve cover.
14. Remove the fan and shroud.
15. Set the engine to TDC of the No. 1 cylinder.
16. Remove the timing belt.
17. Loosen the cylinder head bolts by reversing the torque sequence.
18. Remove the cylinder head.

➡**The cylinder head should be cleaned and inspected prior to installation. For general cylinder head inspection and overhaul procedures, refer to Engine Reconditioning later in this section.**

**To install:**

19. Check the position of the crankshaft. No. 1 piston should be at TDC. Check the position of the camshaft for cylinder No. 1. Both lobes should be in such a position that if the head were installed, the valves would be closed.
20. Install the cylinder head gasket and the cylinder head.
21. Coat a new O-ring for the water pump with coolant and install it in place.
22. Apply a light coat of oil to the head bolts and install.
23. Tighten the head bolts in three steps using the proper sequence.
   a. Step 1—Tighten all bolts to 14 ft. lbs. (20 Nm).
   b. Step 2—Tighten all bolts to 43 ft. lbs. (60 Nm).
   c. Step 3—Angle tighten all bolts an additional 90 degrees.
24. Install the timing belt.
25. Install the shroud and fan.
26. Install the drive belts and pulleys.
27. Install the intake manifold, fuel injection system, throttle cable and valve covers.
28. Install the exhaust manifold and header pipe.
29. Install the air pump assembly.
30. If equipped with a turbocharger, install the turbocharger and related parts.
31. Install the EGR valve, vacuum pump, PCV hoses, distributor cap and wires, and the overflow tank.
32. Connect the negative battery cable.
33. Fill the radiator with coolant, check the engine oil and transmission fluid.
34. Start the engine and allow it to reach operating temperature.
35. Check the timing.

#### 2.8L 6-Cylinder Engine

▶ **See Figures 58, 59 and 60**

1. Disconnect the negative battery cable.
2. Drain the engine oil.
3. Drain the coolant.
4. Remove the air cleaner assembly and all attaching hoses.
5. Disconnect the throttle cable. On automatic transmission equipped vehicles, disconnect the kickdown cable.
6. Disconnect the EGR vacuum hose and remove the pipe between the EGR valve and manifold.
7. Remove the oil filler cap and cover the hole with a rag.
8. Disconnect the PCV pipe(s) from the intake manifold.
9. Remove the front section of the intake manifold.

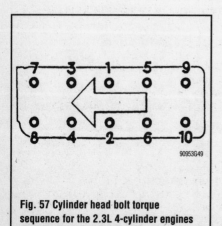

Fig. 57 Cylinder head bolt torque sequence for the 2.3L 4-cylinder engines

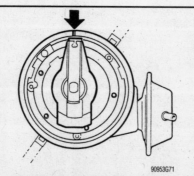

Fig. 58 The engine is at TDC of the No. 1 cylinder when the notch on the distributor aligns with the rotor

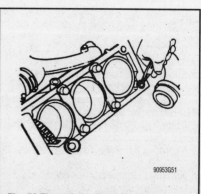

Fig. 59 The cylinder liners must be installed before the cylinder head

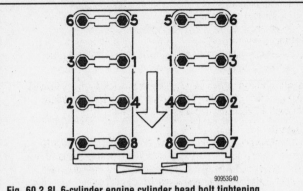

**Fig. 60 2.8L 6-cylinder engine cylinder head bolt tightening sequence**

10. Unplug the electrical connector and fuel line at the cold start injector.

11. Remove the vacuum hose, both fuel lines. and the electrical connector from the control pressure regulator.

12. Remove the hose, pipe and electrical connector from the auxiliary air valve.

13. Remove the auxiliary air valve.

14. Remove the electrical connector from the fuel distributor.

15. Remove the wire loom from the intake manifolds.

16. Remove the spark plug wires.

17. Turn the engine to TDC of the No. 1 cylinder by aligning the notch on the distributor with the rotor.

18. Disconnect the fuel injectors from their holders.

19. Disconnect the distributor vacuum hose, carbon filter hose and diverter valve hose from the intake manifold.

20. Disconnect the power brake hose and heater hose at the intake manifold.

21. Disconnect the throttle control link from it pulley.

22. If equipped with an EGR vacuum amplifier, disconnect the wires from the throttle micro-switch and solenoid valve.

23. At the firewall, disconnect the fuel lines from the fuel filter and return line.

24. Remove the 2 attaching screws and lift out the fuel distributor and throttle housing assembly.

25. If not equipped with an EGR vacuum amplifier, disconnect the EGR valve hose from under the throttle housing.

26. Remove the cold start injector, rubber ring and pipe.

27. Remove the 4 retaining bolts and lift off the intake manifold.

28. Remove the rubber rings.

29. Remove the splash guard under the engine.

30. If removing the left cylinder head, remove the air pump from its bracket.

31. If removing the right cylinder head, disconnect the upper radiator hose.

32. On air conditioned vehicles, remove the air conditioning compressor and secure it aside. Do not disconnect the refrigerant lines.

33. Disconnect the distributor leads and remove the distributor.

34. Remove the EGR valve, bracket and pipe.

35. At the firewall, Remove the electrical connectors at the relays.

36. On air conditioned vehicles, remove the rear compressor bracket.

37. Disconnect the coolant hose(s) from the water pump to the cylinder head(s). If removing the left cylinder head disconnect the lower radiator hose at the water pump.

38. Disconnect the air injection system supply hose from the applicable cylinder head. Separate the air manifold at the rear of the engine. If removing the left cylinder head, remove the backfire valve and air hose.

39. Remove the valve cover(s).

40. On the left cylinder head, remove the Allen head screw and 4 upper bolts to the timing gear cover.

41. On the right cylinder head, remove the 4 upper bolts to the timing gear cover and the front cover plate.

42. From under the vehicle, remove the exhaust pipe clamps for both header pipes.

43. If removing the right cylinder head, remove the retainer bracket bolts and pull the dipstick tube out of the crankcase.

44. Remove the applicable exhaust manifold(s).

45. Remove the cover plate at the rear of the cylinder head.

46. Rotate the camshaft sprocket, for the applicable cylinder head, into position so the large sprocket hole aligns with the rocker arm shaft. With the camshaft in this position, loosen the cylinder head bolts, in sequence, same sequence as tightening, and remove the rocker arm and shaft assembly.

47. Loosen the camshaft retaining fork bolt, directly in back of sprocket, and slide the fork away from the camshaft.

48. Next, it is necessary to hold the cam chain stretched during camshaft removal. Otherwise, the chain tensioner will automatically take up the slack, making it impossible to reinstall the sprocket on the cam without removing the timing chain cover to loosen the tensioner device. To accomplish this, a sprocket retainer tool 999 5104 or equivalent is installed over the sprocket with 2 bolts in the top of the timing chain cover. A bolt is then screwed into the sprocket to hold it in place.

49. Remove the camshaft sprocket center bolt and push the camshaft to the rear, so it clears the sprocket.

50. Remove the cylinder head.

➡**Do not remove the cylinder head by pulling straight up. Instead, lever the head off by inserting 2 spare head bolts into the front and rear inboard cylinder head bolt holes and pulling toward the applicable wheel housing. Otherwise, the cylinder liners may be pulled up, breaking the lower liner seal and leaking coolant into the crankcase. If any do pull up, new liner seals must be used and the crankcase completely drained. If the head(s) seem stuck, gently tap around the edges of the head(s) with a rubber mallet, to break the joint.**

51. Remove the head gasket.

52. Clean the contact surfaces with a plastic scraper and lacquer thinner.

53. If the head is going to be off for any length of time, install liner holders tool 999 5093 or 2 strips of thick stock steel with holes for the head bolts, so the liners stay pressed down against their seals. Install the holders width-wise between the middle 4 head bolt holes.

**To install:**

54. If the dowels at the outboard corners of the block have slipped down, use a pair of needle-nose pliers to retrieve them. Prop them up with an ⅛ inch (3mm). Remember to keep the timing chain taunt during cylinder head installation.

55. Remove the liner holders and install the head gaskets. The left and right head gaskets are different, ensure the correct one is installed.

56. Install the cylinder head.

57. Install the camshaft and remove the timing chain retainer tool.

58. Install the head bolts finger-tight after lubricating with oil.

59. On 1990 asbestos-free gasket, with fixed-washer bolts, tighten all bolts in stages as follows:
   a. Tighten the bolts to 44 ft. lbs. (60 Nm).
   b. Loosen bolts, tighten it to 30 ft. lbs. (40 Nm).
   c. Angle-tighten to 160–180 degrees.

60. Except 1990 asbestos-free gasket, with fixed-washer bolts, tighten all bolts in stages as follows:
   a. Tighten bolts to 43 ft. lbs. (60 Nm).
   b. Loosen bolt 1, then tighten it to 15 ft. lbs. (20 Nm).
   c. Angle-tighten to 106 degrees, using special tool 5098 or equivalent.
   d. Repeat this for remaining bolts in sequence shown. Loosen and tighten each bolt in turn.

➡**After the engine has been warmed-up, angle-tighten each bolt a further 45 degrees.**

61. Install the camshaft center bolt and tighten to 52–66 ft. lbs. (70–89 Nm).

62. Install the timing gear case and rear cylinder head covers.

63. Check and adjust the valve lash.

64. After adjusting valve lash, turn the engine to TDC on No. 1 piston.

65. Install the valve covers, air injection system, exhaust pipes and manifolds.

66. Install all coolant hoses, install the air conditioner compressor brackets, distributor, EGR valve, cold start injector using a new gasket, and intake manifold.

67. Install the vacuum pump and lower splash shield.

68. Fasten all electrical connections previously removed.

69. Install the throttle linkage, fuel injectors and all fuel injection system hoses, lines and electrical connections.

70. Connect the negative battery cable.

71. Fill the radiator with coolant, check the engine and transmission oil.
72. Start the engine and allow it to reach operating temperature.
73. Adjust the timing and check for leaks.

### 2.9L 6-Cylinder Engine

▶ See Figure 61

1. Disconnect the negative battery cable.
2. Drain the engine oil.
3. Drain the cooling system.
4. Remove the front exhaust pipe, heat shield and exhaust manifold(s).
5. Remove the coolant pipe bolts.
6. Set the engine to TDC of the No. 1 cylinder.
7. Remove the timing belt.
8. Remove the transmission mounting plate bolt.
9. Remove the air mass meter and intake hose.
10. Remove the throttle pulley cover, throttle cable and cable bracket.
11. Disconnect the throttle switch lead and vacuum hoses at throttle housing and cruise control servo.
12. Remove the intake manifold outer section.
13. Mark the positions and remove the ignition coils.
14. Mark the camshaft pulleys (intake and exhaust sides) and remove the pulleys, using holding tool 5199 or equivalent.
15. Remove the camshaft sensor, ground terminals and temperature sensor connector.
16. Remove the coolant hose at rear.
17. Carefully tap the top half of the cylinder head upwards, using a soft mallet.
18. Tap the joint lugs and camshaft front ends.
19. Remove the camshafts.
20. Remove the cylinder head bolts, starting at the outside and working inwards.
21. Lift the cylinder head from the engine.
22. Remove the gasket.
23. Clean and inspect the cylinder head and block mating surface.

**To install:**

24. Align the crankshaft timing mark by removing the starter motor and installing the crankshaft locking tool 5451 or equivalent. Turn the crankshaft until it is stopped by the tool.
25. Fit a new cylinder head gasket and install the bottom half of the cylinder head.
26. Oil the cylinder head bolts; install and tighten in sequence as follows:
    a. Stage 1—15 ft. lbs. (20 Nm)
    b. Stage 2—44 ft. lbs. (60 Nm)
    c. Stage 3—angle tighten 130 degrees
27. Install new O-rings in the spark plug wells and oil the camshaft bearing seats.
28. Apply sealing compound (Part No. 1161059-9 or equivalent) to the upper section of the cylinder head.

➡**Do not allow any compound to penetrate the coolant or oil passages.**

29. Install the camshaft.
30. Place the upper section of the cylinder head into position.

31. Install the press tools (5454 or equivalent) and tighten against the lower section.
32. Install the bolts, working from the inside outwards. Tighten to 13 ft. lbs. (17 Nm).
33. Remove the tools.
34. Grease the camshaft front seal and tap the seal into place.
35. Place the upper timing cover into position.
36. Install the camshaft pulleys while aligning the timing marks.
37. Temporarily install and tighten the pulley mounting bolts.
38. Remove the timing cover and install the mounting plate bolt.
39. Install the timing belt.
40. Loosen the camshaft pulley bolts and withdraw the tensioner locking pin.
41. Insert the remaining camshaft pulley bolt.
42. Hold the pulley using the counterhold tool 5199 or equivalent and tighten all bolts alternately to 15 ft. lbs. (20 Nm).
43. Remove the crankshaft locking tool.
44. Install the protective plug and install the starter motor.
45. Install the upper timing cover.
46. Check that the timing marks on the crankshaft and camshaft pulleys are correctly aligned.
47. Install the camshaft sensor, ground terminals and temperature sensor connector.
48. Install the coolant hose at rear.
49. Install the remaining components.
50. Change the engine oil.
51. Fill the cooling system.
52. Connect the negative battery cable.
53. Start the engine and check for leaks.
54. Recheck the cooling system level.

### 2.3L and 2.4L 5-Cylinder Engines

▶ See Figures 62 thru 74

1. Disconnect the negative battery cable.
2. Raise and safely support vehicle.
3. Remove the splash guard below the engine.
4. Drain the coolant into a suitable container.
5. Disconnect the exhaust pipe from the manifold.
6. Remove the exhaust manifold.
7. Set the engine to TDC of the No. 1 cylinder.
8. Remove the timing belt.
9. Disconnect the fuel distribution manifold and lift it and the injectors off to one side. Use 999-5533 holders or equivalent to separate them.
10. Disconnect the two ground straps from the engine.

➡**Make sure that the injectors and needles are not damaged.**

11. Remove the engine cooling fan.
12. Remove the intake manifold.
13. Remove the upper radiator hose from thermostat housing.
14. Remove the camshaft sprockets. Mark them intake or exhaust.
15. Remove the inner timing cover bolt.
16. Remove the air cleaner and hoses.

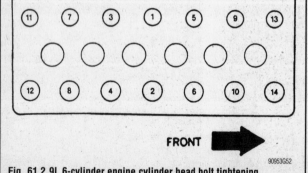

Fig. 61 2.9L 6-cylinder engine cylinder head bolt tightening sequence

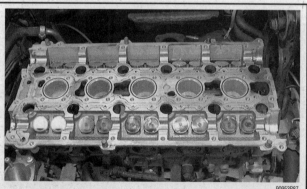

Fig. 62 Remove camshafts to access the cylinder head bolts

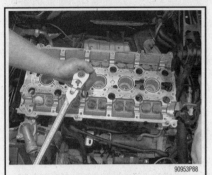

Fig. 63 Loosen the cylinder head bolts starting from the inside and working outward

Fig. 64 Remove the bolts from the cylinder head; if necessary, use a magnet to extract them

Fig. 65 Carefully lift the cylinder head off of the engine block

Fig. 66 After the head is removed, inspect the block for damage, cracks, and obvious wear

Fig. 67 Remove and replace the O-rings around the spark plug holes

Fig. 68 Remove the head gasket . . .

Fig. 69 . . . and thoroughly clean the cylinder head

Fig. 70 View of the combustion chamber, including the intake (larger) valves, exhaust (smaller) valves, and spark plug electrodes

Fig. 71 Carefully place the cylinder head onto the engine block

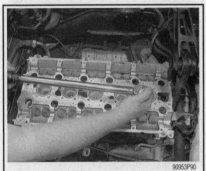

Fig. 72 Tighten the cylinder head bolts in proper sequence to specification using a torque wrench

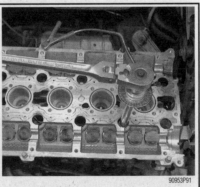

Fig. 73 A torque angle gauge can be helpful when angle-tightening the head bolts

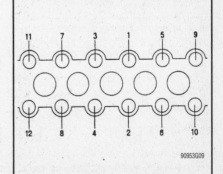

Fig. 74 2.3L and 2.4L 5-cylinder engine head bolt tightening sequence

17. Remove the camshaft position sensor and damper.
18. Remove the distributor cap, wiring and rotor.
19. Remove the extension arm and brackets.
20. Working inwards from each end, loosen the bolts on the upper half of the cylinder head.
21. Gently tap the upper half with a soft mallet on the edges and front of the camshafts.
22. Remove the bolts and upper half of the cylinder head.
23. Mark the camshafts and remove.
24. Remove the coolant pipe bolts.
25. Remove the cylinder head bolts working outward.
26. Remove the lower portion of the cylinder head and head gasket.
27. Clean all mating surfaces thoroughly.

### ✳✳ WARNING

**Do not use a metal scraper. Use a soft putty knife and gasket solvent cleaner with an exhaust fan. The surfaces must be totally clean to assure a tight seal.**

**To install:**
28. Align the crankshaft timing marks.
29. Install crankshaft locking tool 999-5451 or equivalent and turn the crankshaft counterclockwise until it stops.
30. Install a new cylinder head gasket and the lower cylinder head.
31. Apply a small amount of oil to the bolts.
32. Tighten the lower cylinder head in three stages, starting on the inside and working outward as follows:
    a. 15 ft. lbs. (20 Nm)
    b. 44 ft. lbs. (60 Nm)
    c. Angle tighten an additional 130° using an angle gauge
33. Install the coolant pipe using a new gasket.
34. Replace the O-rings in the spark plug wells.
35. Remove No. 1 and No. 5 spark plugs.
36. Using a roller, apply liquid gasket 161-059-9 or equivalent to the upper cylinder head.

➡ **Make sure that no liquid gasket gets into the oil passages. Only a thin coating is required.**

37. Install the camshafts and lock them in place using tools 999-5453 (front) and 999-5452 (rear) or equivalents.
38. Install the upper cylinder head.
39. Pull the head down using press tools 999-5453 or 5454 (2) or equivalents.
40. Tighten the upper half working from the inside outward. Tighten to 13 ft. lbs. (17 Nm).
41. Remove tools 999-5453 and 999-5454 or equivalents.
42. Install the camshaft seals using an appropriate seal driver.
43. Mount the upper timing cover.
44. Install the camshaft sprockets and line up the camshaft timing marks.
45. Install two camshaft sprocket bolts furthest from the timing mark and tighten until they are just touching the sprocket.
46. Remove the upper timing cover.
47. Make sure that the remaining camshaft sprocket bolt hole is centered.
48. Install the tensioner pulley lever and tighten to 18 ft. lbs. (25 Nm).
49. Install the idler pulley and tighten to 18 ft. lbs. (25 Nm).
50. Compress the tensioner by placing in a suitable vise. Tighten the vise slowly and in small increments, stopping every ¼ turn. Install a lock pin 2mm in diameter (a 2mm Allen wrench also will work) in the piston. If the tensioner leaks, has no resistance or will not compress, replace it.
51. Install the timing belt.
52. Install the third camshaft sprocket bolt and tighten the bolts to 15 ft. lbs. (20 Nm).
53. Remove the tensioner lock pin.
54. Remove the crankshaft locking tool from the flywheel end of the block and install the plug in the hole.
55. Install the starter motor.
56. Remove the camshaft locking tool 999-5452 or its equivalent.
57. Turn the crankshaft two complete revolutions and check that the timing marks are lined up.
58. Install the rear camshaft seal using driver 999-5450 or equivalent.

59. Install the upper timing cover.
60. Install the remaining engine components
61. Connect the negative battery cable.
62. Change the engine oil.
63. Fill the cooling system.
64. Start the engine and run it until the thermostat opens.
65. Bleed the cooling system.
66. Check the engine for leaks.

## Oil Pan

### REMOVAL & INSTALLATION

#### 2.3L 4-Cylinder and 2.9L 6-Cylinder Engines

1. Disconnect the negative battery cable.
2. Raise and support the vehicle safely.
3. Drain the engine oil.
4. Remove the splash guard, if equipped.
5. On 2.3L engines, perform the following steps;
    a. Remove the engine mount retaining nuts.
    b. Remove the lower bolt and loosen the top bolt on the steering column yoke.
    c. Slide the yoke assembly up on the steering shaft.
6. Raise and safely support the front of the engine.
7. Remove the retaining bolts for the front axle crossmember.
8. Remove the crossmember.
9. Remove the left engine mount.
10. Remove the pan support bracket.
11. Remove the pan bolts and remove the pan.

**To install:**
12. Clean the gasket mating surfaces thoroughly.
13. Install the oil pan and using new gaskets, tighten the bolts in a criss-cross pattern to 8 ft. lbs. (11 Nm).
14. Lower the engine and install all engine mounts.
15. Install the front crossmember and install the bolts.
16. On 2.3L engines, install the yoke assembly on the steering shaft and tighten the bolts to 18 ft. lbs. (24 Nm).
17. Install the splash guard, if equipped.
18. Lower the vehicle.
19. Connect the negative battery cable.
20. Fill the engine with oil.
21. Start the engine and allow it to reach operating temperature.
22. Check for leaks.

#### 2.8L 6-Cylinder Engine

▶ **See Figure 75**

1. Disconnect the negative battery cable.
2. Raise and support the vehicle safely.
3. Remove the splash guard.

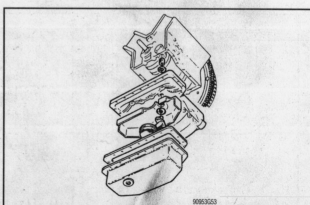

90953G53

**Fig. 75 Oil pan and lower crankcase components—2.8L 6-cylinder engine**

4. Drain the crankcase.
5. Remove the oil pan retaining bolts.
6. Swivel the pan past the stabilizer bar and remove.

**To install:**

7. Clean the gasket mating surfaces thoroughly.
8. Install the oil pan, using a new gasket, and tighten the bolts in a criss-cross pattern to 6–8 ft. lbs. (8–11 Nm).
9. Install the splash guard, lower the vehicle and fill the crankcase with oil.
10. Connect the negative battery cable.
11. Start the engine and allow it to reach operating temperature.
12. Check for leaks.

### 2.3L and 2.4L 5-Cylinder Engines

➡This procedure is performed with the engine removed from the car.

1. Remove the oil filter.
2. Remove the oil pan bolts.
3. Carefully tap the oil pan to break the seal and remove the oil pan.
4. Remove the oil passage O-rings.

**To install:**

5. Thoroughly clean the mating surfaces of the cylinder block and oil pan.
6. Coat new oil passage O-rings with engine oil and install them in the block.
7. Apply a thin layer of gasket sealant to the engine block.
8. Install the oil pan and pan bolts.
9. Tighten the pan bolts in a crisscross pattern to 12 ft. lbs. (17 Nm).
10. Install the oil filter.

## Oil Pump

### REMOVAL & INSTALLATION

#### 2.3L (B230F and B230FT) 4-Cylinder Engine

▶ **See Figure 76**

1. Disconnect the negative battery cable.
2. Drain and recycle the engine oil.
3. Remove the oil pan.
4. Remove the 2 oil pump retaining bolts.
5. Remove the oil pump and pull the delivery tube from the engine block.

**To install:**

6. Coat new sealing rings with engine oil and install them at either end of the delivery tube.
7. Install the pump with the delivery tube attached.
8. Align the pipe to the engine block, so that the seal does not become damaged.
9. Tighten the two oil pump retaining bolts.
10. Attach the clamp for the oil trap drain hose to the oil pump bolts. Make sure the hose is securely clamped behind the oil pump shoulder. Do not shorten the hose.

11. Install the oil pan.
12. Fill the engine with oil.
13. Connect the negative battery cable.
14. Start the vehicle and check the oil level.

#### 2.3L (B234F) 4-Cylinder Engine

▶ **See Figures 77 and 78**

1. Disconnect the negative battery cable.
2. Drain and recycle the engine coolant.
3. Drain and recycle the engine oil.
4. Remove the timing belt.
5. Using a counterholding tool 5039 or similar, remove the oil pump drive pulley.
6. Thoroughly clean the area around the oil pump.
7. Place sheets of newspaper or a container on the splash guard to contain any spillage and remove the oil pump mounting bolts.
8. Remove the pump from the engine.
9. Remove the seal from the groove in the block.
10. Clean the area with solvent, making certain there are no particles of dirt trapped in the pump area.

**To install:**

11. Install the new seal in the groove and install the new oil pump.
12. Lubricate the pump with clean engine oil before installation.
13. Tighten the mounting bolts to 8 ft. lbs. (11 Nm).
14. Using the counterhold, install the drive pulley and tighten the center bolt to 15 ft. lbs. (20 Nm) plug 60 degrees of rotation.
15. Clean the area of any oil spillage; remove the paper or container from the splash guard.
16. Install the timing belt.
17. Fill the engine with coolant.
18. Fill the engine with oil.
19. Connect the negative battery cable.

#### 2.8L 6-Cylinder Engine

▶ **See Figure 79**

The oil pump body is cast integrally with the cylinder block. It is chain driven by a separate sprocket on the crankshaft and is located behind the timing chain cover. The pick-up screen and tube are serviced by removing the oil pan. To check the pump gears or remove the oil pump cover:

1. Disconnect the negative battery cable.
2. Drain and recycle the engine oil.
3. Remove the air cleaner and valve covers.
4. Loosen the fan shroud and remove the fan.
5. Remove the shroud.
6. Loosen the alternator, air pump, power steering pump, air conditioning compressor, if equipped, and remove their drive belts.
7. Block the flywheel from turning and remove the 36mm bolt and the crankshaft pulley.

➡Be careful not to drop key into crankcase.

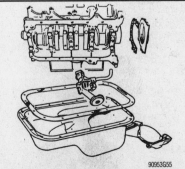

**Fig. 76 Exploded view of the oil pan, rear seal flange, oil pump, and delivery tube on B230F and B230FT engines**

90953G55

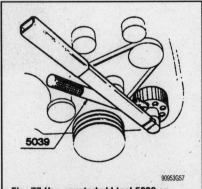

**Fig. 77 Use counterhold tool 5039 or equivalent to remove the pump pulley**

90953G57

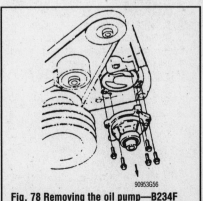

**Fig. 78 Removing the oil pump—B234F engine**

90953G56

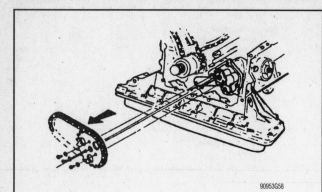

**Fig. 79 Removing the oil pump drive sprocket and chain**

90953G58

8. Remove the timing gear cover (25 bolts).
9. Remove the oil pump drive sprocket and chain.
10. Remove the oil pump cover and gears.

**To install:**

11. Prime the pump, remove all air by filling it with clean engine oil and operating the pump by hands, before installation.
12. Install the oil pump gears and cover.
13. Install the oil pump drive sprocket and chain.
14. Install the timing gear cover, crankshaft pulley, alternator, air pump, power steering pump, air conditioning compressor and all accessory drive belts.
15. Remove the flywheel block and install the valve covers.
16. Fill the engine with oil.
17. Connect the negative battery cable.

### 2.9L 6-Cylinder Engine

1. Disconnect the negative battery cable.
2. Drain the cooling system.
3. Drain the engine oil.
4. Remove the drive belts, front timing belt cover, cooling fan and splashguard.
5. Remove the radiator.
6. Remove the timing belt.
7. Remove the crankshaft pulley, using a suitable puller.
8. Remove the oil pump mounting bolts and remove the oil pump.

**To install:**

9. Before installing the oil pump, thoroughly clean the mating surfaces.
10. Transfer the snow shield.
11. Place a new gasket into position, then install the oil pump using tool 5455 or equivalent. Use the mounting bolts as a guide.
12. Pull in the pump using the crankshaft center nut.
13. Apply threadlocking compound to the pump mounting bolts and install the bolts. Tighten alternately to 84 inch lbs. (10 Nm).
14. Install the crankshaft pulley, using the center bolt and spacer.
15. Install the timing belt.
16. Install the tensioner.
17. Align the timing marks and install the ignition coil cover.
18. Install the radiator.
19. Install the remaining components.
20. Fill the engine with oil.
21. Fill the engine with coolant.
22. Connect the negative battery cable.

### 2.3L and 2.4L 5-Cylinder Engines

The oil pump is on the front of the crankshaft.
1. Disconnect the negative battery cable.
2. Drain and recycle the engine oil.
3. Remove spark plug cover.
4. Remove the drive belts.
5. Remove the front timing cover and timing belt.
6. Raise and safely support the vehicle.

## ✻✻ WARNING

**Do not turn the crankshaft or camshafts once the timing belt has been removed.**

7. Remove the crankshaft damper, using tool 999 5433 or equivalent to counterhold it from moving.
8. Remove the crankshaft sprocket.

## ✻✻ WARNING

**Make sure the puller does not damage the sprocket teeth.**

9. Remove the old front seal using a groove cut chisel.
10. Clean the mating surface where the seal lies.
11. Remove the four bolts retaining the oil pump.

➡There are tabs on the oil pump housing located at the 6 o'clock and 11 o'clock positions.

12. Carefully pry out the oil pump using a groove cut chisel.
13. Clean the surfaces where the pump mates to the engine.

**To install:**

14. Install the new oil pump using tool 999-5455 or equivalent using the bolts to guide it in. Use the crankshaft nut to press it in. Tighten the bolts alternately to 84 inch lbs. (10 Nm).
15. Install the crankshaft timing belt sprocket using the nut and a spacer.
16. Install the timing belt and cover.
17. Install the drive belts.
18. Fill the engine with clean engine oil.
19. Connect the negative battery cable.
20. Start the engine and check for leaks.

## Crankshaft Damper

### REMOVAL & INSTALLATION

#### 2.3L 4-Cylinder Engine

1. Disconnect the negative battery cable.
2. Remove the drive belts and cooling fan.
3. Remove the cooling fan shroud.
4. Remove the center nut on the damper.
5. Remove the damper from the crankshaft.

**To install:**

6. Install the damper on the crankshaft.
7. Tighten the center nut to 44 ft. lbs. (60 Nm) and then an additional 60°.
8. Install the cooling fan shroud.
9. Install the drive belts and cooling fan.
10. Connect the negative battery cable.

#### 2.8L 6-Cylinder Engine

1. Disconnect the negative battery cable.
2. Remove the drive belt(s) and cooling fan.
3. Raise and safely support the vehicle on jackstands.
4. Remove the splashguard from the underside of the vehicle.
5. Remove the starter and install Volvo tool number 5112 or equivalent to keep the crankshaft from turning.
6. Remove the center nut on the crankshaft pulley.

➡Be careful when removing the pulley, the aligning key on the crankshaft can fall out and get lost.

7. Remove the pulley from the crankshaft.

**To install:**

8. Install the pulley onto the crankshaft. Align the key onto the slot on the crankshaft.
9. Tighten the center nut on the pulley to 177–207 ft. lbs. (240–280 Nm).
10. Remove the special tool and install the starter.
11. Install the splashguard.

12. Lower the vehicle.
13. Install the cooling fan and drive belts.
14. Connect the negative battery cable.

## 2.9L 6-Cylinder Engine

1. Disconnect the negative battery cable.
2. Raise and safely support the vehicle on jackstands.
3. Remove the splashguard from the underside of the vehicle.
4. Remove the drive belt(s) and cooling fan.
5. Remove the four vibration damper bolts.
6. Attach Volvo tool number 5433 or equivalent to hold damper. Remove the center nut on damper.
7. Remove the damper from the crankshaft.
**To install:**
8. Install damper onto crankshaft.
9. Attach tool number 5433 or equivalent and tighten center nut to 221 ft. lbs. (300 Nm).
10. Install the four damper bolts and tighten to 26 ft. lbs. (35 Nm).
11. Install the cooling fan and drive belts.
12. Install the splashguard.
13. Lower the vehicle.
14. Connect the negative battery cable.

## 2.3L and 2.4L 5-Cylinder Engines

▶ See Figures 80, 81, 82, 83 and 84

1. Disconnect the negative battery cable.
2. Raise and safely support the vehicle on jackstands.
3. Remove the nut retaining the fenderwell trim in the uppermost corner and bend the trim back to gain access to the front of the engine.
4. Remove the drive belt.
5. Remove the four vibration damper bolts.
6. Attach Volvo tool number 5433 or equivalent to hold the damper stationary.

7. Remove the center nut from the damper.
8. Remove the damper from the crankshaft.
**To install:**
9. Install the damper onto the crankshaft.
10. Attach tool number 5433 or equivalent to hold the damper stationary, and tighten the center nut to 133 ft. lbs. (180 Nm).
11. Install the four damper bolts and tighten to 18 ft. lbs. (25 Nm).
12. Install the drive belt.
13. Install the fenderwell trim.
14. Lower the vehicle.
15. Connect the negative battery cable.

## Timing Belt Cover

### REMOVAL & INSTALLATION

#### 2.3L 4-Cylinder Engine

1. Disconnect the negative battery cable.
2. Remove the cooling fan and shroud.
3. Remove the drive belts.
4. Remove the water pump pulley.
5. Remove the 4 retaining bolts and lift off the timing belt cover.
**To install:**
6. Clean all gasket mating surfaces thoroughly.
7. Install the timing belt cover using a new gasket.
8. Install the water pump pulley, and all drive belts.
9. Install the fan and shroud.
10. Connect the negative battery cable.
11. Start the engine and check for leaks.

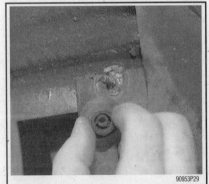

Fig. 80 Remove the nut in the upper left corner of the fenderwell trim . . .

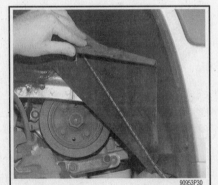

Fig. 81 . . . and bend the trim up to access the crankshaft damper

Fig. 82 While using a suitable tool to keep the crankshaft from rotating, remove the damper retaining bolts

Fig. 83 Keep the damper from turning while you remove the center nut

Fig. 84 Remove the damper from the crankshaft

**B234F 4-Cylinder Engine**

♦ **See Figure 85**

1. Remove the negative battery cable.
2. Remove the drive belts.
3. Remove the radiator fan, its pulley and the fan shroud.
4. Remove the drive belts for the power steering belts and the air conditioning compressor.
5. Beginning with the top cover, remove the retaining bolts and remove the timing belt covers.

**To install:**

6. Clean all gasket mating surfaces thoroughly.
7. Install the timing belt covers using new gaskets.
8. Install the water pump pulley, and all drive belts.
9. Install the fan and shroud.
10. Connect the negative battery cable.
11. Start the engine and check for leaks.

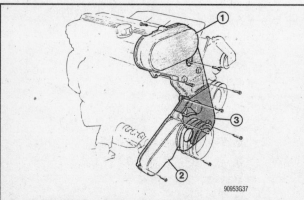

Fig. 85 The B234F engine has a three-piece timing cover

**2.9L 6-Cylinder Engine**

1. Disconnect the negative battery lead.
2. Remove the drive belt.
3. Remove the lower timing belt cover, splash guard and vibration damper guard.
4. Remove the ignition coil cover.
5. Remove the upper timing cover.

**To install:**

6. Install the upper timing belt cover.
7. Install the ignition coil cover.
8. Install the lower timing belt cover, splash guard and vibration damper guard.
9. Install the drive belt.
10. Connect the negative battery cable.

**2.3L and 2.4L 5-Cylinder Engines**

♦ **See Figures 86 thru 93**

1. Disconnect the negative battery cable.
2. Remove the coolant expansion tank and place it on top of the engine.
3. Remove the spark plug cover.
4. Remove the drive belts.
5. Remove the fuel line clips.
6. Remove the right front wheel and loosen the inner fenderwell.
7. Remove the vibration damper guard and turn crankshaft pulley until the marks are lined up.
8. Remove the water pump pulley.
9. Remove the retaining bolts and lift off the timing belt cover.

**To install:**

10. Position the timing belt cover in place and secure with the retainer bolts.
11. Install the water pump pulley, followed by the drive belts.
12. Install the remaining components.
13. Connect the negative battery cable.

Fig. 86 Unplug the connector, disconnect the hose and remove the expansion tank

Fig. 87 Remove the belt and the tensioner

Fig. 88 Remove the spark plug cover to . . .

Fig. 89 . . . access the fuel line clips

Fig. 90 Unfasten the retaining bolts and remove the fuel line clips

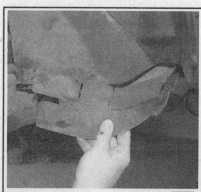

Fig. 91 Remove the fenderwell trim

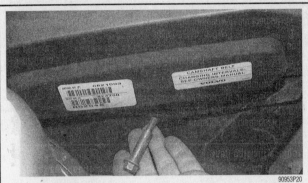

**Fig. 92 Remove the water pump pulley; it is retained by a "shoulder" bolt (shown)**

**Fig. 93 Remove the retaining bolts and carefully remove the timing belt cover**

## Front Crankshaft Seal

### REMOVAL & INSTALLATION

#### 2.3L (B230 and B230FT) 4-Cylinder Engine

1. Disconnect the negative battery cable.
2. Remove the cooling fan and shroud.
3. Remove the drive belts and water pump pulley.
4. Remove upper timing belt cover.
5. Set the crankshaft to TDC and remove the timing belt.

➡**Do not turn the crankshaft or camshaft. Pistons may strike valves.**

6. Carefully pry loose the seal to be replaced. Do not damage the contact face.

**To install:**

7. Clean the contact faces. Lubricate the seal and seat, then press the seal into position.
8. Install the timing belt. Make sure the timing belt is correctly positioned.
9. Install the timing belt cover and vibration damper.
10. Tighten the crankshaft center bolt to 45 ft. lbs. (60 Nm) plus an additional 60 degrees.
11. Install the drive belts and water pump pulley.
12. Install the cooling fan and shroud.
13. Connect the negative battery cable.
14. Start the engine.
15. Check for leaks and proper operation.

#### 2.3L (B234F) 4-Cylinder Engine

1. Disconnect the negative battery cable.
2. Remove the timing/balance shaft belts as described in this section.
3. Remove the timing belt right-side idler.
4. Remove the crankshaft pulley, using a counterhold and guide (Tools

5284 and 5872 or equivalent) between the cylinder head, in the right-hand idler bolt hole.

5. Carefully pry out the seal. Avoid damaging the sealing faces on the shaft and in seating flange.

**To install:**

6. Before installing the new seal, thoroughly clean the crankshaft end and seating flange.
7. Lubricate the new seal and tap the seal into the seating flange.

➡**Face of seal should normally be flush with the chamfered edge in the housing; however, if the shaft end shows sign of wear, seal may be located approximately 3mm further in.**

8. Install the balance shaft drive pulley. Guide must face outwards.
9. Install the timing belt pulley and guides.
10. Install the crankshaft damper/pulley.
11. Tighten the crankshaft bolt in 2-stages. First tighten to 44 ft. lbs. (60 Nm); then tighten an additional 60 degrees.
12. Turn the crankshaft to TDC on No. 1 cylinder.
13. Install the right-hand idler. Tighten to 18.5 ft. lbs. (25 Nm).
14. Install the timing/balance shaft belts as described in this section.
15. Connect the negative battery cable.

#### 2.9L 6-Cylinder Engine

1. Disconnect the negative battery cable.
2. Remove the timing belt.
3. Remove the crankshaft pulley, using a suitable puller.
4. Carefully pry out the old seal.

**To install:**

5. Before installing the new seal, thoroughly clean the crankshaft face.
6. Lubricate the new seal and tap the seal into place, using tool 5455 or equivalent.
7. Install the timing belt.
8. Connect the negative battery cable.

#### 2.3L and 2.4L 5-Cylinder Engines

1. Disconnect the negative battery cable.
2. Remove the fuel line clips.
3. Lift the coolant expansion tank and place it on top of the engine.
4. Remove the drive belts.
5. Remove the front timing cover.
6. Raise and safely support the vehicle.
7. Remove the right front wheel and loosen the inner fender liner.
8. Remove the vibration damper guard and turn crankshaft pulley until all timing marks align.
9. Remove the timing belt.

#### ✳✳ WARNING

**Do not turn the crankshaft or camshafts once the timing belt has been removed.**

10. Install a universal puller so the claws pull against the bolts and not the sprocket. Pull the sprocket off.

#### ✳✳ WARNING

**Make sure that the puller does not damage the sprocket teeth.**

11. Remove the front seal using a groove cut chisel.
12. Clean the mating surface.

**To install:**

13. Install the new seal into place.
14. Install the crankshaft timing belt sprocket using the nut and a spacer.
15. Install the timing belt.
16. Turn the crankshaft two complete revolutions and make sure the timing marks on the crankshaft and camshaft pulleys align properly.
17. Install the two fuel line clips.
18. Install the remaining components.
19. Install the wheel.
20. Connect the negative battery cable.
21. Test run the engine.

## Timing Chain Cover and Seal

### REMOVAL & INSTALLATION

#### 2.8L 6-Cylinder Engine

##### COVER AND SEAL

1. Disconnect the negative battery cable.
2. Remove the air cleaner and valve covers.
3. Loosen the fan shroud and remove the fan.
4. Remove the shroud.
5. Loosen the alternator, air pump, power steering pump, air conditioning compressor, if equipped, and remove their drive belts.
6. Block the flywheel from turning, remove the crankshaft pulley nut (36mm) and the pulley.

➡**Do not drop the pulley key into the crankcase.**

7. Remove the power steering pump and place aside.
8. Remove the pump bracket.
9. Remove the 25 timing chain cover 11mm hex retaining bolts, then tap and remove the cover.

**To install:**

10. Clean the gasket contact surfaces.
11. Place the upper gasket on the cover and the lower gasket on the block.
12. Install the cover and tighten to 7–11 ft. lbs. (10–15 Nm).
13. Trim the gaskets flush with the valve cover.
14. Install a new crankshaft seal.
15. Block the flywheel, install the pulley, key and tighten the 36mm nut to 118–132 ft. lbs. (160–180 Nm).
16. Install the power steering pump, pump bracket, alternator, air pump, power steering pump and air conditioning compressor.
17. Install the fan and shroud.
18. Install the accessory drive belts.
19. Connect the negative battery cable.
20. Start the engine and check for leaks.

##### SEAL ONLY

1. Disconnect the negative battery cable.
2. Remove the air cleaner and valve covers.
3. Loosen the fan shroud and remove the fan.
4. Remove the shroud.
5. Loosen the alternator, air pump, power steering pump, air conditioning compressor, if equipped, and remove their drive belts.
6. Block the flywheel from turning, remove the crankshaft pulley nut (36mm) and the pulley.

➡**Do not drop the pulley key into the crankcase.**

7. Remove the seal, using a suitable puller (Tool 9 995 069-3 or equivalent).

➡**Be careful not to damage the timing chain cover contact surface.**

**To install:**

8. Fill the space between the seal lips with grease and install the new seal, using tool 5103 or equivalent.
9. Block the flywheel, install the pulley, key and tighten the 36mm nut to 118–132 ft. lbs. (160–180 Nm).
10. Install the power steering pump, pump bracket, alternator, air pump, power steering pump and air conditioning compressor.
11. Install the fan and shroud.
12. Install the accessory drive belts.
13. Connect the negative battery cable.
14. Start the engine and check for leaks.

## Timing Belt and Sprockets

### REMOVAL & INSTALLATION

➡**Although not necessary, we at Chilton recommend that you replace the timing belt tensioner when replacing the belt. The tensioner can**

(and often does) leak hydraulic fluid, and can seize, causing the belt to break.

#### B230F and B230FT Engines

1. Disconnect the negative battery cable.
2. Remove the timing belt cover as described in this section.
3. Set the engine to TDC of the No. 1 cylinder.
4. To remove the tension from the belt, loosen the nut for the tensioner and press the idler roller back. The tension spring can be locked in this position by inserting the shank end of a 3mm drill through the pusher rod.
5. Remove the 6 retaining bolts and the crankshaft pulley.
6. Remove the belt, taking care not to bend it at any sharp angles. The belt should be replaced at 45,000 mile (72,500 km) intervals, if it becomes oil soaked or frayed or if it is on a vehicle that has been sitting idle for any length of time.

**To install:**

7. If the crankshaft, idler shaft or camshaft were disturbed while the belt was out, align each shaft with its corresponding index mark to assure proper valve timing and ignition timing, as follows:

   a. Rotate the crankshaft so the notch in the convex crankshaft gear belt guide aligns with the embossed mark on the front cover (12 o'clock position).

   b. Rotate the idler shaft so the dot on the idler shaft drive sprocket aligns with the notch on the timing belt rear cover (4 o'clock position).

   c. Rotate the camshaft so the notch in the camshaft sprocket inner belt guide aligns with the notch in the forward edge of the valve cover (12 o'clock position).

8. Install the timing belt (don't use any sharp tools) over the sprockets and then over the tensioner roller. Some new belts have yellow marks. The 2 lines on the drive belt should fit toward the crankshaft marks. The next mark should then fit toward the intermediate shaft marks, etc.
9. Loosen the tensioner nut and let the spring tension automatically take up the slack. Tighten the tensioner nut to 37 ft. lbs. (51 Nm).
10. Rotate the crankshaft one full revolution clockwise and make sure the timing marks still align.
11. Install the drive belts, radiator fan and shroud.
12. Connect the negative battery cable.

#### B234F Engine

▶ **See Figures 94 thru 101**

➡**The B234F engine has 2 timing belts, one driving the camshafts and one driving the balance shafts. The camshaft belt may be removed separately; the balance shaft belt requires removal of the camshaft belt. During reassembly, the exact placement of the belts and pulleys must be observed.**

1. Remove the negative battery cable.
2. Remove the timing belt covers.
3. Turn the engine to TDC, of the compression stroke, on cylinder No. 1. Make sure the marks on the cam pulleys align with the marks on the backing plate and that the marking on the belt guide plate (on the crankshaft) is opposite the TDC mark on the engine block.
4. Remove the protective cap over the timing belt tensioner locknut. Loosen the locknut, compress the tensioner, to release tension on the belts, and re-tighten the locknut, holding the tensioner in place.
5. Remove the timing belt from the camshafts. Do not crease or fold the belt. Place a mark noting the direction of the belt's rotation if you are reinstalling the same belt.

➡**The camshafts and the crankshaft must not be moved when the belt is removed.**

6. Check the tensioner by spinning it counterclockwise and listening for any bearing noise within. Check also that the belt contact surface is clean and smooth. In the same fashion, check the timing belt idler pulleys. Make sure the bolts are tightened to 18.5 ft. lbs. (25 Nm).
7. If the balance shaft belt is to be removed:

   a. Remove the balance shaft belt idler pulley from the engine.

   b. Loosen the locknut on the tensioner and remove the belt. Slide the belt under the crankshaft pulley assembly. Check the tensioner and idler wheels carefully for any sign of contamination; check the ends of the shafts for any sign of oil leakage.

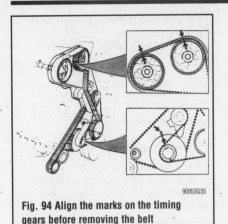

**Fig. 94 Align the marks on the timing gears before removing the belt**

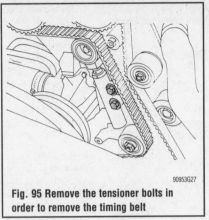

**Fig. 95 Remove the tensioner bolts in order to remove the timing belt**

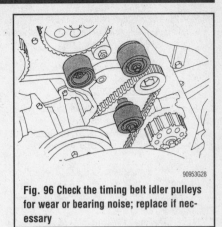

**Fig. 96 Check the timing belt idler pulleys for wear or bearing noise; replace if necessary**

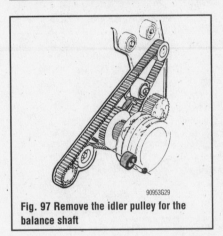

**Fig. 97 Remove the idler pulley for the balance shaft**

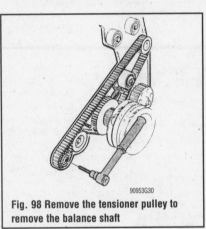

**Fig. 98 Remove the tensioner pulley to remove the balance shaft**

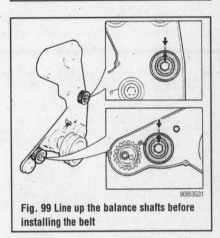

**Fig. 99 Line up the balance shafts before installing the belt**

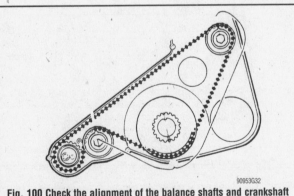

**Fig. 100 Check the alignment of the balance shafts and crankshaft before tightening the tensioner**

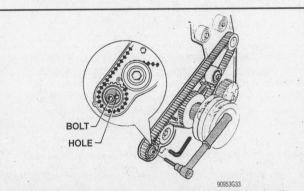

**Fig. 101 Use an Allen wrench as a counterhold when tightening the tensioner pulley**

c. Check the position of the balance shafts and the crankshaft after belt removal. The balance shaft markings on the pulleys should align with the markings on the backing plate and the crankshaft marking should still be aligned with the TDC mark on the engine block.

d. When refitting the balance shaft belt, observe that the belt has colored dots on it. These marks assist in the critical placement of the belt. The yellow dot will align the right lower shaft, the blue dot will align on the crank and the other yellow dot will match to the upper left balance shaft.

e. Carefully work the belt in under the crankshaft pulley. Make sure the blue dot is opposite the bottom (TDC) marking on the belt guide plate at the bottom of the crankshaft. Fit the belt around the left upper balance shaft pulley, making sure the yellow mark is opposite the mark on the pulley. Install the belt around the right lower balance shaft pulley and again check that the mark on the belt aligns with the mark on the pulley.

f. Work the belt around the tensioner. Double check that all the markings are still aligned.

g. Set the belt tension by inserting an Allen key into the adjusting hole in the tensioner. Turn the crankshaft carefully through a few degrees on either side of TDC to check that the belt has properly engaged the pulleys. Return the crank to the TDC position and set the adjusting hole just below the 3 o'clock position when tightening the adjusting bolt. Use the Allen wrench, in the adjusting hole, as a counter hold and tighten the locking bolt to 29.5 ft. lbs. (40 Nm).

h. Check the tension of the belt. If the belt is out of specification, the belt must be readjusted.

**To install:**

8. Reinstall the camshaft belt by aligning the double line marking on the belt with the top marking on the belt guide plate at the top of the crankshaft. Stretch the belt around the crank pulley and place it over the tensioner and the right side idler. Place the belt on the camshaft pulleys. The single line marks on the belt should align exactly with the pulley markings. Route the belt around the oil pump drive pulley and press the belt onto the left side idler.

9. Check that all the markings align and that the engine is still positioned at TDC, of the compression stroke, for cylinder No. 1.

10. Loosen the tensioner locknut.

11. Turn the crankshaft clockwise. The cam pulleys should rotate 1 full turn until the marks again align with the marks on the backing plate.

➡**The engine must not be rotated counterclockwise during this procedure.**

12. Smoothly rotate the crankshaft further clockwise until the cam pulley markings are 1½ teeth beyond the marks on the backing plate.

13. Tighten the tensioner locknut.

14. Check the tension on the balance shaft belt; it should now be 3.8 units. If the tension is too low, adjust the tensioner clockwise. If the tension is too high, repeat Step 7g.

15. Check the belt guide for the balance shaft belt and make sure it is properly seated.

16. Install the center timing belt cover, the one that covers the tensioner, the fan shroud, fan pulley and fan.

17. Install all the drive belts and connect the battery cable.

18. Double check all installation items, paying particular attention to loose hoses or hanging wires, untightened nuts, poor routing of hoses and wires (too tight or rubbing) and tools left in the engine area.

19. Connect the negative battery cable.

20. Start the engine and allow it to run until the thermostat opens.

### ✳✳ CAUTION

**The upper and lower timing belt covers are still removed. The belt and pulleys are exposed and moving at high speed.**

21. Turn the engine **OFF** and bring the engine to TDC, of the compression stroke, on cylinder No. 1.

22. Disconnect the negative battery cable.

23. Check the tension of the camshaft belt. Position the gauge between the right (exhaust) cam pulley and the idler. Belt tension must be 5.5 plus or minus 0.2 units. If the belt needs adjustment, remove the rubber cap over the tensioner locknut, cap is located on the timing belt cover, and loosen the locknut.

24. Insert a suitable tool between the tensioner wheel and the spring carrier pin to hold the tensioner. If the belt needs to be tightened, move the roller to adjust the tension to 6.0 units. If the belt is too tight, adjust to obtain a reading of 5.0 units on the gauge. Tighten the tensioner locknut.

25. Rotate the crankshaft so the cam pulleys move through 1 full revolution and recheck the tension on the camshaft belt. It should now be 5.5 plus or minus 0.2 units. Install the plastic plug over the tensioner bolt.

26. Final check the tension on the balance shaft belt by fitting the gauge and turning the tensioner clockwise. Only small movements are needed. After any needed readjustments, rotate the crankshaft clockwise through 1 full revolution and recheck the balance shaft belt. The tension should now be on the final specification of 4.9 plus or minus 0.2 units.

27. Install the idler pulley for the balance shaft belt.

28. Reinstall the upper and lower timing belt covers.

29. Connect the negative battery cable.

30. Start the engine and final check performance.

### 2.9L 6-Cylinder Engine

◢ See Figure 102

1. Disconnect the negative battery cable.

2. Remove the splashguard, vibration damper guard and ignition coil cover.

3. Remove the auxiliary drive belts.

4. Remove the front timing belt cover.

5. Rotate the crankshaft clockwise, until the timing marks on the camshaft pulleys/timing belt mounting plate and crankshaft pulley/oil pump housing are aligned.

6. Remove the upper timing belt cover.

7. Check the belt tensioner, as outlined in this section. Replace the tensioner, if required.

8. Remove the tensioner upper mounting bolts. Loosen the tensioner lower mounting bolt and twist the tensioner to free the plunger. Remove the lower mounting bolt and remove the tensioner.

9. Remove the timing belt.

➡**Do not rotate the crankshaft while the timing belt is removed.**

10. Check the tensioner and idler pulleys, as follows:
   a. Spin the pulleys and listen for bearing noise.
   b. Check that the pulley surfaces in contact with the belt are clean and smooth.
   c. Check the tensioner pulley arm and idler pulley mountings.
   d. Tighten the tensioner pulley arm to 30 ft. lbs. (40 Nm) and the idler pulley to 18 ft. lbs. (25 Nm).

**To install:**

11. Place the belt around the crankshaft pulley and right-side idler. Place the belt over the camshaft pulleys.

12. Position the belt around the water pump and press over tensioner pulley.

➡**The timing belt lever bushing must be greased every time the belt is replaced or the tensioner pulley removed. This is necessary to help prevent seizure of the bushing, with the possible risk of incorrect belt tension. Service the bushing, using the following procedure:**

   a. Remove the lever mounting bolt, tensioner pulley and sleeve behind the bolt.
   b. Grease the surfaces of the bushing, bolt and sleeve, using high temp grease.
   c. Install the sleeve, tensioner pulley and lever mounting bolt.
   d. Tighten the bolt to 30 ft. lbs. (40 Nm).

13. Insert the tensioner mounting bolts. Tighten to 18 ft. lbs. (25 Nm).

14. Remove the locking pin.

15. Install the front timing belt cover.

16. Turn the crankshaft through 2 revolutions and check that the timing marks on the crankshaft and camshaft pulleys are correctly aligned.

17. Install the ignition coil, front timing belt cover, auxiliaries drive belts, vibration damper guard and splashguard.

18. Connect the negative battery cable.

19. Start and check the engine operation.

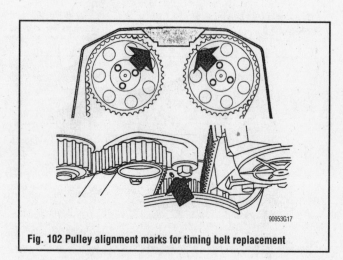

**Fig. 102 Pulley alignment marks for timing belt replacement**

### 2.3L and 2.4L 5-Cylinder Engines

◢ See Figures 103 thru 114

1. Disconnect the negative battery cable.

2. Remove the coolant expansion tank and place it on top of the engine.

3. Remove the spark plug cover and drive belts.

4. Remove the timing belt cover.

5. Align the pulley marks with the marks on the engine mounting plate.

6. Wait five minutes after lining up marks, then install gauge 998 8500 or equivalent between the exhaust camshaft and water pump. Read the gauge using a mirror, while still installed. For 23mm belts, the tension should be 2.7–4.0 units.

➡**If the belt tension is incorrect, the tensioner must be replaced.**

7. Remove the upper tensioner bolt and loosen the lower bolt, turning the tensioner to free up the pulley.

8. Remove the lower bolt and the tensioner.

9. Remove the timing belt.

Fig. 103 Line up the camshaft pulleys with the marks on the engine mounting plate

Fig. 104 If you are not replacing the timing belt, make sure you mark the rotational direction for proper indexing upon installation

Fig. 105 To ease installation, note the belt routing before removal

Fig. 106 The tensioner as mounted on the engine block

Fig. 107 Remove the tensioner pulley from the engine

Fig. 108 Slide the timing belt off the camshaft pulleys and remove it from the engine

Fig. 109 Remove the tensioner from the engine

Fig. 110 Install the tensioner in a vise . . .

Fig. 111 . . . and compress the tensioner piston until . . .

Fig. 112 . . . the holes align . . .

Fig. 113 . . . then install a 2mm lock pin (or 2mm Allen wrench, as used here)

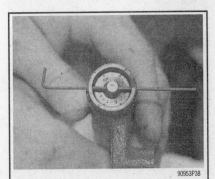

Fig. 114 Remove the tensioner from the vise, leaving the pin or Allen wrench in the piston

**To install:**

10. Turn all the pulleys listening for bearing noise. Check to see that the contact surfaces are clean and smooth.

11. Remove the tensioner pulley lever and idler pulley, lubricate the contact surfaces and bearing with grease. If the tensioner pulley lever or idler is seized replace it.

12. Install the tensioner pulley lever and idler pulley and tighten to 18 ft. lbs. (25 Nm).

13. Compress the tensioner with tool 999 5456 or equivalent and insert a 0.079 in. (2.0mm) lock pin in the piston. If the tensioner leaks, has no resistance, or will not compress, replace it.

14. Install the tensioner and tighten the bolts to 18 ft. lbs. (25 Nm).

15. Install the timing belt in order:
   a. Around the crankshaft sprocket.
   b. Around the right idler pulley
   c. Around the camshaft sprockets
   d. Around the water pump
   e. Onto the tensioner pulley

16. Pull the lock pin out from the tensioner and install the upper timing cover. Turn the crankshaft two complete revolutions and check to see that the timing marks on the crankshaft and camshaft pulleys are lined up.

17. Install the timing belt covers and the fuel line clips.

18. Install the accessory belts.

19. Install the vibration damper guard and the inner fenderwell.

20. Install the spark plug cover.

21. Install the coolant reservoir tank.

22. Connect the negative battery cable.

## ADJUSTMENT

### B234F Engine

▶ **See Figure 115**

1. Place a tension gauge (9988500 or equivalent) between the exhaust camshaft drive pulley and tensioner.

2. Read the gauge. If the belt tension is correct, the gauge should read between 3.2 and 4.2 units.

3. If the reading is incorrect, remove the protective rubber cap in the timing belt cover. Slacken the locknut.

4. Turn the crankshaft clockwise through one revolution. Camshaft pulley markings should again coincide with the markings on the timing belt mounting plate.

➡ **Do not turn the engine counterclockwise during belt tensioning procedure.**

5. Turn the engine further clockwise until the camshaft pulley markings are 1½ teeth past the markings on the timing belt mounting plate. Tighten the tensioner locknut.

6. Turn the crankshaft clockwise to complete one revolution (TDC).

7. Check that all markings coincide.

8. Recheck the belt tension.

9. If the reading is still not correct, proceed as follows:
   a. Slacken the tensioner locknut.
   b. Install the measuring gauge.
   c. Insert a screwdriver between the tensioner pulley and the end of the spring carrier pin.
   d. Re-adjust the belt to obtain the specified tension. Tighten the tensioner locknut to 37 ft. lbs. (50 Nm).

10. Install the protective rubber cap over the tensioner locknut.

11. Install the upper timing belt cover.

### 2.9L 6-Cylinder Engine

1. Place a tension gauge (9988500 or equivalent) between the exhaust camshaft drive pulley and water pump.

2. Read the gauge. If the belt tension is correct, the gauge should read between 3.5 and 4.6 units.

3. If the reading is incorrect, replace the tensioner.

## INSPECTION

▶ **See Figures 116 thru 123**

The timing belt should be periodically inspected for wear. Removal of the timing cover is necessary to visually check the belt for signs of wear or contamination. The belt should show no signs of wear such as cracked teeth, wear on the belt face, wear on one or both sides of the belt, and there should be no foreign materials on the belt or between the teeth. If there is oil, coolant, lubricant, or any other foreign material on the belt, it is a good idea to replace the belt due to the fact that rapid wear can result from this contamination. Usually sticking to the manufacturer's guide for timing belt replacement interval will ensure little problems but it is still a good idea to periodically inspect your belt. If the belt breaks the engine will shut down and serious engine damage can occur. The proper manufacturer recommended timing belt replacement interval can be found in Section 1.

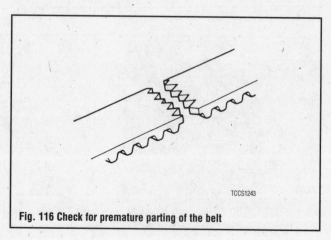
TCCS1243

**Fig. 116 Check for premature parting of the belt**

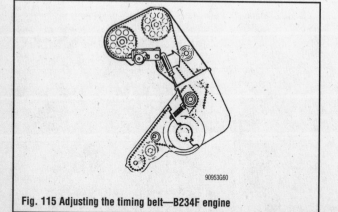
90953G60

**Fig. 115 Adjusting the timing belt—B234F engine**

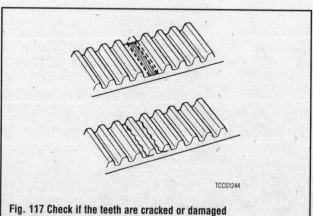
TCCS1244

**Fig. 117 Check if the teeth are cracked or damaged**

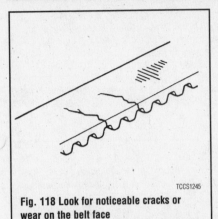

**Fig. 118 Look for noticeable cracks or wear on the belt face**

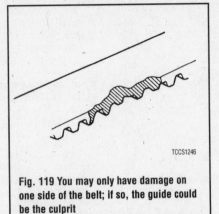

**Fig. 119 You may only have damage on one side of the belt; if so, the guide could be the culprit**

**Fig. 120 Foreign materials can get in between the teeth and cause damage**

**Fig. 121 Inspect the timing belt for cracks, fraying, glazing or damage of any kind**

**Fig. 122 Damage on only one side of the timing belt may indicate a faulty guide**

**Fig. 123 ALWAYS replace the timing belt at the interval specified by the manufacturer**

## Timing Chain and Gears

### REMOVAL & INSTALLATION

**2.8L 6-Cylinder Engine**

▶ See Figures 124, 125, 126 and 127

1. Remove the timing chain cover.
2. Set the engine to TDC of the No. 1 cylinder.
3. Remove the oil pump sprocket and drive chain.
4. Slacken the tension in both camshaft timing chains by rotating each tensioner lock ¼ turn counterclockwise and pushing the rubbing block piston.
5. Remove both chain tensioners.
6. Remove the 2 curved and the 2 straight chain damper/runners.
7. Remove the camshaft sprocket retaining bolt, 10mm Allen head, and the sprocket and chain assembly. Repeat for the other side.

**To install:**

8. Install the chain tensioners and tighten to 60 inch lbs. (7 Nm).
9. Install the curved chain damper/runners and tighten to 7–11 ft. lbs. (10–15 Nm).
10. Install the straight chain damper/runners and tighten to 60 inch lbs. (7 Nm).
11. First install the driver's side camshaft sprocket and chain:
    a. Rotate the crankshaft, using crankshaft nut, if necessary, until the crankshaft key is pointing directly to the driver's side camshaft and the driver's side camshaft key groove is pointing straight-up (12 o'clock).
    b. Place the chain on the driver's side sprocket so the sprocket notch-mark is centered precisely between the 2 white lines on the chain.
    c. Position the chain on the crankshaft sprocket (inner), making sure the other white line on the chain aligns with the crankshaft sprocket notch.
    d. While holding the driver's side chain and sprockets in this position, install the sprocket and chain on the driver's side camshaft, chain stretched on tension side, so the sprocket pin fits into the camshaft recess.

e. Tighten the sprocket center bolt to 51–59 ft. lbs. (69–80 Nm); use a suitable tool to keep the cam from turning.

12. To install the passenger side camshaft sprocket and chain:
    a. Rotate the crankshaft clockwise until the crankshaft key points straight down (6 o'clock).
    b. Align the camshaft key groove so it is pointing halfway between the 8 and 9 o'clock positions; at this position, the No. 6 cylinder rocker arms will rock.
    c. Place the chain on the passenger side sprocket so the sprocket notch-mark is centered precisely between the 2 white lines on the chain.
    d. Then, position the chain on the middle crankshaft sprocket, making sure the other white line aligns with the crankshaft sprocket notch.
    e. Install the sprocket and chain on the camshaft so the sprocket notch fits into the camshaft recess.
    f. Tighten the sprocket nut to 51–59 ft. lbs. (69–80 Nm).

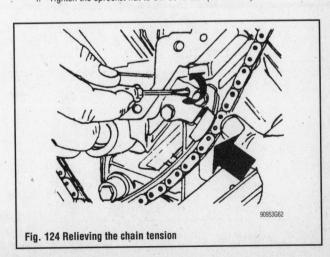

**Fig. 124 Relieving the chain tension**

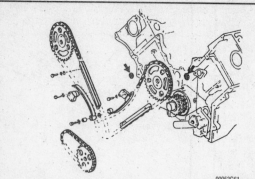

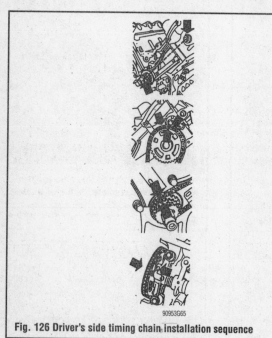

**Fig. 125 Exploded view of timing chain, tensioner and sprocket assembly**

90953G61

90953G65

**Fig. 126 Driver's side timing chain installation sequence**

90953G64

**Fig. 127 Passenger side timing chain installation sequence**

13. Rotate the chain tensioners ¼ turn clockwise each. The chains are tensioned by rotating the crankshaft 2 full turns clockwise. Recheck to make sure the alignment marks coincide.

14. Install the oil pump sprocket and chain.

15. Install the timing chain cover.

## Camshaft, Bearings and Lifters

### REMOVAL & INSTALLATION

The 2.3L 4-cylinder, 2.9L 6-cylinder, and 2.3 and 2.4L 5-cylinder engines all use camshafts that ride directly over the followers (lifters). After camshaft removal, they can be lifted out of their bores and inspected. If removal is necessary, mark the followers to assure their placement in the correct bore.

The 2.8L 6-cylinder engine uses rocker shaft mounted followers. Please refer to Rocker Arm/Shaft removal/installation for their removal.

➡When installing a camshaft, always lubricate the camshaft, seats, and lifters with the proper camshaft lube or moly grease.

**2.3L 4-Cylinder Engines**

1. Disconnect the negative battery cable.
2. Remove the drive belts.
3. Set the engine to TDC of the No. 1 cylinder.
4. Remove the timing belt.
5. Remove the valve cover.
6. Remove the camshaft center bearing cap. Install camshaft press tool 5021 or equivalent over the center bearing journal to hold the camshaft in place while removing the other bearing caps.
7. Remove the 4 remaining bearing caps.
8. Remove the seal from the forward edge of the camshaft.
9. Release camshaft press tool and lift out the camshaft.

### ✳✳ WARNING

**Do not rotate the crankshaft while the camshaft is removed from the cylinder head.**

**To install:**

10. Apply sealant to the outer sealing surfaces of the front and rear caps.
11. Lubricate the camshaft with cam lube or moly grease, and place into position. The guide pin for the timing gear should face up.
12. Install the rear bearing cap.
13. Slide the camshaft back and forth to check the camshaft end-play. End-play should be 0.004–0.016 in. (0.1–0.4mm).
14. Install the camshaft press tool.
15. Install the camshaft seal.
16. Lubricate and install the remaining caps starting in the center and working out.
17. Tighten the bolts to 14 ft. lbs. (20 Nm).
18. Lubricate the front seal and install, using tool 5025 or equivalent.
19. Install the camshaft gear and spacer washer.
20. Remove the tools.
21. Install the timing belt.
22. Install the remaining components.
23. Connect the negative battery cable.

**2.8L 6-Cylinder Engine**

1. Disconnect the negative battery cable.
2. Set the engine to TDC of the No. 1 cylinder.
3. Remove the cylinder head.
4. Remove the camshaft rear cover plate.
5. Remove the camshaft retaining fork at the front of the cylinder head.
6. Pull the camshaft out the rear of the head.

➡The camshaft does not have bearings, the journals in the head are machined to fit the camshaft. The retaining fork is used to adjust end-play to position the camshaft in the correct position.

**To install:**

7. Oil the camshaft and followers and install.
8. Tighten the camshaft retaining bolt to 7–11 ft. lbs. (10–15 Nm).
9. Install the camshaft retaining fork.
10. Install the rear cover plate.
11. Install the cylinder head.
12. Connect the negative battery cable.

## 2.9L 6-Cylinder Engine

1. Disconnect the negative battery cable.
2. Remove the drive belts.
3. Set the engine to TDC of the No. 1 cylinder.
4. Remove the timing belt.

➡**Do not turn the crankshaft while the belt is removed.**

5. Remove the camshaft pulleys, using the holding tool 5199 or equivalent.
6. Remove the top half of the cylinder head.
7. Tap the joint lugs and camshaft front ends lightly.
8. Remove the camshafts.

**To install:**

9. Lubricate the camshafts and bearing seats with cam lube or moly grease.
10. Place the camshafts into position.
11. Install the holding tool 5453 or equivalent to the front end and the locking tool 5452 or equivalent to the rear end of the cylinder head upper section.
12. Install the upper cylinder head section and tighten against the lower section, using the press tools 5454 or equivalent.
13. Install and tighten the retaining bolts to 13 ft. lbs. (17 Nm), starting from the inside and working outwards.
14. Remove the tools.
15. Lubricate the camshaft front seals and tap into place.
16. Install the camshaft pulleys.
17. Tighten the camshaft pulley bolts alternately to 15 ft. lbs. (20 Nm).
18. Install the timing belt.

19. Install the tensioner and tighten the bolts to 18 ft. lbs. (25 Nm). Check that the timing marks on the crankshaft and camshaft pulleys are correctly aligned.
20. Install the remaining components.
21. Install the drive belts.
22. Connect the negative battery cable.

## 2.3L and 2.4L 5-Cylinder Engines

◆ **See Figures 128 thru 138**

1. Disconnect the negative battery cable.
2. Remove the drive belt.
3. Set the engine to TDC of the No. 1 cylinder.
4. Remove the timing belt.
5. Remove the ignition coils cover.

➡**Do not turn the crankshaft while the belt is removed.**

6. Remove the camshaft position sensor and shutter at the right rear of camshaft assembly.
7. Remove the switch holder and shield at the left rear of assembly.
8. Remove the ignition coils. Mark their locations.
9. Mark the pulleys for reference so they can be returned to their original sides, then remove the camshaft pulleys, using holding tool 5199 or equivalent.
10. Remove the top half of the cylinder head.
11. Tap the joint lugs and camshaft front ends lightly.
12. Remove the camshafts.
13. Thoroughly clean the mating surfaces between the upper and lower halves of the cylinder head.

### ✳✳ WARNING

**Do not use a metal scraper. Use a soft putty knife and gasket solvent cleaner with an exhaust fan. The surfaces must be totally clean to assure a tight seal.**

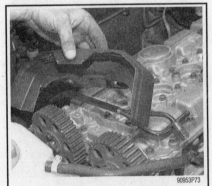

**Fig. 128 Remove the camshaft pulley cover**

**Fig. 129 Prior to removal, mark the exhaust camshaft pulley . . .**

**Fig. 130 . . . and the intake camshaft pulley**

**Fig. 131 Install the pulley holding tool . . .**

**Fig. 132 . . . and remove the pulley retaining bolts**

**Fig. 133 Remove the pulley from the camshaft**

Fig. 134 Carefully lift the intake camshaft from the cylinder head

Fig. 135 Remove the exhaust camshaft

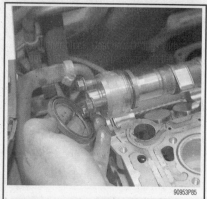

Fig. 136 Remove the camshaft seals

Fig. 137 Inspect the camshaft lobes for wear

Fig. 138 Remove the camshaft followers, noting their position

**To install:**

14. Lubricate the camshafts and bearing seats.
15. Place the camshafts into position.
16. Install the holding tool 5453 or equivalent to the front end and the locking tool 5452 or equivalent to the rear end of the cylinder head upper section.
17. Remove No. 1 and No. 5 spark plugs
18. Using a roller, apply liquid gasket 161 059-9 or equivalent to the upper half of the cylinder head.

➡ Make sure that no liquid gasket gets into the oil passages. Only a thin coating is required.

19. Install the upper cylinder head section and tighten against the lower section, using the press tools 5454 or equivalent.
20. Install and tighten the retaining bolts to 13 ft. lbs. (17 Nm), starting from the inside and working outwards.
21. Remove the tools.

22. Lubricate the camshaft front seals and tap into place.
23. Mount the upper timing cover.
24. Install the camshaft sprockets and line up the camshaft timing marks.
25. Install two camshaft sprocket bolts furthest from the timing mark and tighten until they are just touching the sprocket.
26. Remove the upper timing cover.
27. Make sure that the remaining camshaft sprocket bolt hole is centered.
28. Turn all the idler pulleys listening for bearing noise.
29. Check to see that the contact surfaces are clean and smooth.
30. Remove the tensioner pulley lever and idler pulley, lubricate the contact surfaces and bearing with grease. If the tensioner pulley lever or idler is seized, replace it.
31. Install the tensioner pulley lever and tighten to 18 ft. lbs. (25 Nm).
32. Install the idler pulley and tighten to 18 ft. lbs. (25 Nm).
33. Compress the tensioner fully with tool 999 5456 or equivalent.
34. Install the timing belt.
35. Install the rear camshaft seal using drift 999 5450 or equivalent and press it carefully into position flush with the inner chamfer edge.
36. Install the remaining components
37. Connect the negative battery cable.
38. Start the engine and run it until the thermostat opens.
39. Check the engine for leaks.

## Balance Shafts

### REMOVAL & INSTALLATION

**B234 Engine**

➡ The use of the correct special tools or their equivalent is required for this procedure.

**LEFT SHAFT AND HOUSING**

1. Disconnect the negative battery cable.
2. Set the engine to TDC of the No. 1 cylinder.
3. Remove the timing and balance shaft belts.
4. Use a counterhold tool 5362 and remove the left side balance shaft pulley.
5. Remove the air mass meter and inlet hose.
6. Unfasten the bracket under the intake manifold and remove the bracket holding the alternator and power steering pump. These may be swung aside and tied with wire to the left shock tower.
7. Remove the bolts securing the balance shaft housing to the block. Using an extractor tool 5376 or similar, carefully separate the housing from the block. The housing must be removed evenly from both its front and rear mounts.

**To install:**

8. Clean the joint faces on the cylinder block. Coat new O-rings with engine oil and place them in the grooves around the oil passages on the housing. The rings can be held in place with a light coating of grease.
9. Coat the balance shafts and bearings with cam lube or moly grease.

10. Install the balance shaft housing. Make absolutely sure the housing is evenly mounted on the front and rear mountings. Tighten the bolts alternately in a diagonal pattern. Tighten each bolt ½ turn at a time; tighten them to 15 ft. lbs. (20 Nm). When all the bolts are at 15 ft. lbs. (20 Nm), loosen them individually and tighten each one to 90 inch lbs. (10 Nm) plug 90 degrees of rotation.

➡**Make certain the shaft does not seize within the housing during installation.**

11. If the halves of the housing were split apart during the repair, tighten the joint bolts to 72 inch lbs. (8 Nm).

12. Install the drive pulley. Use a counterholding tool. Note that the pulley has a slot which will align with the guide on the shaft. The shallow side of the pulley faces inward, toward the engine. Tighten the center bolt for the pulley to 37 ft. lbs. (50 Nm).

13. Install the bracket for the alternator and power steering pump. Double check their connections and hoses.

14. Attach the support under the intake manifold and don't forget the wire clamp on the bottom bolt.

15. Install the air mass meter and its intake hose.

16. Install the balance shaft belt and camshaft belt.

17. Connect the negative battery cable.

### RIGHT SHAFT AND HOUSING

1. Disconnect the negative battery cable.
2. Set the engine to TDC of the No. 1 cylinder.
3. Remove the timing and balance shaft belts.
4. Use a counterhold tool 5362 and remove the left side balance shaft pulley.
5. Remove the balance shaft belt tensioner and remove the bolt running through the backing plate to the balance shaft housing.
6. Remove the air mass meter and its air inlet hose.
7. Remove the air preheat hose from the bottom heat shield at the exhaust manifold.
8. Remove the nuts holding the right engine mount to the crossmember.
9. Connect a hoist or engine lift apparatus to the top of the engine.
10. Lift the engine at the right side, being careful to maintain clearance between the brake master cylinder and the intake manifold.
11. Remove the complete motor mount from the block, including the pad and lower mounting plate.
12. Remove the bolts securing the balance shaft housing to the block.
13. Using an extractor tool 5376 or similar, carefully separate the housing from the block. The housing must be removed evenly from both its front and rear mounts.
    **To install:**
14. Clean the joint faces on the cylinder block.
15. Coat new O-rings with engine oil and place them in the grooves around the oil passages on the housing. The rings can be held in place with a light coating of grease.
16. Install the balance shaft housing. Make absolutely sure the housing is evenly mounted on the front and rear mountings. Tighten the bolts alternately in a diagonal pattern. Tighten each bolt ½ turn at a time; tighten them to 15 ft. lbs. (20 Nm). When all the bolts are at 15 ft. lbs. (20 Nm), loosen them individually and tighten each one to 7.5 ft. lbs. (10 Nm) plus 90 degrees of rotation.

➡**Make certain the shaft does not seize within the housing during installation.**

17. If the halves of the housing were split apart during the repair, tighten the joint bolts to 72 inch lbs. (8 Nm).

18. Install the drive pulley. Use a counterholding tool. Note that the pulley has a slot which will align with the guide on the shaft. The shallow side of the pulley faces inward, toward the engine. Tighten the center bolt for the pulley to 37 ft. lbs. (50 Nm).

19. Install the engine mount onto the block.

20. Using the studs on the crossmember as a guide, lower the engine into place on the front crossmember. When the engine is correctly seated, the lifting apparatus may be removed.

21. Reinstall the air mass meter and its air intake hose.

22. Reinstall the motor mount bolts and the air preheat tube at the lower part of the exhaust manifold.

23. Install the bolt through the backing plate and into the balance shaft housing.

24. Reinstall the belt tensioner, tightening the bolt so the pulley is movable when the belt is in position.

25. Reinstall the balance shaft and camshaft belts.

26. Connect the negative battery cable.

## Rear Main Seal

### REMOVAL & INSTALLATION

#### 2.3L 4-Cylinder Engines

1. Disconnect the negative battery cable.
2. Remove the transmission.
3. Remove the clutch and pressure plate, if equipped.
4. Remove the pilot bearing snapring and remove the bearing.
5. Remove the flywheel or driveplate, as equipped.

➡**Be careful not to press in the activator pins for the timing device.**

6. Remove the rear oil pan brace.
7. Remove the 2 center bolts from the pan that bolt into the seal housing.
8. Loosen 2 bolts on either side of the 2 in the seal housing.
9. Remove the 6 seal housing bolts and remove the seal housing.

➡**Be careful not to damage the oil pan gasket when removing the seal housing.**

10. Remove the seal using special tool 2817 or a suitable replacement.
    **To install:**
11. Use a new gasket on the seal housing and coat the seal with oil prior to installation. Install the seal.
12. Install the seal housing and tighten the bolts in a crisscross pattern.
13. Install the rear oil pan brace and flywheel. Tighten the flywheel bolts to 47–54 ft. lbs. (64–73 Nm) in a crisscross pattern. When installing the flywheel turn the crankshaft to bring the No. 1 piston to TDC. The lower flywheel pin should be installed approximately 15 degrees from the horizontal and opposite the starter.
14. Coat the outside of the pilot bearing and install it on the flywheel.
15. Install the clutch assembly and transmission, as required.
16. Connect the negative battery cable.
17. Fill the transmission with fluid.
18. Start the engine and allow it to reach operating temperature.
19. Check for leaks.

#### 2.8L 6-Cylinder Engine

1. Disconnect the negative battery cable.
2. Remove the transmission.
3. Remove the clutch and pressure plate, if equipped.
4. Remove the flywheel or driveplate, on automatic transmissions.

➡**On automatic transmissions remove the crankshaft spacer.**

5. Remove the 2 rear pan bolts.
6. Remove the bolts in the seal housing and then the housing.

➡**Carefully remove the housing so as not to damage the oil pan gasket.**

7. Using tool 5107, remove the old seal.
    **To install:**
8. Coat the new seal with engine oil and using the seal tool, install the new seal.
9. Install the seal housing and tighten the seal housing bolts in a crisscross pattern to 7–11 ft. lbs. (10–15 Nm).
10. Install the rear oil pan bolts.

11. Install the flywheel and clutch assembly, as required.
12. Tighten the flywheel bolts to 33–37 ft. lbs. (45–50 Nm).
13. Install the transmission.
14. Connect the negative battery cable.
15. Fill the transmission with oil.
16. Start the engine and allow it to reach operating temperature.
17. Check for leaks.

### 2.9L 6-Cylinder Engine

1. Disconnect the negative battery cable.
2. Remove the transmission from the vehicle.
3. Remove the flexplate.
4. Carefully pry out the seal, taking care not to damage the sealing faces on the shaft and in seat.
**To install:**
5. Before installing the seal, thoroughly clean the seat and inspect for signs of wear.
6. Lubricate the mating surface between the seat and seal. Oil the seal lips and press the new seal into place, using a suitable seal installer tool 5430 and 1801 or equivalent.
7. Install the flexplate. Use new bolts and threadlocking compound. Tighten the bolts in 2 stages: first to 33 ft. lbs. (45 Nm); then tighten an additional 50 degree turn.
8. Install the transmission.
9. Connect the negative battery cable.

### 2.3L and 2.4L 5-Cylinder Engines

1. Disconnect the negative battery cable.
2. Raise and safely support the vehicle.
3. Remove the transmission as described in Section 7.
4. Remove the flywheel if equipped with manual transaxle, or the flexplate if equipped with automatic transmission.
5. Using a seal puller or other suitable tool, remove the old seal. Take care not to damage the block surface during removal or new seal could leak.
**To install:**
6. Thoroughly clean sealing surface on the block.
7. Using special tools 999-5430 and 999-1801 or equivalent, install the new seal into the engine block.
8. Install the flywheel/flexplate, using threadlocking compound on the bolts.
9. Tighten all the bolts in two stages:
   a. Tighten to 33 ft. lbs. (45 Nm).
   b. Angle tighten 50°.
10. Install the transmission as described in Section 7.
11. Lower the vehicle.
12. Connect the negative battery cable.

## Flywheel/Flexplate

### REMOVAL & INSTALLATION

♦ **See Figures 139 and 140**

The ring gear is contacted by the starter gear during engine start up. If any damage is found on the ring gear (broken or chipped teeth, cracks, etc.) the cause of the failure should be identified and repaired. The starter should be checked as a possible cause.

On vehicles with automatic transmission, the ring gear is an integral part of the flexplate and cannot be replaced. On vehicles with manual gearboxes, the ring gear on the flywheel can be removed and replaced. This replacement involves heating the ring to 450°F, and handling the heated ring. It is usually found to be easier to buy a complete flywheel and ring gear assembly than to attempt the replacement. If you possess the proper equipment for heating and handling the ring gear, the procedure is as follows:

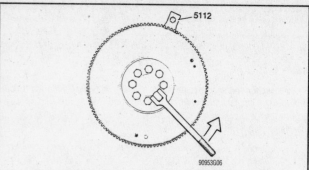

**Fig. 139 The flywheel must be immobilized so that the retaining bolts can be removed; tool 5112 is being used here to hold the flywheel**

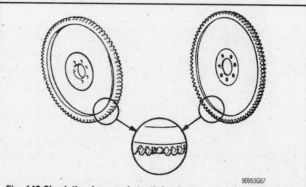

**Fig. 140 Check the ring gear's teeth for damage; if damage is noted, replace the ring gear**

1. Disconnect the negative battery cable.
2. Raise and support the vehicle.
3. Remove the transmission, as described in Section 7.
4. If equipped with a manual transmission/transaxle, remove the clutch plate and disc.
5. Remove the bolts attaching the flywheel or ring gear to the crankshaft flange.
6. Remove the flywheel or ring gear.
7. Inspect the flywheel for cracks, grooves, or bluing and inspect the ring gear for burrs or worn teeth.
8. Replace the flywheel or ring gear if any damage is apparent.
9. Remove burrs with a mill file.
10. To replace a ring gear, use the following steps.
   a. Use a 10mm bit and drill a hole between two cogs (teeth) on the ring gear, being careful not to drill into the flywheel.
   b. Mount the flywheel in a vise protected by soft jaws and split the ring gear at the hole with a chisel.
   c. Heat the new ring gear to approximately 450°F (232°C). When handling the heated ring, wear heavy gloves and use tongs.
   d. Position the ring gear with the beveled side facing the flywheel.
   e. Use a brass drift and tap the ring gear until flush. Allow to air cool before installation; do not attempt to cool the metal with water, oil or other fluids.
11. Install the flywheel.
12. Install the bolts and torque to specification in a crisscross pattern.
13. Install the transmission, as described in Section 7.
14. Lower the vehicle.
15. Connect the negative battery cable.

## EXHAUST SYSTEM

### Inspection

▶ See Figures 141 thru 147

➡Safety glasses should be worn at all times when working on or near the exhaust system. Older exhaust systems will almost always be covered with loose rust particles which will shower you when disturbed. These particles are more than a nuisance and could injure your eye.

### ✳ CAUTION

DO NOT perform exhaust repairs or inspection with the engine or exhaust hot. Allow the system to cool completely before attempting any work. Exhaust systems are noted for sharp edges, flaking metal and rusted bolts. Gloves and eye protection are required. A healthy supply of penetrating oil and rags is highly recommended.

Your vehicle must be raised and supported safely to inspect the exhaust system properly. By placing 4 safety stands under the vehicle for support should provide enough room for you to slide under the vehicle and inspect the system completely. Start the inspection at the exhaust manifold or turbocharger pipe where the header pipe is attached and work your way to the back of the vehicle. On dual exhaust systems, remember to inspect both sides of the vehicle. Check the complete exhaust system for open seams, holes loose connections, or other deterioration which could permit exhaust fumes to seep into the passenger compartment. Inspect all mounting brackets and hangers for deterioration, some models may have rubber O-rings that can be overstretched and non-supportive. These components will need to be replaced if found. It has always been a practice to use a pointed tool to poke up into the exhaust system where the deterioration spots are to see whether or not they crumble. Some models may have heat shield covering certain parts of the exhaust system, it will be necessary to remove these shields to have the exhaust visible for inspection also.

### REPLACEMENT

▶ See Figures 148, 149 and 150

➡Before working on the exhaust system, it is a good idea to soak the retaining hardware with a quality rust penetrant prior to attempting to remove them. After the penetrant is applied wait at least 10–15 minutes to let the penetrant begin to work.

There are basically two types of exhaust systems. One is the flange type where the component ends are attached with bolts and a gasket in-between. The other exhaust system is the slip joint type. These components slip into one another using clamps to retain them together.

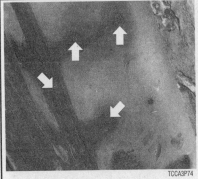

TCCA3P73

Fig. 141 Cracks in the muffler are a guaranteed leak

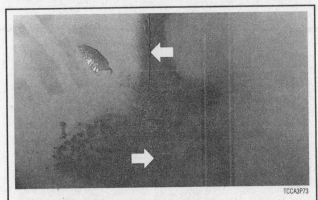

TCCA3P74

Fig. 142 Check the muffler for rotted spot welds and seams

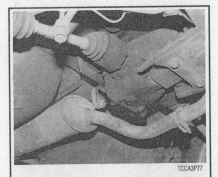

TCCA3P77

Fig. 143 Make sure the exhaust components are not contacting the body or suspension

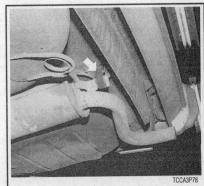

TCCA3P78

Fig. 144 Check for overstretched or torn exhaust hangers

TCCA3P75

Fig. 145 Example of a badly deteriorated exhaust pipe

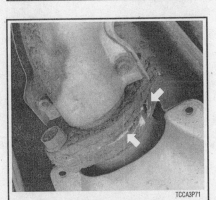

TCCA3P71

Fig. 146 Inspect flanges for gaskets that have deteriorated and need replacement

TCCA3P76

Fig. 147 Some systems, like this one, use large O-rings (donuts) in between the flanges

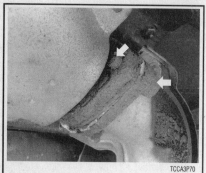

Fig. 148 Nuts and bolts will be extremely difficult to remove when deteriorated with rust

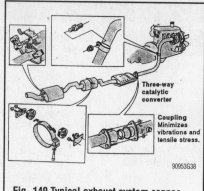

Fig. 149 Typical exhaust system connections—2.3L 4-cylinder engine shown

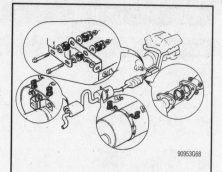

Fig. 150 Exhaust system components, removal and installation—2.8L 6-cylinder engine

> **CAUTION**
>
> Allow the exhaust system to cool sufficiently before spraying a solvent exhaust fasteners. Some solvents are highly flammable and could ignite when sprayed on hot exhaust components.

Before removing any component of the exhaust system, ALWAYS squirt a liquid rust dissolving agent onto the fasteners for ease of removal. A lot of knuckle skin will be saved by following this rule. It may even be wise to spray the fasteners and allow them to sit overnight.

**Flange Type**

▶ See Figure 151

> **CAUTION**
>
> Do NOT perform exhaust repairs or inspection with the engine or exhaust hot. Allow the system to cool completely before attempting any work. Exhaust systems are noted for sharp edges, flaking metal and rusted bolts. Gloves and eye protection are required. A healthy supply of penetrating oil and rags is highly recommended. Never spray liquid rust dissolving agent onto a hot exhaust component.

Before removing any component on a flange type system, ALWAYS squirt a liquid rust dissolving agent onto the fasteners for ease of removal. Start by unbolting the exhaust piece at both ends (if required). When unbolting the headpipe from the manifold, make sure that the bolts are free before trying to remove them. if you snap a stud in the exhaust manifold, the stud will have to be removed with a bolt extractor, which often means removal of the manifold itself. Next, disconnect the component from the mounting; slight twisting and turning may be required to remove the component completely from the vehicle. You may need to tap on the component with a rubber mallet to loosen the component. If all else fails, use a hacksaw to separate the parts. An oxy-acetylene cutting torch may be faster but the sparks are DANGEROUS near the fuel tank, and at the very least, accidents could happen, resulting in damage to the under-car parts, not to mention yourself.

**Slip Joint Type**

▶ See Figure 152

Before removing any component on the slip joint type exhaust system, ALWAYS squirt a liquid rust dissolving agent onto the fasteners for ease of removal. Start by unbolting the exhaust piece at both ends (if required). When unbolting the headpipe from the manifold, make sure that the bolts are free before trying to remove them. if you snap a stud in the exhaust manifold, the stud will have to be removed with a bolt extractor, which often means removal of the manifold itself. Next, remove the mounting U-bolts from around the exhaust pipe you are extracting from the vehicle. Don't be surprised if the U-bolts break while removing the nuts. Loosen the exhaust pipe from any mounting brackets retaining it to the floor pan and separate the components.

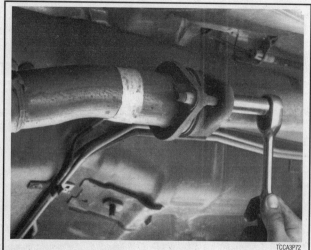

Fig. 151 Example of a flange type exhaust system joint

Fig. 152 Example of a common slip joint type system

## ENGINE RECONDITIONING

### Determining Engine Condition

Anything that generates heat and/or friction will eventually burn or wear out (i.e. a light bulb generates heat, therefore its life span is limited). With this in mind, a running engine generates tremendous amounts of both; friction is encountered by the moving and rotating parts inside the engine and heat is created by friction and combustion of the fuel. However, the engine has systems designed to help reduce the effects of heat and friction and provide added longevity. The oiling system reduces the amount of friction encountered by the moving parts inside the engine, while the cooling system reduces heat created by friction and combustion. If either system is not maintained, a break-down will be inevitable. Therefore, you can see how regular maintenance can affect the service life of your vehicle. If you do not drain, flush and refill your cooling system at the proper intervals, deposits will begin to accumulate in the radiator, thereby reducing the amount of heat it can extract from the coolant. The same applies to your oil and filter; if it is not changed often enough it becomes laden with contaminates and is unable to properly lubricate the engine. This increases friction and wear.

There are a number of methods for evaluating the condition of your engine. A compression test can reveal the condition of your pistons, piston rings, cylinder bores, head gasket(s), valves and valve seats. An oil pressure test can warn you of possible engine bearing, or oil pump failures. Excessive oil consumption, evidence of oil in the engine air intake area and/or bluish smoke from the tail pipe may indicate worn piston rings, worn valve guides and/or valve seals. As a general rule, an engine that uses no more than one quart of oil every 1000 miles is in good condition. Engines that use one quart of oil or more in less than 1000 miles should first be checked for oil leaks. If any oil leaks are present, have them fixed before determining how much oil is consumed by the engine, especially if blue smoke is not visible at the tail pipe.

### COMPRESSION TEST

▶ See Figure 153

A noticeable lack of engine power, excessive oil consumption and/or poor fuel mileage measured over an extended period are all indicators of internal engine wear. Worn piston rings, scored or worn cylinder bores, blown head gaskets, sticking or burnt valves, and worn valve seats are all possible culprits. A check of each cylinder's compression will help locate the problem.

➡A screw-in type compression gauge is more accurate than the type you simply hold against the spark plug hole. Although if takes slightly longer to use, its worth the effort to obtain a more accurate reading.

1. Make sure that the proper amount and viscosity of engine oil is in the crankcase, then ensure the battery is fully charged.
2. Warm-up the engine to normal operating temperature, then shut the engine **OFF**.
3. Disable the ignition system.

**Fig. 153 A screw-in type compression gauge is more accurate and easier to use without an assistant**

TCCS3801

4. Label and disconnect all of the spark plug wires from the plugs.
5. Thoroughly clean the cylinder head area around the spark plug ports, then remove the spark plugs.
6. Set the throttle plate to the fully open (wide-open throttle) position. You can block the accelerator linkage open for this, or you can have an assistant fully depress the accelerator pedal.
7. Install a screw-in type compression gauge into the No. 1 spark plug hole until the fitting is snug.

### ✳✳ WARNING

**Be careful not to crossthread the spark plug hole.**

8. According to the tool manufacturer's instructions, connect a remote starting switch to the starting circuit.
9. With the ignition switch in the **OFF** position, use the remote starting switch to crank the engine through at least five compression strokes (approximately 5 seconds of cranking) and record the highest reading on the gauge.
10. Repeat the test on each cylinder, cranking the engine approximately the same number of compression strokes and/or time as the first.
11. Compare the highest readings from each cylinder to that of the others. The indicated compression pressures are considered within specifications if the lowest reading cylinder is within 75 percent of the pressure recorded for the highest reading cylinder. For example, if your highest reading cylinder pressure was 150 psi (1034 kPa), then 75 percent of that would be 113 psi (779 kPa). So the lowest reading cylinder should be no less than 113 psi (779 kPa).
12. If a cylinder exhibits an unusually low compression reading, pour a tablespoon of clean engine oil into the cylinder through the spark plug hole and repeat the compression test. If the compression rises after adding oil, it means that the cylinder's piston rings and/or cylinder bore are damaged or worn. If the pressure remains low, the valves may not be seating properly (a valve job is needed), or the head gasket may be blown near that cylinder. If compression in any two adjacent cylinders is low, and if the addition of oil doesn't help raise compression, there is leakage past the head gasket. Oil and coolant in the combustion chamber, combined with blue or constant white smoke from the tail pipe, are symptoms of this problem. However, don't be alarmed by the normal white smoke emitted from the tail pipe during engine warm-up or from cold weather driving. There may be evidence of water droplets on the engine dipstick and/or oil droplets in the cooling system if a head gasket is blown.

### OIL PRESSURE TEST

Check for proper oil pressure at the sending unit passage with an externally mounted mechanical oil pressure gauge (as opposed to relying on a factory installed dash-mounted gauge). A tachometer may also be needed, as some specifications may require running the engine at a specific rpm.

1. With the engine cold, locate and remove the oil pressure sending unit.
2. Following the manufacturer's instructions, connect a mechanical oil pressure gauge and, if necessary, a tachometer to the engine.
3. Start the engine and allow it to idle.
4. Check the oil pressure reading when cold and record the number. You may need to run the engine at a specified rpm, so check the specifications chart located earlier in this section.
5. Run the engine until normal operating temperature is reached (upper radiator hose will feel warm).
6. Check the oil pressure reading again with the engine hot and record the number. Turn the engine **OFF**.
7. Compare your hot oil pressure reading to that given in the chart. If the reading is low, check the cold pressure reading against the chart. If the cold pressure is well above the specification, and the hot reading was lower than the specification, you may have the wrong viscosity oil in the engine. Change the oil, making sure to use the proper grade and quantity, then repeat the test.

Low oil pressure readings could be attributed to internal component wear, pump related problems, a low oil level, or oil viscosity that is too low. High oil pressure readings could be caused by an overfilled crankcase, too high of an oil viscosity or a faulty pressure relief valve.

## Buy Or Rebuild?

Now that you have determined that your engine is worn out, you must make some decisions. The question of whether or not an engine is worth rebuilding is largely a subjective matter and one of personal worth. Is the engine a popular one, or is it an obsolete model? Are parts available? Will it get acceptable gas mileage once it is rebuilt? Is the car its being put into worth keeping? Would it be less expensive to buy a new engine, have your engine rebuilt by a pro, rebuild it yourself or buy a used engine from a salvage yard? Or would it be simpler and less expensive to buy another car? If you have considered all these matters and more, and have still decided to rebuild the engine, then it is time to decide how you will rebuild it.

→**The editors at Chilton feel that most engine machining should be performed by a professional machine shop. Don't think of it as wasting money, rather, as an assurance that the job has been done right the first time. There are many expensive and specialized tools required to perform such tasks as boring and honing an engine block or having a valve job done on a cylinder head. Even inspecting the parts requires expensive micrometers and gauges to properly measure wear and clearances. Also, a machine shop can deliver to you clean, and ready to assemble parts, saving you time and aggravation. Your maximum savings will come from performing the removal, disassembly, assembly and installation of the engine and purchasing or renting only the tools required to perform the above tasks. Depending on the particular circumstances, you may save 40 to 60 percent of the cost doing these yourself.**

A complete rebuild or overhaul of an engine involves replacing all of the moving parts (pistons, rods, crankshaft, camshaft, etc.) with new ones and machining the non-moving wearing surfaces of the block and heads. Unfortunately, this may not be cost effective. For instance, your crankshaft may have been damaged or worn, but it can be machined undersize for a minimal fee.

So, as you can see, you can replace everything inside the engine, but, it is wiser to replace only those parts which are really needed, and, if possible, repair the more expensive ones. Later in this section, we will break the engine down into its two main components: the cylinder head and the engine block. We will discuss each component, and the recommended parts to replace during a rebuild on each.

## Engine Overhaul Tips

Most engine overhaul procedures are fairly standard. In addition to specific parts replacement procedures and specifications for your individual engine, this section is also a guide to acceptable rebuilding procedures. Examples of standard rebuilding practice are given and should be used along with specific details concerning your particular engine.

Competent and accurate machine shop services will ensure maximum performance, reliability and engine life. In most instances it is more profitable for the do-it-yourself mechanic to remove, clean and inspect the component, buy the necessary parts and deliver these to a shop for actual machine work.

Much of the assembly work (crankshaft, bearings, piston rods, and other components) is well within the scope of the do-it-yourself mechanic's tools and abilities. You will have to decide for yourself the depth of involvement you desire in an engine repair or rebuild.

## TOOLS

The tools required for an engine overhaul or parts replacement will depend on the depth of your involvement. With a few exceptions, they will be the tools found in a mechanic's tool kit (see Section 1 of this manual). More in-depth work will require some or all of the following:
- A dial indicator (reading in thousandths) mounted on a universal base
- Micrometers and telescope gauges
- Jaw and screw-type pullers
- Scraper
- Valve spring compressor
- Ring groove cleaner
- Piston ring expander and compressor
- Ridge reamer
- Cylinder hone or glaze breaker
- Plastigage®
- Engine stand

The use of most of these tools is illustrated in this section. Many can be rented for a one-time use from a local parts jobber or tool supply house specializing in automotive work.

Occasionally, the use of special tools is called for. See the information on Special Tools and the Safety Notice in the front of this book before substituting another tool.

## OVERHAUL TIPS

Aluminum has become extremely popular for use in engines, due to its low weight. Observe the following precautions when handling aluminum parts:
- Never hot tank aluminum parts (the caustic hot tank solution will eat the aluminum.
- Remove all aluminum parts (identification tag, etc.) from engine parts prior to the tanking.
- Always coat threads lightly with engine oil or anti-seize compounds before installation, to prevent seizure.
- Never overtighten bolts or spark plugs especially in aluminum threads.

When assembling the engine, any parts that will be exposed to frictional contact must be prelubed to provide lubrication at initial start-up. Any product specifically formulated for this purpose can be used, but engine oil is not recommended as a prelube in most cases.

When semi-permanent (locked, but removable) installation of bolts or nuts is desired, threads should be cleaned and coated with Loctite® or another similar, commercial non-hardening sealant.

## CLEANING

▶ **See Figures 154, 155, 156 and 157**

Before the engine and its components are inspected, they must be thoroughly cleaned. You will need to remove any engine varnish, oil sludge and/or carbon deposits from all of the components to insure an accurate inspection. A crack in the engine block or cylinder head can easily become overlooked if hidden by a layer of sludge or carbon.

TCCS3132

**Fig. 154 Use a gasket scraper to remove the old gasket material from the mating surfaces**

TCCS3211

**Fig. 155 Use a ring expander tool to remove the piston rings**

TCCS3208

**Fig. 156 Clean the piston ring grooves using a ring groove cleaner tool, or . . .**

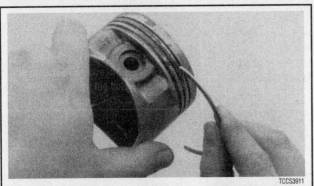

Fig. 157 . . . use a piece of an old ring to clean the grooves. Be careful, the ring can be quite sharp

Most of the cleaning process can be carried out with common hand tools and readily available solvents or solutions. Carbon deposits can be chipped away using a hammer and a hard wooden chisel. Old gasket material and varnish or sludge can usually be removed using a scraper and/or cleaning solvent. Extremely stubborn deposits may require the use of a power drill with a wire brush. If using a wire brush, use extreme care around any critical machined surfaces (such as the gasket surfaces, bearing saddles, cylinder bores, etc.). USE OF A WIRE BRUSH IS NOT RECOMMENDED ON ANY ALUMINUM COMPONENTS. Always follow any safety recommendations given by the manufacturer of the tool and/or solvent. You should always wear eye protection during any cleaning process involving scraping, chipping or spraying of solvents.

An alternative to the mess and hassle of cleaning the parts yourself is to drop them off at a local garage or machine shop. They will, more than likely, have the necessary equipment to properly clean all of the parts for a nominal fee.

### ✳✳ CAUTION

**Always wear eye protection during any cleaning process involving scraping, chipping or spraying of solvents.**

Remove any oil galley plugs, freeze plugs and/or pressed-in bearings and carefully wash and degrease all of the engine components including the fasteners and bolts. Small parts such as the valves, springs, etc., should be placed in a metal basket and allowed to soak. Use pipe cleaner type brushes, and clean all passageways in the components. Use a ring expander and remove the rings from the pistons. Clean the piston ring grooves with a special tool or a piece of broken ring. Scrape the carbon off of the top of the piston. You should never use a wire brush on the pistons. After preparing all of the piston assemblies in this manner, wash and degrease them again.

### ✳✳ WARNING

**Use extreme care when cleaning around the cylinder head valve seats. A mistake or slip may cost you a new seat.**

When cleaning the cylinder head, remove carbon from the combustion chamber with the valves installed. This will avoid damaging the valve seats.

## REPAIRING DAMAGED THREADS

▶ **See Figures 158, 159, 160, 161 and 162**

Several methods of repairing damaged threads are available. Heli-Coil® (shown here), Keenserts® and Microdot® are among the most widely used. All involve basically the same principle—drilling out stripped threads, tapping the hole and installing a prewound insert—making welding, plugging and oversize fasteners unnecessary.

Two types of thread repair inserts are usually supplied: a standard type for most inch coarse, inch fine, metric course and metric fine thread sizes and a spark lug type to fit most spark plug port sizes. Consult the individual tool manufacturer's catalog to determine exact applications. Typical thread repair kits will contain a selection of prewound threaded inserts, a tap (corresponding to the

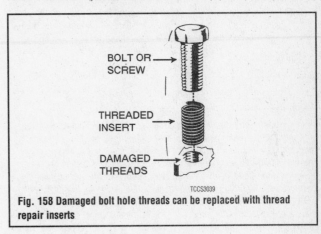

Fig. 158 Damaged bolt hole threads can be replaced with thread repair inserts

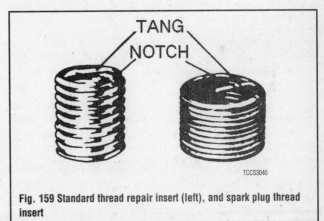

Fig. 159 Standard thread repair insert (left), and spark plug thread insert

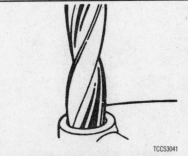

Fig. 160 Drill out the damaged threads with the specified size bit. Be sure to drill completely through the hole or to the bottom of a blind hole

Fig. 161 Using the kit, tap the hole in order to receive the thread insert. Keep the tap well oiled and back it out frequently to avoid clogging the threads

Fig. 162 Screw the insert onto the installer tool until the tang engages the slot. Thread the insert into the hole until it is ¼–½ turn below the top surface, then remove the tool and break off the tang using a punch

outside diameter threads of the insert) and an installation tool. Spark plug inserts usually differ because they require a tap equipped with pilot threads and a combined reamer/tap section. Most manufacturers also supply blister-packed thread repair inserts separately in addition to a master kit containing a variety of taps and inserts plus installation tools.

Before attempting to repair a threaded hole, remove any snapped, broken or damaged bolts or studs. Penetrating oil can be used to free frozen threads. The offending item can usually be removed with locking pliers or using a screw/stud extractor. After the hole is clear, the thread can be repaired, as shown in the series of accompanying illustrations and in the kit manufacturer's instructions.

## Engine Preparation

To properly rebuild an engine, you must first remove it from the vehicle, then disassemble and diagnose it. Ideally you should place your engine on an engine stand. This affords you the best access to the engine components. Follow the manufacturer's directions for using the stand with your particular engine. Remove the flywheel or flexplate before installing the engine to the stand.

Now that you have the engine on a stand, and assuming that you have drained the oil and coolant from the engine, its time to strip it of all but the necessary components. Before you start disassembling the engine, you may want to take a moment to draw some pictures, or fabricate some labels or containers to mark the locations of various components and the bolts and/or studs which fasten them. Modern day engines use a lot of little brackets and clips which hold wiring harnesses and such, and these holders are often mounted on studs and/or bolts that can be easily mixed up. The manufacturer spent a lot of time and money designing your vehicle, and they wouldn't have wasted any of it by haphazardly placing brackets, clips or fasteners on the vehicle. If its present when you disassemble it, put it back when you assemble, you will regret not remembering that little bracket which holds a wire harness out of the path of a rotating part.

You should begin by unbolting any accessories still attached to the engine, such as the water pump, power steering pump, alternator, etc. Then, unfasten any manifolds (intake or exhaust) which were not removed during the engine removal procedure. Finally, remove any covers remaining on the engine such as the rocker arm, front or timing cover and oil pan. Some front covers may require the vibration damper and/or crank pulley to be removed beforehand. The idea is to reduce the engine to the bare necessities (cylinder head(s), valve train, engine block, crankshaft, pistons and connecting rods), plus any other `in block' components such as oil pumps, balance shafts and auxiliary shafts.

Finally, remove the cylinder head(s) from the engine block and carefully place on a bench. Disassembly instructions for each component follow later in this section.

## Cylinder Head

There are two basic types of cylinder heads used on today's automobiles: the Overhead Valve (OHV) and the Overhead Camshaft (OHC). The latter can also be broken down into two subgroups: the Single Overhead Camshaft (SOHC) and the Dual Overhead Camshaft (DOHC). Generally, if there is only a single camshaft on a head, it is just referred to as an OHC head. Also, an engine with an OHV cylinder head is also known as a pushrod engine.

Most cylinder heads these days are made of an aluminum alloy due to its light weight, durability and heat transfer qualities. However, cast iron was the material of choice in the past, and is still used on many vehicles today. Whether made from aluminum or iron, all cylinder heads have valves and seats. Some use two valves per cylinder, while the more hi-tech engines will utilize a multi-valve configuration using 3, 4 and even 5 valves per cylinder. When the valve contacts the seat, it does so on precision machined surfaces, which seals the combustion chamber. All cylinder heads have a valve guide for each valve. The guide centers the valve to the seat and allows it to move up and down within it. The clearance between the valve and guide can be critical. Too much clearance and the engine may consume oil, lose vacuum and/or damage the seat. Too little, and the valve can stick in the guide causing the engine to run poorly if at all, and possibly causing severe damage. The last component all cylinder heads have are valve springs. The spring holds the valve against its seat. It also returns the valve to this position when the valve has been opened by the valve train or camshaft. The spring is fastened to the valve by a retainer and valve locks (sometimes called keepers). Aluminum heads will also have a valve spring shim to keep the spring from wearing away the aluminum.

An ideal method of rebuilding the cylinder head would involve replacing all of the valves, guides, seats, springs, etc. with new ones. However, depending on how the engine was maintained, often this is not necessary. A major cause of valve, guide and seat wear is an improperly tuned engine. An engine that is running too rich, will often wash the lubricating oil out of the guide with gasoline, causing it to wear rapidly. Conversely, an engine which is running too lean will place higher combustion temperatures on the valves and seats allowing them to wear or even burn. Springs fall victim to the driving habits of the individual. A driver who often runs the engine rpm to the redline will wear out or break the springs faster then one that stays well below it. Unfortunately, mileage takes its toll on all of the parts. Generally, the valves, guides, springs and seats in a cylinder head can be machined and re-used, saving you money. However, if a valve is burnt, it may be wise to replace all of the valves, since they were all operating in the same environment. The same goes for any other component on the cylinder head. Think of it as an insurance policy against future problems related to that component.

Unfortunately, the only way to find out which components need replacing, is to disassemble and carefully check each piece. After the cylinder head(s) are disassembled, thoroughly clean all of the components.

### DISASSEMBLY

◗ **See Figures 163 and 164**

Whether it is a single or dual overhead camshaft cylinder head, the disassembly procedure is relatively unchanged. One aspect to pay attention to is careful labeling of the parts on the dual camshaft cylinder head. There will be an intake camshaft and followers as well as an exhaust camshaft and followers and they must be labeled as such. In some cases, the components are identical and could easily be installed incorrectly. DO NOT MIX THEM UP! Determining which is which is very simple; the intake camshaft and components are on the same side of the head as was the intake manifold. Conversely, the exhaust camshaft and components are on the same side of the head as was the exhaust manifold.

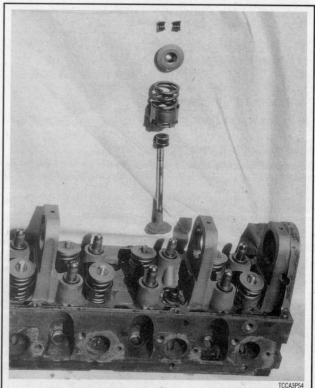

TCCA3P54

**Fig. 163 Exploded view of a valve, seal, spring, retainer and locks from an OHC cylinder head**

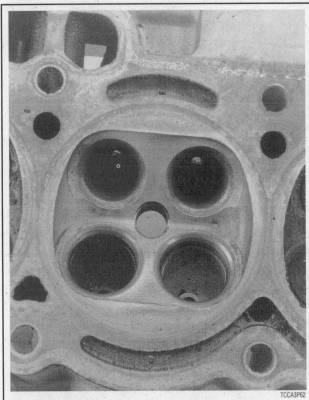

Fig. 164 Example of a multi-valve cylinder head. Note how it has 2 intake and 2 exhaust valve ports

Fig. 166 Most cup type follower cylinder heads retain the camshaft using bolt-on bearing caps

Fig. 167 Position the OHC spring tool in the follower bore, then compress the spring with a C-clamp type tool

## CUP TYPE CAMSHAFT FOLLOWERS

▶ See Figures 165, 166 and 167

Most cylinder heads with cup type camshaft followers will have the valve spring, retainer and locks recessed within the follower's bore. You will need a C-clamp style valve spring compressor tool, an OHC spring removal tool (or equivalent) and a small magnet to disassemble the head.

1. If not already removed, remove the camshaft(s) and/or followers. Mark their positions for assembly.

2. Position the cylinder head to allow use of a C-clamp style valve spring compressor tool.

➡It is preferred to position the cylinder head gasket surface facing you with the valve springs facing the opposite direction and the head laying horizontal.

3. With the OHC spring removal adapter tool positioned inside of the follower bore, compress the valve spring using the C-clamp style valve spring compressor.

Fig. 165 C-clamp type spring compressor and an OHC spring removal tool (center) for cup type followers

4. Remove the valve locks. A small magnetic tool or screwdriver will aid in removal.

5. Release the compressor tool and remove the spring assembly.

6. Withdraw the valve from the cylinder head.

7. If equipped, remove the valve seal.

➡Special valve seal removal tools are available. Regular or needlenose type pliers, if used with care, will work just as well. If using ordinary pliers, be sure not to damage the follower bore. The follower and its bore are machined to close tolerances and any damage to the bore will effect this relationship.

8. If equipped, remove the valve spring shim. A small magnetic tool or screwdriver will aid in removal.

9. Repeat Steps 3 through 8 until all of the valves have been removed.

## ROCKER ARM TYPE CAMSHAFT FOLLOWERS

▶ See Figures 168 thru 176

Most cylinder heads with rocker arm-type camshaft followers are easily disassembled using a standard valve spring compressor. However, certain models may not have enough open space around the spring for the standard tool and may require you to use a C-clamp style compressor tool instead.

Fig. 168 Example of the shaft mounted rocker arms on some OHC heads

Fig. 169 Another example of the rocker arm type OHC head. This model uses a follower under the camshaft

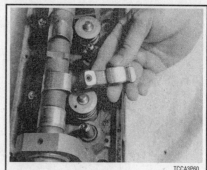

Fig. 170 Before the camshaft can be removed, all of the followers must first be removed . . .

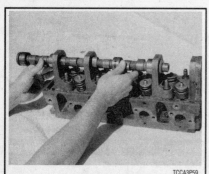

Fig. 171 . . . then the camshaft can be removed by sliding it out (shown), or unbolting a bearing cap (not shown)

Fig. 172 Compress the valve spring . . .

Fig. 173 . . . then remove the valve locks from the valve stem and spring retainer

Fig. 174 Remove the valve spring and retainer from the cylinder head

Fig. 175 Remove the valve seal from the guide. Some gentle prying or pliers may help to remove stubborn ones

Fig. 176 All aluminum and some cast iron heads will have these valve spring shims. Remove all of them as well

1. If not already removed, remove the rocker arms and/or shafts and the camshaft. If applicable, also remove the hydraulic lash adjusters. Mark their positions for assembly.

2. Position the cylinder head to allow access to the valve spring.

3. Use a valve spring compressor tool to relieve the spring tension from the retainer.

➡Due to engine varnish, the retainer may stick to the valve locks. A gentle tap with a hammer may help to break it loose.

4. Remove the valve locks from the valve tip and/or retainer. A small magnet may help in removing the small locks.

5. Lift the valve spring, tool and all, off of the valve stem.

6. If equipped, remove the valve seal. If the seal is difficult to remove with the valve in place, try removing the valve first, then the seal. Follow the steps below for valve removal.

7. Position the head to allow access for withdrawing the valve.

➡Cylinder heads that have seen a lot of miles and/or abuse may have mushroomed the valve lock grove and/or tip, causing difficulty in removal of the valve. If this has happened, use a metal file to carefully remove the high spots around the lock grooves and/or tip. Only file it enough to allow removal.

8. Remove the valve from the cylinder head.

9. If equipped, remove the valve spring shim. A small magnetic tool or screwdriver will aid in removal.

10. Repeat Steps 3 though 9 until all of the valves have been removed.

## INSPECTION

Now that all of the cylinder head components are clean, its time to inspect them for wear and/or damage. To accurately inspect them, you will need some specialized tools:

- A 0–1 in. micrometer for the valves
- A dial indicator or inside diameter gauge for the valve guides
- A spring pressure test gauge

If you do not have access to the proper tools, you may want to bring the components to a shop that does.

### Valves

▶ **See Figures 177 and 178**

The first thing to inspect are the valve heads. Look closely at the head, margin and face for any cracks, excessive wear or burning. The margin is the best place to look for burning. It should have a squared edge with an even width all around the diameter. When a valve burns, the margin will look melted and the edges rounded. Also inspect the valve head for any signs of tulipping. This will show as a lifting of the edges or dishing in the center of the head and will usually not occur to all of the valves. All of the heads should look the same, any that seem dished more than others are probably bad. Next, inspect the valve

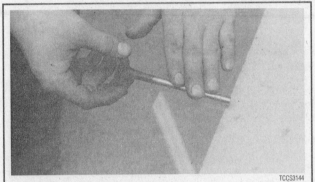

Fig. 177 Valve stems may be rolled on a flat surface to check for bends

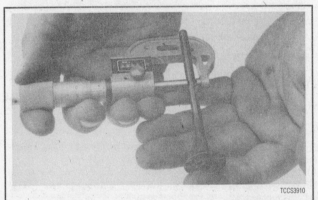

Fig. 178 Use a micrometer to check the valve stem diameter

lock grooves and valve tips. Check for any burrs around the lock grooves, especially if you had to file them to remove the valve. Valve tips should appear flat, although slight rounding with high mileage engines is normal. Slightly worn valve tips will need to be machined flat. Last, measure the valve stem diameter with the micrometer. Measure the area that rides within the guide, especially towards the tip where most of the wear occurs. Take several measurements along its length and compare them to each other. Wear should be even along the length with little to no taper. If no minimum diameter is given in the specifications, then the stem should not read more than 0.001 in. (0.025mm) below the specification. Any valves that fail these inspections should be replaced.

### Springs, Retainers and Valve Locks

▶ **See Figures 179 and 180**

The first thing to check is the most obvious, broken springs. Next check the free length and squareness of each spring. If applicable, insure to distinguish between intake and exhaust springs. Use a ruler and/or carpenters square to measure the length. A carpenters square should be used to check the springs for squareness. If a spring pressure test gauge is available, check each springs rating and compare to the specifications chart. Check the readings against the specifications given. Any springs that fail these inspections should be replaced.

The spring retainers rarely need replacing, however they should still be checked as a precaution. Inspect the spring mating surface and the valve lock retention area for any signs of excessive wear. Also check for any signs of cracking. Replace any retainers that are questionable.

Valve locks should be inspected for excessive wear on the outside contact area as well as on the inner notched surface. Any locks which appear worn or broken and its respective valve should be replaced.

### Cylinder Head

There are several things to check on the cylinder head: valve guides, seats, cylinder head surface flatness, cracks and physical damage.

#### *VALVE GUIDES*

▶ **See Figure 181**

Now that you know the valves are good, you can use them to check the guides, although a new valve, if available, is preferred. Before you measure anything, look at the guides carefully and inspect them for any cracks, chips or breakage. Also if the guide is a removable style (as in most aluminum heads), check them for any looseness or evidence of movement. All of the guides should appear to be at the same height from the spring seat. If any seem lower (or higher) from another, the guide has moved. Mount a dial indicator onto the spring side of the cylinder head. Lightly oil the valve stem and insert it into the cylinder head. Position the dial indicator against the valve stem near the tip and zero the gauge. Grasp the valve stem and wiggle towards and away from the dial indicator and observe the readings. Mount the dial indicator 90 degrees from the initial point and zero the gauge and again take a reading. Compare the two readings for a out of round condition. Check the readings against the specifications given. An Inside Diameter (I.D.) gauge designed for valve guides will give you an accurate valve guide bore measurement. If the I.D. gauge is used, compare the readings with the specifications given. Any guides that fail these inspections should be replaced or machined.

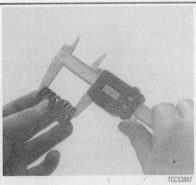

Fig. 179 Use a caliper to check the valve spring free-length

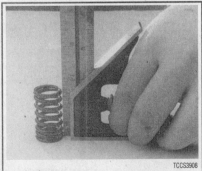

Fig. 180 Check the valve spring for squareness on a flat surface; a carpenter's square can be used

Fig. 181 A dial gauge may be used to check valve stem-to-guide clearance; read the gauge while moving the valve stem

### VALVE SEATS

A visual inspection of the valve seats should show a slightly worn and pitted surface where the valve face contacts the seat. Inspect the seat carefully for severe pitting or cracks. Also, a seat that is badly worn will be recessed into the cylinder head. A severely worn or recessed seat may need to be replaced. All cracked seats must be replaced. A seat concentricity gauge, if available, should be used to check the seat run-out. If run-out exceeds specifications the seat must be machined (if no specification is given use 0.002 in. or 0.051mm).

### CYLINDER HEAD SURFACE FLATNESS

▶ **See Figures 182 and 183**

After you have cleaned the gasket surface of the cylinder head of any old gasket material, check the head for flatness.

Place a straightedge across the gasket surface. Using feeler gauges, determine the clearance at the center of the straightedge and across the cylinder head at several points. Check along the centerline and diagonally on the head surface. If the warpage exceeds 0.003 in. (0.076mm) within a 6.0 in. (15.2cm) span, or 0.006 in. (0.152mm) over the total length of the head, the cylinder head must be resurfaced. After resurfacing the heads of a V-type engine, the intake manifold flange surface should be checked, and if necessary, milled proportionally to allow for the change in its mounting position.

### CRACKS AND PHYSICAL DAMAGE

Generally, cracks are limited to the combustion chamber, however, it is not uncommon for the head to crack in a spark plug hole, port, outside of the head or in the valve spring/rocker arm area. The first area to inspect is always the hottest: the exhaust seat/port area.

A visual inspection should be performed, but just because you don't see a crack does not mean it is not there. Some more reliable methods for inspecting for cracks include Magnaflux®, a magnetic process or Zyglo®, a dye penetrant. Magnaflux® is used only on ferrous metal (cast iron) heads. Zyglo® uses a spray on fluorescent mixture along with a black light to reveal the cracks. It is strongly recommended to have your cylinder head checked professionally for cracks,

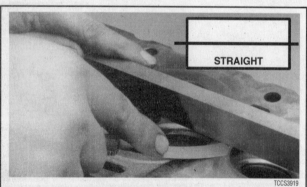

Fig. 182 Check the head for flatness across the center of the head surface using a straightedge and feeler gauge

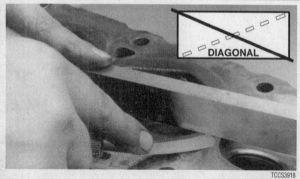

Fig. 183 Checks should also be made along both diagonals of the head surface

especially if the engine was known to have overheated and/or leaked or consumed coolant. Contact a local shop for availability and pricing of these services.

Physical damage is usually very evident. For example, a broken mounting ear from dropping the head or a bent or broken stud and/or bolt. All of these defects should be fixed or, if unrepairable, the head should be replaced.

### Camshaft and Followers

Inspect the camshaft(s) and followers as described earlier in this section.

## REFINISHING & REPAIRING

Many of the procedures given for refinishing and repairing the cylinder head components must be performed by a machine shop. Certain steps, if the inspected part is not worn, can be performed yourself inexpensively. However, you spent a lot of time and effort so far, why risk trying to save a couple bucks if you might have to do it all over again?

### Valves

Any valves that were not replaced should be refaced and the tips ground flat. Unless you have access to a valve grinding machine, this should be done by a machine shop. If the valves are in extremely good condition, as well as the valve seats and guides, they may be lapped in without performing machine work.

It is a recommended practice to lap the valves even after machine work has been performed and/or new valves have been purchased. This insures a positive seal between the valve and seat.

### LAPPING THE VALVES

➡**Before lapping the valves to the seats, read the rest of the cylinder head section to insure that any related parts are in acceptable enough condition to continue.**

➡**Before any valve seat machining and/or lapping can be performed, the guides must be within factory recommended specifications.**

1. Invert the cylinder head.
2. Lightly lubricate the valve stems and insert them into the cylinder head in their numbered order.
3. Raise the valve from the seat and apply a small amount of fine lapping compound to the seat.
4. Moisten the suction head of a hand-lapping tool and attach it to the head of the valve.
5. Rotate the tool between the palms of both hands, changing the position of the valve on the valve seat and lifting the tool often to prevent grooving.
6. Lap the valve until a smooth, polished circle is evident on the valve and seat.
7. Remove the tool and the valve. Wipe away all traces of the grinding compound and store the valve to maintain its lapped location.

### ✳✳ WARNING

**Do not get the valves out of order after they have been lapped. They must be put back with the same valve seat with which they were lapped.**

### Springs, Retainers and Valve Locks

There is no repair or refinishing possible with the springs, retainers and valve locks. If they are found to be worn or defective, they must be replaced with new (or known good) parts.

### Cylinder Head

Most refinishing procedures dealing with the cylinder head must be performed by a machine shop. Read the sections below and review your inspection data to determine whether or not machining is necessary.

### VALVE GUIDE

➡**If any machining or replacements are made to the valve guides, the seats must be machined.**

Unless the valve guides need machining or replacing, the only service to perform is to thoroughly clean them of any dirt or oil residue.

There are only two types of valve guides used on automobile engines: the replaceable-type (all aluminum heads) and the cast-in integral-type (most cast iron heads). There are four recommended methods for repairing worn guides.

- Knurling
- Inserts
- Reaming oversize
- Replacing

Knurling is a process in which metal is displaced and raised, thereby reducing clearance, giving a true center, and providing oil control. It is the least expensive way of repairing the valve guides. However, it is not necessarily the best, and in some cases, a knurled valve guide will not stand up for more than a short time. It requires a special knurlizer and precision reaming tools to obtain proper clearances. It would not be cost effective to purchase these tools, unless you plan on rebuilding several of the same cylinder head.

Installing a guide insert involves machining the guide to accept a bronze insert. One style is the coil-type which is installed into a threaded guide. Another is the thin-walled insert where the guide is reamed oversize to accept a split-sleeve insert. After the insert is installed, a special tool is then run through the guide to expand the insert, locking it to the guide. The insert is then reamed to the standard size for proper valve clearance.

Reaming for oversize valves restores normal clearances and provides a true valve seat. Most cast-in type guides can be reamed to accept an valve with an oversize stem. The cost factor for this can become quite high as you will need to purchase the reamer and new, oversize stem valves for all guides which were reamed. Oversizes are generally 0.003 to 0.030 in. (0.076 to 0.762mm), with 0.015 in. (0.381mm) being the most common.

To replace cast-in type valve guides, they must be drilled out, then reamed to accept replacement guides. This must be done on a fixture which will allow centering and leveling off of the original valve seat or guide, otherwise a serious guide-to-seat misalignment may occur making it impossible to properly machine the seat.

Replaceable-type guides are pressed into the cylinder head. A hammer and a stepped drift or punch may be used to install and remove the guides. Before removing the guides, measure the protrusion on the spring side of the head and record it for installation. Use the stepped drift to hammer out the old guide from the combustion chamber side of the head. When installing, determine whether or not the guide also seals a water jacket in the head, and if it does, use the recommended sealing agent. If there is no water jacket, grease the valve guide and its bore. Use the stepped drift, and hammer the new guide into the cylinder head from the spring side of the cylinder head. A stack of washers the same thickness as the measured protrusion may help the installation process.

### VALVE SEATS

➡**Before any valve seat machining can be performed, the guides must be within factory recommended specifications.**

➡**If any machining or replacements were made to the valve guides, the seats must be machined.**

If the seats are in good condition, the valves can be lapped to the seats, and the cylinder head assembled. See the valves section for instructions on lapping.

If the valve seats are worn, cracked or damaged, they must be serviced by a machine shop. The valve seat must be perfectly centered to the valve guide, which requires very accurate machining.

### CYLINDER HEAD SURFACE

If the cylinder head is warped, it must be machined flat. If the warpage is extremely severe, the head may need to be replaced. In some instances, it may be possible to straighten a warped head enough to allow machining. In either case, contact a professional machine shop for service.

➡**Any OHC cylinder head that shows excessive warpage should have the camshaft bearing journals align bored after the cylinder head has been resurfaced.**

### ❄❄ WARNING

**Failure to align bore the camshaft bearing journals could result in severe engine damage including but not limited to: valve and piston**

damage, connecting rod damage, camshaft and/or crankshaft breakage.

### CRACKS AND PHYSICAL DAMAGE

Certain cracks can be repaired in both cast iron and aluminum heads. For cast iron, a tapered threaded insert is installed along the length of the crack. Aluminum can also use the tapered inserts, however welding is the preferred method. Some physical damage can be repaired through brazing or welding. Contact a machine shop to get expert advice for your particular dilemma.

## ASSEMBLY

The first step for any assembly job is to have a clean area in which to work. Next, thoroughly clean all of the parts and components that are to be assembled. Finally, place all of the components onto a suitable work space and, if necessary, arrange the parts to their respective positions.

### OHC Engines

▶ **See Figure 184**

### CUP TYPE CAMSHAFT FOLLOWERS

To install the springs, retainers and valve locks on heads which have these components recessed into the camshaft follower's bore, you will need a small screwdriver-type tool, some clean white grease and a lot of patience. You will also need the C-clamp style spring compressor and the OHC tool used to disassemble the head.

1. Lightly lubricate the valve stems and insert all of the valves into the cylinder head. If possible, maintain their original locations.
2. If equipped, install any valve spring shims which were removed.
3. If equipped, install the new valve seals, keeping the following in mind:
- If the valve seal presses over the guide, lightly lubricate the outer guide surfaces.
- If the seal is an O-ring type, it is installed just after compressing the spring but before the valve locks.
4. Place the valve spring and retainer over the stem.
5. Position the spring compressor and the OHC tool, then compress the spring.
6. Using a small screwdriver as a spatula, fill the valve stem side of the lock with white grease. Use the excess grease on the screwdriver to fasten the lock to the driver.
7. Carefully install the valve lock, which is stuck to the end of the screwdriver, to the valve stem then press on it with the screwdriver until the grease squeezes out. The valve lock should now be stuck to the stem.
8. Repeat Steps 6 and 7 for the remaining valve lock.
9. Relieve the spring pressure slowly and insure that neither valve lock becomes dislodged by the retainer.
10. Remove the spring compressor tool.
11. Repeat Steps 2 through 10 until all of the springs have been installed.
12. Install the followers, camshaft(s) and any other components that were removed for disassembly.

Fig. 184 Once assembled, check the valve clearance and correct as needed

### ROCKER ARM TYPE CAMSHAFT FOLLOWERS

1. Lightly lubricate the valve stems and insert all of the valves into the cylinder head. If possible, maintain their original locations.

2. If equipped, install any valve spring shims which were removed.

3. If equipped, install the new valve seals, keeping the following in mind:

• If the valve seal presses over the guide, lightly lubricate the outer guide surfaces.

• If the seal is an O-ring type, it is installed just after compressing the spring but before the valve locks.

4. Place the valve spring and retainer over the stem.

5. Position the spring compressor tool and compress the spring.

6. Assemble the valve locks to the stem.

7. Relieve the spring pressure slowly and insure that neither valve lock becomes dislodged by the retainer.

8. Remove the spring compressor tool.

9. Repeat Steps 2 through 8 until all of the springs have been installed.

10. Install the camshaft(s), rockers, shafts and any other components that were removed for disassembly.

## Engine Block

### GENERAL INFORMATION

A thorough overhaul or rebuild of an engine block would include replacing the pistons, rings, bearings, timing belt/chain assembly and oil pump. For OHV engines also include a new camshaft and lifters. The block would then have the cylinders bored and honed oversize (or if using removable cylinder sleeves, new sleeves installed) and the crankshaft would be cut undersize to provide new wearing surfaces and perfect clearances. However, your particular engine may not have everything worn out. What if only the piston rings have worn out and the clearances on everything else are still within factory specifications? Well, you could just replace the rings and put it back together, but this would be a very rare example. Chances are, if one component in your engine is worn, other components are sure to follow, and soon. At the very least, you should always replace the rings, bearings and oil pump. This is what is commonly called a "freshen up".

### Cylinder Ridge Removal

Because the top piston ring does not travel to the very top of the cylinder, a ridge is built up between the end of the travel and the top of the cylinder bore.

Pushing the piston and connecting rod assembly past the ridge can be difficult, and damage to the piston ring lands could occur. If the ridge is not removed before installing a new piston or not removed at all, piston ring breakage and piston damage may occur.

➡️It is always recommended that you remove any cylinder ridges before removing the piston and connecting rod assemblies. If you know that new pistons are going to be installed and the engine block will be bored oversize, you may be able to forego this step. However, some ridges may actually prevent the assemblies from being removed, necessitating its removal.

There are several different types of ridge reamers on the market, none of which are inexpensive. Unless a great deal of engine rebuilding is anticipated, borrow or rent a reamer.

1. Turn the crankshaft until the piston is at the bottom of its travel.

2. Cover the head of the piston with a rag.

3. Follow the tool manufacturers instructions and cut away the ridge, exercising extreme care to avoid cutting too deeply.

4. Remove the ridge reamer, the rag and as many of the cuttings as possible. Continue until all of the cylinder ridges have been removed.

### DISASSEMBLY

▸ **See Figures 185 and 186**

The engine disassembly instructions following assume that you have the engine mounted on an engine stand. If not, it is easiest to disassemble the engine on a bench or the floor with it resting on the bell housing or transmis-

Fig. 185 Place rubber hose over the connecting rod studs to protect the crankshaft and cylinder bores from damage

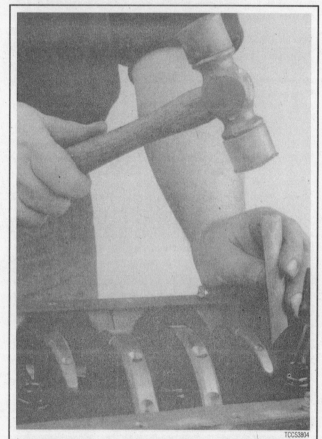

Fig. 186 Carefully tap the piston out of the bore using a wooden dowel

sion mounting surface. You must be able to access the connecting rod fasteners and turn the crankshaft during disassembly. Also, all engine covers (timing, front, side, oil pan, whatever) should have already been removed. Engines which are seized or locked up may not be able to be completely disassembled, and a core (salvage yard) engine should be purchased.

### OHC Engines

If not done during the cylinder head removal, remove the timing chain/belt and/or gear/sprocket assembly. Remove the oil pick-up and pump assembly and, if necessary, the pump drive. If equipped, remove any balance or auxiliary shafts. If necessary, remove the cylinder ridge from the top of the bore. See the cylinder ridge removal procedure earlier in this section.

**All Engines**

Rotate the engine over so that the crankshaft is exposed. Use a number punch or scribe and mark each connecting rod with its respective cylinder number. The cylinder closest to the front of the engine is always No. 1. However, depending on the engine placement, the front of the engine could either be the flywheel or damper/pulley end. Generally the front of the engine faces the front of the vehicle. Use a number punch or scribe and also mark the main bearing caps from front to rear with the frontmost cap being No. 1 (if there are five caps, mark them 1 through 5, front to rear).

### ✳ WARNING

**Take special care when pushing the connecting rod up from the crankshaft because the sharp threads of the rod bolts/studs will score the crankshaft journal. Insure that special plastic caps are installed over them, or cut two pieces of rubber hose to do the same.**

Again, rotate the engine, this time to position the number one cylinder bore (head surface) up. Turn the crankshaft until the number one piston is at the bottom of its travel, this should allow the maximum access to its connecting rod. Remove the number one connecting rods fasteners and cap and place two lengths of rubber hose over the rod bolts/studs to protect the crankshaft from damage. Using a sturdy wooden dowel and a hammer, push the connecting rod up about 1 in. (25mm) from the crankshaft and remove the upper bearing insert. Continue pushing or tapping the connecting rod up until the piston rings are out of the cylinder bore. Remove the piston and rod by hand, put the upper half of the bearing insert back into the rod, install the cap with its bearing insert installed, and hand-tighten the cap fasteners. If the parts are kept in order in this manner, they will not get lost and you will be able to tell which bearings came form what cylinder if any problems are discovered and diagnosis is necessary. Remove all the other piston assemblies in the same manner. On V-style engines, remove all of the pistons from one bank, then reposition the engine with the other cylinder bank head surface up, and remove that banks piston assemblies.

The only remaining component in the engine block should now be the crankshaft. Loosen the main bearing caps evenly until the fasteners can be turned by hand, then remove them and the caps. Remove the crankshaft from the engine block. Thoroughly clean all of the components.

## INSPECTION

Now that the engine block and all of its components are clean, its time to inspect them for wear and/or damage. To accurately inspect them, you will need some specialized tools:
- Two or three separate micrometers to measure the pistons and crankshaft journals
- A dial indicator
- Telescoping gauges for the cylinder bores
- A rod alignment fixture to check for bent connecting rods

If you do not have access to the proper tools, you may want to bring the components to a shop that does.

Generally, you shouldn't expect cracks in the engine block or its components unless it was known to leak, consume or mix engine fluids, it was severely overheated, or there was evidence of bad bearings and/or crankshaft damage. A visual inspection should be performed on all of the components, but just because you don't see a crack does not mean it is not there. Some more reliable methods for inspecting for cracks include Magnaflux®, a magnetic process or Zyglo®, a dye penetrant. Magnaflux® is used only on ferrous metal (cast iron). Zyglo® uses a spray on fluorescent mixture along with a black light to reveal the cracks. It is strongly recommended to have your engine block checked professionally for cracks, especially if the engine was known to have overheated and/or leaked or consumed coolant. Contact a local shop for availability and pricing of these services.

**Engine Block**

### ENGINE BLOCK BEARING ALIGNMENT

Remove the main bearing caps and, if still installed, the main bearing inserts. Inspect all of the main bearing saddles and caps for damage, burrs or high spots. If damage is found, and it is caused from a spun main bearing, the block will need to be align-bored or, if severe enough, replacement. Any burrs or high spots should be carefully removed with a metal file.

Place a straightedge on the bearing saddles, in the engine block, along the centerline of the crankshaft. If any clearance exists between the straightedge and the saddles, the block must be align-bored.

Align-boring consists of machining the main bearing saddles and caps by means of a flycutter that runs through the bearing saddles.

### DECK FLATNESS

The top of the engine block where the cylinder head mounts is called the deck. Insure that the deck surface is clean of dirt, carbon deposits and old gasket material. Place a straightedge across the surface of the deck along its centerline and, using feeler gauges, check the clearance along several points. Repeat the checking procedure with the straightedge placed along both diagonals of the deck surface. If the reading exceeds 0.003 in. (0.076mm) within a 6.0 in. (15.2cm) span, or 0.006 in. (0.152mm) over the total length of the deck, it must be machined.

### CYLINDER BORES

▶ **See Figure 187**

The cylinder bores house the pistons and are slightly larger than the pistons themselves. A common piston-to-bore clearance is 0.0015–0.0025 in. (0.0381–0.0635mm). Inspect and measure the cylinder bores. The bore should be checked for out-of-roundness, taper and size. The results of this inspection will determine whether the cylinder can be used in its existing size and condition, or a rebore to the next oversize is required (or in the case of removable sleeves, have replacements installed).

The amount of cylinder wall wear is always greater at the top of the cylinder than at the bottom. This wear is known as taper. Any cylinder that has a taper of 0.0012 in. (0.305mm) or more, must be rebored. Measurements are taken at a number of positions in each cylinder: at the top, middle and bottom and at two points at each position; that is, at a point 90 degrees from the crankshaft centerline, as well as a point parallel to the crankshaft centerline. The measurements are made with either a special dial indicator or a telescopic gauge and micrometer. If the necessary precision tools to check the bore are not available, take the block to a machine shop and have them mike it. Also if you don't have the tools to check the cylinder bores, chances are you will not have the necessary devices to check the pistons, connecting rods and crankshaft. Take these components with you and save yourself an extra trip.

For our procedures, we will use a telescopic gauge and a micrometer. You will need one of each, with a measuring range which covers your cylinder bore size.

1. Position the telescopic gauge in the cylinder bore, loosen the gauges lock and allow it to expand.

➡ **Your first two readings will be at the top of the cylinder bore, then proceed to the middle and finally the bottom, making a total of six measurements.**

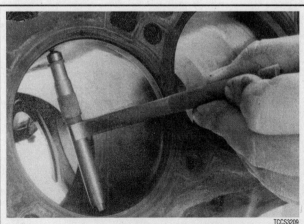

TCCS3209

**Fig. 187 Use a telescoping gauge to measure the cylinder bore diameter—take several readings within the same bore**

2. Hold the gauge square in the bore, 90 degrees from the crankshaft centerline, and gently tighten the lock. Tilt the gauge back to remove it from the bore.

3. Measure the gauge with the micrometer and record the reading.

4. Again, hold the gauge square in the bore, this time parallel to the crankshaft centerline, and gently tighten the lock. Again, you will tilt the gauge back to remove it from the bore.

5. Measure the gauge with the micrometer and record this reading. The difference between these two readings is the out-of-round measurement of the cylinder.

6. Repeat Steps 1 through 5, each time going to the next lower position, until you reach the bottom of the cylinder. Then go to the next cylinder, and continue until all of the cylinders have been measured.

The difference between these measurements will tell you all about the wear in your cylinders. The measurements which were taken 90 degrees from the crankshaft centerline will always reflect the most wear. That is because at this position is where the engine power presses the piston against the cylinder bore the hardest. This is known as thrust wear. Take your top, 90 degree measurement and compare it to your bottom, 90 degree measurement. The difference between them is the taper. When you measure your pistons, you will compare these readings to your piston sizes and determine piston-to-wall clearance.

### Crankshaft

Inspect the crankshaft for visible signs of wear or damage. All of the journals should be perfectly round and smooth. Slight scores are normal for a used crankshaft, but you should hardly feel them with your fingernail. When measuring the crankshaft with a micrometer, you will take readings at the front and rear of each journal, then turn the micrometer 90 degrees and take two more readings, front and rear. The difference between the front-to-rear readings is the journal taper and the first-to-90 degree reading is the out-of-round measurement. Generally, there should be no taper or out-of-roundness found, however, up to 0.0005 in. (0.0127mm) for either can be overlooked. Also, the readings should fall within the factory specifications for journal diameters.

If the crankshaft journals fall within specifications, it is recommended that it be polished before being returned to service. Polishing the crankshaft insures that any minor burrs or high spots are smoothed, thereby reducing the chance of scoring the new bearings.

### Pistons and Connecting Rods

#### PISTONS

▶ See Figure 188

The piston should be visually inspected for any signs of cracking or burning (caused by hot spots or detonation), and scuffing or excessive wear on the skirts. The wrist pin attaches the piston to the connecting rod. The piston should move freely on the wrist pin, both sliding and pivoting. Grasp the connecting rod securely, or mount it in a vise, and try to rock the piston back and forth along the centerline of the wrist pin. There should not be any exces-

sive play evident between the piston and the pin. If there are C-clips retaining the pin in the piston then you have wrist pin bushings in the rods. There should not be any excessive play between the wrist pin and the rod bushing. Normal clearance for the wrist pin is approx. 0.001–0.002 in. (0.025–0.051mm).

Use a micrometer and measure the diameter of the piston, perpendicular to the wrist pin, on the skirt. Compare the reading to its original cylinder measurement obtained earlier. The difference between the two readings is the piston-to-wall clearance. If the clearance is within specifications, the piston may be used as is. If the piston is out of specification, but the bore is not, you will need a new piston. If both are out of specification, you will need the cylinder rebored and oversize pistons installed. Generally if two or more pistons/bores are out of specification, it is best to rebore the entire block and purchase a complete set of oversize pistons.

#### CONNECTING ROD

You should have the connecting rod checked for straightness at a machine shop. If the connecting rod is bent, it will unevenly wear the bearing and piston, as well as place greater stress on these components. Any bent or twisted connecting rods must be replaced. If the rods are straight and the wrist pin clearance is within specifications, then only the bearing end of the rod need be checked. Place the connecting rod into a vice, with the bearing inserts in place, install the cap to the rod and torque the fasteners to specifications. Use a telescoping gauge and carefully measure the inside diameter of the bearings. Compare this reading to the rods original crankshaft journal diameter measurement. The difference is the oil clearance. If the oil clearance is not within specifications, install new bearings in the rod and take another measurement. If the clearance is still out of specifications, and the crankshaft is not, the rod will need to be reconditioned by a machine shop.

➡You can also use Plastigage® to check the bearing clearances. The assembling section has complete instructions on its use.

#### Camshaft

Inspect the camshaft and lifters/followers as described earlier in this section.

#### Bearings

All of the engine bearings should be visually inspected for wear and/or damage. The bearing should look evenly worn all around with no deep scores or pits. If the bearing is severely worn, scored, pitted or heat blued, then the bearing, and the components that use it, should be brought to a machine shop for inspection. Full-circle bearings (used on most camshafts, auxiliary shafts, balance shafts, etc.) require specialized tools for removal and installation, and should be brought to a machine shop for service.

#### Oil Pump

➡The oil pump is responsible for providing constant lubrication to the whole engine and so it is recommended that a new oil pump be installed when rebuilding the engine.

Completely disassemble the oil pump and thoroughly clean all of the components. Inspect the oil pump gears and housing for wear and/or damage. Insure that the pressure relief valve operates properly and there is no binding or sticking due to varnish or debris. If all of the parts are in proper working condition, lubricate the gears and relief valve, and assemble the pump.

### REFINISHING

▶ See Figure 189

Almost all engine block refinishing must be performed by a machine shop. If the cylinders are not to be rebored, then the cylinder glaze can be removed with a ball hone. When removing cylinder glaze with a ball hone, use a light or penetrating type oil to lubricate the hone. Do not allow the hone to run dry as this may cause excessive scoring of the cylinder bores and wear on the hone. If new pistons are required, they will need to be installed to the connecting rods. This should be performed by a machine shop as the pistons must be installed in the correct relationship to the rod or engine damage can occur.

TCCS3210

**Fig. 188 Measure the piston's outer diameter, perpendicular to the wrist pin, with a micrometer**

Fig. 189 Use a ball type cylinder hone to remove any glaze and provide a new surface for seating the piston rings

## Pistons and Connecting Rods

▶ See Figure 190

Only pistons with the wrist pin retained by C-clips are serviceable by the home-mechanic. Press fit pistons require special presses and/or heaters to remove/install the connecting rod and should only be performed by a machine shop.

All pistons will have a mark indicating the direction to the front of the engine and the must be installed into the engine in that manner. Usually it is a notch or arrow on the top of the piston, or it may be the letter F cast or stamped into the piston.

## ASSEMBLY

Before you begin assembling the engine, first give yourself a clean, dirt free work area. Next, clean every engine component again. The key to a good assembly is cleanliness.

Mount the engine block into the engine stand and wash it one last time using water and detergent (dishwashing detergent works well). While washing it, scrub the cylinder bores with a soft bristle brush and thoroughly clean all of the oil passages. Completely dry the engine and spray the entire assembly down with an anti-rust solution such as WD-40® or similar product. Take a clean lint-free rag and wipe up any excess anti-rust solution from the bores, bearing saddles, etc. Repeat the final cleaning process on the crankshaft. Replace any freeze or oil galley plugs which were removed during disassembly.

### Crankshaft

▶ See Figures 191, 192, 193 and 194

1. Remove the main bearing inserts from the block and bearing caps.
2. If the crankshaft main bearing journals have been refinished to a definite undersize, install the correct undersize bearing. Be sure that the bearing inserts and bearing bores are clean. Foreign material under inserts will distort bearing and cause failure.
3. Place the upper main bearing inserts in bores with tang in slot.

➡The oil holes in the bearing inserts must be aligned with the oil holes in the cylinder block.

4. Install the lower main bearing inserts in bearing caps.
5. Clean the mating surfaces of block and rear main bearing cap.

Fig. 190 Most pistons are marked to indicate positioning in the engine (usually a mark means the side facing the front)

Fig. 191 Apply a strip of gauging material to the bearing journal, then install and torque the cap

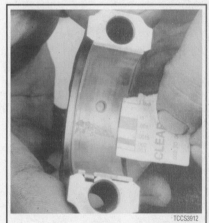

Fig. 192 After the cap is removed again, use the scale supplied with the gauging material to check the clearance

Fig. 193 A dial gauge may be used to check crankshaft end-play

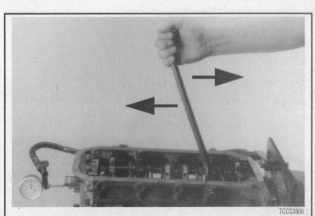

Fig. 194 Carefully pry the crankshaft back and forth while reading the dial gauge for end-play

6. Carefully lower the crankshaft into place. Be careful not to damage bearing surfaces.

7. Check the clearance of each main bearing by using the following procedure:

    a. Place a piece of Plastigage® or its equivalent, on bearing surface across full width of bearing cap and about ¼ in. off center.

    b. Install cap and tighten bolts to specifications. Do not turn crankshaft while Plastigage® is in place.

    c. Remove the cap. Using the supplied Plastigage® scale, check width of Plastigage® at widest point to get maximum clearance. Difference between readings is taper of journal.

    d. If clearance exceeds specified limits, try a 0.001 in. or 0.002 in. undersize bearing in combination with the standard bearing. Bearing clearance must be within specified limits. If standard and 0.002 in. undersize bearing does not bring clearance within desired limits, refinish crankshaft journal, then install undersize bearings.

8. After the bearings have been fitted, apply a light coat of engine oil to the journals and bearings. Install the rear main bearing cap. Install all bearing caps except the thrust bearing cap. Be sure that main bearing caps are installed in original locations. Tighten the bearing cap bolts to specifications.

9. Install the thrust bearing cap with bolts finger-tight.

10. Pry the crankshaft forward against the thrust surface of upper half of bearing.

11. Hold the crankshaft forward and pry the thrust bearing cap to the rear. This aligns the thrust surfaces of both halves of the bearing.

12. Retain the forward pressure on the crankshaft. Tighten the cap bolts to specifications.

13. Measure the crankshaft end-play as follows:

    a. Mount a dial gauge to the engine block and position the tip of the gauge to read from the crankshaft end.

    b. Carefully pry the crankshaft toward the rear of the engine and hold it there while you zero the gauge.

    c. Carefully pry the crankshaft toward the front of the engine and read the gauge.

    d. Confirm that the reading is within specifications. If not, install a new thrust bearing and repeat the procedure. If the reading is still out of specifications with a new bearing, have a machine shop inspect the thrust surfaces of the crankshaft, and if possible, repair it.

14. Rotate the crankshaft so as to position the first rod journal to the bottom of its stroke.

**Pistons and Connecting Rods**

▶ **See Figures 195, 196, 197 and 198**

1. Before installing the piston/connecting rod assembly, oil the pistons, piston rings and the cylinder walls with light engine oil. Install connecting rod bolt protectors or rubber hose onto the connecting rod bolts/studs. Also perform the following:

    a. Select the proper ring set for the size cylinder bore.

    b. Position the ring in the bore in which it is going to be used.

    c. Push the ring down into the bore area where normal ring wear is not encountered.

    d. Use the head of the piston to position the ring in the bore so that the ring is square with the cylinder wall. Use caution to avoid damage to the ring or cylinder bore.

    e. Measure the gap between the ends of the ring with a feeler gauge. Ring gap in a worn cylinder is normally greater than specification. If the ring gap is greater than the specified limits, try an oversize ring set.

    f. Check the ring side clearance of the compression rings with a feeler gauge inserted between the ring and its lower land according to specification. The gauge should slide freely around the entire ring circumference without binding. Any wear that occurs will form a step at the inner portion of the lower land. If the lower lands have high steps, the piston should be replaced.

2. Unless new pistons are installed, be sure to install the pistons in the cylinders from which they were removed. The numbers on the connecting rod and bearing cap must be on the same side when installed in the cylinder bore. If a connecting rod is ever transposed from one engine or cylinder to another, new bearings should be fitted and the connecting rod should be numbered to correspond with the new cylinder number. The notch on the piston head goes toward the front of the engine.

3. Install all of the rod bearing inserts into the rods and caps.

4. Install the rings to the pistons. Install the oil control ring first, then the second compression ring and finally the top compression ring. Use a piston ring expander tool to aid in installation and to help reduce the chance of breakage.

5. Make sure the ring gaps are properly spaced around the circumference of the piston. Fit a piston ring compressor around the piston and slide the piston and connecting rod assembly down into the cylinder bore, pushing it in with

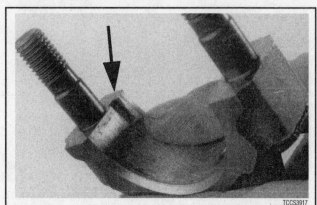

TCCS3923

**Fig. 195 Checking the piston ring-to-ring groove side clearance using the ring and a feeler gauge**

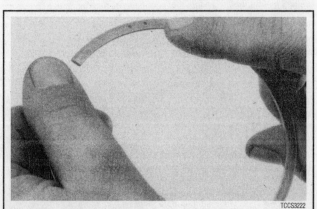

TCCS3917

**Fig. 196 The notch on the side of the bearing cap matches the tang on the bearing insert**

TCCS3222

**Fig. 197 Most rings are marked to show which side of the ring should face up when installed to the piston**

Fig. 198 Install the piston and rod assembly into the block using a ring compressor and the handle of a hammer

the wooden hammer handle. Push the piston down until it is only slightly below the top of the cylinder bore. Guide the connecting rod onto the crankshaft bearing journal carefully, to avoid damaging the crankshaft.

6. Check the bearing clearance of all the rod bearings, fitting them to the crankshaft bearing journals. Follow the procedure in the crankshaft installation above.

7. After the bearings have been fitted, apply a light coating of assembly oil to the journals and bearings.

8. Turn the crankshaft until the appropriate bearing journal is at the bottom of its stroke, then push the piston assembly all the way down until the connecting rod bearing seats on the crankshaft journal. Be careful not to allow the bearing cap screws to strike the crankshaft bearing journals and damage them.

9. After the piston and connecting rod assemblies have been installed, check the connecting rod side clearance on each crankshaft journal.

10. Prime and install the oil pump and the oil pump intake tube.

11. Install the auxiliary/balance shaft(s)/assembly(ies).

## OHC Engines

### CYLINDER HEAD(S)

1. Install the cylinder head(s) using new gaskets.
2. Install the timing sprockets/gears and the belt/chain assemblies.

### Engine Covers and Components

Install the timing cover(s) and oil pan. Refer to your notes and drawings made prior to disassembly and install all of the components that were removed. Install the engine into the vehicle.

## Engine Start-up and Break-in

### STARTING THE ENGINE

Now that the engine is installed and every wire and hose is properly connected, go back and double check that all coolant and vacuum hoses are connected. Check that you oil drain plug is installed and properly tightened. If not already done, install a new oil filter onto the engine. Fill the crankcase with the proper amount and grade of engine oil. Fill the cooling system with a 50/50 mixture of coolant/water.

1. Connect the vehicle battery.
2. Start the engine. Keep your eye on your oil pressure indicator; if it does not indicate oil pressure within 10 seconds of starting, turn the vehicle off.

### ❋❋ WARNING

**Damage to the engine can result if it is allowed to run with no oil pressure. Check the engine oil level to make sure that it is full. Check for any leaks and if found, repair the leaks before continuing. If there is still no indication of oil pressure, you may need to prime the system.**

3. Confirm that there are no fluid leaks (oil or other).
4. Allow the engine to reach normal operating temperature (the upper radiator hose will be hot to the touch).
5. If necessary, set the ignition timing.
6. Install any remaining components such as the air cleaner (if removed for ignition timing) or body panels which were removed.

### BREAKING IT IN

Make the first miles on the new engine, easy ones. Vary the speed but do not accelerate hard. Most importantly, do not lug the engine, and avoid sustained high speeds until at least 100 miles (161 km). Check the engine oil and coolant levels frequently. Expect the engine to use a little oil until the rings seat. Change the oil and filter at 500 miles (805 km), 1500 miles (2415 km), then every 3000 miles (4830 km) past that.

### KEEP IT MAINTAINED

Now that you have just gone through all of that hard work, keep yourself from doing it all over again by thoroughly maintaining it. Not that you may not have maintained it before, heck you could have had one to two hundred thousand miles on it before doing this. However, you may have bought the vehicle used, and the previous owner did not keep up on maintenance. Which is why you just went through all of that hard work. See?

## TORQUE SPECIFICATIONS

| Components | English Specifications | Metric Specifications |
| --- | --- | --- |
| **Camshaft, bearing caps** | | |
| 2.3L 4-cylinder engines | 14 ft. lbs. | 20 Nm |
| **Camshaft, pulleys** | | |
| 2.3L 4-cylinder engines | 37 ft. lbs. | 50 Nm |
| 2.8L 6-cylinder engine | 51-59 ft. lbs. | 69-80 Nm |
| 2.9L 6-cylinder engine | 15 ft. lbs. | 20 Nm |
| 2.3L and 2.4L 5-cylinder engines | 15 ft. lbs. | 20 Nm |
| **Camshaft, retaining bolt** | | |
| 2.8L 6-cylinder engine | 7-11 ft. lbs. | 10-15 Nm |
| **Crankshaft, Damper** | | |
| 2.3L 4-cylinder engines | 44 ft. lbs. * | 60 Nm* |
| 2.8L 6-cylinder engine | 177-207 ft. lbs. | 240-280 Nm |
| 2.9L 6-cylinder engine | | |
| Center nut | 221 ft. lbs. | 300 Nm |
| Retaining bolts | 26 ft. lbs. | 35 Nm |
| 2.3L and 2.4L 5-cylinder engines | | |
| Center nut | 133 ft. lbs. | 180 Nm |
| Retaining bolts | 18 ft. lbs. | 25 Nm |
| **Cylinder head bolts** | | |
| 2.3L 4-cylinder engines | ① | ① |
| 2.8L 6-cylinder engine | ② | ② |
| 2.9L 6-cylinder engine | ③ | ③ |
| 2.3L and 2.4L 5-cylinder engines | ④ | ④ |
| **Engine mounts** | 37 ft. lbs. | 50 Nm |
| **Exhaust manifold** | | |
| 2.3L 4-cylinder engines | 10-20 ft. lbs. | 14-27 Nm |
| 2.8L 6-cylinder engine | 7-11 ft. lbs. | 10-15 Nm |
| 2.9L 6-cylinder engine | 18 ft. lbs. | 25 Nm |
| 2.3L and 2.4L 5-cylinder engines | 18 ft. lbs. | 25 Nm |
| **Flywheel/flexplate** | | |
| 2.3L 4-cylinder engines | 51 ft. lbs. | 70 Nm |
| 2.8L 6-cylinder engine | 51 ft. lbs. | 70 Nm |
| 2.9L 6-cylinder engine | 55 ft. lbs. | 75 Nm |
| 2.3L and 2.4L 5-cylinder engines | 33 ft. lbs. * | 45 Nm* |
| **Intake manifold** | | |
| 2.3L 4-cylinder engines | 15 ft. lbs. | 20 Nm |
| 2.8L 6-cylinder engine | 7-11 ft. lbs. | 10-15 Nm |
| 2.9L 6-cylinder engine | 15 ft. lbs. | 20 Nm |
| 2.3L and 2.4L 5-cylinder engines | 15 ft. lbs. | 20 Nm |
| **Oil pan** | | |
| 2.3L 4-cylinder engines | 8 ft. lbs. | 11 Nm |
| 2.8L 6-cylinder engine | 6-8 ft. lbs. | 8-11 Nm |
| 2.9L 6-cylinder engine | 8 ft. lbs. | 11 Nm |
| 2.3L and 2.4L 5-cylinder engines | 12 ft. lbs. | 17 Nm |
| **Oil pump** | | |
| B230F and B230ft. 4-cylinder engines | 8 ft. lbs. | 11 Nm |
| 2.8L 6-cylinder engine | 8 ft. lbs. | 11 Nm |
| 2.9L 6-cylinder engine | 7 ft. lbs. | 10 Nm |
| 2.3L and 2.4L 5-cylinder engines | 7 ft. lbs. | 10 Nm |
| B234F 4-cylinder engine | 8 ft. lbs. | 11 Nm |
| Drive belt pulley bolt | 15 ft. lbs. * | 20 Nm* |

90953C01

## TORQUE SPECIFICATIONS

| Components | English Specifications | Metric Specifications |
| --- | --- | --- |
| **Thermostat housing** | | |
| 2.3L 4-cylinder engines | 11-15 ft. lbs. | 15-20 Nm |
| 2.8L 6-cylinder engine | 11-15 ft. lbs. | 15-20 Nm |
| 2.9L 6-cylinder engine | 7 ft. lbs. | 10 Nm |
| 2.3L and 2.4L 5-cylinder engines | 15 ft. lbs. | 20 Nm |
| **Timing belt tensioner** | | |
| 2.3L 4-cylinder engines | 37 ft. lbs. | 51 Nm |
| 2.8L 6-cylinder engine | 37 ft. lbs. | 51 Nm |
| 2.9L 6-cylinder engine | 18 ft. lbs. | 25 Nm |
| 2.3L and 2.4L 5-cylinder engines | 18 ft. lbs. | 25 Nm |
| **Timing chain cover** | | |
| 2.8L 6-cylinder engine | 7-11 ft. lbs. | 10-15 Nm |
| **Timing chain tensioner** | | |
| 2.8L 6-cylinder engine | 5 ft. lbs. | 7 Nm |
| **Water pump** | | |
| 2.3L 4-cylinder engines | 11-15 ft. lbs. | 15-20 Nm |
| 2.8L 6-cylinder engine | 11-15 ft. lbs. | 15-20 Nm |
| 2.9L 6-cylinder engine | 15 ft. lbs. | 20 Nm |
| 2.3L and 2.4L 5-cylinder engines | 15 ft. lbs. | 20 Nm |
| **Valve cover** | | |
| 2.3L 4-cylinder engines | 14 ft. lbs. | 20 Nm |
| 2.8L 6-cylinder engine | 11 ft. lbs. | 15 Nm |
| 2.9L 6-cylinder engine | 13 ft. lbs. | 17 Nm |
| 2.3L and 2.4L 5-cylinder engines | 13 ft. lbs. | 17 Nm |

* Plus an additional 60 degrees

① Step 1: Tighten in sequence to 14 ft. lbs. (19 Nm)
Step 1: Tighten in sequence to 43 ft. lbs. (59 Nm)
Step 3: Tighten in sequence an additional 90 degrees

② On 1990 asbestos-free gasket
Step 1: Tighten in sequence to 44 ft. lbs. (60 Nm)
Step 2: Loosen bolts, tighten in sequence to 30 ft. lbs. (40 Nm)
Step 3: Tighten in sequence an additional 160-180 degrees
Except 1990 asbestos-free gasket
Step 1: Tighten in sequence to 43 ft. lbs. (59 Nm)
Step 2: Loosen bolt 1, tighten it to 15 ft. lbs. (20 Nm)
Step 3: Tighten bolt 1 an additional 106 degrees
Step 4: Repeat steps 2 and 3 for the remaining head bolts

③ Step 1: Tighten in sequence to 15 ft. lbs. (20 Nm)
Step 2: Tighten in sequence to 44 ft. lbs. (60 Nm)
Step 3: Tighten in sequence an additional 130 degrees

④ Step 1: Tighten in sequence to 15 ft. lbs. (20 Nm)
Step 2: Tighten in sequence to 44 ft. lbs. (60 Nm)
Step 3: Tighten in sequence an additional 130 degrees

90953C02

## USING A VACUUM GAUGE

*White needle = steady needle      Dark needle = drifting needle*

The vacuum gauge is one of the most useful and easy-to-use diagnostic tools. It is inexpensive, easy to hook up, and provides valuable information about the condition of your engine.

**Indication: Normal engine in good condition**

Gauge reading: Steady, from 17–22 in./Hg.

**Indication: Sticking valve or ignition miss**

Gauge reading: Needle fluctuates from 15–20 in./Hg. at idle

**Indication: Late ignition or valve timing, low compression, stuck throttle valve, leaking carburetor or manifold gasket.**

Gauge reading: Low (15–20 in./Hg.) but steady

**Indication: Improper carburetor adjustment, or minor intake leak at carburetor or manifold**

*NOTE: Bad fuel injector O-rings may also cause this reading.*

Gauge reading: Drifting needle

**Indication: Weak valve springs, worn valve stem guides, or leaky cylinder head gasket (vibrating excessively at all speeds).**

*NOTE: A plugged catalytic converter may also cause this reading.*

Gauge reading: Needle fluctuates as engine speed increases

**Indication: Burnt valve or improper valve clearance. The needle will drop when the defective valve operates.**

Gauge reading: Steady needle, but drops regularly

**Indication: Choked muffler or obstruction in system. Speed up the engine. Choked muffler will exhibit a slow drop of vacuum to zero.**

Gauge reading: Gradual drop in reading at idle

**Indication: Worn valve guides**

Gauge reading: Needle vibrates excessively at idle, but steadies as engine speed increases

TCCS3C01

## Troubleshooting Engine Mechanical Problems

| Problem | Cause | Solution |
|---|---|---|
| External oil leaks | • Cylinder head cover RTV sealant broken or improperly seated | • Replace sealant; inspect cylinder head cover sealant flange and cylinder head sealant surface for distortion and cracks |
| | • Oil filler cap leaking or missing | • Replace cap |
| | • Oil filter gasket broken or improperly seated | • Replace oil filter |
| | • Oil pan side gasket broken, improperly seated or opening in RTV sealant | • Replace gasket or repair opening in sealant; inspect oil pan gasket flange for distortion |
| | • Oil pan front oil seal broken or improperly seated | • Replace seal; inspect timing case cover and oil pan seal flange for distortion |
| | • Oil pan rear oil seal broken or improperly seated | • Replace seal; inspect oil pan rear oil seal flange; inspect rear main bearing cap for cracks, plugged oil return channels, or distortion in seal groove |
| | • Timing case cover oil seal broken or improperly seated | • Replace seal |
| | • Excess oil pressure because of restricted PCV valve | • Replace PCV valve |
| | • Oil pan drain plug loose or has stripped threads | • Repair as necessary and tighten |
| | • Rear oil gallery plug loose | • Use appropriate sealant on gallery plug and tighten |
| | • Rear camshaft plug loose or improperly seated | • Seat camshaft plug or replace and seal, as necessary |
| Excessive oil consumption | • Oil level too high | • Drain oil to specified level |
| | • Oil with wrong viscosity being used | • Replace with specified oil |
| | • PCV valve stuck closed | • Replace PCV valve |
| | • Valve stem oil deflectors (or seals) are damaged, missing, or incorrect type | • Replace valve stem oil deflectors |
| | • Valve stems or valve guides worn | • Measure stem-to-guide clearance and repair as necessary |
| | • Poorly fitted or missing valve cover baffles | • Replace valve cover |
| | • Piston rings broken or missing | • Replace broken or missing rings |
| | • Scuffed piston | • Replace piston |
| | • Incorrect piston ring gap | • Measure ring gap, repair as necessary |
| | • Piston rings sticking or excessively loose in grooves | • Measure ring side clearance, repair as necessary |
| | • Compression rings installed upside down | • Repair as necessary |
| | • Cylinder walls worn, scored, or glazed | • Repair as necessary |

TCCS3002

## Troubleshooting Engine Mechanical Problems

| Problem | Cause | Solution |
|---|---|---|
| Excessive oil consumption (cont.) | • Piston ring gaps not properly staggered | • Repair as necessary |
| | • Excessive main or connecting rod bearing clearance | • Measure bearing clearance, repair as necessary |
| No oil pressure | • Low oil level | • Add oil to correct level |
| | • Oil pressure gauge, warning lamp or sending unit inaccurate | • Replace oil pressure gauge or warning lamp |
| | • Oil pump malfunction | • Replace oil pump |
| | • Oil pressure relief valve sticking | • Remove and inspect oil pressure relief valve assembly |
| | • Oil passages on pressure side of pump obstructed | • Inspect oil passages for obstruction |
| | • Oil pickup screen or tube obstructed | • Inspect oil pickup for obstruction |
| | • Loose oil inlet tube | • Tighten or seal inlet tube |
| Low oil pressure | • Low oil level | • Add oil to correct level |
| | • Inaccurate gauge, warning lamp or sending unit | • Replace oil pressure gauge or warning lamp |
| | • Oil excessively thin because of dilution, poor quality, or improper grade | • Drain and refill crankcase with recommended oil |
| | • Excessive oil temperature | • Correct cause of overheating engine |
| | • Oil pressure relief spring weak or sticking | • Remove and inspect oil pressure relief valve assembly |
| | • Oil inlet tube and screen assembly has restriction or air leak | • Remove and inspect oil inlet tube and screen assembly. (Fill inlet tube with lacquer thinner to locate leaks.) |
| | • Excessive oil pump clearance | • Measure clearances |
| | • Excessive main, rod, or camshaft bearing clearance | • Measure bearing clearances, repair as necessary |
| High oil pressure | • Improper oil viscosity | • Drain and refill crankcase with correct viscosity oil |
| | • Oil pressure gauge or sending unit inaccurate | • Replace oil pressure gauge |
| | • Oil pressure relief valve sticking closed | • Remove and inspect oil pressure relief valve assembly |
| Main bearing noise | • Insufficient oil supply | • Inspect for low oil level and low oil pressure |
| | • Main bearing clearance excessive | • Measure main bearing clearance, repair as necessary |
| | • Bearing insert missing | • Replace missing insert |
| | • Crankshaft end-play excessive | • Measure end-play, repair as necessary |
| | • Improperly tightened main bearing cap bolts | • Tighten bolts with specified torque |
| | • Loose flywheel or drive plate | • Tighten flywheel or drive plate attaching bolts |
| | • Loose or damaged vibration damper | • Repair as necessary |

TCCS3C03

## Troubleshooting Engine Mechanical Problems

| Problem | Cause | Solution |
|---|---|---|
| Connecting rod bearing noise | • Insufficient oil supply | • Inspect for low oil level and low oil pressure |
| | • Carbon build-up on piston | • Remove carbon from piston crown |
| | • Bearing clearance excessive or bearing missing | • Measure clearance, repair as necessary |
| | • Crankshaft connecting rod journal out-of-round | • Measure journal dimensions, repair or replace as necessary |
| | • Misaligned connecting rod or cap | • Repair as necessary |
| | • Connecting rod bolts tightened improperly | • Tighten bolts with specified torque |
| Piston noise | • Piston-to-cylinder wall clearance excessive (scuffed piston) | • Measure clearance and examine piston |
| | • Cylinder walls excessively tapered or out-of-round | • Measure cylinder wall dimensions, rebore cylinder |
| | • Piston ring broken | • Replace all rings on piston |
| | • Loose or seized piston pin | • Measure piston-to-pin clearance, repair as necessary |
| | • Connecting rods misaligned | • Measure rod alignment, straighten or replace |
| | • Piston ring side clearance excessively loose or tight | • Measure ring side clearance, repair as necessary |
| | • Carbon build-up on piston is excessive | • Remove carbon from piston |
| Valve actuating component noise | • Insufficient oil supply | • Check for: <br>(a) Low oil level <br>(b) Low oil pressure <br>(c) Wrong hydraulic tappets <br>(d) Restricted oil gallery <br>(e) Excessive tappet to bore clearance |
| | • Rocker arms or pivots worn | • Replace worn rocker arms or pivots |
| | • Foreign objects or chips in hydraulic tappets | • Clean tappets |
| | • Excessive tappet leak-down | • Replace valve tappet |
| | • Tappet face worn | • Replace tappet; inspect corresponding cam lobe for wear |
| | • Broken or cocked valve springs | • Properly seat cocked springs; replace broken springs |
| | • Stem-to-guide clearance excessive | • Measure stem-to-guide clearance, repair as required |
| | • Valve bent | • Replace valve |
| | • Loose rocker arms | • Check and repair as necessary |
| | • Valve seat runout excessive | • Regrind valve seat/valves |
| | • Missing valve lock | • Install valve lock |
| | • Excessive engine oil | • Correct oil level |

TCCS3C04

## Troubleshooting Engine Performance

| Problem | Cause | Solution |
|---|---|---|
| Hard starting (engine cranks normally) | • Faulty engine control system component | • Repair or replace as necessary |
| | • Faulty fuel pump | • Replace fuel pump |
| | • Faulty fuel system component | • Repair or replace as necessary |
| | • Faulty ignition coil | • Test and replace as necessary |
| | • Improper spark plug gap | • Adjust gap |
| | • Incorrect ignition timing | • Adjust timing |
| | • Incorrect valve timing | • Check valve timing; repair as necessary |
| Rough idle or stalling | • Incorrect curb or fast idle speed | • Adjust curb or fast idle speed (if possible) |
| | • Incorrect ignition timing | • Adjust timing to specification |
| | • Improper feedback system operation | • Refer to Chapter 4 |
| | • Faulty EGR valve operation | • Test EGR system and replace as necessary |
| | • Faulty PCV valve air flow | • Test PCV valve and replace as necessary |
| | • Faulty TAC vacuum motor or valve | • Repair as necessary |
| | • Air leak into manifold vacuum | • Inspect manifold vacuum connections and repair as necessary |
| | • Faulty distributor rotor or cap | • Replace rotor or cap (Distributor systems only) |
| | • Improperly seated valves | • Test cylinder compression, repair as necessary |
| | • Incorrect ignition wiring | • Inspect wiring and correct as necessary |
| | • Faulty ignition coil | • Test coil and replace as necessary |
| | • Restricted air vent or idle passages | • Clean passages |
| | • Restricted air cleaner | • Clean or replace air cleaner filter element |
| Faulty low-speed operation | • Restricted idle air vents and passages | • Clean air vents and passages |
| | • Restricted air cleaner | • Clean or replace air cleaner filter element |
| | • Faulty spark plugs | • Clean or replace spark plugs |
| | • Dirty, corroded, or loose ignition secondary circuit wire connections | • Clean or tighten secondary circuit wire connections |
| | • Improper feedback system operation | • Refer to Chapter 4 |
| | • Faulty ignition coil high voltage wire | • Replace ignition coil high voltage wire (Distributor systems only) |
| | • Faulty distributor cap | • Replace cap (Distributor systems only) |
| Faulty acceleration | • Incorrect ignition timing | • Adjust timing |
| | • Faulty fuel system component | • Repair or replace as necessary |
| | • Faulty spark plug(s) | • Clean or replace spark plug(s) |
| | • Improperly seated valves | • Test cylinder compression, repair as necessary |
| | • Faulty ignition coil | • Test coil and replace as necessary |

TCCS3C05

## Troubleshooting Engine Performance

| Problem | Cause | Solution |
|---|---|---|
| Faulty acceleration (cont.) | • Improper feedback system operation | • Refer to Chapter 4 |
| Faulty high speed operation | • Incorrect ignition timing | • Adjust timing (if possible) |
| | • Faulty advance mechanism | • Check advance mechanism and repair as necessary (Distributor systems only) |
| | • Low fuel pump volume | • Replace fuel pump |
| | • Wrong spark plug air gap or wrong plug | • Adjust air gap or install correct plug |
| | • Partially restricted exhaust manifold, exhaust pipe, catalytic converter, muffler, or tailpipe | • Eliminate restriction |
| | • Restricted vacuum passages | • Clean passages |
| | • Restricted air cleaner | • Cleaner or replace filter element as necessary |
| | • Faulty distributor rotor or cap | • Replace rotor or cap (Distributor systems only) |
| | • Faulty ignition coil | • Test coil and replace as necessary |
| | • Improperly seated valve(s) | • Test cylinder compression, repair as necessary |
| | • Faulty valve spring(s) | • Inspect and test valve spring tension, replace as necessary |
| | • Incorrect valve timing | • Check valve timing and repair as necessary |
| | • Intake manifold restricted | • Remove restriction or replace manifold |
| | • Worn distributor shaft | • Replace shaft (Distributor systems only) |
| | • Improper feedback system operation | • Refer to Chapter 4 |
| Misfire at all speeds | • Faulty spark plug(s) | • Clean or relace spark plug(s) |
| | • Faulty spark plug wire(s) | • Replace as necessary |
| | • Faulty distributor cap or rotor | • Replace cap or rotor (Distributor systems only) |
| | • Faulty ignition coil | • Test coil and replace as necessary |
| | • Primary ignition circuit shorted or open intermittently | • Troubleshoot primary circuit and repair as necessary |
| | • Improperly seated valve(s) | • Test cylinder compression, repair as necessary |
| | • Faulty hydraulic tappet(s) | • Clean or replace tappet(s) |
| | • Improper feedback system operation | • Refer to Chapter 4 |
| | • Faulty valve spring(s) | • Inspect and test valve spring tension, repair as necessary |
| | • Worn camshaft lobes | • Replace camshaft |
| | • Air leak into manifold | • Check manifold vacuum and repair as necessary |
| | • Fuel pump volume or pressure low | • Replace fuel pump |
| | • Blown cylinder head gasket | • Replace gasket |
| | • Intake or exhaust manifold passage(s) restricted | • Pass chain through passage(s) and repair as necessary |
| Power not up to normal | • Incorrect ignition timing | • Adjust timing |
| | • Faulty distributor rotor | • Replace rotor (Distributor systems only) |

TCCS3006

## Troubleshooting Engine Performance

| Problem | Cause | Solution |
|---|---|---|
| Power not up to normal (cont.) | • Incorrect spark plug gap | • Adjust gap |
| | • Faulty fuel pump | • Replace fuel pump |
| | • Faulty fuel pump | • Replace fuel pump |
| | • Incorrect valve timing | • Check valve timing and repair as necessary |
| | • Faulty ignition coil | • Test coil and replace as necessary |
| | • Faulty ignition wires | • Test wires and replace as necessary |
| | • Improperly seated valves | • Test cylinder compression and repair as necessary |
| | • Blown cylinder head gasket | • Replace gasket |
| | • Leaking piston rings | • Test compression and repair as necessary |
| | • Improper feedback system operation | • Refer to Chapter 4 |
| Intake backfire | • Improper ignition timing | • Adjust timing |
| | • Defective EGR component | • Repair as necessary |
| | • Defective TAC vacuum motor or valve | • Repair as necessary |
| Exhaust backfire | • Air leak into manifold vacuum | • Check manifold vacuum and repair as necessary |
| | • Faulty air injection diverter valve | • Test diverter valve and replace as necessary |
| | • Exhaust leak | • Locate and eliminate leak |
| Ping or spark knock | • Incorrect ignition timing | • Adjust timing |
| | • Distributor advance malfunction | • Inspect advance mechanism and repair as necessary (Distributor systems only) |
| | • Excessive combustion chamber deposits | • Remove with combustion chamber cleaner |
| | • Air leak into manifold vacuum | • Check manifold vacuum and repair as necessary |
| | • Excessively high compression | • Test compression and repair as necessary |
| | • Fuel octane rating excessively low | • Try alternate fuel source |
| | • Sharp edges in combustion chamber | • Grind smooth |
| | • EGR valve not functioning properly | • Test EGR system and replace as necessary |
| Surging (at cruising to top speeds) | • Low fuel pump pressure or volume | • Replace fuel pump |
| | • Improper PCV valve air flow | • Test PCV valve and replace as necessary |
| | • Air leak into manifold vacuum | • Check manifold vacuum and repair as necessary |
| | • Incorrect spark advance | • Test and replace as necessary |
| | • Restricted fuel filter | • Replace fuel filter |
| | • Restricted air cleaner | • Clean or replace air cleaner filter element |
| | • EGR valve not functioning properly | • Test EGR system and replace as necessary |
| | • Improper feedback system operation | • Refer to Chapter 4 |

TCCS3C07

## Troubleshooting the Serpentine Drive Belt

| Problem | Cause | Solution |
|---|---|---|
| Tension sheeting fabric failure (woven fabric on outside circumference of belt has cracked or separated from body of belt) | • Grooved or backside idler pulley diameters are less than minimum recommended<br>• Tension sheeting contacting (rubbing) stationary object<br>• Excessive heat causing woven fabric to age<br>• Tension sheeting splice has fractured | • Replace pulley(s) not conforming to specification<br>• Correct rubbing condition<br>• Replace belt<br>• Replace belt |
| Noise (objectional squeal, squeak, or rumble is heard or felt while drive belt is in operation) | • Belt slippage<br>• Bearing noise<br>• Belt misalignment<br>• Belt-to-pulley mismatch<br>• Driven component inducing vibration<br>• System resonant frequency inducing vibration | • Adjust belt<br>• Locate and repair<br>• Align belt/pulley(s)<br>• Install correct belt<br>• Locate defective driven component and repair<br>• Vary belt tension within specifications. Replace belt. |
| Rib chunking (one or more ribs has separated from belt body) | • Foreign objects imbedded in pulley grooves<br>• Installation damage<br>• Drive loads in excess of design specifications<br>• Insufficient internal belt adhesion | • Remove foreign objects from pulley grooves<br>• Replace belt<br>• Adjust belt tension<br>• Replace belt |
| Rib or belt wear (belt ribs contact bottom of pulley grooves) | • Pulley(s) misaligned<br>• Mismatch of belt and pulley groove widths<br>• Abrasive environment<br>• Rusted pulley(s)<br>• Sharp or jagged pulley groove tips<br>• Rubber deteriorated | • Align pulley(s)<br>• Replace belt<br><br>• Replace belt<br>• Clean rust from pulley(s)<br>• Replace pulley<br>• Replace belt |
| Longitudinal belt cracking (cracks between two ribs) | • Belt has mistracked from pulley groove<br>• Pulley groove tip has worn away rubber-to-tensile member | • Replace belt<br>• Replace belt |
| Belt slips | • Belt slipping because of insufficient tension<br>• Belt or pulley subjected to substance (belt dressing, oil, ethylene glycol) that has reduced friction<br>• Driven component bearing failure<br>• Belt glazed and hardened from heat and excessive slippage | • Adjust tension<br>• Replace belt and clean pulleys<br><br>• Replace faulty component bearing<br>• Replace belt |
| "Groove jumping" (belt does not maintain correct position on pulley, or turns over and/or runs off pulleys) | • Insufficient belt tension<br>• Pulley(s) not within design tolerance<br>• Foreign object(s) in grooves | • Adjust belt tension<br>• Replace pulley(s)<br>• Remove foreign objects from grooves |

TCCS3C09

## Troubleshooting the Serpentine Drive Belt

| Problem | Cause | Solution |
|---|---|---|
| "Groove jumping" (belt does not maintain correct position on pulley, or turns over and/or runs off pulleys) | • Excessive belt speed<br>• Pulley misalignment<br>• Belt-to-pulley profile mismatched<br>• Belt cordline is distorted | • Avoid excessive engine acceleration<br>• Align pulley(s)<br>• Install correct belt<br>• Replace belt |
| Belt broken (Note: identify and correct problem before replacement belt is installed) | • Excessive tension<br>• Tensile members damaged during belt installation<br>• Belt turnover<br>• Severe pulley misalignment<br>• Bracket, pulley, or bearing failure | • Replace belt and adjust tension to specification<br>• Replace belt<br><br>• Replace belt<br>• Align pulley(s)<br>• Replace defective component and belt |
| Cord edge failure (tensile member exposed at edges of belt or separated from belt body) | • Excessive tension<br>• Drive pulley misalignment<br>• Belt contacting stationary object<br>• Pulley irregularities<br>• Improper pulley construction<br>• Insufficient adhesion between tensile member and rubber matrix | • Adjust belt tension<br>• Align pulley<br>• Correct as necessary<br>• Replace pulley<br>• Replace pulley<br>• Replace belt and adjust tension to specifications |
| Sporadic rib cracking (multiple cracks in belt ribs at random intervals) | • Ribbed pulley(s) diameter less than minimum specification<br>• Backside bend flat pulley(s) diameter less than minimum<br>• Excessive heat condition causing rubber to harden<br>• Excessive belt thickness<br>• Belt overcured<br>• Excessive tension | • Replace pulley(s)<br>• Replace pulley(s)<br>• Correct heat condition as necessary<br>• Replace belt<br>• Replace belt<br>• Adjust belt tension |

TCCS3C10

## Troubleshooting the Cooling System

| Problem | Cause | Solution |
| --- | --- | --- |
| High temperature gauge indication—overheating | • Coolant level low | • Replenish coolant |
| | • Improper fan operation | • Repair or replace as necessary |
| | • Radiator hose(s) collapsed | • Replace hose(s) |
| | • Radiator airflow blocked | • Remove restriction (bug screen, fog lamps, etc.) |
| | • Faulty pressure cap | • Replace pressure cap |
| | • Ignition timing incorrect | • Adjust ignition timing |
| | • Air trapped in cooling system | • Purge air |
| | • Heavy traffic driving | • Operate at fast idle in neutral intermittently to cool engine |
| | • Incorrect cooling system component(s) installed | • Install proper component(s) |
| | • Faulty thermostat | • Replace thermostat |
| | • Water pump shaft broken or impeller loose | • Replace water pump |
| | • Radiator tubes clogged | • Flush radiator |
| | • Cooling system clogged | • Flush system |
| | • Casting flash in cooling passages | • Repair or replace as necessary. Flash may be visible by removing cooling system components or removing core plugs. |
| | • Brakes dragging | • Repair brakes |
| | • Excessive engine friction | • Repair engine |
| | • Antifreeze concentration over 68% | • Lower antifreeze concentration percentage |
| | • Missing air seals | • Replace air seals |
| | • Faulty gauge or sending unit | • Repair or replace faulty component |
| | • Loss of coolant flow caused by leakage or foaming | • Repair or replace leaking component, replace coolant |
| | • Viscous fan drive failed | • Replace unit |
| Low temperature indication—undercooling | • Thermostat stuck open | • Replace thermostat |
| | • Faulty gauge or sending unit | • Repair or replace faulty component |
| Coolant loss—boilover | • Overfilled cooling system | • Reduce coolant level to proper specification |
| | • Quick shutdown after hard (hot) run | • Allow engine to run at fast idle prior to shutdown |
| | • Air in system resulting in occasional "burping" of coolant | • Purge system |
| | • Insufficient antifreeze allowing coolant boiling point to be too low | • Add antifreeze to raise boiling point |
| | • Antifreeze deteriorated because of age or contamination | • Replace coolant |
| | • Leaks due to loose hose clamps, loose nuts, bolts, drain plugs, faulty hoses, or defective radiator | • Pressure test system to locate source of leak(s) then repair as necessary |

TCCS3C11

## Troubleshooting the Cooling System

| Problem | Cause | Solution |
| --- | --- | --- |
| Coolant loss—boilover | • Faulty head gasket | • Replace head gasket |
| | • Cracked head, manifold, or block | • Replace as necessary |
| | • Faulty radiator cap | • Replace cap |
| Coolant entry into crankcase or cylinder(s) | • Faulty head gasket | • Replace head gasket |
| | • Crack in head, manifold or block | • Replace as necessary |
| Coolant recovery system inoperative | • Coolant level low | • Replenish coolant to FULL mark |
| | • Leak in system | • Pressure test to isolate leak and repair as necessary |
| | • Pressure cap not tight or seal missing, or leaking | • Repair as necessary |
| | • Pressure cap defective | • Replace cap |
| | • Overflow tube clogged or leaking | • Repair as necessary |
| | • Recovery bottle vent restricted | • Remove restriction |
| Noise | • Fan contacting shroud | • Reposition shroud and inspect engine mounts (on electric fans inspect assembly) |
| | • Loose water pump impeller | • Replace pump |
| | • Glazed fan belt | • Apply silicone or replace belt |
| | • Loose fan belt | • Adjust fan belt tension |
| | • Rough surface on drive pulley | • Replace pulley |
| | • Water pump bearing worn | • Remove belt to isolate. Replace pump. |
| | • Belt alignment | • Check pulley alignment. Repair as necessary. |
| No coolant flow through heater core | • Restricted return inlet in water pump | • Remove restriction |
| | • Heater hose collapsed or restricted | • Remove restriction or replace hose |
| | • Restricted heater core | • Remove restriction or replace core |
| | • Restricted outlet in thermostat housing | • Remove flash or restriction |
| | • Intake manifold bypass hole in cylinder head restricted | • Remove restriction |
| | • Faulty heater control valve | • Replace valve |
| | • Intake manifold coolant passage restricted | • Remove restriction or replace intake manifold |

**NOTE:** *Immediately after shutdown, the engine enters a condition known as heat soak. This is caused by the cooling system being inoperative while engine temperature is still high. If coolant temperature rises above boiling point, expansion and pressure may push some coolant out of the radiator overflow tube. If this does not occur frequently it is considered normal.*

TCCS3C12

# 4

# DRIVEABILITY AND EMISSIONS CONTROLS

## AIR POLLUTION

The earth's atmosphere, at or near sea level, consists approximately of 78 percent nitrogen, 21 percent oxygen and 1 percent other gases. If it were possible to remain in this state, 100 percent clean air would result. However, many varied sources allow other gases and particulates to mix with the clean air, causing our atmosphere to become unclean or polluted.

Some of these pollutants are visible while others are invisible, with each having the capability of causing distress to the eyes, ears, throat, skin and respiratory system. Should these pollutants become concentrated in a specific area and under certain conditions, death could result due to the displacement or chemical change of the oxygen content in the air. These pollutants can also cause great damage to the environment and to the many man made objects that are exposed to the elements.

To better understand the causes of air pollution, the pollutants can be categorized into 3 separate types, natural, industrial and automotive.

### Natural Pollutants

Natural pollution has been present on earth since before man appeared and continues to be a factor when discussing air pollution, although it causes only a small percentage of the overall pollution problem. It is the direct result of decaying organic matter, wind born smoke and particulates from such natural events as plain and forest fires (ignited by heat or lightning), volcanic ash, sand and dust which can spread over a large area of the countryside.

Such a phenomenon of natural pollution has been seen in the form of volcanic eruptions, with the resulting plume of smoke, steam and volcanic ash blotting out the sun's rays as it spreads and rises higher into the atmosphere. As it travels into the atmosphere the upper air currents catch and carry the smoke and ash, while condensing the steam back into water vapor. As the water vapor, smoke and ash travel on their journey, the smoke dissipates into the atmosphere while the ash and moisture settle back to earth in a trail hundreds of miles long. In some cases, lives are lost and millions of dollars of property damage result.

### Industrial Pollutants

Industrial pollution is caused primarily by industrial processes, the burning of coal, oil and natural gas, which in turn produce smoke and fumes. Because the burning fuels contain large amounts of sulfur, the principal ingredients of smoke and fumes are sulfur dioxide and particulate matter. This type of pollutant occurs most severely during still, damp and cool weather, such as at night. Even in its less severe form, this pollutant is not confined to just cities. Because of air movements, the pollutants move for miles over the surrounding countryside, leaving in its path a barren and unhealthy environment for all living things.

Working with Federal, State and Local mandated regulations and by carefully monitoring emissions, big business has greatly reduced the amount of pollutant introduced from its industrial sources, striving to obtain an acceptable level. Because of the mandated industrial emission clean up, many land areas and streams in and around the cities that were formerly barren of vegetation and life, have now begun to move back in the direction of nature's intended balance.

### Automotive Pollutants

The third major source of air pollution is automotive emissions. The emissions from the internal combustion engines were not an appreciable problem years ago because of the small number of registered vehicles and the nation's small highway system. However, during the early 1950's, the trend of the American people was to move from the cities to the surrounding suburbs. This caused an immediate problem in transportation because the majority of suburbs were not afforded mass transit conveniences. This lack of transportation created an attractive market for the automobile manufacturers, which resulted in a dramatic increase in the number of vehicles produced and sold, along with a marked increase in highway construction between cities and the suburbs. Multi-vehicle families emerged with a growing emphasis placed on an individual vehicle per family member. As the increase in vehicle ownership and usage occurred, so did pollutant levels in and around the cities, as suburbanites drove daily to their businesses and employment, returning at the end of the day to their homes in the suburbs.

It was noted that a smoke and fog type haze was being formed and at times, remained in suspension over the cities, taking time to dissipate. At first this "smog," derived from the words "smoke" and "fog," was thought to result from industrial pollution but it was determined that automobile emissions shared the blame. It was discovered that when normal automobile emissions were exposed to sunlight for a period of time, complex chemical reactions would take place.

It is now known that smog is a photo chemical layer which develops when certain oxides of nitrogen (NOx) and unburned hydrocarbons (HC) from automobile emissions are exposed to sunlight. Pollution was more severe when smog would become stagnant over an area in which a warm layer of air settled over the top of the cooler air mass, trapping and holding the cooler mass at ground level. The trapped cooler air would keep the emissions from being dispersed and diluted through normal air flows. This type of air stagnation was given the name "Temperature Inversion."

### TEMPERATURE INVERSION

In normal weather situations, surface air is warmed by heat radiating from the earth's surface and the sun's rays. This causes it to rise upward, into the atmosphere. Upon rising it will cool through a convection type heat exchange with the cooler upper air. As warm air rises, the surface pollutants are carried upward and dissipated into the atmosphere.

When a temperature inversion occurs, we find the higher air is no longer cooler, but is warmer than the surface air, causing the cooler surface air to become trapped. This warm air blanket can extend from above ground level to a few hundred or even a few thousand feet into the air. As the surface air is trapped, so are the pollutants, causing a severe smog condition. Should this stagnant air mass extend to a few thousand feet high, enough air movement with the inversion takes place to allow the smog layer to rise above ground level but the pollutants still cannot dissipate. This inversion can remain for days over an area, with the smog level only rising or lowering from ground level to a few hundred feet high. Meanwhile, the pollutant levels increase, causing eye irritation, respiratory problems, reduced visibility, plant damage and in some cases, even disease.

This inversion phenomenon was first noted in the Los Angeles, California area. The city lies in terrain resembling a basin and with certain weather conditions, a cold air mass is held in the basin while a warmer air mass covers it like a lid.

Because this type of condition was first documented as prevalent in the Los Angeles area, this type of trapped pollution was named Los Angeles Smog, although it occurs in other areas where a large concentration of automobiles are used and the air remains stagnant for any length of time.

### HEAT TRANSFER

Consider the internal combustion engine as a machine in which raw materials must be placed so a finished product comes out. As in any machine operation, a certain amount of wasted material is formed. When we relate this to the internal combustion engine, we find that through the input of air and fuel, we obtain power during the combustion process to drive the vehicle. The by-product or waste of this power is, in part, heat and exhaust gases with which we must dispose.

The heat from the combustion process can rise to over 4000°F (2204°C). The dissipation of this heat is controlled by a ram air effect, the use of cooling fans to cause air flow and a liquid coolant solution surrounding the combustion area to transfer the heat of combustion through the cylinder walls and into the coolant. The coolant is then directed to a thin-finned, multi-tubed radiator, from which the excess heat is transferred to the atmosphere by 1 of the 3 heat transfer methods, conduction, convection or radiation.

The cooling of the combustion area is an important part in the control of exhaust emissions. To understand the behavior of the combustion and transfer of its heat, consider the air/fuel charge. It is ignited and the flame front burns progressively across the combustion chamber until the burning charge reaches the cylinder walls. Some of the fuel in contact with the walls is not hot enough to burn, thereby snuffing out or quenching the combustion process. This leaves unburned fuel in the combustion chamber. This unburned fuel is then forced out of the cylinder and into the exhaust system, along with the exhaust gases.

Many attempts have been made to minimize the amount of unburned fuel in the combustion chambers due to quenching, by increasing the coolant temperature and lessening the contact area of the coolant around the combustion area. However, design limitations within the combustion chambers prevent the complete burning of the air/fuel charge, so a certain amount of the unburned fuel is still expelled into the exhaust system, regardless of modifications to the engine.

## AUTOMOTIVE EMISSIONS

Before emission controls were mandated on internal combustion engines, other sources of engine pollutants were discovered along with the exhaust emissions. It was determined that engine combustion exhaust produced approximately 60 percent of the total emission pollutants, fuel evaporation from the fuel tank and carburetor vents produced 20 percent, with the final 20 percent being produced through the crankcase as a by-product of the combustion process.

## Exhaust Gases

The exhaust gases emitted into the atmosphere are a combination of burned and unburned fuel. To understand the exhaust emission and its composition, we must review some basic chemistry.

When the air/fuel mixture is introduced into the engine, we are mixing air, composed of nitrogen (78 percent), oxygen (21 percent) and other gases (1 percent) with the fuel, which is 100 percent hydrocarbons (HC), in a semi-controlled ratio. As the combustion process is accomplished, power is produced to move the vehicle while the heat of combustion is transferred to the cooling system. The exhaust gases are then composed of nitrogen, a diatomic gas ($N_2$), the same as was introduced in the engine, carbon dioxide ($CO_2$), the same gas that is used in beverage carbonation, and water vapor ($H_2O$). The nitrogen ($N_2$), for the most part, passes through the engine unchanged, while the oxygen ($O_2$) reacts (burns) with the hydrocarbons (HC) and produces the carbon dioxide ($CO_2$) and the water vapors ($H_2O$). If this chemical process would be the only process to take place, the exhaust emissions would be harmless. However, during the combustion process, other compounds are formed which are considered dangerous. These pollutants are hydrocarbons (HC), carbon monoxide (CO), oxides of nitrogen (NOx) oxides of sulfur (SOx) and engine particulates.

### HYDROCARBONS

Hydrocarbons (HC) are essentially fuel which was not burned during the combustion process or which has escaped into the atmosphere through fuel evaporation. The main sources of incomplete combustion are rich air/fuel mixtures, low engine temperatures and improper spark timing. The main sources of hydrocarbon emission through fuel evaporation on most vehicles used to be the vehicle's fuel tank and carburetor float bowl.

To reduce combustion hydrocarbon emission, engine modifications were made to minimize dead space and surface area in the combustion chamber. In addition, the air/fuel mixture was made more lean through the improved control which feedback carburetion and fuel injection offers and by the addition of external controls to aid in further combustion of the hydrocarbons outside the engine. Two such methods were the addition of air injection systems, to inject fresh air into the exhaust manifolds and the installation of catalytic converters, units that are able to burn traces of hydrocarbons without affecting the internal combustion process or fuel economy.

To control hydrocarbon emissions through fuel evaporation, modifications were made to the fuel tank to allow storage of the fuel vapors during periods of engine shut-down. Modifications were also made to the air intake system so that at specific times during engine operation, these vapors may be purged and burned by blending them with the air/fuel mixture.

### CARBON MONOXIDE

Carbon monoxide is formed when not enough oxygen is present during the combustion process to convert carbon (C) to carbon dioxide ($CO_2$). An increase in the carbon monoxide (CO) emission is normally accompanied by an increase in the hydrocarbon (HC) emission because of the lack of oxygen to completely burn all of the fuel mixture.

Carbon monoxide (CO) also increases the rate at which the photo chemical smog is formed by speeding up the conversion of nitric oxide (NO) to nitrogen dioxide ($NO_2$). To accomplish this, carbon monoxide (CO) combines with oxygen ($O_2$) and nitric oxide (NO) to produce carbon dioxide ($CO_2$) and nitrogen dioxide ($NO_2$). ($CO + O_2 + NO = CO_2 + NO_2$).

The dangers of carbon monoxide, which is an odorless and colorless toxic gas are many. When carbon monoxide is inhaled into the lungs and passed into the blood stream, oxygen is replaced by the carbon monoxide in the red blood cells, causing a reduction in the amount of oxygen supplied to the many parts of the body. This lack of oxygen causes headaches, lack of coordination, reduced mental alertness and, should the carbon monoxide concentration be high enough, death could result.

### NITROGEN

Normally, nitrogen is an inert gas. When heated to approximately 2500°F (1371°C) through the combustion process, this gas becomes active and causes an increase in the nitric oxide (NO) emission.

Oxides of nitrogen (NOx) are composed of approximately 97–98 percent nitric oxide (NO). Nitric oxide is a colorless gas but when it is passed into the atmosphere, it combines with oxygen and forms nitrogen dioxide ($NO_2$). The nitrogen dioxide then combines with chemically active hydrocarbons (HC) and when in the presence of sunlight, causes the formation of photo-chemical smog.

#### Ozone

To further complicate matters, some of the nitrogen dioxide ($NO_2$) is broken apart by the sunlight to form nitric oxide and oxygen. ($NO_2$ + sunlight = NO + O). This single atom of oxygen then combines with diatomic (meaning 2 atoms) oxygen ($O_2$) to form ozone ($O_3$). Ozone is one of the smells associated with smog. It has a pungent and offensive odor, irritates the eyes and lung tissues, affects the growth of plant life and causes rapid deterioration of rubber products. Ozone can be formed by sunlight as well as electrical discharge into the air.

The most common discharge area on the automobile engine is the secondary ignition electrical system, especially when inferior quality spark plug cables are used. As the surge of high voltage is routed through the secondary cable, the circuit builds up an electrical field around the wire, which acts upon the oxygen in the surrounding air to form the ozone. The faint glow along the cable with the engine running that may be visible on a dark night, is called the "corona discharge." It is the result of the electrical field passing from a high along the cable, to a low in the surrounding air, which forms the ozone gas. The combination of corona and ozone has been a major cause of cable deterioration. Recently, different and better quality insulating materials have lengthened the life of the electrical cables.

Although ozone at ground level can be harmful, ozone is beneficial to the earth's inhabitants. By having a concentrated ozone layer called the "ozonosphere," between 10 and 20 miles (16–32 km) up in the atmosphere, much of the ultra violet radiation from the sun's rays are absorbed and screened. If this ozone layer were not present, much of the earth's surface would be burned, dried and unfit for human life.

### OXIDES OF SULFUR

Oxides of sulfur (SOx) were initially ignored in the exhaust system emissions, since the sulfur content of gasoline as a fuel is less than $\frac{1}{10}$ of 1 percent. Because of this small amount, it was felt that it contributed very little to the overall pollution problem. However, because of the difficulty in solving the sulfur emissions in industrial pollutions and the introduction of catalytic converter to the automobile exhaust systems, a change was mandated. The automobile exhaust system, when equipped with a catalytic converter, changes the sulfur dioxide ($SO_2$) into sulfur trioxide ($SO_3$).

When this combines with water vapors ($H_2O$), a sulfuric acid mist ($H_2SO_4$) is formed and is a very difficult pollutant to handle since it is extremely corrosive. This sulfuric acid mist that is formed, is the same mist that rises from the vents of an automobile battery when an active chemical reaction takes place within the battery cells.

When a large concentration of vehicles equipped with catalytic converters are operating in an area, this acid mist may rise and be distributed over a large ground area causing land, plant, crop, paint and building damage.

### PARTICULATE MATTER

A certain amount of particulate matter is present in the burning of any fuel, with carbon constituting the largest percentage of the particulates. In gasoline, the remaining particulates are the burned remains of the various other compounds used in its manufacture. When a gasoline engine is in good internal condition, the particulate emissions are low but as the engine wears internally, the particulate emissions increase. By visually inspecting the tail pipe emissions, a determination can be made as to where an engine defect may exist. An engine with light gray or blue smoke emitting from the tail pipe normally indicates an increase in the oil consumption through burning due to internal engine wear. Black smoke would indicate a defective fuel delivery system, causing the engine to operate in a rich mode. Regardless of the color of the smoke, the internal part of the engine or the fuel delivery system should be repaired to prevent excess particulate emissions.

Diesel and turbine engines emit a darkened plume of smoke from the exhaust system because of the type of fuel used. Emission control regulations are mandated for this type of emission and more stringent measures are being used to prevent excess emission of the particulate matter. Electronic components are being introduced to control the injection of the fuel at precisely the proper time of piston travel, to achieve the optimum in fuel ignition and fuel usage. Other particulate after-burning components are being tested to achieve a cleaner emission.

Good grades of engine lubricating oils should be used, which meet the manufacturer's specification. Cut-rate oils can contribute to the particulate emission problem because of their low flash or ignition temperature point. Such oils burn prematurely during the combustion process causing emission of particulate matter.

The cooling system is an important factor in the reduction of particulate matter. The optimum combustion will occur, with the cooling system operating at a temperature specified by the manufacturer. The cooling system must be maintained in the same manner as the engine oiling system, as each system is required to perform properly in order for the engine to operate efficiently for a long time.

## Crankcase Emissions

Crankcase emissions are made up of water, acids, unburned fuel, oil fumes and particulates. These emissions are classified as hydrocarbons (HC) and are formed by the small amount of unburned, compressed air/fuel mixture entering the crankcase from the combustion area (between the cylinder walls and piston rings) during the compression and power strokes. The head of the compression and combustion help to form the remaining crankcase emissions.

Since the first engines, crankcase emissions were allowed into the atmosphere through a road draft tube, mounted on the lower side of the engine block. Fresh air came in through an open oil filler cap or breather. The air passed through the crankcase mixing with blow-by gases. The motion of the vehicle and the air blowing past the open end of the road draft tube caused a low pressure area (vacuum) at the end of the tube. Crankcase emissions were simply drawn out of the road draft tube into the air.

To control the crankcase emission, the road draft tube was deleted. A hose and/or tubing was routed from the crankcase to the intake manifold so the blow-by emission could be burned with the air/fuel mixture. However, it was found that intake manifold vacuum, used to draw the crankcase emissions into the manifold, would vary in strength at the wrong time and not allow the proper emission flow. A regulating valve was needed to control the flow of air through the crankcase.

Testing, showed the removal of the blow-by gases from the crankcase as quickly as possible, was most important to the longevity of the engine. Should large accumulations of blow-by gases remain and condense, dilution of the engine oil would occur to form water, soots, resins, acids and lead salts, resulting in the formation of sludge and varnishes. This condensation of the blow-by gases occurs more frequently on vehicles used in numerous starting and stopping conditions, excessive idling and when the engine is not allowed to attain normal operating temperature through short runs.

## Evaporative Emissions

Gasoline fuel is a major source of pollution, before and after it is burned in the automobile engine. From the time the fuel is refined, stored, pumped and transported, again stored until it is pumped into the fuel tank of the vehicle, the gasoline gives off unburned hydrocarbons (HC) into the atmosphere. Through the redesign of storage areas and venting systems, the pollution factor was diminished, but not eliminated, from the refinery standpoint. However, the automobile still remained the primary source of vaporized, unburned hydrocarbon (HC) emissions.

Fuel pumped from an underground storage tank is cool but when exposed to a warmer ambient temperature, will expand. Before controls were mandated, an owner might fill the fuel tank with fuel from an underground storage tank and park the vehicle for some time in warm area, such as a parking lot. As the fuel would warm, it would expand and should no provisions or area be provided for the expansion, the fuel would spill out of the filler neck and onto the ground, causing hydrocarbon (HC) pollution and creating a severe fire hazard. To correct this condition, the vehicle manufacturers added overflow plumbing and/or gasoline tanks with built in expansion areas or domes.

However, this did not control the fuel vapor emission from the fuel tank. It was determined that most of the fuel evaporation occurred when the vehicle was stationary and the engine not operating. Most vehicles carry 5–25 gallons (19–95 liters) of gasoline. Should a large concentration of vehicles be parked in one area, such as a large parking lot, excessive fuel vapor emissions would take place, increasing as the temperature increases.

To prevent the vapor emission from escaping into the atmosphere, the fuel systems were designed to trap the vapors while the vehicle is stationary, by sealing the system from the atmosphere. A storage system is used to collect and hold the fuel vapors from the carburetor (if equipped) and the fuel tank when the engine is not operating. When the engine is started, the storage system is then purged of the fuel vapors, which are drawn into the engine and burned with the air/fuel mixture.

## EMISSION CONTROLS

## Crankcase Ventilation System

### OPERATION

▶ See Figure 1

When the engine is running, a small portion of the gases which are formed in the combustion chamber leak by the piston rings and enter the crankcase. Since these gases are under pressure they tend to escape from the crankcase and enter into the atmosphere. If these gases are allowed to remain in the crankcase for any length of time, they would contaminate the engine oil and cause sludge to build up. If the gases are allowed to escape into the atmosphere, they would pollute the air, as they contain unburned hydrocarbons. The crankcase emission control equipment recycles these gases back into the engine combustion chamber, where they are burned.

Crankcase gases are recycled in the following manner. While the engine is running, clean filtered air is drawn into the crankcase through the intake air filter and then through a hose leading to the oil filler cap or the valve cover. As the air passes through the crankcase it picks up the combustion gases and carries them out of the crankcase, up through the PCV valve, (Volvo calls it the flame guard) and into the intake manifold. After they enter the intake manifold they are drawn into the combustion chamber and are burned.

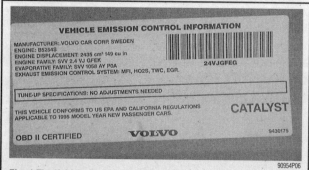

Fig. 1 The Vehicle Emissions Control Information (VECI) label will tell you with what emissions equipment your vehicle is equipped

90954P06

The most critical component of the system is the PCV valve. This vacuum-controlled valve regulates the amount of gases which are recycled into the combustion chamber. At low engine speeds the valve is partially closed, limiting the flow of gases into the intake manifold. As engine speed increases, the valve opens to admit greater quantities of the gases into the intake manifold. If the valve should become blocked or plugged, the gases will be prevented from escaping the crankcase by the normal route. Since these gases are under pressure, they will find their own way out of the crankcase. This alternate route is usually a weak oil seal or gasket in the engine. As the gas escapes by the gasket, it also creates an oil leak. Besides causing oil leaks, a clogged PCV valve also allows these gases to remain in the crankcase for an extended period of time, promoting the formation of sludge in the engine.

## COMPONENT TESTING

Servicing the crankcase ventilation system consists of checking the hoses for cracks or vacuum leaks and checking the hoses, calibrated nipple and flame guard for clogging. Remove the hose from the air inlet tube and with engine running, check for a presence of vacuum. If no vacuum is present, find the restriction in the PCV system.

## REMOVAL & INSTALLATION

Refer to Section 1 for removal and installation of the PCV valve. The PCV nipple should be removed and inspected every 60,000 miles (96,000 km).

## Evaporative Emission Controls

## OPERATION

Changes in atmospheric temperature cause fuel tanks to breathe, that is, the air within the tank expands and contracts with outside temperature changes. If an unsealed system was used, when the temperature rises, air would escape through the tank vent tube or the vent in the tank cap. The air which escapes contains gasoline vapors.

The Evaporative Emission Control System provides a sealed fuel system with the capability to store and condense fuel vapors. When the fuel evaporates in the fuel tank, the vapor passes through vent hoses or tubes to a carbon filled evaporative canister. When the engine is operating the vapors are drawn into the intake manifold.

The vapors are drawn into the engine at idle as well as at operating speeds. This system is called a Bi-level Purge System where there is a dual source of vacuum to remove fuel vapor from the canister. The source of vacuum at idle is a tee in the PCV system.

A sealed, maintenance free evaporative canister is used. The canister is mounted under the vehicle on either side behind the wheel well. The canister is filled with granules of an activated carbon mixture. Fuel vapors entering the canister are absorbed by the charcoal granules.

Fuel tank pressure vents fuel vapors into the canister. They are held in the canister until they can be drawn into the intake manifold. The canister purge valve allows the canister to be purged at a predetermined time and engine operating conditions.

Vacuum for the canister is controlled by the canister purge valve. The valve is operated by the ECM. The ECM regulates the valve by switching the ground circuit on and off based on engine operating conditions. When energized, the valve prevents vacuum from reaching the canister. When not energized the valve allows vacuum to flow through to the canister.

During warm up and for a specified time after hot starts, the ECM energizes (grounds) the valve preventing vacuum from reaching the canister. When the engine temperature reaches the operating level of about 120°F (49°C), the ECM removes the ground from the valve allowing vacuum to flow through the canister and purges vapors through the throttle body. During certain idle conditions, the purge valve may be grounded to control fuel mix calibrations.

The fuel tank is sealed with a pressure-vacuum relief filler cap. The relief valves in the cap are a safety feature, preventing excessive pressure or vacuum in the fuel tank. If the cap is malfunctioning, and needs to be replaced, ensure that the replacement is the identical cap to ensure correct system operation.

During warm up and for a specified time after hot starts, the ECM energizes (grounds) the valve preventing vacuum from reaching the canister. When the engine temperature reaches the operating level of about 120°F (49°C), the ECM removes the ground from the valve allowing vacuum to flow through the canister and purges vapors through the throttle body. During certain idle conditions, the purge valve may be grounded to control fuel mix calibrations.

Some vehicles have added system components due to the EVAP system monitor incorporated in the OBD-II engine control system used on these years. Two, instead of one, EVAP canisters are used and they are mounted on the drivers side of the vehicle. The canister purge valve is located on the bracket with the canisters. A test port for pressurizing the EVAP system is included and located below the brake booster. The test port is used to pressurize the system with a special gas and serious precautions must be taken to avoid damage to the EVAP system and the fuel tank. This is a procedure best suited to a professional shop, due to the precautions and the equipment needed to test this system. The ECM can store trouble codes for EVAP system performance, a list of the codes is provided later in this section. Normal testing procedure can be used for any component listed in EVAP testing in this book.

## COMPONENT TESTING

The majority of the testing of the EVAP system is a visual inspection for damaged, leaking or missing components. Inspect the hoses to the throttle body, the canister, fuel tank, fuel filler pipe, and the filler cap. Any damaged components should be replaced.

### Canister Purge Valve

1. Remove the inlet hose to the valve.
2. Connect a hand-held vacuum pump to the fitting and pump up vacuum.
3. If vacuum holds, valve is ok. If vacuum falls off, valve diaphragm is leaking, replace the valve.

## REMOVAL & INSTALLATION

➡️**To relieve fuel tank pressure, the filler cap must be removed before disconnecting any fuel system component.**

### Evaporative (Carbon) Canister

◆ **See Figures 2, 3, 4 and 5**

1. Disconnect the negative battery cable.
2. Raise and support the vehicle.
3. Remove the retaining bolts from the canister mounting bracket.
4. Remove the canister.
5. Label and disconnect the hoses on the top of the canister.
6. Remove the canister from the mounting bracket.

**To install:**

7. Install the canister in the mounting bracket.
8. Install and tighten the canister brackets retaining bolts.
9. Install the hoses in their proper locations.
10. Lower the vehicle.
11. Connect the negative battery cable.

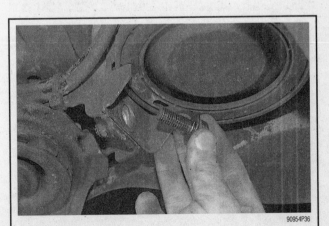

90954P36

**Fig. 2 Remove the bolts from the canister bracket and . . .**

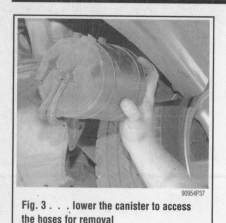

Fig. 3 . . . lower the canister to access the hoses for removal

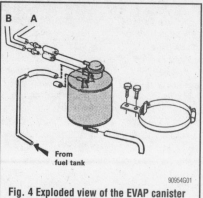

Fig. 4 Exploded view of the EVAP canister and hoses

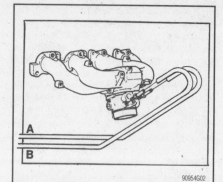

Fig. 5 EVAP system hose connections on the intake manifold

### Canister Purge Valve

➡The valve is located on the top of the canister. When the canister is removed, the valve can be removed from the canister by carefully pulling the valve off of the canister.

## Exhaust Gas Recirculation System

### OPERATION

#### System

▶ See Figure 6

The Exhaust Gas Recirculation (EGR) system is designed to reintroduce exhaust gas into the combustion chambers, thereby lowering combustion temperatures and reducing the formation of oxides of nitrogen ($NO_x$).

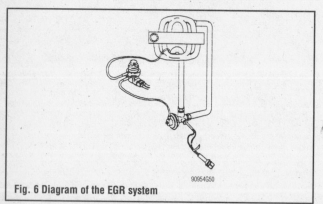

Fig. 6 Diagram of the EGR system

The amount of exhaust gas that is reintroduced into the combustion cycle is determined by several factors, such as: engine speed, engine vacuum, exhaust system backpressure, coolant temperature, throttle position. All EGR valves are vacuum operated. The EGR vacuum diagram for your particular vehicle is displayed on the Vehicle Emission Control Information (VECI) label.

#### EGR Valve

▶ See Figure 7

The EGR valve controls flow of exhaust gases from the exhaust manifold to the intake manifold. The valve is operated by control pressure from the EGR vacuum booster. The EGR valve is located under the intake manifold.

#### EGR Vacuum Controller

▶ See Figure 8

The vacuum controller controls pressure in the vacuum line to the EGR valve by means of the admission valve (lower section). The pressure in the intake manifold is supplied to the reducing valve (upper section). The valve uses an electrical signal to maintain optimum control of the EGR valve. The unit is also designed to allow for ambient air pressure. The vacuum controller valve is located on the left-hand suspension strut tower or on the relay shelf above the electric cooling fan.

#### EGR Temperature Sensor

▶ See Figure 9

The EGR temperature sensor measures the temperature of exhaust gases returned to the intake manifold. This sensor has a positive temperature coefficient, which means that the resistance through the sensor will rise with the temperature. The sensor is designed to measure temperatures up to 930°F (500°C). Detection of temperature variations enables the control unit to determine whether or not the EGR system is working. The sensor is located in the EGR upper pipe, between the intake manifold and EGR valve.

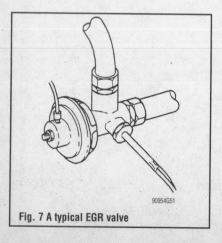

Fig. 7 A typical EGR valve

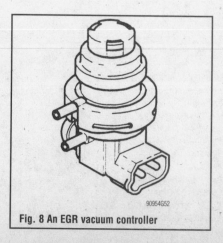

Fig. 8 An EGR vacuum controller

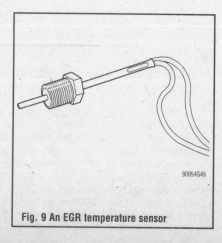

Fig. 9 An EGR temperature sensor

## COMPONENT TESTING

### EGR Temperature Sensor

▶ **See Figure 10**

1. Unplug the temperature sensor connector.
2. Measure the resistance between the terminals of the sensor. The resistance should be 0.1–4000 ohms. Use the temperature-to-resistance chart in this section for reference. If the value is out of range, replace the sensor.

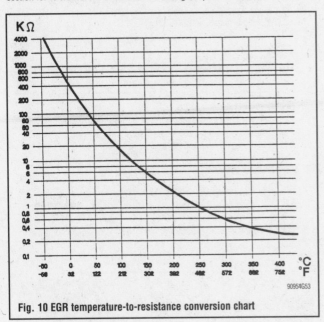

**Fig. 10 EGR temperature-to-resistance conversion chart**

### EGR Gas Flow Test

1. Connect a tachometer to the engine.
2. Remove the vacuum hose or rubber elbow from the EGR valve and connect a hand vacuum pump to the EGR valve vacuum nipple.
3. Start the engine and slowly apply vacuum to the EGR valve diaphragm.
4. The engine speed should drop as vacuum reaches 3–5 in. Hg and continue to drop as more vacuum is applied. The engine may even stall. This means EGR gas is flowing through the system.
5. If the engine speed doesn't drop, check for a failed EGR valve or plugged EGR passage. Remove the EGR valve and inspect/repair as necessary.

### EGR Valve Leakage Test

▶ **See Figure 11**

1. Disconnect the negative battery cable.
2. Disconnect the hose from the fitting from the top of the EGR valve.

3. Connect a hand-held vacuum pump to the fitting and apply 15 inches of vacuum to the valve. Observe the gauge reading on the pump; if vacuum falls off, the diaphragm in the EGR valve has ruptured, and the EGR valve must be replaced. If vacuum remains, proceed to next step.
4. Remove the hose from the bottom of the EGR valve. Using compressed air (if available) and an air nozzle with rubber tip, apply 50 psi of regulated air pressure to the fitting.
5. Using your hand, open the throttle all the way, and listen inside the throttle body; if air is escaping, the poppet valve in the base of the EGR valve is leaking. Replace the EGR valve.

### EGR Vacuum Controller

▶ **See Figures 12, 13 and 14**

1. Remove the inlet hose of the EGR vacuum controller.

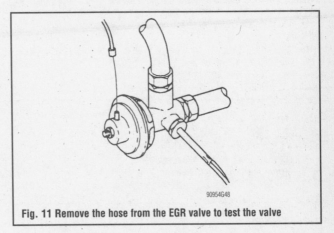

**Fig. 11 Remove the hose from the EGR valve to test the valve**

2. Connect a hand-held vacuum pump to the fitting and apply 10 inches of vacuum. If the vacuum falls off, the controller's diaphragm is leaking. Replace the EGR vacuum controller and retest. If OK, connect hose and proceed to the next step.
3. Remove the hose at the EGR vacuum controller inlet (if reinstalled after last test).
4. Connect a vacuum gauge to this hose.
5. Start the engine and bring it to operating temperature.
6. Hold the engine speed at approximately 1500 RPM. Check for steady manifold vacuum at this hose.

➡ **To figure out what the vacuum should be, remove a vacuum hose directly from the intake manifold and measure the vacuum at 1500 RPM.**

7. If manifold vacuum is not present, check for vacuum leaks in the line or an obstruction. Repair as necessary and retest. If manifold vacuum was OK, shut off engine, connect hose, and proceed to the next step.
8. Disconnect the hose at the vacuum controller outlet fitting.
9. Connect a vacuum gauge to this fitting.

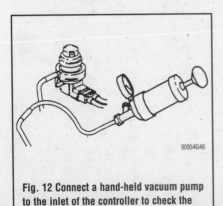

**Fig. 12 Connect a hand-held vacuum pump to the inlet of the controller to check the controller valve diaphragm**

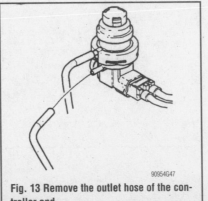

**Fig. 13 Remove the outlet hose of the controller and . . .**

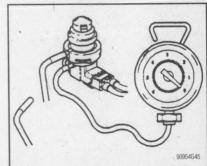

**Fig. 14 . . . connect a vacuum gauge to the port to check operation of the controller valve**

10. Disconnect the electrical connector on the controller. This will simulate an open circuit at the controller.

11. Start the engine and bring it to operating temperature.

12. Hold the engine speed at approximately 2000 RPM while checking for vacuum flow through the vacuum controller.

13. The gauge reading will be low, at idle speed the gauge reading should be erratic. This is normal.

14. To allow full manifold vacuum to flow through the vacuum controller, exhaust backpressure must be present. It must be high enough to hold the bleed valve in the transducer portion of the controller closed. Have a helper momentarily (a few seconds) block the exhaust with a rag or other suitable device.

### ⁂ CAUTION

**Make sure to have the helper wear heavy gloves to reduce the risk of burns from the exhaust gas or exhaust pipes.**

15. As temporary backpressure is built, full manifold vacuum should be observed.

16. If full vacuum was present at the inlet fitting, but is not present at the outlet fitting, replace the valve control.

## REMOVAL & INSTALLATION

### EGR Valve

▶ **See Figures 15, 16, 17, 18 and 19**

1. Disconnect the negative battery cable.
2. Remove any components necessary to access the valve.
3. Unplug the EGR temperature sensor (if equipped).

4. Remove the EGR tube from the valve.
5. Remove the EGR valve mounting bolts.
6. Remove the EGR valve from the vehicle.

**To install:**

7. Clean the valve mounting surface.
8. Install a new gasket on the valve mounting surface.
9. Install the valve into place.
10. Tighten the valve mounting bolts.
11. Insert the EGR tube and tighten the fitting.
12. If equipped, plug in the EGR temperature sensor connector.
13. Install any components removed to access the valve.
14. Connect the negative battery cable.

### EGR Controller Valve

1. Disconnect the negative battery cable.
2. Label and remove the vacuum hoses and electrical connectors from the valve.
3. Remove the fasteners, then remove the valve.

**To install:**

4. Place the new valve into position and secure it with the mounting fasteners.
5. Attach the vacuum lines and wiring connectors to the valve.
6. Connect the negative battery cable.

### EGR Temperature Sensor

1. Disconnect the negative battery cable.
2. Remove any necessary components to access the EGR valve and sensor.
3. Unplug the temperature sensor connector.
4. Using a proper size socket, remove the EGR temperature sensor from the valve.

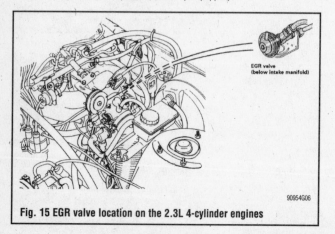

**Fig. 15 EGR valve location on the 2.3L 4-cylinder engines**

**Fig. 16 Location of the EGR valve—850 models**

**Fig. 17 Remove the two valve mounting bolts and . . .**

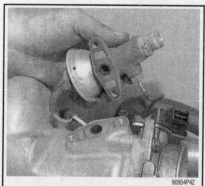

**Fig. 18 . . . lift the valve from the mounting surface**

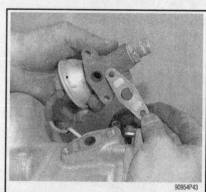

**Fig. 19 Always replace the EGR gasket with a new one when replacing the valve**

**To install:**
5. Install the temperature sensor into the valve and tighten the sensor.
6. Plug the sensor connector in.
7. Install any components removed to access the valve.
8. Connect the negative battery cable.

## Pulsed Secondary Air Injection

### OPERATION

▶ **See Figure 20**

The air injection system is used to inject fresh air into the exhaust manifolds or catalytic converters via an air control valve. The air is created by a air pump that is driven by the engine, it is located in the front of the engine and is propelled by a belt.

The system uses a shut-off valve which is used to prevent backfire in the exhaust system during sudden deceleration. When the throttle is suddenly closed, a too-rich air/fuel mixture may be created which could not normally be burned. This mixture becomes burnable when it reaches the exhaust area and combines with the injected air. The shut-off valve senses the sudden increase in the intake manifold vacuum causing the valve to open, allowing air from the air pump to pass through the valve and silencer into the atmosphere.

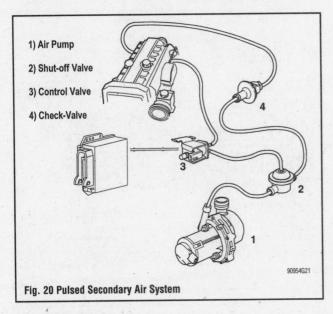

1) Air Pump
2) Shut-off Valve
3) Control Valve
4) Check-Valve

90954G21

**Fig. 20 Pulsed Secondary Air System**

### COMPONENT TESTING

➡ **Do not attempt to correct pump noise by lubricating the air pump. Never lubricate the air pump. Do not assume a pump is bad just because it's noisy.**

#### Control Valve Functional Test

1. Run the engine to normal operating temperature, then increase the speed to 1,500 rpm.
2. Disconnect the vacuum hose at the valve inlet and verify that there is vacuum present.
3. With the engine running at 1,500 rpm, airflow should be felt and heard at the outlet side of the shut-off valve.
4. If the valve is not functioning properly, replace it.

#### Air Supply Pump Functional Check

1. Check and, if necessary, adjust the belt tension. Press at the mid-point of the belt's longest straight run. You should be able to depress the belt about ½ in. (13mm) at most.
2. Run the engine to normal operating temperature and let it idle.
3. Disconnect the air supply hose from the shut-off valve. If the pump is operating properly, airflow should be felt at the hose. The flow should increase as you increase the engine speed. The pump is not serviceable and should be replaced if it is not functioning properly.

### REMOVAL & INSTALLATION

#### Air Pump

1. Disconnect the negative battery cable.
2. Remove the drive belt.
3. Remove the air hose from the air pump.
4. Remove the pivot and adjusting bolts from the pump and bracket.
5. Remove the pump from the vehicle.
**To install:**
6. Install the pump on the mounting bracket and tighten the bolts.
7. Install the air hose onto the pump control valve.
8. Install and adjust the drive belt.
9. Connect the negative battery cable.

## Thermostatic Air Cleaner Assembly

### OPERATION

A thermostatically controlled shutter is housed in the air cleaner. The thermostat senses the intake air temperature and changes the position of the shutter, to vary the proportions of hot and cold air entering the air cleaner.

Intake air preheating provides the engine with nearly constant temperature intake air, regardless of ambient air temperature. This provides for smooth engine running and prevents ice build-up.

### TESTING

1. Remove the air cleaner housing.
2. Remove the shutter housing from the air cleaner.
3. Check the bushings and the mounting of the shutter.
4. Check the shutter position at the following temperatures:
   a. 41°F (5°C) or less
   b. Approximately 50°F (10°C)
   c. 59°F (16°C) or more
5. Replace the thermostat if the shutter does not function as specified.
6. Reassemble and install the air cleaner, making sure the air cleaner housing and ducts are sealing properly.

### REMOVAL & INSTALLATION

1. Remove the air cleaner housing.
2. Remove the retaining clips and remove the shutter housing.
**To install:**
3. Place the shutter into position and install the retaining clips.
4. Install the air cleaner housing.

## Service Reminder Light

### RESETTING

See Section 1 for maintenance light resetting.

## ELECTRONIC ENGINE CONTROLS

### Engine Control Module

#### OPERATION

The Engine Control Module (ECM) performs many functions on your vehicle. The module accepts information from various engine sensors and computes the required fuel flow rate necessary to maintain the correct amount of air/fuel ratio throughout the entire engine operational range.

Based on the information that is received and programmed into the ECM's memory, the ECM generates output signals to control relays, actuators and solenoids. The ECM also sends out a command to the fuel injectors that meters the appropriate quantity of fuel. The module automatically senses and compensates for any changes in altitude when driving your vehicle.

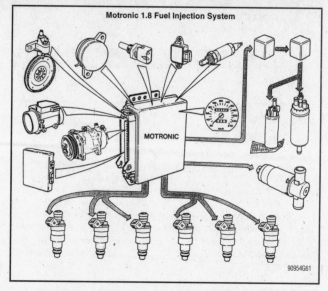

Motronic 1.8 Fuel Injection System

90954G61

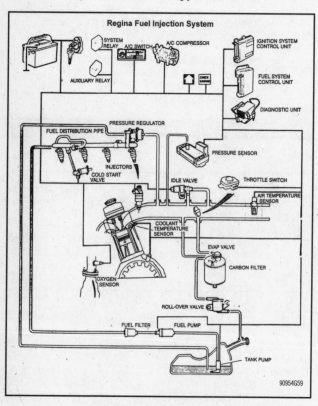

Regina Fuel Injection System

90954G59

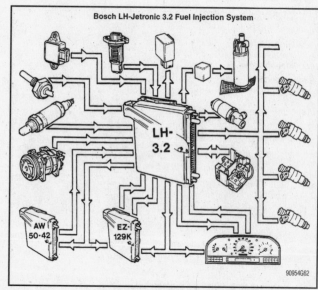

Bosch LH-Jetronic 3.2 Fuel Injection System

90954G62

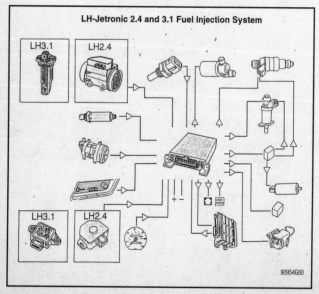

LH-Jetronic 2.4 and 3.1 Fuel Injection System

90954G60

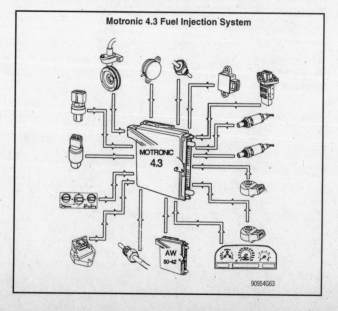

Motronic 4.3 Fuel Injection System

90954G63

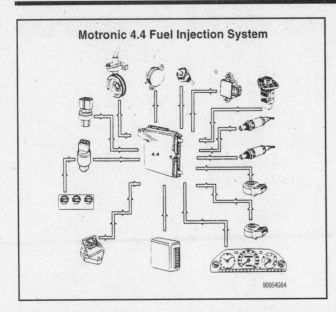

**Motronic 4.4 Fuel Injection System**

90954G64

## REMOVAL & INSTALLATION

➡️If the battery cable(s) is disconnected for longer than 5 minutes, the adaptive fuel factor will be lost. After repair it will be necessary to drive the vehicle at least 10 miles, and as many as 250, to allow the processor to relearn the correct factors. The driving period should include steady-throttle open road driving if possible. During the drive, the vehicle may exhibit driveability symptoms not noticed before. These symptoms should clear as the control module computes the correction factor.

### Coupe, 240, 700 and 940 Series

▶ See Figure 21

➡️The ECM is located on the passenger side footwell under the kickpanel.

1. Disconnect the negative battery cable.
2. Remove the kickpanel to access the ECM.
3. Remove the retaining bolts on the ECM bracket.
4. Carefully lower the ECM and unlatch the harness connector from the ECM.
5. Remove the ECM.

**To install:**

6. Attach the connector to the ECM and carefully place it into position.
7. Tighten the bracket retaining bolts.
8. Install the kickpanel.
9. Connect the negative battery cable.
10. Start the vehicle and check to make sure the "check engine" light on the instrument cluster is operative.

### 960/S90/V90 Series

▶ See Figure 22

➡️The ECM is located behind the driver's side of the dash panel, just beneath the steering column.

1. Disconnect the negative battery cable.
2. Remove the knee bolster panel under the steering column.
3. Remove the retaining bolts on the ECM bracket.
4. Carefully lower the ECM and unlatch the harness connector from the ECM.
5. Remove the ECM.

**To install:**

6. Attach the connector to the ECM and carefully place it into position.
7. Tighten the bracket retaining bolts.
8. Install the knee bolster panel.
9. Connect the negative battery cable.
10. Start the vehicle and check to make sure the "check engine" light on the instrument cluster is operative.

### 850/C70/S70/V70 Series

▶ See Figure 23

➡️The ECM on these models is in the engine compartment in a box similar to the air cleaner box. Air is brought through a pick-up tube from under the car and used to cool the modules as the vehicle drives along. There are sometimes three modules located in this box: an Ignition Control Module (ICM), ECM and, on automatic transaxle vehicles only, a Transmission Control Module (TCM). The ECM is usually the center one.

1. Disconnect the negative battery cable.
2. Remove the lid on the module box behind the passenger side headlamp.
3. Reach down and unsnap the harness connector and remove the ECM from the box.

**To install:**

4. Place the ECM into the box and attach the harness connector to it.
5. Install the lid onto the module box.
6. Connect the negative battery cable.
7. Start the vehicle and check to make sure the "check engine" light on the instrument cluster is operative.

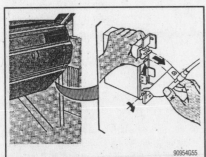

90954G55

Fig. 21 Location of the ECM on Coupe, 240, 700 and 940 series models. Be sure to lift the retaining clip before detaching the connector

90954G05

Fig. 22 On 960/S90/V90 series vehicles, the ECM is located behind the driver's side dash panel

90954P39

Fig. 23 The ECM and transmission module as located in the module box (with the lid removed)

## Heated Oxygen Sensor

### OPERATION

▶ **See Figure 24**

The Oxygen Sensor (O2S) is a device which produces an electrical voltage when exposed to the oxygen present in the exhaust gases. The sensor is mounted in the exhaust manifold. Some oxygen sensors are electrically heated internally for faster switching when the engine is running. The oxygen sensor produces a voltage within 0 and 1 volt. When there is a large amount of oxygen present (lean mixture), the sensor produces a low voltage (less than 0.4v). When there is a lesser amount present (rich mixture) it produces a higher voltage (0.6–1.0v). The stoichiometric or correct fuel to air ratio will read between 0.4 and 0.6v. By monitoring the oxygen content and converting it to electrical voltage, the sensor acts as a rich-lean switch. The voltage is transmitted to the engine controller. The controller signals the power module to trigger the fuel injector.

Later models have two sensors, one before the catalytic converter and one after. This is done for a catalyst efficiency monitor that is a part of the OBD-II engine controls that are on these year vehicles. The one before the catalyst measures the exhaust emissions right out of the engine, and sends the signal to the ECM about the state of the mixture as previously talked about. The second sensor reports the difference in the emissions after the exhaust gases have gone through the catalyst. This sensor reports to the ECM the amount of emissions reduction the catalyst is performing.

The oxygen sensor will not work until a predetermined temperature is reached, until this time the engine controller is running in what as known as OPEN LOOP operation. OPEN LOOP means that the engine controller has not yet begun to correct the air-to-fuel ratio by reading the oxygen sensor. After the engine comes to operating temperature, the engine controller will monitor the oxygen sensor and correct the air/fuel ratio from the sensor's readings. This is what is known as CLOSED LOOP operation.

A Heated Oxygen Sensor (HO2S) has a heating element that keeps the sensor at proper operating temperature during all operating modes. Maintaining correct sensor temperature at all times allows the system to enter into CLOSED LOOP operation sooner.

In CLOSED LOOP operation, the engine controller monitors the sensor input (along with other inputs) and adjusts the injector pulse width accordingly. During OPEN LOOP operation, the engine controller ignores the sensor input and adjusts the injector pulse to a preprogrammed value based on other inputs.

### TESTING

▶ **See Figures 25 and 26**

### ✳✳ WARNING

**Do not pierce the wires when testing this sensor; this can lead to wiring harness damage. Backprobe the connector to properly read the voltage of the HO2S.**

1. Disconnect the HO2S.
2. Check for supply voltage to the heating element by checking the power and ground circuits using the wiring diagrams located in Section 6. Check the heating element by:
   a. Turn the ignition to **RUN** position, with the engine **OFF**.
   b. Using a DVOM, probe the proper circuits connecting the positive lead of the DVOM to the power circuit and the negative lead to the ground circuit.
   c. Battery voltage should be present, if voltage is present but less than 8 volts, perform the following step. If there is no voltage skip the next step.
   d. Remove the connector on the ECM and check the resistance of the HO2S heater's power and ground circuits, if more than 5 ohms, repair the circuit(s). If resistance is less than 5 ohms, replace the ECM.

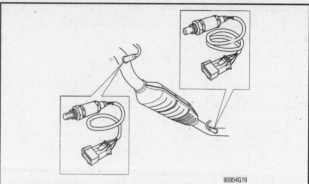
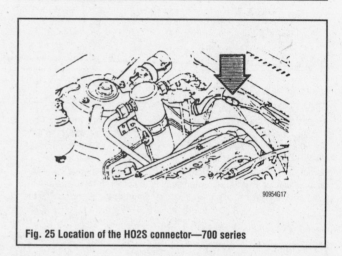

**Fig. 24 OBD-II equipped vehicles have two HO2 sensors, one before and one after the catalyst**

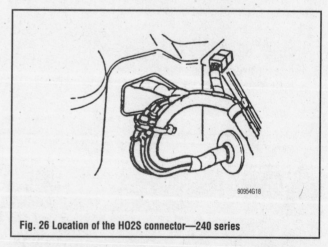

**Fig. 25 Location of the HO2S connector—700 series**

**Fig. 26 Location of the HO2S connector—240 series**

   e. If no voltage is present check for continuity of the HO2S heater's power and ground circuits. If continuity is present and resistance is less than 5 ohms, replace the ECM, if the circuit is open or resistance exceeds 5 ohms repair the circuit(s).
3. Start the vehicle and let it reach operating temperature. With the HO2S connected and engine running, measure the voltage with a Digital Volt-Ohmmeter (DVOM) between terminals **HO2S** and **SIG RTN** (GND) of the oxygen sensor connector. Voltage should fluctuate between 0.01–1.1 volts. If voltage fluctuation is slow or voltage is not within specification, the sensor may be faulty.

## REMOVAL & INSTALLATION

♦ **See Figures 27 thru 35**

1. Disconnect the negative battery cable.
2. Raise and support the vehicle safely.
3. Label and disconnect the HO2S from the engine control wiring harness.

➡ **Lubricate the sensor with penetrating oil prior to removal.**

4. Remove the sensor using an appropriate tool. Special oxygen sensor sockets are available to remove the sensor and can be purchased at many parts stores or where automotive tools are sold. The proper size wrench can be used, most sensors are ⅞ inch or 22mm sizes.

**To install:**

5. Before installing, apply "Never Seez" paste (P/N 1 161 035-9) or equivalent anti-seize compound to the threaded section of the sensor.
6. Install the sensor in the mounting boss and tighten to 40 ft. lbs. (55 Nm).
7. Connect the engine control wiring harness to the sensor.
8. Lower the vehicle.
9. Connect the negative battery cable.
10. Remove the oxygen sensor, using a suitable wrench.

Fig. 27 Location of the front HO2S on an OBD-II equipped 850 model

Fig. 28 The catalyst efficiency monitor HO2S is located under this shield on 850 models

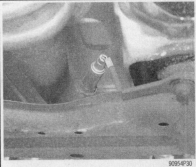

Fig. 29 The sensor can be seen from the side, but the panel must first be removed if the sensor is to be removed

Fig. 30 Unplug the HO2S connectors

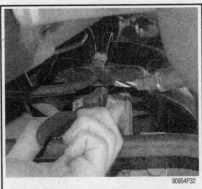

Fig. 31 Remove the clip retaining the harness for the HO2S

Fig. 32 The rear HO2S has an additional clip retaining the harness

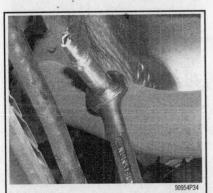

Fig. 33 A proper size open end wrench can be used to remove the HO2S

Fig. 34 Remove the HO2S from the exhaust pipe

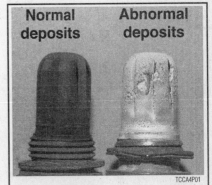

Fig. 35 Inspect the oxygen sensor tip for abnormal deposits

## Idle Air Control Valve

### OPERATION

▶ **See Figure 36**

An Idle Air Control (IAC) valve is incorporated into the system to set the correct air valve opening and constant idle speed. The valve consists of a stepper motor with twin coils, one for opening and one for closing. The ECM delivers pulsed ground signals to both IAC coils. Depending on the signals from the ECM, the motor operates a rotary valve which controls the air flow through the outlet port.

In the event of an electrical fault, a spring maintains the rotary valve in a fixed position and the idling speed is increased to approximately 1200 RPM. The ECM incorporates a self-learning system which enables it to learn the ideal idling speed. Because of this feature, the IAC valve is not adjustable.

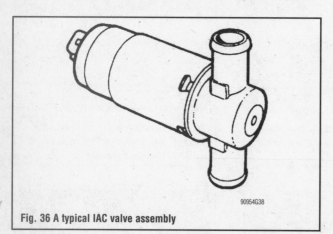

Fig. 36 A typical IAC valve assembly

### TESTING

▶ **See Figures 37, 38, 39, 40 and 41**

1. Disconnect the negative battery cable.
2. Unplug the IAC connector.
3. To test the coil driver circuits in the IAC valve:
   a. Using an ohmmeter, measure the resistance between pins 3 and 2 on the IAC valve.
   b. Resistance should be 10–14 ohms. If resistance is ok, proceed to the next step. If resistance is out of range, replace the IAC and retest.
   c. Using an ohmmeter, measure the resistance between pins 1 and 2 on the IAC valve.
   d. Resistance should be 10–14 ohms. If resistance is ok, proceed to the next step. If resistance is out of range, replace the IAC and retest.
4. To test the voltage lead:
   a. Using an voltmeter, measure the voltage at terminal 2. Turn the ignition **ON**, and measure the voltage between terminal 2 and ground.
   b. Voltage should be battery voltage. If voltage is not present or out of range, repair the circuit. If voltage is ok, proceed to the next step.
5. To test the signal return:
   a. Using an voltmeter, measure the voltage at terminal 1. Turn the ignition **ON**, and measure the voltage between terminal 1 and ground.
   b. Voltage should be around 6.0–8.5v. If voltage is not present or out of range, repair the circuit. If voltage is ok, proceed to the next step.
6. To test the ground circuit:
   a. Using an ohmmeter, measure the resistance at terminal 3. Turn the ignition **ON**, and measure the resistance between terminal 1 and ground.
   b. Resistance should be 0 ohms. If continuity is not present or out of range, repair the circuit. If continuity is ok, replace the CMP sensor and retest.

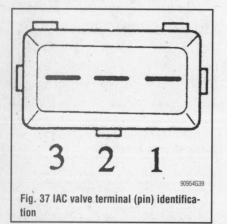

Fig. 37 IAC valve terminal (pin) identification

Fig. 38 IAC valve connector terminal identification

Fig. 39 Testing the coil driver circuit between pins 2 and 3

Fig. 40 Testing the coil driver circuit between pins 2 and 1

Fig. 41 Testing the IAC valve circuit at terminal 2 of the harness connector

## REMOVAL & INSTALLATION

▶ **See Figure 42**

1. Disconnect the negative battery cable.
2. Remove the throttle pulley cover (if equipped).
3. Remove the connector from the IAC.
4. Remove the hoses from the IAC valve.
5. Remove the IAC valve from the mounting hardware.

**To install:**

6. Place the IAC valve in the mounting hardware and secure it.
7. Install the hoses to the IAC.

8. Install the connector on the IAC.
9. Install the throttle pulley cover (if removed).
10. Connect the negative battery cable.

## Engine Coolant Temperature Sensor

### OPERATION

▶ **See Figure 43**

The Engine Coolant Temperature (ECT) sensor resistance changes in response to engine coolant temperature. The sensor resistance decreases as the coolant temperature increases, and increases as the coolant temperature decreases. This provides a reference signal to the ECM, which indicates engine coolant temperature. The signal sent to the ECM by the ECT sensor helps the ECM to determine spark advance, EGR flow rate, air/fuel ratio, and engine temperature. The ECT also is used for temperature gauge operation by sending it's signal to the instrument cluster.

### TESTING

▶ **See Figures 44, 45, 46 and 47**

1. Turn the key to the **ON** position, with the engine **OFF**.
2. Test the resistance of the sensor across the two terminals of the sensor.
3. Using the chart in this section for a cross reference, check the resistance in relationship to the temperature of the engine.
4. If the sensor is not within specifications, replace it.

Fig. 42 Location of the IAC valve—850 models

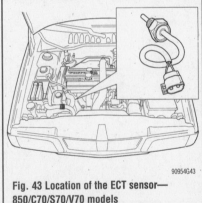

Fig. 43 Location of the ECT sensor—850/C70/S70/V70 models

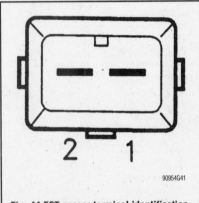

Fig. 44 ECT sensor terminal identification

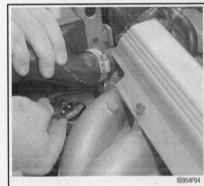

Fig. 45 Unplug the connector from the ECT sensor to test the sensor

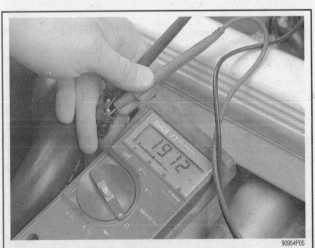

Fig. 46 Use an ohmmeter and check the sensor's resistance based on the temperature of the engine

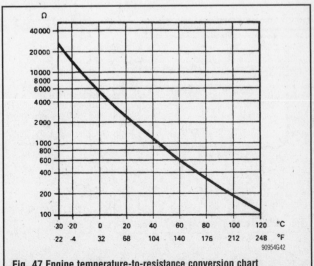

Fig. 47 Engine temperature-to-resistance conversion chart

## REMOVAL & INSTALLATION

1. Disconnect the negative battery cable.

### ❉❉❉ CAUTION

**Never open, service or drain the radiator or cooling system when hot; serious burns can occur from the steam and hot coolant. Also, when draining engine coolant, keep in mind that cats and dogs are attracted to ethylene glycol antifreeze and could drink any that is left in an uncovered container or in puddles on the ground. This will prove fatal in sufficient quantities. Always drain coolant into a sealable container. Coolant should be reused unless it is contaminated or is several years old.**

2. Drain and recycle the engine coolant.
3. Remove any components necessary to access the sensor.
4. Remove the connector from the sensor.
5. Using the proper size socket, unscrew the sensor from its mounting location.

**To install:**

6. Install the sensor in its mounting location and tighten it.
7. Install the connector on the sensor.
8. Install any components removed to access the sensor.
9. Refill and bleed the engine cooling system.
10. Connect the negative battery cable.
11. Inspect for leaks.

### Intake Air Temperature Sensor

#### OPERATION

▶ **See Figure 48**

The Intake Air Temperature (IAT) sensor determines the air temperature inside the intake manifold. Resistance changes in response to the ambient air temperature. The sensor has a negative temperature coefficient. As the temperature of the sensor rises the resistance across the sensor decreases. This provides a signal to the ECM indicating the temperature of the incoming air charge. This sensor helps the ECM to determine spark timing and air/fuel ratio. Information from this sensor is added to the pressure sensor information to calculate the air mass being sent to the cylinders.

#### TESTING

▶ **See Figure 49**

1. Turn the key to the **ON** position, with the engine **OFF**.
2. Test the voltage of the sensor across the two terminals of the sensor.

3. Using the chart in this section for a cross reference, check the voltage in relationship to the temperature of the engine.
4. If the sensor is not within specifications, replace it.

## REMOVAL & INSTALLATION

1. Disconnect the negative battery cable.
2. Unplug the connector from the sensor.
3. The sensor is removed by carefully twisting it out of the intake hose.

**To install:**

4. Twist the sensor into the intake hose.
5. Plug in the connector.
6. Connect the negative battery cable.

### Mass Airflow Meter

#### OPERATION

▶ **See Figures 50 and 51**

The sensor inside the air mass meter consists of a wire which is maintained at 250°F (120°C), above the ambient air temperature of the air entering the engine. As the air mass passing over the wire increases, more current is required to maintain the correct temperature. The amount of current required is used to calculate the air mass taken in.

When the engine is turned off, any dirt on the wire is burned off electrically as the element is heated to a temperature of 1832°F (1000°C) for 1 second. Any dirt remaining on the wire would cause it to send incorrect signals to the control unit and result in an incorrect air/fuel mixture.

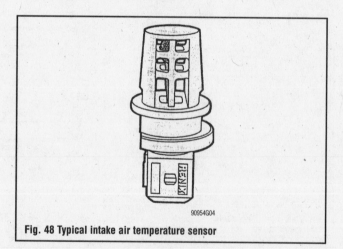

90954G04

**Fig. 48 Typical intake air temperature sensor**

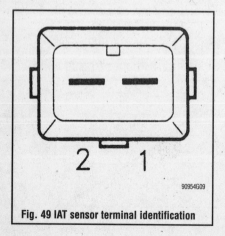

90954G09

**Fig. 49 IAT sensor terminal identification**

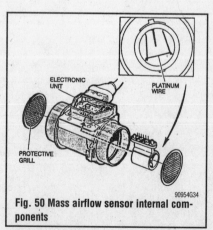

ELECTRONIC UNIT

PLATINUM WIRE

PROTECTIVE GRILL

90954G34

**Fig. 50 Mass airflow sensor internal components**

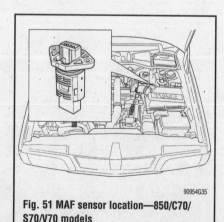

90954G35

**Fig. 51 MAF sensor location—850/C70/ S70/V70 models**

## TESTING

**▶ See Figures 52, 53, 54 and 55**

1. Unplug the connector for the MAF sensor.
2. Using the wiring diagrams found in Section 6, find the signal ground wire. Using a DVOM, connect the leads between the signal ground circuit and a ground. Resistance should be 0 ohms. If the specification is out of spec, repair the wire harness and retest.
3. Using the diagrams, find the signal circuit. Turn the ignition to the **ON** position with the engine **OFF**. Measure the voltage between the signal circuit and ground, voltage should be battery voltage. If voltage is out of spec, repair the open in the wiring and retest.
4. Plug the MAF sensor connector in. Using a DVOM backprobe the signal return and signal ground. With the key in the **ON** position and the engine **OFF**, voltage should be 0.1–0.2v. If voltage is Ok, check all connections to make sure that they have good contact. If voltage is out of specification, replace the MAF sensor.

## REMOVAL & INSTALLATION

**▶ See Figure 56**

1. Disconnect the negative battery cable.
2. Unplug the sensor connector.
3. Remove the two retaining screws for the sensor and remove the sensor.

**To install:**

4. Place the sensor into the air inlet hose.
5. Tighten the retaining screws.
6. Plug in the connector.
7. Connect the negative battery cable.

## Manifold Air Pressure Sensor

### OPERATION

The most important information for measuring engine fuel requirements comes from the pressure sensor. Using the pressure and temperature data, the ECM calculates the intake air mass. It is connected to the engine intake manifold through a hose and takes readings of the absolute pressure. A piezoelectric crystal changes a voltage input to an electrical output which reflects the pressure in the intake manifold.

Atmospheric pressure is measured both when the engine is started and when driving fully loaded, then the pressure sensor information is adjusted accordingly.

The pressure sensor terminal has 3 connectors A, B and C. A is ground, B carries the output signal to the control unit and C provides the pressure sensor with 5 volts of current from the control unit. The output varies between 0.5–5.0 volts depending on intake manifold pressure. When the engine is not running, atmospheric pressure will register at full potential. The sensor is sensitive to electrical disturbances, therefore it is protected by a metal cover. The signal strength should be about 4.4 volts at atmospheric pressure.

### TESTING

**▶ See Figures 57, 58 and 59**

1. Turn the key to the **ON** position, with the engine **OFF**.
2. Test the voltage of the sensor across terminals **A** and **B** of the sensor by backprobing the connector.
3. Adding controlled pressure to the vacuum port on the sensor will help to verify the sensor's operation. A hand-held pump with a gauge (not a vacuum pump) or regulated air pressure can be used.

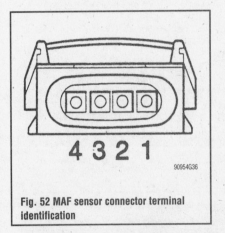

**Fig. 52 MAF sensor connector terminal identification**

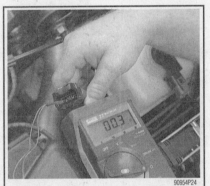

**Fig. 53 Checking the ground circuit of the MAF sensor**

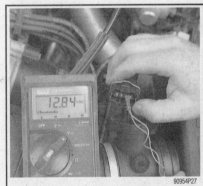

**Fig. 54 Checking the signal circuit of the MAF sensor**

**Fig. 55 Checking the signal return circuit of the MAF sensor**

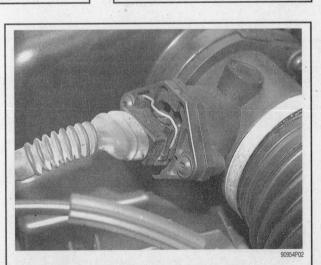

**Fig. 56 Location of the MAF sensor in the air inlet hose**

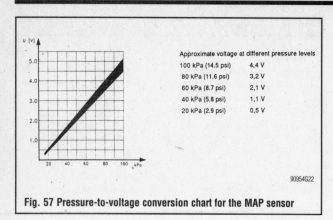

Fig. 57 Pressure-to-voltage conversion chart for the MAP sensor

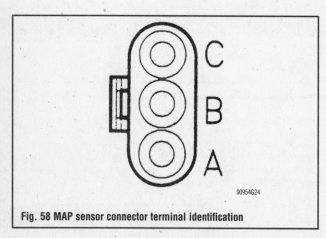

Fig. 58 MAP sensor connector terminal identification

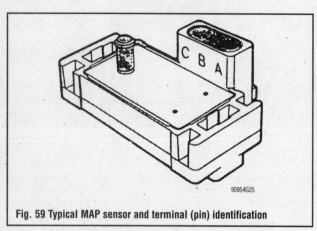

Fig. 59 Typical MAP sensor and terminal (pin) identification

4. Using the chart in this section for a cross reference, check the voltage in relationship to the pressure.

5. If the sensor is not within specifications, replace it.

6. The sensor may also be checked with the engine running; at idle, the sensor should read 1.2–1.6v.

## REMOVAL & INSTALLATION

1. Disconnect the negative battery cable.
2. Remove the bolts securing the bracket to the firewall.
3. Remove the vacuum hose from the sensor.
4. Unplug the connector and remove the sensor.

**To install:**

5. Plug in the sensor connector.
6. Install the vacuum hose.
7. Install the sensor into place and tighten the bracket retaining bolts.
8. Connect the negative battery cable.

## Throttle Switch

### OPERATION

#### ▶ See Figure 60

The throttle switch informs the fuel system and ignition system control units whether the throttle valve is closed or fully opened. The throttle switch is equipped with micro-switches for idling and full load running.

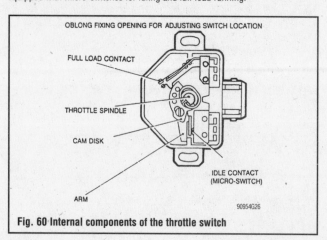

Fig. 60 Internal components of the throttle switch

### TESTING

#### ▶ See Figure 61

1. Unplug the switch connector and connect an ohmmeter to the switch terminals. The center terminal is common, terminal No. 1 is the idle switch, terminal No. 3 is the full load switch.

2. The idle switch should be closed when the throttle is closed. Any movement of the throttle lever will open the switch just before the throttle plate actually opens. Operate the switch by hand, if necessary, to determine a faulty switch or faulty adjustment.

3. Connect the ohmmeter to the full load switch. The switch should close when the throttle lever is 70 degrees off idle, about ⅓ of full stroke.

4. If the switches are good but do not operate at the proper throttle angles, check the throttle cable adjustment.

### REMOVAL & INSTALLATION

1. Disconnect the negative battery cable.
2. Remove any components necessary to access the sensor.
3. Remove the connector from the switch.
4. Remove the mounting screws from the sensor and remove the switch.

**To install:**

5. Install the switch onto the throttle plate shaft.

➡The throttle plate shaft is designed to fit a specific way on the switch, note the position of the shaft before tightening the bolts.

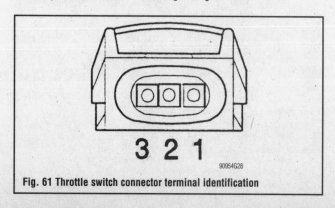

Fig. 61 Throttle switch connector terminal identification

6. Tighten the mounting screws.
7. Install the switch connector.
8. Install any components removed to access the switch.
9. Connect the negative battery cable.

## Throttle Position Sensor

### OPERATION

The Throttle Position (TP) sensor is a potentiometer that provides a signal to the ECM that is directly proportional to the throttle plate position. The TP sensor is mounted on the side of the throttle body and is connected to the throttle plate shaft. The TP sensor monitors throttle plate movement and position, and transmits an appropriate electrical signal to the ECM. These signals are used by the ECM to adjust the air/fuel mixture, spark timing and EGR operation according to engine load at idle, part throttle, or full throttle. The TP sensor is not adjustable.

### TESTING

▶ **See Figures 62, 63 and 64**

1. With the engine **OFF** and the ignition **ON**, check the voltage at the signal return circuit of the TP sensor by carefully backprobing the connector using a DVOM.
2. Voltage should be between 0.2 and 1.4 volts at idle.
3. Slowly move the throttle pulley to the wide open throttle (WOT) position and watch the voltage on the DVOM. The voltage should slowly rise to slightly less than 4.8v at Wide Open Throttle (WOT).
4. If no voltage is present, check the wiring harness for supply voltage (5.0v) and ground (0.3v or less), by referring to your corresponding wiring guide. If supply voltage and ground are present, but no output voltage from TP, replace the TP sensor. If supply voltage and ground do not meet specifications, make necessary repairs to the harness or ECM.

Fig. 62 Checking the signal return of the TP sensor

### REMOVAL & INSTALLATION

▶ **See Figure 65**

1. Disconnect the negative battery cable.
2. Remove any components necessary to access the sensor.
3. Remove the connector from the sensor.
4. Remove the mounting screws from the sensor and remove the sensor.
**To install:**
5. Install the sensor onto the throttle plate shaft.

➡ **The throttle plate shaft is designed to fit a specific way on the sensor, note the position of the shaft before tightening the bolts.**

6. Tighten the mounting screws.
7. Install the sensor connector.
8. Install any components removed to access the sensor.
9. Connect the negative battery cable.

## Knock Sensor

### OPERATION

The operation of the Knock Sensor (KS) is to monitor preignition or "engine knocks" and send the signal to the ECM. The ECM responds by adjusting ignition timing until the "knocks" stop. The sensor works by generating a signal produced by the frequency of the knock as recorded by the piezoelectric ceramic disc inside the KS. The disc absorbs the shock waves from the knocks and exerts a pressure on the metal diaphragm inside the KS. This compresses the crystals inside the disc and the disc generates a voltage signal proportional to the frequency of the knocks ranging from zero to 1 volt.

### TESTING

There is real no tests for this sensor, the sensor produces it's own signal based on information gathered while the engine is running. The sensors also are usually inaccessible without major component removal. The sensors can be monitored with an appropriate scan tool using a data display or other data stream information. Follow the instructions included with the scan tool for information on accessing the data. The only test available is to test the continuity of the harness from the ECM to the sensor.

### REMOVAL & INSTALLATION

▶ **See Figure 66**

➡ **The knock sensors are usually inaccessible without the removal of several components. It is best to locate the knock sensors and figure out what is required to be removed, then proceed to the appropriate section for removal of that component.**

1. Disconnect the negative battery cable.
2. Remove any components necessary to access the sensor(s).

Fig. 63 Checking the signal circuit of the TP sensor

Fig. 64 Checking the ground circuit of the TP sensor

Fig. 65 Location of the TP sensor on the throttle body

**Fig. 66 Knock sensors are located on the engine block under the intake manifold**

3. Unplug the sensor(s).
4. Remove the sensor-to-engine block retaining bolt.
5. Remove the knock sensor(s).
**To install:**
6. Place the sensor(s) into position and tighten the retaining bolt(s).
7. Plug the sensor(s) connector in.
8. Install any components removed for access.
9. Connect the negative battery cable.

## Acceleration Sensor

### OPERATION

▶ **See Figure 67**

The acceleration sensor measures the vertical acceleration of the vehicle, helping the ECM distinguish a bumpy road from a genuine engine "knock". The acceleration sensor works on the same principle as the KS. The acceleration sensor receives a steady voltage signal from the ECM and has a steady return signal. When the vehicle rides over a bumpy terrain, the return signal fluctuates, the fluctuation measuring the deviation of the terrain.

➡ **This sensor is found only on 1995 and later 850 models, 1996 and later 960 models and all 1998 models.**

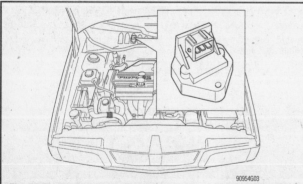

**Fig. 67 The location of the acceleration sensor—850/C70/S70/V70 models**

### TESTING

1. On 850/C70/S70/V70 models, remove the wiper arms and the cowl panel. See Section 6 of this manual for additonal information to access the sensor.

2. Start the vehicle and, using a voltmeter, backprobe the connector's signal return circuit between the connector and ground. Use the wiring diagrams at the end of Section 6.
3. Voltage should be 2.5v. If the there is no voltage, proceed to the next step. If the voltage reading is out of range, replace the sensor.
4. Turn the engine **OFF**, but leave the ignition **ON**.
5. Unplug the connector on the sensor and using a voltmeter, measure the signal from the ECM between the connector and ground. Use the wiring diagrams in the end of Section 6 to help you.
6. Voltage should be 5.0v, if voltage is out of range or there is no voltage repair the circuit. If voltage is ok, proceed to the next step.
7. Turn the ignition **OFF**, using an ohmmeter measure the resistance between the sensor ground and ground. Use the wiring diagrams in the end of Section 6 to help you.
8. Resistance should be 0 ohms, if resistance is out of range repair the circuit.
9. On 850/C70/S70/V70 models install the cowl panel and wiper arms.

### REMOVAL & INSTALLATION

➡ **The sensor is located under the cowl panel on 850/C70/S70/V70 models and adjacent to the driver's side strut tower on 960/S90/V90 models.**

1. Disconnect the negative battery cable.
2. On 850/C70/S70/V70 models remove the wiper arms and the cowl panel, see Section 6 of this manual for more information.
3. Unplug the sensor.
4. Remove the sensor retaining bolts.
5. Remove the sensor from the vehicle.
**To install:**
6. Place the sensor into position and tighten the retaining bolts.
7. Plug the sensor connector in.
8. On 850/C70/S70/V70 models install the cowl panel and wiper arms.
9. Connect the negative battery cable.

## Camshaft Position Sensor

### OPERATION

▶ **See Figure 68**

The function of the Camshaft Position (CMP) sensor is to tell the ECM if the camshaft is on the first or second revolution of an engine cycle. The CMP sensor allows the engine to determine which pistons are approaching TDC. The CMP sensor, in conjunction with the crankshaft position sensor, determine which cylinder requires ignition.

The CMP sensor consists of a trigger rotor and a Hall effect switch. The trigger rotor turns at the same speed as the camshaft. The ECM sends a 5-volt supply to the Hall effect sensor, which is grounded when the rotor passes the Hall effect switch, giving a zero voltage signal. When the sensor is shielded, the sensor returns the 5-volt signal to the ECM.

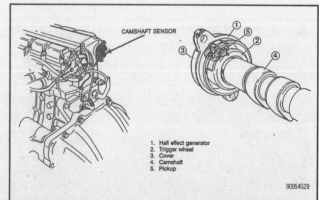

**Fig. 68 Camshaft sensor components and location—960 models**

## TESTING

▶ **See Figures 69, 70 and 71**

1. Disconnect the negative battery cable.
2. Unplug the sensor connector.
3. To test the voltage lead:
   a. Using an voltmeter, measure the voltage at terminal 3. Turn the ignition **ON**, and measure the voltage between terminal 3 and ground.
   b. Voltage should be battery voltage. If voltage is not present or out of range, repair the circuit. If voltage is ok, proceed to the next step.
4. To test the signal return:
   a. Using a voltmeter, measure the voltage at terminal 2. Turn the ignition **ON**, and measure the voltage between terminal 2 and ground.
   b. Voltage should be around 5v. If voltage is not present or out of range, repair the circuit. If voltage is ok, proceed to the next step.
5. To test the ground circuit:

   a. Using an ohmmeter, measure the resistance at terminal 1. Turn the ignition **ON**, and measure the resistance between terminal 1 and ground.
   b. Resistance should be 0 ohms. If continuity is not present or out of range, repair the circuit. If continuity is ok, replace the CMP sensor.

## REMOVAL & INSTALLATION

▶ **See Figures 72, 73 and 74**

1. Disconnect the negative battery cable.
2. Remove the air inlet hose from the air cleaner housing and the throttle body.
3. Unplug the sensor's connector.
4. Remove the two retaining screws and remove the sensor from the engine.

**To install:**

5. Install the sensor into place and tighten the retaining bolts.
6. Plug in the connector.

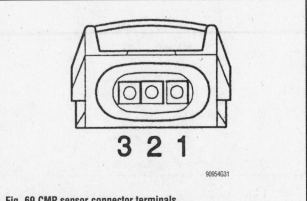

**3 2 1**

90954G31

**Fig. 69 CMP sensor connector terminals**

90954P03

**Fig. 72 Crankshaft position sensor (1) and camshaft position sensor (2)**

90954P09

**Fig. 70 Checking for battery voltage at terminal 3**

90954P44

**Fig. 73 Removing the CMP sensor**

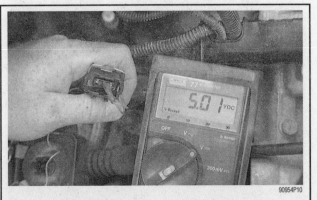

90954P10

**Fig. 71 Checking the signal return circuit of the CMP sensor**

90954P45

**Fig. 74 Inspect the Hall effect switch inside the CMP sensor after removal**

7. Install the air inlet hose onto the throttle body and the air cleaner housing.

8. Connect the negative battery cable.

## Crankshaft Position Sensor

### OPERATION

▶ **See Figure 75**

The Crankshaft Position (CKP) sensor, sometimes called an RPM and/or impulse sensor, is used to determine engine speed and Top Dead Center (TDC). This ensures precise ignition timing. The sensor is located at the rear of the engine block, above the flywheel. Engine speed is transmitted to the fuel control unit. The engine will not start without this signal.

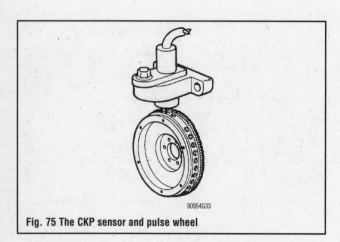

**Fig. 75 The CKP sensor and pulse wheel**

### LH Jetronic and EZK Ignition System Vehicles

On the pulsewheel, there are 60 markings for the CKP sensor, 58 which are drilled holes to provide information to the ignition control unit. There are no holes at 2 of the markings. These are 90 degrees Before Top Dead Center (BTDC), for cylinders No. 1 and No. 4. Ignition timing is based on these markings and other information such as engine load and temperature. This means that ignition timing can be controlled and that there is no need for the ignition setting to be adjusted.

### Regina Engine Control and REX-1 Ignition Systems

On the pulsewheel, there are 44 markings for the CKP sensor, 40 which are drilled holes to provide information to the ignition control unit. There are no holes at 2 of the markings. These are 90 degrees Before Top Dead Center (BTDC), for cylinders No. 1 and No. 4. Ignition timing is based on these markings and other information such as engine load and temperature. This means that ignition timing can be controlled and that there is no need for ignition setting to be adjusted.

### Motronic Engine Control Systems

The flywheel has a series of holes located on the top surface. As the holes pass the CKP sensor, the holes induce a voltage in the coil of the sensor. The passage of several holes generates an A/C signal, the frequency of which is a function of the number of holes passing per second and the voltage of which can vary between 0.1 and 55 vdc, depending on engine speed and temperature.

At 90° TDC for cylinder 1 there is a longer hole. When the longer gap passes the sensor, the voltage stops, and the ECM can calculate camshaft position.

### TESTING

▶ **See Figures 76 and 77**

1. Disconnect the negative battery cable.
2. Unplug the sensor connector.
3. Using an ohmmeter, measure the resistance across the two sensor terminals.
4. Resistance should be between 200–500 ohms. If the resistance is out of range, replace the sensor.

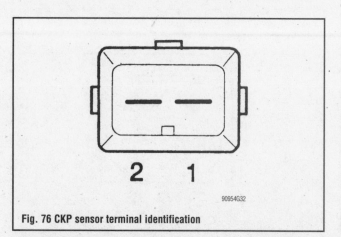

**Fig. 76 CKP sensor terminal identification**

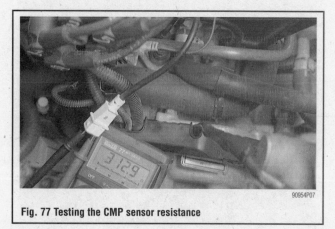

**Fig. 77 Testing the CMP sensor resistance**

### REMOVAL & INSTALLATION

1. Disconnect the negative battery cable.
2. Remove any components necessary to access the sensor.
3. Unplug the sensor's connector.
4. Remove the two retaining screws and remove the sensor from the engine.
**To install:**
5. Install the sensor into place and tighten the retaining bolts.
6. Plug in the connector.
7. Install any components removed to access the sensor.
8. Connect the negative battery cable.

**COMPONENT LOCATIONS**

## TYPICAL ELECTRONIC ENGINE CONTROL COMPONENT LOCATIONS

1. Mass Airflow (MAF) sensor
2. Acceleration sensor (under cowl panel)
3. Module box
4. Data link connector
5. Engine Coolant Temperature (ECT) sensor
6. Idle Air Control (IAC) valve (under cover)
7. Throttle Position (TP) sensor
8. PCV valve

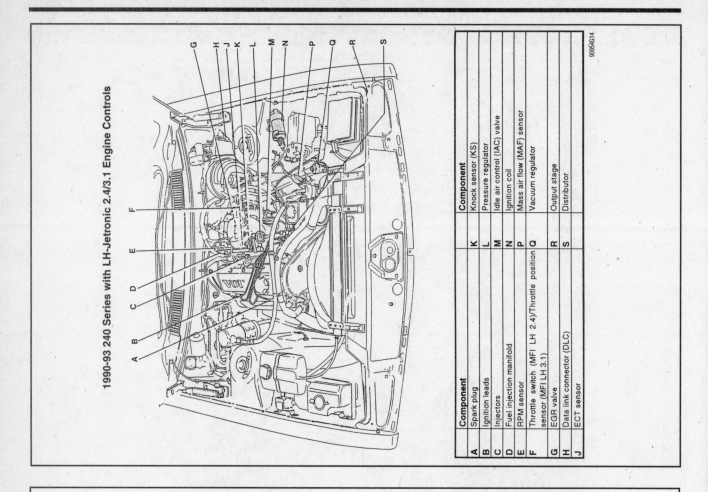

**1990-93 240 Series with LH-Jetronic 2.4/3.1 Engine Controls**

| | Component | | Component |
|---|---|---|---|
| A | Spark plug | K | Knock sensor (KS) |
| B | Ignition leads | L | Pressure regulator |
| C | Injectors | M | Idle air control (IAC) valve |
| D | Fuel injection manifold | N | Ignition coil |
| E | RPM sensor | P | Mass air flow (MAF) sensor |
| F | Throttle switch (MFI LH 2.4)/Throttle position sensor (MFI LH 3.1) | Q | Vacuum regulator |
| G | EGR valve | R | Output stage |
| H | Data link connector (DLC) | S | Distributor |
| J | ECT sensor | | |

9054G14

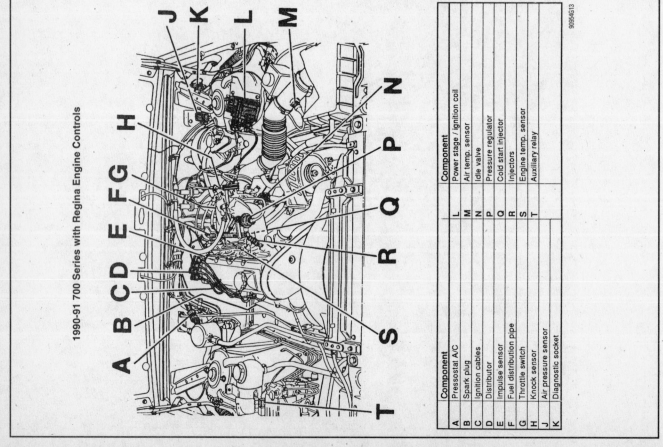

**1990-91 700 Series with Regina Engine Controls**

| | Component | | Component |
|---|---|---|---|
| A | Pressostat A/C | L | Power stage / ignition coil |
| B | Spark plug | M | Air temp. sensor |
| C | Ignition cables | N | Idle valve |
| D | Distributor | P | Pressure regulator |
| E | Impulse sensor | Q | Cold start injector |
| F | Fuel distribution pipe | R | Injectors |
| G | Throttle switch | S | Engine temp. sensor |
| H | Knock sensor | T | Auxiliary relay |
| J | Air pressure sensor | | |
| K | Diagnostic socket | | |

9054G13

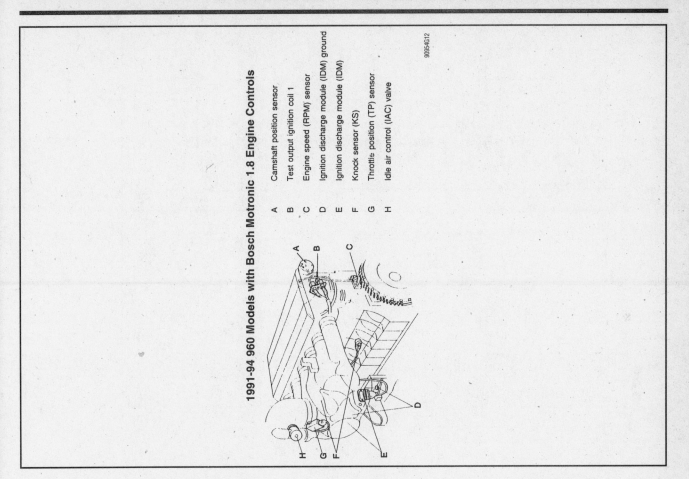

**1991-94 960 Models with Bosch Motronic 1.8 Engine Controls**

| | |
|---|---|
| A | Camshaft position sensor |
| B | Test output ignition coil 1 |
| C | Engine speed (RPM) sensor |
| D | Ignition discharge module (IDM) ground |
| E | Ignition discharge module (IDM) |
| F | Knock sensor (KS) |
| G | Throttle position (TP) sensor |
| H | Idle air control (IAC) valve |

9095G12

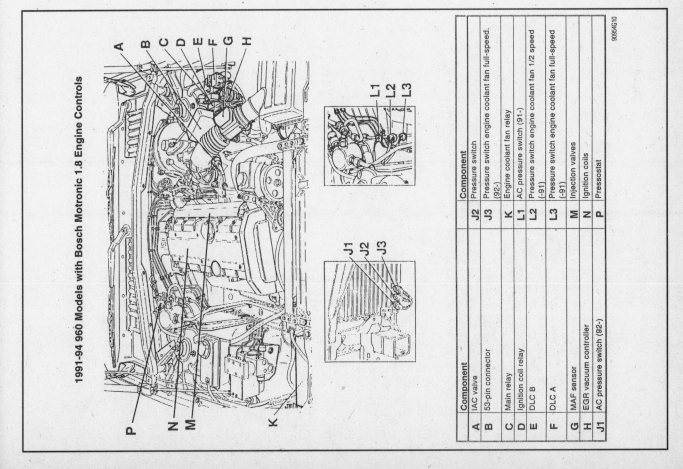

**1991-94 960 Models with Bosch Motronic 1.8 Engine Controls**

| | Component |
|---|---|
| A | IAC valve |
| B | 53-pin connector |
| C | Main relay |
| D | Ignition coil relay |
| E | DLC B |
| F | DLC A |
| G | MAF sensor |
| H | EGR vacuum controller |
| J1 | AC pressure switch (92-) |
| J2 | Pressure switch |
| J3 | Pressure switch engine coolant fan full-speed. (92-) |
| K | Engine coolant fan relay |
| L1 | AC pressure switch (91-) |
| L2 | Pressure switch engine coolant fan 1/2 speed (-91) |
| L3 | Pressure switch engine coolant fan full-speed (-91) |
| M | Injection valves |
| N | Ignition coils |
| P | Pressostat |

9095G10

## 1995-98 850/C70/S70/V70 Models with Bosch Motronic 4.3 Engine Controls

| | |
|---|---|
| A | TCM |
| B | ECM |
| C | MAF sensor |
| D | Injectors |
| E | ECT sensor |
| F | IAC valve |
| G | Main relay |
| H | Ignition coil, power stage |
| I | Relay, engine cooling fan |
| J₁ | Front KS |
| J₂ | Rear KS |
| K | DLC |
| L | Electrical distribution unit |
| M | EVAP valve |
| N | A/C pressure sensor |
| O | Pressostat |
| P | EGR vacuum controller (certain markets only) |
| Q | Acceleration sensor (certain markets only) |
| R | TC control valve (only turbo) |
| S | Pressure servo/wastegate valve (only turbo) |

| | |
|---|---|
| A | Distributor |
| B | RPM sensor |
| C | TP potentiometer |
| D | CMP sensor |
| E | Power ground |
| F | Signal ground |
| G | Pressure regulator |
| H | EGR valve (certain markets only) |
| I | EGR temp. sensor (certain markets only) |

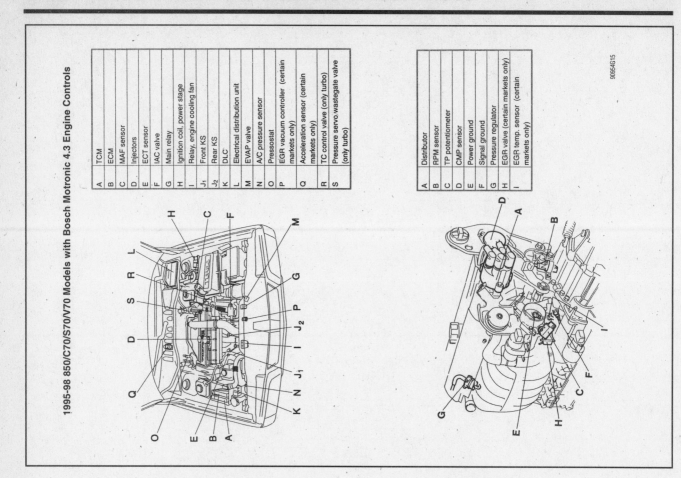

90954G15

## 1993-94 850 Models with Bosch LH-Jetronic 3.2 Engine Controls

| | |
|---|---|
| A | TCM |
| B | MFI module |
| C | ICM |
| D | MAF sensor |
| E | Injectors |
| F | ECT sensor |
| G | IAC valve |
| H | Main relay |
| I | Ignition coil, power stage |
| J | KS |
| K | Relay, engine cooling fan |
| L | DLC |
| M | High-pressure switch |
| N | Electrical distribution unit |
| O | V-VIS solenoid valve |
| P | EGR controller |
| Q | V-VIS vacuum servo |

| | |
|---|---|
| A | Distributor |
| B | RPM sensor |
| C | TP potentiometer |
| D | CMP sensor |
| E | Power ground |
| F | Signal ground |
| G | Pressure regulator |
| H | EGR valve |
| I | EGR-temp. sensor |

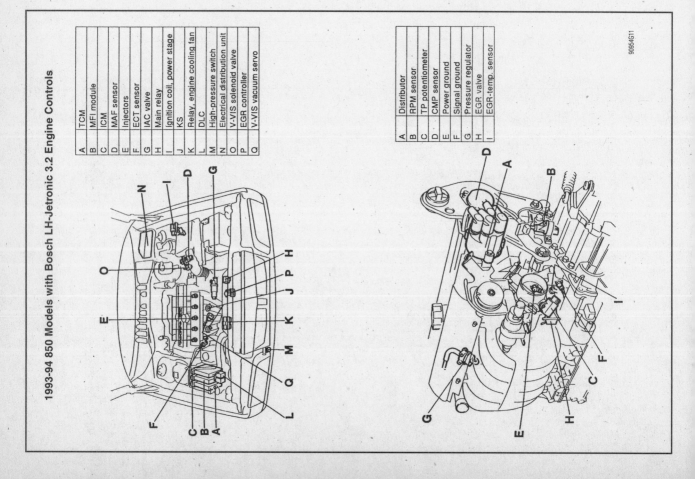

90954G11

## 1995-98 960/S90/V90 Models with Bosch Motronic 4.4 Engine Controls

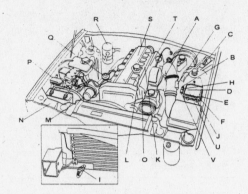

| | |
|---|---|
| A | Idle air control (IAC) valve |
| B | Canister purge (CP) valve |
| C | Accelerometer |
| D | 55–pin connector |
| E | Integrated relay/fusebox |
| F | Pulsed secondary air injection system (PAIR) pump relay |
| G | Mass air flow (MAF) sensor |
| H | Pulsed secondary air injection system (PAIR) solenoid valve |
| I | Air conditioning (A/C) pressure sensor |
| J | Main relay |
| K | Signal ground, |
| L | Power ground |
| M | Pulsed secondary air injection system (PAIR) pump |
| N | Blower fan relay |
| O | Engine coolant temperature (ECT) sensor |
| P | Main fusebox |
| Q | Pulsed secondary air injection system (PAIR) valve |
| R | Pressure switch (Pressostat) |
| S | Ignition coils |
| T | Injectors |
| U | Ignition coil relay |
| V | CO potentiometer (certain markets) |

90954G16

# TROUBLE CODES

## General Information

Volvo vehicles employ the Electronic Engine Control (EEC) system, to manage fuel, ignition and emissions.

The Engine Control Module (ECM) is given responsibility for the operation of the emission control devices, cooling fans, ignition and advance and in some cases, automatic transmission functions. Because the EEC oversees both the ignition timing and the fuel injector operation, a precise air/fuel ratio will be maintained under all operating conditions. The ECM is a microprocessor or small computer which receives electrical inputs from several sensors, switches and relays on and around the engine.

Based on combinations of these inputs, the ECM controls outputs to various devices concerned with engine operation and emissions. The engine control assembly relies on the signals to form a correct picture of current vehicle operation. If any of the input signals is incorrect, the ECM reacts to what ever picture is painted for it. For example, if the coolant temperature sensor is inaccurate and reads too low, the ECM may see a picture of the engine never warming up. Consequently, the engine settings will be maintained as if the engine were cold. Because so many inputs can affect one output, correct diagnostic procedures are essential on these systems.

One part of the ECM is devoted to monitoring both input and output functions within the system. This ability forms the core of the self-diagnostic system. If a problem is detected within a circuit, the controller will recognize the fault, assign it an identification code, and store the code in a memory section. Depending on the year and model, the fault code(s) may be represented by two or three digit numbers. The stored code(s) may be retrieved during diagnosis.

While the EEC system is capable of recognizing many internal faults, certain faults will not be recognized. Because the computer system sees only electrical signals, it cannot sense or react to mechanical or vacuum faults affecting engine operation. Some of these faults may affect another component which will set a code. For example, the ECM monitors the output signal to the fuel injectors, but cannot detect a partially clogged injector. As long as the output driver responds correctly, the computer will read the system as functioning correctly. However, the improper flow of fuel may result in a lean mixture. This would, in turn, be detected by the oxygen sensor and noticed as a constantly lean signal by the ECM. Once the signal falls outside the pre-programmed limits, the engine control assembly would notice the fault and set an identification code.

Additionally, the EEC system employs adaptive fuel logic. This process is used to compensate for normal wear and variability within the fuel system. Once the engine enters steady-state operation, the engine control assembly watches the oxygen sensor signal for a bias or tendency to run slightly rich or lean. If such a bias is detected, the adaptive logic corrects the fuel delivery to bring the air/fuel mixture towards a centered or 14.7:1 ratio. This compensating shift is stored in a non-volatile memory which is retained by battery power even with the ignition switched **OFF**. The correction factor is then available the next time the vehicle is operated.

➡**If the battery cable(s) is disconnected for longer than 5 minutes, the adaptive fuel factor will be lost. After repair it will be necessary to drive the vehicle at least 10 miles to allow the processor to relearn the correct factors. The driving period should include steady-throttle open road driving if possible. During the drive, the vehicle may exhibit driveability symptoms not noticed before. These symptoms should clear as the ECM computes the correction factor.**

## Diagnostic Connector

▶ See Figures 78, 79 and 80

The Data Link Connector (DLC) is located in the engine compartment near the driver's side strut tower on Coupe, 240, 700, and 900 series vehicles without OBD-II. On 850 models the DLC is located in the engine compartment in front of the module box, behind the passenger side headlamp. On OBD-II equipped vehicles, the DLC is located in the interior in center console under a cover.

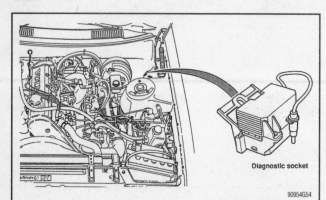

Fig. 78 DLC location for the Coupe, 240, 700, and 900 series

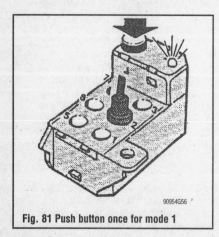

Fig. 79 Lift the cover up to access the OBD-II DLC

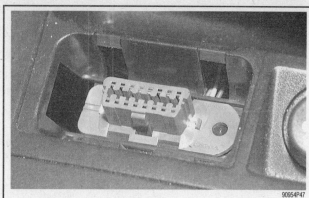

Fig. 80 The OBD-II connector located in the center console with the cover removed

## Reading Codes

**1990–94 Vehicles**

▶ See Figures 81, 82 and 83

1. Open diagnostic socket cover and install selector cable into socket No. 2 for fuel injection codes or socket No. 6 (except Motronic systems) for ignition codes.
2. Turn the ignition switch to the **ON** position.
3. Enter control system 1 by pressing the button once. Hold the button for at least 1 second, but not more than 3.
4. Watch the diode light and count the number of flashes in the 3 flash series indicating a fault code. The flash series are separated by 3 second intervals. Note fault codes.

If there are no fault codes in the diagnostic unit, the diode will flash 1-1-1 and the fuel system is operating correctly.

5. If diode light does not flash when button is pressed, or no code is flashed there is a problem with the soft-diagnostic system, proceed as follows:

a. Check ground connections on the intake manifold, and the ground connection for the Lambda-sond at the right front mudguard.

b. Check the fuses for the pump relay and the primary pump. On 240 models, fuses are located inside the engine compartment on the left side wheel well housing. On 760/780 models, fuses are located in the center console, just below the radio. On 740/940 models, fuses are located behind the ashtray. Access can be gained by removing the ashtray, and pressing upward on the tab marked "electrical fuses press". On 850 models, the fuses are located on the left side of the engine compartment behind the strut mount plate. The fuses on 960 models are located on the far left side of the dashboard. The driver's door must be open to gain access to the fuses.

Fig. 81 Push button once for mode 1

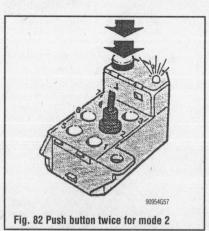

Fig. 82 Push button twice for mode 2

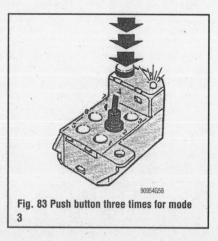

Fig. 83 Push button three times for mode 3

c. Remove glove compartment, and check control unit ground connections.

d. Turn the ignition switch to the **OFF** position. Remove control unit connector and connector protective sleeve.

e. Check diagnostic socket by connecting a voltmeter between ground and No. 4 connection on the control unit connector. Reading should be 12 volts. If no voltage is present, check lead between control unit connector and fuse No. 1 in the fuse/relay box.

f. Turn the ignition to the **ON** position, and install selector cable into the No. 2 socket on the diagnostic socket. Connect a voltmeter between ground and No. 12 connection on the control unit connector. Reading should be 12 volts. Press the button on diagnostic socket and note reading. Reading on the voltmeter should be 0 volts. If no voltage at the control unit is present, take reading at the diagnostic socket connector. If reading remains at 12 volts when button is pressed, check diagnostic socket.

g. Connect a voltmeter between ground and the red/black lead on the diagnostic socket connector. Reading should be 12 volts.

h. Connect a suitable ohmmeter between ground and the brown/black lead in the diagnostic socket connector. Reading should be 0 ohms.

i. Turn the ignition to the **OFF** position. Connect ohmmeter between diagnostic socket selector cable and the pin under selector button. The ohmmeter should read infinity. Press the button and note the reading. The reading should be 0 ohms.

j. Connect a suitable diode/multimeter tester, or equivalent, between the diagnostic socket diode light and the selector cable. Connect red test pin from the tester to pin under diode light and black test pin from tester to selector cable. A reading on the tester indicates correct diode light function.

With no reading on tester, replace diagnostic socket.

k. Check the system relay/primary relay by connecting a voltmeter between ground and the No. 9 connection on the control unit connector, then connect a jumper wire between ground and No. 21 connection on the control unit connector. The relay should activate and the reading should be 12 volts.

6. Press the diagnostic socket button. Note any additional fault codes.

➡**The diagnostic system memory is full when it contains 3 fault codes. Until those codes are corrected and the memory erased, the system cannot give information on any other problems.**

7. Press the diagnostic socket button for the third time to see if a third fault code is stored in the memory. If the diode light flashes the same code 1-1-1, there are no other codes in the memory.

### 1995–98 Vehicles

Reading the control module memory is on of the first steps in OBD-II system diagnostics. This step should be initially performed to determine the general nature of the fault. Subsequent readings will determine if the fault has been cleared.

Reading codes can be performed by any of the methods below:
- Read the control module memory with the Generic Scan Tool (GST)
- Read the control module memory with the vehicle manufacturer's specific tester

To read the fault codes, connect the scan tool or tester according to the manufacturer's instructions. Follow the manufacturer's specified procedure for reading the codes.

### 1990-91 700 Series with Regina Engine and Rex-1 Ignition Systems Trouble Codes

| Fault code | Fault message |
|---|---|
| 1-1-1 | Diagnostic system has not found any faults |
| 1-1-2 | Fault in control unit |
| 1-1-3 | Injectors |
| 2-2-1 | Lambda sond signal absent or faulty |
| 2-3-1 | Adaptive Lambda control too lean / rich in part load range |
| 2-3-2 | Adaptive lambda control too lean / rich when idling |
| 1-2-1 | Pressure sensor signal absent or faulty |
| 1-2-2 | Air temp. sensor signal absent or faulty |
| 1-2-3 | Engine temp. sensor signal absent or faulty |
| 1-3-2 | Battery voltage too high / too low |
| 1-3-3 | Throttle switch at idle position |
| 2-1-3 | Throttle switch in full load position |
| 2-2-2 | System relay signal absent or faulty |
| 2-2-3 | Idling control valve signal absent or faulty |
| 2-3-3 | Adaptive idling control out of limits |
| 3-1-1 | No speedometer signal |
| 3-2-1 | Signal to cold start valve short circuited to ground or missing |

### REX-1 Trouble Codes

| Fault code | Fault message |
|---|---|
| 1-1-1 | Diagnostic system has not found any faults |
| 1-4-2 | Fault in control unit |
| 1-4-3 | Knock sensor signal absent or faulty |
| 1-4-4 | No load signal from fuel system |
| 2-2-4 | Engine temp. sensor signal absent or faulty |

90954C01

## 1990-95 Coupe, 240, 700, and 940 Series with EZ-116K Ignition System Trouble Codes

| DTC | Fault message |
|---|---|
| 1-1-1 | No fault detected |
| 1-4-2 | Control module fault |
| 1-4-3 | KS signal absent or faulty |
| 1-4-4 | Load signal from MFI system absent |
| 1-5-4 | EGR system flow too high |
| 2-1-4 | RPM sensor signal absent intermittently |
| 2-2-4 | ECT sensor signal absent or faulty |
| 2-3-4 | TP switch signal in idling position faulty |
| 2-4-1 | EGR system flow too low (NTC) |
| 2-4-1 | EGR system flow too low (PTC) |
| 4-1-3 | EGR temperature sensor signal absent or faulty (NTC) |
| 4-1-3 | EGR temperature sensor signal absent or faulty (PTC) |

90954C03

## 1990-95 Coupe, 240, 700, and 940 Series with LH-Jetronic 2.4 or 3.1 System Trouble Codes

| DTC | Fault message |
|---|---|
| 1-1-1 | No fault detected |
| 1-1-2 | Control module fault |
| 1-1-3 | Short term fuel trim (Lambda control) too lean/rich |
| 1-2-1 | MAF sensor signal absent or faulty LH 2.4 |
| 1-2-1 | MAF sensor signal absent or faulty LH 3.1 |
| 1-2-3 | ECT signal absent or faulty |
| 1-3-1 | Engine speed signal from DI system absent on starting |
| 1-3-2 | Battery voltage too low or too high |
| 1-3-3 | TP switch signal faulty at idling LH 2.4 |
| 2-1-2 | HO2S signal absent or faulty |
| 2-1-3 | TP switch signal faulty at full load LH 2.4 |
| 2-2-1 | Adaptive fuel trim too lean in part-load range |
| 2-2-3 | IAC valve signal absent or faulty |
| 2-3-1 | Adaptive fuel trim too lean or too rich in part-load range |
| 2-3-2 | Adaptive fuel trim too lean or too rich at idling |
| 3-1-1 | Speedometer signal absent |
| 3-1-2 | No knock enrichment signal from DI system |
| 3-2-2 | MAF sensor burn off signal absent or faulty LH 2.4 |
| 4-1-1 | Throttle position sensor signal absent or faulty LH 3.1 |

90954C02

**1992-95 960 Series with Bosch Motronic 1.8 System Trouble Codes**

| DTC | Fault text |
| --- | --- |
| 1-1-1 | No fault detected by diagnostic system |
| 1-1-2 | ECM fault |
| 1-1-3 | Injector group 1 |
| 1-1-3 | Injector group 2 (earlier models) |
| 1-1-5 | Injector group 2 (later models) |
| 1-2-1 | MAF sensor signal |
| 1-2-3 | ECT sensor signal |
| 1-3-1 | RPM sensor signal |
| 1-3-2 | Battery voltage |
| 1-4-3 | Front KS signal |
| 1-5-4 | EGR system, leakage |
| 2-1-2 | HO2S signal |
| 2-1-4 | RPM sensor signal, intermittent |
| 2-2-1 | Long-term fuel trim, part load |
| 2-2-3 | IAC valve signal |
| 2-3-1 | Long-term fuel trim, part load |
| 2-3-2 | Long-term fuel trim, idle |
| 2-3-3 | Long-term idle air trim |
| 2-4-1 | EGR system |
| 2-4-3 | EGR system, flow malfunction |
| 3-1-1 | TP sensor signal |
| 3-1-4 | VSS signal |
| 3-2-2 | CMP signal |
| 4-1-1 | MAF sensor burnoff |
| 4-1-3 | TP sensor signal |
| 4-3-3 | EGR temperature sensor signal |
|  | Rear KS signal |
| 5-1-1 | Long-term idle air trim, idle |
| 5-1-2 | Short-term fuel trim |

9095AC04

**1993-94 850 Models with LH-Jetronic 3.2 System Trouble Codes**

| DTC | Fault text |
| --- | --- |
| 1-1-1 | No fault detected by diagnostic system |
| 1-1-2 | MFI control module fault |
| 1-1-3 | Short term fuel trim, upper limit |
| 1-2-1 | MAF sensor signal |
| 1-2-3 | ECT sensor signal |
| 1-3-1 | RPM signal from ICM |
| 1-3-2 | Battery voltage |
| 2-1-2 | HO2S signal |
| 2-2-1 | Long term fuel trim part load, upper limit |
| 2-2-3 | IAC valve signal |
| 2-3-1 | Long term fuel trim part load, lower limit |
| 2-3-2 | Long term fuel trim idling, upper limit |
| 3-1-1 | VSS (vehicle speed sensor) signal |
| 4-1-1 | TP potentiometer signal |
| 5-1-1 | Long term fuel trim idling, lower limit |
| 5-1-2 | Short term fuel trim, lower limit |

9095AC05

**1993-94 850 Models with EZ-129K Ignition System Trouble Codes**

| DTC | Fault text |
|-----|------------|
| 1-1-1 | No fault detected by diagnostic system |
| 1-1-2 | Fault in ICM |
| 1-2-3 | ECT sensor signal |
| 1-3-1 | RPM sensor signal |
| 1-4-3 | KS signal front |
| 1-4-4 | Load signal |
| 1-5-4 | EGR system leakage |
| 2-1-4 | RPM sensor signal sporadic |
| 2-4-1 | EGR system flow fault |
| 3-1-1 | VSS signal |
| 3-1-4 | CMP sensor signal |
| 3-2-4 | CMP sensor signal sporadic |
| 4-1-1 | TP potentiometer signal |
| 4-1-3 | EGR temperature sensor signal |
| 4-3-2 | Temperature warning level 1 |
| 4-3-3 | KS sensor signal rear |
| 5-1-3 | Temperature warning level 2 |

90954C06

**1995 850 Models with Bosch Motronic 4.3 System Trouble Codes**

| DTC | Fault text |
|-----|------------|
| 1-1-1 | No faults detected by OBD system |
| 1-1-2 | Fault in ECM |
| 1-1-5 | Injector 1 |
| 1-2-1 | MAF sensor signal |
| 1-2-3 | ECT signal |
| 1-2-5 | Injector 2 |
| 1-3-1 | RPM sensor signal, missing |
| 1-3-2 | Battery voltage |
| 1-3-5 | Injector 3 |
| 1-4-3 | Front KS, signal |
| 1-4-5 | Injector 4 |
| 1-5-3 | Rear HO2S signal |
| 1-5-4 | EGR system, leakage |
| 1-5-5 | Injector 5 |
| 2-1-2 | Front HO2S, signal (only USA/CDN) |
| 2-1-2 | Front HO2S, signal (not USA/CDN) |
| 2-1-4 | RPM sensor signal sporadic |
| 2-2-3 | IAC valve opening signal |
| 2-2-5 | A/C pressure sensor, signal |
| 2-3-1 | Long Term Fuel Trim, part load |
| 2-3-2 | Long Term Fuel Trim, idling |

90954C07

**1995 850 Models with Bosch Motronic 4.3 System Trouble Codes**

| DTC | Fault text |
|-----|-----------|
| 2-3-3 | Long term idle air trim |
| 2-4-1 | EGR system, flow malfunction |
| 2-4-5 | IAC valve closing signal |
| 3-1-1 | VSS signal |
| 3-1-4 | CMP sensor signal |
| 3-1-5 | EVAP system |
| 3-2-5 | Memory failure |
| 3-3-5 | Fault in lead between AW 50-42 and Motronic 4.3 (MIL Request) |
| 4-1-1 | TP sensor signal |
| 4-1-3 | EGR temp. sensor signal |
| 4-1-4 | Boost pressure regulation |
| 4-1-6 | Boost pressure reduction from TCM |
| 4-2-5 | Rear HO2S, regulating |
| 4-3-2 | Temperature warning level 1 |
| 4-3-3 | Rear KS, signal |
| 4-3-5 | Front HO2S slow response |
| 4-3-6 | Rear HO2S, compensation |
| 4-4-3 | TWC efficiency |
| 4-4-4 | Acceleration sensor, signal |
| 4-5-1 | Misfire cyl. 1 |
| 4-5-2 | Misfire cyl. 2 |
| 4-5-3 | Misfire cyl. 3 |
| 4-5-4 | Misfire cyl. 4 |
| 4-5-5 | Misfire cyl. 5 |

90954C08

**1995 850 Models with Bosch Motronic 4.3 System Trouble Codes**

| DTC | Fault text |
|-----|-----------|
| 5-1-3 | Temperature warning level 2 |
| 5-1-4 | Engine cooling fan, low-speed signal |
| 5-2-1 | Front HO2S, preheating |
| 5-2-2 | Rear HO2S, preheating |
| 5-3-1 | Power stage group A |
| 5-3-2 | Power stage group B |
| 5-3-3 | Power stage group C |
| 5-3-4 | Power stage group D |
| 5-3-5 | TC control valve, signal |
| 5-4-1 | EVAP-valve, signal |
| 5-4-2 | Misfire more than 1 cylinder |
| 5-4-3 | Misfire at least 1 cylinder |
| 5-4-4 | Misfire more than 1 cylinder. TWC damage |
| 5-4-5 | Misfire at least 1 cyl. TWC damage |
| 5-5-1 | Misfire cyl. 1. TWC damage |
| 5-5-2 | Misfire cyl. 2. TWC damage |
| 5-5-3 | Misfire cyl. 3. TWC damage |
| 5-5-4 | Misfire cyl. 4. TWC damage |
| 5-5-5 | Misfire cyl. 5. TWC damage |
|  | Verification of repair |

90954C09

## OBD II Trouble Codes

| OBD-II codes | Fault message |
|---|---|
| P0100 | Mass air flow (MAF) sensor, signal |
| P0102 | Mass air flow (MAF) sensor, signal |
| P0103 | Mass air flow (MAF) sensor, signal |
| P0115 | Engine coolant temperature (ECT) sensor, signal |
| P0116 | Engine coolant temperature (ECT) sensor, signal |
| P0117 | Engine coolant temperature (ECT) sensor, signal |
| P0118 | Engine coolant temperature (ECT) sensor, signal |
| P0120 | Throttle position (TP) sensor, signal |
| P0122 | Throttle position (TP) sensor, signal |
| P0123 | Throttle position (TP) sensor, signal |
| P0130 | Front heated oxygen sensor (HO2S), signal |
| P0131 | Front heated oxygen sensor (HO2S), signal |
| P0132 | Front heated oxygen sensor (HO2S), signal |
| P0133 | Front heated oxygen sensor (HO2S), too slow Rear heated oxygen sensor (HO2S), compensation |
| P0135 | front heated oxygen sensor (HO2S), preheating |
| P0136 | Rear heated oxygen sensor (HO2S), signal |
| P0137 | Rear heated oxygen sensor (HO2S), signal |
| P0138 | Rear heated oxygen sensor (HO2S), signal |
| P0140 | Rear heated oxygen sensor (HO2S), check |
| P0141 | rear heated oxygen sensor (HO2S), preheating |
| P0170 | Long-term fuel trim, part load |
| P0171 | Long-term fuel trim, part load Long-term fuel trim, idling |
| P0172 | Long-term fuel trim, part load Long-term fuel trim, idling |
| P0201 | Injector 1 |
| P0202 | Injector 2 |
| P0203 | Injector 3 |
| P0204 | Injector 4 |
| P0205 | Injector 5 |

## OBD II Trouble Codes

| OBD-II codes | Fault message |
|---|---|
| P0206 | Injector 6 |
| P0300 | Misfire emission level from at least 1 cylinder. Misfire with three-way catalytic converter (TWC) damage from at least 1 cylinder |
| P0301 | Misfire emission level cylinder 1 Misfire with three-way catalytic converter (TWC) damage cylinder 1 |
| P0302 | Misfire emission level cylinder 2 Misfire with three-way catalytic converter (TWC) damage cylinder 2 |
| P0303 | Misfire emission level cylinder 3 Misfire with three-way catalytic converter (TWC) damage cylinder 3 |
| P0304 | Misfire emission level cylinder 4 Misfire with three-way catalytic converter (TWC) damage cylinder 4 |
| P0305 | Misfire emission level cylinder 5 Misfire with three-way catalytic converter (TWC) damage cylinder 5 |
| P0306 | Misfire emission level cylinder 6 Misfire with three-way catalytic converter (TWC) damage cylinder 6 |
| P0325 | Front knock sensor (KS), signal |
| P0330 | Rear knock sensor (KS), signal |
| P0340 | Camshaft position (CMP) sensor, signal |
| P0410 | Pulsed secondary air injection system (PAIR), flow fault Pulsed secondary air injection system (PAIR) pump, flow fault Pulsed secondary air injection system (PAIR) valve, leakage Pulsed secondary air injection system (PAIR) pump, signal |
| P0412 | Pulsed secondary air injection system (PAIR) solenoid valve, signal |
| P0413 | Pulsed secondary air injection system (PAIR) solenoid valve, signal |
| P0414 | Pulsed secondary air injection system (PAIR) solenoid valve, signal |
| P0422 | Three-way catalytic converter (TWC) efficiency |
| P0440 | Canister purge (CP) valve, leakage |
| P0443 | Canister purge (CP) valve signal |
| P0444 | Canister purge (CP) valve signal |
| P0445 | Canister purge (CP) valve signal |
| P0500 | Speedometer signal |
| P0505 | Adaptive idle air trim |
| P0530 | Air conditioning (A/C) pressure sensor, signal |
| P0535 | Vehicle speed sensor (VSS), signal |
| P0560 | Battery voltage |
| P0605 | Fault in engine control module (ECM), memory fault |
| P1307 | Accelerometer, signal |
| P1308 | Accelerometer, signal |

90954C10

90954C11

**OBD II Trouble Codes**

| OBD-II codes | Fault message |
|---|---|
| P1326 | Fault in engine control module (ECM), knock control circuit. |
| P1327 | Fault in engine control module (ECM), knock control circuit. |
| P1328 | Fault in engine control module (ECM), knock control circuit. |
| P1329 | Fault in engine control module (ECM), knock control circuit. |
| P1401 | Fault in engine control module (ECM), engine coolant temperature (ECT) sensor circuit NTC switch |
| P1505 | Idle air control (IAC) valve signal opening |
| P1506 | Idle air control (IAC) valve signal opening |
| P1507 | Idle air control (IAC) valve signal closing |
| P1508 | Idle air control (IAC) valve signal closing |
| P1604 | Ignition discharge module (IDM) group D |
| P1605 | Ignition discharge module (IDM) group E |
| P1617 | Cable fault between AW 30–40/43 transmission control module (TCM) and Motronic 4.4 (lamp lights) |
| P1618 | Cable fault between AW 30–40/43 transmission control module (TCM) and Motronic 4.4 (lamp lights) |
| P1619 | engine cooling fan (FC) low-speed |
| P1620 | engine cooling fan (FC) low-speed |
| P1621 | MIL request from another engine control module (ECM) |

90954C12

## Clearing Codes

### 1990–94 Vehicles

1. Turn the ignition switch to the **ON** position.
2. Read fault codes.
3. Press diagnostic socket button 1 time and hold for approximately 5 seconds. Release button. After 3 seconds the diode light should light up. While the light is still lit, press the button again and hold for approximately 5 seconds. After releasing the button, the diode light should go off.
4. To ensure that the memory is erased, press the button 1 time, for 1 second but not more than 3 seconds. The diode light should flash code 1-1-1.
5. Start and run engine. If engine will not start, correct the problem before proceeding and start over with Step 1.
6. Check to see if new fault codes have been stored in the memory by pressing the diagnostic socket button 1 time, for 1 second but not more than 3 seconds.
7. If fault code 1-1-1 flashes, it indicates that there are no additional fault codes stored in its memory.

### 1995–98 Vehicles

Control module reset procedures are a very important part of OBD-II system diagnostics. This step should be done at the end of any fault code repair and at the end of any driveability repair.

Clearing codes can be performed by any of the methods below:
- Clear the control module memory with the Generic Scan Tool (GST)
- Clear the control module memory with the vehicle manufacturer's specific tester
- Turn the ignition off and remove the negative battery cable for at least 1 minute.

Removing the negative battery cable may cause other systems in the vehicle to loose their memory. Prior to removing the cable, ensure you have the proper reset codes for radios and alarms.

➡**The MIL will may also be de-activated for some codes if the vehicle completes three consecutive trips without a fault detected with vehicle conditions similar to those present during the fault.**

# VACUUM DIAGRAMS

▶ **See Figures 84 thru 92**

Following are vacuum diagrams for most of the engine and emissions package combinations covered by this manual. Because vacuum circuits will vary based on various engine and vehicle options, always refer first to the vehicle emission control information label, if present. Should the label be missing, or should the vehicle be equipped with a different engine from the vehicle's original equipment, refer to the diagrams below for the same or similar configuration.

If you wish to obtain a replacement emissions label, most manufacturers make the labels available for purchase. The labels can usually be ordered from a local dealer.

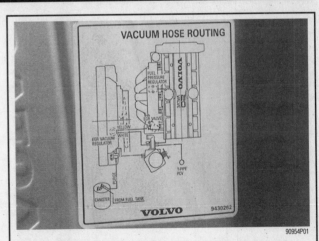

**Fig. 84 The vacuum diagram label on the underside of the hood**

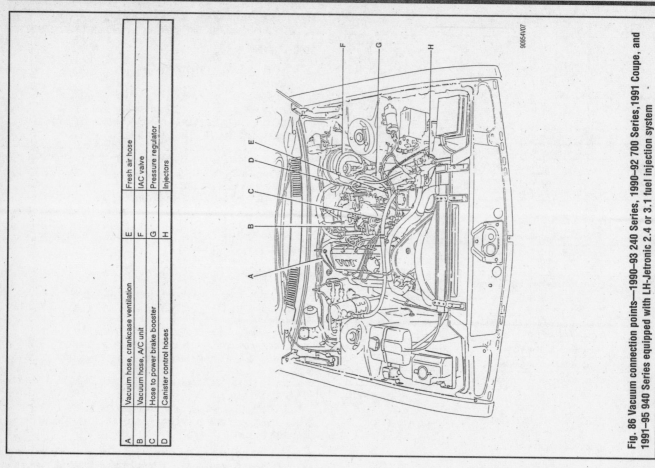

| A | Vacuum hose, crankcase ventilation | E | Fresh air hose |
|---|---|---|---|
| B | Vacuum hose, A/C unit | F | IAC valve |
| C | Hose to power brake booster | G | Pressure regulator |
| D | Canister control hoses | H | Injectors |

Fig. 86 Vacuum connection points—1990–93 240 Series, 1990–92 700 Series, 1991 Coupe, and 1991–95 940 Series equipped with LH-Jetronic 2.4 or 3.1 fuel injection system

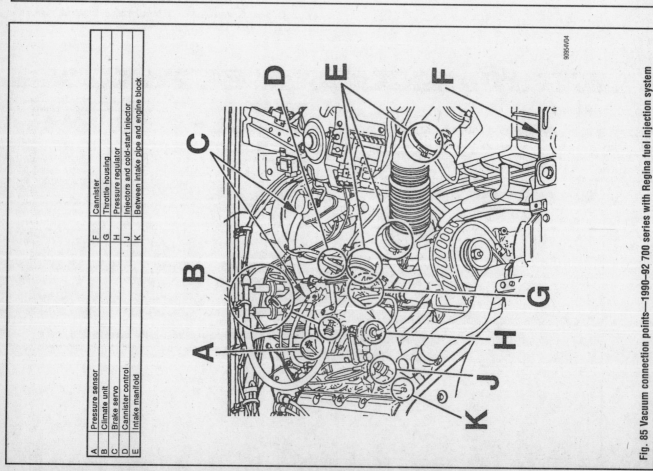

| A | Pressure sensor | F | Cannister |
|---|---|---|---|
| B | Climate unit | G | Throttle housing |
| C | Brake servo | H | Pressure regulator |
| D | Cannister control | J | Injectors and cold-start injector |
| E | Intake manifold | K | Between intake pipe and engine block |

Fig. 85 Vacuum connection points—1990–92 700 series with Regina fuel injection system

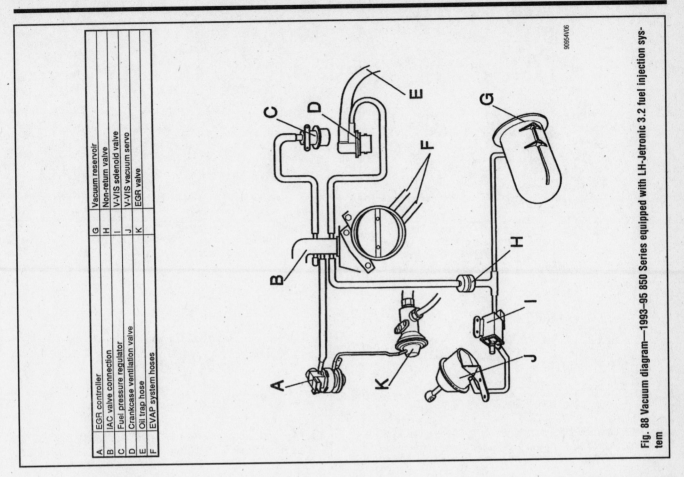

| A | EGR controller | G | Vacuum reservoir |
| B | IAC valve connection | H | Non-return valve |
| C | Fuel pressure regulator | I | V-VIS solenoid valve |
| D | Crankcase ventilation valve | J | V-VIS vacuum servo |
| E | Oil trap hose | K | EGR valve |
| F | EVAP system hoses | | |

Fig. 88 Vacuum diagram—1993–95 850 Series equipped with LH-Jetronic 3.2 fuel injection system

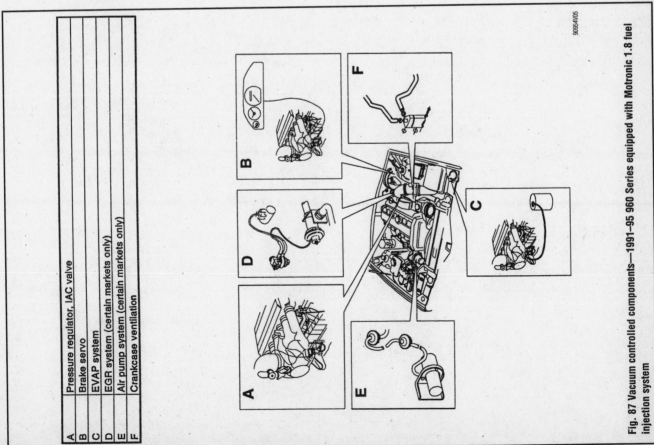

| A | Pressure regulator, IAC valve |
| B | Brake servo |
| C | EVAP system |
| D | EGR system (certain markets only) |
| E | Air pump system (certain markets only) |
| F | Crankcase ventilation |

Fig. 87 Vacuum controlled components—1991–95 960 Series equipped with Motronic 1.8 fuel injection system

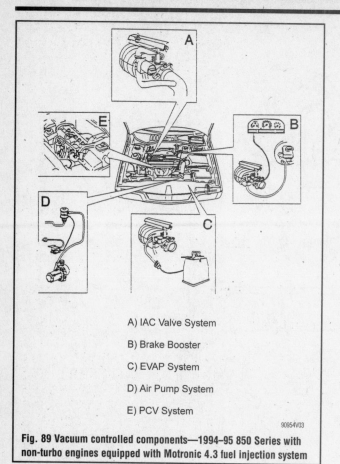

A) IAC Valve System

B) Brake Booster

C) EVAP System

D) Air Pump System

E) PCV System

90954V03

**Fig. 89 Vacuum controlled components—1994–95 850 Series with non-turbo engines equipped with Motronic 4.3 fuel injection system**

A) IAC System

B) Power Brake Booster

C) EVAP System

D) Air Pump System

E) PCV System

90954V02

**Fig. 91 Vacuum controlled components—1996–98 960/S90/V90 models with Motronic 4.4 fuel injection system**

| A | IAC valve pressure regulator |
|---|---|
| B | Turbo Charge Air Cooler (CAC) |
| C | Combined instrument |
| D | TC valve |
| E | EVAP system |
| F | EGR system |
| G | Crankcase ventilation |

90954V01

**Fig. 90 Vacuum controlled components—1994–95 850 Series with turbo engines equipped with Motronic 4.3 fuel injection system**

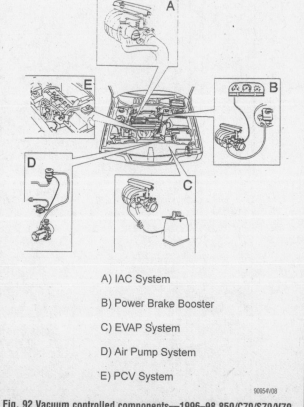

A) IAC System

B) Power Brake Booster

C) EVAP System

D) Air Pump System

E) PCV System

90954V08

**Fig. 92 Vacuum controlled components—1996–98 850/C70/S70/V70 models with Motronic 4.4 fuel injection system**

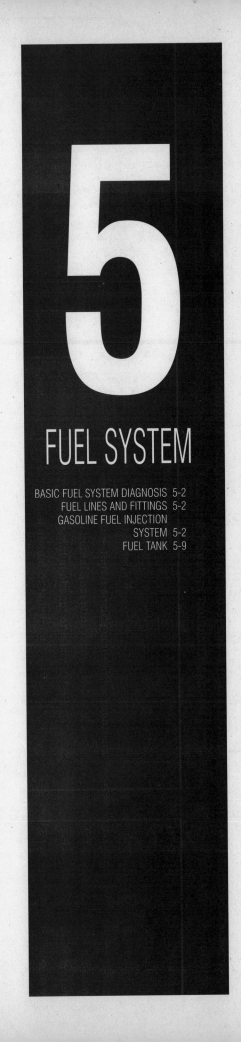

# 5

# FUEL SYSTEM

## BASIC FUEL SYSTEM DIAGNOSIS

When there is a problem starting or driving a vehicle, two of the most important checks involve the ignition and the fuel systems. The questions most mechanics attempt to answer first, "is there spark?" and "is there fuel?" will often lead to solving most basic problems. For ignition system diagnosis and testing, please refer to the information on engine electrical components and ignition systems found earlier in this manual. If the ignition system checks out (there is spark), then you must determine if the fuel system is operating properly (is there fuel?).

## FUEL LINES AND FITTINGS

### Fuel Fittings

REMOVAL & INSTALLATION

Most Volvo fuel lines use threaded-type connections. These connections are removed using the appropriate size flare-nut wrenches. Use one wrench to hold the male fitting, while the other wrench turns the female fitting until the lines are separated.

Some connections do have quick-connect fittings. The fuel filter has a quick-connect fitting; it is removed using a 17mm wrench to depress the tab and remove the line. Other quick-connect fittings have clips which must be removed before the line can be separated.

➡ **For additional information on fuel filter removal and installation, refer to Section 1 of this manual.**

## GASOLINE FUEL INJECTION SYSTEMS

### Bosch LH-Jetronic Fuel Injection System

GENERAL INFORMATION

LH denotes that this is a "hot wire" system. The system is fully electronically controlled and incorporate a number of sensors, whose signals are processed by a control unit. There are several different versions of the LH system, including the 2.2, 2.4, 3.1 and 3.2. The Bosch LH-Jetronic system is used in combination with the EZK ignition system and the turbocharged control system, where applicable. The LH fuel system is characterized by the following:
- Measurement of intake air through the air mass meter of the hot wire type
- Use of a separate cold start valve that supplies extra fuel, at or below 60°F (16°C)
- Knock controlled fuel enrichment system
- Engine speed taken from an inductive transmitter on the flywheel
- Lambda probe (oxygen sensor) providing oxygen content of the exhaust gases
- EVAP system to minimize evaporation from the fuel tank
- Three-way catalytic converter

Several sensors feed the control unit information to precisely control fuel injection. To accomplish this, the control unit evaluates: exhaust gas oxygen content from the oxygen sensor (Lambda-sond), engine RPM and crankshaft position information from the ignition system control unit (if information is not received, the fuel system control unit will not function), engine temperature from the coolant temperature sensor, engine load information from the air mass meter, information from the throttle switch, which indicates if the throttle is closed or wide open, electrical system voltage from the battery current and signals from the A/C switch and clutch, indicating whether they are operating.

### Regina Fuel Injection System

GENERAL INFORMATION

The Regina fuel injection system is a self-diagnosing system that is capable of storing up to 3 fault codes in its memory. It is used in conjunction with the REX-1 ignition system. Both are adaptive systems that are capable of multiple adjustments based on previous driving. If a fault occurs, a warning lamp lights up the instrument panel. Fault tracing can be carried out using the diagnostic program.

The Regina fuel system is characterized by the following:
- A pressure sensor for measuring engine load
- An air mass meter for measuring air intake volume
- A separate cold start valve to ensure starting at low temperatures
- An automatic idle shut-off valve if power is lost
- An induction sensor, mounted on the flywheel, to indicate rpm and crankshaft position through the ignition system control unit

- An electrically heated oxygen sensor (Lambda-sond)
- EVAP system to minimize evaporation from the fuel tank
- Three-way catalytic converter

Various input sensors feed information that is interpreted by the control unit to achieve optimum efficiency. The control unit receives signals from the pressure sensor, air intake temperature sensor and receives crankshaft position information from the ignition control unit, without which the system will not function. The coolant temperature sensor, oxygen sensor and throttle switch also send information to the control unit.

### Bosch Motronic Fuel Injection System

GENERAL INFORMATION

The Bosch Motronic fuel injection system is equipped with a powerful control unit that controls ignition and fuel injection functions by means of individual ignition coils and injectors. There are several different Motronic fuel injection versions. These include the 1.8, 4.3, and 4.4.

In addition to controlling the ignition and fuel injection functions, Motronic also:
- Determines whether the A/C compressor may be switched on
- Reduces the engine torque in response to a signal from the automatic transmission control unit, to insure smooth engagement of the different gears, and also supplies the transmission control unit with information on engine running conditions for computing gear changes
- Controls the operation of the radiator fan

The control unit is provided with adaptive Lambda control and idling control functions, as well as timing retardation function, to eliminate knock. The service requirement is minimal, since neither the carbon monoxide level nor the idling speed require adjustment.

### Fuel System Service Precautions

Safety is the most important factor when performing not only fuel system maintenance, but any type of maintenance. Failure to conduct maintenance and repairs in a safe manner may result in serious personal injury or death. Maintenance and testing of the vehicle's fuel system components can be accomplished safely and effectively by adhering to the following rules and guidelines:
- To avoid the possibility of fire and personal injury, always disconnect the negative battery cable unless the repair or test procedure requires that battery voltage be applied.
- Always relieve the fuel system pressure prior to disconnecting any fuel system component (injector, fuel rail, pressure regulator, etc.), fitting or fuel line connection. Exercise extreme caution whenever relieving fuel system pressure to avoid exposing skin, face and eyes to fuel spray. Please be advised that fuel under pressure may penetrate the skin or any part of the body that it contacts.
- Always place a shop towel or cloth around the fitting or connection prior to loosening to absorb any excess fuel due to spillage. Ensure that all fuel

spillage (should it occur) is quickly removed from engine surfaces. Ensure that all fuel soaked cloths or towels are deposited into a suitable waste container.

- Always keep a dry chemical (Class B) fire extinguisher near the work area.
- Do not allow fuel spray or fuel vapors to come into contact with a spark or open flame.
- Always use a backup wrench when loosening and tightening fuel line connection fittings. This will prevent unnecessary stress and torsion to fuel line piping.
- Always follow the proper torque specifications.
- Always replace worn fuel fitting O-rings with new ones.
- Do not substitute fuel hose or equivalent, where fuel pipe is installed.
- Whenever servicing the fuel system, always work in a well ventilated area.
- Always keep fuel in a container specifically designed for fuel storage; also, always properly seal fuel containers to avoid the possibility of fire or explosion.

## Relieving Fuel System Pressure

▶ **See Figures 1, 2, 3 and 4**

1. Connect adapter 999-5484 or equivalent to fuel drainage unit 981-2270, 2273 or 2282 or suitable equivalent.
2. Remove the protective cap from the valve on the rear of the fuel rail.
3. Connect the adapter in the locked or closed position to the valve on the fuel rail.
4. Start the fuel drainage unit.
5. Unlock or open the adapter valve.
6. Raise and safely support the vehicle.
7. Remove the fuel filter valve cap.
8. Connect vent hose 999 5480 or equivalent to the upstream valve of the fuel filter.
9. Drain the system for approximately 2 minutes.
10. When the system is drained, disconnect vent hose and install the valve cap.
11. Lower the vehicle and disconnect the adapter from the fuel rail.
12. Install the valve cap.
13. Install the protective cap for the fuel rail and throttle pulley cover.

An alternative method is to remove the fuel pump relay or fuse (if equipped) and idle the engine until it stalls, thereby relieving the fuel pressure. Place the ignition key in the **OFF** position and reinstall the fuel pump relay/fuse.

## Fuel Pump

### REMOVAL & INSTALLATION

#### 2.3L 4-Cylinder and 2.8L 6-Cylinder Engines

▶ **See Figures 5 and 6**

1. Properly relieve the fuel system pressure.
2. Disconnect the negative battery cable.
3. Raise and support the vehicle safely.
4. Remove the fuel tank.
5. Loosen the lock ring at the top of the fuel tank and remove the sending unit with the transfer pump attached. Note the direction of the float in the tank.
6. Remove the transfer pump from the sending unit.

**To install:**
7. Install the transfer pump on the sending unit.
8. Install the sending unit in the fuel tank and tighten the lock ring to specification. Do not overtighten the lock ring as the plastic threads on some fuel tanks are easily stripped.
9. Install the fuel tank in the vehicle.
10. Lower the vehicle.
11. Connect the negative battery cable.
12. Start the engine and check for leaks.

#### 2.3L and 2.4L 5-Cylinder, and 2.9L 6-Cylinder Engines

▶ **See Figures 7 thru 20**

1. Relieve the fuel system pressure.
2. Disconnect the negative battery cable.

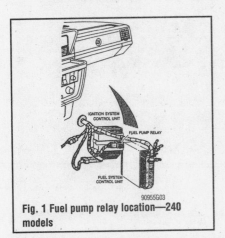

Fig. 1 Fuel pump relay location—240 models

Fig. 2 Fuel pump relay location—940 models

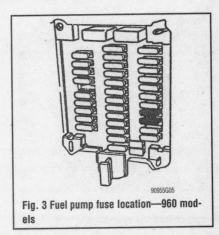

Fig. 3 Fuel pump fuse location—960 models

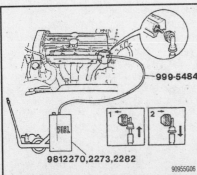

Fig. 4 Connect the adapter to the pressure port, and drain the fuel on 2.3L and 2.4L 5-cylinder engines

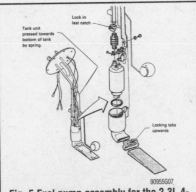

Fig. 5 Fuel pump assembly for the 2.3L 4-cylinder engine

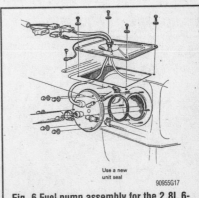

Fig. 6 Fuel pump assembly for the 2.8L 6-cylinder engine

Fig. 7 Remove the clips retaining the carpet . . .

Fig. 8 . . . to expose the fuel pump access cover

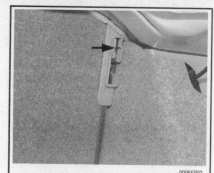

Fig. 9 The rear seats can be folded down from the inside, but this lever must be in the up position

Fig. 10 Release this lever from inside the car to lower the rear seats

Fig. 11 Remove the trim retaining bolt from the bottom of the panel

Fig. 12 Remove the seat back striker using a T30 Torx® bit

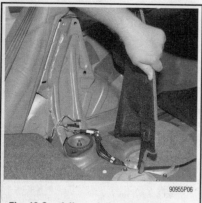

Fig. 13 Carefully push the trim back . . .

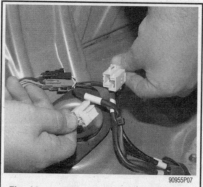

Fig. 14 . . . to access the fuel pump harness connections

Fig. 15 Remove the fuel pump access cover retaining bolts

Fig. 16 When the cover is removed, the fuel pump is visible

Fig. 17 Detach the quick-connect fittings . . .

Fig. 18 . . . and remove the fuel lines from the pump

Fig. 19 Use wrench 5485 or equivalent to remove the fuel pump retaining ring

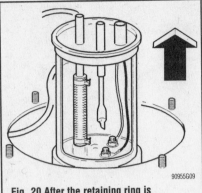

Fig. 20 After the retaining ring is removed, lift the pump out of the tank

Fig. 21 The Schrader valve is located on the fuel rail—remove the protective cap to test fuel pressure

3. Tilt the rear seat forward and remove or fold back the trunk compartment carpet over the right-hand wheel well panel.

4. Disconnect the fuel pump electrical connections.

➡Take note of the color markings on the hoses; colored tape should identify hose locations on the pump.

5. Detach the quick-connect couplers for the fuel delivery and return hoses.

6. Remove the pump unit by unscrewing the retaining nut using tool 999-5485 or equivalent.

7. Lift the pump out carefully and remove the rubber seal. When lifting the pump out, do not grab the connections with pliers or any other sharp tools that might cause damage and result in fuel leakage.

**To install:**

### ❊❊ WARNING

**Install the retaining nut while the pump is removed, otherwise the tank connection may swell and the nut will be difficult to install.**

8. Install a new dry seal, making sure that it is seated properly. Lubricate the top and outer side of the seal with petroleum jelly.

9. Install the pump with the heater connection facing towards the right side of the vehicle.

10. Install the fuel pump retaining nut and tighten it to 30 ft. lbs. (40 Nm) using tool 999-5484 or equivalent.

11. Apply a small amount of petroleum jelly to the delivery and return hose ends and install them on the pump. The delivery line is marked with yellow tape, which should be matched to the yellow marked pump outlet. Make sure that the quick-connectors are properly seated on the pump.

12. Connect the electrical connections, making sure that they are in the correct position. Install the panels and carpets.

13. Connect the negative battery cable.

14. Run the engine and check for leaks.

## PRESSURE TESTING

♦ **See Figures 21 and 22**

1. Relieve the fuel pressure.

2. Connect a fuel pressure gauge 5011 or equivalent, between the fuel line and distribution manifold or Schrader valve if equipped.

➡Position a shop towel in place to catch any spilled fuel when the fuel line connections are removed.

3. On 700 and 900 Series vehicles, remove the seat belt reminder, since this makes the test more easily performed. It is located in the middle of the top row in the fuse box.

4. Start the fuel pump (fuel pump relay removed) by connecting a jumper lead between terminals 30 and 87/2 on the relay socket. Verify the pump operation by removing the fuel cap and listening.

5. Note the gauge reading. The fuel pressure should be approximately 43.5 psi (300 kPa).

6. Remove the jumper lead.

7. Relieve the fuel system pressure and remove the pressure gauge.

8. Re-install the fuel pump relay.

## Throttle Body

### REMOVAL & INSTALLATION

♦ **See Figures 23, 24, 25 and 26**

1. Disconnect the negative battery cable.

2. Remove the throttle pulley cover (if equipped).

3. Remove the throttle body to air cleaner hose.

4. Remove the link between the throttle pulley and the throttle body (if equipped).

5. Remove the throttle cable from the throttle body.

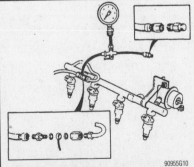

Fig. 22 Install the gauge and adapters between the fuel feed line and fuel rail on models without a Schrader valve

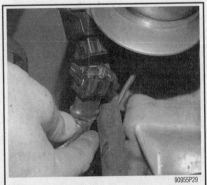

Fig. 23 Unfasten the TP sensor's electrical connector

Fig. 24 Disconnect the accelerator cable

Fig. 25 Unfasten the retaining bolts and remove the throttle body assembly

Fig. 26 Make sure you replace the throttle body gasket to prevent leaks

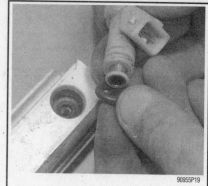

Fig. 27 Remove the injector from the fuel rail and replace the O-ring

6. Remove any necessary hoses.
7. Remove the connector from the Throttle Position (TP) sensor.
8. Remove the four throttle body-to-intake manifold retaining bolts.
9. Remove the throttle body from the intake manifold.

**To install:**

➥If replacing the throttle body, install the TP sensor onto the new throttle body before installing it onto the intake manifold.

10. Thoroughly clean the mounting surfaces of the intake manifold and the throttle body.
11. Install a new gasket onto the throttle body.
12. Install the throttle body onto the intake manifold.
13. Tighten the retaining bolts to 62 inch lbs. (7 Nm).
14. Install the TP sensor connector.
15. Install the throttle cable onto the throttle body.
16. Install the link between the throttle pulley and the throttle body (if equipped).
17. Install any hoses which were removed.
18. Install the throttle body-to-air cleaner hose.
19. Install the throttle pulley cover.
20. Connect the negative battery cable.

## Fuel Injector(s)

### REMOVAL & INSTALLATION

#### 2.3L 4-Cylinder and 2.8L 6-Cylinder Engines

1. Relieve the fuel system pressure.
2. Disconnect the negative battery cable.
3. Disconnect the fuel lines, electrical connectors and vacuum hose from the injection manifold and pressure regulator.
4. Unbolt the pressure regulator from the fuel rail bracket.
5. Remove the injector cover plate, if equipped.
6. Remove the fuel injection manifold retaining bolts. Remove the fuel injection manifold and injectors as one unit.
7. Secure the injection manifold in a suitable holding fixture and remove the fuel injectors.

**To install:**

8. Check the fuel injector O-rings, and replace if necessary.
9. Coat the O-rings with petroleum jelly and install the fuel injectors to the injection manifold.
10. Install the fuel injection manifold and fuel injectors as one unit.
11. Install and tighten the retaining bolts.
12. Install the injector cover plate, if equipped.
13. Connect the pressure regulator to the fuel injection manifold and then attach to the bracket.
14. Connect the vacuum hose, fuel lines and electrical connectors.
15. Connect the negative battery cable.
16. Start the vehicle and check for leaks.

#### 2.9L 6-Cylinder Engine

1. Properly relieve the fuel system pressure.
2. Disconnect the negative battery cable.
3. Remove fuel rail protective cover.
4. Remove the fuel lines from the fuel rail.
5. Label and remove electrical connectors from the injectors.
6. Remove fuel rail retaining bolts.
7. Remove fuel rail assembly by pulling the rail up evenly to ensure the injectors come out of the intake.
8. Remove the injector(s) from the fuel rail.

**To install:**

9. Lubricate the O-rings on the injectors with petroleum jelly or equivalent and place the injectors into the fuel rail, ensuring that the O-rings are seated.
10. Install the fuel rail assembly. Ensure the O-rings seat properly.
11. Tighten the fuel rail retaining bolts.
12. Install the fuel injector connectors.
13. Install the fuel lines on the fuel rail.
14. Install the protective cover on the fuel rail.
15. Connect the negative battery cable.
16. Start the vehicle and check for leaks.
17. Ensure that the fuel pressure is correct.
18. Shut the engine **OFF** and install the protective cover on the fuel rail.

#### 2.3L and 2.4L 5-Cylinder Engines

♦ See Figures 27, 28, 29 and 30

1. Remove the throttle pulley cover and shield over the valve on the fuel rail.
2. Properly relieve the fuel system pressure.
3. Disconnect the negative battery cable.
4. Remove or disconnect the following components:
• Upper air charge pipe
• Fuel rail cover
• Injector connectors
• Fuel line clips
5. Disconnect the vacuum hose from the pressure regulator.
6. Remove the fuel rail retaining bolts and lift the rail off with the injectors.

➥Handle the fuel injectors with care, to avoid damaging the nozzles or needles. Be sure to retain the rubber dampers from the intake manifold.

7. Remove the injector(s) to be replaced and soak up any fuel spillage. Make sure that a spacer is in the fuel rail O-ring seat.

**To install:**

8. Lubricate the O-ring(s) with petroleum jelly, then install the new injector(s) into the rail.
9. Make sure the rubber dampers are installed in the injector ports in the intake manifold.
10. Install the rail into the intake manifold.
11. Install or connect the following:
• New bolts in the fuel rail and tighten to 7.5 ft. lbs. (10 Nm)
• Fuel line clips
• Injector connector with rubber seal

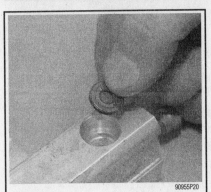

Fig. 28 Make sure the injector spacers are not lost

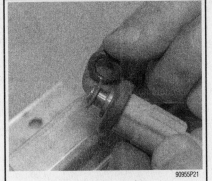

Fig. 29 Replace the O-ring on the intake manifold side of the injector as well

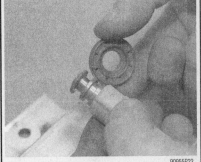

Fig. 30 The rubber dampers for the intake manifold must be installed before the fuel rail is reinstalled

- Fuel rail and throttle pulley covers
- Upper air charge pipe
12. Connect the negative battery cable.
13. Run the car and check for leaks.

## TESTING

The easiest way to test the operation of the fuel injectors is to listen for a clicking sound coming from the injectors while the engine is running. This is accomplished using a mechanic's stethoscope, or a long screwdriver. Place the end of the stethoscope or the screwdriver (tip end, not handle) onto the body of the injector. Place the ear pieces of the stethoscope in your ears, or if using a screwdriver, place your ear on top of the handle. An audible clicking noise should be heard; this is the solenoid operating. If the injector makes this noise, the injector driver circuit and computer are operating as designed. Continue testing all the injectors this way.

### ✳✳ CAUTION

**Be extremely careful while working on an operating engine, make sure you have no dangling jewelry, extremely loose clothes, power tool cords or other items that might get caught in a moving part of the engine.**

### All Injectors Clicking

If all the injectors are clicking, but you have determined that the fuel system is the cause of your driveability problem, continue diagnostics. Make sure that you have checked fuel pump pressure as outlined earlier in this section. An easy way to determine a weak or unproductive cylinder is a cylinder drop test. This is accomplished by removing one spark plug wire at a time, and seeing which cylinder causes the least difference in the idle. The one that causes the least change is the weak cylinder.

If the injectors were all clicking and the ignition system is functioning properly, remove the injector of the suspect cylinder and bench test it. This is accomplished by checking for a spray pattern from the injector itself. Install a fuel supply line to the injector (or rail if the injector is left attached to the rail) and momentarily apply 12 volts DC and a ground to the injector itself; a visible fuel spray should appear. If no spray is achieved, replace the injector and check the running condition of the engine.

### One or More Injectors Are Not Clicking

If one or more injectors are found to be not operating, testing the injector driver circuit and computer can be accomplished using a "noid" light. First, with the engine not running and the ignition key in the **OFF** position, remove the connector from the injector you plan to test, then plug the "noid" light tool into the injector connector. Start the engine and the "noid" light should flash, signaling that the injector driver circuit is working. If the "noid" light flashes, but the injector does not click when plugged in, replace the injector and retest.

If the "noid" light does not flash, the injector driver circuit is faulty. Disconnect the negative battery cable. Unplug the "noid" light from the injector connector and also unplug the ECM. Check the harness between the appropriate pins on the harness side of the ECM connector and the injector connector.

Resistance should be less than 5.0 ohms; if not, repair the circuit. If resistance is within specifications, the injector driver inside the ECM is faulty and replacement of the ECM will be necessary.

### Fuel Injector Rail

## REMOVAL & INSTALLATION

### 2.3L 4-Cylinder and 2.8L 6-Cylinder Engines

#### ◢ See Figures 31 and 32

1. Properly relieve the fuel system pressure.
2. Disconnect the negative battery cable.
3. Label and remove electrical connectors from the injectors.
4. Remove the fuel lines from the fuel rail.
5. Remove the retaining bolts from the fuel rail.

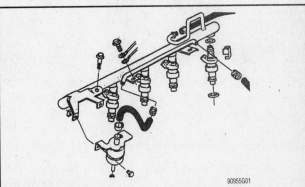

Fig. 31 Exploded view of the 2.3L 4-cylinder fuel rail and pressure regulator assembly

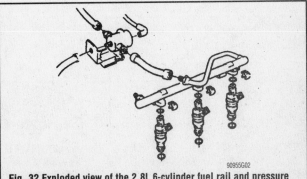

Fig. 32 Exploded view of the 2.8L 6-cylinder fuel rail and pressure regulator assembly

➡On the 2.8L engine, remove one fuel rail at a time.

6. Remove the fuel rail and injectors as an assembly.

**To install:**

7. Lubricate the O-rings on the injectors with petroleum jelly or equivalent.
8. Install the fuel rail assembly. Ensure that the O-rings seat properly.
9. Tighten the fuel rail retaining bolts.
10. Install the fuel lines on the fuel rail.
11. Install the injector connectors.
12. Connect the negative battery cable.
13. Start the vehicle and check for leaks.

### 2.3L and 2.4L 5-Cylinder Engines and 2.9L 6-Cylinder Engine

▶ See Figures 33, 34, 35, 36 and 37

1. Remove the throttle pulley cover and shield over the valve on the fuel rail.
2. Properly relieve the fuel system pressure.
3. Disconnect the negative battery cable.
4. Remove or disconnect the following components:
- Upper air charge pipe
- Fuel rail cover
- Injector connectors
- Fuel line clips
5. Disconnect the vacuum hose from the pressure regulator.
6. Remove the fuel rail retaining bolts and lift the rail off with the injectors.

**To install:**

7. Make sure the rubber dampers are installed in the injector ports in the intake manifold.
8. Install the rail into the intake manifold.
9. Install or connect the following:
- New bolts in the fuel rail and tighten to 7.5 ft. lbs. (10 Nm)
- Fuel line clips
- Injector connector with rubber seal

- Fuel rail and throttle pulley covers
- Upper air charge pipe
10. Connect the negative battery cable.
11. Run car and check for leaks.

## Fuel Pressure Regulator

### REMOVAL & INSTALLATION

#### 2.3L 4-Cylinder and 2.8L 6-Cylinder Engines

1. Properly relieve the fuel system pressure.
2. Disconnect the negative battery cable.
3. Remove the fuel lines from the pressure regulator.
4. Remove the vacuum line from the pressure regulator.
5. Remove the pressure regulator-to-bracket retaining bolts/nuts.

**To install:**

6. Install the pressure regulator in the bracket and tighten the retaining bolts/nuts.
7. Install the vacuum line.
8. Install and tighten the fuel lines.
9. Connect the negative battery cable.
10. Start vehicle and check for leaks.
11. Ensure fuel pressure is correct.
12. Shut engine off and install the protective cover on the fuel rail.

#### 2.9L 6-Cylinder Engine; 2.3L and 2.4L 5-Cylinder Engines

▶ See Figures 38, 39, 40, 41 and 42

1. Properly relieve the fuel system pressure.
2. Disconnect the negative battery cable.
3. Remove the fuel rail assembly.

Fig. 33 Remove the fuel rail cover retaining bolts

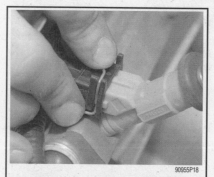

Fig. 34 Unplug the injector connectors by pressing the retaining spring down, and pulling the connector off

Fig. 35 Remove the fuel feed line using the proper size wrenches

Fig. 36 Remove the fuel return line clamp, and make sure both lines are free before removing the fuel rail

Fig. 37 Lift the fuel rail off evenly, taking care not to lose any spacers or O-rings while removing

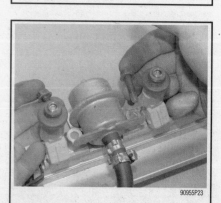

Fig. 38 Remove the pressure regulator retaining bolts

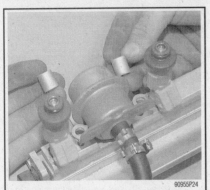

Fig. 39 Remove and safely store the spacers that go under the retaining bolts

Fig. 40 Lift the regulator off of the fuel rail

Fig. 41 Remove the O-ring from the pressure regulator port; install a new O-ring during assembly

Fig. 42 Also replace the copper gasket on the pressure regulator body to prevent leaks

4. Remove the vacuum line from the pressure regulator.
5. Remove the fuel lines from the pressure regulator.
6. Remove the pressure regulator from the fuel rail.

**To install:**

7. Lubricate the O-ring on the pressure regulator and the O-rings on the injectors with petroleum jelly or equivalent.
8. Install new pressure regulator ensuring O-ring seats properly.
9. Install and tighten the fuel lines to the regulator.
10. Install the vacuum line to the pressure regulator.
11. Install the fuel rail assembly. Ensure that the O-rings seat properly.
12. Connect the negative battery cable.
13. Start the vehicle and check for leaks.
14. Check that the fuel pressure is correct.
15. Shut the engine **OFF** and install the protective cover on the fuel rail.

## FUEL TANK

### Tank Assembly

On all vehicles, the fuel tank contains the fuel pump and sending unit assembly.

REMOVAL & INSTALLATION

▶ See Figures 43 thru 48

1. Disconnect the negative battery cable.
2. Properly relieve the fuel system pressure.
3. On the 2.9L 6-cylinder, as well as 2.3 and 2.4L 5-cylinder engine equipped vehicles:
   a. Tilt the rear seat forward and remove or fold back the trunk compartment carpet over the right-hand wheel well panel.
   b. Disconnect the fuel pump electrical connections.

➡Take note of the color markings on the hoses; colored tape should identify hose locations on the pump.

   c. Detach the quick-connect couplers for the fuel delivery and return hoses.
4. Raise and safely support the vehicle on jackstands.
5. Drain the fuel tank completely.

### ✳✳ CAUTION

When performing this procedure, always have a dry-chemical fire extinguisher handy. Fuel vapors are extremely explosive.

6. In the trunk, remove the panels which cover the filler hose.
7. It may be necessary to remove the spare tire on some vehicles.
8. Roll back the carpet and remove the access panel cover.

9. Disconnect the fuel filler pipe connection. Remove the circlip retaining the fuel filler pipe (if equipped).
10. Label and disconnect all fuel lines leading to the fuel tank.
11. Label and remove all electrical connectors at the fuel tank.
12. On some models, it may be necessary to remove the driveshaft.
13. Position a floor jack under the tank, using a large piece of wood as a cushion between the fuel tank and the floor jack.
14. Raise the jack so that it just contacts the tank.
15. Remove any shields or protective covers on the tank.
16. Loosen and remove the tank retaining bolts.
17. Lower the jack slowly and inspect for any obstructions.

**To install:**

18. Install the protective shields and raise the fuel tank into position.
19. Install and tighten the attaching bolts.

Fig. 43 Remove the circlip on the fuel filer pipe to remove the pipe

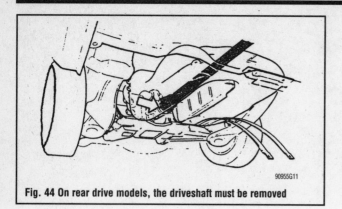

**Fig. 44 On rear drive models, the driveshaft must be removed**

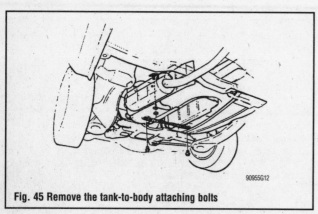

**Fig. 45 Remove the tank-to-body attaching bolts**

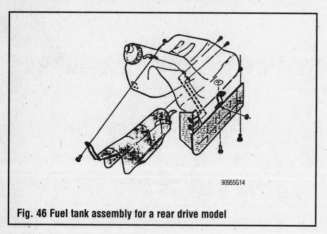

**Fig. 46 Fuel tank assembly for a rear drive model**

20. Remove the floor jack.
21. Fasten the electrical connections, making sure that they are in the correct position.
22. Install the protective panel in the trunk, then replace the spare tire (as required) and the carpet.
23. Lower the vehicle.
24. Connect the negative battery cable.
25. Turn the ignition key **ON** and check for leaks.

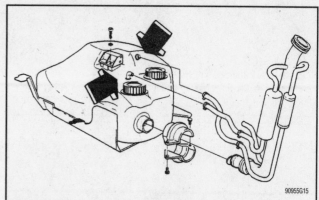

**Fig. 47 Fuel tank assembly—850/C70/S70 and V70 non-AWD models**

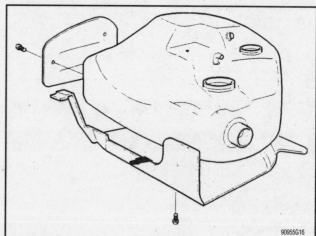

**Fig. 48 If the tank is being replaced, remove and transfer the protective shield**

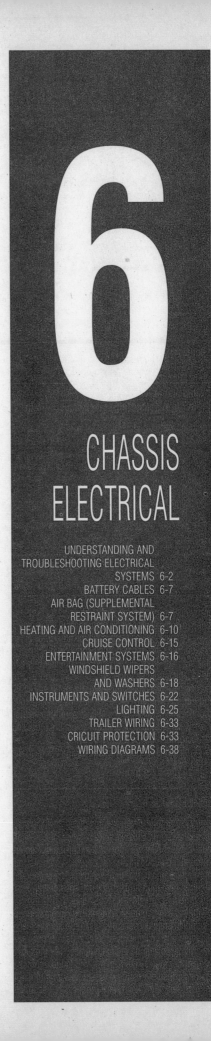

# 6

## CHASSIS
## ELECTRICAL

## UNDERSTANDING AND TROUBLESHOOTING ELECTRICAL SYSTEMS

### Basic Electrical Theory

▶ See Figure 1

For any 12 volt, negative ground, electrical system to operate, the electricity must travel in a complete circuit. This simply means that current (power) from the positive (+) terminal of the battery must eventually return to the negative (-) terminal of the battery. Along the way, this current will travel through wires, fuses, switches and components. If, for any reason, the flow of current through the circuit is interrupted, the component fed by that circuit will cease to function properly.

Perhaps the easiest way to visualize a circuit is to think of connecting a light bulb (with two wires attached to it) to the battery—one wire attached to the negative (-) terminal of the battery and the other wire to the positive (+) terminal. With the two wires touching the battery terminals, the circuit would be complete and the light bulb would illuminate. Electricity would follow a path from the battery to the bulb and back to the battery. It's easy to see that with longer wires on our light bulb, it could be mounted anywhere. Further, one wire could be fitted with a switch so that the light could be turned on and off.

The normal automotive circuit differs from this simple example in two ways. First, instead of having a return wire from the bulb to the battery, the current travels through the frame of the vehicle. Since the negative (-) battery cable is attached to the frame (made of electrically conductive metal), the frame of the vehicle can serve as a ground wire to complete the circuit. Secondly, most automotive circuits contain multiple components which receive power from a single circuit. This lessens the amount of wire needed to power components on the vehicle.

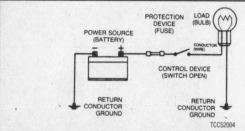

TCCS2004

**Fig. 1 This example illustrates a simple circuit. When the switch is closed, power from the positive (+) battery terminal flows through the fuse and the switch, and then to the light bulb. The light illuminates and the circuit is completed through the ground wire back to the negative (-) battery terminal. In reality, the two ground points shown in the illustration are attached to the metal frame of the vehicle, which completes the circuit back to the battery**

### HOW DOES ELECTRICITY WORK: THE WATER ANALOGY

Electricity is the flow of electrons—the subatomic particles that constitute the outer shell of an atom. Electrons spin in an orbit around the center core of an atom. The center core is comprised of protons (positive charge) and neutrons (neutral charge). Electrons have a negative charge and balance out the positive charge of the protons. When an outside force causes the number of electrons to unbalance the charge of the protons, the electrons will split off the atom and look for another atom to balance out. If this imbalance is kept up, electrons will continue to move and an electrical flow will exist.

Many people have been taught electrical theory using an analogy with water. In a comparison with water flowing through a pipe, the electrons would be the water and the wire is the pipe.

The flow of electricity can be measured much like the flow of water through a pipe. The unit of measurement used is amperes, frequently abbreviated as amps (a). You can compare amperage to the volume of water flowing through a pipe. When connected to a circuit, an ammeter will measure the actual amount of current flowing through the circuit. When relatively few electrons flow through a circuit, the amperage is low. When many electrons flow, the amperage is high.

Water pressure is measured in units such as pounds per square inch (psi); The electrical pressure is measured in units called volts (v). When a voltmeter is connected to a circuit, it is measuring the electrical pressure.

The actual flow of electricity depends not only on voltage and amperage, but also on the resistance of the circuit. The higher the resistance, the higher the force necessary to push the current through the circuit. The standard unit for measuring resistance is an ohm $\Omega$. Resistance in a circuit varies depending on the amount and type of components used in the circuit. The main factors which determine resistance are:
- Material—some materials have more resistance than others. Those with high resistance are said to be insulators. Rubber materials (or rubber-like plastics) are some of the most common insulators used in vehicles as they have a very high resistance to electricity. Very low resistance materials are said to be conductors. Copper wire is among the best conductors. Silver is actually a superior conductor to copper and is used in some relay contacts, but its high cost prohibits its use as common wiring. Most automotive wiring is made of copper.
- Size—the larger the wire size being used, the less resistance the wire will have. This is why components which use large amounts of electricity usually have large wires supplying current to them.
- Length—for a given thickness of wire, the longer the wire, the greater the resistance. The shorter the wire, the less the resistance. When determining the proper wire for a circuit, both size and length must be considered to design a circuit that can handle the current needs of the component.
- Temperature—with many materials, the higher the temperature, the greater the resistance (positive temperature coefficient). Some materials exhibit the opposite trait of lower resistance with higher temperatures (negative temperature coefficient). These principles are used in many of the sensors on the engine.

### OHM'S LAW

There is a direct relationship between current, voltage and resistance. The relationship between current, voltage and resistance can be summed up by a statement known as Ohm's law.

Voltage (E) is equal to amperage (I) times resistance (R): $E = I \times R$

Other forms of the formula are $R = E/I$ and $I = E/R$

In each of these formulas, E is the voltage in volts, I is the current in amps and R is the resistance in ohms. The basic point to remember is that as the resistance of a circuit goes up, the amount of current that flows in the circuit will go down, if voltage remains the same.

The amount of work that the electricity can perform is expressed as power. The unit of power is the watt (w). The relationship between power, voltage and current is expressed as:

Power (w) is equal to amperage (I) times voltage (E): $W = I \times E$

This is only true for direct current (DC) circuits; The alternating current formula is a tad different, but since the electrical circuits in most vehicles are DC type, we need not get into AC circuit theory.

### Electrical Components

### POWER SOURCE

Power is supplied to the vehicle by two devices: The battery and the alternator. The battery supplies electrical power during starting or during periods when the current demand of the vehicle's electrical system exceeds the output capacity of the alternator. The alternator supplies electrical current when the engine is running. Just not does the alternator supply the current needs of the vehicle, but it recharges the battery.

#### The Battery

In most modern vehicles, the battery is a lead/acid electrochemical device consisting of six 2 volt subsections (cells) connected in series, so that the unit is capable of producing approximately 12 volts of electrical pressure. Each subsection consists of a series of positive and negative plates held a short distance apart in a solution of sulfuric acid and water.

The two types of plates are of dissimilar metals. This sets up a chemical reaction, and it is this reaction which produces current flow from the battery when its positive and negative terminals are connected to an electrical load . The power removed from the battery is replaced by the alternator, restoring the battery to its original chemical state.

## The Alternator

On some vehicles there isn't an alternator, but a generator. The difference is that an alternator supplies alternating current which is then changed to direct current for use on the vehicle, while a generator produces direct current. Alternators tend to be more efficient and that is why they are used.

Alternators and generators are devices that consist of coils of wires wound together making big electromagnets. One group of coils spins within another set and the interaction of the magnetic fields causes a current to flow. This current is then drawn off the coils and fed into the vehicles electrical system.

## GROUND

Two types of grounds are used in automotive electric circuits. Direct ground components are grounded to the frame through their mounting points. All other components use some sort of ground wire which is attached to the frame or chassis of the vehicle. The electrical current runs through the chassis of the vehicle and returns to the battery through the ground (-) cable; if you look, you'll see that the battery ground cable connects between the battery and the frame or chassis of the vehicle.

➡It should be noted that a good percentage of electrical problems can be traced to bad grounds.

## PROTECTIVE DEVICES

▶ See Figure 2

It is possible for large surges of current to pass through the electrical system of your vehicle. If this surge of current were to reach the load in the circuit, the surge could burn it out or severely damage it. It can also overload the wiring, causing the harness to get hot and melt the insulation. To prevent this, fuses, circuit breakers and/or fusible links are connected into the supply wires of the electrical system. These items are nothing more than a built-in weak spot in the system. When an abnormal amount of current flows through the system, these protective devices work as follows to protect the circuit:
  • Fuse—when an excessive electrical current passes through a fuse, the fuse "blows" (the conductor melts) and opens the circuit, preventing the passage of current.
  • Circuit Breaker—a circuit breaker is basically a self-repairing fuse. It will open the circuit in the same fashion as a fuse, but when the surge subsides, the circuit breaker can be reset and does not need replacement.
  • Fusible Link—a fusible link (fuse link or main link) is a short length of special, high temperature insulated wire that acts as a fuse. When an excessive electrical current passes through a fusible link, the thin gauge wire inside the link melts, creating an intentional open to protect the circuit. To repair the circuit, the link must be replaced. Some newer type fusible links are housed in plug-in modules, which are simply replaced like a fuse, while older type fusible links must be cut and spliced if they melt. Since this link is very early in the electrical path, it's the first place to look if nothing on the vehicle works, yet the battery seems to be charged and is properly connected.

## ✳✳ CAUTION

Always replace fuses, circuit breakers and fusible links with identically rated components. Under no circumstances should a component of higher or lower amperage rating be substituted.

## SWITCHES & RELAYS

▶ See Figures 3 and 4

Switches are used in electrical circuits to control the passage of current. The most common use is to open and close circuits between the battery and the various electric devices in the system. Switches are rated according to the amount of amperage they can handle. If a sufficient amperage rated switch is not used in a circuit, the switch could overload and cause damage.

Some electrical components which require a large amount of current to operate use a special switch called a relay. Since these circuits carry a large amount of current, the thickness of the wire in the circuit is also greater. If this large wire were connected from the load to the control switch, the switch would have to carry the high amperage load and the fairing or dash would be twice as large to accommodate the increased size of the wiring harness. To prevent these problems, a relay is used.

Relays are composed of a coil and a set of contacts. When the coil has a current passed though it, a magnetic field is formed and this field causes the contacts to move together, completing the circuit. Most relays are normally open, preventing current from passing through the circuit, but they can take any electrical form depending on the job they are intended to do. Relays can be considered "remote control switches." They allow a smaller current to operate devices that require higher amperages. When a small current operates the coil, a larger current is allowed to pass by the contacts. Some common circuits which may use relays are the horn, headlights, starter, electric fuel pump and other high draw circuits.

## LOAD

Every electrical circuit must include a "load" (something to use the electricity coming from the source). Without this load, the battery would attempt to deliver its entire power supply from one pole to another. This is called a "short circuit. "All this electricity would take a short cut to ground and cause a great amount of damage to other components in the circuit by developing a tremendous amount of heat. This condition could develop sufficient heat to melt the insulation on all the surrounding wires and reduce a multiple wire cable to a lump of plastic and copper.

## WIRING & HARNESSES

The average vehicle contains meters and meters of wiring, with hundreds of individual connections. To protect the many wires from damage and to keep them from becoming a confusing tangle, they are organized into bundles, enclosed in plastic or taped together and called wiring harnesses. Different harnesses serve different parts of the vehicle. Individual wires are color coded to help trace them through a harness where sections are hidden from view.

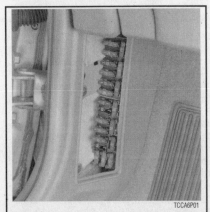

Fig. 2 Most vehicles use one or more fuse panels. This one is located on the driver's side kick panel

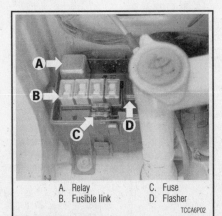

A. Relay          C. Fuse
B. Fusible link   D. Flasher

Fig. 3 The underhood fuse and relay panel usually contains fuses, relays, flashers and fusible links

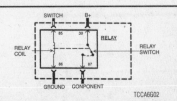

Fig. 4 Relays are composed of a coil and a switch. These two components are linked together so that when one operates, the other operates at the same time. The large wires in the circuit are connected from the battery to one side of the relay switch (B+) and from the opposite side of the relay switch to the load (component). Smaller wires are connected from the relay coil to the control switch for the circuit and from the opposite side of the relay coil to ground

Automotive wiring or circuit conductors can be either single strand wire, multi-strand wire or printed circuitry. Single strand wire has a solid metal core and is usually used inside such components as alternators, motors, relays and other devices. Multi-strand wire has a core made of many small strands of wire twisted together into a single conductor. Most of the wiring in an automotive electrical system is made up of multi-strand wire, either as a single conductor or grouped together in a harness. All wiring is color coded on the insulator, either as a solid color or as a colored wire with an identification stripe. A printed circuit is a thin film of copper or other conductor that is printed on an insulator backing. Occasionally, a printed circuit is sandwiched between two sheets of plastic for more protection and flexibility. A complete printed circuit, consisting of conductors, insulating material and connectors for lamps or other components is called a printed circuit board. Printed circuitry is used in place of individual wires or harnesses in places where space is limited, such as behind instrument panels.

Since automotive electrical systems are very sensitive to changes in resistance, the selection of properly sized wires is critical when systems are repaired. A loose or corroded connection or a replacement wire that is too small for the circuit will add extra resistance and an additional voltage drop to the circuit.

The wire gauge number is an expression of the cross-section area of the conductor. Vehicles from countries that use the metric system will typically describe the wire size as its cross-sectional area in square millimeters. In this method, the larger the wire, the greater the number. Another common system for expressing wire size is the American Wire Gauge (AWG) system. As gauge number increases, area decreases and the wire becomes smaller. An 18 gauge wire is smaller than a 4 gauge wire. A wire with a higher gauge number will carry less current than a wire with a lower gauge number. Gauge wire size refers to the size of the strands of the conductor, not the size of the complete wire with insulator. It is possible, therefore, to have two wires of the same gauge with different diameters because one may have thicker insulation than the other.

It is essential to understand how a circuit works before trying to figure out why it doesn't. An electrical schematic shows the electrical current paths when a circuit is operating properly. Schematics break the entire electrical system down into individual circuits. In a schematic, usually no attempt is made to represent wiring and components as they physically appear on the vehicle; switches and other components are shown as simply as possible. Face views of harness connectors show the cavity or terminal locations in all multi-pin connectors to help locate test points.

## CONNECTORS

▶ See Figures 5 and 6

Three types of connectors are commonly used in automotive applications—weatherproof, molded and hard shell.

- **Weatherproof**—these connectors are most commonly used where the connector is exposed to the elements. Terminals are protected against moisture and dirt by sealing rings which provide a weathertight seal. All repairs require the use of a special terminal and the tool required to service it. Unlike standard blade type terminals, these weatherproof terminals cannot be straightened once they are bent. Make certain that the connectors are properly seated and all of the sealing rings are in place when connecting leads.
- **Molded**—these connectors require complete replacement of the connector if found to be defective. This means splicing a new connector assembly into the harness. All splices should be soldered to insure proper contact. Use care when prob-

**Fig. 5 Hard shell (left) and weatherproof (right) connectors have replaceable terminals**

TCCA6P03

**Fig. 6 Weatherproof connectors are most commonly used in the engine compartment or where the connector is exposed to the elements**

TCCA6P04

ing the connections or replacing terminals in them, as it is possible to create a short circuit between opposite terminals. If this happens to the wrong terminal pair, it is possible to damage certain components. Always use jumper wires between connectors for circuit checking and NEVER probe through weatherproof seals.

- **Hard Shell**—unlike molded connectors, the terminal contacts in hard-shell connectors can be replaced. Replacement usually involves the use of a special terminal removal tool that depresses the locking tangs (barbs) on the connector terminal and allows the connector to be removed from the rear of the shell. The connector shell should be replaced if it shows any evidence of burning, melting, cracks, or breaks. Replace individual terminals that are burnt, corroded, distorted or loose.

## Test Equipment

Pinpointing the exact cause of trouble in an electrical circuit is most times accomplished by the use of special test equipment. The following describes different types of commonly used test equipment and briefly explains how to use them in diagnosis. In addition to the information covered below, the tool manufacturer's instructions booklet (provided with the tester) should be read and clearly understood before attempting any test procedures.

### JUMPER WIRES

#### ✳✳ CAUTION

**Never use jumper wires made from a thinner gauge wire than the circuit being tested. If the jumper wire is of too small a gauge, it may overheat and possibly melt. Never use jumpers to bypass high resistance loads in a circuit. Bypassing resistance, in effect, creates a short circuit. This may, in turn, cause damage and fire. Jumper wires should only be used to bypass lengths of wire or to simulate switches.**

Jumper wires are simple, yet extremely valuable, pieces of test equipment. They are basically test wires which are used to bypass sections of a circuit. Although jumper wires can be purchased, they are usually fabricated from lengths of standard automotive wire and whatever type of connector (alligator clip, spade connector or pin connector) that is required for the particular application being tested. In cramped, hard-to-reach areas, it is advisable to have insulated boots over the jumper wire terminals in order to prevent accidental grounding. It is also advisable to include a standard automotive fuse in any jumper wire. This is commonly referred to as a "fused jumper". By inserting an in-line fuse holder between a set of test leads, a fused jumper wire can be used for bypassing open circuits. Use a 5 amp fuse to provide protection against voltage spikes.

Jumper wires are used primarily to locate open electrical circuits, on either the ground (-) side of the circuit or on the power (+) side. If an electrical component fails to operate, connect the jumper wire between the component and a good ground. If the component operates only with the jumper installed, the ground circuit is open. If the ground circuit is good, but the component does not operate, the circuit between the power feed and component may be open. By moving the jumper wire successively back from the component toward the power source, you can isolate the area of the circuit where the open is located. When the component stops functioning, or the power is cut off, the open is in the segment of wire between the jumper and the point previously tested.

You can sometimes connect the jumper wire directly from the battery to the "hot" terminal of the component, but first make sure the component uses 12 volts in operation. Some electrical components, such as fuel injectors or sensors, are designed to operate on about 4 to 5 volts, and running 12 volts directly to these components will cause damage.

## TEST LIGHTS

▶ **See Figure 7**

The test light is used to check circuits and components while electrical current is flowing through them. It is used for voltage and ground tests. To use a 12 volt test light, connect the ground clip to a good ground and probe wherever necessary with the pick. The test light will illuminate when voltage is detected. This does not necessarily mean that 12 volts (or any particular amount of voltage) is present; it only means that some voltage is present. It is advisable before using the test light to touch its ground clip and probe across the battery posts or terminals to make sure the light is operating properly.

### ✳✳ WARNING

**Do not use a test light to probe electronic ignition, spark plug or coil wires. Never use a pick-type test light to probe wiring on computer controlled systems unless specifically instructed to do so. Any wire insulation that is pierced by the test light probe should be taped and sealed with silicone after testing.**

Like the jumper wire, the 12 volt test light is used to isolate opens in circuits. But, whereas the jumper wire is used to bypass the open to operate the load, the 12 volt test light is used to locate the presence of voltage in a circuit. If the test light illuminates, there is power up to that point in the circuit; if the test light does not illuminate, there is an open circuit (no power). Move the test light in successive steps back toward the power source until the light in the handle illuminates. The open is between the probe and a point which was previously probed.

The self-powered test light is similar in design to the 12 volt test light, but contains a 1.5 volt penlight battery in the handle. It is most often used in place of a multimeter to check for open or short circuits when power is isolated from the circuit (continuity test).

The battery in a self-powered test light does not provide much current. A weak battery may not provide enough power to illuminate the test light even when a complete circuit is made (especially if there is high resistance in the circuit). Always make sure that the test battery is strong. To check the battery, briefly touch the ground clip to the probe; if the light glows brightly, the battery is strong enough for testing.

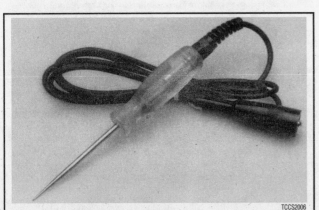

**Fig. 7 A 12 volt test light is used to detect the presence of voltage in a circuit**

TCCS2006

➡**A self-powered test light should not be used on any computer controlled system or component. The small amount of electricity transmitted by the test light is enough to damage many electronic automotive components.**

## MULTIMETERS

Multimeters are an extremely useful tool for troubleshooting electrical problems. They can be purchased in either analog or digital form and have a price range to suit any budget. A multimeter is a voltmeter, ammeter and ohmmeter (along with other features) combined into one instrument. It is often used when testing solid state circuits because of its high input impedance (usually 10 megaohms or more). A brief description of the multimeter main test functions follows:

* Voltmeter—the voltmeter is used to measure voltage at any point in a circuit, or to measure the voltage drop across any part of a circuit. Voltmeters usually have various scales and a selector switch to allow the reading of different voltage ranges. The voltmeter has a positive and a negative lead. To avoid damage to the meter, always connect the negative lead to the negative (-) side of the circuit (to ground or nearest the ground side of the circuit) and connect the positive lead to the positive (+) side of the circuit (to the power source or the nearest power source). Note that the negative voltmeter lead will always be black and that the positive voltmeter will always be some color other than black (usually red).

* Ohmmeter—the ohmmeter is designed to read resistance (measured in ohms) in a circuit or component. Most ohmmeters will have a selector switch which permits the measurement of different ranges of resistance (usually the selector switch allows the multiplication of the meter reading by 10, 100, 1,000 and 10,000). Some ohmmeters are "auto-ranging" which means the meter itself will determine which scale to use. Since the meters are powered by an internal battery, the ohmmeter can be used like a self-powered test light. When the ohmmeter is connected, current from the ohmmeter flows through the circuit or component being tested. Since the ohmmeter's internal resistance and voltage are known values, the amount of current flow through the meter depends on the resistance of the circuit or component being tested. The ohmmeter can also be used to perform a continuity test for suspected open circuits. In using the meter for making continuity checks, do not be concerned with the actual resistance readings. Zero resistance, or any ohm reading, indicates continuity in the circuit. Infinite resistance indicates an opening in the circuit. A high resistance reading where there should be none indicates a problem in the circuit. Checks for short circuits are made in the same manner as checks for open circuits, except that the circuit must be isolated from both power and normal ground. Infinite resistance indicates no continuity, while zero resistance indicates a dead short.

### ✳✳ WARNING

**Never use an ohmmeter to check the resistance of a component or wire while there is voltage applied to the circuit.**

* Ammeter—an ammeter measures the amount of current flowing through a circuit in units called amperes or amps. At normal operating voltage, most circuits have a characteristic amount of amperes, called "current draw" which can be measured using an ammeter. By referring to a specified current draw rating, then measuring the amperes and comparing the two values, one can determine what is happening within the circuit to aid in diagnosis. An open circuit, for example, will not allow any current to flow, so the ammeter reading will be zero. A damaged component or circuit will have an increased current draw, so the reading will be high. The ammeter is always connected in series with the circuit being tested. All of the current that normally flows through the circuit must also flow through the ammeter; if there is any other path for the current to follow, the ammeter reading will not be accurate. The ammeter itself has very little resistance to current flow and, therefore, will not affect the circuit, but it will measure current draw only when the circuit is closed and electricity is flowing. Excessive current draw can blow fuses and drain the battery, while a reduced current draw can cause motors to run slowly, lights to dim and other components to not operate properly.

## Troubleshooting Electrical Systems

When diagnosing a specific problem, organized troubleshooting is a must. The complexity of a modern automotive vehicle demands that you approach any problem in a logical, organized manner. There are certain troubleshooting techniques, however, which are standard:

• Establish when the problem occurs. Does the problem appear only under certain conditions? Were there any noises, odors or other unusual symptoms? Isolate the problem area. To do this, make some simple tests and observations, then eliminate the systems that are working properly. Check for obvious problems, such as broken wires and loose or dirty connections. Always check the obvious before assuming something complicated is the cause.

• Test for problems systematically to determine the cause once the problem area is isolated. Are all the components functioning properly? Is there power going to electrical switches and motors. Performing careful, systematic checks will often turn up most causes on the first inspection, without wasting time checking components that have little or no relationship to the problem.

• Test all repairs after the work is done to make sure that the problem is fixed. Some causes can be traced to more than one component, so a careful verification of repair work is important in order to pick up additional malfunctions that may cause a problem to reappear or a different problem to arise. A blown fuse, for example, is a simple problem that may require more than another fuse to repair. If you don't look for a problem that caused a fuse to blow, a shorted wire (for example) may go undetected.

Experience has shown that most problems tend to be the result of a fairly simple and obvious cause, such as loose or corroded connectors, bad grounds or damaged wire insulation which causes a short. This makes careful visual inspection of components during testing essential to quick and accurate troubleshooting.

## Testing

### OPEN CIRCUITS

#### ◗ See Figure 8

This test already assumes the existence of an open in the circuit and it is used to help locate the open portion.
1. Isolate the circuit from power and ground.
2. Connect the self-powered test light or ohmmeter ground clip to the ground side of the circuit and probe sections of the circuit sequentially.
3. If the light is out or there is infinite resistance, the open is between the probe and the circuit ground.
4. If the light is on or the meter shows continuity, the open is between the probe and the end of the circuit toward the power source.

### SHORT CIRCUITS

➡ **Never use a self-powered test light to perform checks for opens or shorts when power is applied to the circuit under test. The test light can be damaged by outside power.**

1. Isolate the circuit from power and ground.
2. Connect the self-powered test light or ohmmeter ground clip to a good ground and probe any easy-to-reach point in the circuit.
3. If the light comes on or there is continuity, there is a short somewhere in the circuit.
4. To isolate the short, probe a test point at either end of the isolated circuit (the light should be on or the meter should indicate continuity).

5. Leave the test light probe engaged and sequentially open connectors or switches, remove parts, etc. until the light goes out or continuity is broken.
6. When the light goes out, the short is between the last two circuit components which were opened.

### VOLTAGE

This test determines voltage available from the battery and should be the first step in any electrical troubleshooting procedure after visual inspection. Many electrical problems, especially on computer controlled systems, can be caused by a low state of charge in the battery. Excessive corrosion at the battery cable terminals can cause poor contact that will prevent proper charging and full battery current flow.
1. Set the voltmeter selector switch to the 20V position.
2. Connect the multimeter negative lead to the battery's negative (-) post or terminal and the positive lead to the battery's positive (+) post or terminal.
3. Turn the ignition switch **ON** to provide a load.
4. A well charged battery should register over 12 volts. If the meter reads below 11.5 volts, the battery power may be insufficient to operate the electrical system properly.

### VOLTAGE DROP

#### ◗ See Figure 9

When current flows through a load, the voltage beyond the load drops. This voltage drop is due to the resistance created by the load and also by small resistance created by corrosion at the connectors and damaged insulation on the wires. The maximum allowable voltage drop under load is critical, especially if there is more than one load in the circuit, since all voltage drops are cumulative.
1. Set the voltmeter selector switch to the 20 volt position.
2. Connect the multimeter negative lead to a good ground.
3. Operate the circuit and check the voltage prior to the first component (load).
4. There should be little or no voltage drop in the circuit prior to the first component. If a voltage drop exists, the wire or connectors in the circuit are suspect.
5. While operating the first component in the circuit, probe the ground side of the component with the positive meter lead and observe the voltage readings. A small voltage drop should be noticed. This voltage drop is caused by the resistance of the component.
6. Repeat the test for each component (load) down the circuit.
7. If a large voltage drop is noticed, the preceding component, wire or connector is suspect.

### RESISTANCE

#### ◗ See Figures 10 and 11

#### ❊❊ WARNING

**Never use an ohmmeter with power applied to the circuit. The ohmmeter is designed to operate on its own power supply. The normal 12 volt electrical system voltage could damage the meter!**

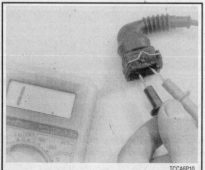
Fig. 8 The infinite reading on this multimeter (1 . ) indicates that the circuit is open
TCCA6P10

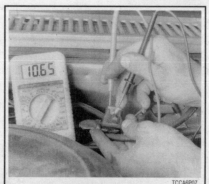
Fig. 9 This voltage drop test revealed high resistance (low voltage) in the circuit
TCCA6P07

Fig. 10 Checking the resistance of a coolant temperature sensor with an ohmmeter. Reading is 1.04 kilohms
TCCA6P08

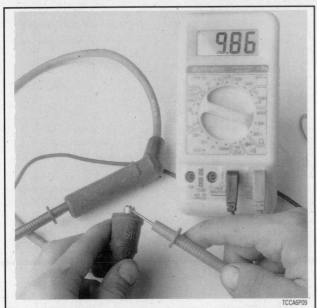

**Fig. 11 Spark plug wires can be checked for excessive resistance using an ohmmeter**

1. Isolate the circuit from the vehicle's power source.
2. Ensure that the ignition key is **OFF** when disconnecting any components or the battery.
3. Where necessary, also isolate at least one side of the circuit to be checked, in order to avoid reading parallel resistance. Parallel circuit resistance will always give a lower reading than the actual resistance of either of the branches.
4. Connect the meter leads to both sides of the circuit (wire or component) and read the actual measured ohms on the meter scale. Make sure the selector switch is set to the proper ohm scale for the circuit being tested, to avoid misreading the ohmmeter test value.

## Wire and Connector Repair

Almost anyone can replace damaged wires, as long as the proper tools and parts are available. Wire and terminals are available to fit almost any need. Even the specialized weatherproof, molded and hard shell connectors are now available from aftermarket suppliers.

Be sure the ends of all the wires are fitted with the proper terminal hardware and connectors. Wrapping a wire around a stud is never a permanent solution and will only cause trouble later. Replace wires one at a time to avoid confusion. Always route wires exactly the same as the factory.

➡**If connector repair is necessary, only attempt it if you have the proper tools. Weatherproof and hard shell connectors require special tools to release the pins inside the connector. Attempting to repair these connectors with conventional hand tools will damage them.**

## BATTERY CABLES

### Disconnecting the Cables

When working on any electrical component on the vehicle, it is always a good idea to disconnect the negative (-) battery cable. This will prevent potential damage to many sensitive electrical components such as the Engine Control Module (ECM), radio, alternator, etc.

➡**Any time you disengage the battery cables, it is recommended that you disconnect the negative (-) battery cable first. This will prevent your accidentally grounding the positive (+) terminal to the body of the vehi-**

cle when disconnecting it, thereby preventing damage to the above mentioned components.

Before you disconnect the cable(s), first turn the ignition to the **OFF** position. This will prevent a draw on the battery which could cause arcing (electricity trying to ground itself to the body of a vehicle, just like a spark plug jumping the gap) and, of course, damaging some components such as the alternator diodes.

When the battery cable(s) are reconnected (negative cable last), be sure to check that your lights, windshield wipers and other electrically operated safety components are all working correctly. If your vehicle contains an Electronically Tuned Radio (ETR), don't forget to also reset your radio stations. Ditto for the clock.

## AIR BAG (SUPPLEMENTAL RESTRAINT SYSTEM)

### General Information

▶ **See Figures 12 and 13**

The air bag system used on Volvo vehicles is referred to as Supplemental Restraint System (SRS). The SRS system provides additional protection for the driver, if a forward collision of sufficient force is encountered. The SRS assists the normal seat belt restraining system by deploying an air bag, via the steering wheel and, on some models, the passenger side of the dashboard.

The system also includes a knee bolster at the lower steering column area. It is used to absorb energy and control the driver's forward movement during an accident by limiting leg movement.

The system also includes a battery voltage check. The SRS warning lamp will illuminate, if the voltage falls below 9 volts. When the voltage rises above 9 volts again, the lamp will be go out after approximately 10 seconds.

The SRS system is monitored continuously by a microprocessor in the crash sensor. Any fault which is detected is stored in the memory and the SRS warning lamp will turn ON.

Some later Volvo models are equipped with a Side Impact Protection System (SIPS). Vehicles equipped with SIPS will contain a decal possibly located on the front windshield, driver's side of the instrument panel, below the seat pocket, or on the driver's side B-pillar.

The object of the SIPS system is to protect the occupants in the event of certain side-impact accidents. An air bag is deployed to cushion the impact against the outer side of the vehicle. This system uses sensor mounted in the seat bottom, just outside the seat track. If an accident occurs, the bag could deploy,

triggered based upon information gathered by the crash sensor measuring the violence of the collision. This sophisticated process occurs in milliseconds.

The SIPS system is not part of the SRS system and has it's own function, in fact unlike the SRS system, the SIPS system can deploy one side without deploying the other, depending on which side the impact occurs.

### SYSTEM OPERATION

Under normal conditions, the SRS warning lamp will come ON when the ignition switch is turned to the **ON** position. If the engine is not started, the lamp will be extinguished after approximately 10 seconds. Failure of the warning lamp to go OFF, while driving, indicates a fault in the SRS system. The warning lamp will remain lit until the fault is corrected and the memory cleared.

The crash sensor records a combination of G-force and prolong deceleration. When a sufficiently high G-force and prolong deceleration are simultaneously recorded, the power unit will deliver a current which will trigger the gas generator of the inflatable bag. The bag will be filled in a few hundredths of a second with non-toxic nitrogen. Immediately after the collision, the gas is released through a ventilation hole and the air bag slowly collapses. The entire sequence of inflation and collapse takes approximately 0.2 milliseconds.

The SIPS system works very similar to the SRS, however the SIPS is completely mechanical. Only three components per side of the vehicle are used. The crash sensor operates very similar to the SRS and activates when an impact of the deformed door hits the sensor at a speed greater than 2 milliseconds or 6.6 ft. per second. No electricity is used, the crash sensor deploys an igniter that uses a charge very similar to the way a shotgun is fired to fill the bag.

Fig. 12 This label is a reminder of the presence of a Supplemental Restraint System (SRS); be sure to heed the information

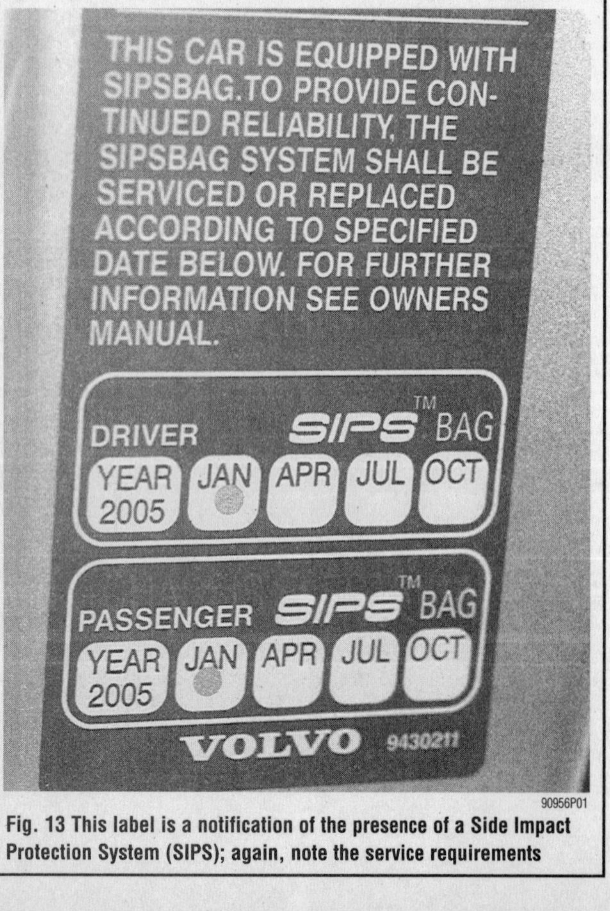

Fig. 13 This label is a notification of the presence of a Side Impact Protection System (SIPS); again, note the service requirements

The SIPS bag deploys and breaks through the seat cushion SIPS module cover. A stitch seam in the seat is strategically placed to aid in this process. The bag deploys toward the door to help protect the driver/passenger's rib cage during a side-impact collision. There is a vent on the underside of the bag which will allow the bag to deflate slowly, acting as a brake on the driver/passenger.

## SERVICE PRECAUTIONS

➡**Since the Supplemental Restraint System (SRS) is such a complex and critical safety system (which requires special precautions when repairs are being made), Volvo recommends that all repairs to the SRS system be performed by Volvo SRS-trained technicians.**

### ❄ CAUTION

**To avoid deployment when servicing the SRS system or components in the immediate area, do not use electrical test equipment such as battery or AC powered voltmeter, ohmmeter, etc. or any type of tester other than specified. Do not use a non-powered probe tester. To avoid personal injury all precautions must be strictly adhered to.**

• All work which includes removing or replacing the air bag assembly must be carried out with the battery disconnected and with the ignition turned **OFF** for the duration of work. This is to ensure that the air bag does not accidentally inflate during service repairs and that no faults codes will register, requiring subsequent cancellation.
• When working around the instrument panel or steering column, take special care to ensure that the SRS wiring are not pinched, chafed or penetrated by bolts/screws, etc. This is most likely to happen when installing the sound insulation, knee bolsters, ignition lock or steering column cover.
• For air bag fault tracing purposes and/or to check the system, use multimeter 999 6525 and test resistor 998 86595 or their equivalents.
• Do not disassemble or tamper with the air bag assembly.
• Always store a removed air bag assembly with the pad surface upwards.
• Never install used SRS parts from another vehicle.
• Never replace the original steering wheel with any other design, since it will make it impossible to properly install the air bag.
• Always detach the yellow SRS connector when performing any diagnostic troubleshooting or service procedure associated with the SRS system.
• When repairs are made to the front suspension and steering, be aware that the contact reel can only withstand being turned 3 turns in either direction.
• Never install an air bag assembly that shows signs of being dropped or improperly handled, such as dents, cracks or deformation.
• When replacing a sensor, the replacement unit should be installed with the directional arrow oriented.
• Do not energize the system until all components are connected. A failure code may appear.
• Always wear gloves and safety glasses when handling the air bag assembly. Wash hands with mild soap and water afterwards.
• Always store the air bag assembly on a secure flat surface, away from high heat source and free of oil, grease, detergent or water.
• Never disconnect any electrical connection with the ignition switch **ON** unless instructed to do so in a test.
• Before disconnecting the negative battery cable, make a record of the contents memorized by each memory system (audio, seats, etc.). Then when service or repairs are completed, make certain to reset these memory systems.

## DISARMING THE SYSTEM

1. Turn the ignition switch to the **OFF** position.
2. Disconnect the negative battery cable AND TAPE the cable end away from the battery.

## ARMING THE SYSTEM

Assuming that the system components (air bag control module, sensors, air bag, etc.) are installed correctly and are in good working order, the system is armed whenever the battery's positive and negative battery cables are connected.

## Air Bag Module

REMOVAL & INSTALLATION

➡In addition to a driver side air bag module, some models contain a passenger side air bag module, located above the glove box.

### Driver Side

▶ See Figures 14, 15 and 16

1. Place the front wheels in a straight-ahead position.
2. Disconnect the negative battery cable AND TAPE the cable end away from the battery.
3. Turn the ignition key to position I so that the steering lock is OFF.
4. On some models, remove the sound insulation knee guard and the side panel from the center console.
5. Turn the steering wheel slightly in order to reach the 2 Torx® bolts in back of the steering wheel.
6. Remove the two attaching bolts.
7. Disconnect the connector and remove the air bag module.

➡Do not turn the ignition switch ON while the air bag assembly is removed, as this will register a fault code.

To install:
8. Rest the bottom of the air bag assembly on the steering wheel and reattach the connector.
9. Place the air bag module in position, being careful not to get the leads caught.
10. Install and tighten the retaining bolts to 53 inch lbs. (6 Nm).

➡When tightening the air bag assembly retaining bolts, tighten the right side bolt first.

11. Install the knee guard (if removed).

12. Connect the negative battery cable.
13. Turn the ignition on and check the SRS system for codes.

### Passenger Side

The passenger side air bag is removed when the instrument panel cover is removed. See the Instrument Cluster Removal and Installation procedure, later in this section, for removal of the cover. After the cover is removed, the air bag module is simply unbolted from the cover. To install, tighten the module retaining bolts and install the cover back onto the instrument panel.

## Contact Reel

REMOVAL & INSTALLATION

1. Place the front wheels in a straight-ahead position.
2. Disconnect the negative battery cable AND TAPE the cable end away from the battery.
3. Remove the air bag assembly.

➡Do not turn the ignition switch ON while the air bag assembly is removed, as this will register a fault code.

4. Unfasten the retaining bolt and remove the steering wheel. On some models, it may be necessary to use a puller; if so, follow the tool manufacturer's instructions.
5. Detach the connector and remove the contact reel.
To install:
6. Set the contact reel to the zero position. If the contact reel must be "zeroed," turn the reel to the far right end and then back 3 revolutions to the left. Lock the contact reel with the screw in the plastic strip.
7. Install the steering wheel.
8. Install the air bag assembly.

9. Reconnect the negative battery cable.
10. Check the vehicle operation and SRS system for fault codes.

Fig. 14 Remove the driver side air bag module's retaining bolts . . .

Fig. 15 . . . and carefully pull the module from the steering wheel

Fig. 16 Unplug the connector from the air bag and remove the module from the car. Handle and store the module safely, as described

## HEATING AND AIR CONDITIONING

### Blower Motor

REMOVAL & INSTALLATION

#### 240 Series and Coupe

1. Disconnect the negative battery cable.
2. Remove the sound insulation and side panels on both sides of the radio, if equipped.
3. Remove the control panel and center console.
4. Remove or disconnect, as required, the center air vents, the cable and electrical connectors from the clock, the glove compartment and air ducts for the center air vents.
5. From the right side, remove the air ducts and disconnect the vacuum hoses from the shutter actuators.
6. Fold back the floor mat, remove the rear floor duct screw and move the duct aside.
7. Remove the outer blower motor casing and the blower motor wheel.

➡It may be necessary to remove the support from under the glove compartment in order to remove the blower motor casing.

8. Disconnect the blower motor switch from the center console and the electrical leads from the switch.
9. From the left side, disconnect the air ducts and the vacuum hoses from the shutter actuators.
10. Remove or disconnect the inner blower motor casing, the vacuum hose from the rear floor shutter actuator, the electrical connector and the blower motor.

➡Should the blower motor need to be replaced, a modified replacement unit is available. Certain modifications must be done and instructions are included with the new assembly.

**To install:**
11. Clean heater housing of all dirt, leaves, etc. before installation.
12. Install the blower motor, the electrical connector, the vacuum hose to the rear floor shutter actuator and the inner blower motor casing.
13. Install the blower motor wheel and the outer blower motor casing.
14. Install the rear floor air duct and the floor mat.
15. At the left side, connect the air ducts and the vacuum hoses to the shutter actuators.
16. Connect the electrical leads to the blower motor switch and the switch to the center console.
17. At the right side, install the air ducts and connect the vacuum hoses to the shutter actuators.
18. Install or connect, as required, the center air vents, the cable and electrical connectors to the clock, the glove compartment and air ducts for the center air vents.
19. Install the control panel and center console.
20. Install the sound insulation and side panels to both sides of the radio.
21. Reconnect the negative battery cable.
22. Check the system for proper operation.

➡On some vehicles, a drum type fan is used which can be balanced by fitting steel clips to the outer edge. On most vehicles, a hose is connected to the fan housing to supply cooling air to avoid damage to the fan motor assembly.

#### 740 Series

1. Disconnect the negative battery cable.
2. Remove the lower glove box panel and the glove box.
3. Unfasten the electrical connector from the blower motor.
4. Remove the blower motor-to-housing screws and the blower motor assembly.
**To install:**
5. Clean the heater housing of all dirt, leaves, etc. before installation.
6. Attach the electrical connector to the blower motor.
7. Install the motor, screws and panel beneath the glove compartment.
8. Connect the negative battery cable.
9. Check the blower motor operation.

#### 760, 780, 900 Series and S90/V90 Models

*WITH AUTOMATIC CLIMATE CONTROL (ACC)*

▶ **See Figure 17**

1. Disconnect the negative battery cable.
2. Remove the lower glove box panel.
3. From the right side, remove the instep molding.
4. Remove the panel from above the control unit, being careful not damage it.
5. Unfasten the electrical connector from the control unit.
6. Remove the control unit-to-bracket bolts and the control unit.
7. Remove the bracket-to-chassis bolts and the bracket.
8. Remove the electrical connector from the blower motor.
9. Remove the ventilation pipe, blower motor-to-housing screws and blower motor.
**To install:**
10. Clean the heater housing of all dirt, leaves, etc. before installation. Install the blower motor and ventilation pipe.
11. Fasten the electrical connector to the blower motor.
12. Install the control unit bracket and control unit.
13. Attach the electrical connector to the control unit.
14. Install the panel above the control unit, the instep panel and the lower glove box panel.
15. Connect the negative battery cable.
16. Check the blower motor operation.

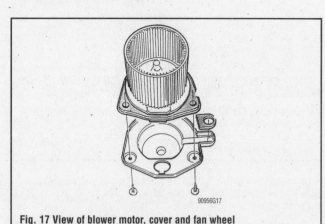

90956G17

**Fig. 17 View of blower motor, cover and fan wheel**

*WITH ELECTRONIC CLIMATE CONTROL (ECC)*

1. Disconnect the negative battery cable.
2. From the right side, remove the lower glove box panel and the glove box.
3. Remove the electrical connector and the mounting bracket from the blower motor housing.
4. Remove the electrical connector from the blower motor.
5. Remove the blower motor-to-housing screws and the motor.
**To install:**
6. Clean the heater housing of all dirt, leaves, etc. before installation.
7. Position the rubber seal to the blower motor and install the assembly.
8. Attach the electrical connector to the blower motor and the positive terminal to the housing.
9. Connect the negative battery cable.
10. Check all blower motor speeds for proper operation.
11. Install the glove box and the lower panel.

#### 850 and C70/S70/V70 Series

▶ **See Figure 18**

1. Disconnect the negative battery cable.
2. Remove the following:
   • Three passenger's side soundproofing panel screws and panel
   • Four glove compartment screws and glove compartment

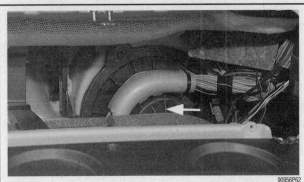

90956P62

**Fig. 18 The blower motor is accessible after the glove box is removed**

- Four glove compartment door screws and door
- On vehicles equipped with a passenger side airbag, remove the support brace for the air bag module
- Fan motor connector
- Cable duct from the fan motor
- Two connectors from the brackets
- Four fan motor screws and fan motor

**To install:**

3. Install the following in order:
- New fan motor and attaching screws
- Two connectors in the brackets
- Cable duct to the fan motor
- The support brace for the air bag module
4. Install the glove compartment and door using the screws.
5. Refit the soundproofing panel and screws.
6. Connect the negative battery cable.
7. Test the fan motor function.

## Heater Core

### REMOVAL & INSTALLATION

➡On vehicles equipped with Automatic Climate Control (ACC), a thermal switch is located on the outlet hose from the heater core. It switches on and starts the fan motor only when the water temperature exceeds approximately 95°F (35°C). This prevents cold air from being blown into the passenger compartment during winter. The thermal switch is bypassed in the defrost position.

#### 240 Series and Coupe

1. Disconnect the negative battery cable.
2. Drain the cooling system.
3. Move the heater controls to the CLOSED position.
4. Remove the soundproofing and side panels from both sides of the center dash console.
5. Remove the radio and the center control panel.
6. Disconnect any necessary cables and move the panel aside.
7. Remove the glove box assembly and the strip below the right air vent by carefully prying it off with a small prybar.
8. Remove the steering wheel casing (column cover) and disconnect the choke control with the cover plate.
9. Remove the strip from under the left air vent, the instrument panel lighting intensity and light switch knobs; do not remove the switch.
10. Detach the speedometer drive cable and any electrical connectors from the instrument panel cover plate, then remove the cover plate.
11. Remove the storage compartment, the center air vents and the instrument panel frame.
12. From the left side, detach the windshield wiper connectors.
13. Disconnect the air duct between the heater and the center air vents.
14. Disconnect the electrical connector from the glove box courtesy light and the rubber straps from the defroster vents.

15. Remove the dashboard unit from the dash assembly, as necessary.
16. Remove or disconnect the rear floor air duct screws and lower the duct slightly.
17. Remove or disconnect the following:
    a. The lower heater mount screws
    b. The vacuum hose from the vacuum tank
    c. The cable from the control valve
    d. The upper and lower center console screws
    e. The center support screws located on the console
    f. The fan motor ground electrical connector
    g. The inlet hose from the control valve
18. Disconnect the upper hose from the heater core tube and the vacuum hoses from the shutter actuators.
19. Loosen the upper housing screws.
20. From the right side, disconnect the vacuum hoses from the shutter actuators.
21. Disconnect and remove the air ducts.
22. Disconnect the hoses from the vacuum tank.
23. Remove the rear floor duct screws and lower the duct slightly.
24. Remove the upper and lower console screws and position it aside.
25. Remove the right support screws and the support.
26. Disconnect the electrical connector from the heater fan switch and the positive lead.
27. Disconnect the REC shutter vacuum hose from the control panel.
28. Disconnect the input vacuum hose from the T connection-to-floor shutter actuators.
29. Remove the upper heater housing retaining assembly screws and remove the assembly from the vehicle.
30. Place the assembly on a cleared area and remove or disconnect the following:
    a. The upper hose from the heater core.
    b. The air inlet rubber seal from the top of the housing.
    c. The REC shutter clips, from the left side.
    d. The rubber seals from both defroster vents.
    e. All outer blower motor casing clips and the casing from the assembly.
31. Remove the blower motor wheel locking clips (from both sides) and the blower motor wheels.
32. Remove the heater core drain hose and the vacuum tank assembly. The vacuum tank bracket screws from the left side. The REC shutter spring and heater housing clips.
33. Remove the blower motor screws and the heater control valve capillary tube from the T-joint.
34. Pull the heater housing apart from the middle.
35. Remove the blower motor and the heater core assembly.

**To install:**

36. Install the blower and heater core in the housing assembly. Make sure that the fan motor is correctly positioned in the housing. Install the fan motor hose.
37. Using a suitable sealant, coat the mating surface of the heater housing and assemble the case.
38. Install the heater control valve capillary tube to the T-joint and the blower motor screws.
39. Install the heater housing clips and REC shutter spring. At the left side, install the vacuum tank assembly, the vacuum tank bracket screws and the heater core drain hose.
40. Install the blower motor wheel and the blower motor wheel locking clips to both sides.
41. Install or connect the following items:
    a. Outer blower motor casing clips to the assembly.
    b. Rubber seals to both defroster vents.
    c. REC shutter clips to the left side.
    d. Air inlet rubber seal to the top of the housing.
    e. Upper hose to the heater core.
42. Install the heater assembly into the vehicle.

➡Before installation, be sure all sealing flanges are correctly sealed to prevent air leakage during the system operation.

43. Install the upper housing retaining screws.
44. Connect the REC shutter vacuum hose to the control panel.
45. Attach the electrical connector to the heater fan switch and the positive lead. Install the protective cover.

46. Install the right support and console.
47. Install the heater assembly lower mount and the rear floor duct.
48. Connect the hoses to the vacuum tank.
49. Install the air ducts.
50. At the right side, connect the vacuum hoses to the shutter actuators.
51. Connect the upper hose to the heater core tube and the vacuum hoses to the shutter actuators.
52. Install or connect the following items:
    a. Inlet hose to the control valve.
    b. Fan motor ground electrical connector.
    c. Console center support and the center console screws.
    d. Cable to the control valve.
    e. Vacuum hose to the vacuum tank.
    f. Lower heater mount screws.
53. Install the rear floor air and the dashboard unit to the dash assembly.
54. Attach the electrical connector to the glove box courtesy light and the rubber straps to the defroster vents.
55. Secure the windshield wiper connectors, the air duct between the heater housing and the center air vents.
56. Install the instrument panel, the storage compartment, the center air vents and the instrument panel frame.
57. Attach the speedometer cable and any electrical connectors to the instrument panel.
58. Install the strip from under the left air vent, the instrument panel lighting intensity and light switch knobs.
59. Install the steering wheel casing and connect the choke control with the cover plate.
60. Install the glove box assembly and the strip below the right air vent.
61. Install the center control panel and the radio.
62. Install the soundproofing and side panels to both sides of the center dash console.
63. Move the heater controls to the OPEN position.
64. Refill the cooling system.
65. Connect the negative battery cable.
66. Start the engine, allow it to reach normal operating temperature, and check for leaks.
67. Check the heating system for proper operation.

## 700 Series

1. Disconnect the negative battery cable.
2. Drain the cooling system.
3. Remove the throttle cable from the pulley assembly.
4. Disconnect all heater hoses.
5. From the left side of the dashboard, remove the lower panel.
6. Remove the hose from the panel air vent.
7. At the control panel, move the selector to the FLOOR position.
8. Remove the following items:
    a. Accelerator pedal.
    b. Ignition system control unit and bracket.
    c. Cruise control connector, if equipped.
    d. Water valve hose and grommet.
9. Remove both hoses from the water valve and the clip from the water valve control cable.
10. To remove the water valve, turn it right, pull it out and disconnect the cable.
11. Remove the heater core cover and the heater core assembly.
**To install:**
12. Clean the heater core housing of all dirt, leaves, etc. before installation.
13. Install the heater core assembly and the cover.
14. Connect the water valve.
15. Install the water valve control cable clip, turn the valve left, adjust the cable and install the clip.
16. Connect the hoses to the water valve and the heater core.
17. Install the following items:
    a. Grommet and water valve.
    b. Cruise control connector, if equipped.
    c. Ignition system bracket and control unit.
    d. Accelerator pedal.
18. Connect the hose to the panel air vent below the dashboard, and attach the lower panel.
19. Reconnect the throttle cable to the pulley assembly.

20. Connect the negative battery cable.
21. Refill the cooling system.
22. Start the vehicle, allow it to reach normal operating temperature, and check for leaks.
23. Check the heating system for proper operation.

## Except Coupe, 240 and 700 Series

### WITH AUTOMATIC CLIMATE CONTROL (ACC) SYSTEM

➡**Before beginning this procedure, have the A/C system discharged by a certified MVAC technician.**

1. Disconnect the negative battery cable.
2. Drain the cooling system.
3. Disconnect the heater hoses from the heater core assembly.
4. Remove the ashtray, ashtray holder, cigarette lighter and console storage compartment.
5. Remove the console assembly from the gearshift lever and parking brake lever.
6. Detach the electrical connector.
7. Remove the rear ashtray, the console and light.
8. Remove the screws beneath the plastic cover in the bottom of the storage compartment and the parking brake console.
9. From the left side of the passenger compartment, remove the panel from under the dashboard. Pull down the floor mat on and remove the side panel screws, at the front and rear edge.
10. From the right side of the passenger compartment, detach the panel from under the glove compartment, then remove the glove compartment box with its lighting. Pull down the floor mat and remove the side panel screws, at the front and rear edge.
11. Remove the radio compartment assembly screws.
12. Remove the screws from the heater control, the radio compartment assembly console and the control panel.
13. Loosen the heater control head assembly retaining screws and remove the assembly and mount from the dashboard.
14. Remove the center dash panel, the distribution duct screw and the air duct-to-panel vents/distribution duct screws.
15. Remove the screws holding the rear seat air ducts and the air distribution duct section to rear seat ducts.
16. Remove the vacuum hoses from the vacuum motors and the hose from the aspirator, if equipped with an ACC unit.
17. Remove the distribution unit housing from the vehicle.
18. Remove the retaining clips and the heater core assembly.
19. If the vacuum motors must be replaced, remove the panel from the distribution unit and replace the vacuum motor.
**To install:**
20. Clean the heater core housing of all dirt, leaves, etc. before installation.
21. Install the heater core assembly and the retaining clips.
22. Install the distribution unit into the vehicle.
23. Connect the vacuum hoses to the vacuum motors and the hose to the aspirator, if equipped with an ACC unit.
24. Install the air ducts top-to-rear seats and the air distribution duct section-to-rear seat ducts.
25. Install the center dash panel, the distribution duct screw and the air duct-to-panel vents/distribution duct screws.
26. Install the heater control head assembly unit and the mount to the dash.
27. Install the heater control, the radio compartment console and the control panel.
28. Install the radio compartment screws.
29. At the right side of the passenger compartment, install the panel under the glove compartment and the glove compartment box with its lighting.
30. Install the side panel screws, at the front and rear edge.
31. At the left side of the passenger compartment, install the panel under the dashboard.
32. Install the plastic cover in the bottom of the storage compartment and the parking brake console.
33. Fasten the electrical connector.
34. Install the rear ashtray, the console and light.
35. Install the console assembly to the gearshift lever and the parking brake.
36. Install the ashtray holder, ashtray, cigarette lighter and console storage compartment.
37. Reconnect the heater core hoses.

38. Refill and bleed the cooling system.
39. Connect the negative battery cable.
40. Start the engine, allow it to reach normal operating temperature, and check for leaks.
41. Check the heating system for proper operation.
42. Have the A/C system charged by a certified MVAC technician.

### WITH ELECTRONIC CLIMATE CONTROL (ECC) SYSTEM

1. Disconnect the negative battery cable.
2. Drain the cooling system.
3. Disconnect the heater hoses from the heater core assembly.
4. Remove the heater core cover plate.
5. Remove the dashboard by performing the following steps:
    a. From the right side, remove the lower glove box panel, glove box, footwell panel and A-post panel.
6. Disconnect the solar sensor electrical connector and cut the cable ties.
    a. From the left side, remove the lower steering wheel soundproofing, knee bolster (leave bracket attached to bolster), footwell panel and A-post panel.
    b. From the left side, remove the defroster grille, plastic fuse box screws, ashtray, dashboard-to-center console screws, parking brake-to-console screws (move console rearward) and lower center console screws (located below the ashtray).

➡Before performing the next step, be sure the front wheels are in the straight ahead position.

    c. If not an SRS equipped vehicle, remove the steering wheel, steering wheel adjustment assembly (with an Allen wrench), upper steering column cover panels and steering column combination switch assembly.
    d. If an SRS equipped vehicle, remove the steering column adjuster (using an Allen wrench), steering column covers, air bag assembly (with a Torx® bit), steering wheel center bolt, plastic tape label screw from the steering wheel hub (use the lock screw, label attached, to lock the contact reel through the steering wheel hub hole), then lift off the steering wheel. Remove the contact reel and the steering column combination switch assembly.

➡After securing the contact reel, do not turn the steering wheel, for it will shear off the contact reel pin.

    e. From the left side of the steering column, push out the light switch panel. Remove the small trim moldings and the light switch.
    f. From the right side of the steering column, push out the switch panel.
    g. Remove the ECC control panel, radio console and small trim molding.
    h. Remove the outer air vent grille by lifting it upwards, grasp it at the bottom and pull it upwards to release it.
    i. Remove the instrument panel cover-to-dashboard screws and the cover.
    j. Remove the combined instrument assembly-to-dashboard screws and the assembly; detach any electrical connectors and/or vacuum hoses.
    k. From the rear of the dashboard, cut the cable ties.
    l. At the dashboard-to-firewall area, turn the retaining clips, pull the dashboard out slightly and pass the fuse box through the opening.
7. Disconnect the cable harnesses from the dashboard and carefully lift it from the vehicle.
8. From the left side of the heater housing, remove the lower duct.
9. Disconnect the vacuum hoses from the diaphragms and the electrical connector. Remove the heater core cover-to-housing screws and the cover.
10. Remove the heater core-to-housing bracket and carefully remove the heater core.
### To install:
11. Clean the heater housing of all dirt, leaves, etc. before installation.
12. Install the heater core and the bracket.
13. Install the heater core cover to the housing.
14. Attach the electrical connector and the vacuum hoses.
15. Install the lower duct to the housing assembly.
16. Install the dashboard by performing the following steps:
    a. Install the dashboard, connect the cable harnesses, and pass the fuse box through the opening. Secure the dash clips by turning them ⅓ turn.
    b. Install the combined instrument assembly to the dashboard.
17. Install the instrument panel cover and the outer air vent grille.
    a. Install the small trim molding, radio console, ECC control panel and right side switch panel.
    b. At the left side of the steering column, install the light switch, the small trim moldings and the light switch panel.

    c. If an SRS equipped vehicle, install the steering column combination switch assembly and the contact reel.
    d. Install the steering wheel and remove the lock screw.
    e. Install the steering wheel center bolt, air bag assembly and steering column adjuster.
    f. If not an SRS equipped vehicle, install the steering column combination switch assembly, steering column covers, steering wheel adjustment assembly and steering wheel.
    g. At the left side, install the lower center console screw, parking brake-to-console screws, dashboard-to-center console screws, ashtray, plastic fuse box screws and defroster grille.
    h. At the left side, install the A-post panel, footwell panel, knee bolster (with bracket) and lower steering wheel soundproofing.
    i. At the right side, fasten the solar sensor electrical connector, then install the A-post panel, footwell panel, glove box and lower glove box panel.
18. Install the heater core cover plate and connect the heater hoses to the heater core.
19. Refill the cooling system.
20. Connect the negative battery cable.
21. Start the engine, allow it to reach normal operating temperature, and check for leaks.
22. Check the heating system for proper operation.

## Heater Water Control Valve

### REMOVAL & INSTALLATION

♦ **See Figure 19**

1. Disconnect the negative battery cable.
2. Drain the cooling system so that the level (of the system) is below the control valve.

### ✳✳ CAUTION

**Never open, service or drain the radiator or cooling system when hot; serious burns can occur from the steam and hot coolant. Also, when draining engine coolant, keep in mind that cats and dogs are attracted to ethylene glycol antifreeze and could drink any that is left in an uncovered container or in puddles on the ground. This will prove fatal in sufficient quantities. Always drain coolant into a sealable container. Coolant should be reused unless it is contaminated or is several years old.**

3. Loosen the heater hose clamps and remove the hoses.
4. Disconnect the cable and/or vacuum line to the valve.
5. Unfasten the mounting screws and remove the valve.
### To install:
6. Place the control in position and secure it.
7. Connect the heater hoses (replace any hoses that show wear) and secure the hose clamps.
8. Connect the cable and/or vacuum line(s).
9. Connect the negative battery cable.
10. Fill the cooling system and check the control valve operation.

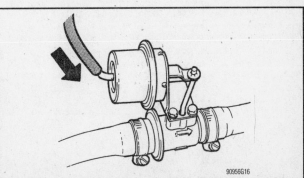

90956G16

**Fig. 19 The water control valve is mounted in the heater core inlet hose**

## Air Conditioning Components

### REMOVAL & INSTALLATION

Repair or service of air conditioning components is not covered by this manual, because of the risk of personal injury or death, and because of the legal ramifications of servicing these components without the proper EPA certification and experience. Cost, personal injury or death, environmental damage, and legal considerations (such as the fact that it is a federal crime to vent refrigerant into the atmosphere), dictate that the A/C components on your vehicle should be serviced only by a Motor Vehicle Air Conditioning (MVAC) trained, and EPA certified automotive technician.

➡️**If your vehicle's A/C system uses R-12 refrigerant and is in need of recharging, the A/C system can be converted over to R-134a refrigerant (less environmentally harmful and expensive). Refer to Section 1 for additional information on R-12 to R-134a conversions, and for additional considerations dealing with your vehicle's A/C system.**

## Control Cables

### REMOVAL & INSTALLATION

#### 240 Series and Coupe

1. Disconnect the negative battery cable.
2. Remove the soundproofing and side panels from both sides of the center dash console.
3. Remove the radio assembly.
4. Remove the center control panel. Position the control assembly as far forward as possible.
5. Remove the cable (upper end) from the lever on the control assembly.
6. Disconnect the cable (lower end) from the proper distribution door. Note its location and position for correct installation.

7. Remove the control cable.

**To install:**

8. Install the cable onto the proper distribution door.
9. Route the control cable in the proper position.
10. Attach the cable to the control panel assembly.
11. Install the center control panel.
12. Verify the cable operation.
13. Adjust the cable, as necessary.
14. Install the radio.
15. Install the soundproofing and side panels.
16. Connect the negative battery cable.

#### Except 240 Series and Coupe

▶ **See Figure 20**

1. Disconnect the negative battery cable.
2. Remove the glove box and panel below the glove box assembly.
3. Position the heater control to the WARM position.
4. Remove the trim panel.
5. Remove the control assembly from the dashboard. Position the control assembly as far forward as possible.
6. Remove the cable (upper end) from the lever on the control assembly.
7. Disconnect the cable (lower end) from the distribution door. Note its location and position for correct installation.
8. Remove the control cable.

**To install:**

9. Install the cable onto the proper distribution door.
10. Route the control cable in the proper position.
11. Attach the cable to the control panel assembly.
12. Install the center control panel.
13. Verify the cable operation.
14. Adjust the cable, as necessary.
15. Install the trim panel.
16. Install the glove box and panel.
17. Connect the negative battery cable.

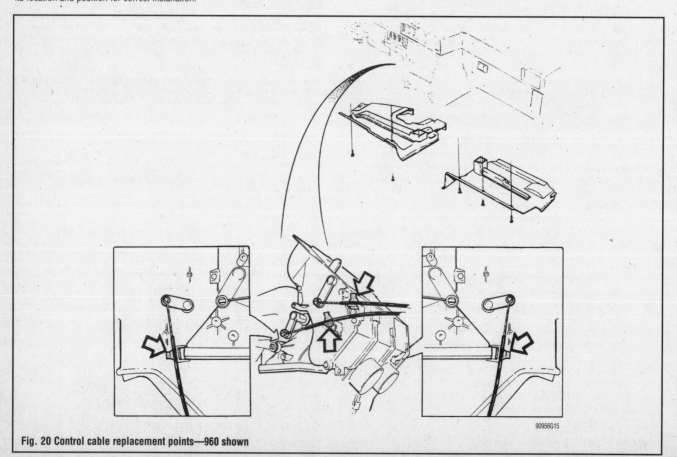

**Fig. 20 Control cable replacement points—960 shown**

90956G15

## ADJUSTMENT

On all vehicles, make sure the air mix shutter assembly touches both end stops when the control cable is moved between the COOL and WARM positions on the manual control head assembly.

## Control Panel

### REMOVAL & INSTALLATION

#### Manual Control Head

##### 240 SERIES AND COUPE

1. Disconnect the negative battery cable.
2. Remove the soundproofing and side panels from both sides of the center dash console.
3. Remove the radio assembly.
4. Remove the center control panel. Position the control assembly as far forward as possible.
5. Remove the lever knob, then detach the cable from the lever and control assembly.

**To install:**

6. Attach the cable to the control panel assembly.
7. Install the center control panel.
8. Install the knob.
9. Verify the cable operation.
10. Adjust the cable, as necessary.
11. Install the radio.
12. Install the soundproofing and side panels.
13. Connect the negative battery cable.
14. Check the system for proper operation.

##### EXCEPT 240 SERIES AND COUPE

1. Disconnect the negative battery cable.
2. Remove the trim panel.
3. Remove the control assembly from the dashboard.
4. Disconnect the control cable clip, vacuum connections and electrical connections.

**To install:**

5. Attach the cable to the control panel assembly.
6. Secure the vacuum and electrical connections.
7. Install the center control panel.
8. Verify the cable operation.
9. Adjust the cable, as necessary.
10. Install the trim panel.
11. Connect the negative battery cable.
12. Check the system for proper operation.

#### Electronic Control Head

▶ **See Figure 21**

1. Disconnect the negative battery cable.
2. Remove the control knobs.
3. Remove the panel retaining screws.
4. Pull the panel out and unplug the electrical connectors.
5. Remove the panel from the dashboard.

**To install:**

6. Plug in the electrical connectors.
7. Position the panel in place and install the retaining screws.
8. Push the knobs onto the shafts.
9. Reconnect the negative battery cable.
10. Check the system for proper operation.

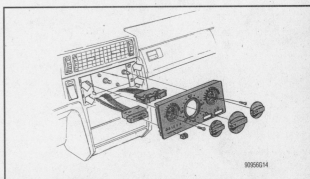

90956G14

**Fig. 21 Exploded view of an electronic control panel assembly**

## CRUISE CONTROL

## General Information

▶ **See Figures 22 and 23**

The cruise control system maintains the vehicle speed at a setting selected by the driver by means of mechanical, electrical, and vacuum operated devices.

The cruise control unit receives an immediate electrical input from the ignition switch; therefore, the cruise circuit is ready for operation whenever the ignition switch is turned on. Actual activation of the cruise control is accomplished by lifting up and holding the control switch in the direction of ACCEL/SET or DECEL/SET until the desired speed is attained. The control unit also receives information about operating conditions from the brake switch, distributor, speed sensor, clutch switch (with manual transmission), or shift lever position switch (with automatic transmission). The cruise control unit, in turn, sends operational signals to the devices that regulate the throttle position. The throttle position maintains the selected vehicle speed. The cruise control compares the actual speed of the vehicle to the selected speed. Then, the control unit uses the result of that comparison to open or close the throttle.

The control unit will disengage the instant the driver depresses the brake pedal. The brake switch sends an electronic signal to the control unit when the brake pedal is depressed; the control unit responds by allowing the throttle to close. The shift lever position switch (automatic transmission) or clutch switch (manual transmission) sends a disengage signal input to the control unit that also allows the throttle to close.

➡**The use of the speed control is not recommended when driving conditions do not permit maintaining a constant speed, such as in heavy traffic or on roads that are winding, icy, snow covered or slippery.**

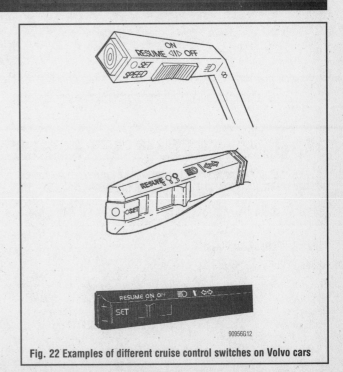

90956G12

**Fig. 22 Examples of different cruise control switches on Volvo cars**

The cruise control system will set and automatically maintain any speed above 25 mph (40 kph). When the desired speed is attained, a brief tapping against the switch toward the ACCEL/SET or DECEL/SET, will keep the speed constant until a new speed is selected or if the brake pedal is depressed. To match this set speed, hold the switch in direction of ACCEL/SET or DECEL/SET until the desired speed is attained. Upon releasing the switch, the new speed is held constant.

Short tapping against the switch towards the OFF position, or depressing the brake or clutch pedal, will switch off the cruise control system. However, the system remains ready for operation until the ignition switch is turned off. If the system is disengaged temporarily by the brake switch, clutch switch or deceleration, and the vehicle speed is still above 25 mph, tap the switch toward RESUME. The vehicle will automatically return to the previous set speed retained in memory.

If the vehicle is accelerated above the set speed, the vehicle will return to the set speed when the pedal is released. While driving with the cruise control system, do not engage the selector lever in **N** position, on vehicles with an automatic transmission, since this will speed up the engine.

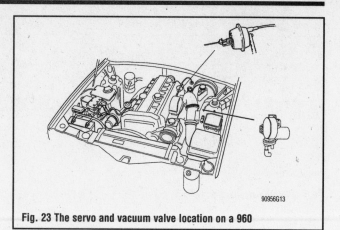

90956G13

**Fig. 23 The servo and vacuum valve location on a 960**

# CRUISE CONTROL TROUBLESHOOTING

| Problem | Possible Cause |
|---|---|
| Will not hold proper speed | Incorrect cable adjustment |
| | Binding throttle linkage |
| | Leaking vacuum servo diaphragm |
| | Leaking vacuum tank |
| | Faulty vacuum or vent valve |
| | Faulty stepper motor |
| | Faulty transducer |
| | Faulty speed sensor |
| | Faulty cruise control module |
| Cruise intermittently cuts out | Clutch or brake switch adjustment too tight |
| | Short or open in the cruise control circuit |
| | Faulty transducer |
| | Faulty cruise control module |
| Vehicle surges | Kinked speedometer cable or casing |
| | Binding throttle linkage |
| | Faulty speed sensor |
| | Faulty cruise control module |
| Cruise control inoperative | Blown fuse |
| | Short or open in the cruise control circuit |
| | Faulty brake or clutch switch |
| | Leaking vacuum circuit |
| | Faulty cruise control switch |
| | Faulty stepper motor |
| | Faulty transducer |
| | Faulty speed sensor |
| | Faulty cruise control module |

Note: Use this chart as a guide. Not all systems will use the components listed.

TCCA6C01

# ENTERTAINMENT SYSTEMS

## Radio Receiver/Amplifier/Tape Player/CD Player

### REMOVAL & INSTALLATION

#### Radio/Tape Deck/CD Player

▶ **See Figures 24, 25 and 26**

On most models, the radio is held in by 2 clips in the console. Remove the side covers and locate the 2 access holes (one on each side) in line with the radio case. Insert a small probe or very small screwdriver into each hole and push gently. This releases the clips and the radio may be removed from the front of the console.

Other models have the same style clips, but they are released by inserting a thin, flat probe down each side of the radio from the front. Again, release the clips and slide the radio free. Disconnect the wiring before pulling the radio too far from the dash.

The radios on some models are designed with the releases built into the front of the case. Simply push the tabs with your fingers and remove the radio.

➡**Although these radios are relatively simple to remove, many have a security code programmed into the circuitry. Once reinstalled, the radio will not work if the correct code is not entered. The radio should not be removed or disconnected if the user code is not available.**

#### Amplifier

1. Disconnect the negative battery cable.
2. Remove the retaining screws from the mounting bracket.
3. Detach the electrical connectors from the amplifier.
4. Remove the amplifier.

Fig. 24 Use a small screwdriver or another suitable tool to gently depress and release the retaining tabs

90956P52

Fig. 25 Grasp the tabs and pull the radio out; be careful not to pull so far that the radio falls

90956P53

Fig. 26 When the connectors are accessible, unplug them. Once the connectors are unplugged, the radio will lose its memory

90956P54

**To install:**
5. Attach the connectors to the amplifier.
6. Place the amplifier in the mounting bracket.
7. Tighten the retaining screws.
8. Connect the negative battery cable.
9. Check the operation of the amplifier.

### CD Changer

The CD changer is located under the package shelf on sedans, above the spare tire on wagons with no third row of seats, and in the well between the second and third row of seats on wagons equipped with a third row.
1. Remove any necessary trim to access the bracket retaining screws.
2. Remove the bracket retaining hardware.
3. Disconnect any wiring attached to the changer.
4. Remove the CD changer from the vehicle.
**To install:**
5. Attach the wiring to the CD changer.
6. Place the changer into position and tighten the retaining hardware.
7. Install any removed trim.

## Speakers

### REMOVAL & INSTALLATION

#### Door Speakers

▶ See Figures 27, 28 and 29

1. Remove the door panel(s).
2. Remove the four retaining screws on the speaker assembly.
3. Pull the speaker out and remove the electrical connector from the back.
**To install:**
4. Install the electrical connector onto the back of the speaker.
5. Place the speaker in the opening in the door.
6. Tighten the four retaining screws.

7. Verify the proper operation of the speaker.
8. Install the door panel.

#### Dashboard Speakers

▶ See Figures 30 thru 35

1. Remove the speaker cover on the top of the dashboard by removing the retaining screws.
2. Remove the speaker retaining screws.
3. Pull the speaker out and remove the electrical connector from the back.
**To install:**
4. Install the electrical connector onto the back of the speaker.
5. Place the speaker in the opening in the dashboard.
6. Tighten the retaining screws.
7. Verify the proper operation of the speaker.
8. Install the speaker cover on the dashboard and tighten the retaining screws.

#### Rear Roof Pillar Speakers (Wagon)

1. Unfasten the grille retaining screws and remove the grille.
2. Remove the speaker retaining screws.
3. Pull the speaker out of the opening and unplug the electrical connector.
**To install:**
4. Plug in the electrical connector.
5. Install the speaker in the opening and tighten the retaining screws.
6. Install the speaker grille and tighten the retaining screws.

#### Rear Deck Speakers (Sedan)

1. From under the package tray, remove the grille retaining screws and remove the grille.
2. Remove the speaker retaining screws.
3. Pull the speaker out of the opening and unplug the electrical connector.
**To install:**
4. Plug in the electrical connector.
5. Install the speaker in the opening and tighten the retaining screws.
6. Install the speaker grille and tighten the retaining screws.

Fig. 27 When the grille is removed, the speaker mounting screws are exposed

90956P98

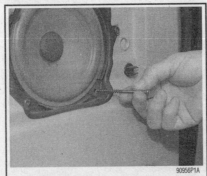

Fig. 28 Unfasten the mounting screws and remove the speaker from the door

90956P1A

Fig. 29 Unplug the speaker connection and set the speaker aside in a safe place

90956P2A

Fig. 30 Carefully pry up the speaker grille and . . .

Fig. 31 . . . remove it from the dashboard

Fig. 32 Remove the speaker retainers; some models have screws while others have plastic push-in type "buttons"

Fig. 33 On this button type retainer, simply depress the center portion so that it pops up before removal

Fig. 34 After the retainers are removed, pull the speaker from the dashboard

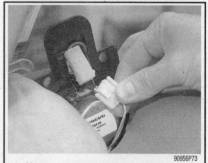
Fig. 35 Unplug the electrical connector and remove the speaker

## WINDSHIELD WIPERS AND WASHERS

### Windshield Wiper Blade and Arm

REMOVAL & INSTALLATION

♦ See Figures 36 and 37

1. Carefully pry up/lift the plastic or metal cover at the base of the wiper arm.
2. Unscrew and remove the retaining nut.
3. Matchmark the arm and pivot for realignment upon installation.
4. Gently lift the blade and arm from the glass and remove the arm from the pivot.

**To install:**

5. Place the arm over the pivot and tighten the retaining nut to 10–13 ft. lbs. (14–18 Nm). Do not overtighten, or the splines will be damaged. Make sure the wiper blade will be in the correct position on the glass before tightening the nut.
6. Install the cover.

➡For wiper blade (element) replacement, refer to Section 1.

Fig. 37 Matchmark the wiper arm to the pivot, and gently lift off the arm

### Windshield Wiper Motor

REMOVAL & INSTALLATION

**Front**

#### COUPE, 240 AND 700 SERIES

1. Disconnect the negative battery cable.
2. Remove the passenger side underdash panel (beneath the glove box).
3. Remove the defroster hoses and remove the glove box.
4. Remove the shaft nut from the motor which attaches the linkage.
5. Remove the wiper linkage.
6. Disconnect the wiper motor assembly and lift it out through the glove box opening.

**To install:**

7. Install the wiper motor and tighten the retaining bolts.

Fig. 36 Remove the wiper arm retaining nut

8. Install the wiper linkage.
9. Tighten the shaft nut on the motor.
10. Attach the defroster hoses and install the glove box.
11. Install the panel under the dashboard.
12. Connect the negative battery cable.

### EXCEPT COUPE, 240 AND 700 SERIES

◆ **See Figures 38 thru 48**

1. Disconnect the negative battery cable.
2. Remove the wiper arms.
3. Lift the hood to its uppermost position by pushing the catch on the hood hinges.
4. Release the washer hoses from the clips along the edge of the cowl.
5. Remove the cowl retaining bolts. Older vehicles may use plastic clips instead of bolts to hold the cowl in place.
6. Remove the clamps securing the vent hoses.
7. Lift the cowl up to gain access to the hoses and remove them.

8. Remove the cowl by pulling it forward and then rotating the front edge upward.
9. Unplug the electrical connectors.
10. Remove the bolts which hold the linkage assembly.
11. Remove the linkage and motor assembly from the vehicle.
12. Remove the spindle nut on the motor.
13. Remove the 3 motor attaching bolts.
14. Lift the motor free of the linkage.
**To install:**

➥**When reassembling, make sure the wipers are in the park position.**

15. Install the motor and tighten the attaching bolts.
16. Install the motor on the linkage and tighten the spindle nut.
17. Install the linkage and motor assembly in the vehicle and tighten the retaining bolts.

➥**After the motor is secure on the linkage and the linkage is mounted on the vehicle, visually check for any possible interference between the moving parts and the wiring.**

**Fig. 38 The bolts retaining the cowl typically have size T25 Torx® heads**

**Fig. 39 Unfasten the retaining bolts with the proper size bit**

**Fig. 40 Remove the clamps that secure the vent hoses**

**Fig. 41 Lift up the cowl slightly and remove the hoses**

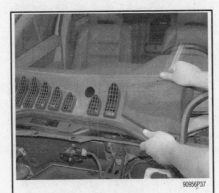

**Fig. 42 Remove the cowl panel**

**Fig. 43 Unplug the electrical connectors**

**Fig. 44 Unfasten the linkage and motor assembly retaining bolts**

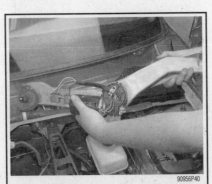

**Fig. 45 Lift the assembly from the vehicle after the retaining bolts are removed**

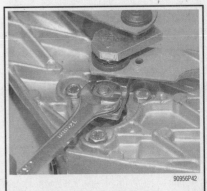

**Fig. 46 Remove the spindle nut**

Fig. 47 Lift the linkage from the motor shaft after the nut is removed

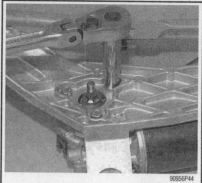

Fig. 48 Remove the motor retaining bolts (typically 3)

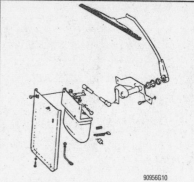

Fig. 49 Exploded view of the rear wiper assembly on a 240 wagon

18. Attach the connectors to the motor.

19. Lower the cowl down, but not all the way, and attach the vent hoses. Install the clamps on the hoses.

20. Install the cowl and make sure the cowl is properly seated before installing the bolts.

21. Install the washer hoses in their clips.

22. Install the wiper arms.

23. Connect the negative battery cable.

## Rear (Wagons)

### 240 SERIES

▶ See Figure 49

1. Disconnect the negative battery cable.
2. Remove the upholstered finish panel on the inside of the liftgate.
3. Remove the bolts for the wiper motor protection plate.
4. Disconnect the ball-and-socket wiper arm link at the motor.
5. Fold the protection plate aside and lift out the wiper motor.
6. Mark the wires and disconnect them at the motor.

➡The brushes in the motor are replaceable. If brush replacement is required, remove the motor cover, unhook the brush springs and remove the brushes from the holders. Be careful not to damage the brush holders. Install the new brushes and attach the springs, then attach the cover.

To install:

➡Make certain that the motor is in the park position before installing.

7. Connect the wiring to the motor, then install the motor and protection plate.
8. Reattach the connecting link to the motor and install the retaining screws for the protection plate.
9. Install the trim panel on the inside of the liftgate.
10. Connect the negative battery cable.

### 700 AND 900 SERIES, S90/V90 MODELS

▶ See Figure 50

1. Disconnect the negative battery cable.
2. Remove the inner trim pad on the liftgate.

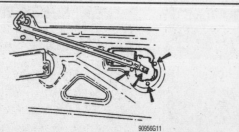

Fig. 50 Location of the rear wiper motor retaining bolts—700 series model shown

3. Loosen and remove the center nut on the motor and remove the linkage from the motor.
4. Unfasten the bolts holding the motor and remove the motor. Disconnect the wiring from the motor.

To install:

5. When reassembling, make certain that the motor is in the park position.
6. Attach the wiring and mount the motor to the liftgate.
7. Attach the linkage to the motor and tighten the center nut.
8. Replace the trim pad.
9. Connect the negative battery cable.

### 850 AND S70/C70/V70 SERIES

➡Refit the radio interference suppression unit if one is present.

1. Disconnect the negative battery cable.
2. Loosen the wiper arm nut a few turns.
3. Remove the wiper arm by holding the nut with locking pliers and pulling the arm off. Remove the nut.
4. Remove the liftgate panel.
5. Remove the wiper motor assembly nuts and detach the electrical connectors.
6. Lift the assembly out.
7. Remove the nut from the wiper motor shaft.
8. Remove the wiper linkage from the motor.
9. Remove the wiper motor.

To install:

10. Install the new wiper motor.
11. Install the wiper linkage and tighten the shaft nut.
12. Install the wiper assembly and attach the electrical connectors. Fasten it with the attaching nuts and tighten them to 7.5 ft. lbs. (10 Nm).
13. Install the liftgate panel.
14. Connect the negative battery cable.
15. Run the motor and allow it to stop by itself when the switch is turned **OFF**.
16. Install the wiper arm and nut hand-tight.
17. Adjust the position of the arm so that it is parallel to the bottom of the rear window.
18. Tighten the nut to 12 ft. lbs. (16 Nm).

## Headlight Wiper Blades

### REMOVAL & INSTALLATION

▶ See Figures 51, 52, 53 and 54

The small blades for the headlight wipers found on some models are removed in the same fashion as the windshield wiper blades. Pull the wiper away from the light, lift the pivot cover, remove the nut, then remove the blade and arm. It is necessary to disconnect the washer tube from the blade assembly when removing the arm.

During installation, place the wiper blade below the park stop on the light. Tighten the retaining nut and reposition the blade above the stop. The blade should rest firmly on the stop. Don't forget to reattach the washer line.

Fig. 51 Lift the pivot cover to access the retaining nut . . .

Fig. 52 . . . then remove the nut

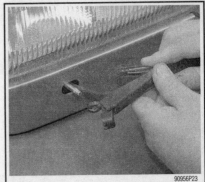

Fig. 53 Lift the arm off of the pivot shaft and . . .

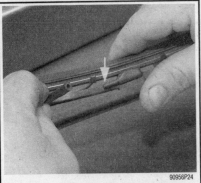

Fig. 54 . . . detach the washer tube from the blade

Fig. 55 The trim under the headlamp is held by two clips; carefully pull outward to release the clips

Fig. 56 The motor is retaining by two bolts

## Headlight Wiper Motor

### REMOVAL & INSTALLATION

#### 700 Series

1. Disconnect the negative battery cable.
2. Remove the wiper arm.
3. Detach the wiring connector and the ground wire (2 separate connectors) for the motor. Connectors for both the left and right motors may be located near the left fender.
4. Loosen the nut on the motor shaft, slide off the plastic tubing and remove the motor.

**To install:**

5. Make sure the motor is in the park position before installation.
6. Install the motor and connect the plastic tubing.
7. Tighten the nut on the motor shaft.

8. Attach the wiring connectors. Insure a secure fit for all wiring connectors.
9. Install the wiper arm.
10. Connect the negative battery cable.

#### Except 700 Series

⬥ See Figures 55, 56, 57, 58 and 59

1. Disconnect the negative battery cable.
2. Remove the wiper arm.
3. Remove the trim under the headlamp.
4. Remove the motor retaining bolts.
5. Unplug the electrical connector(s).
6. Carefully remove the motor from the vehicle.

**To install:**

➡ Make sure the motor is in the park position before installation.

7. Place the motor into position and plug the electrical connector(s) in.
8. Tighten the motor retaining bolts.

Fig. 57 Unplug the electrical connector(s)

Fig. 58 Carefully lift the motor out of the engine compartment

Fig. 59 The motor shaft is extremely long, and is best removed by pulling the motor upward, then out

9. Install the trim under the headlamp.
10. Reinstall the wiper arm.
11. Connect the negative battery cable.

## Windshield Washer Motor

### REMOVAL & INSTALLATION

#### Front

1. Disconnect the negative battery cable.
2. Remove the windshield washer bottle filler pipe.
3. Lift the washer motor out of the washer bottle using needlenose pliers.
4. Undo the wiring connector and the hose from the motor.
5. Remove the washer motor.

**To install:**

6. Install the hose and wiring connector on the washer motor.

➡️**It is a good idea to wet or lubricate the end of the motor and filler pipe which extends into the washer bottle to aid in their installation, and to help avoid pushing the rubber grommet into the bottle.**

## INSTRUMENTS AND SWITCHES

## Instrument Cluster

### REMOVAL & INSTALLATION

#### 240, 700 Series, 940 Models and Coupe

1. Disconnect the negative battery cable.
2. Remove the molded plastic casings from the steering column.
3. Remove the bracket retaining screw and lower the bracket toward the steering column.
4. Remove the cluster attaching screws.
5. Disconnect the speedometer cable.
6. Tilt the cluster out of its snap fitting and disconnect the plug. On vehicles equipped with a tachometer, disconnect the tachometer sending wire.
7. Lift the cluster out of the dashboard.

**To install:**

8. Position the cluster in the dashboard, making sure the wiring and speedometer cable are reconnected before securing the cluster. Also make sure the cluster engages its snap fittings when placed in the dashboard.
9. Install the cluster attaching screws, and replace the bracket and retaining screw.
10. Install the molded plastic casings on the steering column.
11. Connect the negative battery cable.

#### Except 240, 700 Series, 940 Models and Coupe

▶ **See Figures 60 thru 78**

1. Disconnect the negative battery cable.
2. Open the glove compartment.
3. Disconnect the glove compartment swing-down arms from the glove compartment door.
4. Remove the screws attaching the glove compartment lining and remove the lining.

### ✳️ CAUTION

**Refer to the SRS (air bag) system Safety Precautions listed earlier in this section.**

5. Disconnect the passenger side air bag module.
6. Remove the 4 screws over the glove compartment, and under the air bag module.
7. Remove the screws over the instrument cluster.
8. Remove the panel vents.
9. Remove the side demister vents.

7. Install the motor into the opening in the washer bottle, being careful not to disturb the rubber grommet.
8. Install the filler pipe into the washer bottle.
9. Fill the washer bottle with the appropriate mixture of solvent.
10. Connect the negative battery cable.
11. Check the operation of the washer motor.

#### Rear (Wagons)

1. Disconnect the negative battery cable.
2. From underneath the vehicle, remove the washer motor from its bracket.
3. Pull the pump downward to access the wiring connector and hose.
4. Detach the wiring connector and hose.

**To install:**

5. Install the washer pump into the bracket.
6. Attach the wiring connector and hose.
7. Fill the washer bottle with the appropriate mixture of solvent.
8. Connect the negative battery cable.
9. Check the operation of the washer motor.

10. Remove the retaining screws behind the vents.
11. Remove the dash speaker grilles and remove the speakers.
12. Remove the dash panel retaining screws under each speaker grille.

### ✳️ CAUTION

**Refer to the SRS (air bag) system Safety Precautions listed earlier in this section for proper handling and storage.**

13. Remove the instrument panel cover with the attached passenger side air bag module.
14. Undo the retaining clips on the instrument cluster.
15. Lift the instrument cluster away from the dashboard.
16. Unfasten the connectors on the back of the cluster and remove the cluster.

**To install:**

17. If any light bulbs need to be replaced on the instrument cluster, simply twist the bulb(s) ¼ turn counterclockwise and remove. Install and twist the replacement bulb(s) clockwise.
18. Attach the connectors on the back of the cluster assembly.
19. Position the instrument cluster into place and connect the retaining clips.
20. Place the instrument panel cover into place and install the retaining screws.
21. Install the vents, dash speakers, and grilles.
22. Install the air bag module retaining screws.
23. Plug in the air bag module connector.
24. Install the glove compartment lining and lid.
25. Connect the negative battery cable.

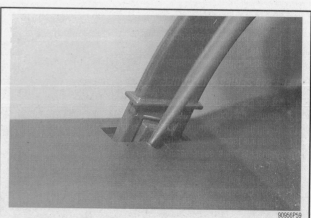

90956P59

**Fig. 60 Release the tabs to disengage the swing-down arms from the glove compartment door**

Fig. 61 Remove the glove compartment lining retaining screws . . .

Fig. 62 . . . and remove the lining

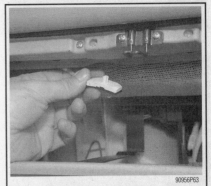

Fig. 63 Unplug the connector from the passenger side air bag module

Fig. 64 Remove the four screws above the glove box . . .

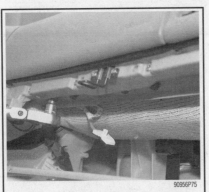

Fig. 65 . . . and the bolts for the air bag support bracket

Fig. 66 Remove the retaining screws over the instrument cluster

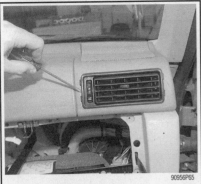

Fig. 67 Gently pry out either side of the passenger vent assembly . . .

Fig. 68 . . . and remove it from the dashboard

Fig. 69 Gently pry out and remove the vent cover on the driver's side

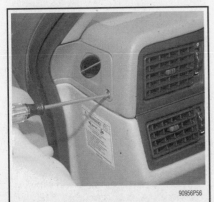

Fig. 70 Unfasten the retaining screw . . .

Fig. 71 . . . and remove the side demister vent (one on each side)

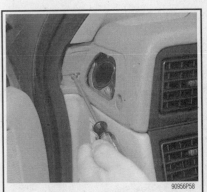

Fig. 72 Remove the dash pad retaining screw behind the demister vent

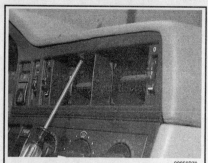

**Fig. 73 After removing the center panel vent covers, unfasten the dash panel retaining screws**

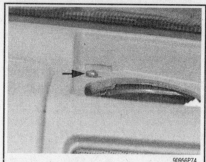

**Fig. 74 Remove this screw from each side after the dashboard speaker grilles are removed**

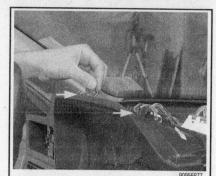

**Fig. 75 Unsnap the retaining clips for the instrument cluster . . .**

**Fig. 76 . . . then unplug the electrical connectors . . .**

**Fig. 77 . . . and lift the instrument cluster out of the dash panel**

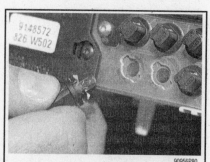

**Fig. 78 The instrument cluster bulbs are easily removed by twisting ¼ turn and pulling them out**

## Gauges

### REMOVAL & INSTALLATION

▶ **See Figures 79, 80 and 81**

The gauges can be replaced individually on some models, but others require replacement of the entire gauge cluster assembly. The instrument cluster contains many components; inside the cluster are modules, printed circuit boards, fuses, and some also contain small microprocessor computers for the clock and driver information center. Diagnosis of this system is complex, and the cost of parts is high; since most parts are special order only, trial and error replacement is just not practical. It is advised to diagnose the failed component before replacement.

On models where the gauges can be replaced, simply remove the instrument cluster as outlined in this section, and remove the cluster cover. Remove the retaining devices (some use bolts, some are held in by tabs, etc.) and remove the gauge from the cluster. To install, reverse this procedure.

On models where the cluster must be replaced, remove the instrument cluster as outlined previously in this section. Remove the printed circuit board and any components necessary to remove the board, then remove the cluster cover. Unfasten the instrument cluster retainers and remove the gauge cluster assembly.

When replacing a speedometer or odometer assembly, or the instrument cluster, federal law requires the odometer reading of the replacement unit to be set to register the same mileage as the prior odometer. If the mileage cannot be set, the law requires that the replacement be set at zero and a proper label be installed on the driver's door frame to show the previous odometer reading and date of replacement.

## Headlight Switch (Lighting Selector)

### REMOVAL & INSTALLATION

#### 240 Series and Coupe

1. Disconnect the negative battery cable.
2. Disconnect the hose from the left side dashboard vent.

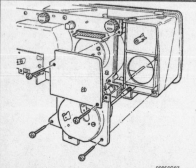

**Fig. 79 This gauge is accessed by removing the cover panel and the retaining screws**

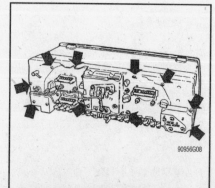

**Fig. 80 Location of the retaining screws for the back of the instrument cluster**

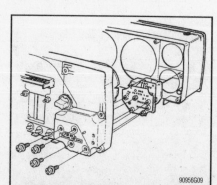

**Fig. 81 After removing the back of the cluster, the gauge is removed by unfastening the retaining screws**

3. Carefully remove the trim below the vent, then unfasten the screws holding the vent in place and remove the vent assembly.

4. Using a very small screwdriver, loosen the setscrew holding the selector knob onto the shaft. If no setscrew is evident, simply pull on the knob until it comes free of the shaft.

5. Unfasten the shaft nut from the switch and remove the switch through the back of the dashboard.

6. Remove the plug from the back of the switch assembly.

7. When reassembling, remember to connect the new switch to the wiring harness and, if equipped, tighten the small setscrew holding the knob to the shaft.

8. Install the switch into dashboard.

9. Tighten the shaft nut.

10. Connect the wiring harness.

11. Install the dashboard trim.

12. Install the vent hose.

13. Install the selector knob.

14. Reconnect the battery and check the switch function.

### Except 240 Series and Coupe

1. Disconnect the negative battery cable.

2. Remove the selector knob by pulling it free of the shaft.

3. Detach the wiring connector by reaching under the dashboard. It may be necessary to loosen or remove the underdash pad to gain access.

4. Unfasten the shaft nut from the switch and remove the switch through the back of the dashboard.

**To install:**

5. Install the switch into dashboard.

6. Tighten the shaft nut.

7. Connect the wiring harness.

8. Install the underdash pad (if removed).

9. Install the selector knob by pressing it onto the shaft.

10. Reconnect the battery and check the switch function.

### Rocker Switches

#### REMOVAL & INSTALLATION

▶ **See Figures 82 and 83**

The dash or console mounted rocker switches are easily removed. Depending on the model, it may be necessary to remove the trim panel surrounding the switch. After this is done, reach behind the switch and disconnect the wire harness running to the switch. While your hand is back there, grasp each side of the switch, compress the retaining clips and remove the switch through the front of the panel.

If length allows, the wire harness may be brought out through the panel (after the switch is removed) for circuit testing. When reinstalling, make sure the wiring is properly routed and not crimped or pinched. The switch should engage the panel with a definite click when in place. Reinstall the trim panel.

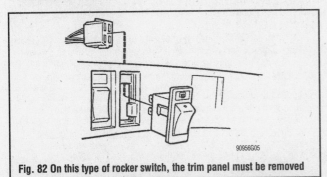

90956G05

**Fig. 82 On this type of rocker switch, the trim panel must be removed**

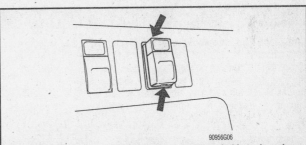

90956G06

**Fig. 83 On this type, a small screwdriver or other suitable tool can be inserted into the groove (indicated by the arrows) to release the switch**

## LIGHTING

### Headlights

#### REMOVAL & INSTALLATION

#### Replaceable Halogen Bulbs

▶ **See Figures 84, 85 and 86**

1. Open the vehicle's hood and secure it in an upright position.

2. If so equipped, remove the headlight bulb and socket assembly's access cover.

➡ **Bulbs with in-line sockets typically utilize separate locking rings, but those with angled sockets do not.**

3. If equipped with a locking ring, twist and remove the ring to expose the bulb and socket assembly. If there is no separate ring, simply twist the bulb socket, then withdraw the assembly rearward.

4. If necessary, gently pry the electrical connector's retaining clip over the projection on the socket (use care not to break the clip.) Remove the bulb and socket assembly from the vehicle.

**To install:**

5. Before installing a light bulb and socket, ensure that all electrical contact surfaces are free of corrosion or dirt.

6. Line up the replacement headlight bulb and socket assembly with the electrical connector. Firmly push the connector onto the socket until the spring clip latches over the socket's projection.

### ✳✳ WARNING

**Do not touch the glass bulb with your fingers. Oil from your fingers can severely shorten the life of the bulb. If necessary, wipe off any dirt or oil from the bulb with rubbing alcohol before completing installation.**

7. To ensure that the replacement bulb functions properly, activate the applicable switch to illuminate the bulb which was just replaced. (If this is a combination low and high beam bulb, be sure to check both intensities.) If the replacement light bulb does not illuminate, either it too is faulty or there is a problem in the bulb circuit or switch. Correct if necessary.

8. Position the replacement headlight bulb; if applicable, secure the locking ring. Also install the access cover, if so equipped.

9. Remove all tools, then close the vehicle's hood.

#### Sealed Beam Units

▶ **See Figure 87**

1. Disconnect the battery cable.

2. Release the headlight trim, using the applicable method. If equipped with plastic screws, rotate them ½ turn, then remove the trim. If equipped with a clip at the top center of the trim panel, squeeze the two sides together, and pull upward to release the trim.

3. Unfasten the 4 small screws holding the retainer, then remove the retainer and the headlamp.

4. Unplug the electrical connector from the rear of the headlamp.

5. Installation is the reverse of removal.

Fig. 84 Remove the access cover to replace the headlamp bulb

Fig. 85 Twist the angled bulb and socket assembly ¼ turn counterclockwise and withdraw it from the lens . . .

Fig. 86 . . . then release the tab and disengage the electrical connector

## AIMING THE HEADLIGHTS

▶ **See Figures 88 thru 92**

The headlights must be properly aimed to provide the best, safest road illumination. The lights should be checked for proper aim and adjusted as necessary. Certain state and local authorities have requirements for headlight aiming; these should be checked before adjustment is made.

**✷✷ CAUTION**

**About once a year, when the headlights are replaced or any time front end work is performed on your vehicle, the headlight should be accurately aimed by a reputable repair shop using the proper equipment. Headlights not properly aimed can make it virtually impossible to see and may blind other drivers on the road, possibly causing an accident. Note that the following procedure is a temporary fix, until you can take your vehicle to a repair shop for a proper adjustment.**

Headlight adjustment may be temporarily made using a wall, as described below, or on the rear of another vehicle. When adjusted, the lights should not glare in oncoming car or truck windshields, nor should they illuminate the passenger compartment of vehicles driving in front of you. These adjustments are rough and should always be fine-tuned by a repair shop which is equipped with headlight aiming tools. Improper adjustments may be both dangerous and illegal.

For most of the vehicles covered by this manual, horizontal and vertical aiming of each sealed beam unit is provided by two adjusting screws which move the retaining ring and adjusting plate against the tension of a coil spring. There is no adjustment for focus; this is done during headlight manufacturing.

➡Because the composite headlight assembly is bolted into position, no adjustment should be necessary or possible. Some applications, how-

Fig. 87 Remove the trim ring while supporting the headlight to prevent it from falling.

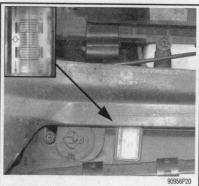

Fig. 88 The headlight aiming levels, as viewed from the top

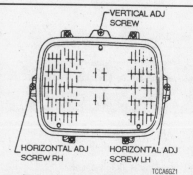

Fig. 89 Location of the aiming screws on most vehicles with sealed beam headlights

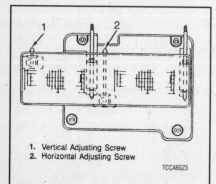

1. Vertical Adjusting Screw
2. Horizontal Adjusting Screw

Fig. 90 Example of headlight adjustment screw location for composite headlamps

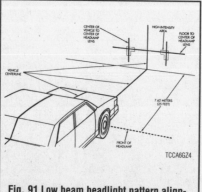

Fig. 91 Low beam headlight pattern alignment

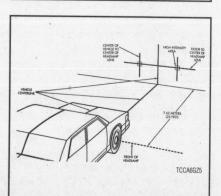

Fig. 92 High beam headlight pattern alignment

ever, may be bolted to an adjuster plate or may be retained by adjusting screws. If so, follow this procedure when adjusting the lights, BUT always have the adjustment checked by a reputable shop.

Before removing the headlight bulb or disturbing the headlamp in any way, note the current settings in order to ease headlight adjustment upon reassembly. If the high or low beam setting of the old lamp still works, this can be done using the wall of a garage or a building:

1. Park the vehicle on a level surface, with the fuel tank about ½ full and with the vehicle empty of all extra cargo (unless normally carried). The vehicle should be facing a wall which is no less than 6 feet (1.8m) high and 12 feet (3.7m) wide. The front of the vehicle should be about 25 feet (7.6m) from the wall.

2. If aiming is to be performed outdoors, it is advisable to wait until dusk in order to properly see the headlight beams on the wall. If done in a garage, darken the area around the wall as much as possible by closing shades or hanging cloth over the windows.

3. Turn the headlights **ON** and mark the wall at the center of each light's low beam, then switch on the high beams and mark the center of each light's high beam. A short length of masking tape which is visible from the front of the vehicle may be used. Although marking all four positions is advisable, marking one position from each light should be sufficient.

4. If neither beam on one side is working, and if another like-sized vehicle is available, park the second one in the exact spot where the vehicle was and mark the beams using the same-side light. Then switch the vehicles so the one to be aimed is back in the original spot. It must be parked no closer to or farther away from the wall than the second vehicle.

5. Perform any necessary repairs, but make sure the vehicle is not moved, or is returned to the exact spot from which the lights were marked. Turn the headlights **ON** and adjust the beams to match the marks on the wall.

6. Have the headlight adjustment checked as soon as possible by a reputable repair shop.

## Signal and Marker Lights

### REMOVAL & INSTALLATION

▶ See Figure 93

**Turn Signal and Parking Lights**

#### 1990–93 MODELS

➡ **Depending on the vehicle and bulb application, either unscrew and remove the lens or disengage the bulb and socket assembly from the rear of the lens housing.**

1. Raise and support the hood.
2. Working from inside the engine compartment, twist the socket ¼ turn counterclockwise, then remove the bulb and socket assembly.

➡ **Do not remove the electrical connector from the socket.**

3. Depress the bulb and twist it ¼ turn counterclockwise, then remove the bulb.

**To install:**
4. Before installing a light bulb into the socket, ensure that all electrical contact surfaces are free of corrosion or dirt.

➡ **Before installing the light bulb, note the positions of the two retaining pins on the bulb. They will likely be at different heights on the bulb, to ensure that the bulb is installed correctly. If, when installing the bulb, it does not turn easily, do not force it. Remove the bulb and rotate it 180 degrees from its former position, then reinsert it into the bulb socket.**

5. Insert the light bulb into the socket and, while depressing the bulb, twist it ⅛ turn clockwise until the two pins on the light bulb are properly engaged in the socket.

6. To ensure that the replacement bulb functions properly, activate the applicable switch to illuminate the bulb which was just replaced. If the replacement light bulb does not illuminate, either it too is faulty or there is a problem in the bulb circuit or switch. Correct if necessary.

7. If applicable, install the socket and bulb assembly into the rear of the lens housing; otherwise, install the lens over the bulb.

#### 1994–98 MODELS

▶ See Figures 94, 95, 96 and 97

1. The lamp assembly is held into place by a retaining spring. Pull the lamp assembly out to access the bulb.

➡ **If you use great care, you can turn the lamp around and wedge it so that it will stay, leaving both your hands free to change the bulb.**

2. Press the tabs and remove the bulb assembly.
3. Remove the bulb by turning it to release the locking tabs.

**To install:**
4. Install a new bulb and place the bulb assembly into the lens, ensuring that the gasket is installed.

5. Push the bulb assembly in until the tabs engage.
6. Pull the lamp assembly out and position it, then release the tension, allowing the spring to pull it back into place; this may require several tries.

**Side Marker Light**

▶ See Figure 98

1. Disengage the bulb and socket assembly from the lens housing.
2. Gently grasp the light bulb and pull it straight out of the socket.

**To install:**
3. Before installing the light bulb into the socket, ensure that all electrical contact surfaces are free of corrosion or dirt.

4. Line up the base of the light bulb with the socket, then insert the light bulb into the socket until it is fully seated.

5. To ensure that the replacement bulb functions properly, activate the applicable switch to illuminate the bulb which was just replaced. If the replacement light bulb does not illuminate, either it too is faulty or there is a problem in the bulb circuit or switch. Correct as necessary.

6. Install the socket and bulb assembly into the lens housing.

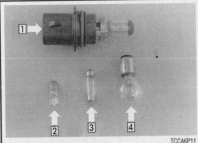

1. Halogen headlight bulb
2. Side marker light bulb
3. Dome light bulb
4. Turn signal/brake light bulb

TCCA6P11

**Fig. 93 Examples of various types of automotive light bulbs**

90956P16

**Fig. 94 Pull out the lamp assembly—note the spring used to retain the lamp**

90956P17

**Fig. 95 Release the tabs and the bulb assembly will come out**

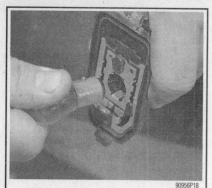

Fig. 96 Free the bulb by turning it to release the retaining tabs

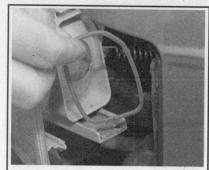

Fig. 97 Be careful to position the gasket properly, or premature bulb failure could result

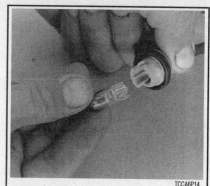

Fig. 98 Simply pull this side marker light bulb straight from its socket

### Rear Turn Signal, Brake and Reverse Lights

#### 240 SEDAN

All tail lamp bulbs are replaced from inside the trunk.

1. Open the trunk. Unscrew and remove the tail lamp inside cover. The cover is hooked at the upper edge. Lift the lower end out and up, then unhook the upper edge.

2. Turn the socket approximately ⅜ inch (1cm) counterclockwise and remove it from the tail lamp lens housing.

3. Depress the bulb in the socket, turn it slightly counterclockwise and remove it.

**To install:**

4. Align the pins on the side of the replacement bulb with the grooves in the socket. Push in the bulb and turn it slightly clockwise.

5. To ensure that the replacement bulb functions properly, activate the applicable switch to illuminate the bulb which was just replaced. If the replacement light bulb does not illuminate, either it too is faulty or there is a problem in the bulb circuit or switch. Correct as necessary.

➟One of the socket's retaining tabs is wider than the other, so the socket must be properly oriented.

6. Install the bulb and socket assembly in the tail lamp lens housing. Turn the socket clockwise to lock it.

7. Position and fasten the tail lamp inside cover.

#### 240 WAGON

All bulbs in the tail light cluster are removed from inside the trunk.

1. To access the left side bulb, remove the spare tire cover and the spare wheel assembly.

2. To access the right side bulb, remove the stowage cover. Loosen the clip and move the panel aside.

3. Depress the bulb and turn it slightly counterclockwise, then remove it.

**To install:**

4. Install the bulb and related components in the reverse order of removal. Be sure to position the socket with the word "Volvo" turned toward the center of the vehicle.

#### EXCEPT 240 SEDAN AND WAGON

▶ See Figures 99, 100, 101 and 102

All bulbs in the tail light cluster are removed from inside the trunk. To avoid confusion, replace bulbs one at a time.

1. Unscrew and remove the tail lamp inside cover. Note that the inside cover is hooked at the lower edge.

2. Remove the plastic screw and remove the bulb and socket as a unit.

3. Depress the bulb in the socket and turn it slightly counterclockwise, then remove it.

**To install:**

4. Align the pins on the side of the bulb with the grooves in the socket, then insert and twist the replacement bulb.

5. To ensure that the replacement bulb functions properly, activate the applicable switch to illuminate the bulb which was just replaced. If the replacement light bulb does not illuminate, either it too is faulty or there is a problem in the bulb circuit or switch. Correct as necessary.

6. Install the bulb and socket assembly in the tail lamp housing.

7. Replace the tail lamp inside cover.

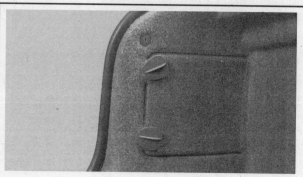

Fig. 99 The tail lamp's access cover is inside the trunk

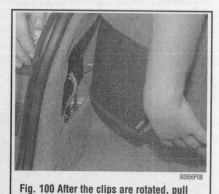

Fig. 100 After the clips are rotated, pull the trim back to reveal the lights

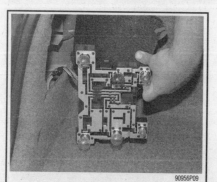

Fig. 101 Press the tabs and the tail lamp light bulb cluster can be removed

Fig. 102 These light bulbs are removed by turning counterclockwise slightly to release their retaining pins

## High-Mounted Brake Light

### 240 SERIES

1. On sedans, use a screwdriver to depress the catch, then pull the plastic cover up and away from the light assembly.

---

**✳✳ WARNING**

When using a screwdriver to pry plastic components, use care to avoid scratching or breaking. If necessary, wear eye protection whenever possible.

---

2. On wagons, depress the marked areas on the side of the housing and pull it away from the light assembly.

3. Press in the reflector catch to release the reflector assembly. Swing out the reflector and remove the bulb.

4. Install a new bulb and snap the reflector into position. Check that the bulb lights when the brake pedal is depressed.

5. Align the light bulb terminals with the holes in the lamp housing, and press the bulb into place.

### EXCEPT 240 SERIES

▶ See Figures 103, 104, 105 and 106

1. Depress the light cover's catch with a screwdriver.

---

**✳✳ WARNING**

When using a screwdriver to pry plastic components, use care and avoid scratching or breaking. If necessary, wear eye protection whenever possible.

---

2. Grasp the cover with both hands and pull it towards you.

3. Gently depress the reflector's tabs and pull off the bulb/socket/reflector assembly.

4. Twist and remove the bulb from the socket.

**To install:**

5. Insert the replacement bulb into the socket and check that the light works.

6. Install the bulb/socket/reflector assembly.

7. On Sedan models, press the cover into position, noting the position of the alignment pin at the top.

8. On Wagon models, align the catches and press the cover into position.

## Spoiler Mounted Brake Light

1. Remove the retaining screws from the lens, then remove the lens.

2. Remove the bulb.

**To install:**

3. Install the replacement bulb into the socket, and check that the light works.

4. Ensure that the gasket is in place.

5. Install the lens onto the housing and tighten the retaining screws.

## Dome Light

▶ See Figures 107, 108, 109, 110 and 111

1. Using a small prytool, carefully remove the cover lens from the lamp assembly.

2. Remove the bulb from its retaining clip contacts. If the bulb has tapered ends, gently depress the spring clip/metal contact and disengage the light bulb, then pull it free of the two metal contacts.

**To install:**

3. Before installing the light bulb into the metal contacts, ensure that all electrical conducting surfaces are free of corrosion or dirt.

4. Position the bulb between the two metal contacts. If the contacts have small holes, be sure that the tapered ends of the bulb are situated in them.

5. To ensure that the replacement bulb functions properly, activate the applicable switch to illuminate the bulb which was just replaced. If the replacement light bulb does not illuminate, either it is faulty or there is a problem in the bulb circuit or switch. Correct as necessary.

6. Install the cover lens until its retaining tabs are properly engaged.

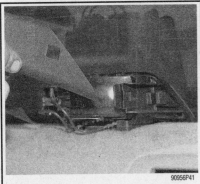

**Fig. 103 Remove the cover to access the bulb**

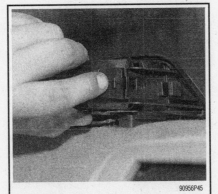

**Fig. 104 Gently squeeze the tabs . . .**

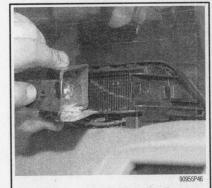

**Fig. 105 . . . and pull the bulb/reflector assembly out to replace the bulb**

**Fig. 106 Lightly depress and twist the bulb counterclockwise to remove it**

**Fig. 107 A small amount of tape around the end of the prytool can help prevent damage to the trim**

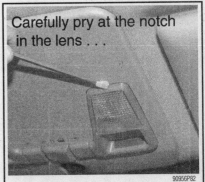

Carefully pry at the notch in the lens . . .

**Fig. 108 The lens is made of plastic and can easily break, so be careful**

Fig. 109 After removal, place the lens in a safe location where it will not be damaged

Fig. 110 With the lens removed, the bulb is accessible

Twist and pull to remove the bulb

Fig. 111 The bulb is retained by 2 small pins on its base which lock it into place

## Interior Light

### 240 SERIES

1. Insert a screwdriver through the opening in the right side of the housing and depress the catch tab.
2. Pull out the housing assembly and remove the bulb.
3. Installation is the reverse of the removal procedure.

### EXCEPT 240 SERIES

1. Take hold of the front section of the light and pull the housing straight down.
2. Replace the bulb and check its operation.
3. Install the bulb housing.

## Door Warning Lamps and Vanity Mirror

1. Insert a screwdriver and gently turn it to remove the lens.
2. Replace the bulb, and check its operation.
3. Press the lens back into place.

## Shift Indicator Lamp

▶ See Figures 112 and 113

1. Disconnect the negative battery cable.
2. Remove the center console, as described in Section 10.
3. Locate the shift lamp bulb, and twist the bulb/socket assembly out of the shifter.
4. Pull the bulb straight out; it is retained by springs located on the side of the bulb socket.

**To install:**

5. Push the new bulb into place.
6. Install the new bulb and socket into the shifter.
7. Install the center console.
8. Connect the negative battery cable.

Fig. 112 The shift indicator lamp is located beneath the shifter assembly

Fig. 113 Remove the socket from the shifter to gain access to the bulb

## Engine Compartment and/or Trunk Light

1. Remove the lamp assembly retaining screws. Lift out and remove the assembly.
2. Replace the bulb, and check its operation.
3. Reinstall by first inserting the guides into one side, then press in the light assembly.
4. Install the retaining screws.

## License Plate Light

### 240 SERIES SEDAN

1. Slide the bulb housing backwards until it is released from the front edge.
2. Pull out the lamp housing and remove the bulb.
3. Install a new bulb.
4. Insert the front edge of the lamp housing and press up the rear edge by hand.

### 240 SERIES WAGON

1. Insert a screwdriver through the opening in the housing and depress the catch tab.

### ✳✳ WARNING

When using a screwdriver to pry plastic components, use care and avoid scratching or breaking. If necessary, wear eye protection whenever possible.

2. Pull out the housing assembly.
3. Installation is the reverse of the removal procedure.

### 780 SERIES

1. Slide the bulb housing backwards until it is released from the front edge.
2. Pull out the lamp housing and remove the bulb.
3. Install a new bulb.

4. Insert the front edge of the lamp housing and press up the rear edge by hand.

### EXCEPT 240 AND 780 SERIES

▶ See Figures 114, 115 and 116

1. Remove the screws from the light housing.
2. Insert a screwdriver and pry off the light assembly.
3. Replace the bulb, and check its operation
4. Reinstall the light housing.

## Fog/Driving Lights

### REMOVAL & INSTALLATION

▶ See Figure 117

1. Remove the fog lamp lens using a small prytool.
2. Remove the light bulb from the fog light housing by twisting it counterclockwise until it is disengaged, then pull it out of the housing.

**To install:**

3. Insert the new bulb into the light housing and twist it clockwise to lock it in place.
4. Install the lens onto the fog lamp assembly by snapping it into place.
5. Test the lights for proper operation. If the bulb does not function properly, determine the source of the problem (defective bulb, dirty socket, faulty wiring, blown fuse, etc.) and correct the situation.

### INSTALLING AFTERMARKET AUXILIARY LIGHTS

▶ See Figure 118

➡Before installing any aftermarket light, make sure it is legal for road use. Most acceptable lights will have a DOT approval number. Also check your local and regional inspection regulations. In certain areas,

aftermarket lights must be installed in a particular manner or they may not be legal for inspection.

1. Disconnect the negative battery cable.
2. Unpack the contents of the light kit purchased. Place the contents in an open space where you can easily retrieve a piece if needed.
3. Choose a location for the lights. If you are installing fog lights, below the bumper and apart from each other is desirable. Most fog lights are mounted below or very close to the headlights. If you are installing driving lights, above the bumper and close together is desirable. Most driving lights are mounted between the headlights.
4. Drill the needed hole(s) to mount the light. Install the light, and secure using the supplied retainer nut and washer. Tighten the light mounting hardware, but not the light adjustment nut or bolt.
5. Install the relay that came with the light kit in the engine compartment, in a rigid area, such as a fender. Always install the relay with the terminals facing down. This will prevent water from entering the relay assembly.
6. Using the wire supplied, locate the ground terminal on the relay, and connect a length of wire from this terminal to a good ground source. You can drill a hole and screw this wire to an inside piece of metal; just scrape the paint away from the hole to ensure a good connection.
7. Locate the light terminal on the relay; and attach a length of wire between this terminal and the fog/driving lamps.
8. Locate the ignition terminal on the relay, and connect a length of wire between this terminal and the light switch.
9. Find a suitable mounting location for the light switch and install. Some examples of mounting areas are a location close to the main light switch, auxiliary light position in the dash panel, if equipped, or in the center of the dash panel.
10. Depending on local and regional regulations, the other end of the switch can be connected to a constant power source such as the battery, an ignition opening in the fuse panel, or a parking or headlight wire.
11. Locate the power terminal on the relay, and connect a wire with an in-line fuse of at least 10 amperes between the terminal and the battery.
12. With all the wires connected and tied up neatly, connect the negative battery cable.
13. Turn the lights ON and adjust the light pattern, if necessary.

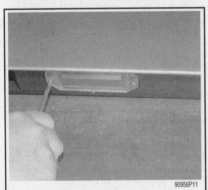

Fig. 114 Remove the lens attaching screws . . .

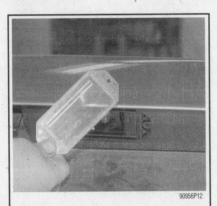

Fig. 115 . . . and remove the lens

Fig. 116 Remove the bulb by pulling it straight out

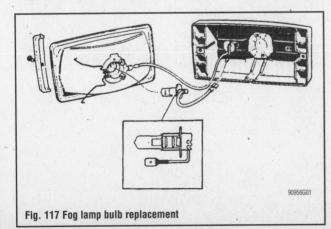

Fig. 117 Fog lamp bulb replacement

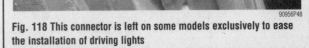

Fig. 118 This connector is left on some models exclusively to ease the installation of driving lights

AIMING

1. Park the vehicle on level ground, so it is perpendicular to and, facing a flat wall about 25 ft. (7.6m) away.

2. Remove any stone shields, if equipped, and switch ON the lights.

3. Loosen the mounting hardware of the lights so you can aim them as follows:

a. The horizontal distance between the light beams on the wall should be the same as between the lights themselves.

b. The vertical height of the light beams above the ground should be 4 in. (10cm) less than the distance between the ground and the center of the lamp lenses for fog lights. For driving lights, the vertical height should be even with the distance between the ground and the center of the lamp.

4. Tighten the mounting hardware.

5. Test to make sure the lights work correctly, and the light pattern is even.

## LIGHT BULB APPLICATIONS

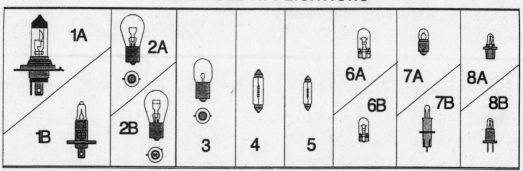

| Bulb to fit | Rating | Fitting | Fig. no. |
|---|---|---|---|
| Ashtray, front | 1.2W | Special | 8B |
| Ashtray, rear | 1.2W | Special | 8B |
| Automatic shift indicator | 1.2W | Special | 7B |
| Rear light | 21W | BA 15s | 2A |
| Trunk light 4-D | 10W | SV 8,5 | 4 |
| Rear light 4-door | 5W | BA 15s | 3 |
| Rear light 5-door | 21/4W | BAZ 15d | 2B |
| Rear courtesy light 5-D | 10W | SV8,5 | 4 |
| Flashers, front | 21W | BA 15s | 2A |
| Flashers, rear | 21W | BA 15s | 2A |
| Flashers, side | 5W | W 2,1x9,5d | 6A |
| Brake light | 21W | BA 15s | 2A |
| Brake light, high-level | 21W | BA 15s | 2A |
| Brake light, spoiler-mounted | 5W | W2,1x9,5d | 6A |
| Cigarette lighter | 1.2W | Special | 7B |
| Dim rear light | 21W | BA 15s | 2A |
| Door warning light | 3W | W 2,1x9,5d | 6A |
| Glove compartment light | 2W | BA 9s | 7A |
| Courtesy light | 5W | W 2,1x9,5d | 6A |
| Dashboard light | 3W | W 2,1x9,5d | 6A |
| Dashboard: Warning and indicator lights | 1.2W | W 2x4,6d | 8A / 6B |
| Rear reading light | 5W | BA 9s | 7A |
| Vanity mirror light | 1.2W | SV 5,5 | 5 |
| License plate light | 5W | W 2.1x9,5d | 6A |
| Parking lights, front | 5W | BA 15s | 3 |
| Control panel light, ECC | 1.2W | Special | 8A |
| Control panel light, AC unit | 1.2W | Special * | |
| Headlights with H4 bulb | 60/55W | P 43t-38 / H4 | 1A |
| Headlights with 2 x 1 H1 bulbs | 55W | P 14s / H1 | 1B |
| Headlights (US/Can), single bulb | HB2 | 9003 | |
| Headlights (US/Can), dual bulb High beam | HB3 | 9005 | |
| Low beam | HB4 | 9006 | |
| Ceiling light, front | 5W | BA 9s | 7A |
| Ceiling light, seatbelt warning light | 1.2W | W 2x4,6d | 6B |

* Replace PCB if bulb blows.

## TRAILER WIRING

Wiring the vehicle for towing is fairly easy. There are a number of good wiring kits available and these should be used, rather than trying to design your own.

All trailers will need brake lights and turn signals as well as tail lights and side marker lights. Most areas require extra marker lights for overwide trailers. Also, most areas have recently required back-up lights for trailers, and most trailer manufacturers have been building trailers with back-up lights for several years.

Additionally, some Class I, most Class II and just about all Class III and IV trailers will have electric brakes. Add to this number an accessories wire, to operate trailer internal equipment or to charge the trailer's battery, and you can have as many as seven wires in the harness.

Determine the equipment on your trailer and buy the wiring kit necessary. The kit will contain all the wires needed, plus a plug adapter set which includes the female plug, mounted on the bumper or hitch, and the male plug, wired into, or plugged into the trailer harness.

When installing the kit, follow the manufacturer's instructions. The color coding of the wires is usually standard throughout the industry. One point to note: some domestic vehicles, and most imported vehicles, have separate turn signals. On most domestic vehicles, the brake lights and rear turn signals operate with the same bulb. For those vehicles without separate turn signals, you can purchase an isolation unit so that the brake lights won't blink whenever the turn signals are operated.

One, final point, the best kits are those with a spring loaded cover on the vehicle mounted socket. This cover prevents dirt and moisture from corroding the terminals. Never let the vehicle socket hang loosely; always mount it securely to the bumper or hitch.

## CIRCUIT PROTECTION

### Fuses

▶ **See Figures 119, 120 and 121**

All electrical equipment is protected from overloading by fuses. Each fuse has an amperage rating that will allow it to transmit a predetermined amount of current before its filament melts, thereby stopping the excessive current flow. By providing this engineered "weak spot" in the circuit, the first failure will occur at a known location (the fuse), eliminating hours of tracing wiring harnesses to locate a problem.

If a fuse blows repeatedly, the trouble is probably in the electrical component that the fuse protects. NEVER replace a fuse with another of a higher ampere rating. Sometimes a fuse will blow when all of the electrical equipment protected by the fuse is operating, especially under severe weather conditions. For this reason, it is wise to carry a few spare fuses of each type in the car.

When tracking down an inoperative electrical circuit, follow a logical pattern. Wiring itself is rarely the problem. Remember that, in some cases, a fuse can look good but not be capable of passing an electrical load. Either remove the fuse and check it with an ohmmeter or simply replace it with a new one. Always

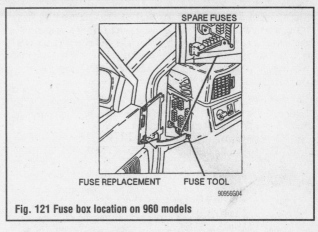

Fig. 121 Fuse box location on 960 models

have the ignition switched **OFF** when removing and replacing fuses. On all models, the circuit that each fuse protects is listed either on the fuse box cover or in the owner's manual.

A blown fuse is indicated by the failure of all units protected by it. It is caused by overloading the circuits. Examine the curved metal wire, on the inside of the fuse, to see if it is broken. If so, replace with a new fuse of the same color and amperage.

### REPLACEMENT

#### 240 and Coupe Models

The fuses and relays on 240 and Coupe models are positioned in the front of the left front door pillar. When installing fuse No. 1, be certain to use an 8 amp fuse.

Fuses and relays on the 760, 780 and 940 models are located in the central electrical unit behind the ashtray in the center console. In addition, a fuse for the ABS braking system is located under the instrument panel, to the left of the steering wheel. When installing fuse No. 5, be certain to use a 15 amp fuse.

Fuses and relays on 740, 850, 960 and all 1998 models are located on the far left side of the dashboard. When installing fuses No. 26 and 33, be certain to use 10 amp fuses.

All vehicles are equipped with a fuse removal tool, located in the fuse box. Grasp the blown fuse with the tool and remove it.

➡**Care must be exercised when replacing fuses. Check to ensure that the ignition switch is OFF.**

#### 700 Series and 940 Models

1. To obtain access to the central electrical unit, remove the ashtray. Pull out and depress the tongue.
2. Press the section marked "electrical fuses-press" and remove the unit.
3. Remove the fuse using the special fuse tool clipped in the fuse box. Pull the fuse straight out.

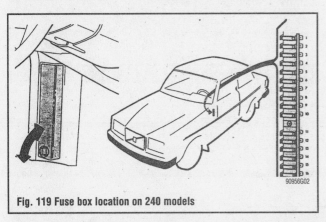

Fig. 119 Fuse box location on 240 models

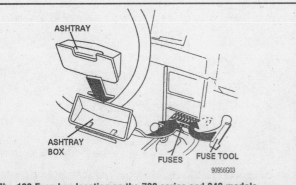

Fig. 120 Fuse box location on the 700 series and 940 models

**Except Coupe, 240, 700 and 940 Series**

▶ **See Figures 122, 123 and 124**

1. Remove the cover to gain access to the fuses.
2. Remove the fuse using the special fuse tool clipped in the fuse box. Pull the fuse straight out.
3. Replace the fuse with the proper amperage rating fuse.
4. When replacing the cover, push in the front edge first and then press into place.

## Fusible Links

### ✳✳ WARNING

**DO NOT replace blown fusible links with standard wire. Use only fusible type wire with Hypalon® insulation, or damage to the electrical system could occur. Also, be sure to use the correct gauge of wire.**

➡**Not all vehicles have fusible links. Most later models use Maxi-fuses in the underhood fuse box to provide circuit protection. An easy way to determine if your vehicle has fusible links is to verify the type of charging system voltage regulator; those models with an external voltage regulator are protected by fusible links, while those models without an external regulator utilize Maxi-fuses.**

When a fusible link blows, it is very important to find out the cause. Do not just replace the link to correct the problem. The fusible links are placed in the system for protection against dead shorts to ground.

In some instances, the link may be blown and it will not show through the insulation. Check the entire length of the fusible wire when the link is suspected of failure.

### REPLACEMENT

To repair any blown fuse link, use the following procedure:

1. Determine which circuit is damaged, its location and the cause of the open fuse link. If the damaged fuse link is one of three fed by a common No. 10 or 12 gauge wire, determine the specific affected circuit.
2. Disconnect the negative battery cable.
3. Cut the damaged fuse link from the wiring harness and discard it. If the fuse link is one of three circuits fed by a single feed wire, cut it out of the harness at each splice end and discard it.
4. Identify and procure the proper fuse link and butt connectors for attaching the fuse link to the harness.
5. To repair any fuse link in a 3-link group with one feed: After cutting the open link out of the harness, cut each of the remaining undamaged fuse links close to the feed wire weld.
6. Strip approximately ½ in. (13mm) of insulation from the detached ends of the two good fuse links. Then insert two wire ends into one end of a butt connector, carefully push one stripped end of the replacement fuse link into the same end of the butt connector and crimp all three firmly together.

➡**Care must be taken when fitting the three fuse links into the butt connector, as the internal diameter is a snug fit for three wires. Make sure to use a proper crimping tool. Pliers, side cutters, etc. will not apply the proper crimp to retain the wires and withstand a pull test.**

7. After crimping the butt connector to the three fuse links, cut the weld portion from the feed wire and strip approximately ½ in. (13mm) of insulation from the cut end. Insert the stripped end into the open end of the butt connector and crimp very firmly.
8. To attach the remaining end of the replacement fuse link, strip approximately ½ in. (13mm) of insulation from the wire end of the circuit from which the blown fuse link was removed, and firmly crimp a butt connector or equivalent to the stripped wire. Then, insert the end of the replacement link into the other end of the butt connector and crimp firmly.
9. Using rosin core solder with a consistency of 60 percent tin and 40 percent lead, solder the connectors and the wires at the repairs and insulate with electrical tape.
10. To replace any fuse link on a single circuit in a harness, cut out the damaged portion, strip approximately ½ in. (13mm) of insulation from the two wire ends and attach the appropriate replacement fuse link to the stripped wire ends with two proper size butt connectors. Solder the connectors and wires and insulate with tape.
11. To repair any fuse link which has an eyelet terminal on one end, such as the charging circuit, cut off the open fuse link behind the weld, strip approximately ½ in. (13mm) of insulation from the cut end and attach the appropriate new eyelet fuse link to the cut stripped wire with an appropriate size butt connector. Solder the connectors and wires at the repair and insulate with tape.
12. Connect the negative battery cable to the battery and test the system for proper operation.

➡**Do not mistake a resistor wire for a fuse link. The resistor wire is generally longer and has print stating, "Resistor: don't cut or splice." DO NOT replace blown fusible links with standard wire. Use only fusible type wire with Hypalon® insulation, or damage to the electrical system could occur. Also, be sure to use the correct gauge of wire.**

## Circuit Breakers

### RESETTING AND/OR REPLACEMENT

Circuit breakers are located inside the fuse panel. They are automatically reset when the problem corrects itself, or the circuit cools down to allow operation again.

## Flashers

### REPLACEMENT

The flasher is self-contained in the turn signal/windshield wiper and washer combination switch. If the flasher becomes inoperative, the switch assembly must be replaced. Refer to the Turn Signal (Combination) Switch removal and installation procedure in Section 8.

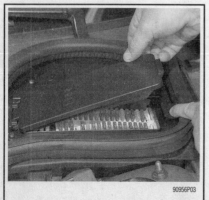

90956P03

**Fig. 122 Lift the lid on the fuse box**

90956P04

**Fig. 123 The fuse location and rating chart is located on the underside of the lid**

90956P05

**Fig. 124 A fuse removal tool is included in the fuse box**

## 240 FUSES

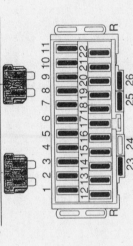

**Some of the equipment listed below is optional**

1 Cigarette lighter, Power mirrors, Radio, Tailgate wiper/washer. ........................ 8 A
2 Windshield wiper/washer, Horn ........ 16 A
3 Heater blower .................................... 25 A
4 Fuel feed (in-tank) pump, Lambda-sond heating element ................................. 8 A
5 Turn signals, Tail lights, Heated mirrors ......................................................... 16 A
6 Main fuel pump relay, Lambda-sond, Fuel injection system .................................. 8 A
7 Brake lights, Shiftlock, ABS .............. 8 A
8 Central locking, Interior and glove compartment lights, Trunk compartment lights, Radio, Power antenna, Clock, Daytime running lights (Canada) .............................................. 8 A
9 Hazard warning flashers ................... 8 A
10 Power windows ............................... 16 A
11 Heated rear window, 4th gear (automatic transmission) ..................................... 16 A
12 Air conditioning (with blower control), Power windows (relay), Heated rear window (relay), Seat belt reminder, Cruise control, Shiftlock ............................... 8 A
13 Heated front seats, Daytime running lights – relay (Canada) ................................ 16 A
14 Rear fog lights ................................. 8 A
15 Parking lights (left side). License plate light ................................................. 8 A
16 Parking lights (right side), Instruments and control panel lights, Shift indicator light ................................................. 8 A

ABS-equipped vehicles: this system is protected by a separate 10A fuse located under the front seat on the passenger's side.

Refer to the fuse location chart at fuse box for fuses specific to your car.

90956C02

## 700 SERIES FUSES

| Location* | Amperage |
|---|---|
| 1 Fuel pump, fuel injection system | 25 |
| 2 Central locking, hazard warning flashers, headlight flashers | 25 |
| 3 Spare | – |
| 4 Brake lights, shift-lock | 30 |
| 5 Glove compartment light, clock, radio, interior light, trunk light, door open warning, power antenna | 15 |
| 6 Heater fan MCC | 30 |
| 7 Extra lights | 30 |
| 8 Electrically operated windows | |
| 9 Warning light, seat belt, turn signals, air conditioning relay, heated front seats, electrically-operated windows, shift-lock | 15 |
| 10 Heated rear window Power-operated sunroof | 30 |
| 11 Tank pump, Lambda-sond | 15 |
| 12 Back-up lights, cruise control, overdrive (manual transmission), disengagement of 4th gear on automatic transmission, bulb failure warning lamp | |
| 13 Hot start valve | 15 |
| 14 Electrically-operated side view mirrors, cigarette lighter, radio, rear wiper (wagon) | 15 |
| 15 Horn, windshield wash/wipe | 25 |

| Location* | Amperage |
|---|---|
| 16 Heater blower, air conditioning | 30 |
| 17 High beam (left) | 15 |
| 18 High beam (right), extra lights | 15 |
| 19 Low beam (left) | 15 |
| 20 Low beam (right) | 15 |
| 21 LH parking lights (front and rear), license plate light, lighting for: ash tray, heater, control panel, switch for heated rear window, sunroof switch, left instrument panel, radio | 15 |
| 22 Seat belt light.RH parking lights (front and rear), center console compartment, foglight relay, lighting for: Heated seat switch, gear selector panel, rear ash tray | 15 |
| 23 Heated front seats | 25 |
| 24 SRS test socket | |
| 25 Rear fog light/lights | 15 |
| 26 Radio | 15 |

*Some of the equipment/systems listed may be available on certain models only and/or as optional items only.

NOTE: On cars equipped with ABS, the system is protected by an additional 10A fuse located under the instrument panel to the left of the steering wheel.

Intact fuse    Defective fuse

90956C03

## 850, C70, S70 AND V70 FUSES

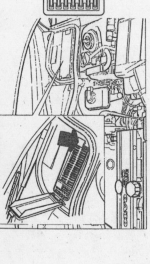

| No. | Function | Amps |
|---|---|---|
| 1 | Control units, Automatic transmission, Fuel and Ignition systems | 15 |
| 2 | Fuel pump | 15 |
| 3 | Courtesy light, Oil gauge, Exhaust temperature gauge (Japan), Speed warning | 10 |
| 4 | Spare | - |
| 5 | Passenger compartment fan, speed 4 | 30 |
| 6 | Central locking system and Alarm | 25 |
| 7 | Audio | 15 |
| 8 | Power antenna and Towing hook (-93), Air pump (94-) | 40 |
| 9 | ABS , TRACS (93-) | 30 |
| 10 | Spare (-93), Heated rear seat (94-) | 15 |
| 11 | Heated rear window & wing mirrors | 30 |
| 12 | Brake light | 10 |
| 13 | Hazard blinkers + High beam flash and Alarm | 15 |
| 14 | ABS , TRACS (93-) | 30 |
| 15 | Radio, Courtesy light, Door warning lights, Oil level-/pressure sensor and Remote-controlled central locking (-93), Seatbelt reminder and OBD-socket (94-) | 10 |
| 16 | Power antenna, Towing bracket contact and Accessories | 30 |
| 17 | Spare (-92), Key reminder (94-), Seatbelt reminder (-93) | 10 |
| 18 | Heated seats (-93), Power door mirrors (93), Spare (94-) | - |
| 19 | High beam, LH | 15 |
| 20 | High beam, RH + high beam check light | 15 |
| 21 | Low beam, LH | 15 |
| 22 | Low beam, RH | 15 |
| 23 | Parking -/tail light, LH, License plate light | 10 |
| 24 | Parking-/tail light, RH | 10 |
| 25 | Dipped rear light + indicator light | 10 |
| 26 | Spare (-93), Heated front seat and heated wing mirrors (94-) | 25 |
| 27 | Flashers and rear light, TRACS (93-) | 15 |
| 28 | Heated rear window, Seatbelt reminder, Cruise control, Shift-lock, Bulb failure warning sensor (Germany), Heated door mirrors (93-) | 10 |
| 29 | ABS , TRACS (93-) | 15 |
| 30 | Cigarette lighter | 10 |
| 31 | Passenger compartment fan, speeds 1 - 3 and AC system | 25 |
| 32 | Radio, Remote-controlled central locking system (93-) | 10 |
| 33 | Diagnostic unit, power seats, Light control motors, Rear window wiper and washer pump (94-) | 15 |
| 34 | Horn, windshield wipers, Headlight wipers and washer pump | 25 |
| 35 | Rheostat, Instrument lighting (94-), Power sunroof (93-) | 10 |
| 36 | Spare | - |
| 37 | Power window winders and Sunroof | automat. |
| 38 | Spare | 20 |
| 39 | Power seat, LH | automat. |
| 40 | Power seat, RH | automat. 20 |

90956205

90956204

## 940 FUSES

*Defective fuse*  *Intact Fuse*

*Fuse removal tool*

| Location* | Amperage |
|---|---|
| 1 Left parking lights, license plate light, rear parking lights | 10 |
| 2 Right parking lights | 10 |
| 3 Left high beam | 15 |
| 4 Right high beam | 15 |
| 5 SRS test | |
| 6 Left low beam | 15 |
| 7 Right low beam | 15 |
| 8 Front fog lights | 15 |
| 9 Rear fog lights | 10 |
| 10 Instrument illumination: ashtray front and rear, heater control panel, switches and seat belt light | 25 |
| 11 Back-up lights, turn signals, cruise control | 15 |
| 12 - | |
| 13 Heated rear window, heated door mirrors | 25 |
| 14 Overdrive, relay for electrically operated sun roof, electrically operated windows | 10 |
| 15 - | |
| 16 - | |
| 17 - | |
| 18 Radio/cassette tape player | 5 |
| 19 ECC, electrically operated side door mirrors, rear window wiper/washer (wagons) | 15 |
| 20 Windshield wipers/washers, horn | 25 |
| 21 Constant idle speed system | 5 |
| 22 - | |
| 23 - | |
| 24 - | |

| Location | Amperage |
|---|---|
| 25 Hazard warning flashers, central locking system | 25 |
| 26 Clock, interior lighting, door open warning lights, glove box, cargo space and vanity mirror | 10 |
| 27 Brake lights, shiftlock release | 15 |
| 28 Heater fan, air conditioning | 30 |
| 29 Electrically operated antenna, electrical connector for trailer | 30 |
| 30 Fuel pump (tank), electrically heated Lambda sond | 10 |
| 31 Fuel injection, fuel pump (main) | 25 |
| 32 Radio/amplifier | 15 |
| 33 Radio/cassette tape player | 10 |
| 34 Electrically operated windows, electrically operated sun roof | 30 |
| 35 Electrically heated front seats, electrically operated front seats | 30 |

Note: The ABS system is protected by an additional 10 A fuse which is located under the instrument panel to the left of the steering wheel.

Note: Refer to fuse box cover label for your vehicle's specific fuse usage.

Note: Fuses No. 34 and 35 are circuit breakers which activate when overloaded. After 20 seconds, the circuits should have cooled down and function normally.

## 960, S90 AND V90 FUSES

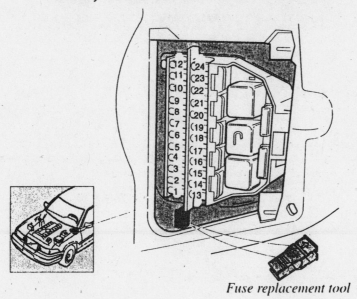

*Fuse replacement tool*

| Location ** | Amperage |
|---|---|
| 1 Heated rear window | 25 |
| 2 Central locking | 20 |
| 3 Brake light. Light switch | 15 |
| 4 Ignition switch, SRS | 10 |
| 5 Spare | |
| 6 Windshield wiper/washer, Headlight wiper. horn relay | 25 |
| 7 Climate unit | 20 |
| 8 Power seats, Power side door mirrors Tailgate wiper/washer (wagons) Instrument lighting, Ambient temp. sensor | 15 |
| 9 Audio system | 15 |
| 10 Cigarette lighter, | 15 |
| 11 Interior lighting. Transmission mode selector | 5 |
| 12 ABS | 5 |
| 13 Clock. Interior/glove compartment lighting. Door open warning lights, Cargo space lighting. Vanity mirror | 10 |
| 14 Alarm, Horn | 10 |

| Location ** | Amperage |
|---|---|
| 15 Power antenna, Headlight flasher, Trailer | 20 |
| 16 Accessories | 20 |
| 17 Hazard warning flasher, Direction indicator, Alarm hazard indication | 20 |
| 18 Audio/amplifier, CD changer | 15 |
| 19 Backup lights, Turn indicators, Cruise control | 15 |
| 20 Light switch, High/low beam relay | 15 |
| 21 Seat belt reminder, Timer- electrically heated rear window | 5 |
| 22 Heated driver's seat | 15 |
| 23 Heated passenger's seat | 15 |
| 24 Rear foglights | 5 |
| 25 Power seats * | 30 |
| 26 Power windows, Power sunroof * | 30 |

* Automatic circuit breakers

** Some of the equipment/systems listed may be available on certain models only and/or as optional items only.

90956C06

# INDEX OF WIRING DIAGRAMS

## WIRING DIAGRAM SYMBOLS

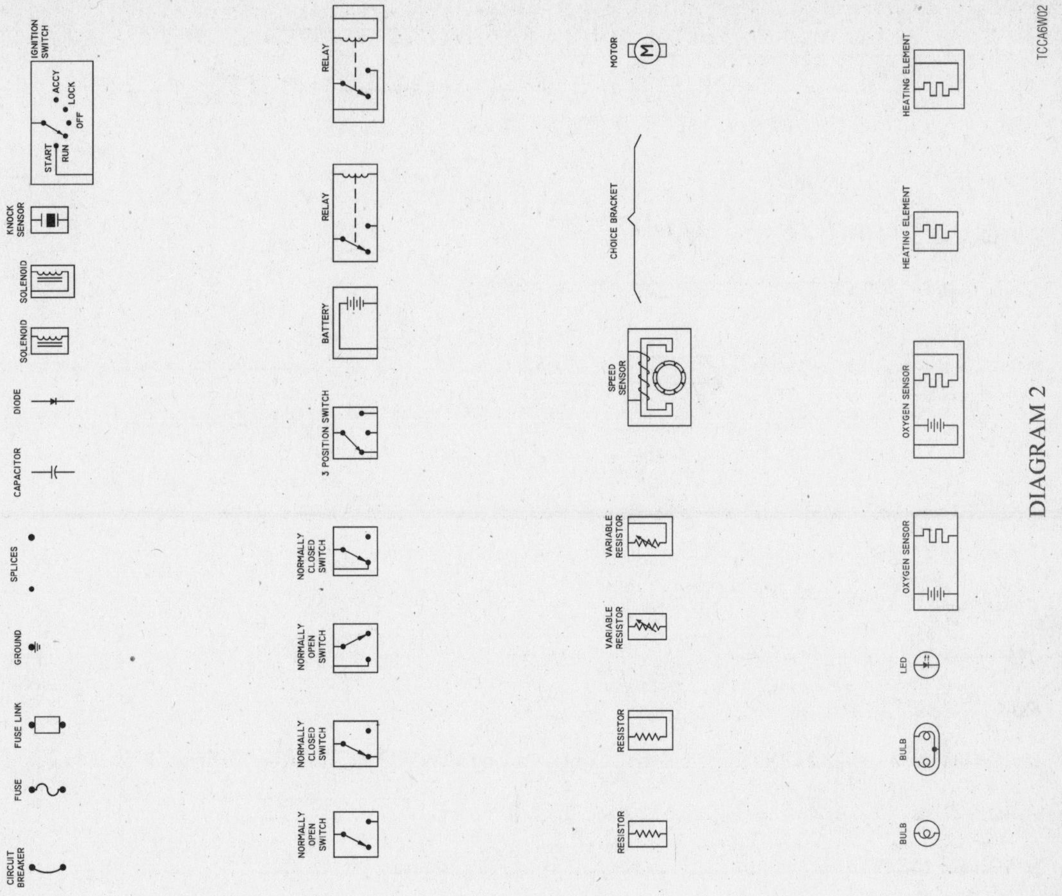

IGNITION SWITCH

KNOCK SENSOR

SOLENOID

SOLENOID

DIODE

CAPACITOR

SPLICES

GROUND

FUSE LINK

FUSE

CIRCUIT BREAKER

RELAY

RELAY

BATTERY

3 POSITION SWITCH

NORMALLY CLOSED SWITCH

NORMALLY OPEN SWITCH

NORMALLY CLOSED SWITCH

NORMALLY OPEN SWITCH

MOTOR

CHOICE BRACKET

SPEED SENSOR

VARIABLE RESISTOR

VARIABLE RESISTOR

RESISTOR

RESISTOR

LED

BULB

BULB

HEATING ELEMENT

HEATING ELEMENT

OXYGEN SENSOR

OXYGEN SENSOR

DIAGRAM 2

TCCA6W02

## SAMPLE DIAGRAM: HOW TO READ & INTERPRET WIRING DIAGRAMS

### WIRE COLOR ABBREVIATIONS

| | | | |
|---|---|---|---|
| BLACK | B | PNK | |
| BROWN | BR | PURPLE | P |
| RED | R | GREEN | G |
| ORANGE | O | WHITE | W |
| YELLOW | Y | LIGHT BLUE | LBL |
| GRAY | GY | LIGHT GREEN | LG |
| BLUE | BL | DARK GREEN | DG |
| VIOLET | V | DARK BLUE | DBL |
| TAN | T | NO COLOR AVAILABLE | NCA |

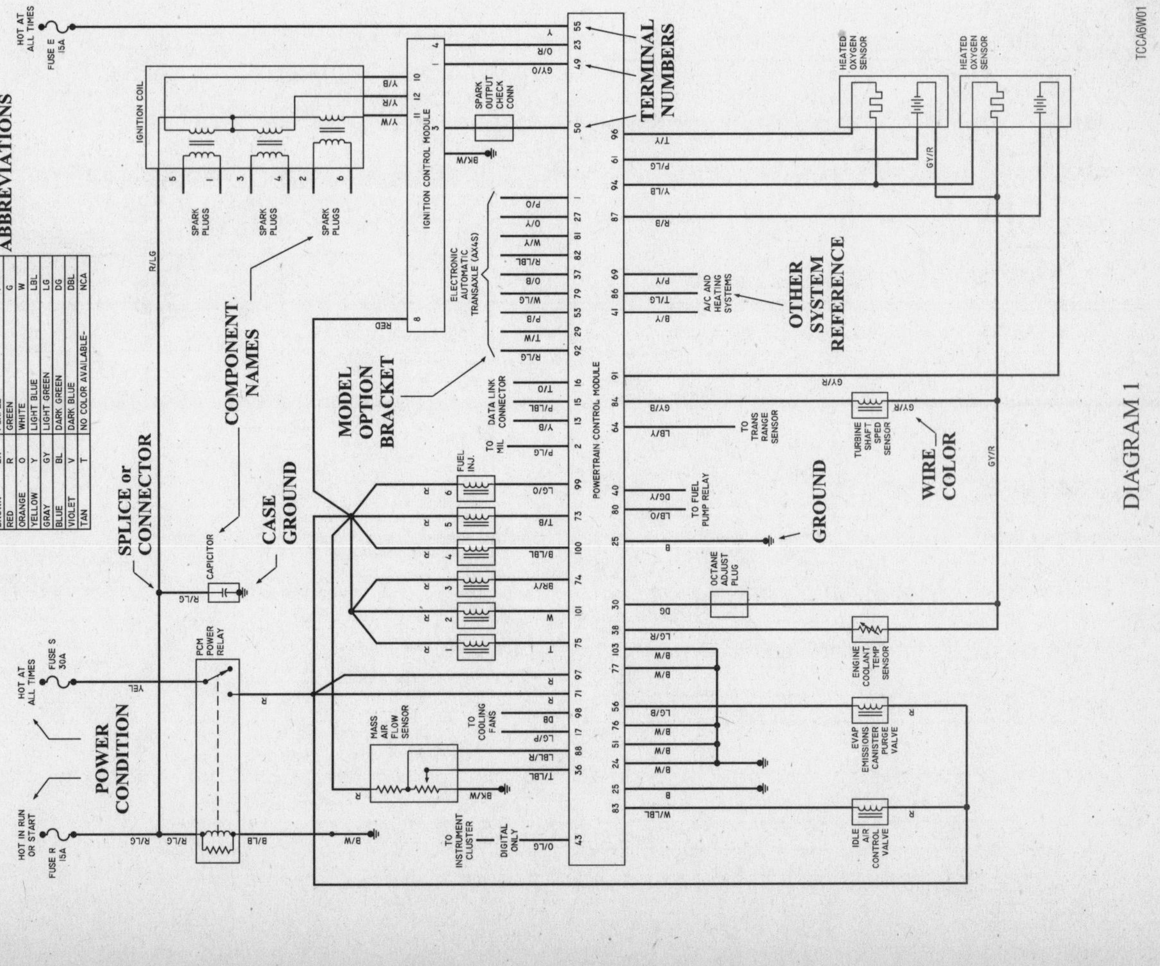

COMPONENT NAMES

SPLICE or CONNECTOR

CASE GROUND

MODEL OPTION BRACKET

POWER CONDITION

HOT AT ALL TIMES
FUSE E 15A

IGNITION COIL

SPARK PLUGS

SPARK PLUGS

SPARK PLUGS

IGNITION CONTROL MODULE

SPARK OUTPUT CHECK CONN

ELECTRONIC AUTOMATIC TRANSAXLE (AX4S)

DATA LINK CONNECTOR

TO MIL

POWERTRAIN CONTROL MODULE

FUEL INJ.

CAPACITOR

PCM POWER RELAY

HOT AT ALL TIMES
FUSE S 30A

HOT IN RUN OR START
FUSE R 15A

MASS AIR FLOW SENSOR

TO COOLING FANS

TO INSTRUMENT CLUSTER

DIGITAL ONLY

TERMINAL NUMBERS

HEATED OXYGEN SENSOR

HEATED OXYGEN SENSOR

OTHER SYSTEM REFERENCE

A/C AND HEATING SYSTEMS

TO TRANS RANGE SENSOR

TURBINE SHAFT SPEED SENSOR

TO FUEL PUMP RELAY

OCTANE ADJUST PLUG

GROUND

WIRE COLOR

ENGINE COOLANT TEMP SENSOR

EVAP EMISSIONS CANISTER PURGE VALVE

IDLE AIR CONTROL VALVE

DIAGRAM 1

TCCA6W01

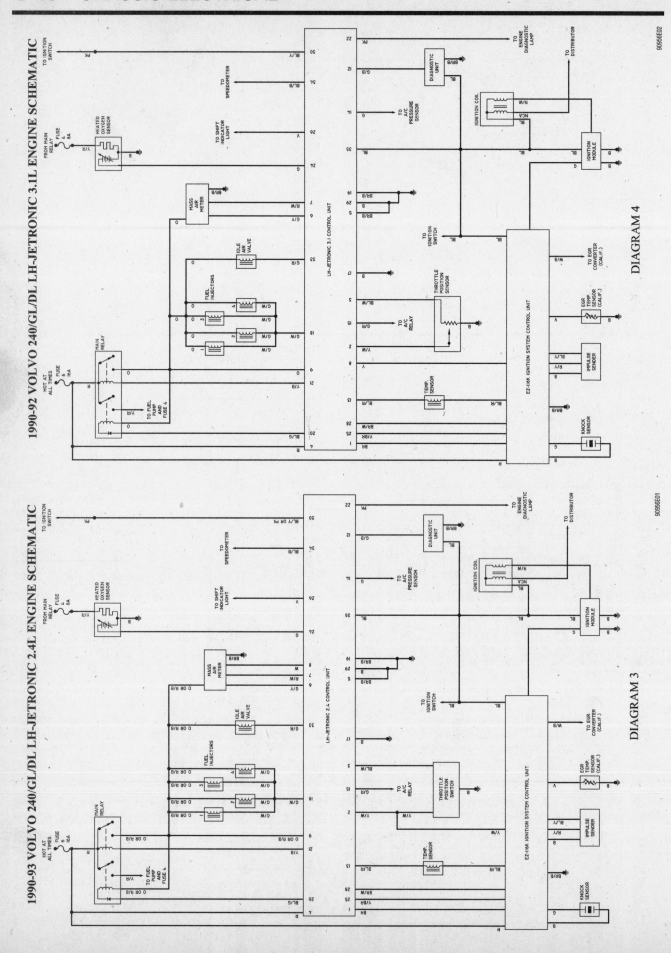

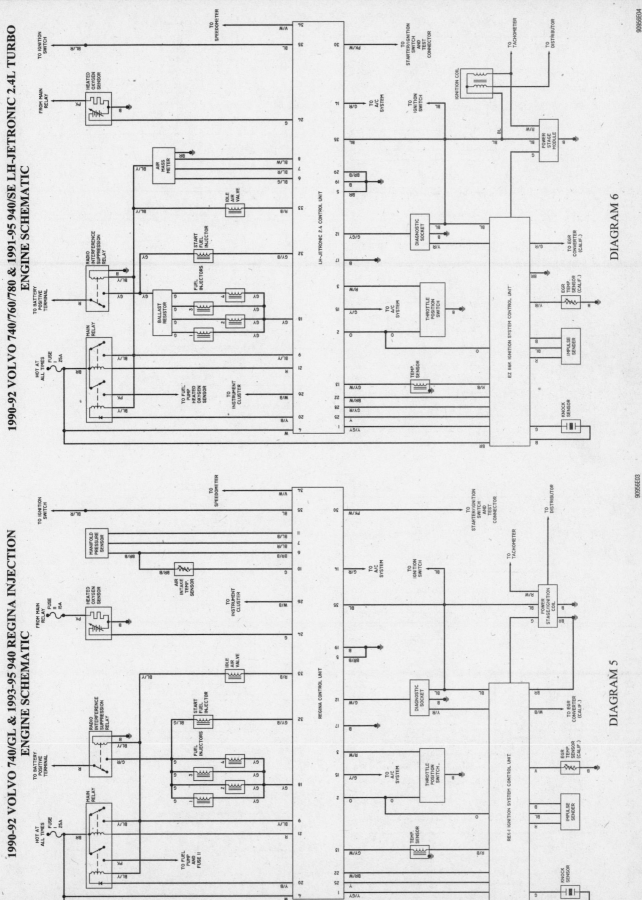

1990-92 VOLVO 740/760/780 & 1991-95 940/SE LH-JETRONIC 2.4L TURBO ENGINE SCHEMATIC

DIAGRAM 6

1990-92 VOLVO 740/GL & 1993-95 940 REGINA INJECTION ENGINE SCHEMATIC

DIAGRAM 5

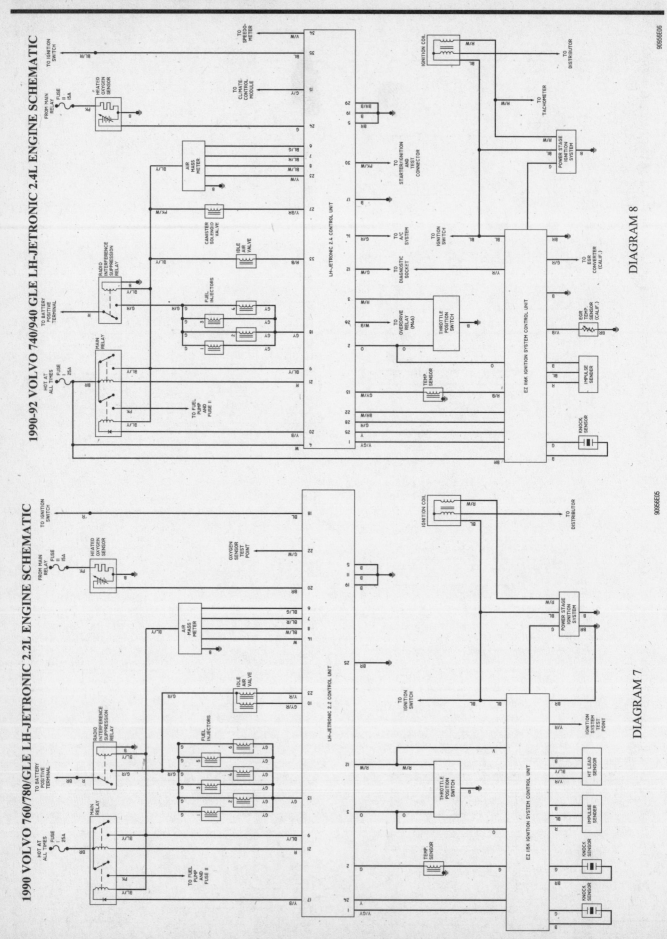

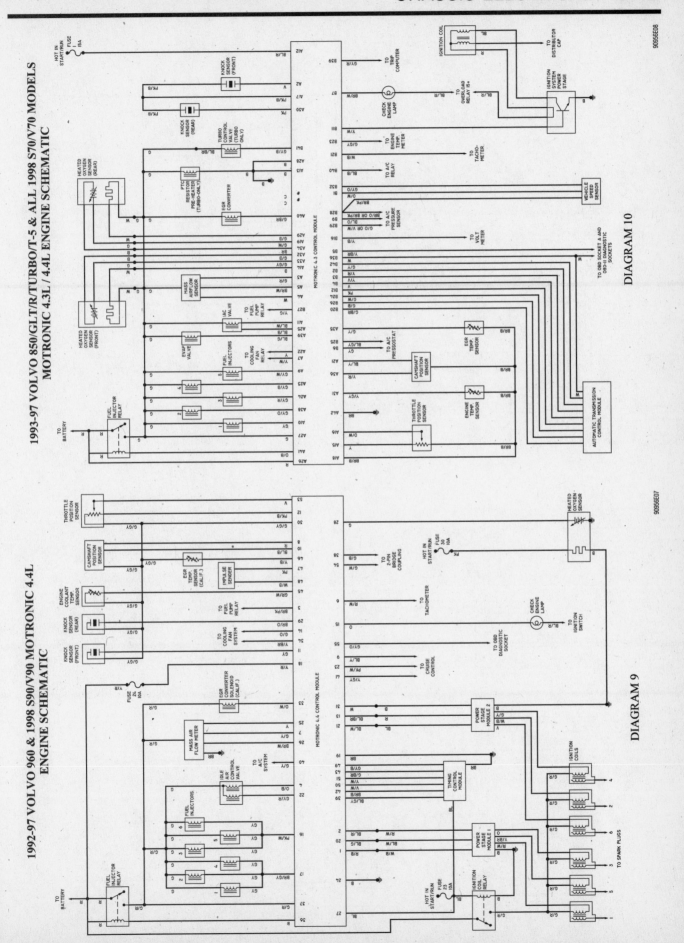

**1993-97 VOLVO 850/GLT/R/TURBO/T-5 & ALL 1998 S70/V70 MODELS
MOTRONIC 4.3L / 4.4L ENGINE SCHEMATIC**

DIAGRAM 10

**1992-97 VOLVO 960 & 1998 S90/V90 MOTRONIC 4.4L
ENGINE SCHEMATIC**

DIAGRAM 9

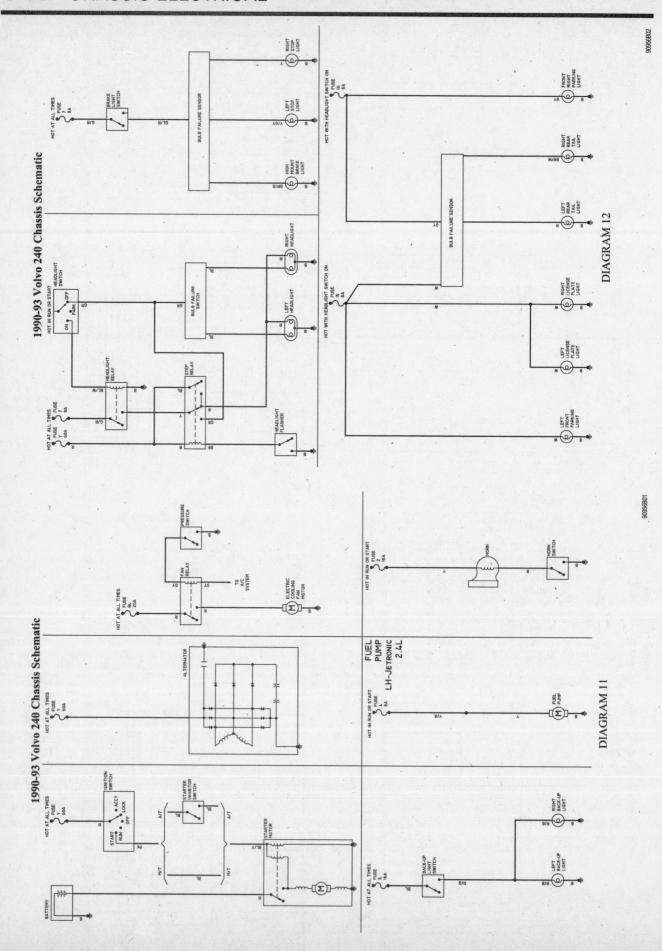

1990-93 Volvo 240 Chassis Schematic

DIAGRAM 12

DIAGRAM 11

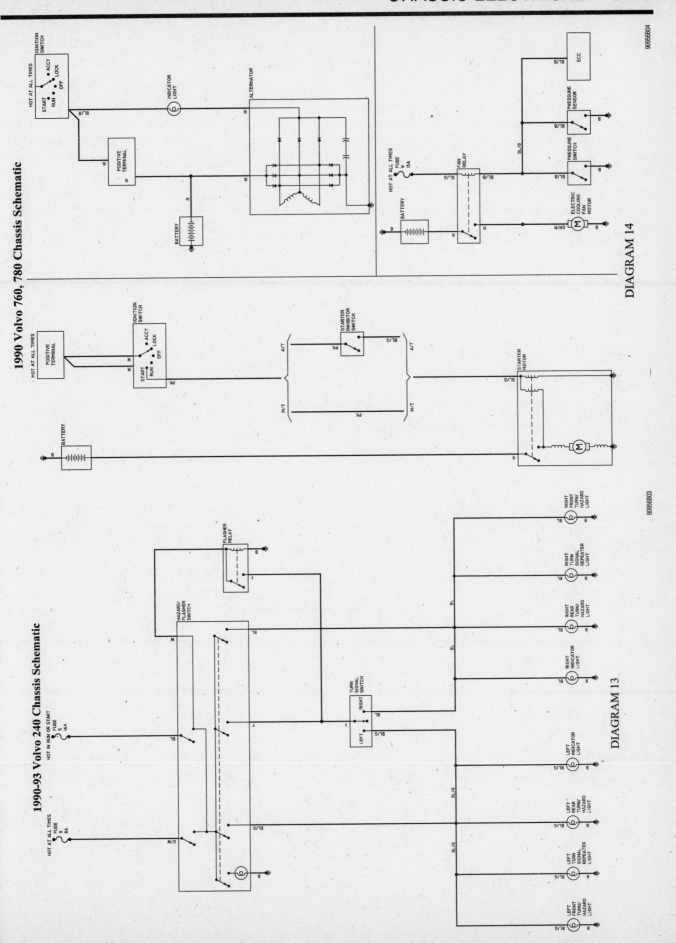

**1990 Volvo 760, 780 Chassis Schematic**

DIAGRAM 14

**1990 Volvo 760, 780 Chassis Schematic**

**1990-93 Volvo 240 Chassis Schematic**

DIAGRAM 13

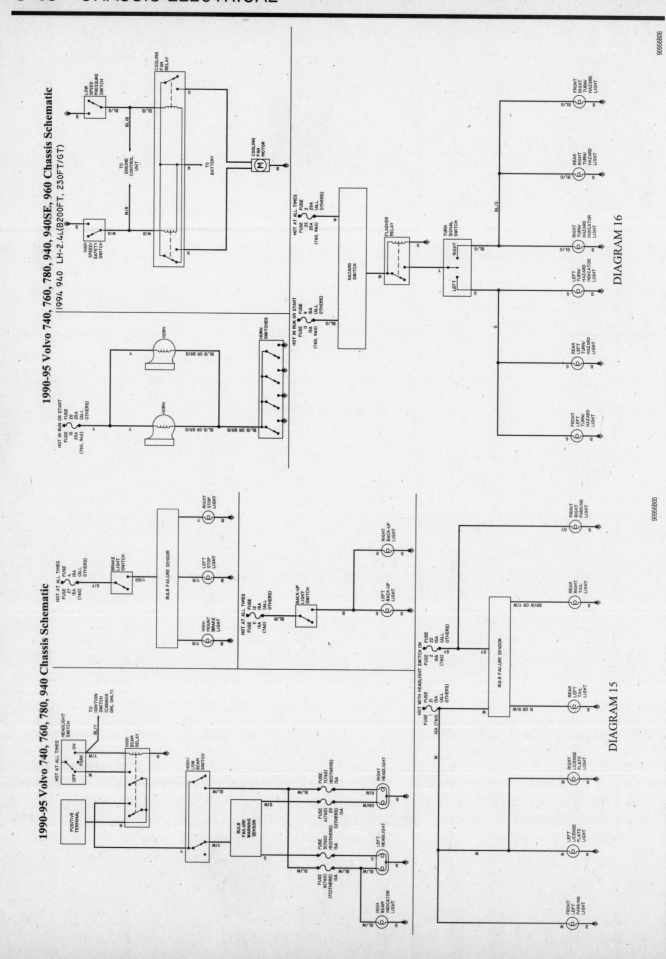

1990-95 Volvo 740, 760, 780, 940, 940SE, 960 Chassis Schematic
(1994 940 LH-2.4L(B200FT, 230FT/GT)

DIAGRAM 16

1990-95 Volvo 740, 760, 780, 940 Chassis Schematic

DIAGRAM 15

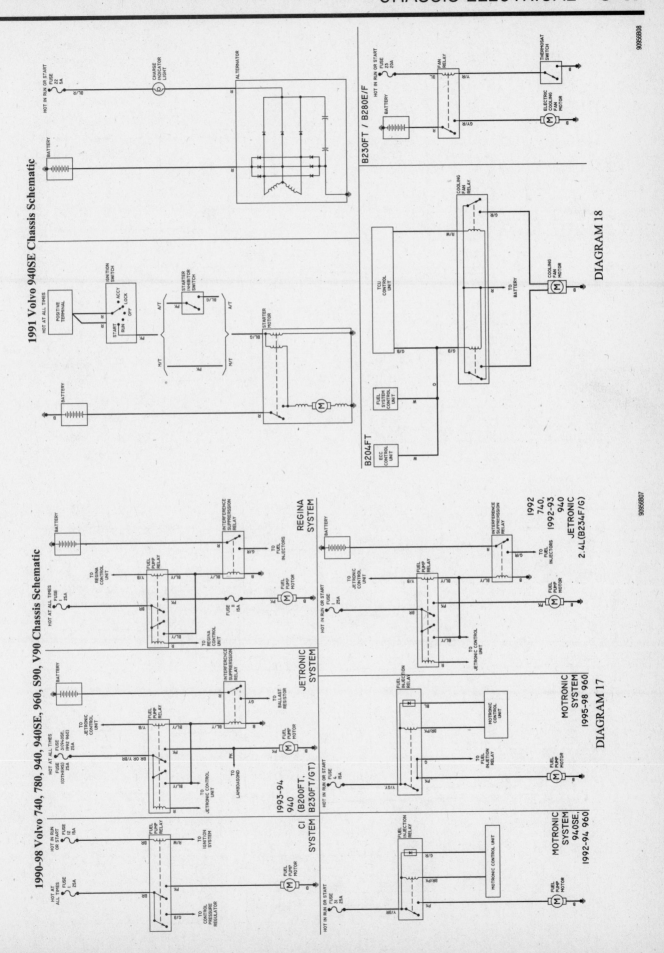

1991 Volvo 940SE Chassis Schematic

1990-98 Volvo 740, 780, 940, 940SE, 960, S90, V90 Chassis Schematic

DIAGRAM 18

DIAGRAM 17

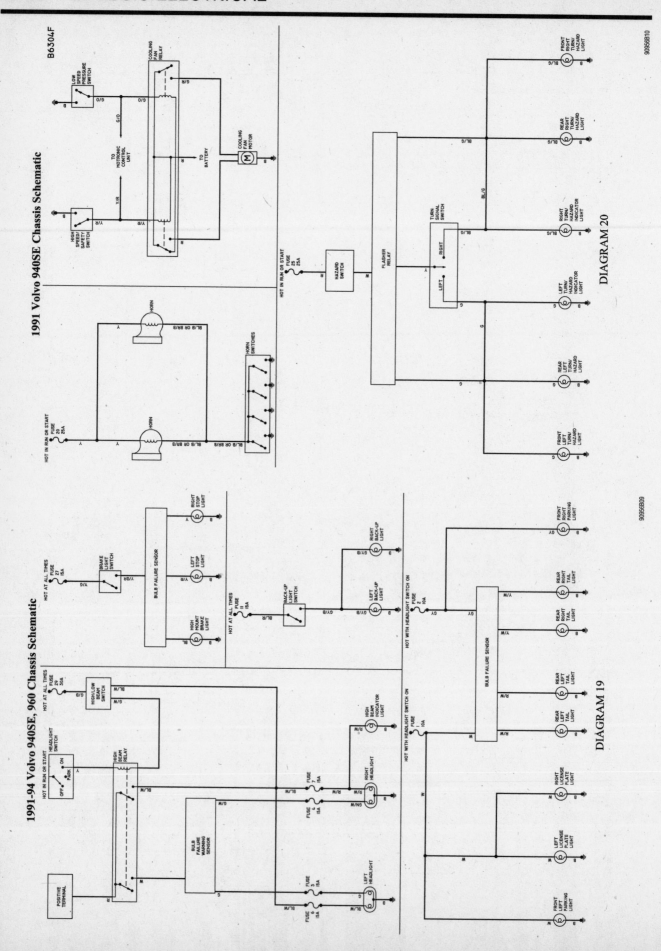

1991 Volvo 940SE Chassis Schematic

1991-94 Volvo 940SE, 960 Chassis Schematic

DIAGRAM 20

DIAGRAM 19

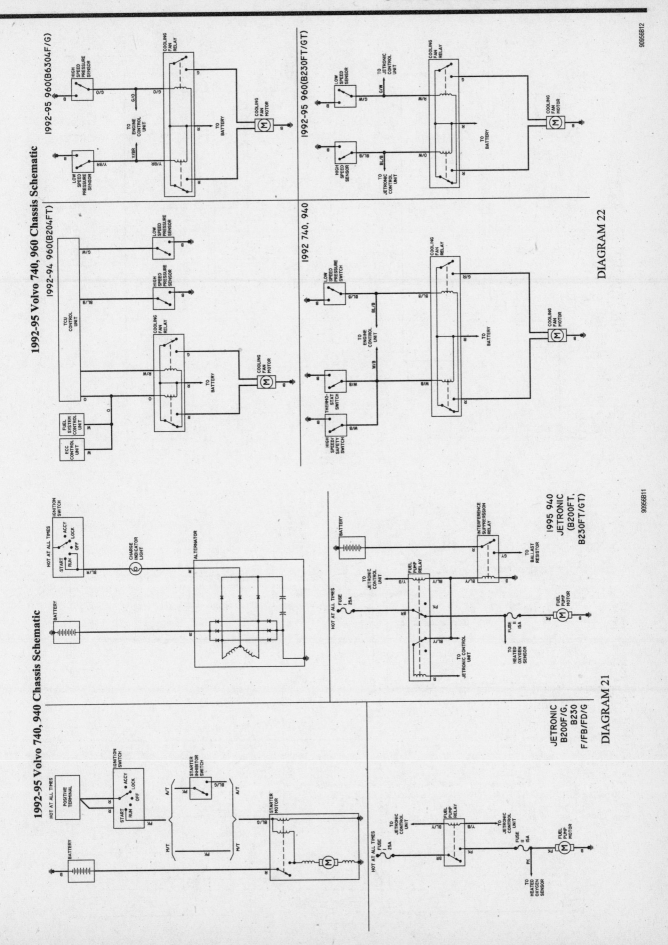

DIAGRAM 22

DIAGRAM 21

**1994 Volvo 940 Chassis Schematic**

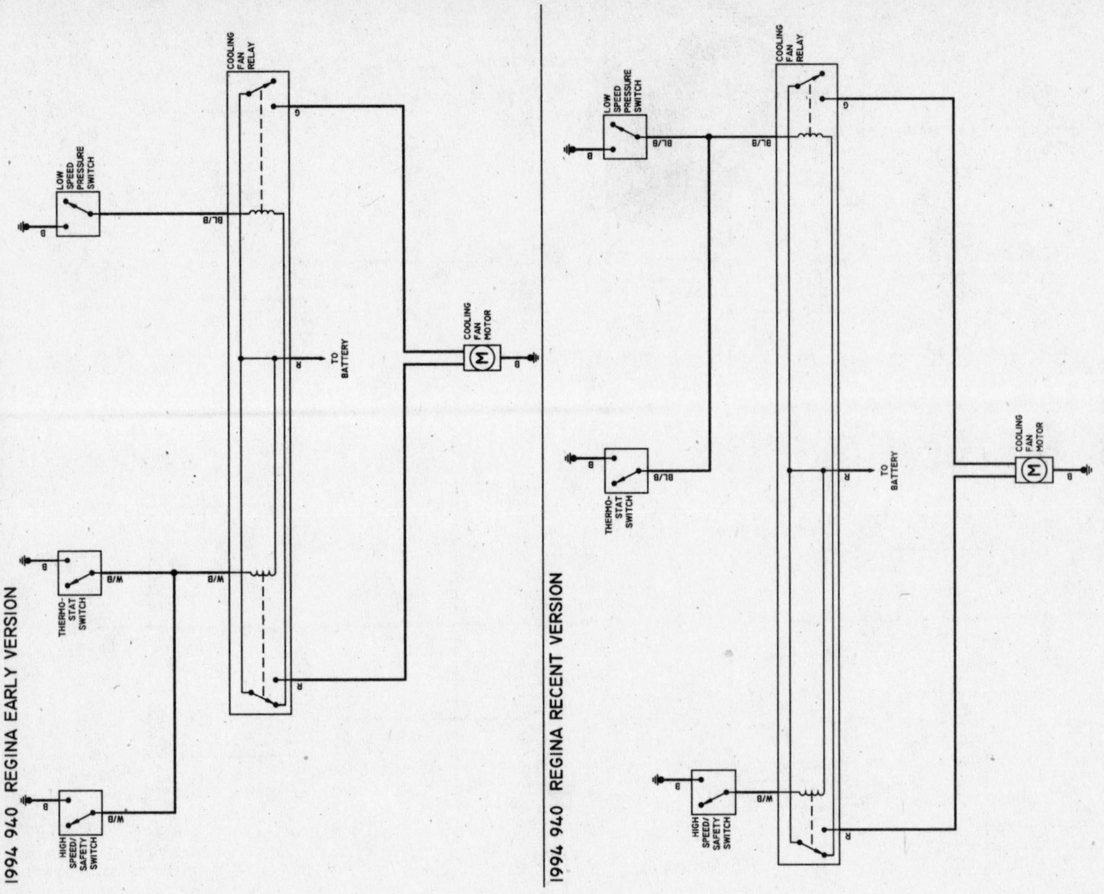

1994 940 REGINA EARLY VERSION

1994 940 REGINA RECENT VERSION

DIAGRAM 24

**1992-98 Volvo 960, S90, V90 Chassis Schematic**

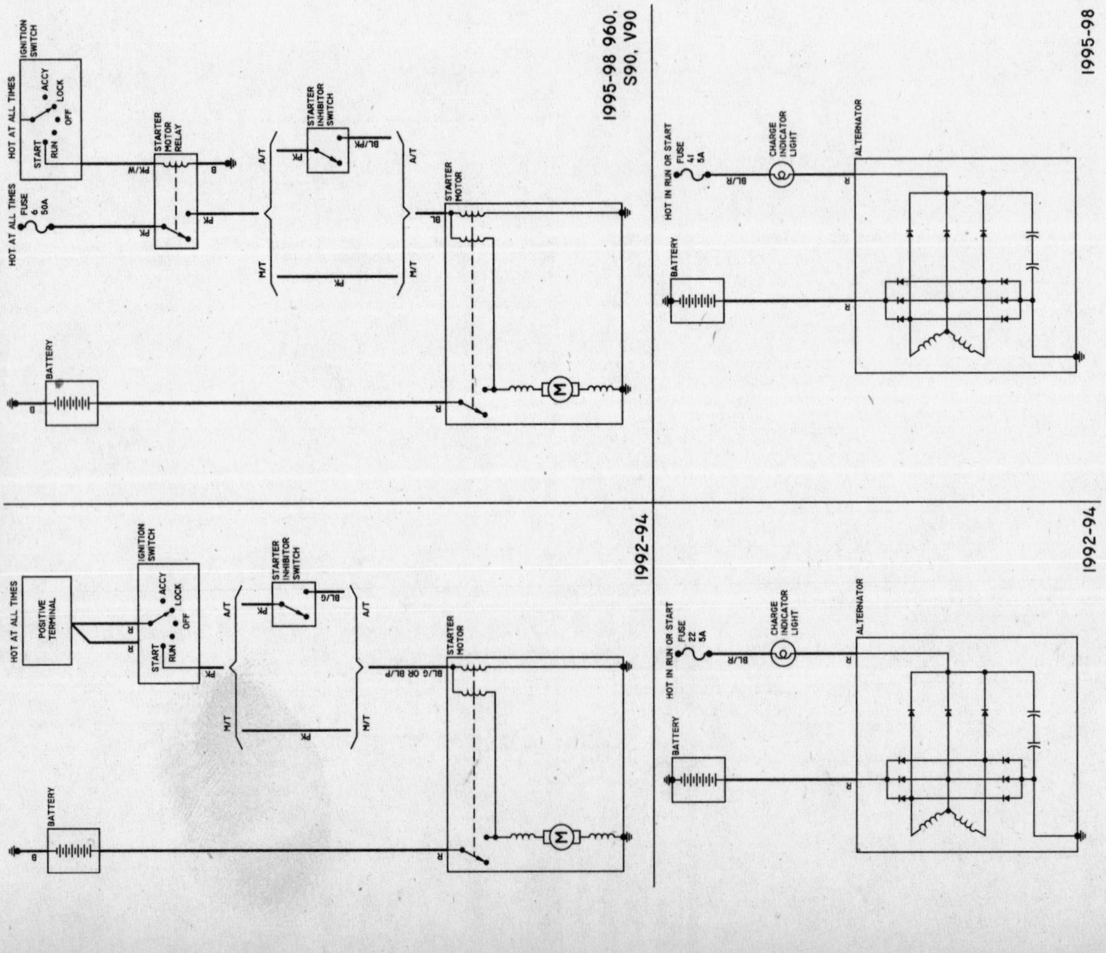

1995-98 960, S90, V90

1992-94

1995-98

1992-94

DIAGRAM 23

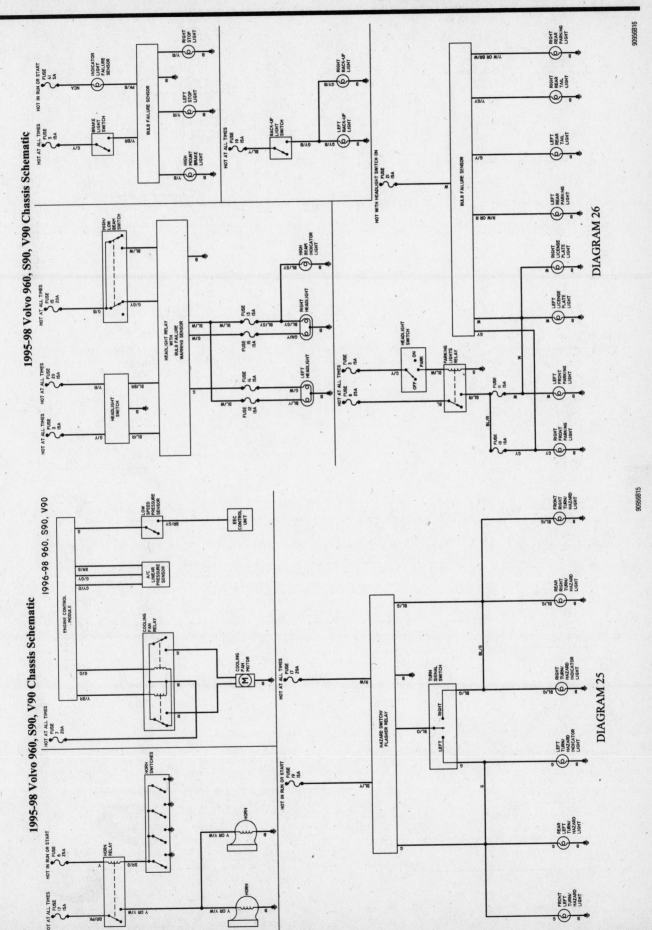

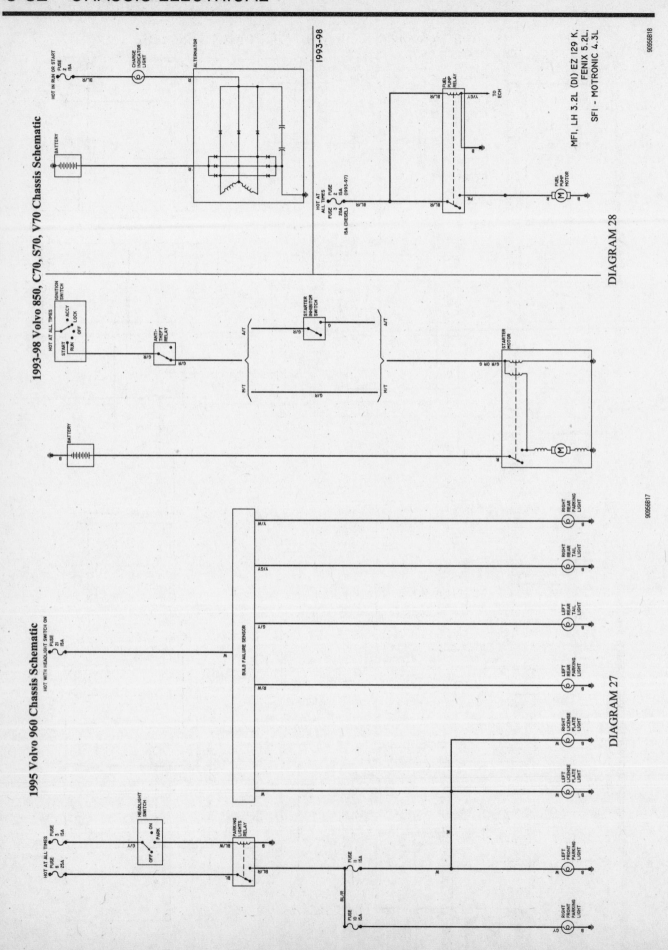

1993-98

MFI, LH 3.2L (DI) EZ 129 K,
FENIX 5.2L,
SFI - MOTRONIC 4.3L

DIAGRAM 28

90956B18

1993-98 Volvo 850, C70, S70, V70 Chassis Schematic

90956B17

1995 Volvo 960 Chassis Schematic

DIAGRAM 27

## 1993-98 Volvo 850, C70, S70, V70 Chassis Schematic

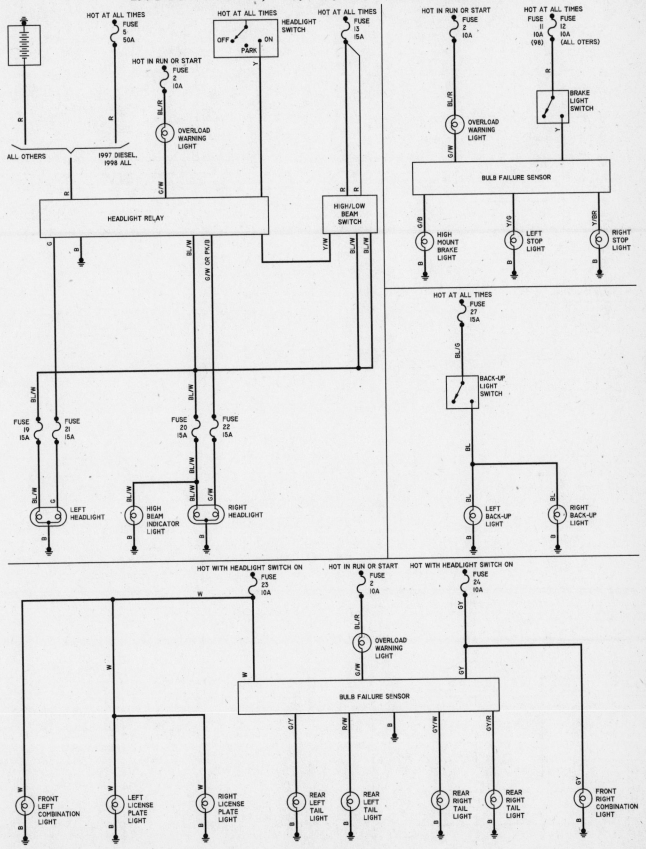

**DIAGRAM 29**

90956B19

## 1993-98 Volvo 850, C70, S70, V70 Chassis Schematic

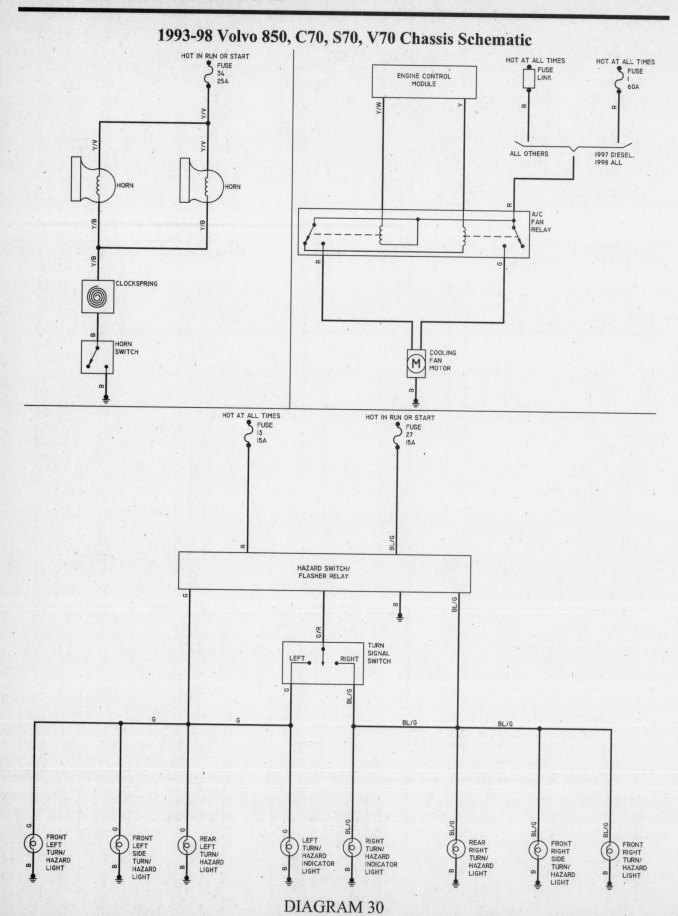

DIAGRAM 30

90956B20

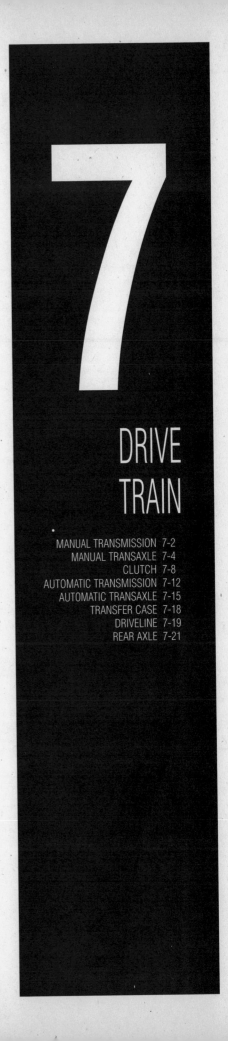

# 7

## DRIVE TRAIN

## MANUAL TRANSMISSION

### Understanding the Manual Transmission

Because of the way an internal combustion engine breathes, it can produce torque (or twisting force) only within a narrow speed range. Most overhead valve pushrod engines must turn at about 2500 rpm to produce their peak torque. Often by 4500 rpm, they are producing so little torque that continued increases in engine speed produce no power increases.

The torque peak on overhead camshaft engines is, generally, much higher, but much narrower.

The manual transmission and clutch are employed to vary the relationship between engine RPM and the speed of the wheels so that adequate power can be produced under all circumstances. The clutch allows engine torque to be applied to the transmission input shaft gradually, due to mechanical slippage. The vehicle can, consequently, be started smoothly from a full stop.

The transmission changes the ratio between the rotating speeds of the engine and the wheels by the use of gears. 4-speed or 5-speed transmissions are most common. The lower gears allow full engine power to be applied to the rear wheels during acceleration at low speeds.

The clutch driveplate is a thin disc, the center of which is splined to the transmission input shaft. Both sides of the disc are covered with a layer of material which is similar to brake lining and which is capable of allowing slippage without roughness or excessive noise.

The clutch cover is bolted to the engine flywheel and incorporates a diaphragm spring which provides the pressure to engage the clutch. The cover also houses the pressure plate. When the clutch pedal is released, the driven disc is sandwiched between the pressure plate and the smooth surface of the flywheel, thus forcing the disc to turn at the same speed as the engine crankshaft.

The transmission contains a mainshaft which passes all the way through the transmission, from the clutch to the driveshaft. This shaft is separated at one point, so that front and rear portions can turn at different speeds.

Power is transmitted by a countershaft in the lower gears and Reverse. The gears of the countershaft mesh with gears on the mainshaft, allowing power to be carried from one to the other. Countershaft gears are often integral with that shaft, while several of the mainshaft gears can either rotate independently of the shaft or be locked to it. Shifting from one gear to the next causes one of the gears to be freed from rotating with the shaft and locks another to it. Gears are locked and unlocked by internal dog clutches which slide between the center of the gear and the shaft. The forward gears usually employ synchronizers; friction members which smoothly bring gear and shaft to the same speed before the toothed dog clutches are engaged.

### Adjustments

Shift linkage adjustments are neither necessary nor possible on Volvo manual transmissions.

### Shift Handle

REMOVAL & INSTALLATION

1. Disconnect the negative battery cable.
2. Raise and safely support the vehicle on jackstands.
3. From under the vehicle:
   a. Loosen the setscrew and drive out the pin for the shifter rod.
   b. Disconnect the shift lever from the rod.
4. From inside the vehicle:
   a. Pull up the shift boot.
   b. Remove the fork for the Reverse gear detent.
   c. Remove the snapring and lift up the shifter.
   d. If overdrive-equipped, disconnect the engaging switch wire.
**To install:**
5. If equipped, connect the overdrive switch.
6. Install the shifter and install the snapring.
7. Install the fork for the Reverse gear detent.
8. Install the shift boot.
9. From under the vehicle:

   a. Connect the shift lever rod.
   b. Install the pin and setscrew.
10. Lower the vehicle.
11. Connect the negative battery cable.

### Back-up Light Switch

REMOVAL & INSTALLATION

▸ **See Figure 1**

1. Disconnect the negative battery cable.
2. Raise the vehicle and support it safely on jackstands.
3. Matchmark and remove the front driveshaft from the transmission or overdrive unit; lower the shaft out of the way.
4. Position and support the transmission with a jack or transmission hoist.
5. Loosen, but do not separate the exhaust joint at the right side of the transmission case.
6. Carefully remove the transmission crossmember from the body.
7. Lower the rear end of the transmission.
8. Disconnect the wiring from the switch. Thoroughly clean the area around the switch before removing it.
9. Remove the switch using a suitable socket (5250 or equivalent).
**To install:**
10. Install the switch into the transmission, and connect the wiring.

➡**After replacing the switch and connecting the wiring, check its function before reassembling everything.**

11. Raise the transmission back into position and install the crossmember.
12. Position and tighten the exhaust joint.
13. Reinstall the driveshaft.
14. Lower the vehicle.
15. Connect the negative battery cable.

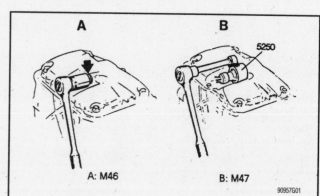

Fig. 1 Removing the back-up light switch on the M46 and M47 manual transmissions

### Extension Housing Seal

REMOVAL & INSTALLATION

➡**This procedure covers removal and installation of the extension housing seal with the transmission mounted in the vehicle.**

1. Disconnect the negative battery cable.
2. Raise and support the vehicle safely.
3. Matchmark the driveshaft with the coupling.
4. Disconnect the driveshaft. Use tool 5244 or equivalent for a round coupling flange.
5. Remove the coupling flange nut. Use spanner 5149 or equivalent to prevent the flange from rotating.

6. Remove the coupling flange, using a suitable puller (tool 2261 or equivalent).

7. Carefully pry the seal from the housing.

**To install:**

8. Clean the sealing areas thoroughly.

9. Install a new seal using a suitable drift (2412 for M46 or 5064 for M47 or their equivalent).

10. Press the coupling flange into place, using tool 1845 or equivalent.

11. Install the coupling flange nut. Tighten to 126 ft. lbs. (175 Nm) on the M46 or 65–80 ft. lbs. (90–110 Nm) on the M47.

12. Install the driveshaft.

13. Lower the vehicle.

14. Connect the negative battery cable.

## Manual Transmission Assembly

### REMOVAL & INSTALLATION

**240**

1. Disconnect the negative battery cable.

2. At the firewall, disconnect the back-up light connector.

3. Raise the front of the vehicle and install jackstands.

4. From under the vehicle:
   a. Loosen the setscrew and drive out the pin for the shifter rod.
   b. Disconnect the shift lever from the rod.

5. From inside the vehicle:
   a. Remove the shifter.

6. Disconnect the clutch cable and return spring at the fork.

7. Disconnect the exhaust pipe bracket(s) from the flywheel cover.

8. Remove the oil pan splash guard.

9. Using a floor jack and a block of wood, support the engine beneath the oil pan.

10. Remove the transmission support crossmember.

11. Disconnect the driveshaft.

12. Disconnect the speedometer cable.

13. If so equipped, disconnect the overdrive wire.

14. Remove the starter retaining bolts and pull the starter free of the flywheel housing. Leave the starter wiring connected and secure the starter out of the way.

### ✳ CAUTION

**The transmission is heavy. Support its weight with a second jack or hoist before removing. Do not allow the transmission to hang partially removed on the shaft.**

15. Support the transmission using another floor jack.

16. Remove the flywheel bell housing-to-engine bolts and remove the transmission by pulling it straight back.

**To install:**

17. Prior to installation, inspect the condition of the clutch and throwout bearing. Replace the bearing if it is scored or has been noisy in operation.

18. After reinstalling the transmission, tighten the mounting bolts to 30 ft. lbs. (41 Nm).

19. Secure the starter to the bell housing.

20. Fill the transmission with fluid to the proper level.

21. Connect the driveshaft, the speedometer cable and if necessary, the overdrive wiring.

22. Reinstall the transmission cross member. When secure, remove the jack from beneath the engine.

23. Replace the splash guard and attach the exhaust bracket to the bell housing.

24. Reconnect the clutch cable and return spring to the fork.

25. Install the shifter.

26. Under the vehicle: Connect the shifter rod to the shift lever. Don't forget to tighten the setscrew.

27. Connect the back-up light wiring.

28. Lower the vehicle.

29. Connect the negative battery cable.

**700 Series Vehicles**

1. If possible, support the engine with a hoist or support apparatus such as Volvo tool 5006 or equivalent. The purpose of supporting the rear of the engine is to prevent damage to the fan, radiator or front engine mounts by limiting the downward travel of the engine when the transmission crossmember is removed. If no lifting apparatus is available, place a jack with a protective wooden block beneath the engine oil pan. Do not place the jack under the flywheel (clutch) housing.

2. Disconnect the battery ground cable.

3. Remove the ashtray and holder assembly.

4. Remove the trim box around the gear shift lever.

5. Disconnect the shift lever cover from the floor.

6. Remove the snapring at the base of the shift lever.

7. Raise the vehicle and safely support it.

8. From underneath the vehicle, disconnect the gear shift rod at the gear shift lever.

9. Remove the lock screw, and press out the pivot pin.

10. Push up on the shift lever, and pull it up and out of the vehicle.

11. Matchmark the driveshaft and transmission flanges for later assembly.

12. Disconnect the driveshaft from the transmission.

13. Separate the exhaust pipe at the joint under the vehicle.

14. Detach the bracket from the front end of the exhaust pipe (near the bend).

15. Unbolt the transmission crossmember; at the same time, detach it from the rear support (rubber bushing).

16. Remove the rear support from the transmission.

17. Lower the transmission, as required.

18. Tag and disconnect the electrical connectors from the overdrive, back-up light connector and the solenoid.

19. Cut the plastic clamp at the gear shift assembly from the wiring harness.

20. Remove the starter motor retaining bolts.

21. Remove the cover plate under the bell housing and the cover plate from the other starter motor opening, as required.

22. Remove the slave cylinder from the bell housing and upper bolts holding the bell housing.

### ✳ CAUTION

**The transmission is heavy. Support its weight with a second jack or hoist before removing. Do not allow the transmission to hang partially removed on the shaft.**

23. Place a transmission jack or a hydraulic floor jack underneath the transmission so that the transmission is resting on the jack pad. If possible, have another person steadying and guiding the transmission on the jack as it is lowered.

24. Remove the lower bolts holding the bell housing, and lower the transmission a few inches as you roll it back so the input shaft will clear. Stop the jack and make sure all wires and linkage are disconnected, then lower the transmission the rest of the way.

**To install:**

25. When installing the transmission, make sure the release bearing is correctly positioned in the shift fork, and that the input shaft is aligned in the clutch disc.

26. Install the upper bolts in the bell housing.

27. Raise the end of the transmission and attach the gear lever.

28. Attach the slave cylinder or clutch cable to its mounts.

29. Reinstall the starter motor.

30. Remount the gear lever to the transmission. Secure the connectors for the back-up lights, the solenoid and (on M46) the overdrive unit.

31. Replace the transmission crossmember.

32. Set the engine back to its normal position.

33. Tighten the exhaust pipe joint, attach its bracket and attach the gear shift rod to the gear shift lever.

34. Install and tighten the driveshaft.

35. Refill the transmission with the proper amount of fluid.

36. Connect the gear shift rod to the gear shift lever.

37. Inside the vehicle, mount and secure the shifter assembly.

38. Double check all installation items, paying particular attention to loose hoses or hanging wires, untightened nuts, poor routing of hoses and wires (too tight or rubbing) and tools left in the work area.

39. Lower the vehicle.

40. Install the ashtray, interior trim and shifter boot.

41. Connect the negative battery cable.

## MANUAL TRANSAXLE

### Understanding the Manual Transaxle

Because of the way an internal combustion engine breathes, it can produce torque, or twisting force, only within a narrow speed range. Most modern, overhead valve pushrod engines must turn at about 2500 rpm to produce their peak torque. By 4500 rpm they are producing so little torque that continued increases in engine speed produce no power increases. The torque peak on overhead camshaft engines is generally much higher, but much narrower.

The manual transaxle and clutch are employed to vary the relationship between engine speed and the speed of the wheels so that adequate engine power can be produced under all circumstances. The clutch allows engine torque to be applied to the transaxle input shaft gradually, due to mechanical slippage. Consequently, the vehicle may be started smoothly from a full stop. The transaxle changes the ratio between the rotating speeds of the engine and the wheels by the use of gears. The gear ratios allow full engine power to be applied to the wheels during acceleration at low speeds and at highway/passing speeds.

In a front wheel drive transaxle, power is usually transmitted from the input shaft to a mainshaft or output shaft located slightly beneath and to the side of the input shaft. The gears of the mainshaft mesh with gears on the input shaft, allowing power to be carried from one to the other. All forward gears are in constant mesh and are free from rotating with the shaft unless the synchronizer and clutch is engaged. Shifting from one gear to the next causes one of the gears to be freed from rotating with the shaft and locks another to it. Gears are locked and unlocked by internal dog clutches which slide between the center of the gear and the shaft. The forward gears employ synchronizers; friction members which smoothly bring gear and shaft to the same speed before the toothed dog clutches are engaged.

### Back-up Light Switch

#### REMOVAL & INSTALLATION

1. Disconnect the negative battery cable.
2. Raise and safely support the vehicle.
3. Unplug the back-up light switch connector.
4. Unscrew the back-up light switch connector from the transaxle and remove it.

**To install:**
5. Thread the switch into the transaxle and tighten.
6. Plug the electrical connector in.
7. Lower the vehicle.
8. Connect the negative battery cable.

### Manual Transaxle Assembly

#### REMOVAL & INSTALLATION

**850**

1. With all four wheels on the ground, loosen the front axle shaft locknuts.
2. Place the transaxle in **N** and set the parking brake.
3. Disconnect and remove the battery, air cleaner air intake ducts.
4. Remove the battery tray.
5. On turbocharged models, disconnect the timing valve from air cleaner and the turbocharger air duct clamp and hose.
6. Disconnect the gear selector cables from the brackets and lever.
7. Remove the selector link plate after tapping out the lock pin.
8. Detach the back-up light switch connector.
9. On turbocharged models remove the control pulley cover.
10. Disconnect the turbocharger inlet pipe and tie it back out of the way.
11. Disconnect the upper coolant hose to the engine oil cooler.
12. Disconnect the clutch slave cylinder and remove the clip.
13. Remove the ground strap from the transaxle.
14. Loosen the rear engine mount and splash guard nut.
15. Remove the bolts connecting the engine, transaxle and starter.

16. Disconnect the transaxle ground strap.
17. Disconnect the ground strap from the firewall.
18. Remove the torque arm bolt.
19. Secure the engine from above with an engine support that rests on the inner edges of the engine compartment.
20. Lift the engine up slightly to take weight off the engine mounts.
21. Raise and safely support the vehicle and remove the wheels.
22. Disconnect the ABS sensor from the left side axle shaft, but do not unfasten the connector.
23. Drain the gear oil from the transaxle.
24. Disconnect all brackets for the front brake lines and ABS wiring for both sides of the vehicle.
25. Remove the plastic inner fender liners on both sides.
26. Remove and discard the axle shaft locknuts.
27. Separate the ball joint from control arm, being careful not to damage the boots.
28. Disconnect the sway bar links on both sides.
29. Remove the mounting screws holding the cable to the front of the subframe and disconnect the cable from the subframe.
30. Disconnect the carbon canister hoses.
31. Disconnect the exhaust pipe clamp behind the catalytic converter.
32. Remove the left and right halfshafts.

➡ **Be careful not to damage the transaxle seal.**

33. Install seal plugs in the transaxle.
34. Loosen the two right side subframe-to-body bolts approximately ½ in. (15mm).
35. Remove the subframe-to-body bolts on the left side.

➡ **Make sure the steering gear bolts come out of the subframe and the control arm is free of the axle shaft boot on the right side.**

36. Remove the jack and let the frame hang down from the right side bolts.
37. Tie the left side of the steering gear to the left side frame rail for support.
38. Remove the steering gear engine mount bolt and nut at the top of the mount and remove.

➡ **Make sure the steering gear is properly secured so the lower steering shaft does not slide out of the steering column.**

39. Disconnect the oxygen sensor wiring clamps from the cover, as well as the connector and wiring to the vehicle speed sensor.
40. Remove the cover at the back of the engine and the mount from the transaxle.
41. Lower the engine and transaxle with the lifting hook.

#### ✳✳ WARNING

If the engine is lowered too far, the exhaust pipe will be crushed against the steering rack. Be careful not to pinch any wiring or hoses and be sure that the engine dipstick tube is free of the fan.

42. Remove the seven remaining transaxle-to-engine bolts. Pull the gearbox away from the engine. Lower the jack and move the transaxle away.

**To install:**
43. Secure the throwout bearing fork to the transaxle.
44. Make sure the mating surfaces on the transaxle and engine are clean and that the dowel pins are in place on the engine.

➡ **Do not grease the primary shaft or throwout bearing sleeve. Make sure there are no breaks in the clutch plate.**

45. Lift the transaxle into place and mate to the engine.
46. Install the seven bolts securing the engine and transaxle and tighten them a little at a time to draw the transaxle into place. Tighten the bolts to 37 ft. lbs. (50 Nm) and remove the transaxle jack.
47. Lift the engine and transaxle up until the distance between the engine support beam and spark plug cover is 0.20 in. (5mm).
48. Install the rear transaxle mount and bolts.
49. Tighten the rear two bolts to 37 ft. lbs. (50 Nm), then remove the front bolt.
50. Install the cover.

51. Install the engine mount by fitting its guide pin into the cover.
52. Install a new nut and hand-tighten.
53. Install the steering rack engine mount bolt, but do not tighten.
54. Remove the support for the steering gear.
55. Reconnect the oxygen sensor wiring and clamps on the cover.
56. Install the vehicle speed sensor connector and wiring and connect the transaxle ground strap.
57. Install the subframe using new 4 x M14 bolts and apply grease to the threads.
58. Starting on the left side, lift the frame with a jack.
59. Mount the support brackets on both sides.
60. Tighten the frame bolts to 78 ft. lbs. (105 Nm), then tighten an additional 120°.
61. Tighten the bracket bolts to 37 ft. lbs. (50 Nm).
62. Remove the jack and repeat the procedure for the right side.
63. Remove the engine support tool and lifting eyelet from engine.
64. Tighten the engine mount nut to 37 ft. lbs. (50 Nm).
65. Install five new nuts on the steering rack and tighten them to 37 ft. lbs. (50 Nm).
66. Install the front engine mount nut, then tighten the front and rear bolts to 37 ft. lbs. (50 Nm).
67. Install the torque rod mount on the transaxle using new bolts. On earlier vehicles equipped with M18 bolts, tighten the bolts to 13 ft. lbs. (18 Nm) and then an additional 90 degrees. On later models with M10 bolts, tighten to 26 ft. lbs. (35 Nm) and then an additional 40 degrees.
68. Install the oil line bracket bolts and tighten to 19 ft. lbs. (25 Nm).
69. Tighten the exhaust pipe clamp while rocking the pipe back and forth to seat it properly.
70. Install the right and left halfshafts.

➡**Make sure the transaxle axle seal and axle boot are not damaged.**

71. Connect the control arms to the ball joints using new nuts.
72. Connect the brake line and ABS cable bracket on both sides.
73. Install the ABS sensor on the axle shaft and clean if needed.
74. Tighten the sensor to 7.4 ft. lbs. (10 Nm).
75. Attach the cable pipe and carbon canister to the subframe.
76. Install the front splash guard.
77. Install the wheels.
78. Install the starter and tighten the bolts to 30 ft. lbs. (40 Nm).
79. Connect the cable conduit and oxygen sensor connectors.
80. Install the dipstick tube with a new O-ring and tighten the bolt to 19 ft. lbs. (25 Nm).
81. Connect the slave cylinder and clips.
82. Fasten the back-up light switch connector.
83. Position the shift lever plate and secure with the lock pin.
84. Install the cables and lubricate the levers, cables, washers and clips with grease.
85. Connect ground strip to the firewall.
86. Install a new bolt and nut for the extension arm and torque rod.
87. Connect the oil cooler hose to the cooler, if equipped.
88. Lower the vehicle.
89. Install the throttle body and cover over control pulley.

90. Connect the intake manifold to the turbocharger.
91. Install the coolant expansion tank, battery tray, air cleaner and connectors.
92. Connect the control valve to air cleaner on turbocharged models.
93. Install the battery and attach leads.
94. Tighten the axle shaft nut to 89 ft. lbs. (120 Nm), then tighten an additional 60 degrees. Lock the axle shaft nut by notching its flange into the axle shaft groove.
95. Fill the transaxle with the specified amount of oil.
96. Reinstall the plug.
97. Check the function of the clutch before driving.

## Halfshafts

### REMOVAL & INSTALLATION

#### 850, C70, S70 and V70 Models

▶ **See Figures 2 thru 8**

1. With the vehicle sitting on all four wheels, loosen the axle shaft nut.
2. Raise and safely support the vehicle.
3. Remove the wheels.
4. Disconnect the ABS sensor from the halfshaft, but do not disconnect the harness.
5. Disconnect all brackets for brake lines and ABS wiring on both sides and let them hang.
6. Remove the axle nut.
7. Push the end of the halfshaft from hub using a soft drift and a mallet.
8. Disconnect the sway bar from the link.
9. Remove all splash guards.
10. Separate the ball joint from control arm, being careful not to damage the boots.
11. For the right side halfshaft, remove the bearing cap and pull the shaft out of the transmission while holding the strut out of the way.
12. Install a plug in the transmission.

➡**Be careful not to damage the transmission seal.**

13. For left side, remove the halfshaft by carefully prying between the transmission and the halfshaft.
14. Hold the strut assembly out of the way.
15. Install a plug in the transmission.
**To install:**
16. Install the right halfshaft and tighten the bearing cap to 19 ft. lbs. (25 Nm).
17. Install the splashguard.

➡**Make sure that the transmission axle seal and axle boot are not damaged.**

18. Clean the ABS wheel if necessary.
19. Apply metal adhesive to the halfshaft splines. Carefully press shaft in so

Fig. 2 Loosening the axle nut will be tough; it is sometimes easier to do with the wheels on the ground

Fig. 3 After loosening, remove the axle nut

Fig. 4 Remove the nut retaining the lower ball joint to the spindle

Fig. 5 After the lower control arm is separated from the spindle, tap the halfshaft out of the hub

Fig. 6 The halfshaft will need to be removed from the transaxle with a prybar or suitable tool

Fig. 7 After the halfshaft is removed, inspect the axle seal and . . .

Fig. 8 . . . the halfshaft retaining ring on the spline shaft

that the lock ring engages with the differential gear. Check it by carefully pulling on the shaft joint housing.

20. Install the axle nut and hand-tighten.
21. Connect the ball joints using new nuts.
22. Install the sway bar link using new nuts.
23. Connect the brake line and ABS cable bracket on both sides.
24. Install the ABS sensor on the halfshaft and clean it with a soft brush.
25. Install the wheels.
26. With all four wheels on the ground, tighten the axle nut to 89 ft. lbs. (120 Nm) plus an additional 60°. Lock the nut by staking its flange into the driveshaft groove.

## CV-JOINTS OVERHAUL

▶ **See Figures 9 thru 22**

These vehicles use several different types of joints. Engine size, transaxle type, whether the joint is an inboard or outboard joint, even which side of the vehicle is being serviced could make a difference in joint type. Be sure to properly identify the joint before attempting joint or boot replacement. Look for identification numbers at the large end of the boots and/or on the end of the metal retainer bands.

The 3 types of joints used are the Birfield Joint, (B.J.), the Tripod Joint (T.J.) and the Double Offset Joint (D.O.J.).

➡**Do not disassemble a Birfield joint. Service with a new joint or clean and repack using a new boot kit.**

The distance between the large and small boot bands is important and should be checked prior to and after boot service. This is so the boot will not be installed either too loose or too tight, which could cause early wear and crackling, allowing the grease to get out and water and dirt in, leading to early joint failure.

➡**The driveshaft joints use special grease; do not add any grease other than that supplied with the kit.**

### Double Offset Joint

The Double Offset Joint (D.O.J.) is bigger than other joints and, in these applications, is normally used as an inboard joint.

1. Remove the halfshaft from the vehicle.
2. Side cutter pliers can be used to cut the metal retaining bands. Remove the boot from the joint outer race.
3. Locate and remove the large circlip at the base of the joint. Remove the outer race (the body of the joint).
4. Remove the small snapring and take off the inner race, cage and balls as an assembly. Clean the inner race, cage and balls without disassembling.
5. If the boot is to be reused, wipe the grease from the splines and wrap the splines in vinyl tape before sliding the boot from the shaft.
6. Remove the inner (D.O.J.) boot from the shaft. If the outer (B.J.) boot is to be replaced, remove the boot retainer rings and slide the boot down and off of the shaft at this time.

**To install:**

7. Be sure to tape the shaft splines before installing the boots. Fill the inside of the boot with the specified grease. Often the grease supplied in the replacement parts kit is meant to be divided in half, with half being used to lubricate the joint and half being used inside the boot.
8. Install the cage onto the halfshaft so the small diameter side of the cage is installed first. With a brass drift pin, tap lightly and evenly around the inner race to install the race until it comes into contact with the rib of the shaft. Apply the specified grease to the inner race and cage and fit them together. Insert the balls into the cage.
9. Install the outer race (the body of the joint) after filling with the specified grease. The outer race should be filled with this grease.
10. Tighten the boot bands securely. Make sure the distance between the boot bands is correct.
11. Install the halfshaft to the vehicle.

### Except Double Offset Joint

1. Disconnect the negative battery cable. Remove the halfshaft.
2. Use side cutter pliers to remove the metal retaining bands from the boot(s) that will be removed. Slide the boot from the T.J. case.
3. Remove the snapring and the tripod joint spider assembly from the halfshaft. Do not disassemble the spider and use care in handling.
4. If the boot is be reused, wrap vinyl tape around the spline part of the shaft so the boot(s) will not be damaged when removed. Remove the dynamic damper, if used, and the boots from the shaft.

**To install:**

5. Double check that the correct replacement parts are being installed. Wrap vinyl tape around the splines to protect the boot and install the boots and damper, if used, in the correct order.
6. Install the joint spider assembly to the shaft and install the snapring.
7. Fill the inside of the boot with the specified grease. Often the grease supplied in the replacement parts kit is meant to be divided in half, with half being used to lubricate the joint and half being used inside the boot. Keep grease off the rubber part of the dynamic damper (if used).
8. Secure the boot bands with the halfshaft in a horizontal position. Make sure distance between boot bands is correct.
9. Install the halfshaft to the vehicle and reconnect the negative battery cable.

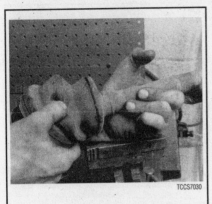

TCCS7030

**Fig. 9 Check the CV-boot for wear**

TCCS7031

**Fig. 10 Removing the outer band from the CV-boot**

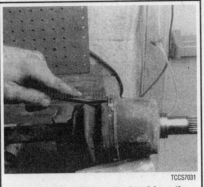

TCCS7032

**Fig. 11 Removing the inner band from the CV-boot**

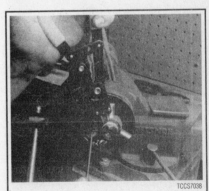

TCCS7033

**Fig. 12 Removing the CV-boot from the joint housing**

TCCS7034

**Fig. 13 Clean the CV-joint housing prior to removing boot**

TCCS7035

**Fig. 14 Removing the CV-joint housing assembly**

TCCS7036

**Fig. 15 Removing the CV-joint**

TCCS7037

**Fig. 16 Inspecting the CV-joint housing**

TCCS7038

**Fig. 17 Removing the CV-joint outer snapring**

TCCS7039

**Fig. 18 Checking the CV-joint snapring for wear**

TCCS7040

**Fig. 19 CV-joint snapring (typical)**

TCCS7041

**Fig. 20 Removing the CV-joint assembly**

Fig. 21 Removing the CV-joint inner snapring

Fig. 22 Installing the CV-joint assembly (typical)

## CLUTCH

### Understanding the Clutch

> ✳✳ **CAUTION**
>
> The clutch driven disc may contain asbestos, which has been determined to be a cancer causing agent. Never clean clutch surfaces with compressed air! Avoid inhaling any dust from any clutch surface! When cleaning clutch surfaces, use a commercially available brake cleaning fluid.

The purpose of the clutch is to disconnect and connect engine power at the transaxle. A vehicle at rest requires a lot of engine torque to get all that weight moving. An internal combustion engine does not develop a high starting torque (unlike steam engines) so it must be allowed to operate without any load until it builds up enough torque to move the vehicle. Torque increases with engine rpm. The clutch allows the engine to build up torque by physically disconnecting the engine from the transaxle, relieving the engine of any load or resistance.

The transfer of engine power to the transaxle (the load) must be smooth and gradual; if it weren't, drive line components would wear out or break quickly. This gradual power transfer is made possible by gradually releasing the clutch pedal. The clutch disc and pressure plate are the connecting link between the engine and transaxle. When the clutch pedal is released, the disc and plate contact each other (the clutch is engaged) physically joining the engine and transaxle. When the pedal is pushed inward, the disc and plate separate (the clutch is disengaged) disconnecting the engine from the transaxle.

Most clutches utilize a single plate, dry friction disc with a diaphragm-style spring pressure plate. The clutch disc has a splined hub which attaches the disc to the input shaft. The disc has friction material where it contacts the flywheel and pressure plate. Torsion springs on the disc help absorb engine torque pulses. The pressure plate applies pressure to the clutch disc, holding it tight against the surface of the flywheel. The clutch operating mechanism consists of a release bearing, fork and cylinder assembly.

The release fork and actuating linkage transfer pedal motion to the release bearing. In the engaged position (pedal released) the diaphragm spring holds the pressure plate against the clutch disc, so engine torque is transmitted to the input shaft. When the clutch pedal is depressed, the release bearing pushes the diaphragm spring center toward the flywheel. The diaphragm spring pivots the fulcrum, relieving the load on the pressure plate. Steel spring straps riveted to the clutch cover lift the pressure plate from the clutch disc, disengaging the engine drive from the transaxle and enabling the gears to be changed.

The clutch is operating properly if:
1. It will stall the engine when released with the vehicle held stationary.
2. The shift lever can be moved freely between 1st and Reverse gears when the vehicle is stationary and the clutch disengaged.

### Driven Disc and Pressure Plate

REMOVAL & INSTALLATION

▶ See Figures 23 thru 38

#### Rear Drive Models

1. Remove the transmission.
2. Scribe alignment marks on the clutch and flywheel.
3. Slowly loosen the bolts holding the clutch to the flywheel in a diagonal pattern.
4. Remove the bolts and lift off the clutch and pressure plate.
5. Inspect the pressure plate for heat damage, cracks, scoring or any other damage.
6. Place a ruler diagonally over the pressure plate friction surface and measure the distance between the straightedge of the ruler and the inner diameter of the pressure plate. This measurement must not be greater than 0.008 inch (0.2mm). In addition, there must be no clearance between the straightedge and the outer diameter of the pressure plate. This check should be made at several points.

**To install:**

7. Clean the pressure plate and flywheel with solvent to remove any traces of oil and wipe them clean with a cloth.
8. Position the clutch assembly with the longest side of the hub facing away from the engine. Fit it to the flywheel and align the bolt holes.
9. Insert centering tool 5111 or equivalent or an input shaft from an old transmission of the same type, through the clutch assembly and flywheel. This centers the assembly and pilot bearing.
10. Install the clutch retaining bolts and tighten them in a diagonal pattern, a few turns at a time. After all the bolts are tightened, remove the centering tool.
11. Install the transmission.

#### Front Drive Models

1. Remove the transaxle.
2. Lock the flywheel in position.
3. Remove the six bolts retaining the pressure plate and disc, loosen them in rotation.
4. Remove the pressure plate and disc.
5. Remove the throwout bearing from the sleeve and fork.
6. Remove the fork and dust cap from the transaxle.
7. Clean and check the throwout bearing, It should rotate freely and quietly.
8. Clean and check the fork for cracks and wear and that the dust cap is intact.
9. Check the pressure plate carefully for signs of overheating, cracks, scor-

ing or other damage to the friction surface. Make sure that the diaphragm spring is not split or damaged. If any part of the pressure plate is damaged, it must be replaced.

10. Check the pressure plate for warpage by laying a straightedge across the contact surface and checking the distance with a feeler gauge. The maximum width is 0.008 in. (0.2mm).

➡**Warpage is permitted in one direction only.**

11. Check the flywheel for cracks and heavy scoring. If it is damaged it must be replaced.
12. Check the clutch disc for oil or dirt and clean if necessary.

**To install:**

13. Install the throwout bearing fork, and lubricate the ball joint with grease.
14. Install the throwout bearing and dust cap.
15. Secure the fork to the transaxle, so that it cannot be moved during installation.
16. Install the clutch disc and pressure plate using centering drift 999 5487 or equivalent clutch alignment tool.
17. Install the clutch bolts, tightening them in rotation so that the clutch slides over the locating pins and lies evenly against the flywheel. Then tighten the bolts to 18 ft. lbs. (25 Nm). Remove the centering drift.

➡**Do not apply any grease to the splines on the transaxle input shaft.**

18. Install the transaxle and check the clutch operation.

## CLUTCH INSPECTION

Check the pressure plate for heat damage, cracks, scoring, or other damage to the friction surface. Check the curvature of the pressure plate with a steel ruler.

Place the ruler diagonally over the pressure plate friction surface and measure the distance between the straight edge of the ruler and the inner diameter of the pressure plate. This measurement must not be greater than 0.008 inch (0.2mm). In addition, there must be no clearance between the straight edge of the ruler and the outer diameter of the pressure plate. This check should be made at several points. Additionally, inspect the tips of the diaphragm springs (fingers) for any sign of wear. Replace the clutch as a unit (disc, pressure plate and throwout bearing) if any fault is found.

Check the throwout bearing by rotating it several times while applying finger pressure, so that the ball bearings roll against the inside of the races. If the bearing does not turn easily or if it binds at any point, replace it as a unit. Also make sure that the bearing slides easily on the guide sleeve from the transmission.

Inspect the clutch disc for signs of slippage (burns) or oil contamination. Make sure the rivets are not loose and that the clutch contact surfaces are well above the rivet heads. The thickness of the disc above the rivet heads is the "remaining life" of the disc; always replace the disc if in doubt.

When reassembling, apply grease to the splines and end shaft, the throwout bearing and the pivot ball and seat of the clutch fork.

## Clutch Cable

### REMOVAL & INSTALLATION

This procedure does not apply to hydraulic clutches.

1. Raise and support the vehicle safely.
2. Disconnect the clutch cable from the clutch fork. Some vehicles are equipped with a release bearing that rotates. These vehicles will have a clutch return spring at the pedal assembly.
3. Disconnect the cable at the pedal assembly.
4. Remove the cable. On some early vehicles, the clutch cable is fitted with a weight. Do not replace the weight when installing the new cable.

**To install:**

5. Install the cable in the vehicle.
6. Connect the clutch cable at the clutch fork and the pedal assembly.
7. Adjust the clutch cable.

Fig. 23 Typical clutch alignment tool, note how the splines match the transmission's input shaft

Fig. 24 Loosen and remove the clutch and pressure plate bolts evenly, a little at a time . . .

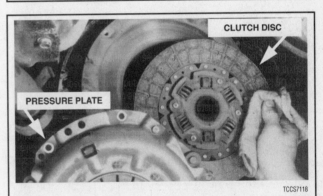

Fig. 25 . . . then carefully removing the clutch and pressure plate assembly from the flywheel

Fig. 26 Check across the flywheel surface, it should be flat

**Fig. 27 If necessary, lock the flywheel in place and remove the retaining bolts . . .**

**Fig. 28 . . . then remove the flywheel from the crankshaft in order replace it or have it machined**

**Fig. 29 Upon installation, it is usually a good idea to apply a threadlocking compound to the flywheel bolts**

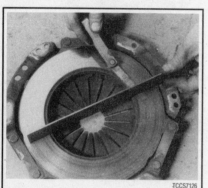

**Fig. 30 Check the pressure plate for excessive wear**

**Fig. 31 Be sure that the flywheel surface is clean, before installing the clutch**

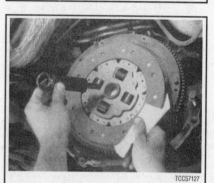

**Fig. 32 Install a clutch alignment arbor, to align the clutch assembly during installation**

**Fig. 33 Clutch plate installed with the arbor in place**

**Fig. 34 Clutch plate and pressure plate installed with the alignment arbor in place**

**Fig. 35 Pressure plate-to-flywheel bolt holes should align**

**Fig. 36 You may want to use a threadlocking compound on the clutch assembly bolts**

**Fig. 37 Install the clutch assembly bolts and tighten in steps, using an X pattern**

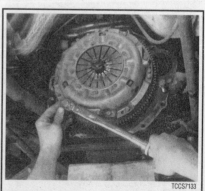

**Fig. 38 Be sure to use a torque wrench to tighten all bolts**

## CLUTCH ADJUSTMENT

#### ▶ See Figures 39 and 40

1. Clutch play is adjusted under the vehicle at the clutch fork.
2. Loosen the locknut on the fork side of the cable bracket and turn the adjust nut until the proper play is achieved.
3. Tighten the locknut.

➡**Vehicles equipped with hydraulic clutch assemblies are not adjustable.**

4. Clutch play for all engines except turbocharged is 0.12–0.20 in. (3–5mm). Turbocharged engine clutch play (free movement rearward) is 0.04–0.12 in. (1–3mm).

### Master Cylinder

On some models, the brake master cylinder incorporates the clutch master cylinder. For those models, refer to Brake Master Cylinder removal and installation in Section 9.

### REMOVAL & INSTALLATION

#### ▶ See Figure 41

1. Disconnect the negative battery cable.
2. Drain the clutch reservoir with a bulb syringe.

### ❊ WARNING

**Be careful not to drip brake fluid on any painted surfaces.**

3. Remove the underdash panel and remove the lockring and pin from the clutch pedal.
4. Remove the hose from the master cylinder. Use a clean jar to collect spillage.
5. Unfasten the retaining bolts and remove the master cylinder.
**To install:**

➡**When reinstalling, make sure that the clearance (free-play) between the pushrod and piston is 0.04 inch (1mm).**

6. Install the master cylinder and tighten the retaining bolts.
7. Install the hose onto the master cylinder. Make certain the hose is correctly threaded and secure.
8. Install the pushrod onto the pedal.
9. Top up the fluid and bleed the system as explained later in this section.
10. Connect the negative battery cable.

### Slave Cylinder

### REMOVAL & INSTALLATION

1. Raise and support the front end on jackstands.
2. Disconnect the fluid line at the cylinder.
3. Unbolt the cylinder from the flywheel housing.
**To install:**
4. Install the cylinder and tighten the retaining bolts.
5. Connect the fluid line.
6. Lower the vehicle.
7. Bleed the clutch system.

### HYDRAULIC SYSTEM BLEEDING

#### ▶ See Figures 42 and 43

The hydraulic clutch system should be bled any time the hoses have been loosened or any component replaced. The bleeding process is quite simple and eliminates any air which has become trapped within the lines. The clutch system may be bleed using Tool 998 5876 or equivalent, or with the help of an assistant.

Add brake fluid to the reservoir. Attach a length of hose to the bleeder nipple on the slave cylinder (at the transmission) and put the other end in a clear glass jar. Put enough brake fluid in the jar to cover the end of the hose.

Have an assistant press the clutch pedal to the floor and open the bleed screw on the slave cylinder. Close off the bleeder while the pedal is still depressed and repeat the process with another application of the clutch pedal. As the bleeder is released each time, observe the fluid in the jar. When no bubbles are coming out of the hose, the system is bled. Secure the fitting, remove the hose and jar, and top up the brake fluid to its proper level.

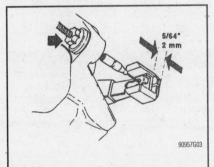

Fig. 39 Checking the clutch negative play

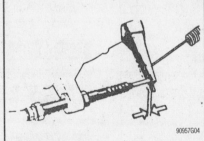

Fig. 40 Adjust the clutch cable by turning the locknut

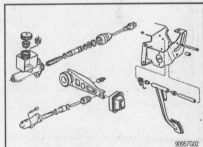

Fig. 41 Exploded view of the hydraulic clutch system

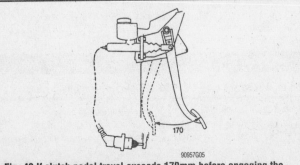

Fig. 42 If clutch pedal travel exceeds 170mm before engaging the clutch, bleed the clutch

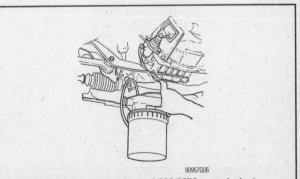

Fig. 43 Bleeding the clutch using tool 998 5876 or equivalent

## AUTOMATIC TRANSMISSION

### Understanding the Automatic Transmission

The automatic transmission allows engine torque and power to be transmitted to the rear wheels within a narrow range of engine operating speeds. It will allow the engine to turn fast enough to produce plenty of power and torque at very low speeds, while keeping it at a sensible rpm at high vehicle speeds (and it does this job without driver assistance). The transmission uses a light fluid as the medium for the transmission of power. This fluid also works in the operation of various hydraulic control circuits and as a lubricant. Because the transmission fluid performs all of these functions, trouble within the unit can easily travel from one part to another. For this reason, and because of the complexity and unusual operating principles of the transmission, a very sound understanding of the basic principles of operation will simplify troubleshooting.

### Neutral Safety Switch/Reverse Light Switch

#### REMOVAL & INSTALLATION

▶ See Figure 44

The start inhibitor (neutral safety switch) also serves to illuminate the back-up lights. The switch is found on the left side of the gear shift selector.
1. Remove the ashtray and panel in the center console.
2. Remove the faceplate with the gear position symbols.
3. Remove the start inhibitor/back-up light switch.
4. Open the connector and lift off the switch.
**To install:**
5. Install the new switch and connect the wiring. Make sure that the tab on the selector lever enters the slot on the switch. Don't forget the prism which fits onto the top of the new switch.
6. Reinstall the holder and the shifter faceplate.
7. Install the panel and the ashtray in the center console.

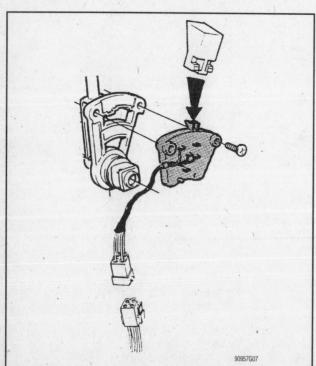

90957G07

Fig. 44 The neutral safety/back-up light switch as mounted on the gear shift selector

#### ADJUSTMENT

There is no adjustment for this switch.

### Extension Housing Seal

#### REMOVAL & INSTALLATION

➡This procedure covers removal and installation of the extension housing seal with the transmission mounted in the vehicle.

1. Disconnect the negative battery cable.
2. Raise and support the vehicle safely.
3. Matchmark the driveshaft with the coupling.
4. Disconnect the driveshaft.
5. Using tool 5244 or equivalent for a round coupling flange, remove the coupling flange nut. Use a spanner (tool 5149 or equivalent) to prevent the flange from rotating.
6. Remove the coupling flange, using a suitable puller (tool 2261 or equivalent).
7. Unfasten the retaining bolts and remove the housing with the governor assembly.
8. Remove the gasket from the housing.
**To install:**
9. Clean the sealing areas thoroughly.
10. Install a new gasket onto the housing.
11. Install the housing with the governor housing attached, and tighten the bolts to 20–35 ft. lbs. (27–47 Nm).
12. Press the coupling flange into place, using tool 1845 or equivalent.
13. Install the coupling flange nut and tighten to 65–85 ft. lbs. (90–110 Nm).
14. Install the driveshaft.
15. Lower the vehicle.
16. Connect the negative battery cable.

### Automatic Transmission Assembly

#### REMOVAL & INSTALLATION

#### ❋❋ CAUTION

**If the vehicle has been driven within the last 3–5 hours, the transmission oil can be scalding hot. Use extreme care when draining the oil or handling components.**

**Except 240 and 960**

▶ See Figure 45

1. Disconnect the battery ground cable.
2. Place the gear selector in the **P** position.
3. Disconnect the kickdown cable at the throttle pulley on the engine.
4. Disconnect the oil filler tube at the oil pan, and drain the transmission oil.

#### ❋❋ CAUTION

**The oil will be scalding hot if the vehicle was recently driven.**

5. Disconnect the control rod at the transmission lever, and disconnect the reaction rod at the transmission housing.
6. On the AW71 transmission, disconnect the wire at the solenoid (slightly to the rear of the transmission-to-driveshaft flange).

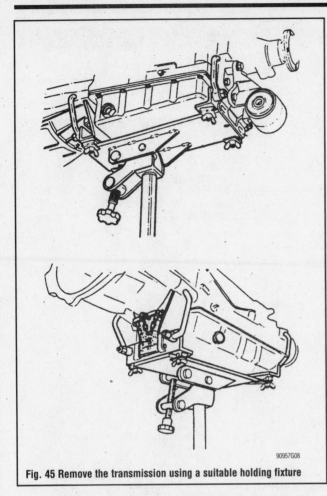

**Fig. 45 Remove the transmission using a suitable holding fixture**

7. Matchmark the transmission-to-driveshaft flange and unbolt the drive-shaft.

8. Place a jack or transmission dolly under the transmission and support the unit. Remember that the transmission will be heavier at the front end than the rear.

9. Remove the transmission crossmember assembly.

10. Disconnect the exhaust pipe at the joint and remove the exhaust pipe bracket from the exhaust pipe.

11. Remove the rear engine mount with the exhaust pipe bracket.

12. Remove the starter motor.

13. Remove the cover plate at the torque converter housing.

14. Disconnect the oil cooler lines at the transmission.

15. Remove the upper bolts at the torque converter cover.

16. Remove the oil filler tube.

➡It is helpful to have another person steadying and guiding the transmission during the removal process.

17. Remove the lower bell housing bolts.

18. Remove the bolts retaining the torque converter to the drive plate.

19. Pry the torque converter back from the drive plate with a small prybar.

20. Slowly lower the transmission as you pull it back to clear the input shaft.

### ✳✳ WARNING

Do not tilt the transmission forward, or the torque converter may slide off.

**To install:**

21. When reinstalling, install the two lower bolts in the casing as soon as the transmission is in place. For the B280 engine, adjust the panel between the starter motor and torque converter casing, and install the bolts for the starter.

22. Mount the oil filler tube at the oil pan, but do not tighten the nut.

23. Install the tube bracket and the two upper bolts in the converter casing.

24. Tighten the nut for the oil tube to 65 ft. lbs. (88 Nm).

25. Install the bolts for the coupling flange; hand-tighten the bolts first, then tighten in a crisscross pattern to 32 ft. lbs. (44 Nm).

26. Reinstall the rear engine mount with the exhaust pipe bracket and reconnect the exhaust system.

27. Reinstall the transmission crossmember; when it is securely bolted in place, the supporting jack may be removed.

28. Reinstall the driveshaft.

29. Making sure that both the transmission linkage and the shift selector in the vehicle are in the **P** position, attach the actuator rod and the reaction rod.

30. Adjust the shift linkage as necessary.

31. Lower the vehicle.

32. On AW71 models, install and connect the wiring to the solenoid valve.

33. Connect the kickdown cable at the throttle pulley. Adjust the cable if necessary.

34. Fill the transmission with oil.

35. Connect the negative battery cable.

36. Apply the parking brake. Start the engine and allow to idle. Move the selector lever through all gear positions.

37. Place the selector lever in **P**. Wait 2 minutes and check the fluid level. Top up, as required.

**240**

1. Disconnect the negative battery cable.

2. Remove the dipstick and filler pipe clamp.

3. Remove the bracket and throttle cable from the dashboard and throttle control.

4. Disconnect the exhaust pipe at the manifold flange.

5. Raise and support the vehicle.

6. Drain the fluid into a clean container.

7. Disconnect the driveshaft from the transmission flange.

8. Disconnect the selector lever controls (shift linkage) and the pan reinforcing bracket.

9. Remove the converter attaching bolts.

10. Support the transmission with a jack or a transmission dolly and holding fixture.

11. Remove the rear crossmember.

12. Disconnect the exhaust pipe brackets and remove the speedometer cable from the case.

13. Remove the filler pipe.

14. Install a wooden block between the engine and firewall; lower the jack until the engine contacts the block.

15. Make sure no tension is put on the battery cable.

16. Disconnect all electrical wiring at the transmission case.

17. Disconnect the starter cable and remove the starter.

18. Remove the converter housing bolts.

19. Pull the transmission backwards to clear the guide pins.

20. Lower and remove the transmission assembly from the vehicle.

**To install:**

21. When reinstalling, load the transmission straight onto the engine and install the converter housing bolts.

22. Tighten the converter-to-drive plate bolts to 35 ft. lbs. (48 Nm).

23. Install the starter and connect its cable; hook up all other wiring to the transmission case.

24. Using the jack, elevate the transmission and engine into their proper position.

25. Install the speedometer cable and the filler pipe.

26. Reconnect the exhaust pipe and the rear engine mount brackets.

27. Install the rear crossmember and tighten its bolts to 18 ft. lbs. (25 Nm). When the crossmember is secure, the jack may be removed.

28. Install the converter attaching bolts.

29. Connect the selector lever controls and the pan reinforcing bracket.

30. Connect the driveshaft to the transmission flange.

31. Lower the vehicle.

32. Reconnect the exhaust pipe at the manifold flange.

33. Reinstall the bracket and throttle cable and adjust if necessary.

34. Install the dipstick and filler pipe.

35. Reconnect the negative battery cable.

36. Fill the transmission to the proper level with fluid.

37. Apply the parking brake. Start the engine and allow to idle. Move the selector lever through all gear positions.

38. Place the selector lever in **P**. Wait 2 minutes and check the fluid level. Top up, as required.

## 960

1. Disconnect the negative battery cable.
2. Support the engine using the special tools (5006, 5033, 5115, 5429 and 5186, or their equivalents).
3. Remove the preheater pipe under the engine. Be careful not to damage the O-ring.
4. Disconnect the front section of the exhaust pipe.
5. Disconnect the transmission cooler lines and plug the openings.
6. Unfasten the 3 transmission connectors.
7. Disconnect the oxygen sensor lead from the transmission unit and support member.
8. Matchmark the driveshaft coupling halves to aid during re-assemble.
9. Disconnect the driveshaft.
10. Remove the clips between the gear selector lever and control rod/reaction arm. Withdraw the rods from the mounting.
11. Disconnect the transmission support member from the transmission bump stop and side members.
12. Position a service jack beneath the transmission.
13. Carefully lower the transmission.
14. Remove the torque converter-to-flexplate retaining bolts.
15. Remove the transmission housing bolts.
16. Separate the torque converter from the flexplate and lower the transmission.

**To install:**

17. Lift the transmission into position, while aligning the torque converter with the flexplate.
18. Install the transmission housing mounting bolts.
19. Install the torque converter retaining bolts and tighten alternately to 22 ft. lbs. (30 Nm).
20. Raise the transmission and secure the support member. Tighten to 37 ft. lbs. (50 Nm).
21. Install the gear selector lever.
22. Install the locking clips.
23. Connect the transmission oil cooler lines.
24. Connect the transmission connectors and oxygen sensor lead.
25. Connect the driveshaft. Check to ensure the matchmarks are aligned.
26. Lubricate the O-ring and install the preheater pipe.
27. Install the front exhaust pipe.
28. Remove the engine support tools.
29. Reconnect the negative battery cable.
30. Fill the transmission to the proper level with the appropriate fluid.
31. Apply the parking brake. Start the engine and allow to idle. Move the selector lever through all gear positions.
32. Place the selector lever in **P**. Wait 2 minutes and check the fluid level. Top up, as required.

## ADJUSTMENTS

Before performing any adjustments, the following checks should be made: Check that the engine can be started, only with the selector lever in position **P** and with the brake pedal depressed. The selector lever should stand vertically when in the **P** position. Check that the back-up lights illuminate only when the selector lever is in the **R** position. On AW 70/71/72 transmissions, check that the clearance from position **D** towards **N** is the same or smaller than the clearance between position **3** towards **2**. On the AW 30-40 transmission, check that there is a noticeable play from position **D** towards **N**; however, that play should not be greater than the play from position **3** towards **L**.

### Shift Control

#### *AW 70/71/72 TRANSMISSIONS*

▶ **See Figure 46**

1. Set the selector lever in position **P**. Loosen the retaining nuts for the shift control rod "A" and retaining arm "B".
2. Check that the lever on the transmission is at position **P** (first step seen from the rear). Turn the transmission output shaft until it locks.
3. Set the lever in the vertical position on the shift control rod, or just facing

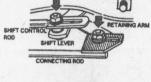

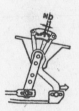

**Fig. 46 Adjusting the shift control on AW 70/71/72 transmissions**

forward; tighten the nut. Push the retaining arm lightly to the rear until slight resistance is felt. Temporarily tighten the retaining nut to 42 inch lbs. (5 Nm).

4. Check that the clearance from position **D** towards **N** is the same or smaller than the clearance between position **3** towards **2**.
5. If incorrect:
   a. If the gear selector lever is stiff in position **D**, move the connecting rod ⁵⁄₆₄ inch (2mm) to the rear.
   b. If the gear selector lever is stiff in position **3**, move the connecting rod ⅛ inch (3mm) to the front.
6. When the adjustment is correct, tighten the retaining nut to 13–17 ft. lbs. (17–23 Nm).
7. After adjustment, check that the engine can be started, only with the selector lever in position **P** and with the brake pedal depressed. The back-up lights should illuminate only when the selector lever is in the **R** position.

#### *AW 30/40 TRANSMISSION*

▶ **See Figure 47**

1. Place the selector lever in position **P**.
2. Loosen the nuts on the control rod and reaction strut.
3. Make sure the selector link arm on the transmission is in position **P** (rearmost gear position).
4. Make sure the gear lever arm "A" is vertical (or slightly forward) and tighten the nut.
5. Press the reaction arm "B" gently backwards until slight resistance is felt. Tighten the nut approximately 48 inch lbs. (5 Nm).
6. Check that the play from position **D** towards **N**; is the same as the play from position **3** towards **L**.
7. If incorrect:
   a. If there is no play in position **D**, move the reaction arm backwards approximately 0.08 inches (2mm).
   b. If there is no play in position **3**, move the reaction arm forwards approximately 0.12 inches (3mm).

8. When the adjustment is correct, tighten the retaining nut to 13–17 ft. lbs. (17–23 Nm).

9. After adjustment, check that the engine can be started, only with the selector lever in positions **P** or **N**. The back-up lights should illuminate only when the selector lever is in the **R** position.

**Kickdown Cable/Throttle Linkage**

*AW 70/71/72 TRANSMISSIONS*

♦ See Figure 48

1. Check that the wire is tensioned at idle setting, without tensioning against the throttle pulley, and that it is in the pulley groove and runs smoothly.

2. Pull the wire out approximately 0.39 inch (10mm) and release suddenly. A mechanical click should be heard from the throttle cam, when it reaches the standby setting. Adjust with the wire tensioner.

   a. If no clicking is heard, the wire is too firmly tensioned.

   b. If no kickdown can be obtained, the wire is too slack.

3. Check the cable sheath adjustment with the throttle pedal in the vehicle depressed, not by actuating the linkage by hand. When depressing the throttle pedal fully, the distance from the cable sheath to the clip should be 2.02 inches (51.5mm), but 1.98–2.06 inches (50.4–52.6mm) is permitted. If required, adjust the distance on the cable sheath.

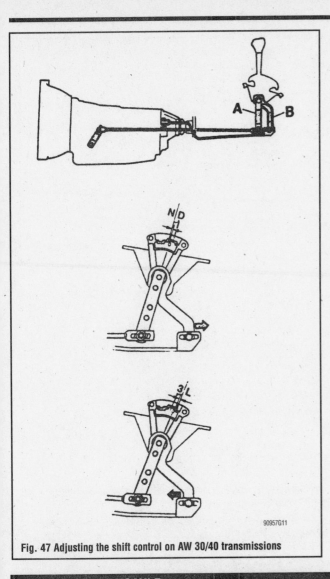

Fig. 47 Adjusting the shift control on AW 30/40 transmissions

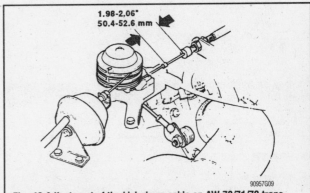

Fig. 48 Adjustment of the kick-down cable on AW 70/71/72 transmissions

## AUTOMATIC TRANSAXLE

### Understanding the Automatic Transaxle

The automatic transaxle allows engine torque and power to be transmitted to the front wheels within a narrow range of engine operating speeds. It will allow the engine to turn fast enough to produce plenty of power and torque at very low speeds, while keeping it at a sensible rpm at high vehicle speeds (and it does this job without driver assistance). The transaxle uses a light fluid as the medium for the transmission of power. This fluid also works in the operation of various hydraulic control circuits and as a lubricant. Because the transaxle fluid performs all of these functions, trouble within the unit can easily travel from one part to another. For this reason, and because of the complexity and unusual operating principles of the transaxle, a very sound understanding of the basic principles of operation will simplify troubleshooting.

### Gear Position Sensor

REMOVAL & INSTALLATION

♦ See Figure 49

1. Make sure the gear selector is in the **N** position.
2. Disconnect the battery cables and remove the battery.
3. Remove the battery tray.
4. Remove the air cleaner assembly and intake hose.
5. Remove the transmission cable from the rod arm.

6. Remove the selector lever.
7. Remove the dipstick pipe bracket.
8. Remove the position sensor's mounting bolts and remove the sensor from the transaxle.
9. Disconnect the clamps and remove the connector from the transaxle.
**To install:**
10. Install the sensor and adjust using procedure outlined below.

Fig. 49 The gear position sensor is visible after the air cleaner is removed

11. Tighten the sensor's mounting bolts.
12. Install the dipstick pipe bracket.
13. Install the selector lever.
14. Install the transmission cable onto the cable arm.
15. Install the air cleaner assembly and intake hose.
16. Install the battery tray.
17. Install the battery and connect the battery cables.

### ADJUSTMENT

1. Make sure the gear selector is in the **N** position.
2. Disconnect the battery cables and remove the battery.
3. Remove the battery tray.
4. Remove the air cleaner assembly and intake hose.
5. Remove the transmission cable from the rod arm.
6. Remove the dipstick pipe bracket.
7. Install tool 5475 on the selector shaft and check that the indentation on the tool aligns with the mark on the sensor. If the sensor requires adjustment, perform the following:
   - Remove the position sensor mounting bolts and the selector shaft nut.
   - Rotate the sensor until the marks align.
   - Tighten the sensor mounting bolts and the selector shaft nut.

**To install:**
8. Install the dipstick pipe bracket.
9. Install the selector lever.
10. Install the transmission cable onto the cable arm.
11. Install the air cleaner assembly and intake hose.
12. Install the battery tray.
13. Install the battery and connect the battery cables.

### Automatic Transaxle Assembly

#### REMOVAL & INSTALLATION

#### 850, C70, S70 and V70 Models

▶ **See Figures 50 and 51**

1. Pull the steering wheel adjustment lever out and adjust the wheel in and up as far as it will go. Then lock it in position.
2. Put the transaxle gear selector in **N** and set the parking brake.
3. Disconnect and remove the battery and air cleaner assembly.
4. Remove the battery tray.
5. On turbo models, disconnect the control valve from air cleaner and the air charge manifold clamp and hose. Also remove the turbocharger air cleaner intake.
6. Detach the transaxle cable and connector from the transaxle. Be careful not to damage the rubber seal.
7. Remove the wiring harness and ground from the control system cover.
8. On early models, disconnect the transaxle vent hose.
9. On later models, disconnect the wiring and oxygen sensor from transaxle brackets.
10. Disconnect the transaxle cooling lines from the quick disconnects and drain the transmission fluid.
11. Remove the dipstick and tube.
12. On vehicles with an EGR valve, disconnect the hoses to the valve.
13. On turbo models, remove the cover over the control pulley, then disconnect the intake to the throttle body and pull it to one side so that the throttle body is free. Seal all oil connections to prevent dirt from entering.
14. Remove the bolts connecting the engine and transaxle and starter.
15. Disconnect the transaxle ground strap.
16. Lift off the radiator overflow tank and let it hang.
17. Remove the torque rod extension arm bolt and swing it out of the way.

➡ **It will be necessary to support the engine from above and still be able raise and lower the car.**

18. Install lifting yoke 999-5534 or equivalent in place of the torque rod extension arm.
19. Install support tool 999-5033 on the inside fender rail, lifting beam support 999-5006 or equivalent placing the beam directly over the eyelet for the lifting yoke.

20. Install the lifting hook 999-5460 or equivalent and pull it up slightly until the load is taken off of the engine mounts. Measure the distance between the beam and spark plug cover and make note of it.
21. Raise and safely support the vehicle.
22. Remove the front wheels.
23. Disconnect the ABS sensor from the left side axle shaft but do not disconnect.
24. Disconnect all brackets for the brake lines and ABS wiring on both sides.
25. Remove the plastic inner fender wells on both sides.
26. Remove the transfer case (V70 AWD models only).
27. Remove the left and right side halfshafts.
28. Install a seal plug in the transaxle.
29. Remove all the splash guards.
30. Separate the ball joints from the control arms, being careful not to damage the boots.
31. Disconnect the sway bar links on both sides.
32. Remove the subframe cable mounting screws and disconnect them from the subframe.
33. Disconnect the carbon canister and hoses from the subframe. Cut the wire tie and hang the holder on the body.
34. Disconnect the exhaust pipe clamp behind the catalytic converter.
35. Remove the oil line bracket screws and torque rod holder mounting screws.
36. Back the engine mounting/steering gear bolt off one turn.
37. Remove the five steering gear mounting nuts in the subframe.
38. Position a jack under the left-hand side of the subframe so that it is barely touching.
39. Remove the subframe bracket bolts on the body. Back the 15mm bolts between the frame and body on the right-hand side several turns. Remove the bolts from the left.

➡ **Make sure the steering gear bolts come out of the subframe.**

40. Remove the jack and let the frame hang down from the right side bolts.
41. Secure the end of the right side driveshaft on the oil lines.
42. Remove the steering gear engine mount bolt and nut at the top of the engine mount and remove the mount.

➡ **Make sure the steering gear is properly secured so the lower steering shaft does not slide out of the steering column.**

43. Disconnect the oxygen sensor wiring clamps from the cover and the connector and wiring to the vehicle speed sensor.
44. Remove the cover at the back of the engine and the mount from the transaxle.
45. Lower the engine and transaxle with the lifting hook until the distance between the beam and spark plug cover is 12.6 in. (320mm).

### ❋❋ WARNING

**If the engine is lowered too far, the exhaust pipe will be crushed against the steering rack. Be careful not to pinch any wiring or hoses and be sure that the engine dipstick tube is free of the fan.**

46. Install transaxle fixture 5463 on the transaxle jack or equivalent, using the torque rod mounting bolts to hold it in place. At the same time, fit support plate tool 5463-1 or equivalent and raise the jack so that it is making light contact.
47. Remove the six torque converter bolts using a TX50 Torx® socket.
48. Remove the lower plastic nut and fold out the inner fender well on the right-hand side.
49. Then turn the crankshaft with a socket and ratchet.
50. Remove the seven bolts between the engine and transaxle.
51. Remove the torque converter bolts from the flywheel.
52. Remove the transaxle making sure the torque converter comes out with it and does not slip off the shaft. Use the hole in the torque converter cover to press the torque converter in to keep it from sliding off.

### ❋❋ WARNING

**Do not pry against carrier plate rim, as damage may result.**

**To install:**
53. Flush the oil lines with clean transmission fluid.
54. Install the line and hose on the transaxle using new O-rings on the quick-connectors.

55. Install the hose on the upper transaxle cooler line catch pan under the return line.

56. Inspect all components before installing.

57. Apply a small amount of grease to the torque converter guide pin and install, making sure the converter is all the way into the transaxle. The distance between the cover and converter bolt flange should be 0.55 in. (14mm).

58. Install the transaxle securing in place with the seven bolts between the engine and transaxle. Tighten them to 37 ft. lbs. (50 Nm).

59. Install new torque converter bolts and tighten to 22 ft. lbs. (30 Nm) using a TX50 Torx® socket.

➡**Remove the socket from the crankshaft.**

60. Install the rear transaxle mount and three bolts. Tighten the rear two bolts to 37 ft. lbs. (50 Nm), then remove the front bolt.

61. Install the cover against the mount and tighten the bolt to 37 ft. lbs. (50 Nm).

62. Install the engine mount guide pin into the cover. Install a new nut and hand-tighten.

63. Install the steering rack engine mount bolt, but do not tighten.

64. Reconnect the oxygen sensor.

65. Install the vehicle speed sensor connector and connect the transaxle ground strap.

66. Install the subframe using new bolts. Apply grease to the threads.

67. Starting on the left, lift the frame with a transaxle jack. Mount the support brackets on both sides.

68. Tighten the frame bolts to 78 ft. lbs. (105 Nm) plus an additional 120 degrees.

69. Tighten the bracket bolts to 37 ft. lbs. (50 Nm).

70. Remove the jack and repeat the procedure for the right side.

71. Install five new nuts on the steering rack and tighten them to 37 ft. lbs. (50 Nm).

72. Install the front engine mount nut, then tighten the front and rear bolts to 37 ft. lbs. (50 Nm).

73. Install the torque rod mount on the transaxle using new bolts, tighten the M18 bolts (early models) to 13 ft. lbs. (18 Nm) plus an additional 90 degrees or M10 bolts (later models) to 26 ft. lbs. (35 Nm) plus an additional 40 degrees.

74. Install the transfer case (if equipped).

75. Install the right and left halfshafts.

➡**Make sure the transaxle axle seal and axle boot are not damaged.**

76. Connect the control arms to the ball joints using new nuts.

77. Install the sway bar link using new nuts and tighten to 37 ft. lbs. (50 Nm).

78. Attach the cable pipe and carbon filter container to the subframe. Tie the hoses with a strip clamp on the subframe.

79. Install engine splash guard on early models.

80. Install the front splash guard by pressing in the guides and installing the screws.

81. Install the five transaxle bolts on top side and tighten to 37 ft. lbs. (50 Nm).

82. Install the starter.

83. Connect the cable conduit and oxygen sensor connectors.

84. Install the dipstick tube with a new O-ring and tighten to 19 ft. lbs. (25 Nm).

85. Connect the wiring harness, ground lead, transaxle connectors.

86. Connect the transaxle vent and EGR hoses.

87. Attach the transaxle cable and adjust.

88. Connect the ground strip to the firewall.

89. Install a new bolt and nut for the extension arm and torque rod.

90. Tighten early model M8 bolts to 13 ft. lbs. (18 Nm) plus an additional 120 degrees. Tighten later model M10 bolts to 26 ft. lbs. (35 Nm) plus an additional 90 degrees.

91. Install the remaining components.

92. Fill the transaxle with fluid.

93. Check the fluid level after the engine has reached normal operating temperature to assure that it is correct.

## ADJUSTMENTS

### Throttle Linkage/Kickdown Switch

◆ **See Figures 52 and 53**

1. Remove the throttle pulley cover.

2. Remove the clip from the kickdown cable.

3. Install a 0.14 inch (3.5mm) spacer between the throttle pulley stop and the bracket stop.

4. Install the clip into the cable making sure it is firmly against the bracket.

5. Adjust until the cable is under light tension.

6. Remove the locking clip.

7. Remove the spacer.

8. Reinstall the locking clip.

9. Install the pulley cover.

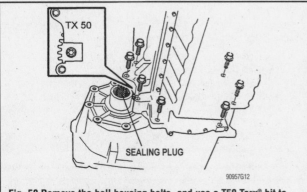

Fig. 50 Remove the bell housing bolts, and use a T50 Torx® bit to remove the torque converter bolts

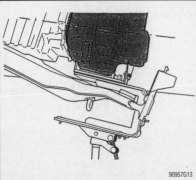

Fig. 51 Use a suitable stand to support the transaxle before removing

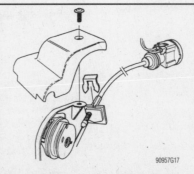

Fig. 52 Remove the throttle pulley cover and cable clip in order to adjust the throttle cable

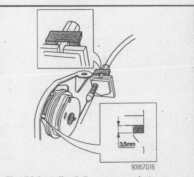

Fig. 53 Install a 3.5mm spacer between the throttle pulley stop and the bracket stop, then adjust the cable

## Halfshafts

### REMOVAL & INSTALLATION

➡The procedure for halfshaft removal is the same for manual transaxle, so refer to the Halfshaft removal and installation procedure in the Manual Transaxle portion of this section.

## TRANSFER CASE

### Rear Output Shaft Seal

#### REMOVAL & INSTALLATION

1. Raise and safely support the vehicle.
2. Mark the flange, and remove the rear driveshaft from the transfer case.
3. Remove the transfer case rear driveshaft flange using counterhold tool 5652 or equivalent. Remove the flange nut.
4. Remove the flange from the transfer case using puller 5304 or equivalent.
5. Remove the pinion spacer sleeve using puller 7693 or equivalent.
6. Remove the seal using puller 5069 or equivalent inside seal puller.

**To install:**
7. Thoroughly clean the sealing surface before installing new seal.
8. Lubricate the new seal with wheel bearing grease.
9. Install the new seal in transfer case, and press seal into place using tools 5653 and 5504 or equivalent seal installer.
10. Install the pinion spacer sleeve.
11. Install the flange and tighten the nut to 133–148 ft. lbs. (180–200 Nm).
12. Install the rear driveshaft.
13. Lower the vehicle.

### Front Output Shaft Seal

#### REMOVAL & INSTALLATION

1. Raise and safely support the vehicle.
2. Remove the right front wheel.
3. Remove the passenger side halfshaft from the transfer case.
4. Remove the old seal from the transfer case using a seal puller or other suitable tool.

### OVERHAUL

Refer to the Halfshaft Overhaul procedure in the Manual Transaxle portion of this section.

**To install:**
5. Thoroughly clean the sealing surface before installing the new seal.
6. Lubricate the new seal with wheel bearing grease.
7. Install the new seal in transfer case, and press seal into place using tool 5564 or an equivalent seal driver.
8. Install the passenger side halfshaft.
9. Install the right front wheel. Tighten the lug nuts to 81 ft. lbs. (110 Nm).
10. Lower the vehicle.

### Transfer Case Assembly

#### REMOVAL & INSTALLATION

▶ See Figures 54 and 55

1. Raise and safely support the vehicle.
2. Remove the right front wheel.
3. Remove the passenger side halfshaft from the transfer case.
4. Remove the transfer case vibration damper with support bracket.
5. Mark the flange, and remove the rear driveshaft from the transfer case.
6. Remove the transfer case-to-transaxle retaining bolts.
7. Remove the transfer case.

**To install:**
8. Install the transfer case on the transaxle. Make sure that the coupling sleeve is between the transaxle and the transfer case.
9. Tighten the retaining bolts to 37 ft. lbs. (50 Nm).
10. Install the rear driveshaft.
11. Install the vibration damper and bracket.
12. Install the passenger side halfshaft.
13. Install the right front wheel. Tighten the lug nuts to 81 ft. lbs. (110 Nm).
14. Lower the vehicle.

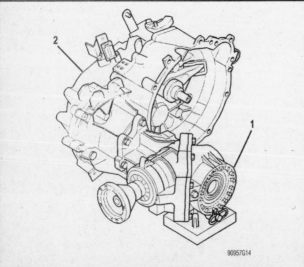

90957G14

**Fig. 54 The transfer case (1) as assembled to the transaxle (2)**

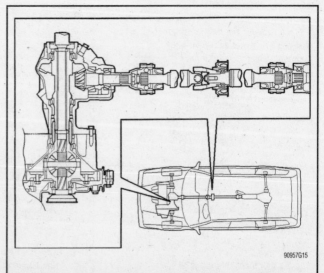

90957G15

**Fig. 55 Cutaway view of power distribution through a transfer case**

## DRIVELINE

**▶ See Figure 56**

The driveshaft is a two-piece tubular unit, connected by an intermediate universal joint. The rear end of the front section of the driveshaft contains a splined sleeve. A splined shaft forming one of the yokes for the intermediate U-joint fits into this sleeve.

The front section is supported by a bearing contained in an insulated rubber housing attached to the bottom of the driveshaft tunnel. The front section is connected to the transmission flange, and the rear section is connected to the differential housing flange by universal joints.

Each joint consists of a spider with 4 ground trunnions in the flange yokes surrounded by needle bearings.

## Driveshaft and U-Joints

### REMOVAL & INSTALLATION

**▶ See Figures 57 and 58**

1. Raise the vehicle and safely support the vehicle.
2. Mark the relative positions of the driveshaft yokes on the transmission and differential housing flanges for purposes of assembly.
3. Remove the nuts and bolts which retain the front and rear driveshaft sections to the transmission and differential housing flanges.
4. Remove the support bearing housing from the driveshaft tunnel, and lower the driveshaft and universal joint assembly as a unit.
5. Pry up the lock washer and remove the support bearing retaining nut.
6. Pull off the rear section of the driveshaft with the intermediate universal joint and splined shaft of the front section. The support bearing may now be pressed off from the driveshaft.
7. Remove the support bearing from its housing.
8. For removal of the universal joints from the driveshaft, refer to "Universal Joint Overhaul" in this section.

9. Inspect the driveshaft sections for straightness. Using a dial indicator, or rolling the shafts along a flat surface, make sure that the driveshaft out-of-round does not exceed 0.010 inches (0.25mm). Do not attempt to straighten a damaged shaft. Any shaft exceeding 0.010 inches (0.25mm) out-of-round will cause substantial vibration, and must be replaced. Also, inspect the support bearing by pressing the races against each other by hand and turning them in opposite directions. If the bearing binds at any point, it must be discarded and replaced.

**To install:**

10. Install the support bearing into its housing.
11. Press the support bearing and housing onto the front driveshaft section.
12. Push the splined shaft of the rear section (with the intermediate universal joint and rear driveshaft section) into the splined sleeve of the front section.
13. Install the retaining nut and lock washer for the support bearing.

**➡ Pay particular attention to the placement of the yokes at the end of the shaft. They must be in the same alignment front and rear or driveline vibration will be induced.**

14. Taking note of the alignment marks made prior to removal, position the driveshaft and universal joint assembly to its flange and install but do not tighten its retaining nuts and bolts.
15. Position the support bearing housing to the driveshaft tunnel and install the retaining nut.
16. Tighten the nuts which retain the driveshaft sections to the transmission and differential housing flanges to 32 ft. lbs. (44 Nm).
17. Lower the vehicle.
18. Road test the vehicle and check for driveline vibrations.

### U-JOINT OVERHAUL

**▶ See Figures 59, 60, 61 and 62**

1. Remove the driveshaft and universal joint assembly as previously outlined.
2. Clean off the dirt from the surrounding area and remove the snaprings,

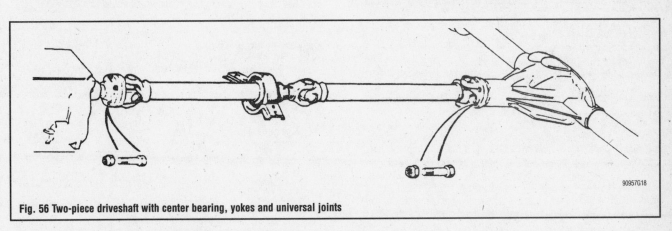

**Fig. 56 Two-piece driveshaft with center bearing, yokes and universal joints**

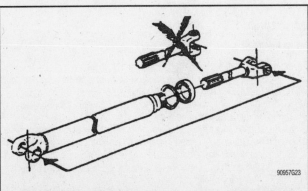

**Fig. 57 Correct relative placement of the yokes is essential to eliminating driveline vibrations**

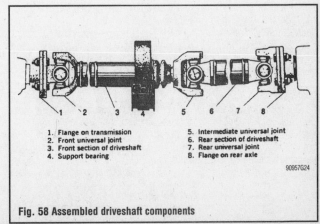

1. Flange on transmission
2. Front universal joint
3. Front section of driveshaft
4. Support bearing
5. Intermediate universal joint
6. Rear section of driveshaft
7. Rear universal joint
8. Flange on rear axle

**Fig. 58 Assembled driveshaft components**

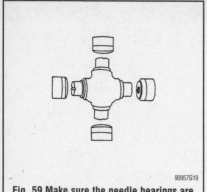

Fig. 59 Make sure the needle bearings are in place inside the cups before installation

90957G19

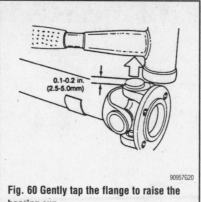

Fig. 60 Gently tap the flange to raise the bearing cup

90957G20

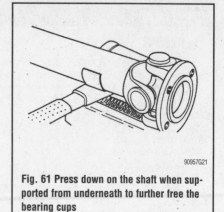

Fig. 61 Press down on the shaft when supported from underneath to further free the bearing cups

90957G21

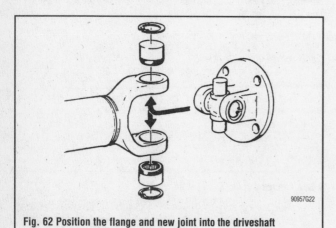

Fig. 62 Position the flange and new joint into the driveshaft

90957G22

which secure the needle bearings in the yokes, with a snapring pliers. If the rings are difficult to loosen, apply rust penetrant and tap the ring lightly with a hammer and punch.

3. Lightly mount the shaft in a vise and adjust its position so that the yoke is supported by the jaws. If at all possible, do not tighten the vise onto the tubular shaft; it can be easily deformed.

4. Using a plastic mallet, tap on the shaft flange until the bearing cup(s) protrude about 0.2 inch (5mm). Do not tap on the tubular shaft.

5. Leaving the flange clamped in the vise, lift the driveshaft and insert a piece of wood or a hammer handle under the shaft. Gently press down on the driveshaft; this will lever the bearing cap upwards. Once all are removed, clean the seats in the driveshaft and flange. Clean the spider and needle bearings completely. Check the contact surfaces for wear. Replace any worn or broken parts. If the old needle bearings and spider are to be reused, fill them with molybdenum disulfide chassis grease, and make sure that the rubber seals are not damaged. If new needle bearings are used, fill them half-way with the grease.

6. Remove the bearing caps and seals from the new spider. Make sure that the needle bearings and seals are in place within the cups.

7. Position the spider into the flange yoke. Place one of the bearing cups on the spider and tap the cup until it is firmly seated.

8. Using the vise and a sleeve of proper size, press the cup into place in the yoke. The cup should project through the yoke about 0.1–0.2 inch (2.5–5.0mm). Install the snapring (circlip). Make sure the spider is centered within the yoke.

9. Repeat the previous pressing operation on the opposite side of the flange yoke. Note that when the second bearing cup is pressed into place, the first bearing cup is pressed against its snapring.

10. Fit the spider into the driveshaft yoke. Place and press each bearing cup into place following the procedures above.

11. Release the assembly from the vise. Check the new joint for free motion in all dimensions. If any stiffness or binding is present, remount the assembly in the vise (as described previously) and LIGHTLY tap the spider ends with a plastic mallet.

## DRIVESHAFT BALANCING

Driveshaft balancing is a process best left for a professional with the proper equipment. Makeshift methods using hose clamps or similar devices can work, but the process of correcting the imbalance in this manner is very tough and extremely time consuming.

Many machine shops can balance driveshafts; some parts stores and jobbers can also balance driveshafts using outside contractors.

## Center Bearing

### REMOVAL & INSTALLATION

The center support bearing must rotate freely with no noise or binding. It not a serviceable component; if it is noisy or binds it must be replaced. Use of a press with the appropriate blocks and sleeves is required for replacement.

**240**

▶ See Figures 63 and 64

1. Remove the front driveshaft and center bearing assembly as previously outlined.

2. Press the bearing out of the rubber mount. The bearing will stay attached to the driveshaft.

3. Using a drift or a press if necessary, remove the bearing from the driveshaft. Take care not to damage the dust cover around the bearing.

4. Install the new bearing by pressing it onto the shaft.

5. Install the rubber mount. Observe correct placement of the bearing within the mount.

6. Reassemble the driveshaft halves. If the splines are dry, lightly coat them with grease.

7. When reinstalling the driveshaft and central bearing in the vehicle, check that the spring and washer are positioned correctly in the rubber mount. Also make sure that the bearing is centered in its mounts before final tightening.

**Except 240**

▶ See Figure 65

1. Raise and safely support the vehicle on jackstands.

2. Mark the relative positions of the driveshaft yokes on the transmission and differential housing flanges for purposes of assembly.

3. Remove the nuts and bolts which retain the front and rear driveshaft sections to the transmission and differential housing flanges.

4. Remove the support bearing housing from the driveshaft tunnel, and lower the driveshaft and universal joint assembly as a unit.

5. Pry up the lock washer and remove the support bearing retaining nut.

6. Pull off the rear section of the driveshaft with the intermediate universal joint and splined shaft of the front section.

7. The support bearing may now be pressed off from the driveshaft.

8. Remove the support bearing from its housing.

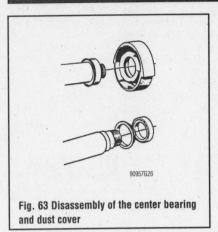

Fig. 63 Disassembly of the center bearing and dust cover

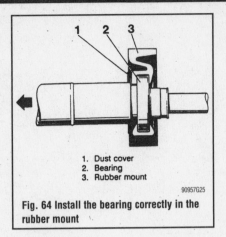

1. Dust cover
2. Bearing
3. Rubber mount

Fig. 64 Install the bearing correctly in the rubber mount

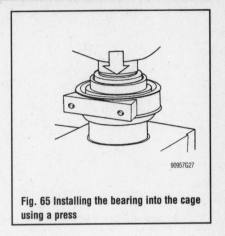

Fig. 65 Installing the bearing into the cage using a press

9. For removal of the universal joints from the driveshaft, refer to "Universal Joint Overhaul" in this section.

10. Inspect the driveshaft sections for straightness. Using a dial indicator, or rolling the shafts along a flat surface, make sure that the driveshaft out-of-round does not exceed 0.010 inches (0.25mm). Do not attempt to straighten a damaged shaft. Any shaft exceeding 0.010 inches (0.25mm) out-of-round will cause substantial vibration, and must be replaced. Also, inspect the support bearing by pressing the races against each other by hand and turning them in opposite directions. If the bearing binds at any point, it must be discarded and replaced.

11. Install the support bearing into its housing.

12. Press the support bearing and housing onto the front driveshaft section. Push the splined shaft of the rear section (with the intermediate universal joint and rear driveshaft section) into the splined sleeve of the front section. Install the retaining nut and lock washer for the support bearing.

➡ **Pay particular attention to the placement of the yokes at the end of the shaft. They must be in the same alignment front and rear or driveline vibration will be induced.**

13. Taking note of the alignment marks made prior to removal, position the driveshaft and universal joint assembly to its flange and install but do not tighten its retaining nuts and bolts. Position the support bearing housing to the driveshaft tunnel and install the retaining nut. Tighten the nuts which retain the driveshaft sections to the transmission and differential housing flanges to 32 ft. lbs. (44 Nm).

14. Remove the safety stands and lower the vehicle.

15. Road test the vehicle and check for driveline vibrations.

## REAR AXLE

### Understanding the Rear Axle

♦ **See Figures 66, 67, 68 and 69**

The rear axle is a special type of transmission that reduces the speed of the drive from the engine and transmission and divides the power to the rear wheels. Power enters the rear axle from the driveshaft via the companion flange. The flange is mounted on the drive pinion shaft. The drive pinion shaft and gear carries the power into the differential. The gear on the end of the pinion shaft drives a large ring gear the axis of rotation of which is 90 degrees away from the of the pinion. The pinion and gear reduce the gear ratio of the axle, and change the direction of rotation to turn the axle shafts which drive both wheels. The rear axle gear ratio is found by dividing the number of pinion gear teeth into the number of ring gear teeth.

The final drive is of the hypoid design, with the drive pinion lying below the ring gear. On solid axle models, each axle shaft is indexed into a splined sleeve for the differential side gears, and supported at its outer end in a tapered roller bearing. Bearing clearance is not adjustable by use of shims, but instead is determined by bearing thickness. Both sides of the axle bearings are protected by oil seals.

On vehicles with a multi-link suspension, the axles are actually halfshafts, bolted to the differential. Each halfshaft has a constant velocity (CV)-joint at each end, allowing a full range of motion as the vehicle passes over bumps and depressions.

The ring gear drives the differential case. The case provides the 2 mounting points for the ends of a pinion shaft on which are mounted two pinion gears. The pinion gears drive the 2 side gears, one of which is located on the inner end of each axle shaft (beam type axle) or inner driveshafts (multi-link axle).

By driving the axle shafts through the arrangement, the differential allows the outer drive wheel to turn faster than the inner drive wheel in a turn.

The main drive pinion and the side bearings, which bear the weight of the differential case, are shimmed to provide proper bearing preload, and to position the pinion and ring gears properly.

➡ **The proper adjustment of the relationship of the ring and pinion gears is critical. It should be attempted only by those with extensive equipment and/or experience.**

Limited-slip differentials include clutches which tend to link each axle shaft to the differential case. Clutches may be engaged either by spring action or by pressure produced by the torque on the axles during a turn. During turning on a dry pavement, the effects of the clutches are overcome, and each wheel turns at the required speed. When slippage occurs at either wheel, however, the clutches will transmit some of the power to the wheel which has the greater amount of traction. Because of the presence of clutches, limited-slip units require a special lubricant.

Type 1041 rear axle (beam type) is attached to the body by support arms, a torque arm and a torque arm frame. A Panhard rod is installed between the rear axle and crossmember. An anti-roll bar is also mounted between the support arms. The 1041 rear axle can be easily identified by its aluminum inspection cover.

Type 1035 and 1045 rear axles (multi-link) is attached to the body by a member consisting of an upper and lower section. The upper links extend from the upper member. The lower links and 2 track rods are mounted between the lower section of the axle member and the wheel bearing housings. The wheel bearing housings and body are connected by the support arms.

Certain rear axle variants are equipped with Automatic Differential Lock. The locking mechanism is controlled by a centrifugal governor. This device operates automatically when one of the drive wheels is spinning and the speed of the vehicle is less than 25 mph (40 km/h). When the vehicle is driven at a steady speed and both driveshafts are rotating at the same speed, the differential functions exactly as a conventional type.

### Determining Axle Ratio

The drive axle is said to have a certain axle ratio. This number (usually a whole number and a decimal fraction) is actually a comparison of the number of gear teeth on the ring gear and the pinion gear. For example, a 4.11 rear means

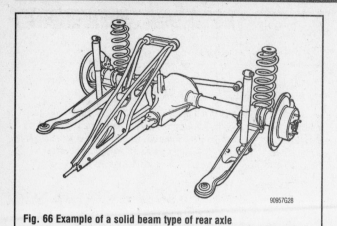

**Fig. 66 Example of a solid beam type of rear axle**

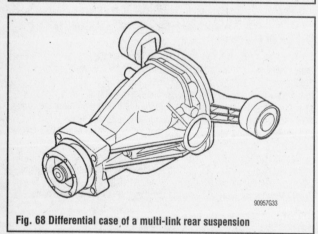

**Fig. 67 Example of a multi-link (independent) suspension rear axle**

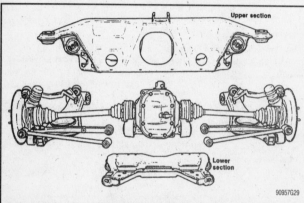

**Fig. 68 Differential case of a multi-link rear suspension**

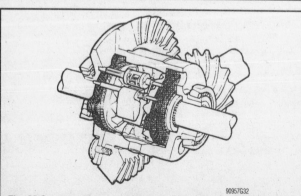

**Fig. 69 Cutaway view of an Automatic Differential Lock rear differential**

that theoretically, there are 4.11 teeth on the ring gear for each tooth on the pinion gear. By dividing the number of teeth on the pinion gear into the number of teeth on the ring gear, the numerical axle ratio (4.11) is obtained. This also provides a good method of ascertaining exactly what axle ratio one is dealing with.

Another method of determining gear ratio is to jack up and support the vehicle so that both rear wheels are off the ground. Make a chalk mark on the rear wheel and the driveshaft. Put the transmission in neutral. Turn the rear wheel one complete turn and count the number of turns that the driveshaft makes. The number of turns that the driveshaft makes in one complete revolution of the rear wheel is an approximation of the rear axle ratio.

## Axle Shaft, Bearing and Seal

REMOVAL & INSTALLATION

> ✳✳ **CAUTION**
>
> **This procedure requires removal of the rear brake pads or shoes. Brake pads and shoes may contain asbestos, which has been determined to a cancer causing agent. Never clean the brake surfaces with compressed air! Avoid inhaling and dust from brake surfaces! When cleaning brakes, use commercially available brake cleaning fluids.**

**Except Multi-Link Suspension**

▶ **See Figure 70**

1. Raise the vehicle and safely support it on jackstands.
2. Remove the applicable wheel.
3. Remove the brake caliper mounting bolts and remove the caliper. Secure the caliper, with a piece of stiff wire, to the rear springs.

➡ **Do not allow the caliper to hang by the brake line.**

4. Remove the brake disc and parking brake shoes.
5. Remove the thrust washer bolts through the holes in the axle shaft flange.
6. Using a puller (slide hammer), remove the axle shaft, bearing and oil seal assembly. If a slide hammer is not available, the brake disc may be bolted onto the axle backwards (remember to mount the nuts tapered side out) and used to pull the axle free.
7. Remove the inner oil seal using a suitable puller or small prybar.
8. Clean the inside of the rear axle tube.
9. Press off the toothed wheel. Use 2 V-blocks.
10. Raise up the seal and pressure plate on the axle shaft so that the divided press plate can be placed on the bearing.
11. Place the press yoke over the press plate.
12. Removing the bearing together with the snapring. Use press tool 5212 or equivalent.

   **To install:**
13. Pack the new bearing with grease before installation. The preferred method is with a bearing packer (a low cost tool available at most automotive supply shops) but it may be done by hand if necessary. The bearing must be packed from one side until the grease comes out the other side.
14. Fill the space between the lips of the new oil seal with wheel bearing grease.
15. Position the new seal on the axle shaft.
16. Using a press, install the bearing with a new locking ring, onto the axle shaft.

> ✳✳ **WARNING**
>
> **When reinstalling the additional toothed gear on axles, the gear must be installed precisely 116mm onto the shaft. The acceptable margin is plus or minus 0.1mm. If at all possible, use Volvo tool 2412 which will allow precise location of this gear. If this gear is not properly located, the vehicle may not run properly.**

17. Install the inner oil seal in the axle shaft housing using a seal installation tool (such as Volvo 5009 or similar) and drift.

18. Install the axle shaft into the housing, rotating it so that it aligns with the differential.

19. Install the bolts for the thrust washer and tighten to 29 ft. lbs. (40 Nm).

20. Install the parking brake shoes, brake disc, caliper and pads. Use new bolts and tighten to 43 ft. lbs. (58 Nm). Make sure the brake disc rotates free of the brake pads.

21. Install the wheel and adjust the parking brake.

22. Lower the vehicle.

## Axle Halfshafts

### REMOVAL & INSTALLATION

#### ♦ See Figures 71 and 72

The following procedure only pertains to axle shafts on vehicles with multi-link rear suspensions.

➡ **On vehicles with a multi-link suspension, the axles are actually half-shafts, bolted to the differential. Each halfshaft has a constant velocity (CV)-joint at each end, allowing a full range of motion as the vehicle passes over bumps and depressions.**

1. Loosen the large halfshaft retaining nut in the center of the wheel bearing housing.

2. Loosen the halfshaft retaining nut.

3. Raise and safely support the vehicle.

4. Remove the wheel(s).

5. At the center of the vehicle, remove the eight bolts holding the upper and lower sections of the final drive housing.

6. Remove the bolts holding the halfshaft to the final drive unit (differential) and remove the shaft from the wheel bearing housing.

7. When the shaft is removed, inspect the rubber boots for any sign of splitting or cracking. The boots must be intact and waterproof or the joint within is at risk. A light coat of silicone or vinyl protectant applied to a CV-boot will extend its life.

**To install:**

8. When reinstalling, fit the threaded end (at the wheel) first, then position and secure the inboard end. Always use new, lightly oiled bolts and tighten them to 70 ft. lbs. (95 Nm).

9. Reinstall the lower section of the final drive housing. Before tightening the eight mounting bolts, install two 12mm long bolts (or 12mm drifts) into the centering holes and align the panel. This is essential to insure correct wheel alignment when finished.

10. Tighten the eight mounting bolts to 52 ft. lbs. (71 Nm) PLUS 30 degrees of rotation.

11. Use a new, lightly oiled halfshaft retaining nut and install it on the threaded end of the shaft. Tighten it until it is snug, but do not final-tighten at this time.

12. Install the wheel(s).

13. Lower the vehicle.

14. Apply the hand brake and tighten the halfshaft nut to 103 ft. lbs. (140 Nm) PLUS 60 degrees of rotation. Double check the wheel lugs for correct tightness.

## Axle Halfshaft Bearings

### REMOVAL & INSTALLATION

The following procedure only pertains to axle shafts on vehicles with multi-link rear suspensions.

➡ **Because of the nature of the multi-link suspension, component position and bolt tightening values (torque) are critical to ride quality and rear wheel alignment. When installing components, exact location must be achieved—close doesn't count. Tightening specifications must be followed exactly or component function will be impaired.**

1. Disconnect the negative battery cable.

2. Raise and support the vehicle safely. Do not allow the rear lifting device to interfere with the support arms.

3. Remove the wheels.

4. Remove the brake caliper mounting bolts and use a piece of wire to hang the caliper out of the way.

5. Mark the position of the brake disc relative to its small locating pin, then remove the disc.

6. Remove the brake shoes.

7. Disconnect and remove the parking brake cable from the wheel bearing housing.

8. Remove the retaining bolt for the support arm at the housing. Tap the support arm loose.

9. Remove the nut and bolt holding the lower link arm to the housing.

10. Remove the retaining bolt for the track rod (Panhard rod) at the bearing housing and use a small claw-type puller to remove the track rod.

11. Loosen and remove the large nut holding the end of the driveshaft within the bearing housing.

12. Remove the retaining nut for the upper link at the bearing housing. The wheel bearing housing can now be removed as a unit.

➡ **There are shims between the bearing housing and the upper link arm. Collect them when the housing is removed.**

13. Mount the housing assembly in a vise.

14. Place a counterhold tool (5340 or equivalent) between the hub and bearing housing.

15. Press out the hub with a proper sized drift.

16. Remove the circlip retaining the bearing in the wheel bearing housing.

17. Press the bearing out of the wheel bearing housing, using a counterhold tool (5341 or equivalent) and a suitable drift. Apply the drift to the inner ring.

18. Use a bearing puller (2722 or equivalent) and a counterhold (5310 or equivalent) to pull the inner ring off the hub.

**To install:**

19. Press in the new bearing using the drift and counterhold. Install the circlip.

20. Using a counterhold below the inner ring, press the hub into place.

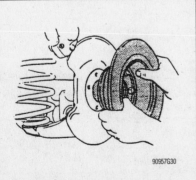

90957G30

**Fig. 70 Removing the axle shaft using the brake disc**

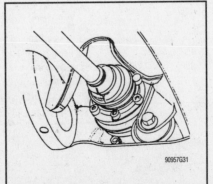

90957G31

**Fig. 71 The axle halfshafts are connected to the differential by retaining bolts**

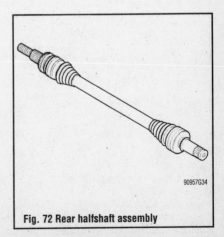

90957G34

**Fig. 72 Rear halfshaft assembly**

**If the counterhold (support) is not applied to the inner ring, the wheel bearing will be destroyed during the hub installation.**

21. Install the wheel bearing housing onto the driveshaft and install the driveshaft retaining nut. Secure the nut, but don't tighten it; that will be done later.

22. Install the shims between the upper link and the wheel bearing housing and then install the retaining nut at the upper link.

23. Pull the wheel bearing housing outwards at the top and tighten the upper link arm nut to 85 ft. lbs. (116 Nm) This pulling out is essential to insure correct wheel alignment when completed.

24. Tilt the bearing housing outwards at the bottom (as necessary) to refit the lower link arm and it's retaining bolt. When in place, pull the bottom of the bearing housing inwards (towards the center of the vehicle) and tighten the link arm to 36 ft. lbs. (49 Nm) PLUS an additional 90 degrees of rotation.

25. Install the support arm and its bolt. Tighten the nut to 44 ft. lbs. (60 Nm) PLUS an additional 90 degrees of rotation.

26. Install the track rod (Panhard rod) and tighten to 63 ft. lbs. (86 Nm).

27. Reinstall the parking brake cable at the bearing housing.

28. Reinstall the brake shoes, the brake disc as marked and the brake caliper. Tighten the caliper mounting bolts to 44 ft. lbs. (60 Nm).

29. Install the wheel, tightening the lugs to 60–62 ft. lbs. (82–85 Nm).

30. Lower the vehicle.

31. Tighten the axle nut to 103 ft. lbs. (140 Nm) PLUS 60 degrees of rotation.

## Pinion Seal

### REMOVAL & INSTALLATION

#### Except Multi-Link Suspension

▶ See Figure 73

1. Raise and safely support the vehicle.
2. Disconnect the driveshaft at the final drive unit (differential).
3. Loosen and remove the large center nut in the center of the pinion flange. The use of a counterhold device is highly recommended (Volvo 5149 or similar).
4. Use a puller to remove the flange from the housing.
5. Remove the old seal from the inside of the casing and discard it.
6. Clean and check the sealing surfaces. Replace the coupling flange if the sealing surface is worn.

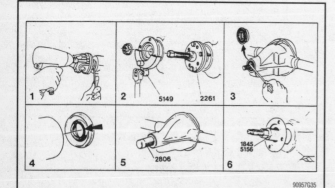

**Fig. 73 Steps to replace the pinion seal**

**To install:**

7. Prepare the new seal by greasing the lip area and greasing the small spring to hold it in place during installation.

8. Install the seal using suitable drivers; do not crimp or gouge the seal during installation.

9. With an installation tool (Volvo 5156 or similar), reinstall the flange in the housing.

10. Install the center nut and tighten it to 145–180 ft. lbs. (197–245 Nm). Use a counterhold device to hold the flange while tightening.

11. Axles denoted by the S prefix in their serial number contain a compression sleeve within the differential housing. On these vehicles, install the center nut and finger-tighten, or carefully tighten to 16 inch lbs. (2 Nm). Make sure that the brakes are not applied and turn the flange at about 1 revolution per second so as to tighten the nut. As an alternative, the nut may be tightened with a wrench to at least 130 ft. lbs. (177 Nm).

12. Reinstall the driveshaft.

13. Check the oil level within the final drive and top up as necessary.

14. Lower the vehicle.

#### Multi-Link Suspension

▶ See Figure 74

1. Raise and safely support the vehicle.
2. Matchmark the driveshaft flange and the final drive (differential) flange.
3. Remove the bolts and separate the shaft from the final drive.
4. Loosen and remove the large center nut in the center of the pinion flange. The use of a counterhold device is highly recommended. (Volvo 5149 or similar). Remove the 1 additional bolt from the flange. This bolt is a weight which serves to balance the rotational forces of the driveshaft.
5. Matchmark the flange and its center shaft for reassembly.
6. Drain the oil from the housing.
7. Use a puller to remove the flange from the housing.
8. Remove the old seal from the inside of the casing and discard it.
9. Clean and check the sealing surfaces. Replace the coupling flange if the sealing surface is worn.

**Fig. 74 Removing the pinion seal using puller 5069 or equivalent**

**To install:**

10. Prepare the new seal by greasing the lip area and greasing the small spring to hold it in place during installation. The use of a seal puller such as Volvo 5069 is highly recommended.

11. Install the seal using suitable drivers; do not crimp or gouge the seal during installation.

12. Position the flange so that the marks align.

13. With an installation tool (Volvo 5156 or similar), reinstall the flange in the housing.

14. Install a new, lightly oiled center nut and tighten it to 132–145 ft. lbs. (180–197 Nm).

**Do not overtighten the center nut. The pinion bearings will become overadjusted and fail prematurely.**

15. Install the bolt for weight in its original position.

16. Install the driveshaft, observing correct placement as shown by the matchmarks. Use new nuts and bolts and tighten them to 36 ft. lbs. (49 Nm).

17. Refill the final drive unit with oil.

18. Lower the vehicle.

## Axle Housing Assembly

### REMOVAL & INSTALLATION

> ※ **WARNING**
>
> **This operation requires removal of a substantial amount of weight from the rear of the vehicle. Position the jackstands at the front end, under the control arm brackets, and at rear, under the jack mounts. If the vehicle is not supported as described, it may become front heavy.**

#### Except Multi-Link Suspension

▶ **See Figure 75**

1. Raise the vehicle and support it safely.

> ※ **WARNING**
>
> **This operation requires removal of a substantial amount of weight from the rear of the vehicle. Position the jackstands at front end, under the control arm brackets and at rear, under the jack mounts. If the vehicle is not supported as described, it may become front heavy.**

2. On the 240 Series, remove the rear axle vent hose and the brake line brackets. Do not loosen any brake lines; they will be left intact.
3. Remove the brake calipers and secure them to the upper spring mount with a piece of stiff wire.
4. Remove the axle shafts, as outlined in this section.
5. Position the jacks or cradle below the rear axle so that the axle is supported.
6. If the exhaust system runs under the axle housing, disconnect the first joint forward of the axle, disconnect any hangers or brackets behind the axle and remove the rear section of the exhaust system.
7. Disconnect the reaction rods or torque rod from the axle housing.
8. Disconnect the Panhard rod from the rear axle.
9. Remove the parking brake cables and mounting brackets from the rear axle.
10. Detach the connector for the speedometer transmitter and, if equipped, the connectors for the ETC system.
11. Loosen and remove the bolts attaching the driveshaft to the pinion flange.
12. Double check that the axle assembly is firmly supported by the jacks or cradle. Remove the bolts which hold the lower mount of the shock absorber.
13. On the 240 Series:
   a. Remove the adjacent bolt which holds the anti-roll bar (sway bar).
   b. Loosen, but do not remove the trailing arm bolts at the front of the trailing arm.

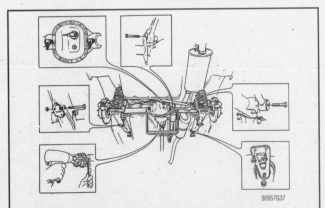

**Fig. 75 Points of reference for solid rear axle removal**

90957G37

c. Lower the jacks or cradle and allow the axle assemble to pivot downwards on the trailing arms. When clear of the vehicle and well supported on the jacks or cradle, remove the trailing arm mounts at the axle housing.
   d. Remove the rear axle assembly.
14. On the 700 and 900 Series:
   a. Remove the front brackets for the support arms. Pry the support arms loose from the front mounts.
   b. Remove the rear axle assembly.
   c. Once the axle assembly is clear of the vehicle, remove the anti-roll bar (sway bar). Mark the support arms for the left and right sides and remove the arms from the axle housing.

**To install:**

15. On the 240 Series:
   a. Position the axle unit under the vehicle and attach the trailing arm mounts. Tighten the bolts only enough to hold and still allow motion.
   b. Raise the axle and align the springs to their upper mounts. Install the anti-roll bar bolts and the bolts for the lower shock absorber mounts
   c. Attach the torque rods to their mounts and attach the Panhard rod to its mount. Tighten these bolts only enough to hold and still allow motion.
16. On the 700 and 900 Series:
   a. Make sure the left and right markings are observed. Fit the bushings within the clamps and fit the clamps.
   b. Tighten the clamps in a crisscross pattern to 33 ft. lbs. (45 Nm) and reinstall the anti-roll bar if so equipped.
   c. Position the axle on its jacks or cradle and elevate it so the support arms align with both their front mounts and the spring seats.
   d. Install the front brackets for the support arms and tighten the two bolts to 35 ft. lbs. (48 Nm). Tighten the nut to 62 ft. lbs. (84 Nm).
   e. Install the lower shock absorber bolts and tighten to 62 ft. lbs. (84 Nm).
17. Reinstall the driveshaft to the pinion flange.
18. Connect the wiring for the ETC sensor and/or the speedometer sensor, as required.
19. Install the parking brake cables and brackets. Adjust the parking brake.
20. Reinstall the exhaust system, as necessary.
21. Complete installation by reversing the removal procedure.
22. Check oil level in differential.
23. Lower the vehicle.

#### Multi-Link Suspension

Because of the nature of the multi-link suspension, component position and bolt tightening values (torque) are critical to ride quality and rear wheel alignment. When installing components, exact location must be achieved; close doesn't count. Tightening specifications must be followed exactly or component function will be impaired.

1. Raise the vehicle and support it firmly with stands. Locate front lifting arms as far forward as possible. Make sure the rear lifting arms do not interfere with the support arms.
2. Remove the rear wheels.
3. On one side only, remove the bolt holding the support arm to the wheel bearing housing.
4. Drive out the support arm.
5. Remove the nut and bolt holding the lower link arm to the wheel bearing housing.
6. Remove the bolts holding the track rod (Panhard rod) to the wheel bearing housing. Use a small claw puller and an M12 bolt 50mm long to move the rod away from the housing.
7. Remove the bolts joining the upper and lower sections of the rear axle housing.
8. Swing the lower part of the wheel bearing housing outwards and swing down the lower part of the axle housing. It will still have the arms attached to it and will be attached to the vehicle by the arms on the opposite side.
9. Matchmark the flanges at the rear of the driveshaft.
10. Remove the four bolts and lower the driveshaft.
11. Place a jack or cradle under the center of the final drive (differential) unit.
12. Raise the jack and support the unit.
13. Remove the bolts holding the final drive to the upper housing.
14. Lower the final drive slightly. Remove the wiring to the impulse sender.
15. Remove the bolts holding the axles to the final drive.

16. Carefully lower the final drive unit and remove it from under the vehicle.

**To install:**

17. Raise the final drive unit almost to its final position under the vehicle and connect the impulse sender cable. Tighten the bolt to 7 ft. lbs. (10 Nm).

18. Raise the unit to its final position and install the three bolts to the upper housing. Tighten the bolts. When the bolts are secure, the jack or cradle may be removed.

19. Attach the halfshafts to the final drive. Tighten the bolts to specifications.

20. Install the driveshaft to the pinion flange. Remember to observe the matchmarks made earlier and position the driveshaft properly.

21. Raise the lower section of the axle housing. Loosely install the bolts which retain it to the upper housing. Before tightening the mounting bolts, install two 12mm long bolts (or 12mm drifts) in the centering holes and align the panel. This is essential to insure correct wheel alignment when finished. Tighten the mounting bolts to specifications.

22. Position and install the lower link arm on the wheel bearing housing. Before tightening the nut and bolt, pull the housing in towards the center of the vehicle. When all the play is out of the mount, tighten the link bolt to specifications.

23. Install the support arm and track rod.
24. Install the wheels.
25. Check the oil level in the final drive and top up as necessary.
26. Lower the vehicle.

## TORQUE SPECIFICATIONS

| Components | English | Metric |
|---|---|---|
| Automatic transmission and M47 output shaft flange nut | 65-85 ft. lbs. | 90-110 Nm |
| Axle shaft-to-multi-link differential retaining bolts | 70 ft. lbs. | 95 Nm |
| Converter-to-flywheel bolts | | |
|    240, 700 Series and Coupe Models | 35 ft. lbs. | 48 Nm |
|    All others | 22 ft. lbs. | 30 Nm |
| Driveshaft flange bolts | 32 ft. lbs. | 44 Nm |
| Extension housing bolts (auto and manual transmissions) | 20-35 ft. lbs. | 27-47 Nm |
| Multi-link rear differential support arm | 44 ft. lbs. | 60 Nm |
| Multi-link rear axle nuts | 103 ft. lbs. | 140 Nm |
| M46 manual transmission output shaft flange nut | 126 ft. lbs. | 175 Nm |
| Pinion retaining nut: | | |
|    Solid rear axle | 145-180 ft. lbs. | 197-245 Nm |
|    Multi-link rear axle | 132-145 ft. lbs. | 180-197 Nm |
| Passenger side transaxle halfshaft support bearing nuts | 19 ft. lbs. | 26 Nm |
| Pressure plate-to-flywheel bolts | 18 ft. lbs. | 25 Nm |
| Rear crossmember mount nuts | | |
|    240, 700 Series and Coupe Models | 18 ft. lbs. | 25 Nm |
|    All others | 37 ft. lbs. | 50 Nm |
| Solid rear axle shaft thrust washer nuts | 29 ft. lbs. | 40 Nm |
| Subframe bolts | 78 ft. lbs.* | 107 Nm* |
| Torque rod transaxle mount with M18 bolts | 13 ft. lbs. | 18 Nm |
|                 with M10 bolts | 26 ft. lbs. | 35 Nm |
| Transaxle bell housing bolts | 37 ft. lbs. | 50 Nm |
| Transaxle halfshaft axle nuts | 89 ft. lbs.** | 120 Nm** |
| Transmission/transaxle mount | 37 ft. lbs. | 50 Nm |
| Transfer case output flange nut | 133-148 ft. lbs. | 181-201 Nm |
| Transfer case-to-transaxle retaining bolts | 37 ft. lbs. | 50 Nm |

\* Plus an additional 120 degrees
\*\* Plus an additional 60 degrees

90957C01

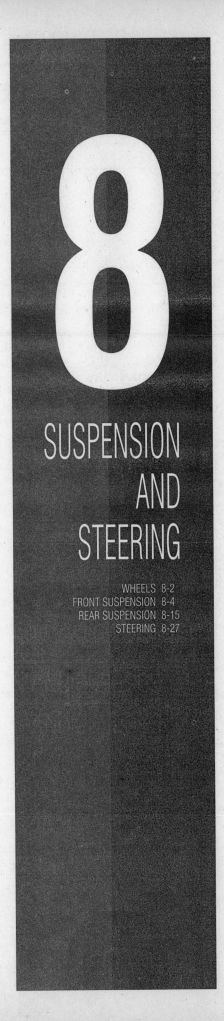

# 8

## SUSPENSION AND STEERING

## WHEELS

### Wheels

#### REMOVAL & INSTALLATION

▶ **See Figures 1 thru 9**

1. Park the vehicle on a level surface.
2. Remove the jack, tire iron and, if necessary, the spare tire from their storage compartments.
3. Check the owner's manual or refer to Section 1 of this manual for the jacking points on your vehicle. Then, place the jack in the proper position.
4. If equipped with lug nut trim caps, remove them by either unscrewing or pulling them off the lug nuts, as appropriate. Consult the owner's manual, if necessary.
5. If equipped with a wheel cover or hub cap, insert the tapered end of the tire iron in the groove and pry off the cover.
6. Apply the parking brake and block the diagonally opposite wheel with a wheel chock or two.

➡**Wheel chocks may be purchased at your local auto parts store, or a block of wood cut into wedges may be used. If possible, keep one or two of the chocks in your tire storage compartment, in case any of the tires has to be removed on the side of the road.**

7. If equipped with an automatic transmission/transaxle, place the selector lever in **P** or Park; with a manual transmission/transaxle, place the shifter in Reverse.
8. With the tires still on the ground, use the tire iron/wrench to break the lug nuts loose.

➡**If a nut is stuck, never use heat to loosen it or damage to the wheel and bearings may occur. If the nuts are seized, one or two heavy ham-** mer blows directly on the end of the bolt usually loosens the rust. Be careful, as continued pounding will likely damage the brake drum or rotor.

9. Using the jack, raise the vehicle until the tire is clear of the ground. Support the vehicle safely using jackstands.
10. Remove the lug nuts, then remove the tire and wheel assembly.

**To install:**

11. Make sure the wheel and hub mating surfaces, as well as the wheel lug studs, are clean and free of all foreign material. Always remove rust from the wheel mounting surface and the brake rotor or drum. Failure to do so may cause the lug nuts to loosen in service.
12. Install the tire and wheel assembly and hand-tighten the lug nuts.
13. Using the tire wrench, tighten all the lug nuts, in a crisscross pattern, until they are snug.
14. Raise the vehicle and withdraw the jackstand, then lower the vehicle.
15. Using a torque wrench, tighten the lug nuts in a crisscross pattern to the proper torque (use the charts at the end of this section). Check your owner's manual or refer to Section 1 of this manual for the proper tightening sequence.

#### ✲✲ WARNING

**Do not overtighten the lug nuts, as this may cause the wheel studs to stretch or the brake disc (rotor) to warp.**

16. If so equipped, install the wheel cover or hub cap. Make sure the valve stem protrudes through the proper opening before tapping the wheel cover into position.
17. If equipped, install the lug nut trim caps by pushing them or screwing them on, as applicable.
18. Remove the jack from under the vehicle, and place the jack and tire iron/wrench in their storage compartments. Remove the wheel chock(s).

Fig. 1 Using a rag or paper towel under the prytool will help prevent scratches to your wheels

Fig. 2 Place the jack at the proper lifting point on your vehicle

Fig. 3 Before jacking the vehicle, block the diagonally opposite wheel with one or, preferably, two chocks

Fig. 4 With the vehicle still on the ground, break the lug nuts loose using the wrench end of the tire iron

Fig. 5 After the lug nuts have been loosened, raise the vehicle using the jack until the tire is clear of the ground

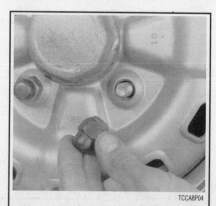

Fig. 6 Remove the lug nuts from the studs

Fig. 7 Remove the wheel and tire assembly from the vehicle

Fig. 8 This pin is used to align the wheel upon installation

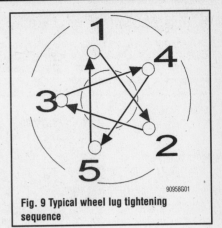

Fig. 9 Typical wheel lug tightening sequence

19. If you have removed a flat or damaged tire, place it in the storage compartment of the vehicle and take it to your local repair station to have it fixed or replaced as soon as possible.

## INSPECTION

Inspect the tires for lacerations, puncture marks, nails and other sharp objects. Repair or replace as necessary. Also check the tires for treadwear and air pressure as outlined in Check the wheel assemblies for dents, cracks, rust and metal fatigue. Repair or replace as necessary.

## Wheel Lug Studs

### REMOVAL & INSTALLATION

▶ **See Figures 10, 11 and 12**

1. Raise and support the appropriate end of the vehicle safely using jackstands, then remove the wheel.
2. Remove the brake pads and caliper. Support the caliper aside using wire or a coat hanger. For details, please refer to Section 9 of this manual.
3. Remove the outer wheel bearing and lift off the rotor.
4. Properly support the rotor using press bars, then drive the stud out using an arbor press.

➡**If a press is not available, CAREFULLY drive the old stud out using a blunt drift MAKE SURE the rotor is properly and evenly supported or it may be damaged.**

**To install:**
5. Clean the stud hole with a wire brush and start the new stud with a hammer and drift pin. Do not use any lubricant or thread sealer.

6. Finish installing the stud with the press.

➡**If a press is not available, start the lug stud through the bore in the hub, then position about 4 flat washers over the stud and thread the lug nut. Hold the hub/rotor while tightening the lug nut, and the stud should be drawn into position. MAKE SURE THE STUD IS FULLY SEATED, then remove the lug nut and washers.**

7. Install the rotor and adjust the wheel bearings.
8. Install the brake caliper and pads.
9. Install the wheel, then remove the jackstands and carefully lower the vehicle.
10. Tighten the lug nuts to the proper torque.

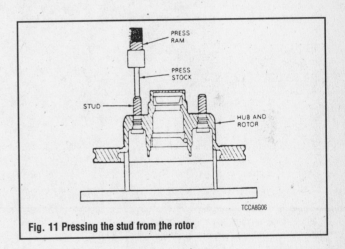

Fig. 11 Pressing the stud from the rotor

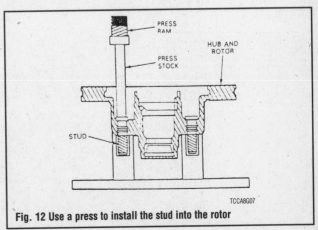

Fig. 10 View of the rotor and stud assembly

Fig. 12 Use a press to install the stud into the rotor

## FRONT SUSPENSION

The front suspension is the MacPherson type, which means that the wheels are independently sprung. The spring is located around the strut assembly, the lower end of which is affixed to the wheel spindle. The strut assembly is retained by a threaded screw in an upper mount, which is fixed to the wheel housing, and by its seating at the bottom. The upper end of the spring is fixed to the wheel arch and rests on the upper mount, through the upper mount seat. The seating for the lower end of the spring is a welded perch on the bottom of the strut tube.

**V70R AWD FRONT SUSPENSION AND STEERING COMPONENTS**

1. Outer tie rod end
2. Sway bar
3. Sway bar link
4. Lower control arm
5. Lower ball joint
6. Strut assembly
7. Sway bar bushing
8. Lower control arm bushing

90958P01

**850 FRONT SUSPENSION AND STEERING COMPONENTS**

1. Sway bar
2. Sway bar bushing
3. Sway bar link
4. Outer tie rod end
5. Lower control arm
6. Lower ball joint
7. Strut assembly
8. Steering rack and pinion

## Coil Springs

### REMOVAL & INSTALLATION

The coil springs are integrated into the strut assembly. See the MacPherson Strut removal and installation and overhaul procedures which follow.

## MacPherson Struts

### REMOVAL & INSTALLATION

#### 240, 700, 900, S90 and V90 Series

▶ **See Figure 13**

1. Raise and safely support vehicle.
2. Remove the wheel.
3. Disconnect the tie rod end.
4. Place a floor jack under the control arm.
5. Disconnect the sway bar link.
6. Unbolt the brake lines from the bracket and detach them from the clips.
7. Remove the cover over the strut nut.
8. Disconnect the coil wire and place it out of the way.
9. Hold the strut shaft with tool 5037 or equivalent and loosen the nut a few turns with tool 5036 or equivalent.
10. Mark the position of the upper mount in the housing, then remove the nuts and washers.
11. Carefully lower the jack and pull the strut and spring out of the housing.

### ✳✳ WARNING

**Be careful not to damage the fender when removing the strut assembly. Use retaining hook 5045 or equivalent attached to the anti-sway bar to prevent it from falling.**

**To install:**
12. Guide the strut assembly into the body.
13. Install the upper mount according to the earlier marking and tighten to 30 ft. lbs. (40 Nm).
14. Tighten the strut nut to 111 ft. lbs. (150 Nm) using socket 5036 and holder 5037 or equivalents.
15. Press nut cover back on and connect the coil wire.
16. Install the sway bar link and tighten it until the distance between the washers is 1.65 in. (42mm).
17. Install the brake line bracket and clips. Make sure that the brake lines are sitting correctly in the wheelwell.

18. Install the tie rod end.
19. Install the wheel.
20. Lower the vehicle and test.

#### 850, C70, S70 and V70 Series

▶ **See Figures 14 thru 20**

1. Raise and safely support vehicle.
2. Remove the wheel.
3. Disconnect the sway bar link from the strut.
4. Remove the ABS sensor lead from the strut and brake bracket, but do not disconnect.
5. Install support tool 5466 or equivalent under the control arm.

### ✳✳ WARNING

**If this tool is not installed, the axle joint may be damaged from excessive downward pressure.**

6. Remove the two nuts and bolts holding the strut to the steering knuckle.
7. Remove the upper nuts attaching the strut attachment to the body.
8. Remove the spring and strut assembly.

**To install:**
9. Install the spring and strut assembly in the spring housing and fasten it using new nuts; tighten them to 18 ft. lbs. (25 Nm).
10. Connect the strut to the steering knuckle using new bolts and nuts.
11. Tighten them to 48 ft. lbs. (65 Nm) and angle tighten 90°.
12. Connect the sway bar to the strut using new nuts.
13. Install the ABS sensor lead to the strut and brake pipe bracket.
14. Remove the support tool.
15. Install the wheel.
16. Lower the vehicle.

### OVERHAUL

### ✳✳ CAUTION

**A coil spring compressor is required to remove the spring. Improper removal procedures may cause serious injury.**

#### 240, 700, 900, S90 and V90 Series

1. Remove the strut from the vehicle.
2. To remove the spring:
   a. Attach spring compressor tool 5040 or equivalent to the spring. The two parts of the tool should be opposite each other and have three coils between the claws.
   b. Compress each side alternately until the strut is loose inside the spring.
   c. Hold the strut shaft with tool 5037 or equivalent and remove the nut with tool 5036 or equivalent and lift off the upper mount, spring retainer, spring and rubber bumper.

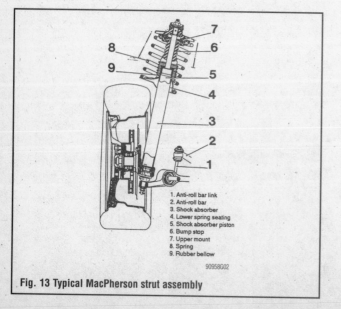

1. Anti-roll bar link
2. Anti-roll bar
3. Shock absorber
4. Lower spring seating
5. Shock absorber piston
6. Bump stop
7. Upper mount
8. Spring
9. Rubber bellow

90958G02

**Fig. 13 Typical MacPherson strut assembly**

90958P23

**Fig. 14 Remove the ABS sensor lead from the strut**

Fig. 15 The strut is attached to the knuckle by two bolts (and nuts)

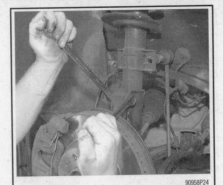

Fig. 16 Remove the two strut-to-knuckle bolts and nuts

Fig. 17 Threading the nut onto the bolt after removal is an easy way to keep track of them

Fig. 18 Separate the strut from the spindle

DO NOT REMOVE

Fig. 19 Remove the three bolts holding the strut to the body, but never remove the large nut in the center while still in the vehicle

Fig. 20 Carefully remove the strut from the vehicle

➡On vehicles equipped with gas pressure struts, the bumper has been replaced by a rubber bellow and disc.

3. To remove the strut, unscrew the retaining nut and pull the shock insert out of the casing, using tool 5039 or equivalent for standard struts, or tool 5173 or equivalent for gas struts.

**To install:**

4. Insert the strut insert into the housing and tighten the retaining nut to 111 ft. lbs. (150 Nm).

5. Install the bumper or bellows and disc on the strut, making sure that the top of the bumper is lower than the top of the strut shaft

6. Install the spring so the compressor tool bolt holes face upwards.

7. Install the upper mount, washer and nut but do not tighten fully.

8. Remove the compressor loosening the bolts alternately and make sure that the ends of the spring fit correctly into the upper and lower plates.

9. Install the strut in the vehicle.

### 850, C70, S70 and V70 Series

▶ See Figures 21 thru 30

1. Remove the strut from the vehicle.

2. Mount the spring and strut assembly in a vise and secure it.

3. Install spring compressing tool 5407 or equivalent and alternately compress the spring.

4. Remove the bolt and washer from the strut attachment using socket 5467 and counterhold 5468 or equivalents.

5. Remove the strut nut using socket 5469 and counterhold 5468 or equivalents.

6. Remove the bearing dustcap and remove the bearing locknut.

7. Remove the spring seat and bearing, rubber stopper, boot, and check them for damage.

8. Remove the compressed spring from the strut.

**To install:**

9. Compress the spring to about 12 in. (30.5cm) in length.

10. Install the rubber stopper.

11. Install the washer.

12. Install the compressed spring.

13. Install the spring seat and bearing.

➡Make sure that the spring ends are properly seated.

14. Install the spring attachment, washer, and nut and tighten it to 52 ft. lbs. (70 Nm) using socket 5467 and counterhold 5468, or their equivalents.

15. Slowly and alternately remove the spring compressor.

16. Install the strut in the vehicle.

Fig. 21 Install the strut spring compressor tool onto the spring

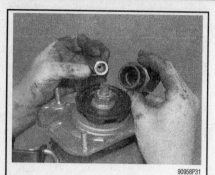

Fig. 22 A tool set, such as this one from Lisle®, is available to aid in the removal of the strut bearing

Fig. 23 One tool fits over the nut, and the other is used to hold the shaft while the retaining nut is removed

Fig. 24 Remove the nut . . .

Fig. 25 . . . followed by the bearing dust cap

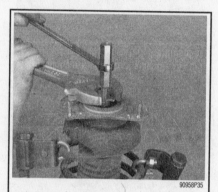

Fig. 26 Use the shaft tool to aid in the removal of the bearing locknut

Fig. 27 Remove the bearing and upper spring seat . . .

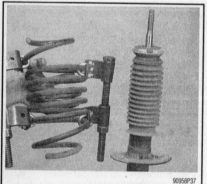

Fig. 28 . . . then remove the compressed spring

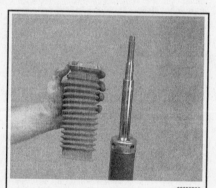

Fig. 29 Don't forget to remove the strut boot if replacing the strut

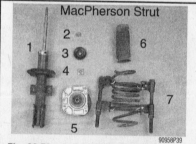

Fig. 30 Disassembled strut components include a strut tube (1), retaining nut (2), bearing dust cap (3) and locknut (4), bearing and upper spring seat (5), boot (6) and compressed spring (7)

## Lower Ball Joint

### INSPECTION

Check the ball joint axial play. Maximum axial play permitted is 0.12 inch (3mm). Check the radial play. Maximum radial play permitted is 0.02 inch (0.5mm).

### REMOVAL & INSTALLATION

#### 240 Series

1. Raise the vehicle and support it safely.
2. Mark the position of the wheel stud nearest to the valve. Wheel is marked to facilitate installation and to avoid the need for rebalancing.

3. Remove the wheel and tire assembly.
4. Remove the ball joint nut from the knuckle.
5. Remove the 4 bolts which retains the ball joint and remove the ball joint from the control arm.
6. Remove the ball joint retaining nut and press the ball joint out of attachment.
**To install:**

➡Ball joints are different for right and left sides. It is therefore important that the correct ball joint is installed on the correct side.

7. Press the ball joint to the attachment, and install the ball joint on the control arm and tighten the bolts to 44 ft. lbs. (60 Nm).
8. Install the ball joint to the knuckle and tighten to 85 ft. lbs. (115 Nm).
9. Install the wheel on the hub assembly, while aligning the marking made earlier. Alternately tighten the nuts to specifications.
10. Lower the vehicle.

**700, 900, S90 and V90 Series**

♦ **See Figure 31**

1. Raise the vehicle and support it safely.
2. Mark the position of the wheel stud nearest to the valve. Wheel is marked to facilitate installation and to avoid the need for rebalancing.
3. Remove the wheel and tire assembly.
4. Remove the bolt which holds the anti-roll bar link to the control arm.
5. Remove the cotter pin, nut and washer for the ball joint stud.
6. Pull the control arm from the ball joint using a suitable puller (5259 or equivalent).
7. Remove the bolts holding the ball joint to the spring strut.
8. Press the control arm downwards and remove the ball joint.

**To install:**

9. Install the new ball joint.
10. Use new bolts and apply sealing fluid to the threads. Check that the bolt heads sit flat on the ball joint. Tighten the bolts to 22 ft. lbs. (30 Nm) PLUS angle tighten 90 degrees.
11. Install the control arm to ball joint.
12. Install the washer and nut.
13. Tighten ball joint stud (nut) to 44 ft. lbs. (60 Nm).
14. Install the cotter pin.
15. Install the anti-roll bar.
16. Install the wheel.
17. Lower the vehicle.

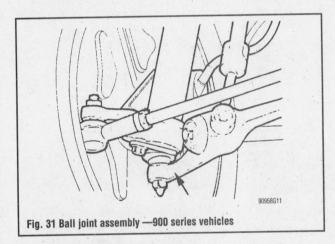

**Fig. 31 Ball joint assembly —900 series vehicles**

**850, C70, S70 and V70 Series**

1. Raise and safely support the vehicle.
2. Remove the wheel.
3. Remove the three nuts holding the ball joint to the lower control arm.
4. Remove the clamping bolt and nut from the steering knuckle where the ball joint is mounted.
5. Spread the ball joint apart and remove it from the hub housing.

**To install:**

6. Clean the control arm and steering knuckle where the new ball joint is fitted.
7. Install the new ball joint with the clamping bolt and nut. Tighten the bolt to 37 ft. lbs. (50 Nm).
8. Connect the ball joint to the lower control arm and fasten it with new nuts. Apply rustproofing compound to the nuts. Starting from inside, working outward, tighten the nuts to 13 ft. lbs. (18 Nm) and then angle tighten 120°.
9. Install the wheel.
10. Lower the car.

## Sway Bar

The sway bar, variously called the anti-roll bar or stabilizer bar, serves to control the sideways roll of the body during cornering. While the bar itself rarely fails, the links and bushings around it are prone to wear. If the bar is not rigidly mounted to the vehicle, it cannot do its job properly.

Sway bars of different diameters (thickness) can stiffen or soften the roll characteristics of a vehicle. Bushings are easily replaced and well worth the effort in terms of restoring proper cornering manners to your vehicle.

### REMOVAL & INSTALLATION

**240 Series**

1. Raise the vehicle and support it safely.
2. Remove the wheels.
3. Remove the underside splash guard panel, if equipped.
4. Remove the upper nut securing the anti-roll bar to the struts.
5. Remove the upper link nut on the opposite side.
6. Remove the bolts for the two retaining brackets and remove the bar.
7. If the link bushings are worn, remove the lower link bolts and remove the entire link.
8. Inspect all the bushings for compression or elongation. Replace as required. The two U-shaped bushings from the front brackets are particularly prone to deforming.

**To install:**

9. Reconnect the lower link to the arms, if removed.
10. Hold the bar in position and install the front brackets with bushings. Make sure the slot in the bushing faces forward.
11. Install the bar to the link on one side of the vehicle but do not tighten more than a few turns.
12. Connect the bar to the link on the opposite side and install the bushings and nut.
13. Tighten each upper link nut until 1.65 inches (42mm) can be measured between the outer surfaces of the upper and lower washers.
14. Reinstall the underside splash panel, if required.
15. Install the wheel.
16. Lower the vehicle.

**700 Series, 940 and 1992–94 960 Models**

♦ **See Figure 32**

1. Raise and safely support vehicle.
2. Remove the wheels.
3. Remove the splashguard from under the engine.
4. Disconnect the anti-sway bar from upper link mounts on both sides.
5. Remove the sway bar clamps on both sides and take the bar off.

**To install:**

6. Install new rubber bushings on sway bar and attach to subframe with clamps.
7. Connect sway bar to upper link mounts and tighten the nut until the distance between bushing washers is 1.65 in. (42mm).
8. Install the splashguard under the engine.
9. Install the wheels.
10. Lower the vehicle.

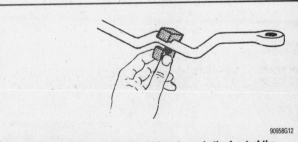

**Fig. 32 The bushing opening should face towards the front of the vehicle when installed**

**1995–98 960/S90/V90 Models**

1. Raise and safely support the vehicle.
2. Remove the wheels.
3. Remove the nuts connecting the sway bar to the axle beam.

4. Remove the bolts connecting the sway bar to the support arms.

5. Remove the sway bar.

**To install:**

6. Attach the sway bar to the axle beam using new nuts. Tighten the nuts to 15 ft. lbs. (20 Nm).

7. Connect the sway bar to the support arms using new bolts. Do not tighten the bolts.

8. Tighten the support arm bolts to 63 ft. lbs. (80 Nm).

9. Install the wheels.

10. Lower the vehicle.

### 850, C70, S70 and V70 Series

▶ **See Figures 33, 34, 35 and 36**

1. Install support rails 5033, bracket 5006 and lifting hook 5115, or suitable equivalents. These make it possible to raise the engine in the vehicle.

2. Raise the engine slightly.

3. Raise and safely support the vehicle.

4. Remove the underengine splashguard.

5. Remove the five nuts holding steering gear to the subframe.

6. Disconnect the power steering line brackets from the subframe at the front and rear edges.

7. Position a suitable jack under the rear crossmember.

8. Remove the bolts holding the subframe brackets to the body on both sides.

9. Remove the two subframe bolts, brackets and washers.

10. Lower the subframe at the rear edge approximately 0.59–0.79 in. (15–20mm). Make sure that the steering gear bolts come away from the frame.

11. Remove the sway bar links and subframe brackets.

12. Remove the sway bar.

**To install:**

13. Install the sway bar and subframe brackets.

14. Install the sway bar links using new nuts and tighten them to 37 ft. lbs. (50 Nm).

15. Raise the subframe up with the jack and push the steering gear mount bolts into the frame.

16. Install the subframe brackets and new M14 bolts, but do not tighten fully.

17. Move the jack to the front edge of the frame and replace the bolts. Do not tighten fully.

18. First tighten the bolts on the left side on the frame to 77 ft. lbs. (105 Nm) and angle tighten 120°. Then do the same to the right side.

19. Tighten the bracket bolts to 37 ft. lbs. (50 Nm).

20. Install new attaching nuts to the steering gear and tighten them to 37 ft. lbs. (50 Nm).

21. Tighten the power steering line brackets on the front and rear edges of the subframe.

22. Install the underengine splashguard.

23. Lower the vehicle.

24. Remove the support rails, bracket and lifting hook.

## Control Arm Strut

The control arm strut, also called the radius rod or strut rod, serve to locate the lower control arm and prevent fore-and-aft movement. Except for impact damage, the rods rarely fail. The rubber bushings on each end are prone to fatigue and wear, and may need to be replaced after a few years. This part is found on all 960/S90/V90 models.

### REMOVAL & INSTALLATION

▶ **See Figure 37**

1. Disconnect the negative battery cable.

2. Raise and safely support the vehicle on jackstands.

3. Loosen the rod-to-bracket bolt but don't remove it.

4. Remove the nut at the control arm. This is sometimes easier said than done; the control arm bolt can be very tight.

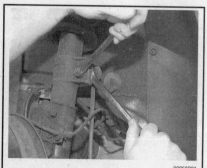

Fig. 33 Hold the hex head on the ball end of the link with an appropriate size wrench, or the nut cannot be removed

Fig. 34 If replacing the link, use a new nut; the old nut can be discarded

Fig. 35 After both nuts are unfastened, remove the link from the vehicle

Fig. 36 The sway bar bushings are located on the subframe

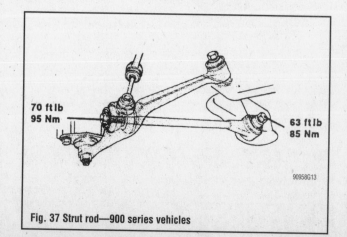

Fig. 37 Strut rod—900 series vehicles

70 ft lb
95 Nm

63 ft lb
85 Nm

5. Once the front nut is loosened, the back mount may be removed and the rod placed on a workbench.

**To install:**

6. If the bushings are to be replaced, press them free of their mounts and install the new ones.

7. Reinstall the rod, attaching the bracket bolt first.

8. Make sure the front bushings seat properly in the control arm and that the front nut draws tight against its washer.

9. Tighten the bracket bolt to 63 ft. lbs. (85 Nm).

10. Tighten the control arm nut to 70 ft. lbs. (95 Nm).

11. Lower the vehicle.

12. Connect the negative battery cable.

## Lower Control Arm

➡On all models, fully install the control arm, bounce the suspension several times, and THEN tighten the control arm-to-crossmember mounting nuts or bolts.

### 240 Series

▶ **See Figure 38**

1. Raise the vehicle and support it safely.

2. Remove the wheel(s).

3. Disconnect the stabilizer (sway bar) link at the control arm.

4. Remove the control arm from the ball joint. Refer to the Lower Ball Joint removal and installation procedure.

5. Remove the control arm rear attachment plate.

6. Remove the control arm front retaining bolt.

7. Remove the control arm.

**To install:**

8. If bushings are to be replaced, note that the right and left bushings are not interchangeable. The right side bushing should be turned so that the small slots point horizontally when installed.

9. Install the bracket onto the control arm. The nut should be tightened only enough to hold securely. The washer should be able to be turned with your fingers after the nut is on.

10. Attach the control arm. Install the front retaining bolt and nut; tighten the nut only a few turns onto the bolt.

11. Guide the stabilizer link into position. Attach it loosely with its nut and bolt.

12. Install the ball joint and its mount. Tighten the 3 mounting bolts to specification.

13. Install the rear bracket to the vehicle. Tighten the three bolts to 25–35 ft. lbs. (34–48 Nm).

14. Tighten the stabilizer link.

15. Install the wheel(s).

16. Lower the vehicle.

17. Jounce the front of the vehicle up and down. This "normalizes" the front suspension and allows the control arm to seek its final position.

18. Tighten the rear mount nut to 38–44 ft. lbs. (52–60 Nm).

19. Tighten the front mount to 55 ft. lbs. (75 Nm).

### 700, 900, S90 and V90 Series

1. Raise the vehicle and support it safely.

2. Remove the wheel(s).

3. Remove the cotter pin from the ball joint and remove the ball joint nut.

4. Disconnect the stabilizer (sway bar) link at the control arm.

5. Disconnect the strut bolt and remove the front bushing.

6. Use a ball joint puller and separate the ball joint from the control arm. Make sure the puller is properly located and that the rubber boot is not damaged during removal.

7. Unbolt the control arm at the crossmember and remove the arm.

8. If the bushings are to be replaced, use a press and support the arm from below. The new bushings should always be pressed in from the front side of the arm.

**To install:**

9. Fit the control arm over the end of the strut rod.

10. Install the arm in the crossmember but do not fully tighten the nut.

11. Install the ball joint in the control arm.

12. Tighten the nut to 44 ft. lbs. (60 Nm), then install a new cotter pin.

13. Install the bushing, washer and bolt for the strut rod. Tighten the bolt to 70 ft. lbs.(95 Nm).

14. Attach the stabilizer link to the control arm and tighten it to 63 ft. lbs. (86 Nm).

15. Install the wheel(s).

16. Lower the vehicle. Jounce the front of the vehicle up and down. This "normalizes" the front suspension and allows the control arm to seek its final position.

17. Tighten the control arm-to-crossmember bolt to 63 ft. lbs.(86 Nm).

### 850, C70, S70 and V70 Series

▶ **See Figures 39 thru 44**

1. Raise and safely support vehicle.

2. Remove the through-bolt securing the ball joint to the spindle.

3. Remove the ball joint from the spindle, an appropriate puller may be necessary.

4. Remove the bolts and nuts holding the lower control arm to the frame.

5. Remove the lower control arm.

**To install:**

6. Clean the ball joint and subframe where the lower control arm mates.

7. Install the lower control arm in the frame and attach with new bolts and nuts. Tighten the lower control arm subframe bolts to 48 ft. lbs. (65 Nm) and then angle tighten 120°.

8. Apply rustproofing compound to the lower control arm nuts.

9. Connect the ball joint to the spindle and tighten the bolt to 13 ft. lbs. (18 Nm).

10. Lower the vehicle.

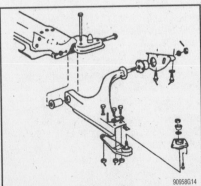

**Fig. 38 Lower control arm—240 series vehicles**

**Fig. 39 You must use two wrenches or ratchets to remove the ball joint through-bolt**

**Fig. 40 Once the bolt is removed, the ball joint is pulled downward from the spindle; however, a puller may be necessary**

**Fig. 41 This groove is where the through-bolt passes and retains the ball joint to the spindle**

**Fig. 42 Remove the control arm-to-subframe bolts and nuts**

**Fig. 43 Threading the nut onto the bolt reduces the chance of losing them or getting the bolts mixed up**

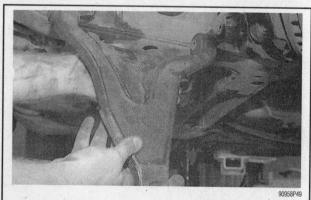

**Fig. 44 Pull the control arm from the subframe to remove it**

## CONTROL ARM BUSHING REPLACEMENT

### 240 Series

1. Raise the vehicle and support it safely.
2. Mark the position of the wheel stud nearest to the valve. This is done to facilitate installation and to avoid the need for rebalancing.
3. Disconnect the stabilizer (sway bar) link at the control arm.
4. Remove the lower control arm.
5. Remove the rear bracket from the control arm.
6. Drive out the old bushings.

**To install:**

7. When replacing the bushings, note that the right and left bushings are not interchangeable. The right side bushing should be turned so that the small slots point horizontally when installed.
8. Install the new bushings onto the control arm.
9. Install the bracket onto the control arm. The nut should be tightened only enough to hold securely. The washer should be able to be turned with your fingers after the nut is on.
10. Install the control arm.
11. Install the stabilizer (sway bar) link at the control arm.
12. Install the wheel.
13. Lower the vehicle.

### 700, 900, S90 and V90 Models

The control arm assembly on these models is connected to the spindle through a ball joint and has one connection to the crossmember.

1. Raise and safely support the vehicle securely on jackstands.
2. Mark the position of the wheel stud nearest to the valve. Wheel is marked to facilitate installation and to avoid the need for rebalancing.
3. Remove the lower control arm.
4. Press out the bushing with a suitable drift.

**To install:**

5. Press in the new bushing with a suitable drift. Use disc 5240 or equivalent as a support. The disc recess should face upwards.

➡ **Press the bushing in from the front side of the control arm.**

6. Install the control arm.
7. Install the wheel.
8. Lower the vehicle.

### 850, C70, S70 and V70 Series

1. Raise and safely support the vehicle.
2. Remove the wheel(s).
3. Remove the control arm.
4. Clean the bushing outer sleeves.
5. Press out the bushings using tool 5481 and 5482 or equivalent.

**To install:**

6. Press in the bushings using tool 5481 and 5482 or equivalent.
7. Install the control arm.
8. Install the wheel(s).
9. Lower the vehicle.

## Knuckle and Spindle

### REMOVAL & INSTALLATION

1. Raise the vehicle and support it safely.
2. Remove the wheel(s).
3. Remove the caliper, and support it out of the way using a piece of wire.
4. Remove the brake rotor.
5. Remove the axle nut (if applicable).
6. Remove any harnesses, lines, etc. that facilitate removal of the spindle.
7. Disconnect the tie rod end from the spindle.
8. Disconnect the lower ball joint from the bottom of the spindle.
9. Disconnect the strut tube from the top of the spindle.
10. Remove the spindle from the vehicle.

**To install:**

➡ **If replacing the spindle with a new one, make sure to transfer the backing plate, hub or any part not attached to the new spindle assembly.**

11. Install the spindle on the vehicle.
12. Connect the strut tube to the spindle and tighten to specification.
13. Connect the lower ball joint to the spindle and tighten to specification.
14. Connect the tie rod end to the spindle and tighten to specification.
15. Reconnect any harnesses, lines, etc. removed.
16. Install the axle nut and tighten to specification.
17. Install the brake rotor.
18. Install the brake caliper.
19. Install the wheel(s).
20. Lower the vehicle.

## Front Wheel Bearings

### INSPECTION

To check wheel bearing play, raise the vehicle and support it safely. Rock the wheel at 12 and 6 o'clock position. If there is movement, the wheel bearing should be serviced.

To check wheel bearing noise, raise the wheel off the ground, then spin the wheel by hand and let it rotate freely after spinning. Check for wheel bearing noise. If the wheel bearing remains noisy after proper adjustment, replace the wheel bearing.

### ADJUSTMENT

#### Except 850, C70, S70 and V70

The front wheel bearings are not adjustable on the rear drive vehicles. If the lateral run-out on the hub with the disc removed exceeds 0.0012 inch (0.030mm), the hub must be replaced.

### REMOVAL & INSTALLATION

#### Except 850, C70, S70 and V70

▶ **See Figures 45, 46 and 47**

1. Raise and support the vehicle safely.
2. Remove the wheel(s).
3. Remove the brake caliper. Hang the caliper out of the way with a piece of stiff wire. Do not let the caliper hang by the brake hose.
4. Pry off the grease cap.
5. Remove the cotter pin and castle nut.
6. Remove the hub and brake disc assembly. Use a bearing puller to remove the inner bearing if it stays on the spindle.

➡**If the vehicle is equipped with separate brake disc and hub, the guide pin and brake disc must be removed from the hub prior to bearing replacement.**

7. Use a brass drift and carefully tap out the grease seal and inner bearing race.
8. Remove the outer bearing race, using a suitable handle and drift.

**To install:**
9. Press in a new inner bearing race, using a suitable handle and drift.
10. Press in a new outer bearing race, using a suitable handle and drift.
11. Pack the wheel bearing between the cage and inner race with as much grease as possible. Also smear grease on the outer side of the bearing and bearing races inside the hub. Fill the space in the hub with grease to a diameter of the smallest ball races.
12. On hubs with integrated brake disc, position the inner bearing seal in the hub and press the seal in so the edge lies in the same plane as the hub.
13. On hub with separate hub and brake disc:
    a. Press the sealing ring onto the spindle, making sure that the seal ring is square. The sealing ring lip should face outwards.
    b. Install the inner bearing in the hub. Press in the sealing washer.
14. Install the hub, outer race and castle nut.

➡**On vehicles with separate hub and brake disc, install the brake disc and guide pin.**

15. To adjust the bearing pre-load:
    a. Spin the hub and simultaneously tighten the center nut to 42 ft. lbs. (57 Nm).
    b. Loosen the nut ½ turn, then tighten the nut by hand, approximately 12 inch lbs. (1.4 Nm).
    c. Install the cotter pin. If the pin hole in the spindle does not align with the pin hole in the nut, unscrew the nut slightly to the nearest pin hole.
    d. Install the protective cap.
16. Install the brake caliper.
17. Install the wheel.
18. Lower the vehicle.

## Front Hub and Bearing

### ADJUSTMENT

#### 850, S70, C70 and V70 Models

The front wheel bearings are not adjustable on front drive vehicles. If the lateral run-out on the hub with the disc removed exceeds 0.0007 inch (0.020mm), the hub must be replaced.

### REMOVAL & INSTALLATION

#### 850, S70, C70 and V70 Models

▶ **See Figures 48 and 49**

1. Raise and safely support vehicle.
2. Remove the wheel.
3. Disconnect the ABS sensor from the axle shaft, but do not detach the sensor connector. Hang the sensor out of the way.
4. Remove the caliper, carrier and rotor. Hang the caliper safely out of the way.
5. Remove the halfshaft.
6. Separate the ball joint from the control arm.
7. Disconnect the sway bar link.
8. Remove the four bolts retaining the hub.
9. Remove the hub.

**To install:**
10. Clean the axle shaft and hub mating surfaces.
11. Clean the ABS sensor with a soft brush.
12. Install the new hub and tighten the bolts alternately to 33 ft. lbs. (45 Nm) plus an additional 60 degrees.
13. Insert the axle shaft into the hub and fit the splines.
14. Tighten the new axle shaft nut by hand.
15. Connect the ball joint to the control arm using new nuts.
16. Connect the sway bar link.
17. Install the brake rotor, carrier and caliper.
18. Tighten the axle nut to 89 ft. lbs. (120 Nm), plus an additional 60 degrees, using tool 5461 or equivalent to counterhold. Lock the axle shaft nut using a chisel to tap the flange into the groove.

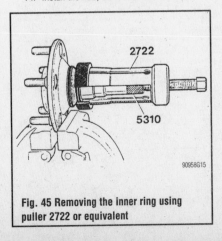

**Fig. 45 Removing the inner ring using puller 2722 or equivalent**

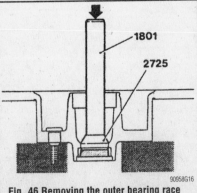

**Fig. 46 Removing the outer bearing race from the hub using drift 2725 or equivalent**

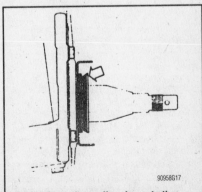

**Fig. 47 Press the sealing ring onto the spindle before installing the hub assembly**

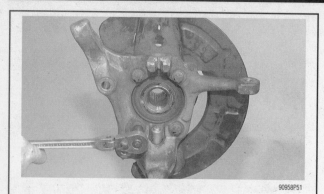

**Fig. 48 Remove the four hub retaining bolts—although shown removed from the spindle, this can be done on the car**

**Fig. 49 Separate the hub from the spindle after the retaining bolts are removed**

19. Clean the ABS sensor and its seat with a soft brush. Tighten the sensor to 84 inch lbs. (10 Nm).
20. Install the wheels.
21. Lower the vehicle.

## Wheel Alignment

If the tires are worn unevenly, if the vehicle is not stable on the highway or if the handling seems uneven in spirited driving, the wheel alignment should be checked. If an alignment problem is suspected, first check for improper tire inflation and other possible causes. These can be worn suspension or steering components, accident damage or even unmatched tires. If any worn or damaged components are found, they must be replaced before the wheels can be properly aligned. Wheel alignment requires very expensive equipment and involves minute adjustments which must be accurate; it should only be performed by a trained technician. Take your vehicle to a properly equipped shop.

Following is a description of the alignment angles which are adjustable on most vehicles and how they affect vehicle handling. Although these angles can apply to both the front and rear wheels, usually only the front suspension is adjustable.

## CASTER

▶ See Figure 50

Looking at a vehicle from the side, caster angle describes the steering axis rather than a wheel angle. The steering knuckle is attached to a control arm or strut at the top and a control arm at the bottom. The wheel pivots around the line between these points to steer the vehicle. When the upper point is tilted back, this is described as positive caster. Having a positive caster tends to make the wheels self-centering, increasing directional stability. Excessive positive caster makes the wheels hard to steer, while an uneven caster will cause a pull to one side. Overloading the vehicle or sagging rear springs will affect caster, as will raising the rear of the vehicle. If the rear of the vehicle is lower than normal, the caster becomes more positive.

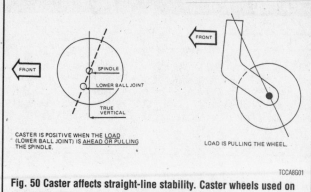

**Fig. 50 Caster affects straight-line stability. Caster wheels used on shopping carts, for example, employ positive caster**

## CAMBER

▶ See Figure 51

Looking from the front of the vehicle, camber is the inward or outward tilt of the top of wheels. When the tops of the wheels are tilted in, this is negative camber; if they are tilted out, it is positive. In a turn, a slight amount of negative camber helps maximize contact of the tire with the road. However, too much negative camber compromises straight-line stability, increases bump steer and torque steer.

## TOE

▶ See Figure 52

Looking down at the wheels from above the vehicle, toe angle is the distance between the front of the wheels, relative to the distance between the back of the wheels. If the wheels are closer at the front, they are said to be toed-in or to have negative toe. A small amount of negative toe enhances directional stability and provides a smoother ride on the highway.

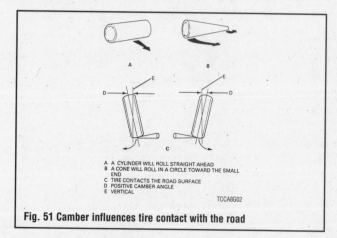

A  A CYLINDER WILL ROLL STRAIGHT AHEAD
B  A CONE WILL ROLL IN A CIRCLE TOWARD THE SMALL END
C  TIRE CONTACTS THE ROAD SURFACE
D  POSITIVE CAMBER ANGLE
E  VERTICAL

**Fig. 51 Camber influences tire contact with the road**

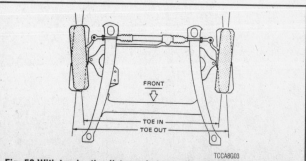

**Fig. 52 With toe-in, the distance between the wheels is closer at the front than at the rear**

**REAR SUSPENSION**

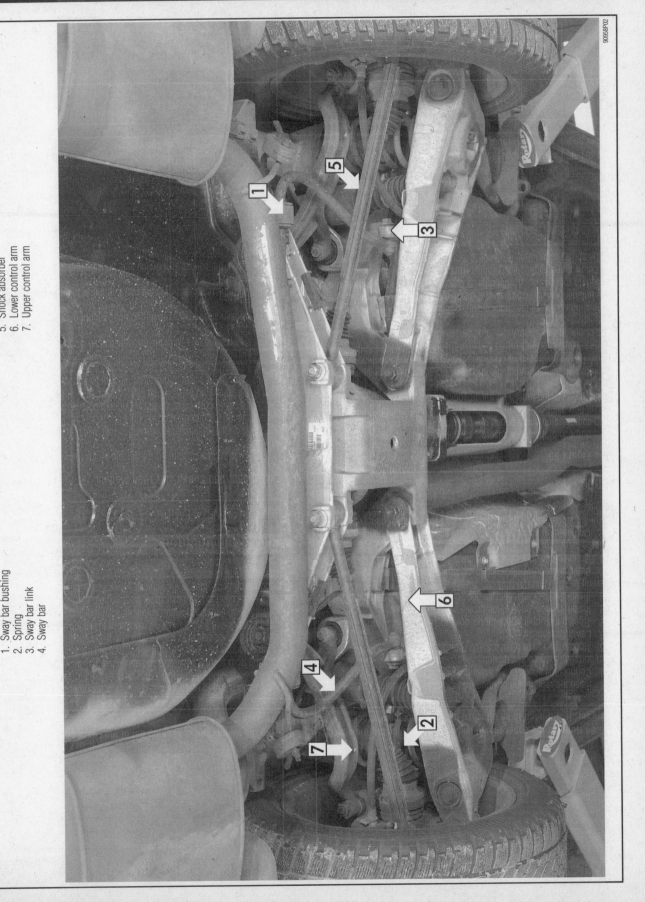

**V70R AWD REAR SUSPENSION COMPONENTS**

1. Sway bar bushing
2. Spring
3. Sway bar link
4. Sway bar

5. Shock absorber
6. Lower control arm
7. Upper control arm

90958P02

**850 REAR SUSPENSION COMPONENTS**

1. Shock absorber
2. Spring
3. Driver side trailing arm
4. Passenger side trailing arm

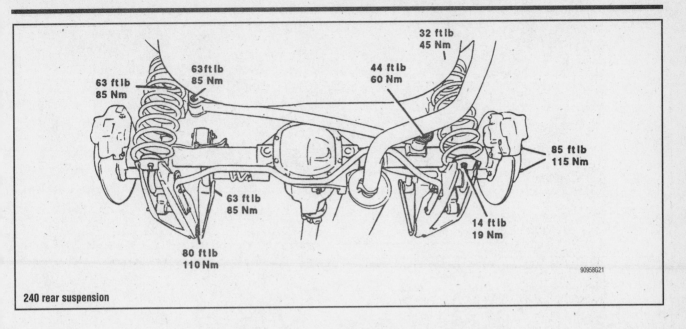

63 ft lb
85 Nm

63 ft lb
85 Nm

32 ft lb
45 Nm

44 ft lb
60 Nm

85 ft lb
115 Nm

63 ft lb
85 Nm

14 ft lb
19 Nm

80 ft lb
110 Nm

90958G21

**240 rear suspension**

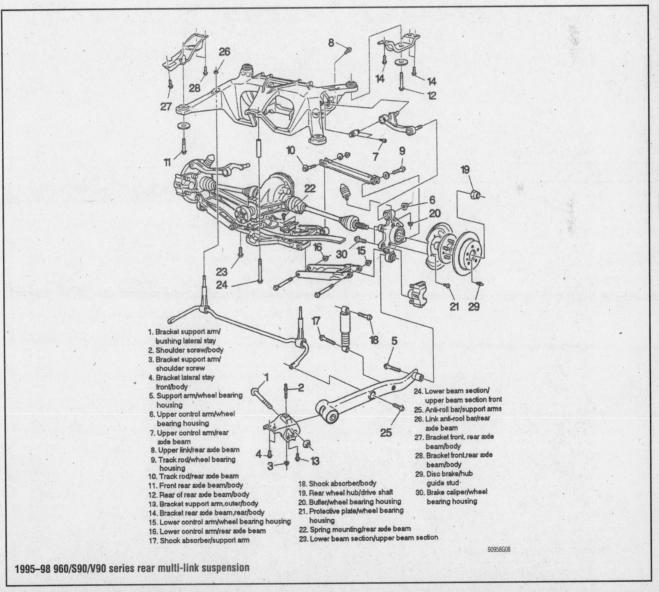

1. Bracket support arm/
   bushing lateral stay
2. Shoulder screw/body
3. Bracket support arm/
   shoulder screw
4. Bracket lateral stay
   front/body
5. Support arm/wheel bearing
   housing
6. Upper control arm/wheel
   bearing housing
7. Upper control arm/rear
   axle beam
8. Upper link/rear axle beam
9. Track rod/wheel bearing
   housing
10. Track rod/rear axle beam
11. Front rear axle beam/body
12. Rear of rear axle beam/body
13. Bracket support arm,outer/body
14. Bracket rear axle beam,rear/body
15. Lower control arm/wheel bearing housing
16. Lower control arm/rear axle beam
17. Shock absorber/support arm

18. Shock absorber/body
19. Rear wheel hub/drive shaft
20. Buffer/wheel bearing housing
21. Protective plate/wheel bearing
    housing
22. Spring mounting/rear axle beam
23. Lower beam section/upper beam section

24. Lower beam section/
    upper beam section front
25. Anti-roll bar/support arms
26. Link anti-roll bar/rear
    axle beam
27. Bracket front, rear axle
    beam/body
28. Bracket front,rear axle
    beam/body
29. Disc brake/hub
    guide stud
30. Brake caliper/wheel
    bearing housing

90958G08

**1995–98 960/S90/V90 series rear multi-link suspension**

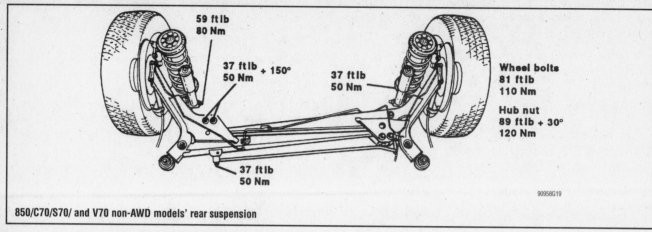

**59 ft lb
80 Nm**

**37 ft lb + 150°
50 Nm**

**37 ft lb
50 Nm**

**Wheel bolts
81 ft lb
110 Nm**

**Hub nut
89 ft lb + 30°
120 Nm**

**37 ft lb
50 Nm**

90958G19

**850/C70/S70/ and V70 non-AWD models' rear suspension**

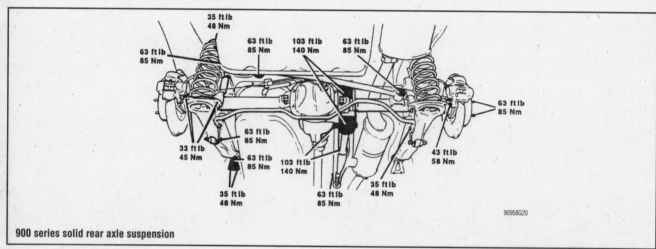

**35 ft lb
48 Nm**

**63 ft lb
85 Nm**

**103 ft lb
140 Nm**

**63 ft lb
85 Nm**

**63 ft lb
85 Nm**

**63 ft lb
85 Nm**

**33 ft lb
45 Nm**

**63 ft lb
85 Nm**

**103 ft lb
140 Nm**

**43 ft lb
58 Nm**

**35 ft lb
48 Nm**

**35 ft lb
48 Nm**

**63 ft lb
85 Nm**

90958G20

**900 series solid rear axle suspension**

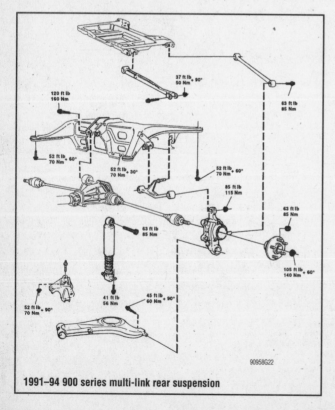

**37 ft lb + 90°
50 Nm**

**120 ft lb
160 Nm**

**63 ft lb
85 Nm**

**52 ft lb + 60°
70 Nm**

**52 ft lb + 30°
70 Nm**

**52 ft lb + 60°
70 Nm**

**85 ft lb
115 Nm**

**63 ft lb
85 Nm**

**63 ft lb
85 Nm**

**105 ft lb + 60°
140 Nm**

**52 ft lb + 90°
70 Nm**

**41 ft lb
56 Nm**

**45 ft lb + 90°
60 Nm + 90°**

90958G22

**1991–94 900 series multi-link rear suspension**

## Coil Spring

REMOVAL & INSTALLATION

**Except 850, 960 Sedan and 1998 Models**

### ❉❉ CAUTION

**A coil spring compressor is required to remove the spring. Improper removal procedures may cause serious injury.**

1. Raise and safely support the vehicle.
2. Remove the rear wheels.
3. Place a hydraulic jack beneath the rear axle housing and raise the housing sufficiently to compress the spring.
4. Install the spring compressor and tighten. Make sure there are at least 3 coils of spring between the attachment points of the compressor.
5. Loosen the nuts for the upper and lower spring attachments.
6. Disconnect the shock absorber at the upper attachment.
7. Lower the jack enough to remove the spring.

**To install:**

8. Make sure the coil spring is compressed.
9. Position the retaining bolt and inner washer for the upper attachment inside the spring.
10. While holding the outer washer and rubber spacer to the upper body attachment, install the spring and inner washer to the upper attachment sandwiching the rubber spacer.

11. Tighten the retaining bolt to 35 ft. lbs. (48 Nm).

12. Raise the jack and secure the bottom of the spring to the lower attachment with the washer and retaining bolt tightened to 63 ft. lbs. (85 Nm).

13. Slowly remove the spring compressor.

14. Connect the shock absorber to its upper attachment.

15. Install the wheels.

16. Lower the vehicle.

### 1992–94 960 Sedan

➡**To properly remove and install the rear coil springs, the rear support arm assembly must be removed.**

1. Raise and support the vehicle safely.

2. Remove the rear wheels and support the arm guards.

3. Remove the retaining bolts at the front and rear of the support arm.

4. Separate the rear end of the support arm from the wheel bearing housing.

5. Place a jack with fixture 5972 or equivalent under the support arm and raise into place.

6. Remove the retaining bolts at the top of the shock and lower the support arm complete with the spring and shock.

**To install:**

7. Lift the assembly into place and tighten the upper damper bolt to 62 ft. lbs. (85 Nm).

8. Replace the mounting bolt and nut at the front of the support arm. Tighten the large nut to 51 ft. lbs. (70 Nm), plus 90 degrees of rotation. Tighten the other bolts to 35 ft. lbs. (48 Nm).

9. Tap the support arm in at the rear and tighten the bolt to 44 ft. lbs. (60 Nm), plus 90 degrees rotation.

10. Replace the control arm guard.

11. Install the wheels.

12. Lower the vehicle.

### 850, C70, S70, and V70 Series Except AWD

◆ **See Figures 53 thru 59**

1. Raise and safely support vehicle.

2. Remove the wheels.

3. Use a jack to press the trailing arm up to unload the shock absorber.

4. Remove the shock lower mount bolt and pull the shock off of its mount,

5. Lower the jack and remove the spring mounting nut.

6. Remove the spring from the car.

**To install:**

7. Transfer the rubber spring spacer and lower mount if installing a new spring.

8. Install the spring in the trailing arm recess and center the mount washer guide pin in the hole.

9. Install a new nut and tighten it to 30 ft. lbs. (40 Nm).

10. Position the jack under the trailing and lift it up.

11. Install the shock on the lower mount, making sure that the spring is correctly seated in the upper mount.

12. Tighten the shock nut to 59 ft. lbs. (80 Nm).

13. Install the wheels.

14. Lower the car.

### V70 AWD Models

1. Raise and safely support the vehicle.

2. Press lower control arm using jack or suitable tool to unload the pressure.

3. Remove the rear shocks.

4. Remove the sway bar.

**Fig. 53 Support the bottom of the spring perch or the trailing arm before disconnecting the shock absorber**

**Fig. 54 Remove the shock absorber lower mount retaining nut**

**Fig. 55 Make sure the washer does not stick to the shock absorber after the shock is removed**

**Fig. 56 Pull the shock absorber off of the lower mount**

**Fig. 57 Remove the spring retaining nut**

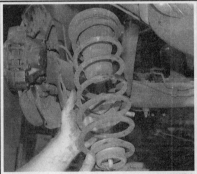

**Fig. 58 Carefully lower the support device and remove the spring from the vehicle**

90958P11

**Fig. 59 Make sure you transfer the shock spacer if you are replacing the spring**

5. Remove the control arm inner and outer mounting nuts.
6. Using a suitable tool, knock the mounting bolts out.
7. Remove the front support arm bolts.
8. Remove the jacking point.
9. Lower the control arm to release the support arm and bracket.
10. Install the jacking point to protect the brake lines.
11. Lower the control arm until spring is fully relieved of pressure, and remove the spring.

**To install:**
12. Replce the spring rubber inserts if worn.
13. Install the spring in the control arm.
14. Raise the control arm up slightly.
15. Remove the jacking point.
16. Raise the control arm all the way and install the support arm bracket, tighten the bolts to 48 ft. lbs. (65 Nm).
17. Install the jacking point, tighten the bolt to 78 ft. lbs. (105 Nm).
18. Install the outer and inner control arm mounting bolts, tighten the nuts to 59 ft. lbs. (80 Nm).
19. Install the sway bar.
20. Install the shocks.
21. Remove the jack from under the control arm.
22. Lower the vehicle.

## Leaf Spring

### REMOVAL & INSTALLATION

#### 1995–98 960/S90/V90

▶ See Figure 60

➡**Multi-Link suspensions require alignment any time the suspension components are disassembled. Installation tightening and torque procedures are critical to correct alignment.**

1. Raise and support the vehicle safely. Make sure the front supports are placed as far forward as possible. Check that the rear supports will not interfere with the support arm.
2. Remove the rear wheels.
3. Remove the sway bar from the vehicle.
4. Install compression tool Kent-Moore® No. J-41470 (or equivalent) as follows:
   a. Attach one end of the tool yoke into the boss on one side of the axle support beam.

➡**There is a boss cast into the support on either side of where the spring is visible from underneath.**

   b. Slide the tool into the boss on the other side of the axle support beam to fully engage the yoke.
   c. Make sure the tool is seated between the retaining tabs before any suspension components can be removed.
   d. Make sure the rollers on the ends of the tool are positioned inside the lower control arms.
   e. Turn the handle to raise the control arms and compress the leaf spring.

**Do not tighten the tool after the pegs have contacted the axle support beam.**

5. Once the spring is compressed, components can be removed.
6. Compress the suspension slightly.
7. Removed the shock absorber mounting bolt from the rear support arm.
8. Press the suspension up to normal position, as if the vehicle were on the ground.
9. Remove the bolts at the front of the support arm bracket.
10. Remove the support arm-to-wheel bearing housing bolt.
11. Loosen the support arm bracket nut a few turns.
12. Tap the support arm off the wheel bearing housing.
13. Remove the support arm bracket nut and the support arm with the bracket attached. Do not remove the support arm-to-bracket through bolt.
14. Remove the track rod-to-wheel bearing housing bolt.
15. Tap the track rod off the wheel bearing housing.
16. Remove the lower control arm-to-wheel bearing housing nut. Tap out the bolt with a brass punch.
17. Loosen the inboard lower control arm mounting nut until approximately 0.04–0.08 in. (1–2mm) of the bolt still protrudes from the nut. Tap the bolt with a brass punch until the nut contacts the lower control arm.
18. Repeat Steps 6–14 to disassemble the opposite side of the suspension.
19. Lower the compression tool and control arms completely. Inspect the spring mountings in the lower control arms. Retain the mountings in the control arms for assembly.
20. Loosen all the lower rear axle support bolts one turn.
21. Remove the two front bolts at the pinion flange.
22. Remove the spacers.
23. Install rear axle retainer 5580 (or equivalent) to the front edge of the differential. Install rear axle retainer 5579 (or equivalent) to the rear edge of the differential.
24. Position a lift or jack against the lower axle support beam.
25. Remove the lower support beam mounting bolts and lower the support beam.

➡**Before removing the spring mounting plates, take note of the positioning. Installation must be in the same positions.**

26. Remove the spring mounting plates and remove the spring.
27. Check all spring mountings for damage or wear.
**To install:**
28. Install the spring. Install the spring mounting plates using new bolts.

➡**The leaf spring is marked with a center line.**

29. Make sure the spring is centered. Tighten the spring mounting plate bolts alternately to 37 ft. lbs. (50 Nm).
30. Position the lower axle support beam on a lift or jack.
31. Make sure the lower axle support beam contact surfaces are clean and that the lower differential bushing is in place.
32. Make sure the lower differential bushings are inside the guide flanges of the lower axle support beam.
33. Raise the lower axle support beam into position.
34. Install new mounting bolts except at the pinion flange. Tighten the bolts until there is approximately 0.08–0.16 in. (2–4mm) clearance between the support surfaces.

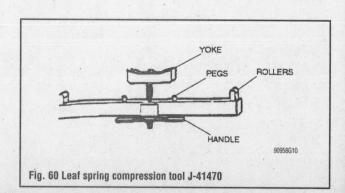

90958G10

**Fig. 60 Leaf spring compression tool J-41470**

35.  Remove the lift or jack.

36.  Remove the differential retainers 5579 and 5580 (or equivalents) from the differential.

37.  Install the 2 front spacers between the upper and lower axle support beams.

38.  Install new bolts at the pinion flange.

39.  Tighten all lower axle support bolts diagonally until snug. Tighten the bolts diagonally to 59 ft. lbs. (80 Nm).

40.  Install the compression tool.

41.  Install the spring into the mounting in the control arms.

42.  Raise the control arms up to their normal position.

43.  Install the lower control arm to the wheel bearing housing,

44.  Install the track rod to the wheel bearing housing using a new nut and tighten to 59 ft. lbs. (80 Nm).

45.  Install the rear support arm using new bolts and nut, but do not yet tighten the bolts and nut.

46.  Tighten the rear bolt and front nut to 59 ft. lbs. (80 Nm).

47.  Tighten the front bolts to 37 ft. lbs. (50 Nm).

48.  Install the shock absorbers.

49.  Make sure the washers and bushings on the sway bar links are in place.

50.  Raise the sway bar into position and install.

51.  Install the wheels.

52.  Lower the vehicle.

53.  Check wheel alignment.

## Shock Absorber

### REMOVAL & INSTALLATION

#### Except 850, 960 Sedan and 1998 Models

1.  Raise and safely support the vehicle.

2.  Place a jack under the lower arm and lift the rear suspension to unload the shock.

3.  Remove the lower nut and bolt securing the shock to the rear axle.

4.  Lower the vehicle enough to remove the shock.

5.  Remove the upper shock absorber through-bolt.

6.  Remove the old shock absorber.

**To install:**

7.  Install the shock absorber in the upper mount and hand-tighten the through-bolt.

8.  Raise the rear end and attach the shock using the lower mount bolt. Hand-tighten the nut.

9.  Tighten the lower bolt to 63 ft. lbs. (85 Nm).

10.  Remove the jack.

11.  Lower the vehicle.

12.  Tighten the upper bolt to 63 ft. lbs. (85 Nm).

#### 1992–94 960 Sedan

➡Multi-link suspensions require alignment any time the suspension components are disassembled. Installation and tightening procedures are critical to correct alignment.

1.  Raise and support the vehicle safely. Make sure the jackstands are placed as far forward as possible. Check that the rear jackstands will not interfere with the floor jack.

2.  Remove the wheels.

3.  Remove the bolts holding the protective guard to the control arm, and remove the guard.

4.  At the front of the arm, remove the two retaining bolts which hold the bracket (for the support arm) to the frame. Do not attempt to remove the through-bolt.

5.  Remove the retaining bolt at the rear of the support arm.

6.  Separate the rear end of the support arm from the wheel bearing housing.

7.  Using either Volvo tool 5972 or two floor jacks, support the arm at the front and rear ends. Raise the jacks just enough to unload the shock.

8.  Remove the retaining bolt at the top of the shock absorber.

9.  Lower the jacks slowly; the arm will come free with the spring and shock attached.

10.  Remove the spring with the upper and lower rubber seats.

11.  Unbolt the shock absorber from the arm.

**To install:**

12.  Install the shock absorber on the arm and tighten the bottom mount to 41 ft. lbs. (56 Nm).

13.  Install the bottom spring rubber seat on the support arm. Take care to properly locate the grooves in the rubber seat.

14.  Install the spring and the top rubber seat.

15.  Place the assembled support arm on the jacks and raise into position.

16.  Compress the spring until the shock absorber is in the correct position. The shock may be held in place temporarily with a drift in the hole.

17.  Insert the bolt, and tighten to 62 ft. lbs. (85 Nm).

18.  Reinstall the mounting bolts at the front of the support arm bracket and tighten to 35 ft. lbs. (48 Nm). Tighten the large nut to 51 ft. lbs. (70 Nm) plus an additional 90 degrees of rotation.

19.  At the rear of the support arm, tap the arm into place on the wheel bearing housing. Tighten the bolt to 44 ft. lbs. (60 Nm) plus an additional 90 degrees of rotation. Do not overtighten.

20.  Reinstall the protective cover on the control arm.

21.  Install the wheel.

22.  Lower the vehicle.

23.  Roll the vehicle several feet forwards and backwards before adjusting the rear wheel alignment.

#### 1995–98 960/S90/V90 and AWD V70 Series

1.  Raise and safely support the rear of the vehicle with jackstands. Place the jackstands so they do not interfere with the support arm of the vehicle.

2.  Remove the wheel.

3.  Use a floor jack and raise up the support arm.

4.  Disconnect the shock absorber from the support arm.

5.  Disconnect the shock absorber from the body. Remove the shock absorber.

**To install:**

6.  Install the shock absorber and connect it to the body using a new bolt. Tighten the bolt to 59 ft. lbs. (80 Nm).

7.  With the support arm raised, connect the shock absorber to the support arm and install a new bolt. Tighten the bolt to 59 ft. lbs. (80 Nm).

8.  Carefully lower the lift from the support arm.

9.  Install the wheels.

10.  Lower the vehicle.

#### 850, C70, S70 and V70, Except AWD Models

▶ **See Figures 61, 62, 63 and 64**

1.  On early four door Series, remove the plastic side panel, then fold the back seat forward and fold back the trunk carpet. Remove the support panel under the edge of the carpet and detach the side panels at the front and fold them over. Remove the back seat catch and panel mounting clip.

2.  On later four-door series, remove the support panel over the shock mount. Make small cuts in the panel if necessary to fold it up.

3.  On five-door series, remove the front floor panel bolts and pull the panel back to free it from the front mount.

4.  Remove the panel.

5.  Raise and safely support the vehicle.

6.  Remove the two upper shock mount bolts.

7.  Using a floor jack, press the trailing arm up to unload the shock absorber.

8.  Disconnect the shock absorber from the lower mount, then pull it off of the trailing arm.

9.  Lower the vehicle and lift the shock assembly out from the top.

10.  Check the shock upper mount bushing for damage and replace if necessary.

**To install:**

11.  Install the upper mount on the new shock as follows:

- standard shock absorbers to 30 ft. lbs. (40 Nm)
- gas shock absorber M12 nuts to 30 ft. lbs. (40 Nm)
- gas shock absorber M10 nuts to 15 ft. lbs. (20 Nm), plus an additional 90 degrees

12.  Install the shock absorber in the vehicle and turn the upper mount bolts a few turns.

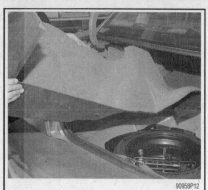

Fig. 61 Remove the carpet to access the upper shock absorber mount

Fig. 62 Remove the two upper shock absorber mounting bolts

Fig. 63 Remove the shock absorber from the vehicle

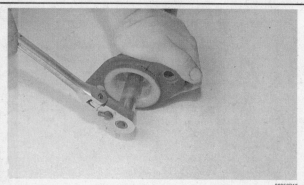

Fig. 64 Remove the upper mount and bushing if replacing the shock absorber; it will need to be attached to the replacement shock

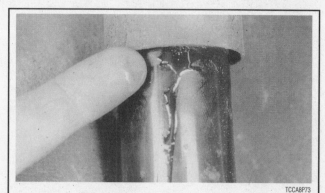

Fig. 65 When fluid is seeping out of the shock absorber, it's time to replace it

13. Raise the vehicle and position the jack under the trailing arm and lift up.

14. Connect the shock to the lower mount, making sure that the shock is seated correctly in the upper mount.

15. Tighten the nut to 59 ft. lbs. (80 Nm).

16. Lower the vehicle.

17. Tighten the upper shock mount bolts to 18 ft. lbs. (25 Nm).

18. Install the front edge of the panels using the clips.

19. Install the back seat catches and bolts with thread locking compound, tightening to 15 ft. lbs. (20 Nm).

20. Replace the cover plate and trunk carpet.

21. On later four-door series, fold down the cover over the shock mount and install the carpeting.

22. On five-door series, line up the front edge of the floor panel and install the bolt at the rear edge. Line up the panel with the rear floor panel and tighten the bolts.

## TESTING

▶ See Figure 65

The purpose of the shock absorber is simply to limit the motion of the spring during compression and rebound cycles. If the vehicle is not equipped with these motion dampers, the up and down motion would multiply until the vehicle was alternately trying to leap off the ground and to pound itself into the pavement.

Contrary to popular rumor, the shocks do not affect the ride height of the vehicle. This is controlled by other suspension components such as springs and tires. Worn shock absorbers can affect handling; if the front of the vehicle is rising or falling excessively, the "footprint" of the tires changes on the pavement and steering is affected.

The simplest test of the shock absorber is simply push down on one corner of the unladen vehicle and release it. Observe the motion of the body as it is released. In most cases, it will come up beyond it original rest position, dip back below it and settle quickly to rest. This shows that the damper is controlling the spring action. Any tendency to excessive pitch (up-and-down) motion

or failure to return to rest within 2–3 cycles is a sign of poor function within the shock absorber. Oil-filled shocks may have a light film of oil around the seal, resulting from normal breathing and air exchange. This should NOT be taken as a sign of failure, but any sign of thick or running oil definitely indicates failure. Gas filled shocks may also show some film at the shaft; if the gas has leaked out, the shock will have almost no resistance to motion.

While each shock absorber can be replaced individually, it is recommended that they be changed as a pair (both front or both rear) to maintain equal response on both sides of the vehicle. Chances are quite good that if one has failed, its mate is weak also.

## Lower Control Arms

### REMOVAL & INSTALLATION

**Except 850, 960 Sedan and 1998 Models**

1. Raise and safely support the vehicle on the frame and remove the rear wheels.

2. Place a hydraulic jack beneath the rear axle housing and raise the housing sufficiently to compress the spring and shock.

3. Install a compressor on the spring and tighten. Make sure there are at least 3 coils of spring between the attachment points of the compressor.

4. Remove the lower shock attachment bolts and nut.

5. Lower the rear axle and remove the spring.

6. Remove the sway bar from the trailing arms, if equipped.

7. Remove the axle-to frame through-bolt securing the trailing arm to the vehicle body.

8. Loosen and remove the through bolt securing the trailing arm to the rear axle.

9. With the rear axle firmly supported, remove the trailing arm.

**To install:**

10. Install the control arm on the axle housing and tighten the bolt finger-tight.

11. Raise the assembly into position and install the axle-to-frame bolts finger-tight.

12. Install the shock and coil spring.

13. Tighten all control arm bolts to 85 ft. lbs. (115 Nm).

14. Install the wheels.

15. Lower the vehicle.

### 1992–94 960 Sedan

➡Multi-Link suspensions require alignment any time the suspension components are disassembled. Installation tightening and torque procedures are critical to correct alignment.

1. Raise and support the vehicle safely. Make sure the front supports are placed as far forward as possible. Check that the rear supports will not interfere with the support arm.

2. Remove the wheels.

3. Loosen and remove the bolts holding the protective guard to the arm and remove the guard.

4. At the front of the arm, remove the two retaining bolts which hold the bracket (for the control arm) to the frame. Do not attempt to remove the through-bolt.

5. Remove the retaining bolt at the rear of the control arm.

6. Separate the rear end of the control arm from the wheel bearing housing.

7. Using either Volvo tool 5972 or two floor jacks, support the arm at the front and rear ends. Raise the jacks just enough to relieve the tension on the shock absorber.

8. Remove the retaining bolt at the top of the shock absorber.

9. Lower the jacks slowly; the arm will come free with the spring and shock attached.

10. Unbolt the shock absorber from the arm, then unbolt and remove the bracket at the front of the arm. Take note of the relationship between the bracket and the arm: the bracket correctly mounts one way only.

**To install:**

11. Install the control arm bracket in the correct position and tighten the nut to 91 ft. lbs. (125 Nm) plus and additional 120 degrees of rotation.

12. Install the shock absorber on the arm and tighten the bottom mount to 41 ft. lbs. (56 Nm).

13. Install the bottom spring seat on the control arm. Take care to properly locate the grooves in the seat.

14. Install the spring and the top rubber seat. Place the assembled support arm on the jacks and raise into position.

15. Gently raise the jacks and compress the spring until the shock absorber is in the correct position. Install the shock.

16. Reinstall the mounting bolts at the front of the control arm bracket. Tighten the bolts to 35 ft. lbs. (48 Nm) and the large nut to 51 ft. lbs. (70 Nm) plus an additional 90 degrees of rotation.

17. At the rear of the control arm, tap the arm into place on the wheel bearing housing. Tighten the bolt to 44 ft. lbs. (60 Nm) plus an additional 90 degrees of rotation. Do not overtighten this fitting.

18. Reinstall the protective cover on the control arm. Install the wheel.

19. Lower the vehicle to the ground and final tighten the lugs to 62 ft. lbs. (85 Nm).

20. Roll the vehicle several feet forwards and backwards before adjusting the rear wheel alignment.

### 1995–98 960/S90/V90

➡Multi-Link suspensions require alignment any time the suspension components are disassembled. Installation tightening and torque procedures are critical to correct alignment.

1. Raise and support the vehicle safely. Make sure the front supports are placed as far forward as possible. Check that the rear supports will not interfere with the support arm.

2. Install compression tool Kent-Moore® No. J-41470 (or equivalent):

a. Attach one end of the tool yoke into the boss on one side of the axle support beam.

➡There is a boss cast into the support on either side of where the spring is visible from underneath.

b. Slide the tool into the boss on the other side of the axle support beam to fully engage the yoke.

c. Make sure the tool is seated between the retaining tabs before any suspension components can be removed.

d. Make sure the rollers on the ends of the tool are positioned inside the lower control arms.

e. Turn the handle to raise the control arms and compress the leaf spring.

### ✳✳ CAUTION

**Do not tighten the tool after the pegs have contacted the axle support beam.**

f. Once the spring is compressed, components can be removed.

3. Compress the suspension slightly.

4. Removed the shock absorber mounting bolt from the rear support arm.

5. Remove the sway bar-to-support arm bolts on both sides. Press the sway bar up away from the rear support arms.

6. Press the suspension up to normal position, as if the vehicle were on the ground.

7. Remove the bolt s at the front of the support arm bracket.

8. Remove the support arm-to-wheel bearing housing bolt.

9. Loosen the support arm bracket nut a few turns. Tap the support arm off the wheel bearing housing.

10. Remove the support arm bracket nut and the support arm with the bracket attached. Do not remove the support arm-to-bracket through-bolt.

11. Remove the brake caliper and hang it up with steel wire. Do not allow the caliper to hang by the brake hose.

12. Remove the lower control arm-to-wheel bearing housing nut. Tap out the bolt with a brass punch.

13. Loosen the inboard lower control arm mounting nut until approximately 0.04–0.08 in. (1–2mm) of the bolt still protrudes from the nut. Tap the bolt with a brass punch until the nut contacts the lower control arm.

14. Lower the compression tool and control arm completely. Inspect the spring mounting in the lower control arm. Retain the mountings in the control arm for assembly.

15. Remove the inboard lower control arm mounting nut. Tap out the bolt with a brass punch. Tap the lower control arm off the lower rear axle support beam.

16. Inspect the lower control arm bushings for damage or wear.

**To install:**

17. Install the lower control arm onto the lower rear axle support beam with a new nut and bolt. Do not tighten. Install the spring into the mounting in the control arm.

18. Use the compression tool to raise the control arms up to their normal position.

19. Install the lower control arm to the wheel bearing housing, using a new nut. Tighten both ends of the control arm to 59 ft. lbs. (80 Nm).

20. Install the brake caliper with new bolts and tighten to 44 ft. lbs. (60 Nm).

21. Install the rear support arm using new bolts and nut. Do not tighten bolts and nut.

22. Tighten the rear bolt and front nut to 59 ft. lbs. (80 Nm). Tighten the front bolts to 37 ft. lbs. (50 Nm).

23. Install the shock absorber:

a. If equipped with standard shock absorbers, compress the shock by hand. Install a new bolt and tighten to 59 ft. lbs. (80 Nm).

b. If equipped with self-leveling shock absorbers, lower the compression tool. Install a new bolt and tighten to 59 ft. lbs. (80 Nm).

24. Lower the sway bar into position and install new sway bar-to-support arm bolts, but do not tighten.

25. Install the wheels.

26. Lower the vehicle.

27. Tighten the sway bar bolts to 59 ft. lbs. (80 Nm).

28. Check wheel alignment and test drive vehicle.

### V70 AWD Models

1. Raise and safely support the vehicle.

2. Remove the shocks.

3. Remove the spring.

4. Remove the support arm from the control arm.

5. Remove the control arm from the vehicle.

**To install:**

6. Install the control arm.

7. Install the support arm onto the control arm and tighten the bolt to 59 ft. lbs. (80 Nm).

8. Install the spring.

9. Install the shocks.

10. Lower the vehicle.

## Upper Control Arm

### REMOVAL & INSTALLATION

#### 1992–94 960 Sedan

1. Raise and support the vehicle safely. Make sure the front supports are placed as far forward as possible.

2. Remove the wheels.

3. Remove the brake caliper without disconnecting the brake hose. Tie it with wire out of the way. Do not allow it to hang by the hose.

4. Remove the bolt holding the lower support arm to the wheel bearing housing and tap the support arm loose.

5. Remove the nut and bolt holding the lower control arm (intermediate arm) to the wheel bearing housing.

6. Remove the bolt attaching the track rod to the wheel bearing housing.

7. Use a small bearing puller to disconnect the track rod.

8. Remove the nut which holds the upper control arm to the wheel bearing housing.

9. Collect and note the location of the spacers between the upper control arm and the bearing housing. They are alignment shims and must be reinstalled properly.

10. Remove the nut holding the rear upper control arm to the rear axle member (support).

11. At the front of the upper control arm, remove the nut and bolt which holds it to the rear axle member.

12. Use a pair of adjustable pliers to remove the control arm from the vehicle.

**To install:**

13. Install the arm to the rear axle member and secure with nut and bolt.

14. Install both the front and rear mounts.

15. Install the spacers at the wheel bearing housing, and install the nut holding the arm to the housing.

16. Inboard at the rear axle support, tighten the rearmost nut to 62 ft. lbs. (85 Nm).

17. Tighten the front nut and bolt to 51 ft. lbs. (70 Nm) plus an additional 60 degrees of rotation.

18. Pull the top of the wheel bearing housing outwards away from the center of the vehicle. This is essential for correct wheel alignment. Tighten the upper control arm nut at the bearing housing to 84 ft. lbs. (115 Nm).

19. Pull the wheel bearing housing outward and install the lower control arm with the bolt and nut, but do not tighten it.

20. Pull the wheel bearing housing inwards towards the center of the vehicle. Tighten the control arm nut to 37 ft. lbs. (50 Nm) plus and additional 90 degrees of rotation.

21. Reinstall the support arm; tighten the mount to 44 ft. lbs. (60 Nm) plus an additional 90 degrees of rotation.

22. Install the track rod and tighten to 62 ft. lbs. (85 Nm).

23. Install the brake caliper.

24. Install the wheels.

25. Lower the vehicle.

26. Check and adjust the rear alignment if necessary.

#### 1995–98 960/S90/V90

1. Raise and safely support the vehicle.

2. Remove the wheel.

3. Install compression tool J-41470 or a suitable equivalent. Apply light pressure to the link arm.

4. Disconnect the shock absorber from the support arm.

5. Remove the sway bar bolts from support arm on both sides.

6. Turn the compression tool up to its fully compressed position.

7. Remove the brake caliper and hang it safely out of the way so that the brake hose is not damaged.

8. Remove the nut connecting the upper control arm to the wheel bearing housing.

9. Using a brass drift, tap the bolt out to release the upper control arm bushing from the wheel bearing housing.

10. Remove the bolt connecting the track rod to the wheel bearing housing.

11. Separate the track rod from the wheel bearing housing.

12. Remove the nut connecting the lower control arm to the wheel bearing housing. Use a brass drift to tap out the bolt.

13. Separate the wheel bearing housing from the upper control arm. Allow the wheel bearing housing to rest on the lower control arm.

14. Remove the front and rear bolts from the upper control arm.

15. Pull the upper control from the rear axle beam and remove it.

**To install:**

16. Install the upper control arm in the rear axle beam and attach it with new front and rear bolts. Tighten the bolts to 18 ft. lbs. (25 Nm).

17. Push the wheel bearing housing up and connect it to the upper control arm.

18. Install a new attaching nut, but do not tighten.

19. Connect the support arm to the wheel bearing housing and install a new attaching bolt, but do not tighten.

20. Connect the lower control arm to the wheel bearing housing. Install the through bolt and a new nut, but do not tighten.

21. Install the track rod and attaching bolt, but do not tighten.

22. Tighten the attaching bolts and nuts in the following sequence to the indicated specifications:

- upper control arm nut—92 ft. lbs. (120 Nm)
- lower control arm nut—63 ft. lbs. (80 Nm)
- support arm bolts—63 ft. lbs. (80 Nm)
- track rod bolt—63 ft. lbs. (80 Nm)

23. Install the brake caliper and new attaching bolts. Tighten the bolts to 47 ft. lbs. (60 Nm).

24. Install the shock absorber and a new attaching bolt. Tighten the bolt to 63 ft. lbs. (80 Nm).

25. Release the pressure on the compression tool.

26. Connect the sway bar to the support arm using new bolts, but do not tighten.

27. Install the wheels.

28. Lower the vehicle.

## Trailing Arms

### REMOVAL & INSTALLATION

♦ **See Figures 66, 67, 68 and 69**

Trailing arms are found only on the 850 series.

1. Raise and safely support the vehicle.

2. Undo the brake line and the ABS speed sensor wiring bracket on the right rear trailing arm.

3. Remove the wheels.

4. Remove the shock absorbers.

5. Remove the springs.

6. Remove the sway bar.

7. Position a jack or suitable tool under the left trailing arm.

8. Raise the left trailing arm to release the trailing arm mounting.

9. Press the right trailing arm from the left trailing arm.

10. Remove the right trailing arm body mounting bolts.

11. Remove the right trailing arm.

12. If necessary, remove the left trailing arm body mounting bolts and remove the trailing arm.

**To install:**

13. Install new trailing arm mountings.

14. Align the left and right trailing arms.

15. Tighten the left and right trailing arm mounting to 59 ft. lbs. (80 Nm).

16. Tighten the trailing arm-to-body bolts to the following specifications:

- Bolt through the trailing arm bracket and rear axle link—78 ft. lbs. (105 Nm) and angle tighten an additional 90°.
- Bracket bolts to 48 ft. lbs. (65 Nm) and angle tighten an additional 60°.

17. Install the sway bar.

18. Install the springs.

19. Install the shock absorbers.

20. Install the brake line and ABS wiring bracket.

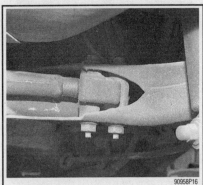

Fig. 66 Passenger side trailing arm mounting

Fig. 67 Sway bar mounting

Fig. 68 Driver side trailing arm mounting

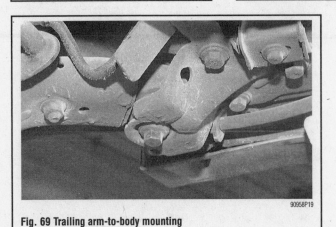

Fig. 69 Trailing arm-to-body mounting

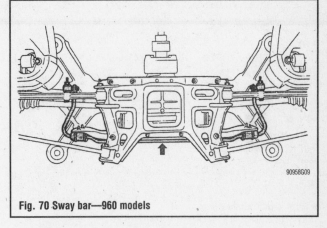

Fig. 70 Sway bar—960 models

21. Install the wheels.
22. Lower the vehicle.

## Sway Bar

### REMOVAL & INSTALLATION

#### Except 850, 1995–97 960 and 1998 Models

1. Raise the vehicle and support it safely. Place the stands at the rear jacking points.
2. Remove the wheels.
3. Use a floor jack to raise the rear axle just enough to unload the shock absorbers.
4. Remove the lower shock retaining bolts.
5. Remove the nuts holding the sway bar to the brackets.
6. Remove the sway bar.
**To install:**
7. When installing the sway bar, attach both the bracket nut and the lower shock retaining bolt hand-tight.
8. Once all four mounting points are snug, tighten the bracket nuts to 35 ft. lbs. (48 Nm) and the shock absorber bolts to 63 ft. lbs. (86 Nm).
9. Remove the jack from the axle.
10. Install the wheels, if removed.
11. Lower the vehicle.

#### 1995–98 960/S90/V90 and AWD V70 Series Models

♦ See Figure 70

1. Raise and safely support the vehicle.
2. Remove the wheels.
3. Remove the nut and through-bolt securing the sway bar to the support arm.

4. Remove the nuts securing the bracket retainer to the axle beam.
5. Lower the sway bar.
**To install:**
6. Install the sway bar to the axle beam and secure in place using the nuts. Tighten the nuts to 15 ft. lbs. (20 Nm).
7. Connect the sway bar to the support arm and attach the through-bolt and nut. Do not tighten at this time.
8. Install the wheels.
9. Lower the vehicle.
10. With all four wheels on the ground, Tighten the support arm bolts to 63 ft. lbs. (80 Nm).

#### 850, C70, S70 and V70 Series

1. Raise and safely support the vehicle.
2. Remove the left-hand rubber silencer mount and hang it up as high as possible with a tie wrap.
3. Remove the outer transverse arm mount nut and bolt.
4. Mark the position of the right side transverse arm mount in relation to the left-hand trailing arm hole. Punch a mark on the edge of the hole and remove the other mount bolt.

➡It is important that this mark is made properly, otherwise the toe-in will be incorrect.

5. Remove the anti-sway bar mount bolts, then the bar.
**To install:**
6. Install the anti-sway bar using new nuts and bolts, but do not tighten completely.
7. Connect the transverse arm mount to the trailing arm with new bolts and nuts. Install the inner bolt first and line up the mark with the outer hole, tighten it enough to keep it in position. Then install the outer bolt and nut and tighten to 37 ft. lbs. (50 Nm) and angle tighten 120°.
8. Tighten the anti-sway bar bolts as follows:
- right side bolts to 37 ft. lbs. (50 Nm)
- left side forward bolt to 37 ft. lbs. (50 Nm) and angle tighten 90°

- left side rear bolt to 48 ft. lbs. (65 Nm) and angle tighten 90°
9. Cut the tie wrap holding the silencer and install the rubber mount.
10. Lower the vehicle.

## Wheel Bearings

### ADJUSTMENT

The rear wheel bearings are sealed, pressed-in units, and no adjustment is possible.

### REMOVAL & INSTALLATION

#### Except 850, 960 Sedan and 1998 Models

1. With the vehicle sitting on all four wheels, loosen the rear axle nut.
2. Raise and support the vehicle safely. Do not allow the lifting arms to interfere with the support arms.
3. Remove the wheels.
4. Remove the brake caliper and use a piece of wire to hang the caliper out of the way.
5. Remove the brake disc and parking brake shoes.
6. Disconnect and remove the parking brake cable from the wheel bearing housing.
7. Remove the retaining bolt for the support arm at the housing. Tap the support arm loose.
8. Remove the nut and bolt holding the lower link arm to the housing.
9. Remove the retaining bolt for the track rod at the bearing housing and use a small claw-type puller to remove the track rod.
10. Remove the axle nut.
11. Remove the retaining nut for the upper link at the bearing housing. The wheel bearing housing can now be removed as a unit.

➡ There are shims between the bearing housing and the upper link arm. Collect them when the housing is removed.

12. Mount the housing assembly in a vise.
13. Place counterhold tool 5340 or equivalent between the hub and bearing housing. Press out the hub with a proper sized drift
14. Remove the circlip retaining the bearing in the wheel bearing housing and press the bearing out. Press against the inner race.
15. Use bearing puller 2722 or equivalent to pull the inner race off the hub.
**To install:**
16. Press the new bearing into the housing. Make sure the press tool contacts only the outer bearing race or the bearing will be damaged. Install the circlip.
17. Support the inner race and press the hub into the bearing. If the inner race is not properly supported, the bearing will be damaged.
18. Install the wheel bearing housing onto the housing and install the axle nut hand-tight.
19. Install the shims between the upper link and the wheel bearing housing and then install the retaining nut at the upper link.
20. Pull the wheel bearing housing outwards at the top and tighten the upper link arm nut to 85 ft. lbs. (110 Nm). This is essential to insure correct wheel alignment when completed.
21. Tilt the bearing housing outwards at the bottom as necessary to refit the lower link arm and its retaining bolt. When in place, pull the bottom of the bearing housing in towards the center of the vehicle and tighten the link arm to 36 ft. lbs. (47 Nm) plus an additional 90 degrees of rotation.
22. Install the support arm and its bolt.
23. Install the track rod and tighten to 63 ft. lbs. (82 Nm).
24. Reinstall the parking brake cable at the bearing housing.
25. Reinstall the parking brake shoes, the brake disc as marked and the brake caliper.
26. Install the wheels.
27. Lower the vehicle.
28. With all four wheels on the ground, tighten the axle nut to 103 ft. lbs. (134 Nm) plus an additional 60 degrees of rotation.

#### 1990–94 940 and 960

1. With the vehicle sitting on all four wheels, loosen the rear axle nut.
2. Raise and support the vehicle safely. Do not allow the rear lifting arms to interfere with the support arms.
3. Remove the wheels.
4. Remove the brake caliper and use a piece of wire to hang the caliper out of the way.
5. Mark the position of the brake disc relative to its small locating pin, then remove the disc. Remove the brake shoes.
6. Disconnect and remove the parking brake cable from the wheel bearing housing.
7. Remove the retaining bolt for the support arm at the housing. Tap the support arm loose.
8. Remove the nut and bolt holding the lower link arm to the housing.
9. Remove the retaining bolt for the track rod at the bearing housing and use a small claw-type puller to remove the track rod.
10. Remove the axle nut.
11. Remove the retaining nut for the upper link at the bearing housing. The wheel bearing housing can now be removed as unit.

➡ There are shims between the bearing housing and the upper link arm. Collect them when the housing is removed.

12. Mount the housing assembly in a vise.
13. Place a counterhold tool 5340 or equivalent between the hub and bearing housing. Press out the hub with a proper sized drift
14. Remove the circlip retaining the bearing in the wheel bearing housing and press the bearing out. Press against the inner race.
15. Use a bearing puller 2722 or equivalent to pull the inner race off the hub.
**To install:**
16. Press the new bearing into the bearing housing. Make sure the press tool contacts only the outer bearing race or the bearing will be damaged. Install the circlip.
17. Support the inner race and press the hub into the bearing. If the inner race is not properly supported, the bearing will be damaged.
18. Install the wheel bearing housing onto the halfshaft and install the axle nut hand-tight.
19. Install the shims between the upper link and the wheel bearing housing and then install the retaining nut at the upper link.
20. Pull the wheel bearing housing outwards at the top and tighten the upper link arm nut to 85 ft. lbs. (116 Nm). This is essential to insure correct wheel alignment when completed.
21. Tilt the bearing housing outwards at the bottom as necessary to refit the lower link arm and retaining bolt. When in place, pull the bottom of the bearing housing in towards the center of the vehicle and tighten the link arm to 36 ft. lbs. (49 Nm) plus an additional 90 degrees of rotation.
22. Install the support arm and bolt. Tighten the nut to 44 ft. lbs. (60 Nm) plus an additional 90 degrees of rotation.
23. Install the track rod and tighten to 63 ft. lbs. (86 Nm).
24. Reinstall the parking brake cable at the bearing housing.
25. Reinstall the brake shoes, the brake disc as marked and the brake caliper.
26. Install the wheels.
27. Lower the vehicle.
28. With all four wheels on the ground, tighten the axle nut to 103 ft. lbs. (140 Nm) plus an additional 60 degrees of rotation.

#### 1995–98 960/S90 Sedan and AWD V70 Series Models

1. With the vehicle sitting on all four wheels, loosen the rear axle nut.
2. Raise and safely support vehicle. Position a lift or jackstands so they do not interfere with the suspension arms. Remove the wheel.
3. Use tool 999 5577 or equivalent to compress the suspension slightly against the spring.
4. Remove the damper bolt and pull the damper from the support arm.
5. Remove the anti-sway bolts in both of the support arms.
6. Raise the suspension up into normal position.
7. Remove the axle shaft nut.
8. Remove the brake caliper and support it safely out of the way.

9. Mark the position of the brake disc and remove the disc.

10. Remove the parking brake shoes and disconnect the adjuster from the parking brake cable.

11. Disconnect the parking brake cable from the wheel bearing housing and remove the nut for the upper link bushing.

12. Tap the bushing bolt free of the wheel bearing housing.

13. Remove the bolt to the track rod and separate the rod from the wheel bearing housing.

14. Remove the support arm bolt and tap if free of the bushing.

15. Remove the link nut and tap the bolt out using a brass drift

16. Remove the wheel bearing housing.

➡ **The bearing must be replaced any time the hub is pressed out.**

17. Position the wheel bearing housing in a press so the hub can be pressed out. Using an appropriate sized drift, press the hub off.

18. Remove the circlip holding the bearing in the housing and press the bearing out.

19. Position the drift in the inner bearing race. Using the puller 999 2722 and counter hold 999 5310, or their equivalents, pull the inner race out of the hub.

**To install:**

20. Properly support the bearing housing and press the new bearing in. Make sure the press tool contacts only the outer bearing race or the bearing will be damaged. Install the circlip.

21. Support the inner bearing race on the press table and press the hub into the bearing. Make sure the inner bearing race is supported or the bearing will be damaged.

22. Fit the wheel bearing housing to the upper link and driveshaft Then install all the nuts and bolts before tightening any of them. Tighten the nut for the upper link to 85 ft. lbs. (115 Nm) and all others to 63 ft. lbs. (80 Nm).

23. Connect the parking brake cable to the wheel bearing housing and fasten with clip.

24. Install the adjuster for the cable with arrow on the upper side pointing up.

25. Install the parking brake shoes, retainers, and spring.

26. Install the brake disc.

27. Install a new axle nut but do not tighten it yet.

28. Install the brake caliper using new bolts.

29. Install new anti-sway bolts on both sides, but do not tighten them fully.

30. Clean the face of the brake disc and the back side of the wheel where the two mate. Lubricate the guide pin with rustproofing compound.

31. Install the wheels.

32. Lower the car.

33. Tighten the anti-sway bar bolts on both sides to 63 ft. lbs. (80 Nm).

34. With all four wheels on the ground, tighten the axle nut to 130 ft. lbs. (140 Nm) plus an additional 60°.

## Hub and Bearings

### REMOVAL & INSTALLATION

#### 850, S70, C70 and V70, Except AWD V70 Series

➡ **The bearing and hub are replaced as a single component. The bearing is not available separately.**

1. Raise and safely support vehicle.

2. Remove the wheels.

3. Remove the caliper and the brake line from the mounting clip. When the left brake caliper is removed, the three-way brake line connector mounting bolt must also be removed. Remove the caliper and hang it from the spring to prevent brake hose damage.

4. Back off the parking brake adjustment, so the rotor can be removed.

5. Remove the rotor.

6. Remove the cap, hub nut and hub.

**To install:**

7. Clean the stub axle thoroughly.

8. Install the hub using a new nut and tighten it to 89 ft. lbs. (120 Nm) plus an additional 30 degrees. Make sure that there is no play in the bearings after installation.

9. Install the dust cap using an appropriate tool.

10. Clean the face of the hub and back side of the rotor where the two mate.

11. Install the rotor and guide pin. Tighten the pin to 7 ft. lbs. (9 Nm).

12. Adjust the parking brake shoes until the disc cannot be turned, then back it off four to six notches.

13. Install the brake caliper.

14. Install the brake line and mounting clips, and the three-way connector on the left-hand side, if applicable.

15. Install the wheels.

16. Lower the vehicle.

## STEERING

All 1990–98 Volvos are equipped with a servo operated steering system. The steering gear is of the rack and pinion type. A vane-type servo pump is belt-driven from the crankshaft. Wheel deflection is limited by a stop in the steering gear and cannot be adjusted.

In addition, these vehicles are equipped with a Supplemental Restraint System (SRS). The SRS system consists of an inflatable bag located in the center of the steering wheel. The bag is normally folded up, but is instantly inflated in the event of certain types of collision. The SRS provides extra safety, in addition to the seat belts.

### ❊❊ WARNING

**All work which includes removing or replacing the air bag assembly must be carried out with the battery disconnected and with the ignition turned OFF for the duration of work. This is to ensure that the air bag does not accidentally inflate during service repairs and that no faults codes will register, requiring subsequent cancellation.**

## Safety Precautions

• Before beginning work which could affect the SRS system, always turn the ignition **OFF**, disconnect the negative battery cable AND TAPE the end of the cable.

• When working around the instrument panel or steering column, take special care to ensure that the SRS wiring are not pinched, chafed or penetrated by

bolts/screws, etc. This is most likely to happen when installing the sound insulation, knee bolsters, ignition lock or steering column cover.

• When repairs are made to the front suspension and steering, be aware that the contact reel can only withstand being turned 3 turns in either direction.

• Never service the steering shaft or steering gear without first locking the contact reel and removing the steering wheel.

• When fault tracing the SRS system with the air bag assembly in place, install the special tool 998 8695 or equivalent. This tool has the same resistance as the air bag assembly. The use of this tool prevent accidental air bag inflation and fault code registration during work.

## Steering Wheel

### REMOVAL & INSTALLATION

◆ **See Figures 71, 72 and 73**

### ❊❊ WARNING

**Before working the steering system, read the SRS service precautions in Section 6.**

1. Drive the vehicle forward on a level surface so that the wheels are straight.

2. Disconnect the negative battery cable AND TAPE the cable end.

**Fig. 71 Remove the steering wheel mounting bolt**

**Fig. 72 Lock the contact reel down before removing the steering wheel**

**Fig. 73 View of the contact reel with the wheel removed**

3. Turn the ignition key to position **I** so that the steering lock is OFF.
4. Remove the air bag assembly, as described in Section 6.
5. Remove the steering wheel mounting bolt.
6. Lock the contact reel: Release the locking screw in the end of the plastic strip from its "parking hole" in the steering wheel. Screw must always remain in plastic strip. Attach the locking screw to the contact reel pin. The contact reel is now locked in the zero position.

### ✳✳ WARNING

**Do not turn the steering wheel, as this will cause the pin to snap, requiring replacement of the contact reel.**

Remove the steering wheel, being careful to pull the lead and plastic strip with the screw through the hole in the middle.

**To install:**

7. Install the steering wheel.
8. Set the steering wheel so that the contact reel pin is in the center of the steering wheel hole.
9. Install the steering wheel nut finger-tight.
10. Remove the screw in the contact reel plastic strip and install in its parking hole in steering wheel.
11. Tighten the steering wheel nut to 42 ft. lbs. (60 Nm).
12. Install the air bag assembly.

### ✳✳ CAUTION

**When connecting the battery, make sure that no one is in the vehicle in case of an SRS malfunction causing accidental air bag deployment.**

13. Connect the negative battery cable.
14. Check the vehicle operation and SRS system for fault codes.

## Turn Signal/Windshield Wiper Switch

REMOVAL & INSTALLATION

▶ See Figure 74

### ✳✳ CAUTION

**This procedure requires removal of the steering wheel. If the vehicle is equipped with the SRS (air bag) system, refer to the safety precautions listed earlier in this section. DO NOT remove the wheel until these precautions have been followed.**

1. Disconnect the negative battery cable.
2. Turn the steering wheel to the straight ahead position.
3. Remove the center pad from the wheel.

4. Remove the steering wheel retaining bolt. If possible, matchmark the wheel and steering shaft. If the vehicle is equipped with SRS, pull out the locking screw and the long tape label from its station in the steering wheel hub. Use the lock screw (with the tape flag attached) to lock the contact reel through the hole in the steering wheel hub. Do not turn the steering wheel once the bolt is removed; the pin in the contact reel will shear.
5. Remove the steering wheel and the upper and lower steering column casings.
6. To remove the switch, simply remove the retaining screws holding it to the column and unplug the connector.

**To install:**

➡**When reassembling, remember to check the position of all the wires so that nothing is pinched in casings.**

7. Install the switch in the column, attach the electrical connectors, and tighten the retaining screws.
8. Reinstall the column casings.
9. Install the steering wheel. Check that the steering wheel position is true to the position of the wheels. If the vehicle is SRS equipped, do not turn the steering wheel until the center bolt is reinstalled and tight; doing so will shear the pin in the contact reel. Remove the locking bolt with its flag and store it in the extra hole on the left side of the wheel.
10. Tighten the steering wheel bolt to 42 ft. lbs. (60 Nm).
11. Reinstall the center pad.
12. Connect the negative battery cable.
13. Start the vehicle and check the SRS system for faults.

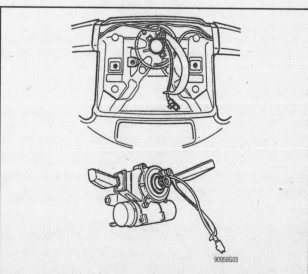

**Fig. 74 Typical turn signal/windshield wiper switch assembly**

## Rear Window Wiper Switch

The tailgate washer/wiper controls are mounted on the same control stalk as the front wipers. The components are not individually replaceable for the rear system. To replace the switch assembly, follow the directions given for Turn Signal/Windshield Wiper Switch.

## Ignition Lock Cylinder/Switch

The ignition lock cylinder/switch is an integral unit. The lock cylinder turns inside the switch assembly, and makes contact with terminals inside the switch, determining which circuit to energize. Replacement of the separate components is not possible; they are replaced as an assembly.

### REMOVAL & INSTALLATION

#### 240 Series

The ignition lock cylinder is mounted on the steering column and incorporates a steering wheel lock to deter vehicle theft Removal of the lock assembly requires the removal of the steering column assembly.

1. Disconnect the negative battery cable AND TAPE the cable end.
2. Remove the air bag assembly.
3. Remove the steering wheel.
4. Remove the contact reel.
5. Pull up the cover from the lower steering shaft joint, if required.
6. Loosen the upper bolts in the upper and lower joints.
7. Pull down the lower steering shaft so that the upper joint is freed from the upper steering shaft
8. Remove the upper and lower steering column covers.
9. Disconnect the connector for the wiper control.
10. Remove the retaining bolts for the wiper and indicator controls holder.
11. Lift the holder over the steering shaft and remove. Note the position of the indicator switch lead and remove.
12. Remove the connector from the starter switch, if required.
13. Remove the steering column's lower retaining bracket, seal in the firewall and defroster hose from the heater unit.
14. Tap the shearing bolts so that the bolts and plastic washers slide out of their slots in member.
15. Carefully remove the steering column with steering lock. Avoid getting the steering column caught while passing through the firewall.
16. Mount the steering column in a vise.
17. Break off the washers from the rear end edge of the shearing bolts, then using a pair of channel locks, remove the shearing bolts.
18. Press the ignition lock assembly from the steering column, using a suitable drift and counterhold tool (5295 or equivalent).
19. Install the key in the lock and turn.

**To install:**

20. Install the key in the lock and turn.
21. Press the new ignition lock assembly onto the steering column, using a suitable drift and counterhold tool (5295 or equivalent). The lock assembly, when installed, should be positioned as follows: Measure the distance from the top of the lock assembly to the end of the steering column, above splined area. The distance should be 5.98 inches (152mm).
22. Remove the key form the lock.
23. Turn the steering shaft and check that the lock barrel locks it.
24. Before installing the steering column, check that the upper steering shaft's collapsible coupling is intact. Its upper end (A) should not be able to move axially in relation to its lower end (B). Also, check the total length; it should be 27.38–28.18 inches (69.5–71.5cm). If the measurement is incorrect, replace the complete steering column.
25. Install the plastic guides in the column support. Turn the guides so that the washers faces downwards.
26. Install the steering column into position, but do not tighten the shearing bolts completely.
27. Pull the steering column towards the rear as far as possible; tighten the bolts further, but do not shear them yet.
28. Install the rubber grommets.
29. Install the lower retaining bracket and tighten the bolts lightly.
30. Coat the firewall rubber seals with petroleum jelly.

31. Install the seal on the steering column (cone turned inward) from the engine compartment side.
32. Tighten the upper bolts, but do not shear them yet.
33. Tighten the lower retaining bolts to 11–17 ft. lbs. (15–25 Nm).
34. Attach the defroster hose and reconnect the ignition lock connector.
35. Attach the universal joint to the upper steering column shafts. First tighten the upper bolt, then the lower.
36. Install the locking pins.
37. Checking and adjusting steering shaft:

   a. When checking, the distance (A) between the upper steering shaft joint and shoulder on the lower steering shaft should be 0.39–0.75 inch (10–19mm).

   b. If incorrect, loosen the upper bolted at (B) the lower joint. Loosen the lower bolt (C) of the upper shaft universal joint. Adjust the distance (A), by moving the shaft up or down. Tighten the bolts (B and C) to 14–20 ft. lbs. (18–28 Nm).

➡**Make sure the position of the upper steering shaft does not change, as this can affect the distance between the steering wheel and the steering column cover.**

38. Install the holder for the combination switch control and connect the leads.
39. Connect the ground lead to one of the retaining bolts.
40. Install the upper and lower steering column covers.
41. Set contact reel to zero position: If contact reel must be zero, turn the reel to the far right end and then back 3 revolution to the left. Lock the contact reel with the screw in the plastic strip.
42. Ensure the front wheels are perfectly in straight-ahead position.
43. Install the contact reel bracket and contact reel.
44. Reconnect and properly position the lead.

### ❊❊ WARNING

**Do not turn the steering, as this will cause the pin to snap, requiring replacement of the contact reel.**

45. Install the steering wheel. Set the steering wheel so that the contact reel pin is in the center of the steering wheel hole.
46. Install the steering wheel nut finger-tight.
47. Remove the screw in the contact reel plastic strip and install in its parking hole in steering wheel.
48. Tighten the steering wheel nut to 42 ft. lbs. (60 Nm).

### ❊❊ CAUTION

**When connecting the battery, make sure that no one is in the vehicle in case of an SRS malfunction causing accidental air bag deployment.**

49. Connect the negative battery cable.
50. Check the SRS lamp operation and that no fault codes have been registered.

#### Except 240 Series

◆ **See Figures 75 and 76**

### ❊❊ WARNING

**Before working the steering system, read the SRS service precautions in Section 6.**

1. Place the front wheels in straight-ahead position.
2. Disconnect the negative battery cable AND TAPE the cable end.
3. Remove the air bag assembly.
4. Remove the steering wheel.
5. Remove the contact reel assembly.
6. Remove the combination switch.
7. Remove the steering column rake adjustment lever using a 0.12 in. (3mm) hex wrench.
8. Remove the parking plate around the steering tube (4 screws).
9. Disconnect the ignition lock connector.

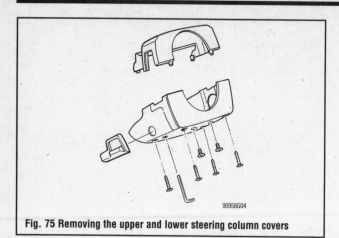

90958G04

**Fig. 75 Removing the upper and lower steering column covers**

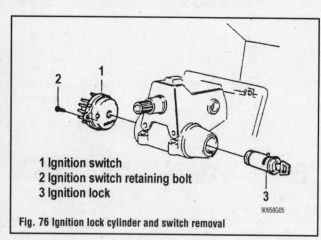

**1 Ignition switch**
**2 Ignition switch retaining bolt**
**3 Ignition lock**

90958G05

**Fig. 76 Ignition lock cylinder and switch removal**

10. Turn the ignition switch to position **I**.
11. Take a 0.079 inch (2mm) drift and press down the tumblers in the cylinder.
12. Remove the lock assembly.
**To install:**
13. Install the steering lock assembly.
14. Turn the ignition switch to position **I** and press down the tumblers with a suitable drift
15. Install the lock assembly.
16. Install the combination switch assembly.
17. Install the contact reel.
18. Install the steering wheel.
19. Install the air bag assembly.

### ✳✳ CAUTION

**When connecting the battery, make sure that no one is in the vehicle in case of an SRS malfunction causing accidental air bag deployment.**

20. Reconnect the negative battery cable.
21. Check the vehicle operation and SRS system for fault codes.

### Steering Linkage

#### REMOVAL & INSTALLATION

All vehicles are equipped with rack and pinion steering (manual or power). Rack and pinion systems save space and weight, improve steering response and eliminate most of the rods and linkage under the vehicle.

### Tie Rod Ends

◆ **See Figures 77 thru 82**

1. Raise and safely support the vehicle.
2. Remove the wheel(s).
3. Measure the length between the end of the tie rod and the steering rack housing, and mark the position of the tie rod end on the rack.

➡**Another way to remove the tie rod end and not drastically change the alignment is to loosen the locknut on the steering rack, but do not turn it any more than the initial loosening. Remove the tie rod end from the spindle as usual, but unthread the tie rod end from the steering rack without moving the locknut. When installing the tie rod end, thread the tie rod end onto the rack until it bottoms against the locknut, then turn the tie rod end so that the ball joint is ready to be connected to the spindle. Place the tie rod end in the spindle and tighten the retaining nut, then install the cotter pin. Tighten the locknut on the steering rack; the toe on the side you worked on should be very close, if not the same, as when you started.**

4. Loosen the locknut on the steering rack and pinion.
5. Remove the cotter pin (if equipped) and the retaining nut from the spindle.
6. Separate the tie rod end from the steering arm using an appropriate puller.
7. Unthread the tie rod end from the steering rack.
**To install:**
8. Thread the tie rod end onto the steering rack until it aligns with the marking made earlier.
9. Tighten the tie rod locknut to 52 ft. lbs. (70 Nm).
10. Connect the tie rod end to the steering arm.
11. Tighten the retaining nut.
   a. 850 series and C70/S70/V70: tighten to 52 ft. lbs. (70 Nm).
   b. 240, 700, 940 and 960 series, and S90/V90: tighten to 44 ft. lbs. (60 Nm).
12. Install the cotter pin (if equipped).
13. Install the wheels.
14. Lower the vehicle and check the front wheel alignment.

### Inner Tie Rod

➡**If a steering boot or inner rod is damaged on the rack and pinion assembly, they are easily replaced after tie rod end removal. DO NOT allow a torn boot to go unattended, as steering rack damage will likely occur.**

1. Raise and safely support the vehicle.
2. Remove the wheel.
3. Remove the outer tie rod end from the spindle.
4. Remove the steering rack boot.
5. Using appropriate tools, hold the rack and loosen the inner tie rod by turning the hex on the ball.
6. Remove the inner tie rod assembly with the tie rod end attached.
**To install:**
7. Mark the position of the tie rod end on the inner tie rod, and remove the tie rod end.

➡**An alternative method is to measure the length of the assembled inner tie rod and tie rod end before removal. Then, assemble the new inner tie rod and tie rod end to the same length.**

8. Install the tie rod end onto the inner tie rod.
9. Compare the marks and assemble to the same length.
10. Clean the tie rod threads on the rack assembly.
11. Thread the new inner tie rod end onto the rack and tighten.
12. Using a punch, stake the inner tie rod assembly to the rack by hitting the inner tie rod lip.
13. Install the steering rack boot.
14. Fasten the tie rod end to the spindle.
15. Install the wheel.
16. Lower the vehicle.

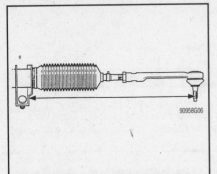

Fig. 77 Measuring the distance from the steering rack housing to the tie rod end's ball joint

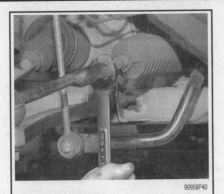

Fig. 78 Loosen the locknut on the steering rack

Fig. 79 Remove the retaining nut from the tie rod end where it fastens to the spindle

Fig. 80 The use of an appropriate puller is recommended, especially if the tie rod end is only being removed and not replaced

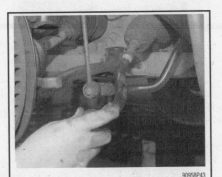

Fig. 81 After the tie rod end is separated from the spindle, unthread it from the rack and pinion

Fig. 82 After the tie rod end is removed, inspect the threads on the steering rack's inner tie rod

## Manual Rack and Pinion

This procedure applies only to 240 series vehicles with manual rack and pinion assemblies. All other models of the 240 series, as well as all other vehicles covered by this manual, have a power rack and pinion; for those vehicles, refer to the procedure later in this section.

### REMOVAL & INSTALLATION

1. Disconnect the negative battery cable.
2. Remove the lockbolt and nut from the column flange.
3. Bend apart the flange slightly with a screwdriver.
4. Raise and support the vehicle safely.
5. Remove the front wheels.
6. Disconnect the tie rod ends, using a ball joint puller.
7. Remove the splash guard.
8. Disconnect the steering gear from the front axle member (beam).
9. Disconnect the steering gear at the steering shaft flange.
10. Remove the steering gear. Save the dowel pins.

**To install:**

11. Install rubber spacers and plates for the steering gear attachment points.
12. Position the steering gear and guide the pinion shaft into the steering shaft The recess on the pinion shaft should be aligned towards the lockbolt opening in the shaft
13. Attach the steering gear to the front axle member.
14. Check that the U-bolts are aligned in the plate slots. Install flat washers and nuts. Tighten the nuts to 10–18 ft. lbs. (14–25 Nm).
15. Install the splash guard.
16. Connect the steering rods to the steering arms. Tighten the nuts to 44 ft. lbs. (60 Nm).
17. Install the front wheels.
18. Lower the vehicle.
19. Install the lockbolt for the steering shaft flange. Tighten the bolt to 18 ft. lbs. (25 Nm).
20. Have the alignment checked and reset if needed.
21. Connect the negative battery cable.

## Power Rack and Pinion

### REMOVAL & INSTALLATION

**240 Series and Coupe**

### ✳✳ CAUTION

**On vehicles with air bags, the front wheels must be pointing straight ahead with the steering wheel locked. If this is not done, the contact reel of the air bag system will reach its end position and deploy the air bag.**

1. Disconnect the negative battery cable. Disarm the air bag system, if equipped.
2. Raise and support the vehicle safely on jackstands.
3. Remove the front wheels
4. From under the vehicle, remove the splashguard.
5. With the wheels pointed straight ahead, measure the length from one tie rod end to the steering rack housing.
6. Remove the steering column U-joint by scribing an alignment mark on the shaft.
7. Remove the cotter pin and loosen the nut and bolt securing the joint to the column shaft.
8. Separate the joint and steering shaft.
9. Remove the tie rod ends.

10. With a drip pan placed below the hoses to the steering rack, tag then remove the hoses. Discard the copper sealing washers.

11. Remove the sway bar if equipped.

12. Remove the two steering rack fixing bolts and nuts.

13. Lower the steering rack down from the vehicle frame and out.

**To install:**

14. Position the steering rack in the vehicle and secure the rack with the fixing nuts and bolts. Tighten the nuts and bolts to 32 ft. lbs. (44 Nm).

15. Install the sway bar if removed.

16. Install the hoses to the rack using new sealing washers. Tighten the hose bolts to 30 ft. lbs. (42 Nm).

17. Install the tie rod ends.

18. Connect the steering shaft and U-joint by aligning the scribe mark on the steering shaft with the mark on the U-joint. Tighten the retainer nut and bolt to 15 ft. lbs. (20 Nm). Install a new cotter pin.

19. Install the splashguard.

20. Fill the steering reservoir and bleed the system.

21. Lower the vehicle.

### 700 Series, 900 Series and S90/V90

♦ **See Figure 83**

1. Disconnect the negative battery cable.

2. Raise and support the vehicle safely.

3. Remove the splash guard and the small jacking panel on the front crossmember.

4. Disconnect the lower steering shaft from the steering gear.

5. At the lower universal joint, remove the snaprings and loosen the upper clamp bolt.

6. Remove the lower clamp bolt and slide the joint up on the shaft

7. Use a ball joint separator and disconnect the tie rods at the outer ends.

8. Disconnect the fluid lines from the steering gear. Catch the spilled fluid in a pan and install plugs in the lines.

9. Remove the sway bar mounting brackets from the side members and move them out of the way.

10. Remove the steering gear retaining bolts and lower the assembly out of the vehicle.

**To install:**

11. When reinstalling, position the rack in position and install the retaining bolts. Tighten them to 32 ft. lbs. (44 Nm).

12. Install the sway bar mounting brackets.

13. Use new copper washers and connect the fluid lines to the assembly.

14. Connect the tie rods and tighten their nuts to 44 ft. lbs. (60 Nm).

15. Slide the lower universal joint down the shaft and into position.

16. Tighten the lower clamp bolt first, then the upper. Both bolts are tightened to 15 ft. lbs. (20 Nm).

17. Install the snaprings.

18. Reinstall the jacking plate and the splash guard.

19. Fill the reservoir with the appropriate type of Automatic Transmission Fluid (ATF). For further information, refer to Section 1.

20. Start the engine and smoothly turn the steering wheel from lock to lock 3 or 4 times.

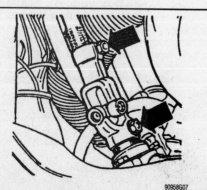

90958G07

**Fig. 83 Unfasten the two attaching nuts/bolts to remove the lower shaft from the steering gear**

21. Bleed the system and recheck the fluid level in the reservoir.

22. Lower the vehicle.

### 850, C70, S70 and V70 Series

**✳✳ CAUTION**

**On vehicles with air bags, the front wheels must be pointing straight ahead with the steering wheel locked. If this is not done, the contact reel of the air bag system will reach its end position and deploy the air bag.**

➡**The front subframe must be lowered. The bolts cannot be used again once loosened: new subframe bolts are required.**

1. Disconnect the negative battery cable. Disarm the air bag system, if equipped.

2. Install support rail 5033, bracket 5006 and lifting hook, or their equivalents, over the engine.

3. Lift the engine up slightly so that there is no pressure on the engine mounts.

4. Raise and safely support the vehicle.

5. Remove the front wheels.

6. Disconnect the tie rod ends.

7. Remove the splash guard from below the engine.

8. Disconnect the power steering fluid lines brackets and clamps from the front and rear of the subframe.

9. Remove the five nuts holding the steering rack to the subframe.

10. Position a jack below the rear part of the subframe and remove the following:

- 4 bolts holding the subframe to the body on both sides
- 2 bolts and washers holding the bracket to the subframe

11. Loosen the front subframe bolts so the frame lowers 0.59–0.79 in. (15–20mm).

12. Lower the subframe using the jack, and place a spacer between the frame and the body at the rear edge so the frame will not pop up.

13. Position a catch pan under the steering rack and disconnect the power steering lines from the rack.

14. Remove the steering column joint bolt and press it up from the steering rack.

15. Remove the bolt holding the rack to the engine mount.

16. Remove rack from the right side.

**To install:**

17. Transfer the thermal protection plate and center attachment mount, but do not tighten the mounting bolts.

18. Install the protective plugs in the line connection holes.

19. Install the tie rod ends.

20. Install the steering rack from the right side and let it rest on the rear engine mount.

21. Raise the rack up on the right side so that it is straight in relation to the frame and tighten the engine mount bolt to 37 ft. lbs. (50 Nm).

22. Connect the fluid lines and brackets loosely using new O-rings on the lines.

23. Align the fluid lines in the bracket and tighten them in the steering rack.

24. Fit the steering rack onto the steering shaft joint and tighten the bolt to 15 ft. lbs. (20 Nm).

25. Install the bolt lock clip.

26. Lift the rear of the subframe up using a jack and line up the steering rack mount bolts in the frame.

27. Install new subframe bolts loosely.

28. Move the jack to the front and replace the bolts with new ones, but do not tighten.

29. Tighten the bolts on the left side of the subframe to 77 ft. lbs. (105 Nm) plus an additional 120 degrees.

30. Tighten the right side bolts the same way.

31. Finally, tighten the bracket bolts on both sides to 37 ft. lbs. (50 Nm).

32. Install new nuts on the steering rack and tighten them to 37 ft. lbs. (50 Nm).

33. Tighten the steering rack center bolt to 59 ft. lbs. (80 Nm).

34. Install the front and rear steering fluid line brackets and tighten them.

35. Install the engine splashguard below the engine.

36. Install the wheels.
37. Fill the power steering fluid reservoir with fluid.
38. Connect the negative battery cable.
39. Start the vehicle and bleed the steering system.
40. Check the fluid level once again.
41. Lower the vehicle and check the toe-in.

## Power Steering Pump

### REMOVAL & INSTALLATION

#### 240 Series, 700 Series and Coupe

1. Disconnect the negative battery cable.
2. Remove all dirt and grease from around the line connections at the pump.
3. Using a container to catch any fluid that might run out, disconnect the power steering lines and plug them to prevent dirt from entering the system.
4. Remove the tensioner locking screws on both sides of the pump and remove the drive belt.
5. Turn the pump up and remove the three bolts holding the bracket to the engine block.
6. Remove the pump and bracket.
7. If the pump is being replaced with a new one, remove the nut and pulley from the old pump and transfer it to the new one. Separate the bracket and tensioner from the pump and install them loosely on the new pump.

**To install:**
8. Place the pump in position on the engine and install the retaining bolts and spacer. tighten the bolts to 18 ft. lbs. (25 Nm).
9. Install the drive belt.
10. Adjust the belt tension and then tighten the nuts of the long bolts.
11. Use new copper washers, and reconnect the fluid lines to the pump.
12. Fill the reservoir with Type A or Dexron®III automatic transmission fluid and bleed the system.
13. Connect the negative battery cable.

#### 940, 960, S90 and V90 Series

1. Disconnect the negative battery cable.
2. Loosen the belt tensioner.
3. Remove the mounting bracket and bolt.
4. Disconnect the lines at or near the pump. Depending on the type of pump, it may be necessary to disconnect the rubber hoses from the metal pipes instead of removing the lines at the pump body. Use a catch pan under the vehicle for spillage. Plug the lines and fittings immediately to avoid contamination.
5. Remove the large retaining bolt and remove the drive belt from the pump.
6. Lower the pump slightly and disconnect the filler hose from the pump.
7. Remove the pump from the vehicle.

**To install:**
8. If the pump is to be replaced with a new one, transfer the pulley, the mounting bracket and the washers to the new pump.
9. Install the mounting bracket on the new pump; make sure the thick washer is between the bracket and the pump body.
10. Install the pulley with the conical face of the washer must be to the outside.
11. Connect the filler hose to the pump.
12. Position the pump and install the retaining bolts loosely.
13. Install the mounting bracket and belt.
14. Adjust the belt tension.
15. Tighten the lower retaining bolts to 18 ft. lbs. (25 Nm).
16. Connect the fluid hoses to the pump. Use new copper washers and/or hose clamps. Tighten the banjo fittings to 31 ft. lbs. (40 Nm).

17. Connect the negative battery cable.
18. Fill the fluid reservoir and start the engine.
19. Bleed the steering system.

#### 850, C70, S70 and V70 Series

1. Disconnect the negative battery cable.
2. Remove the radiator reservoir cap.
3. Open the radiator draincock on the left side under the radiator and drain out about 3.2 qts. (3 liters) of coolant.
4. Disconnect the radiator hose from the thermostat housing.
5. Remove the oil hose holder from the dipstick tube and the air cooler hose from the control module box.
6. Using the proper sized ratchet, release the tension from the drive belt tensioner and remove the belt from the power steering pump.
7. Remove the long bolt and spacer from the plate.
8. Loosen the pressure side hose a quarter turn and the lower plate mount nut a few turns.
9. Remove all of the pump mounting bolts.
10. Lift the pump straight up and disconnect the pressure hose and old O-ring. Collect any fluid that spills.
11. Carefully make a small cut in the end of the return line no longer than the mark on the hose itself.
12. Remove the pump.
13. Raise and safely support the vehicle.
14. Turn the steering wheel from lock to lock and collect the fluid from the lines. Make sure no oil gets into the alternator.
15. Place the old pump in a vise and remove the pulley using an appropriate puller.

**To install:**
16. Install the pulley on the new pump, using an appropriate pressing tool. Apply a small amount of oil to the shaft to ease the installation.
17. Install the pump and five mounting bolts, tighten them to 18 ft. lbs. (25 Nm).
18. Install the long bolt and cover plate spacer, tighten it to 18 ft. lbs. (25 Nm).
19. Tighten the lower attachment to 18 ft. lbs. (25 Nm).
20. Install the following:
- pressure hose with a new O-ring
- return hose
- hose bracket for power steering hoses to dipstick tube
- radiator hose
- pump drive belt
- cooling hose to the control module box.
21. Connect the negative battery cable.
22. Fill the cooling system with coolant.
23. Fill the power steering pump reservoir with new fluid.
24. Bleed the steering system.

### BLEEDING

1. Fill the reservoir with the proper type of fluid.
2. Raise and support the vehicle safely.
3. Place the transmission in **N** and apply the parking brake.
4. Start the engine and fill the reservoir as the level drops.
5. When the reservoir level has stopped dropping, slowly turn the steering wheel from lock to lock several times. Fill the reservoir if necessary.
6. Continue to turn the steering wheel slowly until the fluid in the reservoir is free of air bubbles.
7. Stop the engine and observe the oil level in the reservoir. If the oil level rises more than ¼ in. (6mm) past the level mark, air still remains in the system. Continue bleeding until the level rise is correct.
8. Lower the vehicle.

## FRONT SUSPENSION TORQUE SPECIFICATIONS

| Components | English | Metric |
|---|---|---|
| **Axle nut** | | |
| 850/C70/S70/V70 | 89 ft. lbs. | 120 Nm |
| **Control arm strut** | | |
| Bracket bolt | 63 ft. lbs. | 85 Nm |
| Control arm nut | 70 ft. lbs. | 95 Nm |
| **Lower ball joint** | | |
| 240 Series | | |
| Retaining nut | 85 ft. lbs. | 115 Nm |
| Ball joint-to-control arm bolts | 44 ft. lbs. | 60 Nm |
| Coupe, 700 and 900 series, and S90/V90 | | |
| Retaining nut | 44 ft. lbs. | 60 Nm |
| 850/C70/S70/V70 | | |
| Retaining nut | 12 ft. lbs. | 18 Nm |
| **Lower control arm** | | |
| 240 Series | | |
| Front mount | 38 ft. lbs. | 44 Nm |
| Rear mount | 55 ft. lbs. | 75 Nm |
| Coupe, 700 and 900 series, and S90/V90 | | |
| Subframe mount | 63 ft. lbs. | 86 Nm |
| 850/C70/S70/V70 | | |
| Subframe mount | 48 ft. lbs. | 65 Nm |
| **Strut nut** | | |
| Coupe, 240, 700 and 900 series, and S90/V90 | 111 ft. lbs. | 150 Nm |
| 850/C70/S70/V70 | 52 ft. lbs. | 70 Nm |
| **Strut-to-knuckle** | | |
| Coupe, 240, 700 and 900 series, and S90/V90 | 63 ft. lbs. | 85 Nm |
| 850/C70/S70/V70 | 48 ft. lbs.* | 65 Nm* |
| **Upper strut mount** | | |
| Coupe, 240, 700 and 900 series, and S90/V90 | 30 ft. lbs. | 40 Nm |
| 850/C70/S70/V70 | 18 ft. lbs. | 25 Nm |
| **Wheels** | | |
| 240 Series | 85 ft. lbs. | 115 Nm |
| Coupe, 700 and 900 series, and S90/V90 | 63 ft. lbs. | 85 Nm |
| 850/C70/S70/V70 | 81 ft. lbs. | 110 Nm |

* Plus an additional 60 degrees

90958C01

## REAR SUSPENSION TORQUE SPECIFICATIONS

| Components | English | Metric |
|---|---|---|
| **Axle nut** | | |
| 1991-94 900 series | 103 ft. lbs.** | 140 Nm** |
| 1995-98 960/S90/V90 and V70 AWD | 103 ft. lbs.** | 140 Nm** |
| 850/C70/S70/V70 | 89 ft. lbs.* | 120 Nm* |
| **Coil spring retaining nut** | | |
| Coupe, 240 and 700 series,and 940 | | |
| Upper nut | 35 ft. lbs. | 48 Nm |
| Lower nut | 63 ft. lbs. | 85 Nm |
| 850/C70/S70/V70 except AWD | 30 ft. lbs. | 40 Nm |
| 1992-94 960 | | |
| Upper mount | 62 ft. lbs. | 85 Nm |
| Lower mount | 44 ft. lbs.*** | 60 Nm*** |
| **Leaf spring** | | |
| Mounting plate bolts | 37 ft. lbs. | 50 Nm |
| **Lower control arm** | | |
| Coupe, 240, 700series, and 940 | 85 ft. lbs. | 115 Nm |
| 1992-94 960 | 91 ft. lbs.*** | 125 Nm*** |
| 1995-98 960/S90/V90 | 59 ft. lbs. | 80 Nm |
| V70 AWD | 59 ft. lbs. | 80 Nm |
| **Shock mounts** | | |
| Coupe, A48240, 700series, and 940 | 63 ft. lbs. | 85 Nm |
| 1992-94 960 | | |
| Upper mount | 62 ft. lbs.C50 | 85 Nm |
| Lower mount | 41 ft. lbs. | 56 Nm |
| 1995-98 960/S90/V90 and V70 AWD | 59 ft. lbs. | 80 Nm |
| 850/C70/S70/V70 except AWD | | |
| Upper mount | 18 ft. lbs. | 25 Nm |
| Lower mount | 59 ft. lbs. | 80 Nm |
| **Sway bar mounts** | | |
| Coupe, 240, 700series, and 1991-94 900 series | 35 ft. lbs. | 48 Nm |
| 1995-98 960/S90/V90 and V70 AWD | 15 ft. lbs. | 20 Nm |
| 850/C70/S70/V70 except AWD | | |
| Passenger side | 37 ft. lbs. | 50 Nm |
| Driver's side forward bolt | 35 ft. lbs.*** | 48 Nm*** |
| Driver's side rear bolt | 48 ft. lbs. | 68 Nm |
| **Trailing arm** | | |
| Mounting bolt | 59 ft. lbs. | 80 Nm |
| Bracket bolt | 48 ft. lbs. | 65 Nm |
| **Upper control arm** | | |
| 1992-94 960 | | |
| Rear nut | 62 ft. lbs. | 85 Nm |
| Front nut | 51 ft. lbs.** | 70 Nm** |
| 1995-98 960/S90/V90 and V70 AWD | | |
| Arm-to-axle | 18 ft. lbs. | 25 Nm |
| Mounting bolt | 92 ft. lbs. | 120 Nm |

\* Plus an additional 30 degrees

\** Plus an additional 60 degrees

\*** Plus an additional 90 degrees

90958C02

## STEERING SYSTEM TORQUE SPECIFICATIONS

| Components | English | Metric |
|---|---|---|
| **Manual rack and pinion** | | |
| Mounting nuts | 10 -18 ft. lbs. | 14-25 Nm |
| Steering rods | 44 ft. lbs. | 60 Nm |
| Steering shaft flange | 18 ft. lbs. | 25 Nm |
| **Power rack and pinion** | | |
| Coupe and 240 | | |
| Mounting nuts | 32 ft. lbs. | 44 Nm |
| Steering shaft flange | 15 ft. lbs. | 20 Nm |
| 700 series, 900 series, and S90/V90 | | |
| Mounting nuts | 32 ft. lbs. | 44 Nm |
| Steering shaft flange | 15 ft. lbs. | 20 Nm |
| 850/C70/S70/V70 | | |
| Mounting nuts | 37 ft. lbs. | 50 Nm |
| Steering shaft flange | 15 ft. lbs. | 20 Nm |
| **Power steering pump** | | |
| Mounting bolts | 18 ft. lbs. | 25 Nm |
| Line banjo fittings | 31 ft. lbs. | 42 Nm |
| **Steering wheel** | | |
| Retaining nut | 42 ft. lbs. | 60 Nm |
| **Tie rod end** | | |
| 850/C70/S70/V70 | 52 ft. lbs. | 70 Nm |
| All others | 44 ft. lbs. | 60 Nm |

90958C03

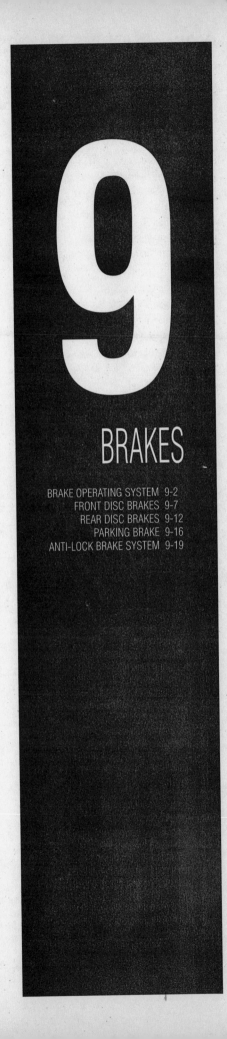

# 9

## BRAKES

## BRAKE OPERATING SYSTEM

### Basic Operating Principles

Hydraulic systems are used to actuate the brakes of all modern automobiles. The system transports the power required to force the frictional surfaces of the braking system together from the pedal to the individual brake units at each wheel. A hydraulic system is used for two reasons.

First, fluid under pressure can be carried to all parts of an automobile by small pipes and flexible hoses without taking up a significant amount of room or posing routing problems.

Second, a great mechanical advantage can be given to the brake pedal end of the system, and the foot pressure required to actuate the brakes can be reduced by making the surface area of the master cylinder pistons smaller than that of any of the pistons in the wheel cylinders or calipers.

The master cylinder consists of a fluid reservoir along with a double cylinder and piston assembly. Double type master cylinders are designed to separate the front and rear braking systems hydraulically in case of a leak. The master cylinder coverts mechanical motion from the pedal into hydraulic pressure within the lines. This pressure is translated back into mechanical motion at the wheels by either the wheel cylinder (drum brakes) or the caliper (disc brakes).

Steel lines carry the brake fluid to a point on the vehicle's frame near each of the vehicle's wheels. The fluid is then carried to the calipers and wheel cylinders by flexible tubes in order to allow for suspension and steering movements.

All Volvos are equipped with a four wheel power-assisted disc brake system. Disc brakes offer better stopping, ease of repair and simplified construction.

In disc brake systems, the cylinders are part of the calipers. At least one cylinder in each caliper is used to force the brake pads against the disc.

All pistons employ some type of seal, usually made of rubber, to minimize fluid leakage. A rubber dust boot seals the outer end of the cylinder against dust and dirt. The boot fits around the outer end of the piston on disc brake calipers, and around the brake actuating rod on wheel cylinders.

The hydraulic system operates as follows: When at rest, the entire system, from the piston(s) in the master cylinder to those in the wheel cylinders or calipers, is full of brake fluid. Upon application of the brake pedal, fluid trapped in front of the master cylinder piston(s) is forced through the lines to the wheel cylinders. Here, it forces the pistons outward, in the case of drum brakes, and inward toward the disc, in the case of disc brakes. The motion of the pistons is opposed by return springs mounted outside the cylinders in drum brakes, and by spring seals, in disc brakes.

Upon release of the brake pedal, a spring located inside the master cylinder immediately returns the master cylinder pistons to the normal position. The pistons contain check valves and the master cylinder has compensating ports drilled in it. These are uncovered as the pistons reach their normal position. The piston check valves allow fluid to flow toward the wheel cylinders or calipers as the pistons withdraw. Then, as the return springs force the brake pads or shoes into the released position, the excess fluid reservoir through the compensating ports. It is during the time the pedal is in the released position that any fluid that has leaked out of the system will be replaced through the compensating ports.

Dual circuit master cylinders employ two pistons, located one behind the other, in the same cylinder. The primary piston is actuated directly by mechanical linkage from the brake pedal through the power booster. The secondary piston is actuated by fluid trapped between the two pistons. If a leak develops in front of the secondary piston, it moves forward until it bottoms against the front of the master cylinder, and the fluid trapped between the pistons will operate the rear brakes. If the rear brakes develop a leak, the primary piston will move forward until direct contact with the secondary piston takes place, and it will force the secondary piston to actuate the front brakes. In either case, the brake pedal moves farther when the brakes are applied, and less braking power is available.

All dual circuit systems use a switch to warn the driver when only half of the brake system is operational. This switch is usually located in a valve body which is mounted on the firewall or the frame below the master cylinder. A hydraulic piston receives pressure from both circuits, each circuit's pressure being applied to one end of the piston. When the pressures are in balance, the piston remains stationary. When one circuit has a leak, however, the greater pressure in that circuit during application of the brakes will push the piston to one side, closing the switch and activating the brake warning light.

In disc brake systems, this valve body also contains a metering valve and, in some cases, a proportioning valve. The metering valve keeps pressure from traveling to the disc brakes on the front wheels until the brake shoes on the rear wheels have contacted the drums, ensuring that the front brakes will never be used alone. The proportioning valve controls the pressure to the rear brakes to lessen the chance of rear wheel lock-up during very hard braking.

Warning lights may be tested by depressing the brake pedal and holding it while opening one of the wheel cylinder bleeder screws. If this does not cause the light to go on, substitute a new lamp, make continuity checks, and, finally, replace the switch as necessary.

The hydraulic system may be checked for leaks by applying pressure to the pedal gradually and steadily. If the pedal sinks very slowly to the floor, the system has a leak. This is not to be confused with a springy or spongy feel due to the compression of air within the lines. If the system leaks, there will be a gradual change in the position of the pedal with a constant pressure.

Check for leaks along all lines and at wheel cylinders. If no external leaks are apparent, the problem is inside the master cylinder.

### DISC BRAKES

Instead of the traditional expanding brakes that press outward against a circular drum, disc brake systems utilize a disc (rotor) with brake pads positioned on either side of it. An easily-seen analogy is the hand brake arrangement on a bicycle. The pads squeeze onto the rim of the bike wheel, slowing its motion. Automobile disc brakes use the identical principle but apply the braking effort to a separate disc instead of the wheel.

The disc (rotor) is a casting, usually equipped with cooling fins between the two braking surfaces. This enables air to circulate between the braking surfaces making them less sensitive to heat build-up and more resistant to fade. Dirt and water do not drastically affect braking action since contaminants are thrown off by the centrifugal action of the rotor or scraped off the by the pads. Also, the equal clamping action of the two brake pads tends to ensure uniform, straight line stops. Disc brakes are inherently self-adjusting. There are three general types of disc brake:

- Fixed caliper
- Floating caliper
- Sliding caliper

The fixed caliper design uses two pistons mounted on either side of the rotor (in each side of the caliper). The caliper is mounted rigidly and does not move.

The sliding and floating designs are quite similar. In fact, these two types are often lumped together. In both designs, the pad on the inside of the rotor is moved into contact with the rotor by hydraulic force. The caliper, which is not held in a fixed position, moves slightly, bringing the outside pad into contact with the rotor. There are various methods of attaching floating calipers. Some pivot at the bottom or top, and some slide on mounting bolts. In any event, the end result is the same.

### POWER BOOSTERS

Virtually all modern vehicles use a vacuum assisted power brake system to multiply the braking force and reduce pedal effort. Since vacuum is always available when the engine is operating, the system is simple and efficient. A vacuum diaphragm is located on the front of the master cylinder and assists the driver in applying the brakes, reducing both the effort and travel he must put into moving the brake pedal.

The vacuum diaphragm housing is normally connected to the intake manifold by a vacuum hose. A check valve is placed at the point where the hose enters the diaphragm housing, so that during periods of low manifold vacuum brakes assist will not be lost.

Depressing the brake pedal closes off the vacuum source and allows atmospheric pressure to enter on one side of the diaphragm. This causes the master cylinder pistons to move and apply the brakes. When the brake pedal is released, vacuum is applied to both sides of the diaphragm and springs return the diaphragm and master cylinder pistons to the released position.

If the vacuum supply fails, the brake pedal rod will contact the end of the master cylinder actuator rod and the system will apply the brakes without any power assistance. The driver will notice that much higher pedal effort is needed to stop the car and that the pedal feels harder than usual.

## Vacuum Leak Test

1.  Operate the engine at idle without touching the brake pedal for at least one minute.
2.  Turn off the engine and wait one minute.
3.  Test for the presence of assist vacuum by depressing the brake pedal and releasing it several times. If vacuum is present in the system, light application will produce less and less pedal travel. If there is no vacuum, air is leaking into the system.

## System Operation Test

1.  With the engine **OFF**, pump the brake pedal until the supply vacuum is entirely gone.
2.  Put light, steady pressure on the brake pedal.
3.  Start the engine and let it idle. If the system is operating correctly, the brake pedal should fall toward the floor if the constant pressure is maintained.
    Power brake systems may be tested for hydraulic leaks just as ordinary systems are tested.

### ✳✳ WARNING

**Clean, high quality brake fluid is essential to the safe and proper operation of the brake system. You should always buy the highest quality brake fluid that is available. If the brake fluid becomes contaminated, drain and flush the system, then refill the master cylinder with new fluid. Never reuse any brake fluid. Any brake fluid that is removed from the system should be discarded.**

## Brake Light Switch

The switch controlling the brake lights is located at the brake pedal. As the pedal moves from its rest position, the switch engages and turns on the brake lights.

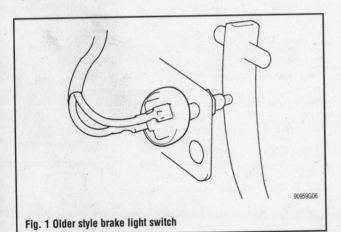

Fig. 1 Older style brake light switch

## REMOVAL & INSTALLATION

▶ **See Figures 1 and 2**

1.  Remove the soundproofing.
2.  Detach the electrical connectors at the switch
3.  Unscrew the locknut and remove the switch.

**To install:**

4.  Place the new switch into position.
5.  Install the locknut and electrical connectors.
6.  After installing the new switch, it must be adjusted so that the brake lights comes ON when the brake pedal is depressed approximately ⅜–½ inches (8–14mm).

## Master Cylinder

### REMOVAL & INSTALLATION

▶ **See Figures 3 thru 10**

1.  Disconnect the negative battery cable.
2.  To prevent brake fluid from spilling onto and damaging the paint, place a protective cover over the fender apron, and rags beneath the master cylinder.
3.  Unplug the electrical connector for the brake fluid level sensor.
4.  Empty out and discard the brake fluid.
5.  Label and disconnect the brake lines from the master cylinder and plug them immediately.
6.  Label and remove any hoses from the master cylinder.

➡ **It may be easier to remove the hoses when the master cylinder is loosened and partially removed.**

7.  If the vehicle has a hydraulic clutch, disconnect its line from the fluid reservoir. Plug it and secure the line out of the way.
8.  Remove the two nuts which retain the master cylinder and reservoir assembly to the vacuum booster, and lift the assembly forward, being careful not to spill any fluid on the fender.

### ✳✳ WARNING

**Do not depress the brake pedal while the master cylinder is removed!**

**To install:**

9.  Place a new sealing rim (if equipped) onto the sealing flange of the master cylinder.
10. Position the master cylinder and reservoir assembly onto the booster studs, and install the washer and nuts.
11. Tighten the nuts to 103–130 inch lbs. (12–15 Nm).
12. Remove the plugs and loosely connect the brake lines. Have a helper depress the brake pedal to remove air from the cylinder. Tighten the nuts for the lines when the brake fluid (free of air bubbles) is forced out.
13. Reconnect the lines for the hydraulic clutch (if so equipped) and any hoses which were removed.

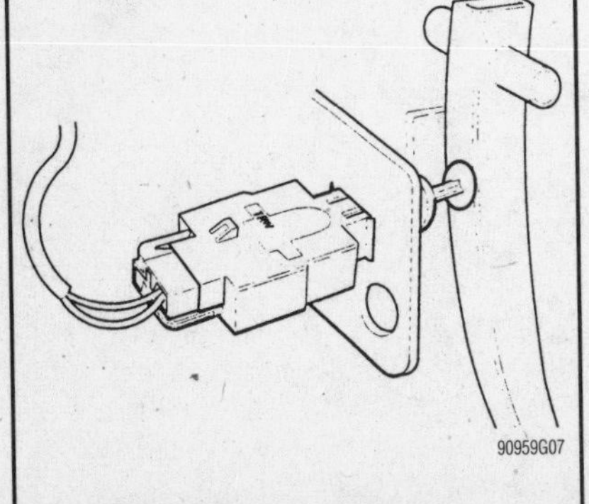

Fig. 3 The brake fluid level sensor is located on the reservoir cap

Fig. 4 A vacuum pump is useful to draw brake fluid out of the master cylinder reservoir

Fig. 2 Newer style brake light switch

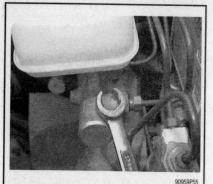

Fig. 5 A flare nut or "line" wrench should be used to detach the brake lines

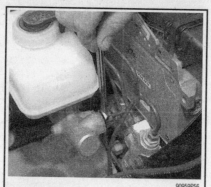

Fig. 6 Label and disconnect the brake lines

Fig. 7 Remove the two master cylinder retaining nuts

Fig. 8 Slowly rotate and remove the master cylinder from the booster assembly

Fig. 9 The hoses are usually more accessible after the master cylinder is moved

Fig. 10 The pushrod end should be inspected after the master cylinder is removed

14. Fasten the electrical connector for the brake fluid level sensor.

15. Bleed the entire brake system and, where applicable, the clutch system. Refer to the bleeding procedure later in this section.

16. Connect the negative battery cable.

## Power Brake Booster

### CHECKING POWER BRAKE FUNCTION

Remove the vacuum by depressing the brake pedal approximately 5 times. Depress the brake pedal and start the engine. The pedal position should drop slightly if the power brake is functioning properly.

### PRESSURE TESTING THE SYSTEM

Apply moderate pressure on the brake pedal for approximately 20 seconds. Then, repeat with high pedal pressure for 5 seconds. The pedal position must not drop. A drop indicates brake fluid leakage or booster vacuum leak.

### REMOVAL & INSTALLATION

▶ See Figures 11 and 12

1. Disconnect the negative battery cable.
2. Remove the master cylinder.
3. Disconnect the vacuum hose and check valve from the booster.
4. If required, disconnect the fuel filter and vacuum pump. Position them aside.

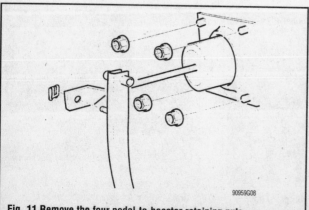

Fig. 11 Remove the four pedal-to-booster retaining nuts

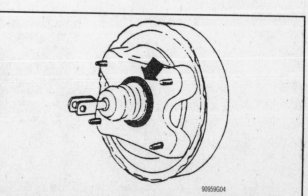

Fig. 12 Remember to install the check valve seal when replacing the booster

5. From inside the vehicle, remove the soundproofing and disconnect the brake pedal rod.

6. Remove the power booster retaining nuts.

7. Remove the power booster from the vehicle.

**To install:**

8. Before installing the booster, check the valve seal. Replace it if necessary. When installing the new check valve seal, ensure that the flange of the seal is in the correct position.

9. On the 2 x 8 inch booster, install the sealing washer and seal onto the booster.

10. Install the booster to the vehicle.

11. Reconnect the brake pedal to the booster rod.

12. Refit the soundproofing.

13. Install the master cylinder, check valve and vacuum hose.

14. Bleed the brakes and clutch, if so equipped.

15. Connect the negative battery cable.

## Proportioning Valve

➡The proportioning valve is also known as a pressure differential warning valve.

Each of the brake circuits has a proportioning (relief) valve located inline between the rear wheels. The purpose of this valve is to ensure that brake pressure on all four wheels compensates for the change in weight distribution under varied braking conditions.

The harder the brakes are applied, the more weight there is on the front wheels. The valve regulates hydraulic pressure to the rear wheels, so that under hard braking conditions they receive a smaller percentage of the total braking effort. This prevents premature rear wheel lockup and possible skidding or loss of control.

### VALVE RESETTING

1. Disconnect the plug contact and screw out the warning switch so the pistons inside the valve may return to their normal position.

2. Repair and bleed the faulty hydraulic circuit.

3. Screw in the warning switch and tighten it to 10–14 ft. lbs. (14–19 Nm).

4. Connect the plug contact.

### REMOVAL & INSTALLATION

1. Place a rag under the valve to catch the brake fluid.

2. Detach the electrical connector from the switch and slacken the brake pipe connections.

3. Unfasten the bolt(s) which retain the valve to the underbody and unscrew the brake pipe connections.

4. Remove the differential warning valve.

**To install:**

5. Place a new seal on it, then screw the valve onto the rear brake hose and hand-tighten.

6. Secure the valve to the underbody with the retaining bolt(s).

7. Connect the brake pipe and tighten both connections, making sure there is no tension on the flexible rear hose.

8. Bleed the brake system.

## Brake Hoses and Pipes

Metal lines and rubber brake hoses should be checked frequently for leaks and external damage. Metal lines are particularly prone to crushing and kinking under the vehicle. Any such deformation can restrict the proper flow of fluid and therefore impair braking at the wheels. Rubber hoses should be checked for cracking or scraping; such damage can create a weak spot in the hose and it could fail under pressure.

Any time the lines are removed or disconnected, extreme cleanliness must be observed. Clean all joints and connections before disassembly (use a stiff bristle brush and clean brake fluid); be sure to plug the lines and ports as soon as they are opened. New lines and hoses should be flushed clean with brake fluid before installation to remove any contamination.

### REMOVAL & INSTALLATION

♦ **See Figures 13, 14, 15 and 16**

1. Disconnect the negative battery cable.

2. Raise and safely support the vehicle on jackstands.

3. Remove any wheel and tire assemblies necessary for access to the particular line you are removing.

4. Thoroughly clean the surrounding area at the joints to be disconnected.

5. Place a suitable catch pan under the joint to be disconnected.

6. Using two wrenches (one to hold the joint and one to turn the fitting), disconnect the hose or line to be replaced.

7. Disconnect the other end of the line or hose, moving the drain pan if necessary. Always use a back-up wrench to avoid damaging the fitting.

8. Disconnect any retaining clips or brackets holding the line and remove the line from the vehicle.

➡**If the brake system is to remain open for more time than it takes to swap lines, tape or plug each remaining clip and port to keep contaminants out and fluid in.**

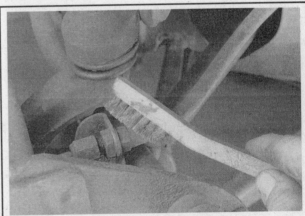

TCCA9P09

**Fig. 13 Use a brush to clean the fittings of any debris**

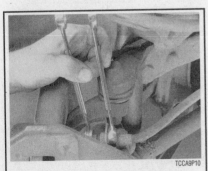

TCCA9P10

**Fig. 14 Use two wrenches to loosen the fitting. If available, use flare nut type wrenches**

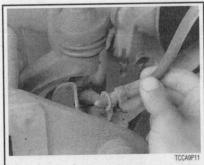

TCCA9P11

**Fig. 15 Any gaskets/crush washers should be replaced with new ones during installation**

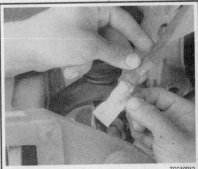

TCCA9P12

**Fig. 16 Tape or plug the line to prevent contamination**

**To install:**

9. Install the new line or hose, starting with the end farthest from the master cylinder. Connect the other end, then confirm that both fittings are correctly threaded and turn smoothly using finger pressure. Make sure the new line will not rub against any other part. Brake lines must be at least ½ in. (13mm) from the steering column and other moving parts. Any protective shielding or insulators must be reinstalled in the original location.

### ✳✳ WARNING

**Make sure the hose is NOT kinked or touching any part of the frame or suspension after installation. These conditions may cause the hose to fail prematurely.**

10. Using two wrenches as before, tighten each fitting.
11. Install any retaining clips or brackets on the lines.
12. If removed, install the wheel and tire assemblies, then carefully lower the vehicle to the ground.
13. Refill the brake master cylinder reservoir with clean, fresh brake fluid, meeting DOT 3 specifications. Properly bleed the brake system.
14. Connect the negative battery cable.

### Bleeding the Brake System

▶ **See Figures 17 and 18**

Whenever a spongy brake pedal indicates that there is air in the system, or when any part of the hydraulic system has been removed for service, the system must be bled. In addition, if the level in the master cylinder reservoir is allowed to drop below the minimum mark for too long a period of time, air may enter the system, necessitating bleeding.

If only one caliper is removed for servicing, it is usually necessary to bleed only that unit. If, however, the master cylinder, warning valve, or any of the main system lines are removed, the entire system must be bled.

Be careful not to spill any brake fluid onto the brake surfaces or the paint. When bleeding the entire system, the rear of the car should be raised higher than the front. Only use brake fluid bearing the designation DOT 3.

The following procedure is acceptable for use on vehicles with and without ABS.

1. Check to make sure that floor mats are not obstructing pedal travel. Full pedal travel should be 6 inches (15cm).
2. Clean the cap and top of the master cylinder reservoir, and make sure that the vent hole in the cap is open. Fill the reservoir to the maximum mark.

➥ **Never allow the level to drop below the minimum mark during bleeding.**

3. If only one brake caliper or line was removed, it will usually suffice to bleed only that wheel. Otherwise, prepare to bleed the entire system beginning at the passenger side rear wheel.
4. Raise the vehicle and support it safely.
5. Remove the protective cap for the bleeder and fit a suitable line wrench on the nipple.

➥ **The calipers, on some models, are equipped with 2 bleeder screws. Attach one hose to each screw and submerge in brake fluid.**

6. Install a tight plastic hose onto the nipple and insert the other end of the hose into a glass bottle containing clean brake fluid. The hose must hang down below the surface of the fluid, or air will be sucked into the system when the brake pedal is released.
7. Open the bleeder nipple and pump the brake pedal 5 times. Keep the brake pedal depressed and close the nipple. Release the brake pedal and check the brake fluid. This should be repeated until the fluid flowing into the bottle is completely free of air bubbles. Continue to bleed the system in the following manner.
   - driver's side rear wheel
   - passenger side front wheel
   - driver's side front wheel

➥ **During this procedure, check the master cylinder reservoir frequently.**

8. When completed, press the pedal to the bottom of its stroke and tighten the bleeder screw.
9. Install the protective cap. If the pedal still feels spongy after bleeding the entire system, repeat the bleeding sequence.
10. Fill the reservoir to the maximum line.
11. Turn the ignition **ON** but do not start the engine. Apply moderate force to the brake pedal. The pedal must travel no more than 2.4 inches (61mm) without ABS; 2.17 inches (55mm) with ABS. The brake warning light (and ABS warning light) must not be on.

➥ **After bleeding the brake system, pressure test the brake system, by depressing the brake pedal with a force corresponding to an abrupt halt, almost sufficient to lock the wheels, for 30 seconds. Then check whether there has been any leakage of brake fluid from the master cylinder.**

12. Lower the vehicle.

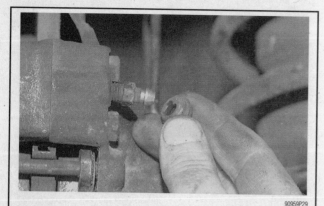

**Fig. 17 Remove the nipple exposing the bleeder valve**

90959P29

**Fig. 18 Install a clear tube on the bleeder valve to visually inspect for air bubbles**

90959P30

## FRONT DISC BRAKES

### Brake Pads

REMOVAL & INSTALLATION

### ❄ CAUTION

**Older brake pads or shoes may contain asbestos, which has been determined to be cancer causing agent. Never clean the brake surfaces with compressed air! Avoid inhaling any dust from any brake surface! When cleaning brake surfaces, use a commercially available brake cleaning fluid.**

#### 240 Series

1. Raise and safely support the vehicle.
2. Remove the front wheels.
3. Remove the spring clips and retaining pins. Remove the retaining springs and brake pads.

➡If the brake pads are difficult to remove, tool 2917 or equivalent can be used to collapse the caliper pistons to ease removal.

4. Clean the caliper where the brake pads sit and inspect the dust caps for damage, and replace if necessary.
5. Check the brake rotor surface for signs of wear, warping or variations in thickness.
6. Compress the caliper pistons using a large pair of pliers or a C-clamp.

➡It may be necessary to remove some brake fluid from the reservoir when depressing the piston.

**To install:**
7. Before replacing the pads:
    a. Check the rubber dust caps for the brake pistons, replace if defective. If dirt has penetrated into the cylinders, due to a defective dust cap, recondition the caliper.
    b. Check the friction surface of the disc, if required, replace or machine the rotor surface.
    c. Check the rubber seals on the guide pins, replace them if they are defective.
8. Install the brake pads, retaining springs, retaining pins, and spring clips.
9. Check the brake fluid level and pump the brake pedal several times. It may be necessary to bleed the brake system.
10. Install the wheels.
11. Check the brake pedal operation before driving the vehicle.

#### 700 Series, 900 Series, S90 and V90 Models

1. Raise and safely support the vehicle.
2. Remove the wheels.
3. Remove the lower caliper guide pin bolt and swing the caliper upwards.
4. Remove the brake pads.

➡Do not depress the brake pedal while pads are removed.

**To install:**
➡The fluid level can rise in the reservoir when the piston is compressed.

5. Remove some brake fluid to prevent spillage. Air may be trapped in the dust seal of the piston. To avoid damage to the boot, it may be necessary to release the trapped air.
6. Press the piston back into the caliper.
7. Inspect the piston dust cap, if it is damaged, the caliper must be overhauled or replaced.
8. Check the disc brake surface for distortion or variation in thickness. Replace if not within specification.
9. Check to see that the metal guide plates are in position and install the pads. Check the guide pin boots for damage and replace them if necessary.

10. Swing the caliper down into position, being careful not to damage the guide pin boots. Tighten the guide pin bolt to 20 ft. lbs. (27 Nm).
11. Check the reservoir fluid level and add as necessary.
12. Operate the brake pedal repeatedly.
13. Install the wheels.

#### 850, S70, C70 and V70 Series

▶ **See Figures 19 thru 29**

1. Raise and safely support the vehicle.
2. Remove the front wheels.
3. Carefully remove retaining spring, without bending.
4. Remove the protective caps from the guide pin bolts.
5. Use an appropriate size Allen wrench (typically 7mm) to remove the guide pins.
6. Remove caliper from the carrier.
7. Remove the brake pads. Hang the caliper from the spring so that the hose is not damaged.

### ❄ WARNING

**Do not depress the brake pedal while the pads are removed.**

8. Clean the caliper carrier where the brake pads sit.
9. Check the piston dust boot for damage or dirt. If the boot is damaged, the caliper should be overhauled or replaced.
10. Check the brake rotor for signs of wear or damage.
11. Check the guide pin bolt rubber sleeves for damage and replace if necessary.
**To install:**
12. Press the piston back into the caliper cylinder using a suitable tool.
13. Lubricate the caliper guide pins with silicone grease.
14. Insert the brake pads and slide the caliper on over them.

Fig. 19 Remove the retaining spring

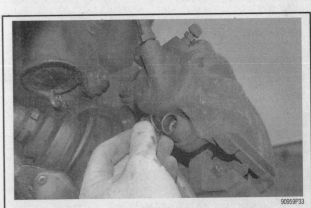

Fig. 20 Remove the protective caps over the caliper guide pins . . .

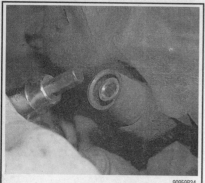

Fig. 21 . . . and use an appropriate size Allen wrench (typically 7mm) . . .

Fig. 22 . . . to loosen and remove the caliper guide pins

Fig. 23 A large C-clamp is a useful tool to compress the piston

Fig. 24 Pull the caliper off and remove the brake pads

Fig. 25 The inboard pad is held into the caliper by metal tabs

Fig. 26 Thoroughly brush and clean the caliper carrier before replacing the pads

Fig. 27 Volvo recommends that a high temperature grease be applied to the pad contact points on the caliper carrier . . .

Fig. 28 . . . and caliper pins prior to pad installation

Fig. 29 Inspect the rubber sleeves for damage and cracking

15. Tighten the guide pins to 22 ft. lbs. (30 Nm) and replace the dust caps.
16. Install the retaining spring.
17. Install the wheels.
18. Lower the vehicle.
19. Depress the brake pedal several times and check the brake fluid reservoir level.
20. Check brake pedal function before driving vehicle.

## INSPECTION

▶ See Figure 30

### ❊❊ CAUTION

Older brake pads or shoes may contain asbestos, which has been determined to be cancer causing agent. Never clean the brake surfaces with compressed air! Avoid inhaling any dust from any brake

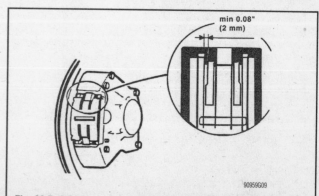

Fig. 30 Pad thickness is measured from the disc to the edge of the pad

surface! When cleaning brake surfaces, use a commercially available brake cleaning fluid.

Check the width of the brake pads using a thickness gauge, available at most auto parts stores. Minimum brake pad thickness is 0.08 inch (2mm).

## Brake Caliper

### REMOVAL & INSTALLATION

#### 240 Series

1. Raise and safely support the vehicle.
2. Remove the front wheel(s).
3. Disconnect any ABS wires, if equipped.
4. Clean the caliper to ensure that no dirt gets into the brake line.
5. Disconnect the brake lines, and remove the two caliper mounting bolts.

➡ If the brake line is seized to the caliper, it should be replaced.

**To install:**

6. Install the caliper using new mounting bolts.
7. Check the location of the caliper in relation to the disc.
   a. Use feeler gauges to check the distance between the disc and the caliper support stubs on both sides.
   b. The difference between the two measurements must not exceed 0.001 in. (0.25mm).
   c. Repeat the measurements using the upper and lower support stubs to check if the caliper is mounted parallel to the disc.
   d. If the caliper is not correctly aligned, shims can be used to adjust its position.
8. Install the brake pads and make sure that the disc can rotate freely between the pads.
9. Connect any ABS wires unfasten during removal.
10. Bleed the brake system.
11. Install the wheels.
12. Lower the vehicle.
13. Check the brake pedal function before driving vehicle.

#### 700 Series, 900 Series, S90 and V90 Models

1. Raise and safely support the vehicle.
2. Remove the wheels.
3. Disconnect the ABS lead and brake hose from their clips.
4. Clean the brake hose and line connection.
5. Disconnect the hose from the line.
6. Disconnect the hose from the caliper.
7. Remove the lower caliper guide pin bolt, swing the caliper up and remove the brake pads.
8. Remove the caliper mounting bolts and lift the caliper off.
9. Remove the upper caliper guide pin bolt to separate the caliper from the mounting bracket.
10. Clean the guide pins and inspect for wear or damage. Replace as necessary.

**To install:**

11. Lubricate the guide pins with silicone grease.
12. Reassemble the caliper and mounting bracket using one guide pin bolt, but do not tighten.
13. Install the bleed nipple and brake hose.
14. Mount the caliper with new bolts and tighten to 74 ft. lbs. (100 Nm).
15. Install the brake pads and guide pin bolt.
16. Tighten the guide pin bolts to 20 ft. lbs. (27 Nm).
17. Reconnect brake hose to line and ABS lead to the hose.

➡ Make sure that the brake hoses are not twisted.

18. Bleed the brake system.
19. Install the wheels.
20. Lower the vehicle.
21. Check brake pedal function before driving vehicle.

#### 850, S70, C70 and V70 Series

▶ See Figures 31 and 32

1. Turn the ignition switch **OFF** and, if equipped with ABS, remove the key to prevent accidental pump activation.
2. Raise and safely support the vehicle.
3. Remove the wheel(s).
4. Disconnect any ABS wires, if equipped.
5. Loosen the brake hose a half turn.
6. Remove the caliper bolts, lift the caliper off and unscrew the caliper from the hose.
7. Drain the remaining brake fluid from the caliper.
8. Remove the brake pads.

**To install:**

9. Grease the caliper bolts with lithium grease and insert them into the sleeves.
10. Screw the caliper onto the brake hose.
11. Install the brake pads and mount the caliper.
12. Tighten the caliper bolts to 22 ft. lbs. (30 Nm) and install the dust caps.
13. Install the retaining clip.
14. Tighten the brake hose to 13 ft. lbs. (18 Nm).

➡ Make sure that the brakes hose is not twisted.

15. Fill the master cylinder and bleed the brake system. Check the system for leaks and proper function.
16. Connect any ABS wires which were previously removed.
17. Install the wheels.
18. Lower the vehicle.
19. Check the brake function before driving the car.

90959P43

**Fig. 31 Loosen and remove the caliper carrier retaining bolts, usually using a 17mm socket or wrench . . .**

90959P44

**Fig. 32 . . . and remove the caliper carrier**

### OVERHAUL

▶ **See Figures 33 thru 40**

➡ Some vehicles may be equipped dual piston calipers. The procedure to overhaul the caliper is essentially the same with the exception of multiple pistons, O-rings and dust boots.

1. Remove the caliper from the vehicle and place on a clean workbench.

### ✳✳ CAUTION

**NEVER place your fingers in front of the pistons in an attempt to catch or protect the pistons when applying compressed air. This could result in personal injury!**

➡ Depending upon the vehicle, there are two different ways to remove the piston from the caliper. Refer to the brake pad replacement procedure to make sure you have the correct procedure for your vehicle.

2. The first method is as follows:
   a. Stuff a shop towel or a block of wood into the caliper to catch the piston.
   b. Remove the caliper piston using compressed air applied into the caliper inlet hole. Inspect the piston for scoring, nicks, corrosion and/or worn or damaged chrome plating. The piston must be replaced if any of these conditions are found.
3. For the second method, you must rotate the piston to retract it from the caliper.
4. If equipped, remove the anti-rattle clip.
5. Use a prytool to remove the caliper boot, being careful not to scratch the housing bore.
6. Remove the piston seals from the groove in the caliper bore.
7. Carefully loosen the brake bleeder valve cap and valve from the caliper housing.

8. Inspect the caliper bores, pistons and mounting threads for scoring or excessive wear.
9. Use crocus cloth to polish out light corrosion from the piston and bore.
10. Clean all parts with denatured alcohol and dry with compressed air.

**To assemble:**

11. Lubricate and install the bleeder valve and cap.
12. Install the new seals into the caliper bore grooves, making sure they are not twisted.
13. Lubricate the piston bore.
14. Install the pistons and boots into the bores of the calipers and push to the bottom of the bores.
15. Use a suitable driving tool to seat the boots in the housing.
16. Install the caliper in the vehicle.
17. Install the wheel and tire assembly, then carefully lower the vehicle.
18. Properly bleed the brake system.

### Brake Disc (Rotor)

### REMOVAL & INSTALLATION

#### 240 Series

1. Raise and safely support vehicle.
2. remove the front wheel(s).
3. Remove the brake caliper and hang it from the spring with a piece of wire.
4. Remove the two screws securing the disc.
5. Lift the disc off, it may be necessary to tap on the disc with a soft headed hammer.

**To install:**

6. Install the new disc, make sure the mating surfaces of the disc and hub are clean and dry.
7. Install the caliper using new mounting bolts.

Fig. 33 For some types of calipers, use compressed air to drive the piston out of the caliper, but be sure to keep your fingers clear

TCCA9P01

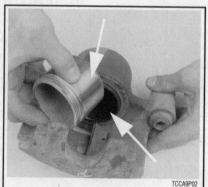

Fig. 34 Withdraw the piston from the caliper bore

TCCA9P02

Fig. 35 On some vehicles, you must remove the anti-rattle clip

TCCA9P03

Fig. 36 Use a prytool to carefully pry around the edge of the boot . . .

TCCSA9P04

Fig. 37 . . . then remove the boot from the caliper housing, taking care not to score or damage the bore

TCCA9P05

Fig. 38 Use extreme caution when removing the piston seal; DO NOT scratch the caliper bore

TCCA9P06

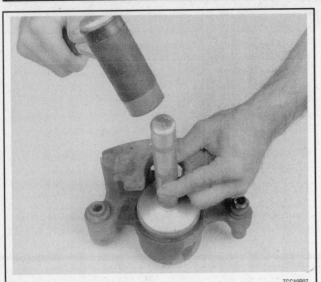

Fig. 39 Use the proper size driving tool and a mallet to properly seal the boots in the caliper housing

8. Check the location of the caliper in relation to the disc. Use feeler gauges to check the distance between the disc and the caliper support stubs on both sides. The difference between the two measurements must not exceed 0.001 in. (0.0013mm). Repeat the measurements using the upper and lower support stubs to check if the caliper is mounted parallel to the disc. If the caliper is not correctly aligned, shims can be used to adjust the caliper's position.

9. Install the brake pads and make sure that the disc can rotate freely between the pads.

10. Install the disc securing screws.

11. Install the wheels.

12. Check brake pedal function before driving vehicle.

### 700 Series, 900 Series, S90 and V90 Models

1. Raise and safely support the vehicle.

2. Remove the wheels.

3. Remove the caliper and brake pads.

4. Hang the caliper from the spring, to avoid damaging the brake hose.

5. Remove the wheel pin guide and brake disc.

6. Clean the hub flange, remove the corrosion with a scraper and or wire brush.

7. Clean the ABS pick-up and toothed wheel using a soft brush.

**To install:**

8. Ensure that the mating surfaces on the hub and disc are clean.

9. Insert guide pin and tighten to 6 ft. lbs. (8 Nm). Reinstall the ring gauge and cross tighten the lug nuts to 63 ft. lbs. (85 Nm).

10. Measure disc run-out. Measure on the disc surface 0.60 in. (15mm) in from the edge. Maximum run-out is 0.0023 in. (0.060mm). Remove the measuring equipment.

11. Install the caliper carrier using new mounting bolts, then install the caliper and brake pads.

12. Operate the brake pedal several times and check the fluid level.

13. Install the wheels.

14. Check brake function before driving vehicle. Limit hard braking whenever possible during the 500 miles (800 km) after pad replacement.

### 850, S70, C70 and V70 Series

♦ **See Figures 41 and 42**

1. Raise and safely support the vehicle.

2. Remove the wheels.

3. Remove the brake caliper and brake pads.

4. Remove the carrier.

5. Remove the guide pin bolt.

6. Remove the rotor and clean the hug flange of all corrosion and dirt.

7. Check the hub run-out by mounting gauge ring (Volvo tool 5419 from tool kit 5418) or equivalent.

8. Install the dial indicator on the spindle (using the caliper bracket bolt holes). Place the probe end to the gauge ring.

9. Turn hub slowly and identify the highest point. If the run-out exceeds 0.0007 in. (0.020mm), the hub must be replaced.

10. Remove the measuring equipment.

**To install:**

11. Install the brake rotor.

12. Tighten the guide pin bolt to 72 inch lbs. (8 Nm).

13. Install the caliper carrier using new bolts.

14. Install the brake caliper and brake pads.

15. Depress the brake pedal several times and check the brake fluid reservoir.

16. Install the wheels.

17. Check the brake function before driving vehicle.

## INSPECTION

Inspect the brake rotor for scoring and wear; minor scoring or disc pad lining build-up does not require rotor machining or replacement. If heavy scoring, cracks or other damage is evident, replace or have the rotor machined, as necessary.

Glaze on the rotor can be removed by hand-sanding it with medium grit garnet paper or aluminum oxide sandpaper.

The minimum thickness of each brake rotor is indicated on the rotor itself. Do not utilize a rotor which is worn below the minimum allowable thickness. If rotor damage cannot be corrected by grinding to these minimums, the rotor must be replaced.

Rotor lateral run-out must not be more than 0.001 in. (0.035mm).

Fig. 40 There are tools, such as this Mighty-Vac, available to assist in proper brake system bleeding

Fig. 41 Remove the wheel guide pin bolt . . .

Fig. 42 . . . and remove the brake disc from the hub

## REAR DISC BRAKES

### Brake Pads

REMOVAL & INSTALLATION

#### 240 Series

##### *WITH ATE CALIPER*

1. Raise and safely support vehicle.
2. Remove the wheel(s).
3. Drive the retaining pins out using a 3mm punch.
4. Remove the retaining spring and brake pads.

➡**If the brake pads are difficult to remove, tool 2917 or equivalent can be used to compress the caliper pistons to ease removal.**

5. Clean the brake caliper and inspect the dust caps for damage, replace if necessary.
6. Check the rotor for signs of wear, warping or variations in thickness.
7. Compress the piston into the caliper using a large pair of pliers, or tool 2809 or equivalent.

➡**It may be necessary to remove some fluid from the master cylinder, to prevent spilling when compressing the piston.**

**To install:**

8. Caliper piston position must be checked before installation:
   a. To check the position of the piston and prevent brake squeal, rotate the piston 20° in relation to the lower surface of the brake caliper.
   b. Use tool 2919 or equivalent to position the piston. The allowable tolerance is 18–22° when the template is pressed against one of the shoulders, the distance to the other (A) should be a maximum of 0.04 in. (1mm).
   c. If necessary, use tool 2918 or equivalent to rotate the piston. The tool should be placed against the piston, and tightened by turning the handle. The correct clearance is obtained by moving the handle up or down.
9. Install the brake pads and one retaining pin.
10. Install a new retaining spring and the other retaining pin.
11. Tap the retaining pins into place.
12. Check the brake fluid level and pump brake pedal repeatedly. It may be necessary to bleed the brake system.
13. Install the rear wheels.
14. Lower the vehicle.
15. Check the brake pedal operation before driving the vehicle.

##### *WITH GIRLING CALIPER*

1. Raise and safely support vehicle.
2. Remove the rear wheels.
3. Remove the spring clips and retaining pins.
4. Remove the retaining springs and brake pads.

➡**If the brake pads are difficult to remove tool 2917 or equivalent can be used to collapse the caliper pistons to ease removal.**

5. Clean the brake caliper and inspect the dust caps for damage, replace if necessary.
6. Check the rotor for signs of wear, warping or variations in thickness.
7. Compress the piston into the caliper using a large pair of pliers or tool 2809 or equivalent.

➡**It may be necessary to remove some fluid from the master cylinder, to prevent spilling when compressing the piston.**

**To install:**

8. Install the brake pads, retaining springs, retaining pins, and spring clips.
9. Check the brake fluid level and pump brake pedal repeatedly. It may be necessary to bleed the brake system.
10. Install the rear wheels.
11. Lower the vehicle.
12. Check the brake pedal operation before driving the vehicle.

#### 700 Series, 900 Series, S90 and V90 Models

1. Raise and safely support the vehicle.
2. Remove the wheels.

3. On models with an independent rear axle, do the following;
   a. Remove the lower caliper guide bolt.
   b. Swing the caliper up and tie it back with a piece of wire. Remove the brake pads.
4. On models with solid rear axles, remove the brake pads in this sequence:
   a. Using a 3mm punch, drive out the guide pins.
   b. Remove spring plate.
   c. Remove the brake pads and shims.

➡**If the brake pads are difficult to remove, extractor 2917 or equivalent can be used to remove them.**

➡**Do not operate the brake pedal while the pads are removed.**

5. Clean the caliper where the pads rest.
6. Inspect the piston dust boot for damage of dirt. If dirt has entered the caliper, it must be reconditioned or replaced.
7. Press the piston back into the caliper using large adjustable pliers, taking care not to damage the dust boot. If the piston is difficult to compress, this could indicate that oxidation has occurred. The caliper must be reconditioned or replaced in this case.
8. Inspect the rubber guide pin boots and replace if necessary.
9. Check the disc brake surface for distortion or variation in thickness. Replace if needed.

**To install:**

10. On models with an independent rear axle, install the new pads and lower the piston housing and tighten the lower guide pin bolt to 25 ft. lbs. (34 Nm).
11. On models with a solid rear axle;
    a. Check the piston position with tool 2918 or equivalent to minimize brake noise.
    b. To check the position of the piston and prevent brake squeal, rotate the piston 20° in relation to the lower surface of the brake caliper.
    c. Use tool 2919 or equivalent to position the piston. The allowable tolerance is 18–22° when the template is pressed against one of the shoulders, the distance to the other (A) should be a maximum of 0.04 in. (1mm).
    d. If necessary, use tool 2918 or equivalent to rotate the piston. The tool should be placed against the piston and tightened by turning the handle. The correct clearance is obtained by moving the handle up or down.
    e. Coat the anti-squeal shim with a thin coating of silicone grease on both sides. Then install the shims and brake pads in the order they where removed.
    f. Install one guide pin, a new spring plate, then the other guide pin.
12. Install the wheels.
13. Lower the vehicle.
14. Check the brake fluid reservoir level.
15. Operate the brake pedal repeatedly.

#### 850, S70, C70 and V70 Series

▶ **See Figures 43 thru 50**

1. Raise and safely support the vehicle.
2. Remove the wheels.
3. Drive out the retaining pins with a 3mm drift and remove the retaining spring.
4. Clean the brake caliper surfaces where the pads lie.
5. Check and clean the piston dust boot for dirt or damage and replace if necessary.
6. Check the brake disc surface for damage, if it is warped or distorted, replace it or check the run-out.

**To install:**

7. Press the pistons back into their housing using a suitable tool. Make sure that they are seated properly.
8. Grease the pad shims on both sides with a thin layer of silicone grease.
9. Install the shims on the pads,
10. Install the pads in the caliper.
11. Install one retaining pin, the retaining spring and then the other pin.
12. Depress the brake pedal several times and check the brake fluid reservoir level.
13. Install the wheels.
14. Lower the vehicle.
15. Check the brake function before driving the car.

Fig. 43 The rear pads are retained by two pins

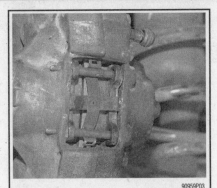

Fig. 44 A spring is also used to retain the springs

Fig. 45 Use a punch and hammer to lightly tap out the retaining pins

Fig. 46 Slide the pads out through the opening in the rear of the caliper

Fig. 47 Remember to transfer the shims to the new pads

Fig. 48 An easy way to compress the piston is to use a prybar and the old pad, but take care not to damage the rotor

Fig. 49 Install the retaining pins and drive them into place using a hammer and punch, or other suitable tool

Fig. 50 A light tap with a hammer will ensure that the pins are seated

## INSPECTION

The rear disc brake pads are checked for thickness in the same manner as the front. Refer to the Front Disc Brake Pad inspection procedure.

## Brake Caliper

### REMOVAL & INSTALLATION

#### 240 Series

1. Raise and safely support the vehicle.
2. Remove the wheels.
3. Remove the guard plate, if equipped.

4. Disconnect any ABS wires, if equipped.
5. Disconnect the brake line from the rear axle and remove the mounting bolts for the caliper.
6. Disconnect the brake line from the caliper and remove the caliper.
7. Remove the brake pads.

**To install:**

8. Attach the brake line loosely to the caliper.
9. Install the caliper using new mounting bolts.
10. Check the position of the caliper in relation to the disc as follows:
    a. Use feeler gauges to check the distance between the disc and the caliper support stubs on both sides.
    b. The difference between the two measurements must not exceed 0.001 in. (0.25mm).
    c. Repeat the measurements using the upper and lower support stubs to check if the caliper is mounted parallel to the disc.

d. If the caliper is not correctly aligned, shims can be used to adjust its position.

11. Tighten the bleed screw and line.
12. Attach the brake line to the rear axle.
13. Install the brake pads.
14. Connect any ABS wires unfastened earlier.
15. Bleed the brake system.
16. Install the wheels.
17. Lower the vehicle.
18. Check brake function before driving the vehicle.

### 700 Series, 900 Series, S90 and V90 Models

1. Raise and safely support the vehicle.
2. Remove the wheels.
3. Disconnect any ABS wires, if equipped.
4. Clean the brake hose and line connection. Disconnect the hose from the line. Disconnect the hose from the caliper.
5. Disconnect the parking brake cable from the bracket.
6. On models with an independent rear axle, do the following;
    a. Remove the caliper retaining bolt and swing the caliper up. Remove the brake pads.
    b. Unfasten the two caliper bolts and remove the caliper.
    c. Mount the caliper in a vise. Remove the remaining guide pin retaining bolt and separate the caliper from its retainer.
7. On models with a solid rear axle, do the following;
    a. Remove the guide pins using a 3mm punch.
    b. Remove the dampening spring, and brake pads.
    c. Unfasten the caliper mounting bolts and remove the caliper.

**To install:**

8. On models with an independent rear axle, do the following;
    a. Clean the caliper retainer and install new rubber sleeves. Lubricate the guide pins with silicone grease. Reassemble the caliper and retainer using one retainer bolt, but do not tighten.
    b. Install the caliper using new bolts and tighten them to 43 ft. lbs. (58

Nm). Install the brake pads. Swing the caliper down and install the lower caliper guide pin retaining bolt and tighten them both to 25 ft. lbs. (34 Nm).
9. On models with a solid rear axle, do the following;
    a. Lubricate the shims and install the brake pads.
    b. Install one fluid pin, and a new dampening plate. Then install the other guide pin.
10. Connect the brake hose, caliper and brake line.
11. Connect the parking brake cable to the bracket.
12. Connect any ABS wires, unfastened earlier.

➡ **Make sure the hose is not twisted between the caliper and line.**

13. Bleed the brake system using upper nipple.
14. Install the wheels.
15. Lower the vehicle.

### 850, S70, C70 and V70 Series

◆ **See Figures 51 thru 56**

1. Turn the ignition switch **OFF** and, if equipped with ABS, remove the key to prevent accidental pump activation.
2. Raise and safely support the vehicle.
3. Remove the wheel(s).
4. Disconnect any ABS wires, if equipped.
5. Clean the brake caliper thoroughly and remove the dust caps from the bleeder nipple.
6. Open the bleed nipple and lock the brake pedal the depressed position. Collect the brake fluid spillage in a suitable container.
7. Remove the brake pads and disconnect the brake pipes from the caliper.
8. Remove caliper mounting bolts and lift the caliper off.
9. Drain the remaining brake fluid in the caliper into suitable container.

**To install:**

10. Clean the caliper mount where the caliper lies.
11. Install the caliper and new mounting bolts. Tighten the bolts to 44 ft. lbs. (60 Nm).

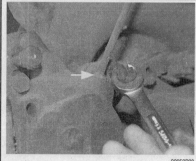

Fig. 51 To avoid damaging the fastener, be sure to use the correct size flare nut or "line wrench" to disconnect the brake line

Fig. 52 After the brake line is loosened, remove it from the caliper . . .

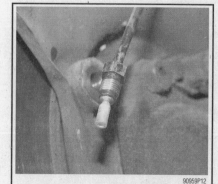

Fig. 53 . . . and plug the brake line to prevent dirt from entering

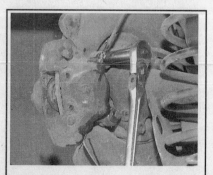

Fig. 54 Unfasten the brake caliper mounting bolts . . .

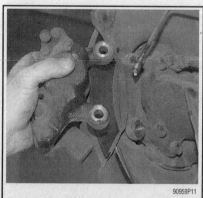

Fig. 55 . . . then remove the caliper

Fig. 56 Volvo recommends that you spread a small amount of threadlocking compound on the caliper mounting bolts

12. Connect the brake line to the caliper and tighten to 10 ft. lbs. (14 Nm).

13. Grease the brake pad shims with a thin layer of silicon grease. Put the shims on the back of the pads and install them in the caliper.

14. Install one retaining pin, spring then the other retaining pin.

15. Fill the brake master cylinder and bleed the brake system.

16. Connect any ABS wires, unfastened earlier.

17. Install the wheels.

18. Lower the vehicle and check the brake function before driving.

## OVERHAUL

See the Front Brake Caliper overhaul procedure, earlier in this section.

## Brake Disc (Rotor)

### REMOVAL & INSTALLATION

#### 240 Series

1. Raise and safely support vehicle.

2. Remove the wheel(s).

3. Remove the brake caliper and hang it from the spring with a piece of wire.

4. Remove the two screws securing the disc.

5. Lift off the disc; it may be necessary to tap on the disc with a soft-faced hammer.

**To install:**

6. Install the new disc, make sure the mating surfaces of the disc and hub are clean and dry.

7. Install the caliper using new mounting bolts.

8. Check the location of the caliper in relation to the disc. Use feeler gauges to check the distance between the disc and the caliper support stubs on both sides. The difference between the two measurements must not exceed 0.001 in. (0.0013mm). Repeat the measurements using the upper and lower support stubs to check if the caliper is mounted parallel to the disc. If the caliper is not correctly aligned, shims can be used to adjust the caliper's position.

9. Install the brake pads and make sure that the disc can rotate freely between the pads.

10. Install the disc securing screws.

11. Install the wheels.

12. Lower the vehicle.

13. Check brake pedal function before driving vehicle.

#### 700 Series, 900 Series, S90 and V90 Models

1. Raise and safely support vehicle.

2. Remove the wheel(s).

3. Remove the caliper and brake pads.

4. Hang the caliper on the spring to prevent damaging the brake hose.

5. Remove the locating pin and tap the disc off with a plastic mallet if stuck.

6. Clean the axle shaft flange, remove all corrosion and dirt.

**To install:**

7. Install the new disc making sure that the friction surfaces on both sides are clean.

8. Install the locating stud and tighten to 72 inch lbs. (8 Nm).

9. Install the caliper using new bolts, then install the brake pads.

10. Install the wheels.

11. Lower the vehicle.

#### 850, S70, C70 and V70 Series

▶ **See Figures 57, 58 and 59**

1. Raise and safely support the vehicle.

2. Remove the wheel(s).

3. Remove the brake pads and shims.

4. Remove the two caliper and disconnect the brake line from its clip.

5. Remove the brake caliper and hang it from the spring to prevent damaging the line.

6. Loosen the parking brake adjuster slightly so the disc a can be removed.

7. Remove the wheel guide pin bolt and disc.

**To install:**

8. Clean the face of the hub and check it for signs of damage. If the hub shows signs of damage, check the run-out by:

    a. Mounting a dial indicator and rotating the hub with sensor tip on the face of the hub.

    b. If the highest spot on the hub is higher than 0.007 in. (0.20mm), the hub must be replaced.

9. Carefully brush the ABS pulse wheel off with a soft brush.

10. Install the brake disc and guide pin bolt.

11. Tighten the bolt to 72 inch lbs. (8 Nm).

12. Install the caliper and pads, using new mounting bolts.

13. Install the brake line and mounting clip.

14. Depress the brake pedal several times and check the brake fluid reservoir.

15. Adjust the parking brake.

16. Install the wheels.

17. Lower the vehicle.

18. Check the brake function before driving the vehicle.

### INSPECTION

Inspect the brake rotor for scoring and wear; minor scoring or disc pad lining build-ups does not require rotor machining or replacement. If heavy scoring, cracks or other damage is evident, replace or have the rotor machined, as necessary.

Glaze on the rotor can be removed by hand-sanding it with medium grit garnet paper or aluminum oxide sandpaper.

The minimum thickness of each brake rotor is indicated on the rotor itself. Do not utilize a rotor which is worn below the minimum allowable thickness. If rotor damage cannot be corrected by grinding to these minimums, the rotor must be replaced.

Rotor lateral run-out must not be more than 0.001 in. (0.035mm).

90959P13

**Fig. 57 Use the appropriate size wrench to loosen . . .**

90959P14

**Fig. 58 . . . and remove the wheel guide pin bolt**

90959P15

**Fig. 59 Remove the brake disc; if stuck, lightly tap with a soft-faced hammer to loosen it**

## PARKING BRAKE

The cable operated emergency brake is a complete separate brake system acting only on the rear wheels. When the lever in the vehicle is pulled up, cables running to the rear of the vehicle actuate 2 sets of brake shoes. These shoes expand against the machined surface inside the rear brake disc. The system must, however, remain in proper repair and adjustment so that it will hold the vehicle when parked and be available for emergency use if needed.

## Cables

### REMOVAL & INSTALLATION

#### 240 Series

1. Apply the parking brake.
2. Remove the hub caps for the rear wheels and loosen the lug nuts a few turns.
3. Raise and safely support the vehicle.
4. Remove the wheel and tire assembly.
5. Release the parking brake.
6. Remove the bolt and the wheel from the pulley.
7. Remove the rubber cover for the front attachment of the cable sleeve and nut, as well as the attachment for the rubber suspension ring on the frame.
8. Remove the cable from the other side of the attachment in the same manner.
9. Hold the return spring in position. Pry up the lock and remove the lock pin so the cable releases form the lever.
10. Remove the return spring with washers.
11. Loosen the nut for the rear attachment of the cable sleeve.
12. Lift the cable forward after loosening both side of the attachments and remove it.

**To install:**

13. Adjust the rear brake shoes of the parking brake by removing the rear ashtray between the front seat backs.
14. Tighten the parking brake cable adjusting screw so the brake is fully applied when pulled up 2–3 notches.
15. If one cable is stretched more than the other, they can be individually adjusted by removing the parking brake cover (2 screws) and turning the individual cable adjusting nut at the front of each yoke pivot.
16. Install the ashtray and parking brake cover, if equipped.
17. Install new rubber cable guides for the cable suspension.
18. Place the cable in position in the rear attachment and tighten the nut.
19. Install the washers and return spring.
20. Oil the lock pin and install it, together with the cable, on the lever.
21. Install the attachment and rubber cable guide on the frame.
22. Install the cable in the same manner on the side of the vehicle.
23. Place the cable sleeve in position in the front attachments and install the rubber covers.
24. Lubricate and install the pulley on the pull rod.
25. Adjust the pulley so the parking brake is fully engaged with the lever at the 3rd or 4th notch.
26. Install the wheel and tire assemblies.
27. Lower the vehicle.

#### Except 240 Series

##### SHORT CABLE—RIGHT SIDE

1. Raise and safely support the vehicle.
2. Remove the passenger side rear wheel.
3. Remove the right brake caliper and hang it from the coil spring with a wire.
4. Remove the brake disc.
5. Unhook the rear return spring and remove the brake shoes.
6. Push out the pin holding the cable to the brake lever.
7. Remove the rubber bellows (boot) from the backing plate and remove the bellows from the cable.
8. Remove the spring clip, pin and cable from the back of the differential housing.

9. Remove the cable guide on the differential by removing the top bolt from the housing cover.
10. Remove the cable.

**To install:**

11. Install the cable guide on the new cable.
12. Check the rubber bellows for wear or damage and replace if necessary. Install the bellows and position it through the hole in the backing plate. Make sure the bellows sits correctly on the backing plate.
13. Smear the contact surfaces of the brake levers with a thin layer of heat resistant graphite grease.
14. Connect the cable to the lever and install the pin.

➡ **The arrow stamped on the lever should point upward and outwards.**

15. Push the cable through and place the lever in position behind the rear axle flange.
16. Install the cable guide on the axle.
17. Connect the cable to the equalizer using the pin and spring clip.
18. Install the brake shoes and rear return spring.
19. Install the brake disc and caliper. Use new bolts. and tighten to 43 ft. lbs. (58 Nm). Make sure the disc rotates freely.
20. Adjust the parking brake.
21. Install the wheel.
22. Lower the vehicle.

##### LONG CABLE—LEFT SIDE

▶ **See Figures 60 and 61**

1. Remove the center console.
2. Slacken the parking brake adjusting screw.
3. Remove the cable lock ring and remove the cable.
4. Pull out the cable from the spring sleeve.
5. Raise and safely support the vehicle.
6. Remove the driver side rear wheel.
7. Remove the left rear brake caliper and hang it from the coil spring with a piece of wire.
8. Remove the brake disc and rear return spring.
9. Remove the brake shoes.
10. Push out the pin holding the cable to the lever.
11. Remove the rubber bellows from the backing plate and remove the bellows from the cable.
12. Pull out the cable from the backing plate and the equalizer on top of the rear axle.
13. Remove the cable clamp on the sub-frame, above the driveshaft, and the cable.

**To install:**

14. Install the new cable through the grommet in the floor; check that the grommet sits correctly.
15. Clamp the cable to the sub-frame.
16. Smear the contact surfaces of the brake levers with a thin layer of heat resistant graphite grease.
17. Connect the cable to the lever and install the pin.

➡ **The arrow stamped on the lever should point upward and outwards.**

18. Push the cable through and place the lever in position behind the rear axle flange.
19. Install the cable guide on the axle.
20. Connect the cable to the equalizer using the pin and spring clip.
21. Install the brake shoes and rear return spring.
22. Install the brake disc and caliper. Use new bolts. and tighten to 43 ft. lbs. (58 Nm). Make sure the disc rotates freely.
23. Adjust the parking brake.
24. Install the wheel.
25. Lower the vehicle.

### ADJUSTMENT

▶ **See Figures 62, 63 and 64**

1. The parking brake should be fully applied when the handle is moved no more than ten notches. If adjustment is required, adjust the brake shoes first.

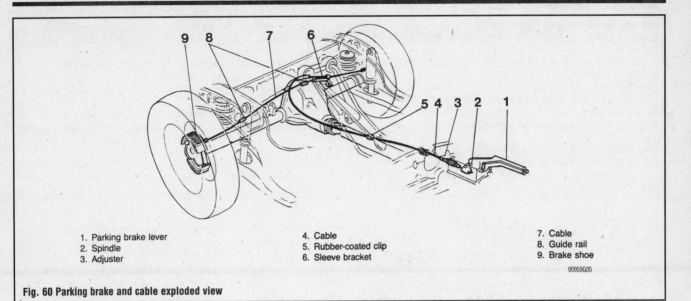

1. Parking brake lever
2. Spindle
3. Adjuster
4. Cable
5. Rubber-coated clip
6. Sleeve bracket
7. Cable
8. Guide rail
9. Brake shoe

90959G05

**Fig. 60 Parking brake and cable exploded view**

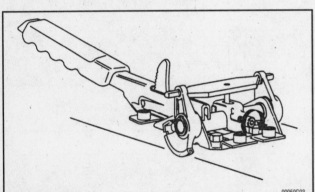

90959G03

**Fig. 61 Release the tension on the cable by backing off the bolt on the handle**

2. For 850 models, full braking should be reached when the handle is raised about five notches. If cable adjustment is required:

a. Remove the square cover plate under the armrest in the middle console.

b. Turn the adjustment screw so that full braking is obtained between the second and eighth notch.

c. Replace the square cover plate.

3. Raise and safely support the vehicle.

4. Remove the rear wheels.

5. With the brake handle released, install a brake adjusting tool through the hole in the rotor between the studs.

6. Turn the adjuster wheel until the rotor will not turn.

7. Loosen the adjuster wheel 4–5 notches.

8. Make sure the rotor turns freely. If the shoes are binding inside the rotor even after loosening the adjuster more, remove the rotor to repair the problem.

9. Move the handle again: adequate braking power should be obtained at 3–7 notches with a normal pull force of approximately 65 lbs. (84 Nm). If cable adjustment is required, remove the access panel behind the brake handle and adjust through the opening in the rear console.

10. The yoke on top of the brake handle should be at right angles to the parking brake lever. If the yoke is out of alignment, lower the handle and turn the nuts at the cable ends to adjust. There should always be at least 0.1 inch (2mm) thread protruding.

11. Make sure the indicator light on the instrument panel illuminates when the brake is applied.

## Brake Shoes

REMOVAL & INSTALLATION

◆ See Figures 65 thru 72

1. Using the appropriate parking brake cable adjustment procedure, gain access to the adjuster and loosen it so that the tension is removed from the cable.

2. Raise and safely support the vehicle safely

3. Remove the brake line-to-axle clamp, as required.

4. Remove the caliper and hang it out of the way. Be careful not to crimp hoses or lines.

90959P25

**Fig. 62 The parking brake is adjusted through an opening in the rotor on 850/C70/S70/V70 models**

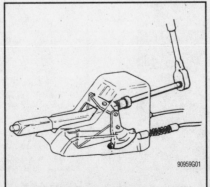

90959G01

**Fig. 63 Parking brake adjustment on 240, Coupe and 700 series models**

90959G02

**Fig. 64 Parking brake adjustment on 900 series models**

5. Remove the disc. Don't attempt to remove the hub.

6. Using brake spring pliers, remove one retaining spring from the shoe assembly.

7. Remove the shoes from the vehicle, taking note of the location and placement of the adjuster.

**To install:**

8. Check for hydraulic leaks, worn components, and the brake shoes contact surface for signs of wear.

9. Thoroughly clean the hardware, surfaces, and backing plate with an appropriate brake cleaner.

10. Assemble the shoes with one spring and install onto the vehicle.

11. Install the other retaining spring.

12. Place adjuster in position and align shoes for disc reinstallation.

13. Install the brake disc. Check that the disc turns freely without binding on the shoes.

14. Reinstall the brake caliper. Always use new retaining bolts and tighten them to 42 ft. lbs. (57 Nm).

15. Reinstall the brake line-to-axle clamp, as required.

16. Adjust the brake shoes (except 700 series) and then the cables, as described earlier in this section.

17. Reinstall the wheels.

18. Lower the vehicle.

19. Check the emergency brake for proper holding and adjust the cables as necessary. Full braking effect must be possible within 3–5 notches, after adjustment.

## ADJUSTMENT

Refer to the Parking Brake Cable adjustment procedure, earlier in this section.

Fig. 65 The parking brake shoes are retained by two springs, one at the top . . .

Fig. 66 . . . and one at the bottom

Fig. 67 A pair of needlenose pliers works very well to remove the springs

Fig. 68 After the top spring is removed, take out the adjuster

Fig. 69 When the top spring has been removed, the shoes can be removed with the bottom spring still attached

Fig. 70 Thoroughly clean the parking brake backing plate prior to installation

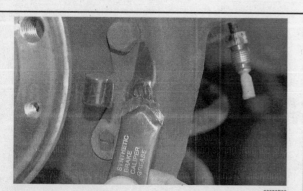

Fig. 71 Use a proper high temperature grease to lubricate the backing plates

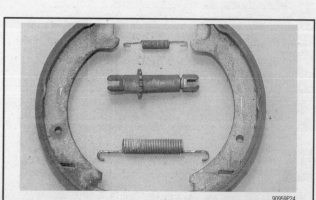

Fig. 72 Disassembled view of the parking brake shoes and associated hardware

## ANTI-LOCK BRAKE SYSTEM

### General Information

#### ▶ See Figures 73 and 74

The Anti-lock Braking System, designated ABS, prevents wheel lock-up. The ABS provides the shortest possible braking distance while maintaining full directional stability. The ABS controls the front wheels individually and the rear wheels together. The rear piston in the master cylinder operates the front brakes and the front piston operates the rear axle brakes.

Under normal conditions, the ABS system functions in the same manner as a standard brake system and is transparent to the operator. The system is a combination of electrical and hydraulic components, working together to control the flow of brake fluid to the wheels when necessary.

The Control Unit (CU) is the electronic brain of the system, receiving and interpreting signals from the wheel speed sensors. The unit will enter anti-lock mode when it senses impending wheel lock at any wheel and immediately control the brake line pressures to the affected wheel(s) by issuing output signals to the hydraulic modulator.

The hydraulic modulator contains solenoids which react to the signals from the CU. When not activated, the solenoids allow brake line pressure to be modulated by the brake pedal in the normal fashion. At the direction of the (CU), the solenoids move to positions either isolating the brake line from pedal pressure (pressure hold) or isolating the line and opening a passage to relieve line pressure (pressure release). In this manner, brake application is controlled or actually lessened, dependent on the locking tendency of each wheel.

The decisions regarding these functions are made very rapidly and each solenoid can be cycled several times per second. Volvo employs a 3-channel control system. The front wheels are controlled separately; the rears are watched by a single sensor on all models except the 850/C70/S70/V70 which have two, and the common feed line to the rear brakes is controlled by one output on the hydraulic modulator.

The operator may feel a slight pulsing in the brake pedal and/or hear popping or clicking noises when the system engages. These sensations are due to the valves cycling and the pressures being changed rapidly within the brake system. While completely normal and not a sign of system failure, these sensations can be disconcerting to an operator unfamiliar with the system.

Although the ABS system prevents wheel lock-up under hard braking, as brake pressure increases, wheel slip is allowed to increase as well. This slip will result in some tire chirp during ABS operation. The sound should not be interpreted as lock-up but rather as an indication of the system holding the wheel(s) just outside the locking point. Additionally, the final few feet of an ABS-engaged stop may be completed with the wheels locked; the system is inoperative below 3 mph.

When the ignition is ON and vehicle speed is over 3 mph (5 kph), the CU monitors the function of the system. Should a fault be noted, such a loss of signal from a sensor, the ABS system is immediately disabled by the CU. The ANTI-LOCK dashboard warning lamp is illuminated to inform the operator. When the ABS system is disabled, the vehicle retains normal braking capacity without the benefits of anti-lock.

Some vehicles have a Traction Control System (TRACS) incorporated into the ABS system. The CU monitors the speed sensors just as it does for the ABS, and if one of the drive wheels is detected moving faster than the other, it engages that wheel's brakes to reduce the power to the wheel. This is accomplished by closing and opening the solenoids in the hydraulic modulator, causing the brake fluid to be "pumped" to that wheel, slowing the wheel rotation down and applying power equally.

### System Components

#### DESCRIPTION

**Wheel Speed Sensors**

#### ▶ See Figure 75

The speed signal is sent to the control unit via a sensor and pulse wheel assembly. Each front wheel has its own assembly. Rear wheel speed is measured by one sensor and pulse wheel assembly on all vehicles except for the 850/C70/S70/V70 models which have one on each wheel.

As the teeth of the pulse generator pass the tip of the sensor, the changes from peak to valley to peak generate a small AC voltage in the sensor. The frequency of the voltage—which increases with wheel speed—is used by the CU to determine wheel speed. By comparing wheel speed during braking, the control unit determines impending wheel lock.

**Electronic Control Unit (CU)**

The CU is located below the left dashboard, above the left kick panel on the 240 and most of the 700 series. It is located on the right front wheel housing on 760 models with a B280 engine. On most other models, it is attached to the hydraulic modulator and is alongside the brake master cylinder. The unit is a microprocessor that receives and processes signals according to predetermined logic, and supplies a control signal to the solenoid valves located on the hydraulic modulator.

The control unit contains the safety or monitor circuitry which will disable the ABS system if any electrical fault is detected. The safety circuit also monitors battery voltage and will disable the system if voltage becomes too high or too low.

The electronic control unit cannot be repaired or serviced; if an internal fault is detected, the unit must be replaced.

**Hydraulic Modulator**

#### ▶ See Figure 76

Usually located under or near the brake master cylinder in the engine compartment, the hydraulic modulator contains the solenoid valves, the system recirculation pump, the solenoid control relay and the pump control relay. Cer-

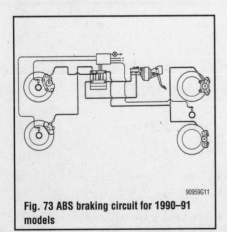

**Fig. 73 ABS braking circuit for 1990–91 models**

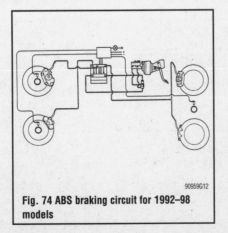

**Fig. 74 ABS braking circuit for 1992–98 models**

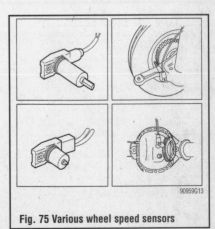

**Fig. 75 Various wheel speed sensors**

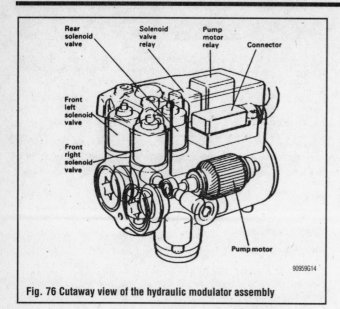

Fig. 76 Cutaway view of the hydraulic modulator assembly

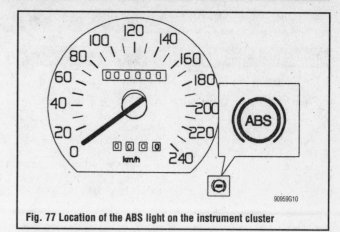

Fig. 77 Location of the ABS light on the instrument cluster

tain engine and body combinations will locate the hydraulic modulator on the left wheel arch.

The 3 internal solenoids are electrically operated valves. When no current is applied, the valves are in the normal or open position, allowing brake fluid pressure to be controlled by the brake pedal. Engagement of ABS causes the solenoid to move through part of its travel, blocking the brake fluid passage. This puts the valve in the hold position, maintaining existing brake line pressure. If the CU still senses a wheel locking or about to lock, the solenoid is moved to the full extent of its travel, opening the pressure relief passage. Brake fluid in the circuit is allowed to escape, reducing line pressure and releasing the brake. The released fluid is momentarily held in a pressure accumulator which serves to reduce the pedal pounding sensation to the operator. Once released from the accumulator, the fluid is pumped back into the system for reuse.

With the exception of the two relays mounted on the unit, the hydraulic unit has no serviceable parts and cannot be repaired. If an internal fault is found, the unit must be replaced.

### Brake Lamp

The red dashboard BRAKE warning lamp functions in a manner identical to non-ABS vehicles. If the fluid level should drop below an acceptable level, the lamp will light as a warning to the operator. If the BRAKE lamp is lit, braking function on the vehicle may be impaired; do not operate the vehicle until the status and reliability of the braking system is determined.

### Anti-lock Lamp

♦ See Figure 77

The Anti-lock Braking System (ABS) warning lamp is coupled to the ABS CU. The lamp will light briefly during engine start-up as the CU performs an initial check of the system. If no faults are found, the CU will extinguish the lamp within a few seconds. After this initial test, the lamp should not come on during vehicle operation.

If the ABS lamp does come on during operation, the CU has detected a fault and disabled the system. If only the ABS warning lamp is lit, the vehicle retains normal braking characteristics and may be safely driven. If both warning lamps are lit, the braking capacity of the vehicle may be impaired.

### SYSTEM PRECAUTIONS

• If the vehicle is equipped with an air bag system, always properly disable the system before commencing work on the ABS system. Refer to Section 6 for the correct disabling procedure.
• Certain components within the ABS system are not intended to be serviced or repaired individually. Only those components with removal and installation procedures should be serviced.
• Do not use rubber hoses or other parts not specifically specified for the

ABS system. When using repair kits, replace all parts included in the kit. Partial or incorrect repair may lead to functional problems and require the replacement of other components.
• Lubricate rubber parts with clean, fresh brake fluid to ease assembly. Do not use lubricated shop air to clean parts; damage to rubber components may result.
• Use only brake fluid from an unopened container. Use of suspect or contaminated brake fluid can reduce system performance and/or durability.
• A clean repair area is essential. Perform repairs after components have been thoroughly cleaned. Do not allow ABS components to come into contact with any substance containing mineral oil; this includes used shop rags.
• The control unit is a microprocessor similar to other computer units in the vehicle. Insure that the ignition switch is **OFF** before removing or installing controller harnesses. Avoid static electricity discharge at or near the controller.
• Never disconnect any electrical connection with the ignition switch **ON** unless instructed to do so in a test.
• Avoid touching connector pins with fingers.
• Leave new components and modules in the shipping package until ready to install them.
• To avoid static discharge, always touch a vehicle ground after sliding across a vehicle seat or walking across carpeted or vinyl floors.
• If any arc welding is to be done on the vehicle, the ABS control unit should be disconnected before welding operations begin.
• Never allow welding cables to lie on, near or across any vehicle electrical wiring.
• If the vehicle is to be baked after paint repairs, disconnect and remove the control unit from the vehicle.

### REMOVAL & INSTALLATION

#### Hydraulic Modulator

1. Disconnect the negative battery cable.
2. Remove the cover (if equipped) from the hydraulic modulator.
3. Remove both relays (if equipped) from the top of the unit; disconnect the wiring connector at the unit.
4. Remove the air inlet hose.
5. Unplug any connectors from the unit.
6. Place rags or towels around the unit to absorb brake fluid which will be spilled.
7. Clean the line connections thoroughly.
8. Label each line for installation.
9. Remove the brake lines from the modulator.
10. Remove the bolts from the modulator support and push the support to the right.
11. Remove the hydraulic modulator.
**To install:**
12. If a new modulator is being installed, remove the hexagonal plugs from the old unit and install on the new unit. Check that the rubber pads are not damaged; install the rubber pads onto the hexagonal plugs.
13. Install the modulator and tighten the support. If installing a new unit, remove the plugs from the brake line ports.

14. Reconnect the brake lines according to the labels made at removal. The lines must be in their exact original positions.

15. Remove the rags from the work area and dispose of them properly.

16. Plug in any removed connectors.

17. Install the air inlet hose.

18. Install the relays (if equipped) on the hydraulic modulator.

19. Install the cover on the unit.

20. Bleed the brake system. Vehicles with hydraulic clutches may require bleeding of the clutch system as well.

21. When bleeding is complete, test the brake system by having an assistant press hard on the brake pedal; keep it depressed for 30 seconds. During the 30 second period, check that no leakage occurs at the brake line connections on the hydraulic modulator.

22. Connect the negative battery cable.

23. Test drive the vehicle, confirming system function.

### Control Unit

#### 1990–93 MODELS

▶ See Figure 78

The control unit is located under the steering wheel, behind the knee bolster panel.

1. Disconnect the negative battery cable.

2. Remove the knee bolster panel under the steering wheel..

3. Loosen or remove the clips and retainers holding the control unit.

4. Lift out the unit.

5. Remove the electrical harness from the unit.

**To install:**

6. Attach the harness to the control module.

7. Place the control module into place and install the clips and retainers.

8. Install the knee bolster panel.

9. Connect the negative battery cable.

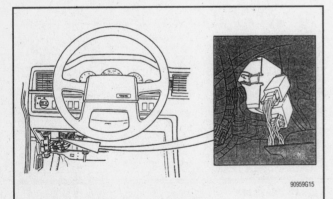

**Fig. 78 Control unit location on 1990–93 vehicles**

90959G15

#### 1994–98 MODELS

▶ See Figure 79

The control unit is located in the engine compartment, near the master cylinder/brake booster.

1. Disconnect the negative battery cable.

2. Clean the connector of any dirt, grime and/or oil.

3. Remove the connector from the control unit.

4. Remove the control unit retaining bolts.

5. Lift the control unit out of the engine compartment.

**To install:**

6. Lower the control unit into place aligning the bolts holes.

7. Tighten the retaining bolts.

8. Install the connector on the control unit.

9. Connect the negative battery cable.

### Wheel Speed Sensors

#### FRONT

▶ See Figures 80, 81, 82 and 83

1. Raise and safely support the front of the vehicle.

2. Remove the tire and wheel.

3. With the ignition switch **OFF**, disconnect the wheel speed sensor lead from the ABS harness. Remove any retaining bolts or clips holding the harness in place.

➡**Clips and retainers must be reinstalled in their exact original location. Take careful note of the position of each retainer and of the correct harness routing during removal.**

4. Remove the single bolt holding the speed sensor.

5. Carefully remove the sensor straight out of its mount. Do not subject the sensor to shock or vibration; protect the tip of the sensor at all times.

**To install:**

6. Fit the sensor into position. Make certain the sensor sits flush against the mounting surface; it must not be crooked.

7. Install the retaining bolt.

8. Route the sensor cable correctly and install the harness clips and retainers. The cable must be in its original position and completely clear of moving components.

9. Connect the sensor cable to the ABS harness.

10. Install the wheel.

11. Lower the vehicle to the ground.

#### REAR WITHOUT MULTI-LINK SUSPENSION—EXCEPT 850

▶ See Figure 84

1. Raise and safely support the vehicle.

2. Disconnect the sensor connector from the harness.

3. Remove the clips and retainers holding the sensor wire to the axle. Take note of the routing of the sensor wire; exact reinstallation is required.

4. Remove the retaining bolt holding the sensor to the differential housing.

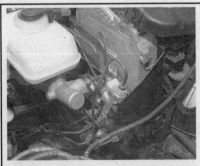

**Fig. 79 The control unit and hydraulic modulator assembly—850 series model shown**

90959P01

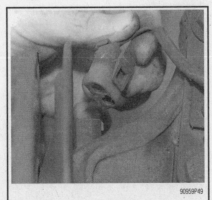

**Fig. 80 Unplug the sensor connector**

90959P49

**Fig. 81 Remove the sensor retaining bolt**

90959P50

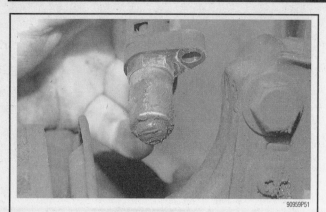

**Fig. 82 Carefully lift the sensor straight up and remove it**

**Fig. 83 If the sensor is going to be reused, clean the tip off before installing**

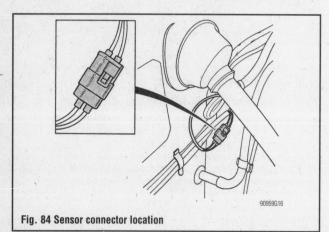

**Fig. 84 Sensor connector location**

5. Remove the sensor straight from its housing; protect the tip from impact.

**To install:**

6. Install the sensor into the housing.
7. Tighten the retaining bolt.
8. Route the wire harness and attach the connectors.
9. Install the clips and retainers to the harness.
10. Lower the vehicle.

### REAR WITH MULTI-LINK SUSPENSION—EXCEPT 850

1. Remove the spare tire and fold back the trunk carpet to expose the fuel filler pipe.
2. Remove the cover(s) from the filler pipe.
3. Break the seal on the speed sensor harness connector and disconnect the sensor from the ABS harness.
4. Press the rubber grommet free of the bodywork and feed the sensor harness to the outside of the vehicle.
5. Raise and safely support the vehicle.
6. Install a jack with support fixture 5972 or its equivalent under the rear axle.
7. Remove the 2 bolts on each side of the rear axle assembly which hold the member to the body.
8. Lower the rear axle slightly, but do not allow the drive shaft to press against the fuel tank.
9. Disconnect the right brake wire from its attachment.
10. Remove the sensor cable from the retaining clips and clamps. Take note of the routing of the cable; it must be reinstalled in its exact original position.
11. Clean the sensor area; remove the retaining bolts and remove the sensor. Protect the tip from damage or impact.

**To install:**

12. Apply a light coat of oil to the O-ring on the new sensor.
13. Fit the sensor into place without damaging the tip.
14. Tighten the retaining bolts to 90 inch lbs. (10 Nm).
15. Install the sensor harness into the cable retainers, making certain it is routed correctly and out of the way of all moving parts.
16. Feed the cable through the body and secure the grommet.
17. Connect the right brake wire.
18. Raise the rear axle assembly and install the 4 bolts. Tighten each bolt to 52 ft. lbs. (70 Nm), then angle tighten each an additional 60 degrees.
19. Lower the vehicle.
20. Connect the sensor wiring harness to the ABS harness in the trunk and reseal the connector.
21. Clamp the cable to the filler pipe.
22. Install the filler covers, reposition the carpet and install the spare tire.
23. Test drive the vehicle, confirming correct function of the ABS system and the dashboard warning lamp.

### 850/C70/S70/V70 REAR SENSORS

▶ See Figure 85

1. Disconnect the negative battery cable.
2. On sedans and the C70:
   a. Fold the passenger side rear seat forward.
   b. Remove the luggage compartment mat.
   c. Remove the fuel pump and level sensor covers.
3. On wagons:
   a. Fold up the floor panel, and bend mat back to access the fuel pump and level sensor covers.
4. Remove the wheel sensor connector.
5. Raise and safely support the vehicle.
6. Note the direction and installation of the sensor harness for reinstallation. Pull the wheel sensor harness through from underneath the vehicle.
7. Remove the wheel(s).
8. Remove the sensor attaching bolt, and remove the sensor.

**To install:**

9. Install the new sensor into place, and tighten the retaining bolt.
10. Route the harness through the suspension and place into opening in floor.
11. Install the wheel(s).
12. Lower the vehicle.
13. Attach the sensor connector.
14. Install the removed covers and trim.
15. Connect the negative battery cable.

Fig. 85 The rear wheel speed sensor as viewed with the brake disc removed

## Pulse Wheel

### INTEGRAL WITH THE ROTOR

1. Raise and safely support the vehicle.
2. Remove the wheel(s) of the pulse wheel being replaced.
3. Remove the brake rotor.
4. Remove the grease seal and the wheel bearings from the rotor.
5. Place the rotor in a shop vise or other suitable holding fixture.
6. Using a suitable puller, remove the pulse wheel from the rotor.

**To install:**

7. Install the new pulse wheel onto the rotor, and using handle 1801 and driver 5276 or equivalent bearing/race/seal driver, press the pulse wheel onto the rotor.
8. Repack wheel bearings and install them into the rotor, and install a new grease seal.
9. Install the brake rotor onto the vehicle.
10. Install the wheel(s).
11. Lower the vehicle.

### INTEGRAL WITH THE HUB

1. Raise and safely support the vehicle.
2. Remove the wheel(s) of the pulse wheel being replaced.
3. Remove the brake rotor.
4. Remove the hub from the vehicle.
5. Place the hub in a vise or other suitable holding fixture.
6. Using a suitable puller, remove the pulse wheel from the hub.

**To install:**

7. Place the hub into a shop press, and using the suitable adapter press the new wheel onto the hub.
8. Install the hub onto the vehicle.
9. Install the brake rotor.
10. Install the wheel(s).
11. Lower the vehicle.

### INTEGRAL WITH THE AXLE SHAFT

1. Raise and safely support the vehicle.
2. Remove the wheel(s) of the pulse wheel being replaced.
3. Remove the brake rotor.
4. Remove the axle shaft from the vehicle.
5. Install the axle shaft in a vise or suitable fixture, ensuring not to damage the axle, or rip the CV-joint boot.
6. Using a suitable puller, remove the pulse wheel from the outer CV-joint.

**To install:**

7. Place the axle shaft into a shop press and, using the suitable adapter, press the new wheel onto the outer joint.

8. Install the axle shaft into the vehicle.
9. Install the brake rotor.
10. Install the wheel(s).
11. Lower the vehicle.

### ON THE DIFFERENTIAL

The pulse wheel is located on the ring gear inside the differential. Teardown of the differential is necessary to replace the pulse wheel. This job requires many special tools and is not recommended for the do-it-yourselfer.

## Diagnosis

### VISUAL CHECK

Before diagnosing an apparent ABS problem, make absolutely certain that the regular service braking system is in correct working order. Many common brake problems (dragging parking brake, seepage, etc.) will affect the ABS system. A visual check of specific system components may reveal problems creating an apparent ABS malfunction.

Performing this inspection may reveal a simple failure, thus eliminating extended diagnostic time.

• Inspect the tire pressures; they must be approximately equal for the system to operate correctly.
• Inspect the brake fluid level in the reservoir.
• Inspect brake lines, hoses, master cylinder assembly and brake calipers for leakage.
• Visually check brake lines and hoses for excessive wear, heat damage, punctures, contact with other parts, missing clips or holders, blockage or crimping.
• Check the calipers for rust or corrosion. Check for proper sliding action if applicable.
• Check the calipers for freedom of motion during application and release.
• Inspect the wheel speed sensors for proper mounting and connections.
• Inspect the sensor wheels for broken teeth or poor mounting.
• Inspect the wheels and tires on the vehicle. They must be of the same size and type to generate accurate speed signals.
• Confirm the fault occurrence with the operator. Certain driver induced faults, such as not releasing the parking brake fully, spinning the wheels under acceleration, sliding due to excessive cornering speed or driving on extremely rough surfaces may fool the system and trigger the dash warning light. These induced faults are not system failures but examples of vehicle performance outside the parameters of the control unit.
• Many system shut-downs are due to loss of sensor signals to or from the controller. The most common cause is not a failed sensor but a loose, corroded or dirty connector. Check harness and component connectors carefully.

If the ANTI-LOCK warning lamp is on during vehicle operation, the control unit has detected a fault and disabled the system.

If the monitoring circuit detects a fault, the control unit will disable the ABS system and light the warning lamp on the dashboard. If the light comes on during vehicle operation, perform diagnostics.

### RETRIEVING DIAGNOSTIC TROUBLE CODES

#### 1990–92 Vehicles

On pre-1993 vehicles, the control unit does not store diagnostic codes; therefore diagnosis must be made in a progressive and logical order. The control unit contains a monitoring circuit to detect any internal faults within the control unit as well as electrical faults in the sensors, solenoids, modulator unit, etc. Refer to the fault tracing procedure, later in this section.

## 1993–95 900 Series Diagnostic Trouble Code Chart

| DTC | Fault detected | ABS light | ABS system |
|---|---|---|---|
| (1-1-1) | No fault detected | - | |
| 1-2-5 | Faulty signal from at least one wheel sensor | on | off |
| 1-3-5 | Fault in control module | on | off |
| 1-4-2 | Brake light switch, open circuit | off | on |
| 1-5-1 | L/H front wheel sensor, open or short-circ. to supply | on | off |
| 1-5-2 | R/H front wheel sensor, open or short-circ. to supply | on | off |
| 1-5-5 | Rear axle sensor, open or short-circ. to supply | on | off |
| 2-1-5 | Valve relay, open-circuit or short-circuit | on | off |
| 2-3-1 | L/H front wheel sensor, signal absent | on | off |
| 2-3-2 | R/H front wheel sensor, signal absent | on | off |
| 2-3-5 | Rear axle sensor, signal absent | on | off |
| 4-1-1 | L/H front wheel valve, open or short-circ. | on | off |
| 4-1-3 | R/H front wheel valve, open or short-circ. | on | off |
| 4-1-5 | Rear valve open or short-circ. | on | off |
| 4-4-3 | Pump motor/relay electrical or mechanical fault | on | off |

90959C02

## 1993–95 850 Series ABS Diagnostic Trouble Code Chart

| DTC | Fault text | Notes |
|---|---|---|
| 1-1-1 | No faults detected by diagnostic system | |
| 1-2-1 | LH front wheel sensor, faulty signal at speed less than 40 km/h (25 mph) | Switches ABS warning indicator on / Switches TRACS warning indicator on |
| 1-2-2 | RH front wheel sensor, faulty signal at speed less than 40 km/h (25 mph) | Switches ABS warning indicator on / Switches TRACS warning indicator on |
| 1-2-3 | LH rear wheel sensor, faulty signal at speed less than 40 km/h (25 mph) | Switches ABS warning indicator on / Switches TRACS warning indicator on |
| 1-2-4 | RH rear wheel sensor, faulty signal at speed less than 40 km/h (25 mph) | Switches ABS warning indicator on / Switches TRACS warning indicator on |
| 1-4-1 | Faulty pedal sensor, shorted to ground or supply | Switches ABS warning indicator on / Switches TRACS warning indicator on |
| 1-4-2 | Faulty brake light switch, open circuit or short circuit | |
| 1-4-3 | Fault in control module | |
| 1-4-4 | Brake discs overheated | Cars with TRACS only / Switches TRACS warning indicator on |
| 2-1-1 | LH front wheel sensor, no signal on moving off | Switches ABS warning indicator on / Switches TRACS warning indicator on |
| 2-1-2 | RH front wheel sensor, no signal on moving off | Switches ABS warning indicator on / Switches TRACS warning indicator on |
| 2-1-3 | LH rear wheel sensor, no signal on moving off | Switches ABS warning indicator on / Switches TRACS warning indicator on |
| 2-1-4 | RH rear wheel sensor, no signal on moving off | Switches ABS warning indicator on / Switches TRACS warning indicator on |
| 2-2-1 | LH front wheel sensor, no signal from ABS system | Switches ABS warning indicator on / Switches TRACS warning indicator on |
| 2-2-2 | RH front wheel sensor, no signal from ABS system | Switches ABS warning indicator on / Switches TRACS warning indicator on |
| 2-2-3 | LH rear wheel sensor, no signal from ABS system | Switches ABS warning indicator on / Switches TRACS warning indicator on |
| 2-2-4 | RH rear wheel sensor, no signal from ABS system | Switches ABS warning indicator on / Switches TRACS warning indicator on |
| 3-1-1 | LH front wheel sensor, open circuit or short circuit | Switches ABS warning indicator on / Switches TRACS warning indicator on |
| 3-1-2 | RH front wheel sensor, open circuit or short circuit | Switches ABS warning indicator on / Switches TRACS warning indicator on |
| 3-1-3 | LH rear wheel sensor, open circuit or short circuit | Switches ABS warning indicator on / Switches TRACS warning indicator on |
| 3-1-4 | RH rear wheel sensor, open circuit or short circuit | Switches ABS warning indicator on / Switches TRACS warning indicator on |

90959C03

## 1993–95 850 Series ABS Diagnostic Trouble Code Chart

| DTC | Fault text | Notes |
|---|---|---|
| 3-2-1 | LH front wheel sensor, intermittent signal problems at speeds over 40 km/h (25 mph) | Switches ABS warning indicator on / Switches TRACS warning indicator on |
| 3-2-2 | RH front wheel sensor, intermittent signal problems at speeds over 40 km/h (25 mph) | Switches ABS warning indicator on / Switches TRACS warning indicator on |
| 3-2-3 | LH rear wheel sensor, intermittent signal problems at speeds over 40 km/h (25 mph) | Switches ABS warning indicator on / Switches TRACS warning indicator on |
| 3-2-4 | RH rear wheel sensor, intermittent signal problems at speeds over 40 km/h (25 mph) | Switches ABS warning indicator on / Switches TRACS warning indicator on |
| 4-1-1 | Inlet valve for LH front wheel, open circuit or short circuit | Switches ABS warning indicator on / Switches TRACS warning indicator on |
| 4-1-2 | Return valve, LH front wheel, open circuit or short circuit | Switches ABS warning indicator on / Switches TRACS warning indicator on |
| 4-1-3 | Inlet valve, RH front wheel, open circuit or short circuit | Switches ABS warning indicator on / Switches TRACS warning indicator on |
| 4-1-4 | Return valve, RH front wheel, open circuit or short circuit | Switches ABS warning indicator on / Switches TRACS warning indicator on |
| 4-2-1 | Inlet valve, rear wheel circuit, open circuit or short circuit | Switches ABS warning indicator on / Switches TRACS warning indicator on |
| 4-2-2 | Return valve, rear wheel circuit, open circuit or short circuit | Switches ABS warning indicator on / Switches TRACS warning indicator on |
| 4-2-3 | TRACS valve, open circuit or short circuit | Cars with TRACS only / Switches ABS warning indicator on / Switches TRACS warning indicator on |
| 4-2-4 | TRACS pressure sensor, faulty or short circuit | Cars with TRACS only / Switches TRACS warning indicator on |
| 4-4-1 | Faulty control module | Switches ABS warning indicator on / Switches TRACS warning indicator on |
| 4-4-2 | Pump pressure low | Switches ABS warning indicator on / Switches TRACS warning indicator on |
| 4-4-3 | Pump motor, electrical or mechanical fault | Switches ABS warning indicator on / Switches TRACS warning indicator on |
| 4-4-4 | No power supply to valves in hydraulic unit | Switches ABS warning indicator on / Switches TRACS warning indicator on |

90969Q04

## 1996 and Later ABS Diagnostic Trouble Code Chart

| DTC | Fault text | Note |
|---|---|---|
| ABS-141 | EBD-pressure sensor signal, circuit fault | Switches on warning light ABS / Switches on warning light TRACS |
| ABS-142 | Brake light switch signal | |
| ABS-143 | Road speed signal, circuit fault | |
| ABS-144 | Brake discs on front wheels overheating | Cars with TRACS only Switches on TRACS warning light Only while temperature is still high |
| ABS-211 | Wheel sensor signal LH front wheel wheel speed incorrect | Switches on ABS warning light / Switches on TRACS warning light |
| ABS-212 | Wheel sensor signal RH front wheel wheel speed incorrect | Switches on ABS warning light / Switches on TRACS warning light |
| ABS-213 | Wheel sensor signal LH rear wheel wheel speed incorrect | Switches on ABS warning light / Switches on TRACS warning light |
| ABS-214 | Wheel sensor signal RH rear wheel wheel speed incorrect | Switches on ABS warning light / Switches on TRACS warning light |
| ABS-221 | Wheel sensor signal LH front wheel ABS control phase too long | Switches on ABS warning light / Switches on TRACS warning light |
| ABS-222 | Wheel sensor signal RH front wheel ABS control phase too long | Switches on ABS warning light / Switches on TRACS warning light |
| ABS-223 | Wheel sensor signal LH rear wheel ABS control phase too long | Switches on ABS warning light / Switches on TRACS warning light |
| ABS-224 | Wheel sensor signal RH rear wheel ABS control phase too long | Switches on ABS warning light / Switches on TRACS warning light |
| ABS-311 | Wheel sensor signal LH front wheel circuit fault | Switches on ABS warning light / Switches on TRACS warning light |
| ABS-312 | Wheel sensor signal RH front wheel circuit fault | Switches on ABS warning light / Switches on TRACS warning light |
| ABS-313 | Wheel sensor signal LH rear wheel circuit fault | Switches on ABS warning light / Switches on TRACS warning light |
| ABS-314 | Wheel sensor signal RH rear wheel circuit fault | Switches on ABS warning light / Switches on TRACS warning light |
| ABS-321 | Wheel sensor signal LH front wheel extrapolation counter | Switches on ABS warning light / Switches on TRACS warning light |
| ABS-322 | Wheel sensor signal RH front wheel extrapolation counter | Switches on ABS warning light / Switches on TRACS warning light |
| ABS-323 | Wheel sensor signal LH rear wheel extrapolation counter | Switches on ABS warning light / Switches on TRACS warning light |
| ABS-324 | Wheel sensor signal RH rear wheel extrapolation counter | Switches on ABS warning light / Switches on TRACS warning light |

90959Q05

### 1996 and Later ABS Diagnostic Trouble Code Chart

| DTC | Fault text | Note |
|---|---|---|
| ABS-411 | Inlet valve LH front wheel, fault in valve terminal circuit | Switches on ABS warning light<br>Switches on TRACS warning light |
| ABS-412 | Outlet valve LH front wheel, fault in valve terminal circuit | Switches on ABS warning light<br>Switches on TRACS warning light |
| ABS-413 | Inlet valve RH front wheel, fault in valve terminal circuit | Switches on ABS warning light<br>Switches on TRACS warning light |
| ABS-414 | Outlet valve HR front wheel, fault in valve terminal circuit | Switches on ABS warning light<br>Switches on TRACS warning light |
| ABS-421 | Inlet valve rear wheel, fault in valve terminal circuit | Switches on ABS warning light<br>Switches on TRACS warning light |
| ABS-422 | Outlet valve rear wheel, fault in valve terminal circuit | Switches on ABS warning light<br>Switches on TRACS warning light |
| ABS-423 | Inlet valve TRACS, fault in valve terminal circuit | Cars with TRACS only |
| ABS-431 | Control module - general hardware fault | Switches on ABS warning light<br>Switches on TRACS warning light |
| ABS-432 | Control module - general interference fault | Switches on ABS warning light<br>Switches on TRACS warning light |
| ABS-433 | Battery voltage<br>too high | Switches on ABS warning light<br>Switches on TRACS warning light |
| ABS-441 | Main control module relay | Switches on ABS warning light<br>Switches on TRACS warning light |
| ABS-442 | Control module - creeping powers | Switches on ABS warning light<br>Switches on TRACS warning light |
| ABS-443 | Pump motor<br>electrical or mechanical fault | Switches on ABS warning light<br>Switches on TRACS warning light |
| ABS-444 | Control module - valve reference power | Switches on ABS warning light<br>Switches on TRACS warning light |
| ABS-445 | Control module - general valve fault | Switches on ABS warning light<br>Switches on TRACS warning light |

90959C06

### 1993–95 Vehicles

▶ See Figure 86

The CU stores trouble codes when a fault is detected. These DTCs can be retrieved using the Data Link Connector (DLC) located on the driver's side of the engine compartment. Connect the selector cable to the DLC terminal 3. Turn the ignition to the **ON** position with the engine off. Press the button on the DLC and hold it down for about one second. Then press the button once, pausing then four times, the Light Emitting Diode (LED) on the DLC will then flash the code. The LED will pause after each number. The codes are three-digit numbers; for example, flash, pause, flash, flash, pause, flash, pause, would indicate code 121.

### 1996–98 Vehicles

▶ See Figure 87

1996 and later Volvos are equipped with OBD-II diagnostic capability. Codes are retrieved via the Data Link Connector (DLC), located in the console. The codes can be read after hooking up the Volvo Scan tool or equivalent Diagnostic tool. Follow the menu on the scan tool to retrieve the DTCs.

## FAULT TRACING

### 1990–93 Vehicles

The Control Unit (CU) contains a monitoring circuit to detect any internal faults within the control unit, as well as electrical faults in the sensors, solenoids, modulator unit, etc.

If the monitoring circuit detects a fault, the control unit will disable the ABS system and light the warning lamp on the dashboard. If the light comes on during vehicle operation, perform the following checks. All tests must be performed, in order.

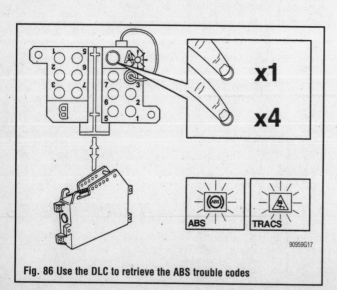

90959G17

**Fig. 86 Use the DLC to retrieve the ABS trouble codes**

**Fig. 87 The DLC is located on the center console, in front of the shifter handle**

1. Remove the soundproofing under the left side of the dashboard. Inspect the 10 amp fuse on the transient surge protector, located adjacent to the ABS control unit.

2. Check all connectors, wires and ground connections for the ABS system. Inspect the connectors at each component.

3. Insure that the ignition is switched **OFF**.

   a. At the CU under the dashboard, depress the lock spring and swing out the connector, disconnecting it from the CU.

   b. Remove the cover from the connector. Remove the white protective moldings from the sides of the connector.

   c. Use an ohmmeter to check ground circuits. Terminal numbers are stamped into the side of the connector. The ABS wiring grounds at the left A-pillar. Test between ground and terminals 10, 20, 32 and 34.

➡**Never check connectors from the front or terminal side; damage may be caused. Always check through the holes in the side of the connector without using excessive force to make contact.**

   d. Resistance should be 0 ohms in all cases. If any other reading is encountered, check for damaged wiring or improper connections. Wires are grounded on the left A-post.

   e. If a fault is found at terminal 32, replace the solenoid relay on the hydraulic modulator and retest.

4. Check the transient surge protector:

   a. Turn the ignition switch **ON**.

   b. Connect a voltmeter between ground and terminal 1 on the control unit connector; 12 volts should be present.

   c. If no voltage is present, measure voltage directly at the transient surge protector connector. Terminals 1, 2 and 4 should be energized and terminal 3 should be grounded.

   d. If only terminal 1 and 4 are energized when terminal 3 is grounded, the transient surge protector has failed and must be replaced.

5. Check the power supply to the control unit connector:

   a. Connect the voltmeter to a known good ground. Depress the brake pedal and at the same time, connect the meter to terminals 25, 27, 28 and 29.

   b. The voltmeter should read 12 volts at all terminals, except terminal 29.

   c. Voltage should read 0.5—1.0 volt at terminal 29.

6. Start the engine. The voltmeter should read 12 volts at terminal 25.

7. If no voltage or incorrect voltage is found in the above tests, proceed as follows. For a problem at:

   a. Terminal 25: Check brake lamp switch and replace if needed. Inspect brake light bulbs and replace as needed.

   b. Terminal 27: Replace defective solenoid relay.

   c. Terminal 28: Replace defective pump relay.

   d. Terminal 29: If reading at 27 is correct, voltage at 29 should be 0.5–1.0 volts. If not, replace solenoid relay.

8. Turn the ignition switch **OFF**.

9. Check voltage to the hydraulic modulator:

   a. Remove the cover from the hydraulic modulator. Detach the connector from the hydraulic modulator.

   b. Switch the ignition **ON**.

   c. Connect the voltmeter to a know good ground and to terminals 6, 7, 10 and 12. Voltage in all cases should be 12 volts.

10. If there is no voltage or improper voltage to any terminal, proceed as follows. For a problem at:

   a. Terminal 6: Inspect wiring for shorts and/or poor connections.

   b. Terminal 7: Attach the connector to the hydraulic modulator with the ignition **OFF**. Turn the ignition **ON** when connected; the ABS warning lamp on the dashboard should come on. If not, replace the warning lamp bulb.

   c. Terminal 10: Transient surge protector failed.

   d. Terminal 12: Inspect wiring for shorts and/or poor connections.

11. Turn the ignition **OFF**; attach the connector to the hydraulic modulator.

12. At the control unit connector, use an ohmmeter to measure the resistance of each wheel speed sensor.

   a. Test the left front sensor between terminals 4 and 6. Test the right front sensor between terminals 11 and 21.

   b. Resistance for the front sensors must be 900–2200 ohms (0.9–2.2 kilohms). If the resistance is not within specifications, unfasten the harness connectors in the engine compartment and measure resistance directly at the sensor. If the readings still differ, inspect the wiring and/or replace the sensor. Also, check the pulse wheels for defects or damage; maximum radial run-out is 0.006 inch (0.15mm).

   c. Measure resistance of the rear speed sensor by testing at terminals 7 and 9. Resistance should be 600–1600 ohms (0.6–1.6 kilohms).

   d. If resistance is not correct, detach the sensor connector on the fuel filler pipe in the trunk. It will be necessary to break the connector seal; do so without damaging the wiring. If readings are still not within specification, inspect wiring and/or replace the sensor.

13. Check the wiring to each sensor.

   a. Raise and safely support the vehicle.

   b. Connect an ohmmeter to the pairs of terminals use in Step 11.

   c. As each pair is tested, have an assistant turn the correct wheel on the vehicle including the rear. Rotate the wheel(s) about one revolution per second; the resistance should vary as the wheel spins.

14. Test the hydraulic modulator solenoid valves: Connect one ohmmeter lead to terminal 32 on the control unit connector. Connect the other test lead to terminal 2 (LF solenoid), then 35 (RF) and then 18 (rear); Resistance should be 0.7–1.7 ohms.

15. Test the pump relay in the hydraulic modulator:

   a. Turn the ignition **ON**.

   b. Connect a jumper between terminal 28 on the control unit connector and ground. The pump should run.

➡**Do not maintain the connection longer than 2 seconds; damage can occur.**

   c. Repeat the test. Simultaneously, measure the voltage between terminal 14 and ground. With the jumper grounding terminal 28, 12 volts should be present.

   d. If the modulator does not start, inspect the wiring and connectors. If no fault is found, replace the pump relay and retest.

16. Test the valve relay in the hydraulic modulator:

   a. Connect the voltmeter between terminal 32 on the control unit connector and ground. Use a jumper wire to connect terminal 27 to ground. The valve relay on the hydraulic modulator should activate (listen for distinct click) and the voltmeter should show 12 volts.

   b. If the relay does not energize, or the correct voltage is not present, inspect the wiring and connectors carefully.

   c. If no wiring fault is found, replace the valve relay.

17. Turn the ignition switch **OFF**. Disconnect all test equipment.

18. If no faults were found during testing, replace the ABS control unit and retest.

19. Reinstall the hydraulic modulator cover and the soundproofing at the left side of the dashboard.

20. Road test the vehicle and confirm proper system operation.

## Bleeding the ABS System

The ABS system is bled the same way as a conventional system; refer to Bleeding the Brake System, earlier in this section.

## BRAKE SPECIFICATIONS
All measurements in inches unless noted

| Year | Model | Master Cylinder Bore | Front Brake Disc | | | Rear Brake Disc | | | Minimum Lining Thickness | |
|---|---|---|---|---|---|---|---|---|---|---|
| | | | Original Thickness | Minimum Thickness | Maximum Run-out | Original Thickness | Minimum Thickness | Maximum Run-out | Front | Rear |
| 1990 | 240 Series | 0.880 | 0.870 | 0.790 | 0.0024 | 0.393 | 0.314 | 0.003 | 0.120 | 0.075 |
| | 740 Series | 0.937 | 0.870 | 0.790 | 0.0024 | 0.378 | 0.330 | 0.003 | 0.120 | 0.075 |
| | 760 Series | 0.937 | 0.870 | 0.790 | 0.0024 | 0.393 | 0.314 | 0.003 | 0.120 | 0.075 |
| | 780 Series | 0.937 | 0.870 | 0.790 | 0.0024 | 0.393 | 0.314 | 0.003 | 0.120 | 0.075 |
| 1991 | 240 Series | 0.880 | 0.870 | 0.790 | 0.0024 | 0.393 | 0.314 | 0.003 | 0.120 | 0.075 |
| | 740 Series | 0.937 | 0.870 | 0.790 | 0.0024 | 0.378 | 0.330 | 0.003 | 0.120 | 0.075 |
| | 940 Series | 0.937 | ① | ② | 0.0024 | ③ | ④ | 0.003 | 0.120 | 0.075 |
| | Coupe | 0.937 | 0.870 | 0.790 | 0.0024 | 0.378 | 0.330 | 0.003 | 0.120 | 0.075 |
| 1992 | 240 Series | 0.880 | 0.870 | 0.790 | 0.0024 | 0.393 | 0.314 | 0.003 | 0.120 | 0.075 |
| | 740 Series | 0.937 | 0.870 | 0.790 | 0.0024 | 0.378 | 0.330 | 0.003 | 0.120 | 0.075 |
| | 940 Series | 0.937 | ① | ② | 0.0024 | ③ | ④ | 0.003 | 0.120 | 0.075 |
| | 960 Series | 0.937 | ① | ② | 0.0024 | ③ | ④ | 0.003 | 0.120 | 0.075 |
| 1993 | 240 Series | 0.880 | 0.870 | 0.790 | 0.0024 | 0.393 | 0.314 | 0.003 | 0.120 | 0.075 |
| | 850 Series | 0.937 | 1.024 | 0.906 | 0.0024 | 0.378 | 0.330 | 0.003 | 0.120 | 0.075 |
| | 940 Series | 0.937 | ① | ② | 0.0024 | ③ | ④ | 0.003 | 0.120 | 0.075 |
| | 960 Series | 0.937 | ① | ② | 0.0024 | ③ | ④ | 0.003 | 0.120 | 0.075 |
| 1994 | 850 Series | 0.937 | 1.024 | 0.906 | 0.0024 | 0.378 | 0.330 | 0.003 | 0.120 | 0.075 |
| | 940 Series | 0.937 | ① | ② | 0.0024 | ③ | ④ | 0.003 | 0.120 | 0.075 |
| | 960 Series | 0.937 | ① | ② | 0.0024 | ③ | ④ | 0.003 | 0.120 | 0.075 |
| 1995 | 850 Series | 0.937 | 1.024 | 0.906 | 0.0024 | 0.378 | 0.330 | 0.003 | 0.120 | 0.075 |
| | 940 Series | 0.937 | ① | ② | 0.0024 | ③ | ④ | 0.003 | 0.120 | 0.075 |
| | 960 Series | 0.937 | ① | ② | 0.0024 | ③ | ④ | 0.003 | 0.120 | 0.075 |
| 1996 | 850 Series | 0.937 | 1.024 | 0.906 | 0.0024 | 0.378 | 0.330 | 0.003 | 0.120 | 0.075 |
| | 960 Series | 0.937 | ① | ② | 0.0024 | ③ | ④ | 0.003 | 0.120 | 0.075 |
| 1997 | 850 Series | 0.937 | 1.024 | 0.906 | 0.0024 | 0.378 | 0.330 | 0.003 | 0.120 | 0.075 |
| | 960 Series | 0.937 | ① | ② | 0.0024 | ③ | ④ | 0.003 | 0.120 | 0.075 |
| 1998 | C70 Series | 0.937 | 1.024 | 0.906 | 0.0024 | 0.378 | 0.330 | 0.003 | 0.120 | 0.075 |
| | S70 Series | 0.937 | 1.024 | 0.906 | 0.0024 | 0.378 | 0.330 | 0.003 | 0.120 | 0.075 |
| | V70 Series | 0.937 | 1.024 | 0.906 | 0.0024 | 0.378 | 0.330 | 0.003 | 0.120 | 0.075 |
| | S90 Series | 0.937 | ① | ② | 0.0024 | ③ | ④ | 0.003 | 0.120 | 0.075 |
| | V90 | 0.937 | ① | ② | 0.0024 | ③ | ④ | 0.003 | 0.120 | 0.075 |

① With standard vented rotor: 0.870
   With heavy duty rotor: 1.024
② With standard vented rotor: 0.790
   With heavy duty rotor: 0.906

③ With standard rear axle: 0.378
   With multi-link rear axle: 0.393
④ With standard rear axle: 0.330
   With multi-link rear axle: 0.314

90959C01

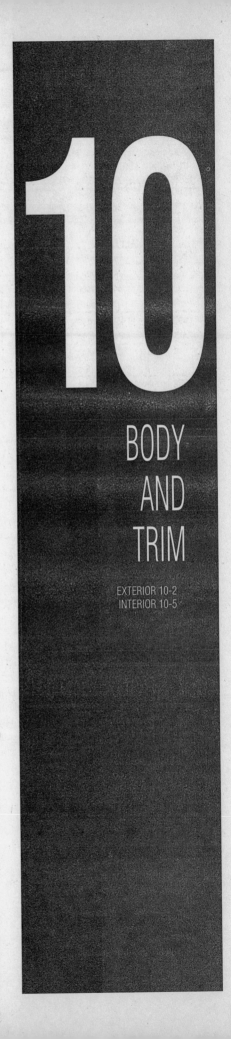

# 10

## BODY AND TRIM

## EXTERIOR

### ✳✳ WARNING

To avoid damage to the Electronic Control Module (ECM) and/or other electronic components, always disconnect the negative battery cable before using any electric welding equipment on the vehicle.

## Doors

### REMOVAL & INSTALLATION

➡ The doors are heavy! Provide proper support for the door when removing. Do not allow the door to sag while partially attached and do not subject the door to impact or twisting movements.

1. Disconnect the negative battery cable.
2. Disconnect any wiring harnesses running into the door. This may be done either inside the door (remove the door panel) or under the dashboard, inside the pillar. Make sure the wiring harness will not catch or bind as the door is removed from the vehicle.
3. Scribe marks around the hinges to facilitate door installation.
4. Support the door with a jack. Place a piece of wood on the jack to protect the paintwork.
5. Have a helper support the door, then loosen and remove the hinge mounting bolts and remove the door from the vehicle.

**To install:**
6. With an assistant, position the door and install the hinge bolts. Do not fully tighten the hinge mounting bolts at this time.
7. Check the door for proper alignment. If required, loosen the mounting bolts just enough to allow the door to be moved into position.
8. Tighten all the hinge bolts and check the final fit.
9. If the door stop bracket was removed, reinstall it.
10. Connect the wiring harness and check the function of electrical components in the door. Install the door panel if removed.
11. Connect the negative battery cable.

### ADJUSTMENT

▸ **See Figure 1**

The primary door adjustments are carried out at the hinge bolts at the forward end of each door. Further adjustment for the closed position and for latching smoothness may be made at the latch plate or striker. This piece is located at the rear edge of the door and is attached to the bodywork of the vehicle; it is the piece which the door engages when closed.

Although the striker or latchplate is different on various models, the adjustment procedure is the same:
1. Adjust the position of the door by moving the striker plate sideways.
2. If further adjustments are necessary, first slacken the upper door hinge bolts, then, if necessary, the lower 2 bolts. Push the door toward the body.

➡ Never loosen more than 3 bolts at a time or the door may drop. Do not attempt to correct height variations (sag) by adjusting the striker.

3. After the striker bolts have been tightened, open and close the door several times. Observe the motion of the door as it engages the striker; it should continue its straight-in motion and not deflect up or down as it hits the striker.
4. Check the feel of the latch during opening and closing. It must be smooth and linear, without any trace of grinding or binding during engagement and release.

➡ It may be necessary to repeat the striker adjustment procedure several times (and possibly adjust the hinges) before the proper door-to-body alignment is corrected.

## Hood

### REMOVAL & INSTALLATION

▸ **See Figures 2, 3, 4, 5 and 6**

1. Raise the hood.
2. Disconnect any electrical or fluid lines between the hood and the body.
3. Scribe marks around the hinges to facilitate hood installation. Have a helper support the hood so it doesn't damage the body during removal.
4. Remove the hinge-to-hood bolts on each side and lift the hood clear of the vehicle.

➡ The hood can be easily damaged; take great care not to bend or dimple the hood. Store it on pads and cover it to protect it while off the vehicle.

**To install:**
5. Position the hood and install the bolts just tight enough to hold it in position.
6. Lower the hood and check the alignment; the gap should be even all around.
7. Tighten the bolts.
8. Attach any electrical connections or fluid lines which were removed.

### ALIGNMENT

➡ Hoods can be easily damaged; take great care not to bend or dimple the hood.

1. Front height adjustment: adjust the guide pins or rubber bump stops on the front panel.
2. Left and right adjustment: loosen the hood and move the hood in the desired direction.
3. Hood length: loosen the hood hinges and move the hood in the desired direction. (The hinges are provided with oval holes.)
4. Rear height adjustment: adjust the hinge mountings near the wheel arch.

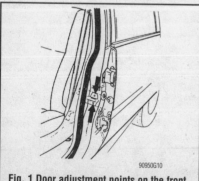

90950G10

**Fig. 1 Door adjustment points on the front door—700 series models shown, others similar**

90950P01

**Fig. 2 Locate the washer jet hoses . . .**

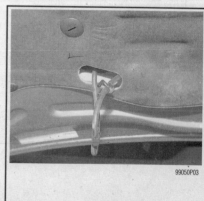

99050P03

**Fig. 3 . . . and disconnect them**

Fig. 4 Remove the clips retaining the hose

Fig. 5 Matchmark the hood and hinges to ease installation

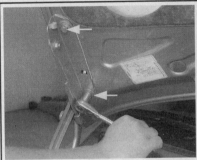

Fig. 6 Remove the two retaining bolts from each side and, with the help of an assistant, remove the hood

## Trunk Lid or Liftgate

### REMOVAL & INSTALLATION

#### 2 and 4-Door Models

1. Open the trunk lid. Have a helper support the lid; remove the retaining clip for the gas shock (which holds the lid open) and disconnect it from the lid.
2. Detach any wiring to the trunk lid at the nearest connector. Make sure the wiring will not bind when the lid is removed.
3. Scribe marks around the hinges to facilitate trunk lid installation.
4. Remove the bolts which hold the hinges to the trunk lid and lift the lid clear of the vehicle.

➡Trunk lids can be easily damaged; take great care not to bend or dimple the trunk lid. Store it on pads and cover it to protect it while off the vehicle.

**To install:**
5. Place the lid into position and lightly tighten the bolts until snug.
6. Check the lid-to-body alignment and adjust the trunk lid as necessary.
7. Final-tighten the bolts.
8. Reattach the gas shock to the trunk lid and reconnect the wiring, if any.

#### Wagon (5-Door Model)

➡Because of the size and weight of the liftgate, this procedure requires 2 people during removal and installation.

1. Remove the inner cover panel on the liftgate.
2. Detach any electrical connectors within the liftgate. Tag or identify the connectors for ease of reassembly.
3. Pull the harness through the hole in the top of the liftgate.
4. While your helper supports the liftgate, disconnect the gas shock(s).
5. With the liftgate safely supported, remove the liftgate-to-hinge bolts on each side at the top. On the 740, one of the bolts is beneath a rubber plug which must be removed.
6. Remove the liftgate from the vehicle and store it on pads.

**To install:**
7. Place the liftgate into position and loosely tighten the bolts until snug.
8. Check the alignment of the liftgate in relation to the body, and adjust it as necessary.
9. When the alignment is correct, final-tighten the hinge bolts. Left-right alignment is critical. Take your time and work for an even fit.
10. Connect the gas shock(s) to the liftgate.
11. Feed the wire harness through the hole at the top of the liftgate and into position.
12. Connect the wires to the proper points.

### ALIGNMENT

#### All Models

Both trunk lids and wagon liftgates are adjustable on their hinges due to slotted holes. The trunk lids are also adjustable by loosening the hinge-to-body bolts and repositioning the hinge vertically.

Wagon liftgates have additional adjusters on the sides. Loosen their screws a few turns and close the liftgate. The adjuster should seek the correct position for smooth operation. Because of the curve of the body and roofline, the wagon liftgate needs to be checked carefully for alignment to the body. Seams should be straight and even, and panels should be flush with no obvious high or low points.

Final adjustments are made at the latch (on the lid) and the striker (on the body). Each can be loosened and moved on its mounts to control tightness and ease of operation. It is recommended to start by loosening the striker only; close the lid or liftgate and let the striker seek its position. Continue adjusting until the latch has no binding in its operation, the key turns freely and the weatherstrip is evenly compressed around the lid/liftgate.

## Grille

### REMOVAL & INSTALLATION

The plastic grilles on these vehicles are retained by a variety of plastic clips and screws. With the hood raised, remove all the retaining hardware and lift the grille clear of the vehicle. Be careful of any wires and/or tubing running between the grille and the radiator. Do not force the grille into position or it will crack; work carefully and make sure everything lines up before tightening the mounting hardware.

On some models, the grille is an integral part of the hood and removal of the hood also removes the grille. This can be verified when the hood is opened; if the grille is attached, it will raise with the hood.

## Outside Mirrors

### REMOVAL & INSTALLATION

#### Mirror Assembly
◆ See Figures 7, 8, 9 and 10

1. Remove the door panel, as described later in this section.
2. Unplug the mirror electrical connector.
3. Remove the trim panel and rubber cover (if equipped).
4. Remove the screws and clips.
5. Remove the mirror assembly.

**To install:**
6. Position the mirror assembly.
7. Tighten the screws and attach the clips.

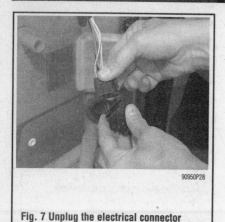

Fig. 7 Unplug the electrical connector

Fig. 8 Remove the trim cover . . .

Fig. 9 . . . to access the retaining screws

Fig. 10 Remove the mirror assembly

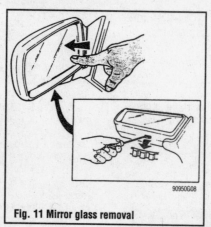

Fig. 11 Mirror glass removal

Fig. 12 Location of the power mirror motor retaining bolts

8. Install the rubber cover.
9. Plug in the electrical connector.
10. Install the door panel.

## Mirror Glass

▶ See Figure 11

1. Press on the lower edge of the mirror so that the gear is revealed in the slot in the bottom of the mirror.
2. Move the cogs to the right with a small screwdriver and remove the mirror glass.

**To install:**
3. Align the assembly lugs on the rear of the mirror glass.
4. Depress the lower edge of the glass and move the cogs to the left.
5. Check to ensure that the new glass is firmly installed.

## Power Mirror Motor

### REMOVAL & INSTALLATION

▶ See Figure 12

1. Remove the mirror glass, as described in the previous procedure.
2. Remove the retaining screws and lift out the motor.
3. Unplug the electrical connector.
4. Remove the motor from the vehicle.

**To install:**
5. Plug in the electrical connector.
6. Position the motor and tighten its retaining screws.
7. Install the mirror glass.

## Power Antenna

The power antenna extends when the radio is turned **ON**. The mast will retract when the radio is turned **OFF**. The 700 and 900 Series vehicles have a switch that allows the antenna to be retracted with the radio **ON**. The switch will also prevent the mast from extending when the radio is first turned **ON**. There are 3 leads to the power antenna unit. There is a ground lead that is electrically connected to the chassis and a green or green and red power lead connected to the fuse box to provide operating voltage. The third lead is connected to the radio (through a switch for the 700 and 900 series vehicles) to provide the signal for antenna operation. When there is power on this lead, the antenna extends; when the power is removed, by turning **OFF** the radio or turning **OFF** the antenna switch on 700 and 900 series vehicles, the antenna retracts.

### REMOVAL & INSTALLATION

1. Disconnect the negative battery cable.
2. Remove the trim panel covering the antenna assembly.
3. Disconnect the electrical leads and ground strap, if used.
4. Unscrew the upper antenna retaining nut around the base on the body.
5. Unbolt the antenna assembly securing fasteners.
6. Remove the antenna assembly from the underside.

**To install:**
7. Install the antenna from the underside and tighten the retaining bolts.
8. Install the upper antenna retaining nut.
9. Connect the electrical leads and the ground strap.
10. Install the trim panel.
11. Connect the negative battery cable.

## Fenders

### REMOVAL & INSTALLATION

1. Remove the windshield wiper arms.
2. Remove the cowl trim.
3. Unfasten the air inlet grille bolts and remove the grille.
4. Remove the bumper end-piece, headlight and turn signal lens assemblies.
5. Remove the wheel well trim.
6. Remove the fender retaining bolts and carefully remove the fender from the vehicle.

**To install:**

➡ **Before installing the retaining bolts at the wheel arch joint, apply sealer (P/N 591278-7 or equivalent).**

7. Install the fender into place and tighten the retaining bolts.
8. Install the wheel well trim.
9. Install the headlight and turn signal lens assemblies, and the bumper end-piece.
10. Install the air inlet grille and tighten the retaining bolts.
11. Install the cowl trim.
12. Install the windshield wiper arms.

## Power Sunroof

The power sunroof is controlled by a switch that selects the direction of travel of the sunroof. The switch changes the polarity of the voltage going to the sunroof motor. This changes the rotation of the motor, thereby changing the direction of sunroof travel.

### REMOVAL & INSTALLATION

◗ **See Figure 13**

1. Open the sunroof to the ventilation position.
2. Disconnect the battery ground cable.
3. Push down the sunroof headlining with a finger. Unhook the retaining springs with a bent piece of wire.
4. Pull down on the headlining sufficiently to pass beneath the gutter rail. At the same time, slide the sunroof to the rear to release the catches at the front.

➡ **Do not pull the sunroof too far to the rear; otherwise, it will be difficult to remove again.**

## INTERIOR

## Instrument Panel and Pad

### REMOVAL & INSTALLATION

◗ **See Figure 14**

1. Disconnect the negative battery cable.
2. Remove the windshield wiper arms and cowl panel.
3. Remove the outer dashboard retaining bolts.
4. Remove the steering wheel.

### ❊❊ CAUTION

**Some models covered by this manual are equipped with a Supplemental Restraint System (SRS), which uses an air bag. Whenever working near any SRS components, such as the impact sensors, air bag module, steering column or instrument panel, disable the SRS, as described in Section 6.**

5. Remove the knee bolster panel under the steering column.
6. Remove the steering column covers.
7. Remove any applicable steering column electrical connectors.

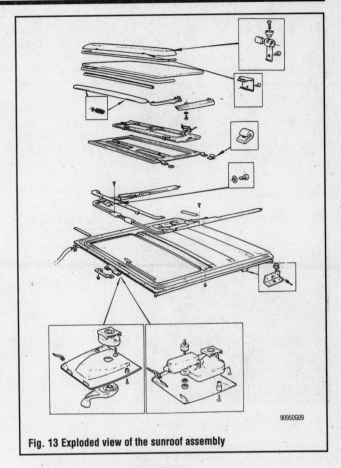

**Fig. 13 Exploded view of the sunroof assembly**

90950G09

5. Unhook the spring retaining brackets.
6. Remove the retaining screws from the sides and front.
7. Remove the sunroof.

**To install:**

8. Fit the sunroof into position and install the retaining screws.
9. Install the spring retaining brackets.
10. Slide the sunroof forward to engage the catches in the front.
11. Install or reposition any trim moved for access.
12. Connect the negative battery cable.

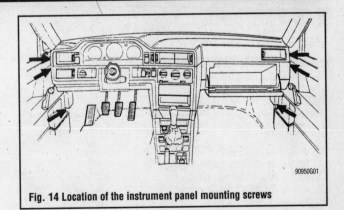

**Fig. 14 Location of the instrument panel mounting screws**

90950G01

8. Remove the steering column retaining bolts and lower the column to the floor.
9. Remove the side demister vents.
10. Detach the dash speaker grilles and remove the speakers.
11. Remove the panel vents.
12. Remove the glove box.

13. Remove the heater control panel.
14. Remove the radio.
15. Remove the center console.
16. Unfasten the dashboard mounting screws.
17. Remove the dashboard from the vehicle.

**To install:**

18. Position the dashboard into place and tighten the mounting screws.
19. Install the center console.
20. Install the radio, heater control panel, glove box, and vents.
21. Raise the steering column and tighten the retaining bolts.
22. Plug the column electrical connectors in and install the column covers.
23. Install the knee bolster panel.
24. Install the steering wheel.
25. Tighten the outer dashboard retaining bolts.
26. Install the cowl panel and the wiper arms.
27. Connect the negative battery cable.

## Center Console

### REMOVAL & INSTALLATION

◆ **See Figures 15 thru 24**

1. Disconnect the negative battery cable.
2. Remove the front panel with the cigarette lighter and diagnostic connector (if equipped), then unplug the connectors.
3. Remove the two retaining bolts under the panel.
4. Open the armrest and remove the two retaining screws under the small access cover.
5. Unplug the console harness connections under the ashtray.
6. Remove the access cover under the parking brake handle.
7. Slowly and carefully remove the console.

Fig. 15 Remove the front console retaining screws

Fig. 16 Separate the cigarette lighter lamp . . .

Fig. 17 . . . and detach the lighter element plug . . .

Fig. 18 . . . then slide out the diagnostic connector and remove the panel

Fig. 19 Lift up the armrest and remove the access cover for the rear retaining screws

Fig. 20 Remove the two rear retaining screws

Fig. 21 Location of the console wiring harness connections

Fig. 22 Unplug the connectors and ensure that they are free of obstructions for console removal

Fig. 23 Lift off the cover beneath the parking brake handle

Fig. 24 Carefully lift the console up and remove

**To install:**

8. Carefully place the console into place.
9. Install the four retaining screws.
10. Plug in the wiring harnesses under the ashtray.
11. Install the front cover.
12. Install the access cover under the armrest.
13. Install the cover under the parking brake handle.
14. Connect the negative battery cable.

## Door Panels

### REMOVAL & INSTALLATION

◆ **See Figures 25 thru 33**

The following procedure applies to both the front and rear door panels.
1. Disconnect the negative battery cable.
2. Remove all necessary retaining screws and clips; some are hidden by small access covers.
3. On some models, it may be necessary to remove the door pocket. Remove it by turning the 3 studs 90 degrees and lifting off the pocket.
4. On some models, it is necessary to remove the armrest. The screws may be concealed behind plastic covers.
5. Remove the plastic housing around the inner latch release (door handle).
6. If equipped with manual windows, remove the window crank handle. Do this by lifting up the small trim strip at the base of the winder. Remove the concealed screw and the handle may be pulled free.
7. Remove the door speaker mounting screws and pull the speaker out of the door, then unplug the connector and remove the speaker.
8. Unscrew the lock button from the shaft.
9. The door panel is removed by gently prying the edge away from the door. Use a broad, flat tool inserted between the panel and the metal of the door. The idea is to separate the clips without damage so they may be reused.
10. Proceed around the door until all the clips are released.

➡ **If the door panel is tight or stuck in one spot, be careful and do not pull hard. First ensure that you have all necessary retaining hardware removed.**

11. Remove the door panel by lifting up to free the lip at the window edge. Be prepared to disconnect any wiring encountered within the door (courtesy lights, speakers, etc.) during removal.

Fig. 25 Door panels can look intimidating, but are often quite easy when care is taken

Fig. 26 Remove the release handle from the lever

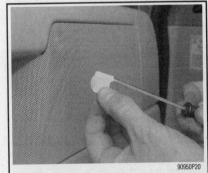

Fig. 27 Applying tape to the end of your screwdriver can help reduce the chance of scratching or damaging the panels

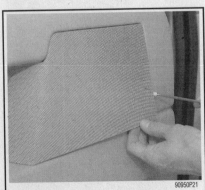

Fig. 28 Remove the speaker grille by gently prying it off

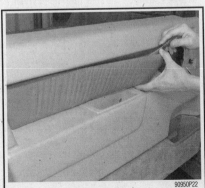

Fig. 29 Remove the trim panel above the armrest by gently prying it off . . .

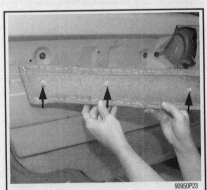

Fig. 30 . . . to release the three retaining clips on the back of the panel

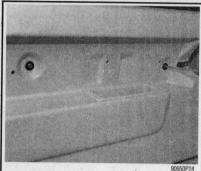

**Fig. 31 Unfasten the retaining screws which are revealed after trim panel removal**

**Fig. 32 Remove the retaining screws from the bottom of the door panel; there are usually 5 screws**

**Fig. 33 Carefully and gently lift the door panel off of the door**

➡️Inside the door is a plastic moisture barrier. It may be removed for access to the door parts, but it must not be ripped or torn. Should it become damaged, either replace it or repair it with waterproof tape. It must be reinstalled intact after any door repairs.

**To install**

12. Before reinstalling the door panel, check every clip to insure that they are properly located and not damaged. Replace any that are unusable.

13. Position the door panel onto the top of the door and seat the lip at the window rail. It may require gentle tapping to seat properly.

14. Making sure each clip aligns with its hole, proceed around the door and tap each clip into place.

15. Install all the retaining hardware and access covers.

16. Plug in the speaker and tighten the retaining bolts.

17. Install the lock button, release handle and window crank handle (if removed).

18. Install the trim around the door release handle.

19. If removed, install the armrest and the door pocket.

20. Connect the negative battery cable.

## Door Locks

### REMOVAL & INSTALLATION

▶ **See Figures 34 and 35**

1. Disconnect the negative battery cable.
2. Remove the inner door panel and the moisture barrier.

➡️For vehicles with manual locks, the lock cylinder is held within the door by a clip which slides across the back of the cylinder, or by two retaining bolts and a bracket, depending on the model.

➡️On vehicles with electric locks, the left door lock has a collar surrounding it. This electrical fitting causes all the doors to lock when the key is used in the driver's door. The retainer on this switch may be opened by prying up the plastic catch; the switch may then be removed from the lock cylinder.

3. Remove the clip or the retaining bolts.
4. Disconnect the lock rod(s) from the lock cylinder.
5. Remove the lock.

**To install:**

6. Connect the lock rod(s) to the lock cylinder.
7. Place the lock cylinder into place in the door and attach the clip or the retaining bolts and bracket.
8. Ensure that the lock cylinder engages the latch mechanism properly.
9. If the vehicle has electric locks, make sure the switch collar is in its correct position and the clip is secure.
10. Reinstall the moisture barrier and the inner door panel.
11. Connect the negative battery cable.

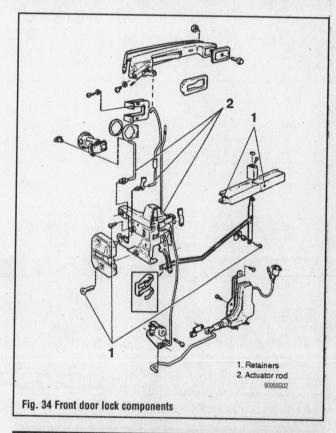

1. Retainers
2. Actuator rod

**Fig. 34 Front door lock components**

## Trunk/Liftgate Lock

### REMOVAL & INSTALLATION

1. Disconnect the negative battery cable.
2. On 4-door models:
   a. Open the trunk lid and remove the clips in the lower right corner of the trunk lid trim.
   b. Bend the trim back carefully to expose the lock cylinder.
3. On wagon models:
   a. Remove the liftgate trim panel.
   b. Remove any necessary trim to access the lock cylinder.
4. Disconnect the lock rod(s) from the lock cylinder.
5. Remove the retaining bolt for the bracket on the lock cylinder.
6. Remove the retaining clip from the lock cylinder.
7. Remove the lock.

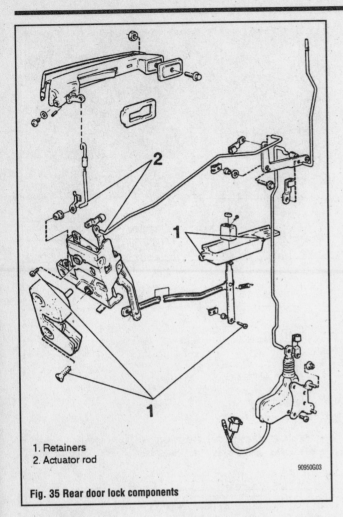

1. Retainers
2. Actuator rod

90950G03

**Fig. 35 Rear door lock components**

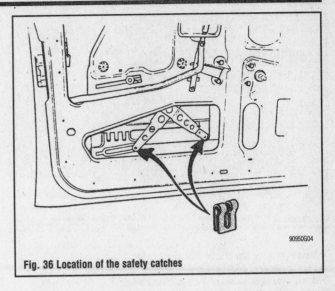

**Fig. 36 Location of the safety catches**

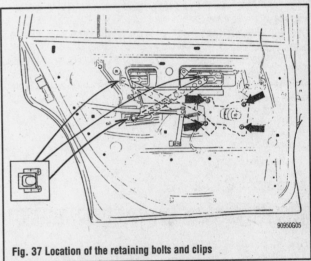

**Fig. 37 Location of the retaining bolts and clips**

### To install:

8. Place the lock cylinder into place and attach the clip.
9. Install the bracket and tighten the retaining bolt.
10. Attach the lock rod to the lock cylinder.
11. Ensure the lock cylinder engages the latch mechanism properly.
12. Install any trim removed.
13. Connect the negative battery cable.

## Door Glass and Regulator

### REMOVAL & INSTALLATION

#### 200 Series, 700 Series and Coupe

##### WITH MANUAL WINDOWS

▶ See Figures 36 and 37

1. Disconnect the negative battery cable.
2. Remove the door panel and the moisture barrier.
3. If the glass is to be replaced or removed, remove the safety catches from the pins on the 2 lower arms and lift out the glass. The regulator can be removed without removing the glass, but the glass must be supported within the door.
4. To remove the regulator, remove the safety clips from the pins on the 2 lower arms.
5. Remove the five bolts holding the regulator to the door and remove the regulator.
   **To install:**
6. Position the regulator into place and tighten the 5 retaining bolts.
7. Attach the door glass and install the safety pins on the lower arms.

8. Install the window crank handle onto the regulator shaft, and ensure the windows moves smoothly without binding. If the window is binding while moving up or down, and assuming that the regulator and glass are installed correctly, you might need to lubricate the run channels. There are specific lubricants for windows, however a good lubricating fluid or silicone spray lubricant will do the job.
9. Remove the crank handle, and install the moisture barrier and door panel.
10. Connect the negative battery cable.

##### WITH ELECTRIC WINDOWS

▶ See Figure 38

1. Disconnect the negative battery cable.
2. Remove the door panel and the moisture barrier.
3. If the glass is to be replaced or removed, remove the safety catches from the pins on the 2 lower arms and lift out the glass. The regulator can be removed without removing the glass, but the glass must be supported within the door.
4. Disconnect the wiring for the motor.
5. Remove the bolts holding the regulator and remove the regulator from the door.
   **To install:**
6. When reinstalling, tighten the mounting screws just enough to hold position and no more. Attach the glass to the regulator with the safety clips and make sure they are properly seated.

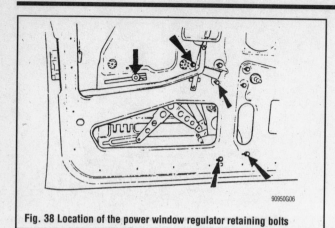

**Fig. 38 Location of the power window regulator retaining bolts**

7. The 4 frontmost mounting bolts can be loosened to eliminate binding. Loosen the screws and operate the window up and down. As the regulator seeks its best position, tighten the bolts to hold it in place. It should take 5 seconds for the window to open fully.

8. Raise the window to its stopped position. Loosen the stop (at the forward edge of the regulator) and raise the window as far as it will go. Readjust the stop to mesh with the gears and tighten it in place.

9. Operate the window and ensure it moves smoothly without binding. If the window is binding while moving up or down, and assuming that the regulator and glass are installed correctly, you might need to lubricate the run channels. There are specific lubricants for windows, however a good lubricating fluid or silicone spray lubricant will do the job.

10. Install the moisture barrier and the door pad.

11. Connect the negative battery cable.

### Except 200 Series, 700 Series and Coupe

1. Disconnect the negative battery cable.
2. Ensure window is in the fully **UP** position.
3. Remove the door panel and the moisture barrier.
4. Support the window so that it does not fall down inside the door. A block of wood under the window wedged in the door will work; however, there are special tools available such as two large suction cups attached to a heavy gauge wire.
5. Remove the window motor.
6. Remove the 3 retaining screws in the inner handle bracket.
7. Remove the 8 regulator mounting bolts.
8. Remove the window regulator.

**To install:**

9. Position the regulator and tighten the 8 retaining bolts.
10. Install the 3 retaining screws in the inner handle bracket.
11. Install the window motor.
12. Install the locking clips for the rail slides. Remove the support for the window.
13. Connect the negative battery cable.
14. Operate the window and ensure it moves smoothly without binding. If the window is binding while moving up or down, and assuming that the regulator and glass are installed correctly, you might need to lubricate the run channels. There are specific lubricants for this, however a good lubricating fluid or silicone spray lubricant will do the job.
15. Install the moisture barrier and the door pad.

## Electric Window Motor

### REMOVAL & INSTALLATION

▶ **See Figure 39**

1. Disconnect the negative battery cable.
2. Remove the door panel.
3. Remove any necessary trim to access the motor assembly.
4. Unplug the electrical connectors.
5. Remove the motor retaining bolts.
6. Remove the motor from the regulator.

**Fig. 39 Remove the three motor retaining bolts**

**To install:**

7. Install the regulator into position, make sure the aligning pin is correctly positioned.
8. Tighten the motor retaining bolts.
9. Plug in the electrical connectors.
10. Install any removed trim from the door.
11. Install the door panel.
12. Connect the negative battery cable.

## Windshield and Fixed Glass

### REMOVAL & INSTALLATION

If your windshield, or other fixed window, is cracked or chipped, you may decide to replace it with a new one yourself. However, there are two main reasons why replacement windshields and other window glass should be installed only by a professional automotive glass technician: safety and cost.

The most important reason a professional should install automotive glass is for safety. The glass in the vehicle, especially the windshield, is designed with safety in mind in case of a collision. The windshield is specially manufactured from two panes of specially-tempered glass with a thin layer of transparent plastic between them. This construction allows the glass to "give" in the event that a part of your body hits the windshield during the collision, and prevents the glass from shattering, which could cause lacerations, blinding and other harm to passengers of the vehicle. The other fixed windows are designed to be tempered so that if they break during a collision, they shatter in such a way that there are no large pointed glass pieces. The professional automotive glass technician knows how to install the glass in a vehicle so that it will function optimally during a collision. Without the proper experience, knowledge and tools, installing a piece of automotive glass yourself could lead to additional harm if an accident should ever occur.

Cost is also a factor when deciding to install automotive glass yourself. Performing this could cost you much more than a professional may charge for the same job. Since the windshield is designed to break under stress, an often life saving characteristic, windshields tend to break VERY easily when an inexperienced person attempts to install one. Do-it-yourselfers buying two, three or even four windshields from a salvage yard because they have broken them during installation are common stories. Also, since the automotive glass is designed to prevent the outside elements from entering your vehicle, improper installation can lead to water and air leaks. Annoying whining noises at highway speeds from air leaks or inside body panel rusting from water leaks can add to your stress level and subtract from your wallet. After buying two or three windshields, installing them and ending up with a leak that produces a noise while driving and water damage during rainstorms, the cost of having a professional do it correctly the first time may be much more alluring. We here at Chilton, therefore, advise that you have a professional automotive glass technician service any broken glass on your vehicle.

## WINDSHIELD CHIP REPAIR

▶ **See Figures 40 thru 54**

➡️**Check with your state and local authorities on the laws for state safety inspection. Some states or municipalities may not allow chip repair as a viable option for correcting stone damage to your windshield.**

Although severely cracked or damaged windshields must be replaced, there is something that you can do to prolong or even prevent the need for replacement of a chipped windshield. There are many companies which offer windshield chip repair products, such as Loctite's® Bullseye™ windshield repair kit. These kits usually consist of a syringe, pedestal and a sealing adhesive. The syringe is mounted on the pedestal and is used to create a vacuum which pulls the plastic layer against the glass. This helps make the chip transparent. The adhesive is then injected which seals the chip and helps to prevent further stress cracks from developing. Refer to the sequence of photos to get a general idea of what windshield chip repair involves.

➡️**Always follow the specific manufacturer's instructions.**

Fig. 40 Small chips on your windshield can be fixed with an aftermarket repair kit, such as the one from Loctite®

Fig. 41 To repair a chip, clean the windshield with glass cleaner and dry it completely

Fig. 42 Remove the center from the adhesive disc and peel off the backing from one side of the disc . . .

Fig. 43 . . . then press it on the windshield so that the chip is centered in the hole

Fig. 44 Be sure that the tab points upward on the windshield

Fig. 45 Peel the backing off the exposed side of the adhesive disc . . .

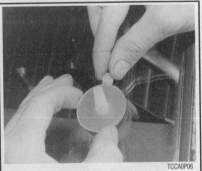

Fig. 46 . . . then position the plastic pedestal on the adhesive disc, ensuring that the tabs are aligned

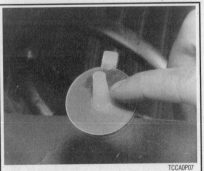

Fig. 47 Press the pedestal firmly on the adhesive disc to create an adequate seal . . .

Fig. 48 . . . then install the applicator syringe nipple in the pedestal's hole

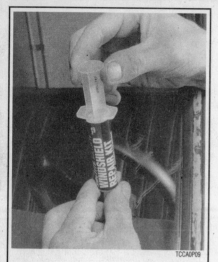

Fig. 49 Hold the syringe with one hand while pulling the plunger back with the other hand

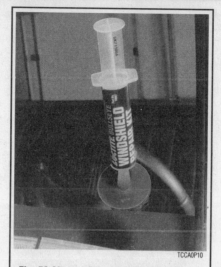

Fig. 50 After applying the solution, allow the entire assembly to sit until it has set completely

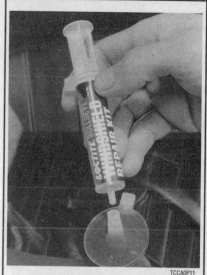

Fig. 51 After the solution has set, remove the syringe from the pedestal . . .

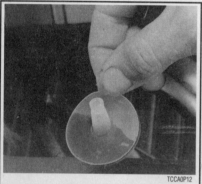

Fig. 52 . . . then peel the pedestal off of the adhesive disc . . .

Fig. 53 . . . and peel the adhesive disc off of the windshield

Fig. 54 The chip will still be slightly visible, but it should be filled with the hardened solution

## Inside Rear View Mirror

### REPLACEMENT

▶ **See Figure 55**

1. Remove the dome light panel.
2. Remove the two mirror mount attaching bolts and remove the rear view mirror and mount assembly.
3. Remove the mirror to mount retaining bolt and remove the mirror from the mount.

**To install:**

4. Position the mirror on the mount and tighten the retaining bolt.
5. Position the mirror and mount assembly onto the roof and tighten the attaching bolts.
6. Install the dome light panel.

Fig. 55 Unfasten the two retaining screws and remove the mirror with the mount

## Seats

REMOVAL & INSTALLATION

### Manual Seats

The front seat and its rails may be unbolted from the floor of the vehicle. Many vehicles have heated seats; it will be necessary to disconnect the wiring harness for this system before removing the seat.

It is necessary to remove the seat belt anchor from the side of the seat. Remove the screw in the rear of the side pocket, lift the pocket out of the way and remove the seat belt bolt.

After all the retaining bolts are removed, the front seat is removed by sliding the seat to the rear of its track and lifting upwards to free the seat from the catches.

The rear seat cushion is removed by pressing down directly over the retaining clips (freeing the hook from the loop) and lifting the cushion clear. The rear seat backrest is held by catches which hold the upper bar in place. These catches can be released with a screwdriver; don't bend them anymore than needed or reassembly will be very difficult.

When reassembling the rear seat, always install the backrest first. Make sure that every clip engages properly and is firmly closed.

### Power Front Seats

1. Disconnect the negative battery cable.
2. Remove the plastic rail covers as necessary and remove the front bolts holding the seat tracks to the vehicle. Loosen but do not remove the bolts at the rear of the tracks.
3. Gently elevate the front of the seat; identify and label the wiring running to the seat components. Disconnect the seat wiring connectors.

### ❋❋ WARNING

Do not disconnect any wiring for other components. Many other units may be found under the seat—leave them connected at all times.

4. Remove the rear mounting bolts and lift the seat clear of the vehicle. It will be heavy—a helper inside the vehicle can ease removal.
5. Either support the seat on crates or a clean workbench or place the seat on a clean blanket to protect it.

**To install:**
6. Position the seat onto the floor and attach the wiring harnesses.
7. Align the mounting holes and tighten the seat mounting bolts.
8. Install the rail covers.
9. Connect the negative battery cable.

## Power Seat Motors

REMOVAL & INSTALLATION

1. Disconnect the negative battery cable.
2. Remove the seat from the vehicle following the procedure outlined previously.
3. Turn the seat upside down and remove the 4 screws holding the motor to its bracket.
4. Lift out the motor and remove the drive cable from the motor. Use care not to kink or crease the cable.
5. Disconnect the wiring to the motor. Remove the pins from the connector case, if required. To remove the fore-and-aft motor, remove the middle connector from the control unit. Open the connector and remove the wiring at the terminals.

**To install:**
6. Properly route the harness and attach the connector to the seat motor.
7. Install the motor and tighten the retaining bolts and final check the wiring. Make sure it is out of the way of any moving parts.
8. Reinstall the seat in the vehicle, connect the wiring harnesses.
9. Connect the negative battery cable.
10. Check the operation of the seat.

➡The motor controlling the seatback tilt is within the seatback. Access to this motor involves removal of the seatback and disassembly of upholstery pieces. If trouble is experienced with this motor, repair by trained personnel is recommended.

## GLOSSARY

**AIR/FUEL RATIO:** The ratio of air-to-gasoline by weight in the fuel mixture drawn into the engine.

**AIR INJECTION:** One method of reducing harmful exhaust emissions by injecting air into each of the exhaust ports of an engine. The fresh air entering the hot exhaust manifold causes any remaining fuel to be burned before it can exit the tailpipe.

**ALTERNATOR:** A device used for converting mechanical energy into electrical energy.

**AMMETER:** An instrument, calibrated in amperes, used to measure the flow of an electrical current in a circuit. Ammeters are always connected in series with the circuit being tested.

**AMPERE:** The rate of flow of electrical current present when one volt of electrical pressure is applied against one ohm of electrical resistance.

**ANALOG COMPUTER:** Any microprocessor that uses similar (analogous) electrical signals to make its calculations.

**ARMATURE:** A laminated, soft iron core wrapped by a wire that converts electrical energy to mechanical energy as in a motor or relay. When rotated in a magnetic field, it changes mechanical energy into electrical energy as in a generator.

**ATMOSPHERIC PRESSURE:** The pressure on the Earth's surface caused by the weight of the air in the atmosphere. At sea level, this pressure is 14.7 psi at 32°F (101 kPa at 0°C).

**ATOMIZATION:** The breaking down of a liquid into a fine mist that can be suspended in air.

**AXIAL PLAY:** Movement parallel to a shaft or bearing bore.

**BACKFIRE:** The sudden combustion of gases in the intake or exhaust system that results in a loud explosion.

**BACKLASH:** The clearance or play between two parts, such as meshed gears.

**BACKPRESSURE:** Restrictions in the exhaust system that slow the exit of exhaust gases from the combustion chamber.

**BAKELITE:** A heat resistant, plastic insulator material commonly used in printed circuit boards and transistorized components.

**BALL BEARING:** A bearing made up of hardened inner and outer races between which hardened steel balls roll.

**BALLAST RESISTOR:** A resistor in the primary ignition circuit that lowers voltage after the engine is started to reduce wear on ignition components.

**BEARING:** A friction reducing, supportive device usually located between a stationary part and a moving part.

**BIMETAL TEMPERATURE SENSOR:** Any sensor or switch made of two dissimilar types of metal that bend when heated or cooled due to the different expansion rates of the alloys. These types of sensors usually function as an on/off switch.

**BLOWBY:** Combustion gases, composed of water vapor and unburned fuel, that leak past the piston rings into the crankcase during normal engine operation. These gases are removed by the PCV system to prevent the buildup of harmful acids in the crankcase.

**BRAKE PAD:** A brake shoe and lining assembly used with disc brakes.

**BRAKE SHOE:** The backing for the brake lining. The term is, however, usually applied to the assembly of the brake backing and lining.

**BUSHING:** A liner, usually removable, for a bearing; an anti-friction liner used in place of a bearing.

**CALIPER:** A hydraulically activated device in a disc brake system, which is mounted straddling the brake rotor (disc). The caliper contains at least one piston and two brake pads. Hydraulic pressure on the piston(s) forces the pads against the rotor.

**CAMSHAFT:** A shaft in the engine on which are the lobes (cams) which operate the valves. The camshaft is driven by the crankshaft, via a belt, chain or gears, at one half the crankshaft speed.

**CAPACITOR:** A device which stores an electrical charge.

**CARBON MONOXIDE (CO):** A colorless, odorless gas given off as a normal byproduct of combustion. It is poisonous and extremely dangerous in confined areas, building up slowly to toxic levels without warning if adequate ventilation is not available.

**CARBURETOR:** A device, usually mounted on the intake manifold of an engine, which mixes the air and fuel in the proper proportion to allow even combustion.

**CATALYTIC CONVERTER:** A device installed in the exhaust system, like a muffler, that converts harmful byproducts of combustion into carbon dioxide and water vapor by means of a heat-producing chemical reaction.

**CENTRIFUGAL ADVANCE:** A mechanical method of advancing the spark timing by using flyweights in the distributor that react to centrifugal force generated by the distributor shaft rotation.

**CHECK VALVE:** Any one-way valve installed to permit the flow of air, fuel or vacuum in one direction only.

**CHOKE:** A device, usually a moveable valve, placed in the intake path of a carburetor to restrict the flow of air.

**CIRCUIT:** Any unbroken path through which an electrical current can flow. Also used to describe fuel flow in some instances.

**CIRCUIT BREAKER:** A switch which protects an electrical circuit from overload by opening the circuit when the current flow exceeds a predetermined level. Some circuit breakers must be reset manually, while most reset automatically.

**COIL (IGNITION):** A transformer in the ignition circuit which steps up the voltage provided to the spark plugs.

**COMBINATION MANIFOLD:** An assembly which includes both the intake and exhaust manifolds in one casting.

**COMBINATION VALVE:** A device used in some fuel systems that routes fuel vapors to a charcoal storage canister instead of venting them into the atmosphere. The valve relieves fuel tank pressure and allows fresh air into the tank as the fuel level drops to prevent a vapor lock situation.

**COMPRESSION RATIO:** The comparison of the total volume of the cylinder and combustion chamber with the piston at BDC and the piston at TDC.

**CONDENSER:** 1. An electrical device which acts to store an electrical charge, preventing voltage surges. 2. A radiator-like device in the air conditioning system in which refrigerant gas condenses into a liquid, giving off heat.

**CONDUCTOR:** Any material through which an electrical current can be transmitted easily.

**CONTINUITY:** Continuous or complete circuit. Can be checked with an ohmmeter.

**COUNTERSHAFT:** An intermediate shaft which is rotated by a mainshaft and transmits, in turn, that rotation to a working part.

**CRANKCASE:** The lower part of an engine in which the crankshaft and related parts operate.

**CRANKSHAFT:** The main driving shaft of an engine which receives reciprocating motion from the pistons and converts it to rotary motion.

**CYLINDER:** In an engine, the round hole in the engine block in which the piston(s) ride.

**CYLINDER BLOCK:** The main structural member of an engine in which is found the cylinders, crankshaft and other principal parts.

**CYLINDER HEAD:** The detachable portion of the engine, usually fastened to the top of the cylinder block and containing all or most of the combustion chambers. On overhead valve engines, it contains the valves and their operating parts. On overhead cam engines, it contains the camshaft as well.

**DEAD CENTER:** The extreme top or bottom of the piston stroke.

**DETONATION:** An unwanted explosion of the air/fuel mixture in the combustion chamber caused by excess heat and compression, advanced timing, or an overly lean mixture. Also referred to as "ping".

**DIAPHRAGM:** A thin, flexible wall separating two cavities, such as in a vacuum advance unit.

**DIESELING:** A condition in which hot spots in the combustion chamber cause the engine to run on after the key is turned off.

**DIFFERENTIAL:** A geared assembly which allows the transmission of motion between drive axles, giving one axle the ability to turn faster than the other.

**DIODE:** An electrical device that will allow current to flow in one direction only.

**DISC BRAKE:** A hydraulic braking assembly consisting of a brake disc, or rotor, mounted on an axle, and a caliper assembly containing, usually two brake pads which are activated by hydraulic pressure. The pads are forced against the sides of the disc, creating friction which slows the vehicle.

**DISTRIBUTOR:** A mechanically driven device on an engine which is responsible for electrically firing the spark plug at a predetermined point of the piston stroke.

**DOWEL PIN:** A pin, inserted in mating holes in two different parts allowing those parts to maintain a fixed relationship.

**DRUM BRAKE:** A braking system which consists of two brake shoes and one or two wheel cylinders, mounted on a fixed backing plate, and a brake drum, mounted on an axle, which revolves around the assembly.

**DWELL:** The rate, measured in degrees of shaft rotation, at which an electrical circuit cycles on and off.

**ELECTRONIC CONTROL UNIT (ECU):** Ignition module, module, amplifier or igniter. See Module for definition.

**ELECTRONIC IGNITION:** A system in which the timing and firing of the spark plugs is controlled by an electronic control unit, usually called a module. These systems have no points or condenser.

**END-PLAY:** The measured amount of axial movement in a shaft.

**ENGINE:** A device that converts heat into mechanical energy.

**EXHAUST MANIFOLD:** A set of cast passages or pipes which conduct exhaust gases from the engine.

**FEELER GAUGE:** A blade, usually metal, or precisely predetermined thickness, used to measure the clearance between two parts.

**FIRING ORDER:** The order in which combustion occurs in the cylinders of an engine. Also the order in which spark is distributed to the plugs by the distributor.

**FLOODING:** The presence of too much fuel in the intake manifold and combustion chamber which prevents the air/fuel mixture from firing, thereby causing a no-start situation.

**FLYWHEEL:** A disc shaped part bolted to the rear end of the crankshaft. Around the outer perimeter is affixed the ring gear. The starter drive engages the ring gear, turning the flywheel, which rotates the crankshaft, imparting the initial starting motion to the engine.

**FOOT POUND (ft. lbs. or sometimes, ft.lb.):** The amount of energy or work needed to raise an item weighing one pound, a distance of one foot.

**FUSE:** A protective device in a circuit which prevents circuit overload by breaking the circuit when a specific amperage is present. The device is constructed around a strip or wire of a lower amperage rating than the circuit it is designed to protect. When an amperage higher than that stamped on the fuse is present in the circuit, the strip or wire melts, opening the circuit.

**GEAR RATIO:** The ratio between the number of teeth on meshing gears.

**GENERATOR:** A device which converts mechanical energy into electrical energy.

**HEAT RANGE:** The measure of a spark plug's ability to dissipate heat from its firing end. The higher the heat range, the hotter the plug fires.

**HUB:** The center part of a wheel or gear.

**HYDROCARBON (HC):** Any chemical compound made up of hydrogen and carbon. A major pollutant formed by the engine as a byproduct of combustion.

**HYDROMETER:** An instrument used to measure the specific gravity of a solution.

**INCH POUND (inch lbs.; sometimes in.lb. or in. lbs.):** One twelfth of a foot pound.

**INDUCTION:** A means of transferring electrical energy in the form of a magnetic field. Principle used in the ignition coil to increase voltage.

**INJECTOR:** A device which receives metered fuel under relatively low pressure and is activated to inject the fuel into the engine under relatively high pressure at a predetermined time.

**INPUT SHAFT:** The shaft to which torque is applied, usually carrying the driving gear or gears.

**INTAKE MANIFOLD:** A casting of passages or pipes used to conduct air or a fuel/air mixture to the cylinders.

**JOURNAL:** The bearing surface within which a shaft operates.

**KEY:** A small block usually fitted in a notch between a shaft and a hub to prevent slippage of the two parts.

**MANIFOLD:** A casting of passages or set of pipes which connect the cylinders to an inlet or outlet source.

**MANIFOLD VACUUM:** Low pressure in an engine intake manifold formed just below the throttle plates. Manifold vacuum is highest at idle and drops under acceleration.

**MASTER CYLINDER:** The primary fluid pressurizing device in a hydraulic system. In automotive use, it is found in brake and hydraulic clutch systems and is pedal activated, either directly or, in a power brake system, through the power booster.

**MODULE:** Electronic control unit, amplifier or igniter of solid state or integrated design which controls the current flow in the ignition primary circuit based on input from the pick-up coil. When the module opens the primary circuit, high secondary voltage is induced in the coil.

**NEEDLE BEARING:** A bearing which consists of a number (usually a large number) of long, thin rollers.

**OHM:** ($\Omega$) The unit used to measure the resistance of conductor-to-electrical flow. One ohm is the amount of resistance that limits current flow to one ampere in a circuit with one volt of pressure.

**OHMMETER:** An instrument used for measuring the resistance, in ohms, in an electrical circuit.

**OUTPUT SHAFT:** The shaft which transmits torque from a device, such as a transmission.

**OVERDRIVE:** A gear assembly which produces more shaft revolutions than that transmitted to it.

**OVERHEAD CAMSHAFT (OHC):** An engine configuration in which the camshaft is mounted on top of the cylinder head and operates the valve either directly or by means of rocker arms.

**OVERHEAD VALVE (OHV):** An engine configuration in which all of the valves are located in the cylinder head and the camshaft is located in the cylinder block. The camshaft operates the valves via lifters and pushrods.

**OXIDES OF NITROGEN (NOx):** Chemical compounds of nitrogen produced as a byproduct of combustion. They combine with hydrocarbons to produce smog.

**OXYGEN SENSOR:** Use with the feedback system to sense the presence of oxygen in the exhaust gas and signal the computer which can reference the voltage signal to an air/fuel ratio.

**PINION:** The smaller of two meshing gears.

**PISTON RING:** An open-ended ring with fits into a groove on the outer diameter of the piston. Its chief function is to form a seal between the piston and cylinder wall. Most automotive pistons have three rings: two for compression sealing; one for oil sealing.

**PRELOAD:** A predetermined load placed on a bearing during assembly or by adjustment.

**PRIMARY CIRCUIT:** the low voltage side of the ignition system which consists of the ignition switch, ballast resistor or resistance wire, bypass, coil, electronic control unit and pick-up coil as well as the connecting wires and harnesses.

**PRESS FIT:** The mating of two parts under pressure, due to the inner diameter of one being smaller than the outer diameter of the other, or vice versa; an interference fit.

**RACE:** The surface on the inner or outer ring of a bearing on which the balls, needles or rollers move.

**REGULATOR:** A device which maintains the amperage and/or voltage levels of a circuit at predetermined values.

**RELAY:** A switch which automatically opens and/or closes a circuit.

**RESISTANCE:** The opposition to the flow of current through a circuit or electrical device, and is measured in ohms. Resistance is equal to the voltage divided by the amperage.

**RESISTOR:** A device, usually made of wire, which offers a preset amount of resistance in an electrical circuit.

**RING GEAR:** The name given to a ring-shaped gear attached to a differential case, or affixed to a flywheel or as part of a planetary gear set.

**ROLLER BEARING:** A bearing made up of hardened inner and outer races between which hardened steel rollers move.

**ROTOR:** 1. The disc-shaped part of a disc brake assembly, upon which the brake pads bear; also called, brake disc. 2. The device mounted atop the distributor shaft, which passes current to the distributor cap tower contacts.

**SECONDARY CIRCUIT:** The high voltage side of the ignition system, usually above 20,000 volts. The secondary includes the ignition coil, coil wire, distributor cap and rotor, spark plug wires and spark plugs.

**SENDING UNIT:** A mechanical, electrical, hydraulic or electro-magnetic device which transmits information to a gauge.

**SENSOR:** Any device designed to measure engine operating conditions or ambient pressures and temperatures. Usually electronic in nature and designed to send a voltage signal to an on-board computer, some sensors may operate as a simple on/off switch or they may provide a variable voltage signal (like a potentiometer) as conditions or measured parameters change.

**SHIM:** Spacers of precise, predetermined thickness used between parts to establish a proper working relationship.

**SLAVE CYLINDER:** In automotive use, a device in the hydraulic clutch system which is activated by hydraulic force, disengaging the clutch.

**SOLENOID:** A coil used to produce a magnetic field, the effect of which is to produce work.

**SPARK PLUG:** A device screwed into the combustion chamber of a spark ignition engine. The basic construction is a conductive core inside of a ceramic insulator, mounted in an outer conductive base. An electrical charge from the spark plug wire travels along the conductive core and jumps a preset air gap to a grounding point or points at the end of the conductive base. The resultant spark ignites the fuel/air mixture in the combustion chamber.

**SPLINES:** Ridges machined or cast onto the outer diameter of a shaft or inner diameter of a bore to enable parts to mate without rotation.

**TACHOMETER:** A device used to measure the rotary speed of an engine, shaft, gear, etc., usually in rotations per minute.

**THERMOSTAT:** A valve, located in the cooling system of an engine, which is closed when cold and opens gradually in response to engine heating, controlling the temperature of the coolant and rate of coolant flow.

**TOP DEAD CENTER (TDC):** The point at which the piston reaches the top of its travel on the compression stroke.

**TORQUE:** The twisting force applied to an object.

**TORQUE CONVERTER:** A turbine used to transmit power from a driving member to a driven member via hydraulic action, providing changes in drive ratio and torque. In automotive use, it links the driveplate at the rear of the engine to the automatic transmission.

**TRANSDUCER:** A device used to change a force into an electrical signal.

**TRANSISTOR:** A semi-conductor component which can be actuated by a small voltage to perform an electrical switching function.

**TUNE-UP:** A regular maintenance function, usually associated with the replacement and adjustment of parts and components in the electrical and fuel systems of a vehicle for the purpose of attaining optimum performance.

**TURBOCHARGER:** An exhaust driven pump which compresses intake air and forces it into the combustion chambers at higher than atmospheric pressures. The increased air pressure allows more fuel to be burned and results in increased horsepower being produced.

**VACUUM ADVANCE:** A device which advances the ignition timing in response to increased engine vacuum.

**VACUUM GAUGE:** An instrument used to measure the presence of vacuum in a chamber.

**VALVE:** A device which control the pressure, direction of flow or rate of flow of a liquid or gas.

**VALVE CLEARANCE:** The measured gap between the end of the valve stem and the rocker arm, cam lobe or follower that activates the valve.

**VISCOSITY:** The rating of a liquid's internal resistance to flow.

**VOLTMETER:** An instrument used for measuring electrical force in units called volts. Voltmeters are always connected parallel with the circuit being tested.

**WHEEL CYLINDER:** Found in the automotive drum brake assembly, it is a device, actuated by hydraulic pressure, which, through internal pistons, pushes the brake shoes outward against the drums.

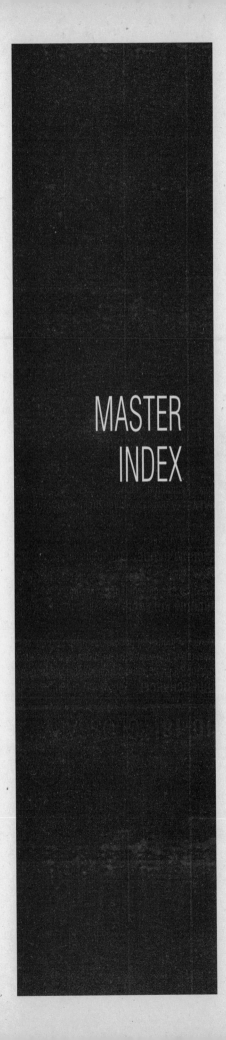

MASTER

INDEX